SCOTTISH LEAGUE PLAYERS' RECORDS

SCOTTISH FOOTBALL LEAGUE DIVISION ONE 1890/91 to 1938/39

Steve Emms & Richard Wells

with the assistance of Jim Creasy

A SoccerData Publication from Tony Brown

Published in Great Britain by Tony Brown,
4 Adrian Close, Beeston, Nottingham NG9 6FL.
Telephone 0115 973 6086. E-mail soccer@innotts.co.uk
www.soccerdata.com

First published 2007

Cover design by Bob Budd.

SoccerData is a specialist publisher of books on association football. Publications include "Definitive" club histories and season-by-season guides from 1888/89 to the 1960s. Please write to the address above for a catalogue or visit the web site.

Printed by 4edge Ltd, Hockley, Essex
www.4edge.co.uk

ISBN 978-1-899468-66-9

INTRODUCTION

This volume completes a trilogy of books covering every player that has appeared in the top division of the Scottish Football League since 1890. Wherever possible we have included details of each man's career elsewhere, for example the Football League, lower divisions of the Scottish League, and (in this volume) the American Soccer League.

Basic information on appearances and goals has been taken from contemporary Athletic News annuals, and wherever possible, club histories and who's who publications. Unfortunately the Athletic News did not include goalscorers during some wartime seasons. Several people have contributed information on their specialist clubs or areas of expertise (Peter McLeish, Jim Jeffrey, Jim Stewart, George Glass, John Henderson) and their assistance is acknowledged with thanks. We have also benefited from Richard Wells' research into Arbroath FC players. Also two men, Bill Hume and Jim Creasy, deserve particular thanks:

Bill Hume spent a great deal of time at Scottish Football League headquarters tracking down players' first names when we only had their initials. Thanks are also due to David C. Thompson of the Scottish Football League for giving us access to their records.

Since Jim Creasy heard about our project he has carried out many hours trawling through Scottish newspapers finding details of player transfers. He has also researched a large number of places and dates of birth. This is information that has not previously been generally available.

Finally we must thank Tony Brown for his advice and support in publishing the series.

Although this book is much larger than we ever envisaged, it can still be regarded as "work in progress". If anyone can fill in any of the gaps that appear in these pages we would be happy to hear from them, either via the publisher, or direct to me at 28, Briar Close, Evesham, WR11 4JQ.

Steve Emms, October 2007

PUBLISHER'S NOTE

Steve and his team are to be congratulated on a magnificent piece of work. I know that this final volume of three was particularly difficult to compile and it is perhaps not surprising that the publication date has slipped by the odd year or two! I have forgotten the exact starting date of the project, but I know Steve has been working on the task for at least six years, which makes me wonder what he will do with his time now that the book is finished.

As Steve says in his introduction, a work of this sort is never really finished. We have reached a point where we have done as much as we can. We feel it is the right moment to publish the data, much of it for the very first time. We trust that readers will find it a valuable source of reference. We will continue to maintain the database that lies behind the book.

There are many areas of interest raised by the following pages that you may wish to study further. For example, of the 7,200 players, some 150 of them made the trip across the Atlantic to play in the American Soccer League, earning salaries well above what they were paid in Scotland. You will be able to find more details of their adventures in North America on the internet. In the 19th century particularly, Scottish players were as common in English football as the foreign stars are in today's Premier League. We have included details of their playing careers both sides of the border.

I am delighted to see the book in print. It is an important addition to the documentation of the game.

Tony Brown, October 2007

KEY TO THE STATISTICS

The "Macs" will be found separately at the end of the list of players whose surnames begin with the letter "M".

Under each player's name the first line gives (where known) their place and date of birth and similar information for their death. "K.I.A." indicates that the man was killed in action during one of the two World Wars of the 20th century. Details of Scottish international caps are shown. Beneath these headings, the information is divided into six columns.

The first column lists the clubs played for. Non-league and junior clubs are listed when known. The next column shows the seasons spent at each club, using the last two digits of the season. "90/91" (for example) refers to 1890/91. An "L" or "T" against the season indicates that the player was either on loan or on trial at the club. The next columns give the number of appearances that season and the number of goals scored. All figures relate to League games only.

The final column shows in which division or league the appearances were made (other than for clubs in Scottish League Division One, which should be taken as read). "D2" and "D3" are the Scottish divisions two and three. Others are:

ASL	American Soccer League	IL	Irish League
BDL	Birmingham & District	LC	Lancashire Combination
CCL	Cheshire County League	LI	League of Ireland
CL	Cheshire League	LL	Lancashire League
ESL	Eastern Soccer League (USA)	ML	Midland League
FA	Football Alliance	NL	Northern League
FL	Football League	SA	Scottish Alliance
HL	Highland League	SL	Southern League

In some places an asterisk appears against a club's name. This indicates that although a player of the same name (or at least with the same initials) made the appearances listed, we have not been able to confirm that it is the same player. Again, correspondence will be welcome.

Please remember that Queen's Park were not members of Division One until 1900/01. Consequently, a number of their well-known players do not appear in these pages.

ABBIE James Lockhart
b. Burntisland 13.11.1919 d. Cupar 1953
Crossgates Primrose
Partick T 36/37 3
37/38
38/39
Alloa A 46/47 D2

ABBOTT James

Inverkeithing U
Raith R 15/16 14 1
16/17 21 5
17/18
Heart of Midlothian 18/19 6
Raith R 19/20 3

ABBOTT Joseph

Third Lanark 95/96 1
Galston 95/96
96/97
97/98
98/99
99/00
00/01

ABERCROMBIE

Kilsyth St Patricks
Hibernian 18/19 4 ?

ABERNETHY Samuel
b. Lugar 1888
Lugar Boswell
Ayr U 18/19 1
Royal Albert 19/20
Hamilton A 19/20 9
20/21 21
Dykehead 21/22
Arthurlie 22/23

ABRAHAM Joseph
b. 1876 d. USA 1965
Partick T 97/98 6
98/99
Belfast Celtic 99/00 IL
Linfield 00/01 IL
Glentoran 00/01 IL
01/02 IL

ABRAM

Renton 91/92 2

ABRAM Robert Lawrence
b. Banks 14.5.1889 d. Southport 20.3.1966
Southport Central
Colne
Stockport Co 08/09 23 2 FL
09/10 28 5 FL
10/11 16 1 FL
Heart of Midlothian 10/11 13
11/12 31 6
12/13 25 1
13/14 38 1
Chelsea 14/15 31 5 FL
19/20 13 2 FL
Cardiff C 20/21 1 FL
Southport 21/22 36 7 FL
22/23 12 FL

ABRINES James Watson
b. Renfrew 31.12.1900 d. Troon 24.12.1976
Muirpark Amateurs
Glengarnock Vale
Parkhead
Albion R 21/22 6
22/23 5
Dundee
Sittingbourne T
Barrow 23/24 7 FL
Kings Park 24/25 D2
25/26 D2
26/27 D2
Duntochter Hibs

ADAM

St Mirren 90/91 2

ADAM Hugh T
b. c1911
Banks o'Dee
Aberdeen 31/32 7 1
32/33 5 1
33/34
34/35 4 1
St Johnstone 35/36 29 5
Arbroath 36/37 31 9
37/38 15 6

ADAM James
b. Larkhall
Hibernian 12/13 4 1
13/14 5 1
Abercorn 13/14 D2

ADAM William
b. Paisley
St Mirren 22/23 2 1
J & P Coats 23/24 23 13 ASL
24/25 34 3 ASL
25/26 30 18 ASL
26/27 18 7 ASL
27/28 43 7 ASL
28/29 30 ASL
Pawtucket Rangers 29A 18 4 ASL
29/30 23 3 ASL
30A 27 2 ASL
31S 1 ASL

ADAMS Andrew

Rutherglen Glencairn
Arbroath 35/36 21 1
36/37 36 2
37/38 38 1
38/39 38 10

ADAMS David Robertson
b. Oathlaw 14.5.1883 d. Edinburgh 29.11.1948
Avonbridge
Vale of Carron
Dunipace Jnrs
Celtic 02/03
03/04 21
04/05 26
05/06 30
06/07 28
07/08 34
08/09 31
09/10 25
10/11 34
11/12 18

ADAMS Francis

St Bernards 93/94 1
Cowlairs 94/95 D2

ADAMS Harry

Kirkcaldy U
Dundee 13/14 8 1
14/15 4 1

ADAMS James 3 caps
b. Edinburgh 1864 d. New Jersey 24.4.1943
Norton Park
Heart of Midlothian 85/86
86/87
87/88
88/89
89/90
90/91 18
91/92 22
92/93 17
93/94 18
Everton 94/95 12 FL
95/96 28 1 FL
Heart of Midlothian 96/97 4 2
St Bernards 96/97
97/98 3

ADAMS James
b. Glasgow 1903
St Rochs
Kilmarnock 23/24 8 1
24/25 3
Queen of the South 25/26 D2
Alloa A 26/27 D2
Airdrieonians 26/27
Queen of the South 26/27 D2

ADAMS James C

East Stirlingshire
Queen's Park 05/06 10
06/07 22
07/08 15
08/09 16
09/10 7

ADAMS James Hendry

Parkhead A
Motherwell 02/03 D2
03/04 2
Lochee U

ADAMS John

Manchester C
Hibernian 06/07 18 1
Royal Albert

ADAMS Joseph

Petershill
Cowdenbeath 32/33 25
Queen of the South 33/34
Coleraine T 33/34 IL
Shelbourne 33/34 LI

ADAMS Nathaniel
b. Belfast 29.9.1891
Distillery 10/11 IL
11/12 IL
12/13 IL
13/14 IL
14/15 IL
Cliftonville 15/16 IL
16/17 IL
17/18 IL
Motherwell 18/19 1
Cliftonville 19/20 IL
20/21 IL
21/22 IL
22/23 IL
23/24 IL
24/25 IL
Portadown 25/26 IL

ADAMS Peter M
b. Perth
Heart of Midlothian 37/38 1
38/39 1

ADAMS Thomas

Rutherglen Glencairn
Queen's Park 11/12 15
Partick T 12/13 25
13/14 23
14/15 30
15/16 34
16/17 26
17/18 32
18/19 7
19/20 22
Broxburn U 20/21
21/22 D2
22/23 D2
23/24 D2

ADAMSON

Hamilton A 06/07 2

ADAMSON Robert McLellan
b. Balbeggie 21.5.1914 d. Perth 27.8.1995
Perth Craigie
Dundee Violet
Heart of Midlothian 34/35
Dundee 35/36 5 3
36/37 2
37/38 3
Wrexham 38/39 35 13 FL
Carlisle U 39/40 2 FL
Dundee U
East Fife 46/47 8 2 D2

ADEY Wilfred
b. Dinnington 6.7.1909 d. Worksop ?.2.1975
Thurcroft Church
Thurcroft Main
Huddersfield T 30/31 FL
Thurcroft Main 31/32
Norton Woodseats 31/32
Sheffield U 31/32 1 FL
32/33 1 FL
33/34 FL
Barnsley 34/35 37 FL
35/36 26 FL
36/37 3 FL
Carlisle U 36/37 35 3 FL
37/38 39 2 FL
Aberdeen 38/39 26

ADSHEAD

Hibernian 17/18 2 ?

AFFLECK James

St Ninians Thistle
Airdrieonians 10/11 6

AGAR Alfred
b. Esh Winning 28.8.1904 d. Carlisle 23.3.1989
Esh Winning
Shildon
West Stanley 25/26
Dundee 26/27 3 1
Barrow 27/28 31 7 FL
Carlisle U 28/29 36 9 FL
29/30 14 2 FL
Accrington S 30/31 35 13 FL
31/32 38 14 FL
Oldham A 32/33 32 10 FL
33/34 20 8 FL
34/35 30 6 FL
35/36 14 3 FL
York C 36/37 24 4 FL
Scarborough 37/38
38/39

AGNEW William
b. Pollokshaws 9.1.1898
Pollok Jnrs
Ayr U 18/19 17 10
19/20 8 6
Falkirk 19/20 7 2
20/21 14 5
Bo'ness L 20/21
Port Vale 21/22 31 4 FL
22/23 11 1 FL
Arthurlie 23/24 D2
24/25 D2
Luton T 25/26 23 8 FL
26/27 12 FL
Providence Clamdiggers 27/28 24 7 ASL

AGNEW William Barbour 3 caps
b. Kilmarnock 16.12.1880 d. Moffat 20.8.1936
Afton Lads
Kilmarnock 00/01 4
01/02 18
Newcastle U 02/03 34 FL
03/04 9 FL
Middlesbrough 04/05 28 1 FL
05/06 37 FL
Kilmarnock 06/07 26 5
07/08 30 5
Sunderland 08/09 19 FL
09/10 9 FL
Falkirk 10/11 22 4
11/12 16 1
Third Lanark
East Stirlingshire

AIMER George Anderson
b. Dundee 27.10.1897 d. Dundee 5.6.1935
Glenisla
Dundee Celtic
Dundee Hibs
Dundee 21/22 13
22/23 16
Fulham 23/24 11 FL
24/25 5 FL
Third Lanark 25/26 D2
26/27 D2
Providence Clamdiggers 27/28 52 ASL
28/29 51 2 ASL
29/30 4 ASL
30A 23 ASL
Fall River Marksmen 31S 1 ASL
New York Giants 31S 2 ASL

AIRD Hugh
Vale of Leithen
Airdrieonians 19/20 6 1
20/21 14 3
St Mirren 20/21 6
Peebles R 21/22
22/23
USA

AITCHISON Alexander
Benburb
Morton 07/08 6 1

AITCHISON James
b. 1880
Rugby XI
Third Lanark 00/01 2

AITKEN
Clyde 92/93 1

AITKEN
Port Glasgow A 02/03 1 1

AITKEN Alexander
Dundee 12/13 25
13/14 27
14/15 25
15/16 16
16/17 10

AITKEN Alexander
Heart of Midlothian 15/16 1
16/17 4

AITKEN Alexander
b. c1864 d. Ayr 7.2.1938
Ayr U 15/16 1

AITKEN Andrew 14 caps
b. Ayr 27.4.1877 d. Ponteland 15.2.1955
Annbank
Ayr Thistle
Ayr Parkhouse
Newcastle U 95/96 27 10 FL
96/97 29 12 FL
97/98 22 4 FL
98/99 25 3 FL
Kilmarnock L 98/99
Newcastle U 99/00 34 FL
00/01 32 1 FL
01/02 29 FL
02/03 32 FL
03/04 32 FL
04/05 28 2 FL
05/06 15 FL
06/07 3 FL
Middlesbrough 06/07 27 FL
07/08 31 1 FL
08/09 17 1 FL
Leicester F 08/09 13 FL
09/10 31 FL
10/11 20 1 FL
Dundee 11/12 29
Kilmarnock 12/13 8
Gateshead T 13/14

AITKEN Daniel
b. Dalry 20.9.1882 d. Tarbolton 27.2.1948
Beith
Ardeer Thistle
Kilmarnock 04/05 26
05/06 30
Millwall A 06/07 18 SL
Swindon T 07/08 1 SL

AITKEN Fergus McKenna
b. Glasgow 5.6.1896 d. Kilmarnock 13.7.1989
Petershill 15/16
Benburb 16/17
Third Lanark 17/18 25 ?
18/19 6 ?
Bury 19/20 42 2 FL
20/21 34 2 FL
Blackburn R 21/22 8 1 FL
Cardiff C 22/23 2 FL
Birmingham 22/23 FL
Southport 23/24 7 FL
24/25 42 1 FL
25/26 29 2 FL
Bradford PA 26/27 11 FL

AITKEN John
b. c1894
Perth Violet
Hibernian 13/14 8 1
14/15 10 1
Broxburn U 14/15

AITKEN John Gordon
b. Govan 17.9.1897 d. Govan 1.12.1967
St Anthonys
St Rochs
Clyde 19/20 8
20/21 1
Bury 21/22 41 7 FL
22/23 38 3 FL
23/24 1 FL
Preston NE 23/24 FL
Southport 24/25 42 1 FL
Crewe A 25/26 26 3 FL
Norwich C 26/27 42 8 FL
Northampton T 27/28 9 5 FL
Kilmarnock 28/29 9 3
29/30 14 1
30/31 32 9
31/32 35 14
32/33 36 4
St Mirren 33/34 3
Morton 33/34 D2

AITKEN Robert Alexander Graham
b. St Ninians 1881
St Ninians Thistle
Kilmarnock 08/09 33
09/10 16
10/11
St Johnstone 11/12 20 D2
12/13 21 D2

AITKEN Samuel
b. Ayr 1878 d. Ayr 7.3.1930
Ayr Parkhouse
Ayr 00/01 16 ? D2
01/02 ? ? D2
02/03 ? ? D2
Middlesbrough 03/04 19 FL
04/05 30 FL
05/06 37 2 FL
06/07 35 2 FL
07/08 38 1 FL
08/09 33 FL
09/10 35 FL
Raith R 10/11 30 1
11/12 32 1

AITKEN W
Yoker A
Dumbarton 21/22 1

AITKEN William
Arniston R
Heart of Midlothian 13/14 2

AITKEN William B
Queen's Park 01/02 4

AITKEN William John
b. Peterhead 2.2.1894 d. Gateshead 9.8.1973
Kirkintilloch Harp
Kirkintilloch Rob Roy
Kilsyth R
Queen's Park 16/17 29 4
17/18 33 10
Rangers 18/19 21 2
Port Vale L 19/20 8 4 CL
19/20 30 4 FL
Newcastle U 20/21 35 3 FL
21/22 16 FL
22/23 25 4 FL
23/24 28 3 FL
Preston NE 24/25 41 5 FL
25/26 15 5 FL
Chorley 26/27
Norwich C 26/27 14 FL
Bideford T
Juventus
AS Cannes
Stade de Reims 34/35
35/36
36/37
Antibes 37/38

AITKENHEAD Walter Campbell Allison 1 cap
b. Maryhill 21.5.1887 d. Pleasington 19.7.1966
Maryhill Harp
Partick T 06/07 4
Blackburn R 06/07 16 1 FL
07/08 7 1 FL
08/09 9 5 FL
09/10 38 12 FL
10/11 35 13 FL
11/12 29 16 FL
12/13 24 12 FL
13/14 17 7 FL
14/15 35 9 FL

AITON James
Cowdenbeath 31/32 10 2

ALEXANDER
St Mirren 90/91 3

ALEXANDER
Heart of Midlothian 96/97 1

ALEXANDER
St Bernards 96/97 4

ALEXANDER Allan
Partick T 98/99 1
99/00
00/01
01/02
02/03 3 1
03/04 1

ALEXANDER Francis Pirie Wilson
b. Gamrie 8.5.1898
Aberdeen University
Aberdeen 21/22 9

ALEXANDER J
Queen's Park 17/18 1

ALEXANDER James
b. Ayrshire c1897
Dumbarton 21/22 12 5
22/23 D2
Alloa A 23/24 D2

ALEXANDER John Woodburn
b. Galston 26.12.1914
Galston
Ayr U 34/35 6
Kilmarnock 35/36 2
36/37 5
Queen of the South 37/38 1

ALEXANDER Robert
Parkhead Jnrs
Hibernian 15/16 27 2
16/17 13 6

ALEXANDER William T
Queen's Park 12/13 1

ALEXANDER William Thomson
Queen's Park 06/07 1

ALLAN Adam B
b. Newtongrange
Newtongrange Star
Queen's Park 30/31 3

ALLAN Adam McIlroy
b. Newarthill 12.9.1904
Regent Star
Rutherglen Glencairn
Falkirk 25/26 18 2
26/27 7
Sunderland 27/28 20 FL
28/29 29 FL
29/30 14 FL
Reading 30/31 30 1 FL
31/32 39 2 FL
32/33 38 FL
Queen of the South 33/34 24 2
34/35 36 1
35/36 36
36/37 27
37/38 38

ALLAN Alexander
Glasgow Perthshire
Queen's Park 15/16 13
16/17 2

ALLAN Alexander
Falkirk 37/38 11
38/39 2

ALLAN Frank
Dundee 09/10 1

ALLAN George
b. Mauchline d. 14.3.1916
Partick T 97/98 5 4
98/99 5 1
99/00
00/01
01/02
02/03
03/04
04/05
05/06 6
06/07 26 1
07/08 19 1
Hamilton A

ALLAN George Horsburgh 1 cap
b. Linlithgow Bridge 23.4.1875 d. Earlsferry 9.10.1899
Vale of Avon
Linlithgow A
Broxburn Shamrock
Bo'ness
Leith A 94/95 5 1
95/96 1 ? D2
Liverpool 95/96 20 26 FL
96/97 29 16 FL
Celtic 97/98 17 14
Liverpool 98/99 30 8 FL

ALLAN Henry Hogg 1 cap
b. Elbury 5.9.1877
Dunfermline Jnrs
Cowdenbeath 95/96
Heart of Midlothian 95/96
96/97 1
97/98 18 1
98/99 17
99/00 16
00/01 18
01/02 14
02/03 14
East Fife 03/04

ALLAN J
Third Lanark 92/93 4

ALLAN James
Beith
Morton 01/02 11 2
02/03 18
03/04 5
Beith

ALLAN James
Wallsend Park Villa
St Mirren 08/09 14
09/10 14

ALLAN James
b. Airdrie 29.8.1899
Glasgow Ashfield
Airdrieonians 21/22 5
22/23
23/24 6
24/25 21
Leeds U 25/26 35 FL
26/27 22 FL
27/28 13 FL
Third Lanark 28/29 33
29/30

ALLAN John
Rangers 91/92 3 1

ALLAN John
Heart of Midlothian 98/99 2 2

ALLAN John
b. Bonhill 1891
Darvel Jnrs
Newmilns
Kilmarnock 09/10 1
10/11 10 5
11/12 15
Galston 12/13
Kilmarnock 13/14

ALLAN John
b. Cardenden c1891
Bowhill Thistle
Hibernian 10/11 2
East Fife 11/12
12/13
Bury 13/14 16 FL
14/15 30 1 FL
19/20 42 FL
20/21 30 FL
21/22 14 FL
Reading 22/23 42 FL
J & P Coats 23/24 3 ASL
24/25 39 ASL
25/26 32 ASL
26/27 33 ASL
27/28 13 ASL

ALLAN John
Blantyre Celtic
Hamilton A 32/33 8 2
33/34 7

ALLAN John
Coltness U
Heart of Midlothian 33/34 1
Clydebank Jnrs 34/35

ALLAN Joseph
St Bernards 97/98 7 1
Heart of Midlothian

ALLAN Joseph
Blantyre Celtic
Leith A 31/32 11
32/33 D2
33/34 D2
Dunfermline A 34/35 1
St Bernards 34/35 D2
35/36 D2
36/37 D2
37/38 D2
38/39 D2

ALLAN Patrick
b. Perth c1893
Perth Violet
Clyde 11/12 6 4
12/13 16 8
13/14 27 9
14/15 35 12
15/16 3
Shelbourne * 15/16 IL
Clyde 16/17
17/18
18/19
19/20 2 1
20/21 20 7
21/22 12 4
Hibernian 22/23 8
Dumbarton Harp

ALLAN Richard
b. Preston
Preston NE 94/95 2 1 FL
Chorley 95/96
Dundee 96/97 8 1
Newcastle U 97/98 24 4 FL
Bristol St Georges

ALLAN Robert
St Monance Swifts
Raith R 37/38 32 1 D2
38/39 38
Dundee

ALLAN Russell
b. Cleland
Renfrew Jnrs
Dykehead
Third Lanark 18/19 33 ?
19/20 38 10
20/21 36 7
21/22 14 9
Motherwell 21/22 12
22/23
23/24
24/25
25/26
Dykehead 25/26 D3

ALLAN Samuel
Beith
Port Glasgow A 04/05 19 1
05/06 30 3
06/07 22
Petershill
Hibernian 07/08 27
08/09 34
09/10 29
10/11 29
11/12 5
Rangers 11/12 1
Broxburn Shamrock 12/13

ALLAN Thomas
b. Carluke 9.10.1891
Law Volunteers
Carluke Milton R
Celtic 09/10 2
Ayr L 09/10 D2
Airdrieonians L 10/11 7
Vale of Leven L 11/12 D2

ALLAN Thomas E
b. Glasgow
Wellwood Star
Rutherglen Glencairn
Heart of Midlothian 06/07 33
07/08 26
Sunderland 08/09 3 FL
09/10 7 FL
10/11 14 FL
Heart of Midlothian 11/12 31
12/13 32
13/14 36
Motherwell 14/15 36
15/16 2

ALLAN Vincent
b. Bellshill
Thornliewood U
Shettleston 32/33
33/34
Airdrieonians 34/35 13

ALLAN W T

Queen's Park 16/17 2

ALLAN William
b. c1889
Kilsyth Emmet
Kirkintilloch Rob Roy
Queen's Park 09/10
Port Glasgow A 09/10 19 3
Partick T 10/11 8 1
11/12 12 1
Ayr U 12/13 D2
Partick T 12/13

ALLAN William
b. Kilbarchan
Kilbarchan A
Morton 21/22 14
22/23 11
Johnstone 22/23 D2
Morton 23/24 34
24/25 22
Bethlehem Steel 25/26 35 ASL
26/27 22 ASL
27/28 19 ASL
28/29 4 ASL
29/30 2 ASL
30/31 ASL
Hartlepools U 31/32 1 FL
St Mirren
Dunfermline A

ALLAN William
b. Strathaven
Burnbank A
Hamilton A 28/29 38
29/30 33
30/31 37
31/32 38
32/33 36
33/34 9
Motherwell 33/34 11
34/35 19
35/36
Partick T 36/37 11
Dalbeattie Star L 36/37
Partick T 37/38
Albion R 38/39 1

ALLAN William R
b. Falkirk
Woodbine R
Vale of Carron
East Stirlingshire
Falkirk
Rangers 04/05 8
Albion R 04/05
05/06
Falkirk 06/07 32
07/08 32
Hibernian 08/09 33
09/10 34
10/11 31
11/12 30
12/13 27
13/14 31
14/15 34
15/16 20
Falkirk 15/16 1
16/17 3
17/18 34
18/19
19/20 1
20/21 3

ALLISON

Abercorn 90/01 1

ALLISON

St Mirren 90/91 1

ALLISON

St Mirren 93/94 2

ALLISON J

Clyde 33/34 1

ALLISON J L

Renton 91/92 13
92/93 18
93/94 14
94/95 3 D2

ALLISON John
b. Glasgow
Parkhead Jnrs
Kilmarnock 23/24 1
St Johnstone
Stenhousemuir
East Stirlingshire 25/26
Airdrieonians 26/27 12 4
27/28 24 2
Queen of the South L
Cowdenbeath 28/29 4
Morton
Barrow 29/30 11 FL
Armadale 29/30 D2
30/31 D2
Shelbourne 31/32

ALLISON Robert

Ardeer Thistle
Kilmarnock 07/08 2
Hurlford
Bathgate
Galston
Stevenston U
Galston

ALLISON W

Airdrieonians 23/24 1

ALLISON William S
b. Camelon
Dunipace
Kettering T 25/26
Raith R 25/26 17 6
26/27 D2
27/28 26 7

ALSTON David

Rothesay Royal Victoria
Partick T 33/34 10 1
Arthurlie 34/35
35/36
36/37
Partick T 37/38 10 5
38/39 2
St Mirren 38/39

AMBLER Harry

Strathclyde
Aberdeen 16/17 32 9
Hibernian L 16/17 1
Aberdeen 17/18
Heart of Midlothian 18/19 2
Abercorn 18/19
19/20
Hall Russells 20/21

AMOS

Heart of Midlothian 92/93 1

ANCELL Robert Francis Dudgeon 2 caps
b. Dumfries 16.6.1911 d. Monifieth 5.7.1987
Mid Annandale
St Mirren 30/31 28
31/32 31
Queen of the South L 31/32 D2
St Mirren 32/33 26
33/34 33
34/35 38
35/36 D2
36/37 2
Newcastle U 36/37 26 FL
37/38 29 FL
38/39 42 1 FL
39/40 3 FL
Dundee 45/46 24
46/47 27
47/48 7
48/49 6
Aberdeen 48/49 15
Berwick R

ANDERSON

Third Lanark 95/96 1

ANDERSON

Abercorn 96/97 1

ANDERSON

Clyde 06/07 1

ANDERSON

Heart of Midlothian 06/07 1

ANDERSON

Port Glasgow A 07/08 1

ANDERSON

Port Glasgow A 09/10 1

ANDERSON

Rangers 16/17 2

ANDERSON

St Mirren 16/17 1

ANDERSON

Ayr U 17/18 2 ?

ANDERSON

Hibernian 27/28 1

ANDERSON Alexander
b. Gorbals 8.1.1922 d. Southport 10.10.1984
Murrayfield Amateurs
Queen's Park 32/33 32 9
33/34 28 10
Heart of Midlothian 34/35 14 3
35/36 17 10
36/37 3 3
37/38 4
Third Lanark 38/39 9 3 D2
46/47
47/48
Rochdale 47/48 FL
Dundalk 48/49 LI
Southport
Bangor C

ANDERSON Alfred James
b. Cumnock 1914
Yoker A
Hibernian 34/35 26 4
35/36 33 3
36/37 15 1
Bolton W 36/37 13 1 FL
37/38 34 2 FL
38/39 5 1 FL

ANDERSON Andrew 23 caps
b. Airdrie 21.2.1909 d. 1991
Coatbridge Juveniles
Baillieston Jnrs
Heart of Midlothian 29/30 12
30/31 33
31/32 25
32/33 34 1
33/34 32 1
34/35 36 1
35/36 35
36/37 37 1
37/38 35
38/39 34

ANDERSON Andrew Lyle
b. Milton 27.2.1885
Glasgow Ashfield
St Mirren 04/05 18 2
05/06 28 6
06/07 32 9
07/08 27 11
Newcastle U 08/09 19 3 FL
09/10 19 1 FL
10/11 18 FL
11/12 5 1 FL
Third Lanark 12/13 12 1
13/14
Leicester F 14/15 25 1 FL
Abercorn

ANDERSON David

Cambuslang Hibs
Clydebank Jnrs
Airdrieonians 06/07 10 4
07/08 3
Ayr

ANDERSON David

Dumbarton
Hibernian 10/11 32 7
11/12 14 4
12/13 21 4
13/14
14/15
Third Lanark 15/16 7 2

ANDERSON David L
b. Edinburgh
Newtongrange Star
Hibernian 19/20 10 1
20/21 35 17
21/22 4 4
St Johnstone 22/23 29 18 D2
St Bernards 22/23 D2

ANDERSON Douglas Nicol
b. Stonehaven 25.3.1914 d. Garstang 9.11.1989
Stonehaven
Aberdeen 34/35 1
Dundee U 35/36 27 6 D2
Hibernian 36/37 8 1
Brentford 37/38 FL
38/39 1 FL
Derry C * 42/43 IL

ANDERSON Edward
b. Beith 27.1.1879 d. Beith 12.4.1954
Beith 99/00
St Mirren 99/00
Beith 00/01
01/02
St Mirren 02/03 4
Woolwich Arsenal 03/04 2 FL
Fulham 03/04 6 SL

ANDERSON Francis

Partick T 16/17 1

ANDERSON Frank
b. Glasgow
Yoker A
Clyde 16/17 1

ANDERSON G

Clydebank 25/26 3 2

ANDERSON George 1 cap
b. Kilmarnock 6.1.1877 d. Canada 20.5.1930
Kilmarnock Rugby XI
Kilmarnock 96/97 6 D2
97/98 16 5 D2
98/99 16 2 D2
99/00 18 1
00/01 16 1
01/02 18 1
02/03 22
03/04 20
04/05 17
Luton T T 05/06 SL
Hurlford 05/06
Kilmarnock 06/07 22
Ayr Parkhouse L 06/07
Kilmarnock 07/08 23
08/09 1

ANDERSON George

St Mirren 98/99 1

ANDERSON George

Dundee 99/00 2 1
00/01
Raith R * 01/02

ANDERSON George

Stewarton Thistle
Alloa A 22/23 1

ANDERSON George Albert
b. Haydon Bridge 1887 d. Dundee 1954
Haydon Bridge
Mickley Colliery
Sunderland 11/12 8 FL
12/13 2 FL
13/14 FL
Aberdeen 14/15 29
15/16 33
16/17 38
Dundee 17/18
18/19
Aberdeen 19/20 42
20/21 38
21/22 25

ANDERSON George E

Leith A 91/92 20 2
92/93 7 3
Blackburn R 92/93 22 2 FL
93/94 27 3 FL
94/95 28 4 FL
95/96 28 1 FL
96/97 27 1 FL
New Brighton Tower 97/98
Blackburn R L 97/98 2 FL
New Brighton Tower 98/99 8 FL
Blackburn R 98/99 26 7 FL
99/00 18 1 FL
Blackpool 00/01 9 2 FL
01/02 28 12 FL
02/03 28 7 FL
03/04 24 8 FL

ANDERSON George Russell
b. Saltcoats 29.10.1904 d. Cambridge 9.11.1974
Dalry Thistle
Airdrieonians 25/26 11 9
Brentford 26/27 8 2 FL
Chelsea 27/28 5 FL
28/29 4 FL
Norwich C 29/30 28 12 FL
Carlisle U T 30/31 2 1 FL
Gillingham T 30/31
Cowdenbeath 30/31 16 2
31/32 19 5
Yeovil T 32/33
Bury 33/34 21 9 FL
34/35 4 1 FL
Huddersfield T 34/35 14 4 FL
Mansfield T 35/36 17 8 FL
36/37 19 8 FL
Ayr U
Saltcoats Victoria

ANDERSON H C

Queen's Park 19/20 1

ANDERSON Harry

Elgin C
Morton 08/09 4 2

ANDERSON Harry A 1 cap
b. Glasgow
Hibernian 09/10 2 1
10/11 19 2
11/12 23 10
Raith R 12/13 33 4
13/14 34 2
14/15 35 2
Third Lanark 15/16 31
Vale of Clyde 15/16
Raith R 16/17
17/18
18/19
St Mirren 18/19 5 ?
Raith R 19/20 37 3
St Mirren 20/21 27 2
Clydebank 21/22 29 1

ANDERSON J M

Queen's Park 08/09 5

ANDERSON James

Clyde 98/99 1
99/00 8
00/01 12 ? D2

ANDERSON James
b. Glasgow
Overton A
Kilmarnock 33/34 12
34/35 14
35/36
36/37 18
37/38 4
Airdrieonians 38/39 30 D2

ANDERSON James
b. Pelaw 26.5.1913
Blyth Spartans
Darlington 33/34 FL
Wigan A 33/34
Blyth Spartans 34/35
Queen of the South 35/36 5 1
36/37 10
37/38 38
38/39 38
Brentford 39/40 3 FL
Carlisle U 46/47 10 FL

ANDERSON John
b. Crieff 6.5.1881
Dunfermline A
Heart of Midlothian 02/03 10
03/04 16
04/05 8
Falkirk 05/06 26
06/07 32
07/08 34 3
08/09 33 1
09/10 33 2
10/11 26
11/12 24
12/13 3
13/14 1 1

ANDERSON John

Vale of Clyde
Port Glasgow A 02/03 2
03/04 26
Notts Co 04/05 9 FL
Port Glasgow A 05/06
06/07
07/08
Hamilton A 08/09 4

ANDERSON John

Queen's Park 10/11 14 1
11/12 26 2
12/13 10 1

ANDERSON John

Heart of Midlothian 16/17 1

ANDERSON John
b. Hamilton
Bent Royal Oak
Blantyre V
Larkhall Thistle
Hamilton A 18/19 10

ANDERSON John

Kilwinning R
Ayr U 24/25
Dundee 25/26 3 2

ANDERSON John
b. Carmuirs
Camelon Jnrs
Forthbank
Queen of the South 33/34 16
34/35 18
35/36 31
36/37 21

ANDERSON John A

Muirkirk Thistle
Glenbuck Cherrypickers
Kilmarnock 15/16 11 1

ANDERSON John McL

Vale of Leven
Rangers 14/15 3 1
Vale of Leven

ANDERSON Joseph
b. Bishopton 1895
Thornliebank
Vale of Leven
Airdrieonians 15/16 15 6
Royal Scots Fusiliers
Dumbarton Harp 18/19
Clydebank 19/20 33 31
Burnley 19/20 8 6 FL
20/21 41 25 FL
21/22 36 20 FL
22/23 28 8 FL
23/24 8 5 FL
Clydebank 23/24 22 14
Pollok 24/25
25/26
Vale of Leven 26/27
Pollok

ANDERSON K

Third Lanark 93/94 11

ANDERSON Neil P

Raith R 38/39 1
East Stirlingshire

ANDERSON Oliver
b. Glasgow 13.5.1919
Glasgow 216 Co BB
Arthurlie
Celtic 37/38
38/39 11 3
Alloa A 46/47 D2
Third Lanark T 47/48
Airdrieonians 47/48 7
Falkirk 48/49 9
49/50
Cowdenbeath 49/50 D2
Ards T 49/50 IL
Arbroath 50/51 D2
Kilmarnock T 50/51 1 D2

ANDERSON R
Hibernian 13/14 6

ANDERSON Robert
b. Clydebank c1883 d. Alloa 21.5.1932
Yoker A
Clydebank Jnrs
Queen's Park 08/09 31 3
Kilmarnock 09/10 29 2
10/11 32 1
11/12 18
Queen's Park 12/13 5

ANDERSON Robert
b. c1905
Arniston R
Third Lanark 23/24 2

ANDERSON Robert
West Calder
Waterford
Arbroath 38/39 12

ANDERSON Samuel
b. Glasgow
Shettleston
Hamilton A 12/13 32 2
South Shields 13/14
Hamilton A 14/15
Bradford C 14/15 14 3 FL
Bathgate
Airdrieonians 16/17 34 6
17/18 22 5
Hamilton A 17/18 4
18/19 23 4
Third Lanark 19/20 15
20/21 33 5
21/22 9
St Bernards 22/23 D2
Nithsdale W 23/24 D3

ANDERSON Smith
Petershill
Yoker A
Queen's Park 19/20 6
20/21 12

ANDERSON T
Queen's Park 10/11 1 1

ANDERSON Thomas
b. Coatbridge
New Stevenston
Hamilton A 21/22 12
Bo'ness 22/23 38 D2
23/24 D2
24/25 D2
25/26 D2
26/27 D2

ANDERSON Thomas Coldwell
b. Shettleston 12.1.1895
Shettleston
Hamilton A 13/14 20 9
Johnstone 14/15
Bathgate
Albion R 19/20 1
Bradford C 20/21 1 FL
21/22 1 FL
Third Lanark 22/23
Bathgate

ANDERSON William
b. c1869 d. ?.1.1919
Sheffield W
Leith A 91/92 22 1
92/93 14
93/94 11

ANDERSON William
Motherwell 04/05 24 1
05/06 4

ANDERSON William
Cambuslang Hibs
Port Glasgow A 05/06 17 1

ANDERSON William
Benvie
St Mirren 07/08 2

ANDERSON William
University College, Dundee
Montrose
Dundee 14/15 1

ANDERSON William
Ashfield
Airdrieonians 16/17 5
Albion R 17/18
Airdrieonians 18/19 8
Albion R
Armadale
Peebles R 22/23

ANDERSON William
Motherwell 18/19 29
19/20 8

ANDERSON William
Denny Hibs
Morton 29/30 6 1
30/31 30 2
31/32 11 2
Falkirk 32/33 23 5
33/34 23 6
Albion R 34/35 31 4
35/36 28
36/37 22

ANDERSON William
Annan A
Queen of the South 30/31 D2
31/32 D2
32/33 D2
33/34 31 3
34/35 37 3
35/36 27 3
36/37 14 4

ANDERSON William George
Falkirk 36/37 7 1
37/38 17 8
38/39 17 7

ANDREW David
Galston
Ayr U 37/38 3

ANDREWS
Dumbarton 93/94 10

ANDREWS Alexander
Kirkintilloch Rob Roy
Clyde 06/07 10 4
07/08 16

ANDREWS N
Queen's Park 10/11 3 1

ANTHONY Thomas
St Ninians Thistle
Wemyss A
Airdrieonians 11/12 17

ARCHER
Abercorn 92/93 1

ARCHIBALD Alexander 8 caps
b. Aberdour 6.8.1897 d. Dalgety 29.11.1946
Dunfermline A
Raith R 15/16 4
16/17 31 4
Rangers 17/18 34 8
18/19 15 3
19/20 38 11
20/21 38 14
21/22 40 9
22/23 34 4
23/24 34 4
24/25 38 10
25/26 18 2
26/27 28 6
27/28 38 16
28/29 32 12
29/30 34 12
30/31 28 6
31/32 21 3
32/33 28 4
33/34 15 2

ARCHIBALD C
Camelon
Falkirk 31/32 6

ARCHIBALD David Kerr
b. Glasgow 20.9.1902
Parkhead
Morton 26/27 33 1
27/28
New York Nationals 28/29 4 ASL
Clyde T 29/30
York C 29/30 17 FL
30/31 9 FL
31/32 30 FL
32/33 29 FL
Shelbourne 33/34 LI

ARCHIBALD George
Edinburgh Myrtle
Third Lanark 03/04 1
04/05 2

ARCHIBALD James Mitchell
b. Falkirk 18.9.1892 d. Waltham Forest 25.1.1975
Cambuslang R
Bellshill A
Motherwell 14/15 13 8
15/16 27 9
16/17 5 1
17/18 7 1
18/19
Tottenham H 19/20 13 FL
20/21 6 1 FL
21/22 5 FL
Aberdare A 22/23 30 2 FL
Clapton Orient 23/24 36 FL
24/25 6 FL
25/26 7 1 FL
26/27 FL
Southend U 27/28 FL
Margate 27/28
28/29
Tunbridge Wells R 29/30
Ashford T

ARCHIBALD Robert Fleming
b. Larkhall 6.11.1894 d. Cambuslang 27.11.1966
Rutherglen Glencairn
Albion R 12/13 D2
Hibernian L 12/13 1 1
Third Lanark 13/14 2
Aberdeen 14/15 31 3
15/16 38 7
Rangers L 16/17 12 3
Ayr U L 17/18 1 ?
Albion R 18/19
Dumbarton 18/19 4 ?
Aberdeen 19/20 40 6
Raith R 20/21 42 2
21/22 42 5
22/23 31 1
23/24 31 2
Third Lanark 24/25 38 2
Stoke C 25/26 42 10 FL
26/27 37 6 FL
27/28 41 6 FL
28/29 41 7 FL
29/30 40 4 FL
30/31 40 3 FL
31/32 21 1 FL
Barnsley 32/33 7 1 FL

ARMORY Wilfred
b. Hunwick 23.1.1911 d. Folkestone 21.12.1996

New Brancepath					
Norwich C					
Spennymoor U					
Ayr U		30/31	9	2	
		31/32	17	2	
Aldershot		32/33	3		FL
Spennymoor U		32/33			
Nuneaton T		33/34			
		34/35			
Folkestone					

ARMOUR Andrew
b. Irvine 24.7.1883 d. Kilmarnock 4.3.1955

Irvine Meadow					
Queen's Park		05/06	22	2	
		06/07	26	11	
		07/08	3		
Kilmarnock		07/08	17	4	
		08/09	30	4	
		09/10	24	4	
Queen's Park		09/10	5	2	
Kilmarnock		10/11	29		
		11/12	13	1	
Huddersfield T		11/12	19	2	FL
		12/13	36	2	FL
		13/14			FL
Clydebank	L	13/14	38	4	
Kilmarnock		14/15	27	5	
		15/16	14	2	

ARMOUR Daniel
b. Johnstone

Johnstone					
Kilmarnock		08/09	34		
		09/10	10		
Ayr U		11/12			D2
St Johnstone		12/13			D2
Kilmarnock					
Johnstone					

ARMOUR J

Queen's Park		05/06	1		

ARMSTRONG Francis

Saltcoats V					
Pollokshaws					
Kilmarnock		14/15	2		
		15/16	26	4	
		16/17	12	5	
Clyde		17/18	4	?	
Clydebank		18/19	2	?	

ARMSTRONG James

Queen's Park		12/13	2		

ARMSTRONG James L

Partick T		14/15	1		

ARMSTRONG James Rae
d. Rouen 10.10.1915

Kilmarnock		12/13	2	2	
St Mirren		13/14	2		
Girvan A					

ARMSTRONG John

Cambuslang R					
Motherwell		05/06	10		

ARMSTRONG John

Grimsby T					
Hibernian		16/17	4	1	

ARMSTRONG Matthew 3 caps
b. Newton Stewart 12.11.1911

Port Glasgow Jnrs					
Celtic					
Aberdeen		31/32	9	2	
		32/33	7	3	
		33/34	12	14	
		34/35	36	31	
		35/36	30	30	
		36/37	36	24	
		37/38	34	19	
		38/39	27	13	
Queen of the South		46/47	27	13	
Elgin C		47/48	?	52	HL
		48/49	?	36	HL
		49/50	?	38	HL
Peterhead					

ARMSTRONG Robert

Clydebank	T				
Dennistoun Established					
Clydebank		20/21	4		

ARMSTRONG Thomas H

Thornliebank					
Arthurlie		25/26			D2
Morton		26/27	9	3	

ARMSTRONG Thomas Hart
b. Cathcart 11.5.1906

Potch Jnrs					
Airdrieonians		31/32	38	33	
		32/33	19	8	
Cowdenbeath	L	32/33	10	10	
Swindon T		33/34	31	21	FL
		34/35	33	9	FL
Crewe A		35/36	34	5	FL
		36/37	33	5	FL
Hyde U					

ARMSTRONG William

Petershill					
Third Lanark		10/11	20	1	
		11/12	17		
		12/13	30		
		13/14	21		

ARMSTRONG William H

Queens Island *					
Aberdeen		23/24	4		
		24/25	2		
Elgin C		25/26			

ARNOTT Alexander
b. Johnstone

St Mirren		22/23	11		
		23/24	11		
		24/25	8		
		25/26	1		
		26/27	21		
		27/28	8		

ARNOTT Archibald

Linthouse					
Partick T		04/05	1		
Renton		05/06			

ARNOTT James

Leicester C					
Dumbarton		15/16	1		

ARNOTT John

Stranraer					
Newcastle U					FL
Hamilton A		07/08	24	9	
Stranraer		08/09			
Dumfries		09/10			

ARNOTT John

Queen's Park		32/33	1		
Stranraer *					
Larne *		34/35			IL

ARNOTT Walter 14 caps
b. Pollokshields 12.5.1861 d. Clarkston 18.5.1931

Pollokshields A					
Ashfield					
Queen's Park					
Pollokshields A					
Queen's Park					
Kilmarnock A					
Corinthians					
Ballina					
Newcastle WE					
Linfield A		91/92			
Third Lanark		92/93	1		
Queen's Park					
St Bernards		93/94	15	1	
Celtic	L	94/95	1		
Notts Co		94/95	1		FL
Corinthians					

ARTHUR Robert B

Morton		05/06	1		

ASHE Thomas
b. c1921

Mossvale Strollers					
St Mirren		37/38			
		38/39	1		
Dumbarton		46/47			D2

ASHFORD Herbert Edwin
b. Fulham 18.2.1896 d. Worthing 5.8.1978

Southall					
Brentford		19/20	9		SL
QPR		20/21	5		FL
		21/22	5		FL
Notts Co		22/23			FL
Ayr U	T	23/24	2		
Dartford		23/24			
		24/25			
		25/26			
		26/27			
Guildford C		27/28			
		28/29			
Tunbridge Wells R					

ASKEW Hubert Frank
b. Rugby 23.7.1908 d. Coventry ?.10.1988

Lord St Jnrs					
Warwick T					
Coventry C		26/27	1		FL
		27/28	6		FL
Morton		28/29			
		29/30	1		
Hinckley U		29/30			
Birmingham		30/31			
Warwick T		30/31			
		31/32			
Coventry Strollers					

ATHERTON Robert William
b. Bethesda 29.7.1876 K.I.A., English Channel

Dalry Primrose					
Heart of Midlothian		97/98			
Hibernian		97/98	5		
		98/99	12	5	
		99/00	13	7	
		00/01	16	5	
		01/02	7	3	
		02/03	22	5	
Middlesbrough		03/04	32	8	FL
		04/05	27	4	FL
Chelsea					

ATHERTON Thomas Henry
b. West Derby 1879 d. 1950s

Dunfermline Jnrs					
Dundee					
Hibernian					
Tottenham H		98/99	2		SL
St Bernards		99/00			
Raith R		99/00			
Partick T		00/01	18	4	
Dundee		01/02	8	2	
Grimsby T		02/03	2		FL
Brentford		03/04	22	2	SL
Motherwell		04/05	12		

ATKINSON John
b. Cambuslang 5.12.1884 d. At sea, W Africa 26.11.1914

Scottish Amateurs					
Hamilton A					
Queen's Park		04/05	4	1	
Hamilton A		05/06	?	?	D2
		06/07	24	4	
		07/08	32	9	
		08/09	3		
Celtic	L	08/09	1	2	
Hamilton A		09/10	21	4	
Partick T	L	09/10	4	1	
Hamilton A					

ATKINSON John

Motherwell		09/10	10	3	

AUCHINCLOSS James
b. Barrhead c1883

Arthurlie					
Partick T		96/97	17		D2
		97/98	18	1	
		98/99	17		
St Mirren		99/00	7		

AUCHINCLOSS John Buchanan
b. Barrhead 1910

Beith					
East Stirlingshire		32/33	15		

AXFORD David (David John or David Hepburn)
b. Arbroath 1882

Arbroath					
Heart of Midlothian		02/03			
		03/04	14	10	
Portsmouth		04/05	4		SL
USA					
Heart of Midlothian		06/07	9	1	
Raith R		07/08			D2
		08/09			D2
Arbroath		09/10			

BAGAN John Francis
b. Rutherglen 25.10.1897 d. Rutherglen 20.9.1925
Mosshill U
Rutherglen Glencairn
Kilmarnock 19/20 32
20/21 11
Beith

BAIGRIE Hugh Wallace
b. Nigg 1912
Aberdeen Woodside
Partick T 33/34 1
34/35 22
35/36 2
Ayr U L 35/36 16
Partick T 36/37 14
37/38 6
Ayr U 37/38 1

BAILEY Wilfred W
b. Leiston
Ipswich T 21/22
Kilmarnock 21/22 2 1
Chesterfield 22/23 3 FL
Stockport Co

BAILLIE James
b. Hamilton 18.2.1900 d. Maryhill 23.3.1966
Motherwell Boys Brigade
Wishaw Thistle
Cardiff C 26/27 4 FL
27/28 1 FL
New York Giants 28/29 ASL
29/30 ASL
Derry C 29/30 IL
Fulham 30/31 2 FL
Dundee U T 31/32 5
Falkirk T 31/32
Preston N E T 31/32
Lille 32/33

BAILLIE Joseph
b. c1898
Lochore
Crosshill U
Hibernian 20/21 3
21/22
East Stirlingshire 22/23 D2

BAILLIE Thomas

Bathgate R
Heart of Midlothian 92/93 3

BAILLIE Victor M

Port Glasgow A 09/10 5
Kings Park 10/11

BAIN Alexander

Buckie Thistle
Raith R 27/28 1

BAIN David
b. Leslie 1882 d. Lochgelly 8.1.1930
Lochgelly U 00/01
01/02
Heart of Midlothian 02/03 5
Lochgelly U 03/04
Cowdenbeath 03/04 D2
Lochgelly U 04/05
Heart of Midlothian 05/06 18
Lochgelly U 06/07

BAIN George

Lochgelly Albert
Dundee U 30/31 10 2 D2
31/32 9 1
Brechin C

BAIN J

Vale of Leven 91/92 4

BAIN James

Fraserburgh
Raith R 27/28
28/29 1

BAIN John

Peebles R
Hamilton A 13/14 26 10
Armadale 14/15
Royal Albert

BAIN John
b. Lochgelly (?)
Inverkeithing Jnrs
Dunfermline A 26/27 22 1
Dundee U 27/28 38 3 D2
28/29 36 4 D2
29/30 11
St Johnstone 30/31 25 1 D2
Raith R
Lochgelly Amateurs

BAIN Peter
b. Portsoy c1909 d. Portsoy 25.10.2001
Buckie Thistle
Elgin C
Aberdeen University
Raith R
Keith
Partick T 33/34 16 7
34/35 30 6
35/36 19 2
Dundee U 36/37 10 3 D2
Raith R T 36/37
Elgin C
Buckie T

BAIN Robert B

Queen's Park 09/10 3 1

BAIN Robert B

Falkirk 10/11 5 1
11/12 1
12/13 1

BAINBRIDGE Simpson
b. Silksworth 3.4.1895 d. Sunderland 12.11.1988
Seaton Delaval
Leeds C 12/13 24 4 FL
13/14 15 4 FL
14/15 18 4 FL
19/20 7 3 FL
Preston NE 19/20 14 1 FL
South Shields 20/21 13 3 FL
Aberdeen 21/22 22 1
Wheatley Hill Alliance
Shildon
Hylton Colliery

BAIRD

Vale of Leven 90/91 1

BAIRD

St Mirren 91/92 1

BAIRD

Leith A 92/93 1

BAIRD

Renton 92/93 2

BAIRD Alexander

Parkhead
St Bernards 01/02 D2
02/03 D2
Port Glasgow A 02/03 3
03/04 15
04/05 13
Beith 05/06

BAIRD David 3 caps
b. Dalry c1868 d. Loanhead 19.3.1946
Dalry Primrose
Heart of Midlothian 88/89
89/90
90/91 8 2
91/92 20 12
92/93 13 2
Nottingham F
Heart of Midlothian 93/94 16 5
94/95 5 2
95/96 14 15
96/97 15 3
97/98 6 1
98/99 1 1
99/00 9 2
00/01 14 1
01/02 8
02/03 11
Motherwell 03/04 1

BAIRD George

Clydebank Jnrs
Rangers 14/15 1
Renton 15/16
Dumbarton 16/17 14
Clydebank 17/18 1
Forth R

BAIRD Henry

Heart of Midlothian 09/10 2

BAIRD John

Kilwinning R
St Mirren 11/12 14 5
12/13 1

BAIRD R H

Heart of Midlothian 00/01 1

BAIRD Thomas Skinner
b. Lugar 7.6.1911
Cumnock Townhead
Lugar Boswell
St Mirren 30/31 3
31/32 32
32/33 7
33/34 11
34/35 25
35/36 D2
36/37 15
Rochdale 37/38 42 FL
38/39 37 FL

BAIRD Walter Young
b. Gourock 3.1.1913 d. 1958
Lesmahagow
Partick T 32/33
Larkhall Thistle
Sheffield W 34/35 1 FL
Hamilton A 35/36 2
Morton 36/37 D2
37/38 23 3
Doncaster R 38/39

BAIRD William Urquhart 1 cap
b. Leith 1.10.1874
The Wilfred
Alva
Dundee
St Bernards 93/94 15
94/95 14 1
95/96 7
96/97 16 2
97/98 16 1
98/99 5
Rangers 98/99
St Bernards 98/99
Dundee 99/00 17
00/01 18

BAKER

Cowlairs 90/91 1

BAKER Jack Francis
b. c1891
Newcastle district
Heart of Midlothian 08/09 1 2
Bradford C

BAKER Joseph

Partick T 98/99 3 1

BALDIE James

Raith R 19/20 6 4
Clackmannan 20/21

BALFOUR David

Brechin C
Dundee 12/13 8
13/14 16
14/15 14
15/16 18

BALFOUR David

Dundee 30/31 6 6
31/32 24 21
32/33 12 10
Cowdenbeath 33/34 2

BALFOUR J A

Queen's Park 08/09 3

BALFOUR James C

Dundee
Third Lanark 33/34 3

BALLANTYNE

Third Lanark 07/08 1

BALLANTYNE

Ayr U 18/19 3 ?

BALLANTYNE Charles
b. Dumbarton c1914
Kilpatrick Jnrs
Dumbarton 31/32
32/33
33/34
34/35
Clyde 35/36 27 13
36/37 11

BALLANTYNE Hugh

Bellshill
Clyde 18/19 5
19/20 3
Arthurlie 20/21
21/22
22/23

BALLANTYNE John
b. Riccarton 30.6.1892 K.I.A. ?
Kenmuirhill A
Kilmarnock 11/12 6 1
Vale of Leven 12/13 D2
Birmingham 12/13 1 FL
13/14 19 3 FL
Vale of Leven 14/15 D2
Rangers 15/16 1
Vale of Leven 15/16
Dumfries

BALLANTYNE John
b. Maryhill 27.10.1899
Glasgow Ashfield
Partick T 21/22 12 2
22/23 34 5
23/24 26 6
Boston Wonder Workers 24/25 40 12 ASL
25/26 35 10 ASL
26/27 39 16 ASL
27/28 32 12 ASL
Partick T 28/29 33 11
29/30 32 12
30/31 32 8
31/32 33 2
32/33 25 7
33/34 28 10
34/35 16 2
Falkirk L 34/35 4
QPR 35/36 15 3 FL
36/37 10 FL

BALLANTYNE John W

Bellshill A
Motherwell 07/08 1
Albion R

BALLANTYNE Robert
b. Scotland
Glasgow Ashfield
Boston Wonder Workers 25/26 36 ASL
26/27 41 2 ASL
27/28 50 ASL
28/29 49 2 ASL
29A 17 ASL
29/30 4 ASL
Fall River Marksmen 29/30 21 1 ASL
30A 26 1 ASL
New York Yankees 31S 14 1 ASL
31A 10 2 ASL
Aberdeen 31/32 11
St Johnstone 32/33 23 3

BALLANTYNE Thomas

Armadale
Partick T 07/08 18 3
08/09 30 5
09/10 18 1
10/11
Dunfermline A 11/12
Armadale 12/13

BALLANTYNE William
b. Glasgow
Shettleston
Clyde 22/23 8 2
23/24 30 7
24/25 30 5
Boston Wonder Workers 24/25 35 2 ASL
Clyde 25/26 D2
26/27
New Bedford Whalers 27/28 51 15 ASL
28/29 22 8 ASL
New York Giants 29/30 30 11 ASL
Brooklyn Wanderers 30A 19 5 ASL
31S 16 2 ASL
New York Americans
Kearny Scots-Americans

BALLANTYNE William
b. Glasgow
Rothesay Royal V
Morton 28/29
29/30 21 3

BALLOCH James
b. Glencraig c1896
Heart of Midlothian
Armadale
Hamilton A 20/21 25 6
Clackmannan 21/22
22/23
Dundee Hibs 22/23
Clackmannan

BANKS George
b. Dreghorn
Stewarton Thistle
Motherwell 25/26 3 1
26/27 2

BANKS Herbert Ernest
b. Coventry 1874 d. Smethwick 1947
72nd Seaforth Highlanders
Everton 96/97 2 FL
St Mirren L 96/97
Third Lanark 97/98 15 3
98/99 13
Millwall 98/99 2 SL
99/00 24 11 SL
00/01
Aston Villa 01/02 5 FL
Bristol C 02/03 20 10 FL
02/03 20 8 FL
Watford 03/04 19 21 SL
Coventry C 04/05 18 12 BDL
Stafford R 05/06
Veritys A

BANKS Samuel G

Glasgow Tramways
Strathclyde
Morton 31/32 11 1

BANKS William
b. Riccarton 2.11.1880
Glenbuck A
Rugby XI
Kilmarnock 03/04 21 4
04/05 25 3
05/06 14 3
Manchester C 05/06 21 1 FL
06/07 4 FL
Atherton Combe
Hurlford 08/09
Portsmouth 08/09 6 SL
Alberta
Manchester C
Kilmarnock 11/12
Nithsdale W

BANNISTER Ernest

Buxton
Manchester C 07/08 1 FL
Preston NE
Darlington
Heart of Midlothian 12/13 23
Ayr U 13/14 6

BARBER Thomas
b. West Stanley 22.7.1886 d. Nuneaton 21.9.1925
Shankhouse
West Stanley
Bolton W 08/09 20 2 FL
09/10 15 1 FL
10/11 17 5 FL
11/12 38 4 FL
12/13 12 2 FL
Aston Villa 12/13 15 2 FL
13/14 28 4 FL
14/15 14 3 FL
Belfast Celtic L 18/19 IL
Celtic L 18/19 5
Partick T L 18/19 1 1
Linfield L 18/19 IL
Distillery L 18/19 IL
Stalybridge C
Crystal Palace 19/20 19 7 SL
Merthyr T 20/21 2 FL
Ton Pentre
Walsall 21/22 5 2 FL
Darlaston
Hinckley U
Barwell

BARBOUR

Renton 93/94 2

BARBOUR J R

Third Lanark 93/94 9

BARBOUR James

Clyde 15/16 16 3
? 16/17
17/18
18/19
Linfield 19/20 IL
Distillery 19/20 IL

BARBOUR John R
K.I.A. ?.7.1916
Glasgow Perthshire
Queen's Park 10/11 10 2
11/12 20 4
12/13 3
Dundee 13/14 17 2
Preston NE 14/15 12 2 FL

BARBOUR Robert

Third Lanark 94/95 16 3
95/96 15 1
96/97 16
97/98 1

BARCLAY Alex S

Aberdeen 13/14 2

BARCLAY Hugh

Thornliebank
Third Lanark 03/04 1

BARCLAY John

St Bernards 98/99 3
99/00 7
00/01 1 D2

BARCLAY John Birrell
b. Thornton 22.1.1904 d. Slough 1978
Wellesley Jnrs
Dundee 24/25 2
Forfar A L 24/25 D2
Dundee 25/26 9 3
Reading 26/27 3 FL
Accrington S 27/28 37 6 FL
28/29 39 5 FL
Yeovil T
Guildford C
Armadale
Albion R 32/33 D2
33/34 D2
34/35 23 5
Boston U 35/36

BARCLAY Thomas

Stewarton Thistle
St Mirren 20/21 5 1
21/22
22/23 4
23/24 18
24/25 17 1
25/26 10 1
26/27 14
27/28 4 1

BARCLAY Thomas

Falkirk 28/29 3

BARKER John Bell 2 caps

b. Govan 28.6.1869
Linthouse
Rangers 91/92 8 5
92/93 11 3
93/94 13 7
94/95 15 9
95/96 12 6

BARNES Hugh

Clyde 94/95 2 1
Airdrieonians *

BARNES James

Heart of Midlothian 17/18 16 3
Broxburn U
Dalkeith Thistle

BARR

Dumbarton 91/92 10
92/93 2
93/94 3

BARR John

St Mirren 04/05 1

BARR John

Lanemark
Partick T 06/07 3

BARR John Millar

b. Bridge of Weir 9.9.1917
Strathclyde
Third Lanark 37/38 9
38/39 18
QPR 46/47 4 FL
Dundee U 47/48

BARR Matthew

Clyde 14/15 11
15/16 1

BARR Matthew

Kilbarchan A
Clyde 13/14
14/15 4 1

These are separate players

BARR Matthew

(one of the above!)
Clyde 18/19 1 ?
19/20 4

BARR R

Cowdenbeath 26/27 1

BARR Robert

b. Kilmarnock 1865
Hurlford
Stoke 88/89 2 FL
89/90
Abercorn 90/91
91/92
92/93 8 3
93/94 16 ? D2
Preston NE 94/95 28 10 FL
95/96 1 FL
Bury 95/96 15 2 FL

BARR Robert

Abercorn 96/97 1

BARR Robert

b. 1874
Black Watch
Third Lanark 97/98 16 1
98/99 14
99/00 14
00/01 20
01/02 3
02/03 21
03/04 24
04/05 24
05/06 28
06/07 24
07/08 19
08/09 16
09/10 16
Abercorn 10/11 6 D2

BARR Robert

Irvine Meadow
St Mirren 20/21 19

BARR Robert R

Queen's Park 25/26 22 15
Hibernian 25/26 1

BARR William

Ayr U 16/17 5
17/18 1 ?

BARRETT Francis 2 caps

b. Dundee 2.8.1872 d. Dundee ?.8.1907
Dundee Harp
Dundee 93/94 6
94/95 18
95/96 17
Newton Heath 96/97 23 FL
97/98 28 FL
98/99 34 FL
99/00 34 FL
New Brighton Tower 00/01 34 FL
Arbroath
Manchester C 01/02 5 FL
Dundee W
Aberdeen 04/05 1 D2

BARRETT Peter

b. Edinburgh 27.6.1909
Edinburgh Emmet
East Fife 22/23 37 10 D2
23/24 35 6 D2
24/25 35 9 D2
25/26 37 10 D2
26/27 32 11 D2
Newport Co 27/28 18 4 FL
Dundee 28/29 15
East Fife 29/30 15 3 D2
Arbroath T 30/31 1 D2

BARRIE Alexander W

b. Parkhead c1881 d. WW1
Parkhead
St Bernards 01/02
Sunderland 02/03 3 FL
03/04 15 FL
04/05 13 FL
05/06 23 FL
06/07 10 FL
Rangers 07/08 11 1
Kilmarnock 08/09 31 1
09/10 31 2
10/11 32 3
11/12 27
Abercorn 12/13 D2

BARRIE James

b. Old Kilpatrick 20.10.1902
Duntochter Hibs
Kirkintilloch Rob Roy
Duntochter Hibs
Dumbarton T
Queen's Park 23/24 1
24/25 10
25/26 19
Clydebank 26/27 D2
Boston Wonder Workers 27/28 1 ASL
Bethlehem Steel 27/28 1 ASL
28/29 4 ASL
New Bedford Whalers 28/29 19 ASL
Boston Wonder Workers 28/29 1 ASL
New Bedford Whalers 29A 9 ASL
Fall River Marksmen 29A 8 ASL
Providence Gold Bugs 29/30 4 ASL
Celtic T 29/30 1
Halifax T 30/31 38 FL
31/32 17 FL
32/33 35 FL
Worcester C 33/34
Cowdenbeath T 33/34 2

BARRIE William S

Arthurlie
Clydebank 23/24 10
Cowdenbeath 24/25
25/26
Bathgate 25/26
Bethlehem Steel 26/27 29 ASL
27/28 9 ASL
28/29 4 ASL
New Bedford Whalers 28/29 20 1 ASL
29A 4 ASL
29/30 28 2 ASL
30/31
Derry C 31/32 IL
32/33 IL
Glenavon 33/34 IL
Dumbarton 34/35 D2

BARRINGTON James

b. Lower Ince 15.12.1901 d. Basford 1968
Wigan U
Bradford C 20/21 1 FL
21/22 1 FL
Hamilton A 22/23 23
23/24
24/25
Wigan B 25/26 37 FL
26/27 34 1 FL
Winsford U L 26/27
Wigan B 27/28 FL
28/29 FL
Nottingham F 29/30 36 FL
30/31 42 FL
31/32 30 FL
32/33 10 FL
33/34 24 1 FL
34/35 36 FL
35/36 32 FL
36/37 1 FL
Ollerton Colliery

BARRON John

Orion
Dundee 01/02 3 1
Orion
Aberdeen

BARRY

Ayr U 17/18 5 ?

BARRY

Clyde 17/18 1 ?

BARRY John George

Queen's Park 15/16 21 1
16/17 33
Third Lanark 17/18 9 ?

BARTON George McIntosh

b. Newtongrange 15.10.1899
d. Weston Super Mare c 8.1970
Newbattle
Midlothian U
Newtongrange Star
Raith R 21/22 8
22/23 25
23/24 18
24/25 35 1
25/26 4
26/27 D2
27/28 29
Bristol R 28/29 25 5 FL
29/30 27 1 FL
30/31 16 FL
Bedminster Down Sports

BARTON Robert C

b. Glasgow
Royal Albert
Queen's Park
Royal Albert
Kilmarnock 06/07 18
07/08 22 3
08/09 5 2
Royal Albert
Ayr Parkhouse
Galston
Kilmarnock 10/11

BARTON Robert C

Heart of Midlothian 08/09 1

BARTRAM James Leslie

b. South Shields 8.3.1911 d. Bristol ?.7.1987
Boldon CW
Portsmouth 30/31
31/32
North Shields 32/33
Falkirk 32/33 15 17
33/34 24 24
34/35 29 20
Northampton T 35/36 12 3 FL
Queen of the South 35/36 14 7
North Shields
South Shields

BATCHELOR Thomas
b. Newburgh
Newburgh WE
Raith R 26/27 D2
27/28 33
28/29 25 2
29/30 D2
30/31 D2
31/32 D2
Falkirk 32/33 36 3
33/34 34 6
34/35 38 2
35/36 D2
36/37 20 1

BATES William
b. West Bromwich (?)
Royal Worcester Regt
Dumbarton 18/19 1 ?

BATTLES Bernard 3 caps
b. Springburn 13.1.1875 d. Glasgow 9.2.1905
Linlithgow Jnrs
Bathgate R
Broxburn Shamrock
Bathgate
Heart of Midlothian 94/95 16
Celtic 95/96 16 2
Liverpool L 95/96 3 FL
Celtic 96/97 12 1
Dundee 97/98 15 1
Liverpool 97/98 1 FL
Celtic 98/99 8 2
99/00 14
00/01 15 1
01/02 13 1
02/03 10
03/04 22
Kilmarnock 04/05 23

BATTLES Bernard Joseph 1 cap
b. Musselburgh 12.10.1905 d. ?.10.1979
Boston Celtics
Boston Wonder Workers 24/25 18 7 ASL
25/26 20 12 ASL
26/27 34 7 ASL
27/28 43 15 ASL
Edinburgh Emmet
Heart of Midlothian 28/29 28 30
29/30 29 25
30/31 34 44
31/32 26 17
32/33 4 3
33/34 22 13
34/35
35/36 5 3

BAUCHOP James Rae
b. Sauchie 22.5.1886 d. Bradford 13.6.1968
Sauchie
Alloa A 03/04
04/05
Celtic 05/06 4 2
06/07 8 3
Norwich C 07/08 22 11 SL
Crystal Palace 07/08 7 6 SL
08/09 35 16 SL
Derby Co 09/10 38 21 FL
10/11 33 19 FL
11/12 31 16 FL
12/13 24 12 FL
Tottenham H 13/14 10 6 FL
Bradford PA 13/14 21 11 FL
14/15 35 26 FL
Celtic L 17/18 1
Bradford PA 19/20 42 11 FL
20/21 35 4 FL
21/22 24 14 FL
Doncaster R 22/23
Lincoln C 23/24 28 11 FL

BAUCHOP William Fotheringham
b. Alloa 18.1.1882 d. USA 1948
Abercorn 00/01 16 ? D2
East Stirlingshire 01/02 D2
Alloa A 01/02
02/03
03/04
04/05
Plymouth A 05/06 3 SL
Heart of Midlothian 06/07 13 3
Carlisle U 07/08
08/09
Stockport Co 09/10 11 2 FL
10/11 29 4 FL
Leicester F 11/12 18 1 FL
Norwich C 12/13 32 1 SL
Fulham 13/14
Grimsby T
Alloa A

BAULD Robert
b. Cowdenbeath 14.3.1902
Glencraig Celtic
Tottenham H T
Cowdenbeath T
Raith R 20/21 16 4
21/22 39 10
22/23 14 2
Dundee U 23/24 26 6 D2
24/25 37 10 D2
25/26 37 3
26/27 34 8
Bradford C 27/28 24 7 FL
28/29 22 8 FL
29/30 28 3 FL
30/31 33 FL
31/32 39 4 FL
32/33 39 6 FL
33/34 27 4 FL
34/35 5 2 FL
Chesterfield 35/36 2 FL

BAXENDALE Frank
b. Leyland 28.12.1913 d. Preston 30.12.1990
Dick Kerrs
Preston NE
Leyland Motors
Blackburn R 35/36 3 FL
36/37 9 3 FL
Falkirk 37/38 7 2
38/39 3
Carlisle U

BAXTER
Leith A 93/94 2

BAXTER Arthur George
b. Dundee 28.12.1911 d. K.I.A,Gradara 5.9.1944
Dundee EE
Portsmouth
Falkirk 34/35 28 9
Dundee 35/36 8 4
36/37 38 12
37/38 36 23
38/39 14 4
Barnsley 38/39 6 2 FL

BAXTER David S S
Bowhill R
St Johnstone 33/34 1
34/35 9
35/36 10
Raith R 36/37 D2
37/38 30 2 D2
38/39 16

BAXTER Davis
Clyde 96/97 6 2

BAXTER John
Dundee 16/17 10

BAXTER Thomas
b. Dunfermline
St Andrews U
Hamilton A 28/29 9
29/30 1

BAXTER William
Motherwell
Ayr U 13/14 8

BEATH John R
Raith R 27/28 18 5
28/29 16 2
29/30 D2
30/31 D2
31/32 D2
32/33 D2
Albion R 33/34 D2
34/35 7 1
Leith A L 34/35 D2

BEATH Robert
Albion R 32/33 D2
33/34 D2
34/35 37 1
35/36 38
36/37 25
37/38 D2
38/39 33 2
46/47 D2
47/48 D2

BEATH Robert H
Kilsyth R
Falkirk 31/32 9 1

BEATON Harry
Royal Albert
Clyde 33/34 7
34/35 34 1
35/36 35 1
36/37 31 3
37/38 35 7
38/39 24 6

BEATTIE
Renton 92/93 1

BEATTIE James Falconer
b. Montrose 15.5.1916 d. Brechin 1965
Forfar Academy
Forfar WE
Forfar V
St Johnstone 32/33 1
33/34
34/35 10 8
35/36 23 14
36/37 18 11
Portsmouth 36/37 5 1 FL
37/38 36 21 FL
38/39 16 5 FL
Millwall 39/40 3 FL

BEATTIE John
Vale of Clyde
Clyde 17/18 12 ?
18/19 31 ?
? 19/20
20/21
21/22
22/23
23/24
Armadale 24/25 D2

BEATTIE John Murdoch
b. Newhills 28.5.1912 d. Wolverhampton 15.1.1992
St Machars
Hall Russells
Aberdeen 31/32 17 2
32/33 38 9
33/34 5 1
Wolverhampton W 33/34 26 7 FL
34/35 18 6 FL
Blackburn R 34/35 23 6 FL
35/36 33 5 FL
36/37 20 6 FL
Birmingham 36/37 17 6 FL
37/38 19 4 FL
Huddersfield T 37/38 3 FL
Grimsby T 37/38 14 2 FL
38/39 42 11 FL
39/40 3 FL
Walsall

BEATTIE Robert 1 cap
b. Stevenston 24.1.1916 d. Irvine 21.9.2002
Ardeer Mission
Kilwinning R
Kilmarnock 32/33 2
33/34 2
34/35 32 16
35/36 38 19
36/37 37 8
37/38 9
Preston NE 37/38 31 9 FL
38/39 42 8 FL
39/40 3 FL
46/47 37 6 FL
47/48 30 5 FL
48/49 37 9 FL
49/50 14 5 FL
50/51 27 4 FL
51/52 3 6 FL
52/53 12 2 FL
53/54 1 FL
54/55 FL
Wigan A 55/56 19 5 LC

BECCI Attilio
b. Borgotoro
Woodside
Arbroath 31/32 1 D2
Woodside 32/33
Arbroath 33/34 20 1 D2
34/35 30 1 D2
35/36 38
36/37 38
37/38 38
38/39 35
Forres Mechanics

BEEDIE William

Clyde 16/17 1

BEGBIE Isaac 4 caps
b. Gorgie 4.6.1868 d. Edinburgh 30.9.1958
Pentland Star
Western
Dalry Albert
Heart of Midlothian 88/89
89/90
90/91 8 1
91/92 22
St Bernards 92/93
Heart of Midlothian 92/93 16
93/94 14 1
94/95 9
95/96 16 1
96/97 13 1
97/98 14
98/99 16
99/00 14
Leith A 00/01
Bathgate 01/02
02/03

BELL

Vale of Leven 90/91 1

BELL

St Mirren 91/92 1

BELL

St Mirren 93/94 12 4

BELL

Dumbarton 95/96 12 6
96/97 1 ? D2

BELL Adam
b. Barrhead
Croy Celtic
Hibernian 11/12 5 2
12/13 7 2
Albion R 13/14 D2
Vale of Leven 14/15 D2
Abercorn 15/16

BELL Alan

Dundee 02/03 21 6
03/04 21 3
04/05 24 3
05/06 22 3
Heart of Midlothian 06/07 1

BELL David

Third Lanark 94/95 14 6
95/96 4 1
St Bernards 96/97 4

BELL Duncan
b. Hamilton
St Anthonys
Motherwell 20/21 4
Hamilton A 21/22 11
Dunfermline A 22/23 D2
23/24 D2
Clydebank 23/24 6
24/25 D2
25/26 9
Vale of Leven 26/27
Beith 27/28

BELL Francis William Clark

Queen's Park 38/39 2

BELL James
b. Mauchline 30.3.1866
Hurlford
Mauchline
Ayr
Mauchline
Dumbarton
Celtic 90/91 15
Hurlford
Kilmarnock

BELL John

Dumbarton 87/88
88/89
89/90
90/91 18 20
91/92 19 23
92/93 11 8

BELL John
b. Dundee 25.9.1872 d. Lewisham 1926
Dundee W
Renton 92/93 15 5
93/94 9 2
Bacup B
Wolverhampton W 94/95 6 3 FL
Grimsby T 95/96 29 5 FL
96/97 20 5 FL
97/98 10 1 FL
98/99 18 2 FL
Chesterfield 99/00 33 1 FL
00/01 21 FL
Millwall A 01/02 29 6 SL
02/03 22 1 SL
Leicester F 03/04 21 FL

BELL John

Rangers 95/96 7

BELL John 10 caps
b. Dumbarton 6.10.1869
Dumbarton Union
Dumbarton 90/91 18 20
91/92 19 23
92/93 11 8
Everton 92/93 3 FL
93/94 24 9 FL
94/95 27 15 FL
95/96 27 9 FL
96/97 27 4 FL
97/98 22 4 FL
Celtic 98/99 17 13
99/00 18 6
New Brighton Tower 00/01 22 9 FL
Everton 01/02 23 5 FL
02/03 22 5 FL
Preston NE 03/04 32 12 FL
04/05 13 3 FL
05/06 30 11 FL
06/07 26 1 FL
07/08 7 2 FL

BELL John

Clyde 08/09 2 1

BELL John
b. Stranraer 1890
Shettleston
Vale of Clyde
Port Glasgow A 07/08 6
08/09
Rangers 09/10 1
Port Glasgow A 10/11 D2
Cowdenbeath 11/12 D2
12/13 D2
Ayr U 13/14 33
14/15 29 1
15/16 38
16/17 27
Clydebank 16/17
Ayr U 17/18 16 ?
Morton 17/18 1
Motherwell 18/19 21
Albion R 19/20 26
Morton 20/21 13

BELL John Barr
b. Barrow 5.4.1901 d. St Leonards 31.5.1973
Dumbarton Academy
Queen's Park 15/16 1
16/17
17/18
18/19 30 13
19/20 31 25
Chelsea 20/21 6 2 FL
21/22 24 5 FL
22/23 13 2 FL
23/24 FL
Hamilton A 24/25 10
25/26
Cowdenbeath 26/27 3
Lovells A *

BELL John Greenhorn
b. Hamilton 14.7.1909 d. Blackpool 3.8.1983
Beith
Ayr U 28/29 2
Beith 29/30
30/31
31/32
Queen of the South 32/33 D2
33/34 18 7
Preston NE 33/34 14 4 FL
34/35 7 1 FL
Queen of the South 35/36 8
Beith 36/37
Albion R 37/38 D2
38/39 31 10

BELL John James
b. Dundee 1891
Ashfield
West Ham U
Army
Heart of Midlothian 15/16 7 3
Third Lanark 16/17 5
17/18
18/19
Dundee 19/20 28 28
20/21 36 25
21/22 17 3
22/23 6 1
Albion R 22/23 9 1
Hamilton A 22/23 2
Newport Co 23/24 21 9 FL
Watford 24/25 18 6 FL
25/26 2 FL
Arbroath 26/27 6 4 D2

BELL Mark Dickson 1 cap
b. Edinburgh 8.2.1881 d. Edinburgh 22.10.1961
Rosebery Jnrs
St Bernards 98/99 3
99/00 16 1
Heart of Midlothian 99/00
St Bernards 00/01 5 D2
Heart of Midlothian 00/01 8 4
01/02 10
Southampton 02/03 10 6 SL
Heart of Midlothian 03/04 17 3
Fulham 04/05 27 4 SL
05/06 26 1 SL
06/07 6 SL
Southampton * 06/07 2 SL
Clapton Orient 07/08 36 1 FL
08/09 28 1 FL
09/10 24 FL
Leyton 10/11 32 1 SL
11/12 33 SL
Gillingham 12/13 SL

BELL Peter
b. Ferryhill 3.3.1895
Willington A
Durham C
Oldham A 19/20 2 FL
20/21 1 FL
21/22 15 2 FL
Darlington 22/23 16 4 FL
Raith R 23/24 35
24/25 37 1
25/26 36 1
Manchester C 26/27 26 4 FL
27/28 16 3 FL
Falkirk 28/29 33 3
Burton T 29/30
Darlington 30/31 11 1 FL

BELL Richard

Parkhead Jnrs
Rangers 16/17 14 1
17/18 1
Dumbarton 17/18 1
18/19 6 ?

BELL Stanley Lawrence Thomas
b. Langbank 5.5.1875 d. 1955
Langbank School
Dumbarton 92/93 13 8
93/94 18 2
Third Lanark 94/95 13 7
Sheffield W 95/96 24 8 FL
96/97 22 5 FL
Everton 97/98 23 11 FL
98/99 18 5 FL
Bolton W 99/00 32 23 FL
00/01 33 8 FL
01/02 22 8 FL
02/03 12 4 FL
Brentford 03/04 25 4 SL
04/05 16 6 SL

BELL W

Dumbarton 91/92 1

BELL William

Motherwell 05/06 2

BELL William

Rosslyn
Raith R 20/21 6
21/22 1 1
22/23 14 1

BELL William
b. Dreghorn 16.12.1905 d. 20.10.1978
Ardeer Thistle
Saltcoats V
Kilmarnock 31/32 20
32/33 9
Galston

BELLAMY James Francis
b. Bethnal Green 11.9.1881 d. Chadwell Heath 30.3.1969
Barking
Grays U 02/03
Reading 02/03 3 2 SL
Woolwich Arsenal 03/04 FL
04/05 1 FL
05/06 17 3 FL
06/07 12 1 FL
Portsmouth 07/08 16 5 SL
Norwich C 07/08 6 3 SL
Dundee 08/09 30 12
09/10 27 13
10/11 31 7
11/12 30 12
Motherwell 12/13 8 1
Burnley 12/13 17 2 FL
13/14 4 1 FL
Fulham 14/15 16 1 FL
Southend U 19/20 6 SL
Ebbw Vale
Barking T

BENNETT
Hibernian 17/18 4 ?

BENNETT Alex J
Queen's Park 07/08 2 1
Hamilton A 07/08 6

BENNETT Alexander 11 caps
b. Glasgow 20.10.1881 d. Cathcart 9.1.1940
Rutherglen Woodburn
Rutherglen Glencairn
Queen's Park T
Heart of Midlothian T
Celtic 03/04 18 13
04/05 21 10
05/06 28 14
06/07 26 5
07/08 32 7
Rangers 08/09 28 13
09/10 22 6
10/11 23 6
11/12 25 11
12/13 22 4
13/14 27 5
14/15 17 3
15/16 17 2
16/17 7 1
Scottish Rifles
Rangers
Ayr U L 17/18 3 ?
18/19 2 ?
Dumbarton 18/19 6 ?
19/20 37 7
Albion R 20/21 30 3
(matches for Ayr U played under the name Thomson)

BENNETT Colvin
Dundee Fairfield
Dundee U 30/31 24 11 D2
31/32 26 6
Montrose 32/33 D2

BENNETT G
Parkhead
Dumbarton
St Mirren 12/13 1

BENNETT George
Gala Fairydean
Heart of Midlothian 10/11 1
11/12
St Johnstone 12/13 24 1 D2

BENNETT James
Dunblane
Partick T 09/10 17
Dunblane

BENNETT James
Queen's Park 09/10 3
10/11 1

BENNETT James B
Queen's Park 13/14 2

BENNETT Patrick
Mossend Hibs
Motherwell 15/16 26 1
Albion R 16/17
Motherwell 17/18 1
18/19 6
Airdrieonians 18/19 8 1

BENNETT Reuben Mitchell
b. Partick 21.12.1913 d. Liverpool ?.12.1989
Aberdeen East End
Hull C 35/36 3 FL
Queen of the South 36/37 3
37/38
38/39
Dundee 46/47 18 D2
47/48
48/49 3
Ayr U

BENNIE John
b. Polmont 30.11.1896
Slamannan
Falkirk 19/20 1
20/21 13 1
Bo'ness 21/22 34 D2
Nelson 21/22 12 5 FL
Bo'ness 22/23 D2

BENNIE P
St Mirren 97/98 5 1
Dunipace

BENNIE Peter
b. Carluke 20.3.1896
Larkhall Thistle
Bellshill A
Royal Albert
Albion R 20/21 6 1
21/22 23 3
22/23 36 1
Burnley 23/24 36 7 FL
Bradford C 24/25 35 2 FL
25/26 21 1 FL
26/27 17 FL

BENNIE Robert Brown
b. Polmont 1873 d. Newcastle 1.10.1945
Airdrieonians
Heart of Midlothian
St Mirren 96/97 11
97/98 18
98/99 15
99/00 10
00/01 17
Newcastle U 01/02 28 FL
02/03 6 FL
03/04 1 FL
Morpeth H

BENNIE Robert Hunter Brown 1 cap
b. Slamannan 27.3.1900 d. 27.7.1972
Holytown U
Parkhead Jnrs
Third Lanark 17/18 15 ?
18/19 16 ?
19/20 29 8
20/21 11 1
Airdrieonians 20/21 16
21/22 29 3
22/23 37
23/24 36 1
24/25 37
25/26 37 3
26/27 28
27/28 32
Heart of Midlothian 28/29 36 2
29/30 27
30/31 32 2
31/32 35 1
32/33 7
Montrose T 33/34 D2
Raith R 33/34 1 D2

BENSON James R
b. Markinch c1914
Markinch Victoria R
St Johnstone 31/32 31 38 D2
32/33 12 8
Brechin C L 32/33 D2
Blackburn R 33/34 FL
34/35 1 1 FL
35/36 1 FL
East Fife 35/36 D2
Falkirk 36/37 10 5
Dunfermline A L 36/37 2
Dundee U

BENZIE William
b. c1911
Burnbank A
St Johnstone 32/33 15
33/34 2
Hamilton A 33/34 15 3
34/35
35/36
36/37
Morton 37/38 7
Kings Park 37/38 D2
Dundee U 38/39 29 15 D2

BERNARD John Robertson
b. Bo'ness 12.4.1908 d. Bo'ness 3.11.2003
Dunipace Jnrs
Kilmarnock 28/29 6
East Fife 29/30 39 D2
30/31 28
Bo'ness 31/32 D2
32/33 D2

BERNARD Robert
b. Bo'ness
Armadale
Airdrieonians 16/17 38
17/18 34
18/19 28
Partick T 19/20 32
20/21 4 1
21/22 8
East Fife 22/23 19 D2
Albion R 23/24 D2

BERRY Richard
Kinglassie Hearts
Raith R 19/20 7
20/21 9

BERTRAM
St Mirren 92/93 1

BERTRAM George Thoirs Geddes
b. Govan 1908
Govan Avondale
Petershill
Dreghorn Jnrs
Airdrieonians 27/28 6 4
28/29 14 4
29/30 28 3
30/31 34 5
31/32 36 6
32/33 6
Hamilton A 32/33 3
Birmingham T 33/34
Partick T T 33/34 1
Brechin C 33/34 D2
Queen of the South 34/35 6 1

BETHUNE John
b. Milngarvie 19.10.1888 d. Sittingbourne 23.1.1955
Milngarvie Alexander
Vale of Clyde
Glasgow Ashfield
Heart of Midlothian 11/12 3
Darlington
Barnsley 12/13 12 FL
13/14 36 FL
14/15 36 FL
Dumbarton Harp 15/16
Barnsley 19/20 16 1 FL
Fulham T
Bristol R 20/21 29 FL
Brentford 21/22 10 FL
Sittingbourne
Sittingbourne Paper Mills

BETT John
Dundee 98/99 5

BEVERIDGE Robert
b. Polmadie 24.6.1877 d. 11.10.1901
Maryhill Harp
Third Lanark 95/96 12 5
96/97 18 7
97/98 17 3
98/99 11 7
Nottingham F 99/00 26 7 FL
00/01 1 FL
Everton 00/01 4 FL

BEVERIDGE William
St Bernards 98/99 2

BEVERIDGE William
Hibernian 16/17 5 1

BEYNON John Alfred
b. Pontypridd 1909 d. Johannesburg 26.6.1937
Great Western Colliery
WBA
Halifax T 28/29 20 4 FL
Scunthorpe U 29/30
30/31
Rotherham U 30/31 13 4 FL
31/32 37 5 FL
Doncaster R 32/33 23 12 FL
Aberdeen 32/33 5 2
33/34 35 11
34/35 32 4
35/36 29 8
36/37 25 9

BICKERSTAFFE Thomas
Nithsdale Royal V
Morton 22/23 8
23/24
24/25
25/26
East Fife 26/27 D2

BIGGS Arthur Gilbert
b. Wootton 26.5.1915 d. Luton 15.1.1996
Wootton
Arsenal 33/34 FL
34/35 FL
35/36 FL
36/37 1 FL
37/38 2 FL
Heart of Midlothian 37/38 15 8
38/39 4 4
Aberdeen 38/39 23 8

BINGHAM David B
Crossgates Primrose
Cowdenbeath 33/34 13

BINKS
Cowlairs 90/91 2

BINNIE Alexander
b. Kilsyth 1905
Kilsyth Rovers
Kilsyth Rangers
Partick T 24/25 2
25/26 5
Port Vale 26/27 4 FL
Hamilton A 26/27 23
27/28 21

BINNIE John
Burnbank
Airdrieonians 03/04 4
Albion R

BIRD Walter Smith
b. Hugglescote c 8.1891 d. Ellistown 2.3.1965
Coalville Swifts
Notts Co 12/13 1 FL
13/14 1 FL
14/15 6 1 FL
Grimsby T 19/20 7 2 FL
Bristol R 20/21 21 5 FL
Dundee 21/22 35 14
22/23 12 1
23/24 8 2
Heart of Midlothian 23/24 9 6
Kilmarnock 24/25 14 2

BIRKENSHAW W
Camelon
Falkirk 32/33 6

BIRRELL James
b. Dunfermline 19.9.1916
Blairhall Colliery
Third Lanark T
Celtic 38/39 6 2
East Fife L
Dunfermline A

BIRRELL Robert
b. Crossgates 1890 d. Halbeath 1956
Kingseat A
Cowdenbeath 10/11 17 D2
11/12 D2
12/13 D2
13/14 D2
14/15 D2
15/16
16/17
17/18
Heart of Midlothian 18/19 27
19/20 26
20/21 29
21/22 31
St Mirren 22/23 2

BIRRELL Thomas A
Hibernian 06/07 1
07/08 2 1
08/09 15 1
09/10 15
10/11 19
11/12 14
12/13 3 1
13/14 5

BIRRELL William
b. Dunfermline d. ?.12.1968
Inverkeithing U
Cowdenbeath 13/14 D2
14/15 D2
15/16
16/17
17/18
18/19
19/20
20/21
21/22 D2
22/23 D2
23/24 D2
24/25 10 1
St Bernards 25/26 D2

BIRRELL William
b. Cellardyke 13.3.1897 d. Ruislip 29.11.1968
Inverkeithing U
Raith R 15/16 13 4
16/17 1
19/20 35 6
20/21 28 7
Middlesbrough 20/21 14 2 FL
21/22 35 9 FL
22/23 38 9 FL
23/24 22 2 FL
24/25 27 3 FL
25/26 42 17 FL
26/27 41 16 FL
27/28 7 1 FL
Raith R 27/28 15 4

BIRSE Charlie D Valentine
b. Dundee 1916
Broughty Ex-Servicemen
Hibernian 37/38 29
38/39 11

BISHOP
Hibernian 17/18 2 ?

BISHOP Andrew Bain
b. Largs c1861 d. Springburn ?.8.1922
Possil Blue Bel
Cowlairs 90/91 4

BISHOP William R
Falkirk 28/29 9

BISLAND
Abercorn 90/91 8
91/92 1

BISSETT George
b. Cowdenbeath 25.1.1896
Glencraig Thistle
Third Lanark 16/17 38 4
17/18 20 ?
St Mirren L 17/18 4
Manchester U 19/20 22 6 FL
20/21 12 4 FL
21/22 6 FL
Wolverhampton W 21/22 25 9 FL
22/23 16 1 FL
Pontypridd 23/24
Southend U 24/25 29 8 FL
25/26 29 6 FL
Lochgelly U 26/27
Dunfermline A 26/27

BLACK
Dumbarton 95/96 2 1

BLACK Adam
Benburb
Partick T 17/18 15
18/19 30 1
19/20 22
Lochgelly U
Bathgate
Leicester C 20/21
Royal Albert 21/22
East Stirlingshire 22/23 D2

BLACK Alexander
Dundee 95/96 1

BLACK Alexander
Dundee 98/99 1

BLACK Andrew 3 caps
b. Stirling 23.9.1917
West End Rangers
Shawfield Jnrs
Heart of Midlothian 34/35 1
35/36 29 16
36/37 34 29
37/38 38 40
38/39 34 20
Manchester C 46/47 34 13 FL
47/48 37 16 FL
48/49 35 11 FL
49/50 33 7 FL
Stockport Co 50/51 42 17 FL
51/52 27 9 FL
52/53 25 12 FL

BLACK Arthur Richard
b. Airdrie 18.2.1907
Gartsherrie Jnrs
Stenhousemuir 26/27 D2
Blantyre V
Morton 31/32 37 38
Manchester U 31/32 3 2 FL
32/33 1 FL
33/34 4 1 FL
St Mirren 34/35 8 2
35/36 D2
36/37 15 8
Morton 37/38 29 23
Queen of the South 38/39 D2
Portadown * 38/39 IL

BLACK David
Heart of Midlothian 94/95 1

BLACK George
Johnstone
Port Glasgow A 00/01 D2
01/02 D2
02/03 6
Raith R 03/04 D2

BLACK George
Port Glasgow A 06/07 17
Partick T 07/08 1

BLACK George
Troon R
Airdrieonians T
Kilmarnock T
Rangers T
Third Lanark 06/07 3

BLACK Hugh
Morton 02/03 2
03/04 12 2
Abercorn 04/05

BLACK Hugh
b. Hurlford
Hurlford
Kilmarnock 05/06 4
06/07 15
Johnstone
Carlisle U 07/08

BLACK James
Westmarch
Port Glasgow A 01/02 D2
02/03 10
Abercorn

BLACK James
b. Motherwell 4.5.1906

Carluke R					
St Johnstone		24/25	5		
		25/26	32	8	
		26/27	25	7	
		27/28	16	4	
		28/29	14	1	
Cowdenbeath		29/30	3	17	
		30/31	29	7	
Charlton A		31/32	23	3	FL
		32/33	8		FL
Burton T		33/34			
Aldershot		34/35	33	3	FL
Cheltenham T		35/36			
Cowdenbeath		35/36			D2

BLACK James McF
b. Glasgow

Yoker A					
Kilmarnock		34/35	26	7	
		35/36	2		
Dumbarton		35/36			D2
		36/37			D2

BLACK James Sneddon
b. Newtongrange c1900 d. Edinburgh 13.4.1933

Newtongrange Star					
Cowdenbeath		23/24			
		24/25	3		
		25/26			
Springfield Babes		26/27	27		ASL
Providence Clamdiggers		26/27	15		ASL
Aberdeen		27/28	29	1	
		28/29	38		
		29/30	37	1	
		30/31	35	1	
		31/32	16	1	
Newtongrange Star					

BLACK John
b. Glasgow

Govanhill Avondale					
Benburb					
Celtic		11/12	4		
Thornliebank	L				
Abercorn	L				
Belfast Celtic		12/13			
		13/14			
Clyde		14/15	27	1	
		15/16	22	8	
Wishaw T	L				
Abercorn	L				
Clydebank	L				
St Mirren	L	17/18	1		
Abercorn	L	17/18			
		18/19			
Dumbarton Harp		18/19			
Dumbarton		19/20	15	1	
Albion R		19/20	10		
Abertillery T					
Bathgate					
Dumbarton Harp		23/24			

BLACK John A S P

Glasgow Perthshire					
Third Lanark		34/35			
		35/36	4		
		36/37			
		37/38	23		
		38/39	34	1	

BLACK Robert

Glasgow Perthshire					
Third Lanark		15/16	23		
Abercorn		15/16			

BLACK William
b. Flemington 16.5.1878

Enfield Star					
Dalziel R					
Queen's Park		03/04	11		
Celtic		04/05	10		
Everton		05/06	13		FL
		06/07	7		FL
Broxburn	L				
Kilmarnock		08/09	1		
Hamilton A		09/10	17		
		10/11	24		
Airdrieonians		11/12	10		
Annbank					
Thornhill					

BLACK William

Bathgate					
Heart of Midlothian		16/17	37		
		17/18	33		
		18/19	31		
		19/20	2		
		20/21	3		
Raith R		21/22			
Bathgate		22/23			D2

BLACK William
b. Airdrie 15.1.1915

Airdrie Academy					
Wishaw Jnrs					
Airdrieonians		32/33	1		
		33/34			
Blantyre V		33/34			
Wishaw Jnrs		34/35			
Hibernian		34/35	23	10	
		35/36	33	15	
		36/37	22	12	
Watford		37/38	16	3	FL
Dunfermline A		38/39			

BLACK William

Forfar A					
Morton		37/38	13	3	
Dundee U		38/39			D2

BLACK William F
b. Linlithgow 1905

Linlithgow Rose					
Heart of Midlothian		25/26	8	6	
		26/27	4	1	
Hamilton A		27/28	10	3	
Swansea T		28/29	11	1	FL
Bo'ness		29/30			D2
Morton		30/31	22	1	
East Stirlingshire		31/32			D2
		32/33	25		
Raith R					

BLACK William N

Arthurlie					
St Johnstone		35/36	6	2	
Alloa A		36/37			D2

BLACKBURN

Abercorn		91/92	1		

BLACKBURN Robert
b. Edinburgh 1885

Raith R					
Hamilton A					
Leith A					
Newcastle U		06/07	3		FL
		07/08	2		FL
Aberdeen		08/09	22	10	
Grimsby T		09/10	6		FL

BLACKHALL Colin Douglas

Musselburgh A					
Heart of Midlothian		15/16	7	1	
		16/17	12		

BLACKSTOCK

Queen's Park		06/07	1		

BLACKWELL Clifford Harry
b. Sheffield 1902

Heeley Friends					
Scunthorpe U					
Aberdeen		21/22	17		
		22/23	38		
		23/24	38		
		24/25	37		
		25/26	36		
		26/27	18		
		27/28	26		
		28/29	4		
		29/30	2		
Scunthorpe U					
Clapton Orient		30/31	12		FL
		31/32	3		FL
Preston NE		32/33			FL
Forfar A					

BLACKWOOD Donaldson G

Bridgeton Waverley					
Albion R		36/37	16	4	

BLACKWOOD John
b. Maine 1875

Petershill		95/96			
		96/97			
		97/98			
		98/99			
Celtic		99/00	1		
Partick T	L	99/00	8	7	D2
Celtic		00/01			
Woolwich Arsenal		00/01	16	6	FL
		01/02	23	9	FL
Reading		02/03	23	9	SL
QPR		02/03	15	10	SL
		03/04	24	20	SL
		04/05	7	3	SL
West Ham U		04/05	4	1	SL
Royal Albert					

BLACKWOOD Robert M

Johnstone					
Kilbirnie Ladeside					
St Mirren		16/17	5		

BLAIR

Abercorn		91/92	2		

BLAIR

Falkirk		18/19	1	?	

BLAIR

Albion R		19/20	1		

BLAIR Daniel 8 caps
b. Parkhead 2.2.1905 d. Blackpool 5.8.1985

Rasharkin					
Cullybacky					
Devonport A					
Toronto Scottish					
Willys Overland Motor Works					
Providence Clamdiggers		24/25	36	5	ASL
Parkhead Jnrs					
Clyde		26/27	21		
		27/28	33		
		28/29	33		
		29/30	33	2	
		30/31	25		
		31/32	11		
Aston Villa		31/32	10		FL
		32/33	37		FL
		33/34	33		FL
		34/35	37		FL
		35/36	12		FL
Blackpool		36/37	42		FL
		37/38	41		FL
		38/39	38		FL
Cardiff C					

BLAIR Daniel D
b. Glasgow 2.2.1905

St Anthonys					
Celtic		24/25	2		
		25/26			
		26/27	1		
Ayr U	L	26/27	7	1	D2
Glasgow Perthshire					

BLAIR J

St Mirren		11/12	1		

BLAIR James

Port Glasgow A		02/03	6		

BLAIR James
b. Dumfries 1885 d. Dumfries 24.3.1913

Dumfries Volunteers					
5th KO Highlanders					
Kilmarnock		03/04	24	5	
		04/05	26	8	
Woolwich Arsenal		05/06	12	3	FL
		06/07	1		FL
Manchester C		06/07	9		FL
		07/08	34		FL
		08/09	31		FL
		09/10	2		FL
Bradford C		10/11	18		FL
		11/12	21	4	FL
Stockport Co		12/13	23	1	FL

BLAIR James 8 caps
b. Glenboig 11.5.1888 d. Cardiff 28.2.1964
Bonnyrigg Thistle
Glasgow Ashfield
Clyde 08/09 30
09/10 17
10/11 27 1
11/12 31
12/13 24 1
13/14 29 2
Sheffield W 14/15 18 FL
Clydebank L 15/16
Alloa A L
Rangers L 16/17 35 3
17/18 27 1
18/19 29 3
Sheffield W 19/20 25 FL
20/21 14 FL
Cardiff C 20/21 24 FL
21/22 31 FL
22/23 33 FL
23/24 36 FL
24/25 37 FL
25/26 16 FL
Bournemouth 26/27 23 FL
27/28 38 FL

BLAIR James
b. Springburn
Civil Service Strollers
Heart of Midlothian
Broxburn U 21/22
Airdrieonians 21/22 1 1

BLAIR James

Third Lanark 31/32 17 4
32/33 5
33/34 38
34/35 D2
35/36 36
36/37 33
37/38 38
38/39 35 2

BLAIR John

Clyde 98/99 5

BLAIR John

Heart of Midlothian 98/99 10 3
99/00 6 1

BLAIR John
b. Ardrossan
Saltcoats V
Partick T 19/20 13 1
20/21 38 11
21/22 40 12
22/23 29 6
23/24 12 1
24/25 8 1
Saltcoats V 25/26
26/27
27/28
Morton 28/29 D2
29/30
Saltcoats V 30/31

BLAIR John 1 cap
b. Pollokshields c1910 d. c1975
Yoker A
Motherwell 31/32 4
32/33 26 1
33/34 35 1
34/35 38
35/36 37
36/37 38
37/38 33
38/39 35

BLAIR John Guthrie
b. Neilston 23.8.1905 d. Kilmarnock 1.1.1972
Thornliebank
Neilston Park Villa
Neilston V
Pollok
Third Lanark 23/24 28 4
24/25 21 10
25/26
Tottenham H 26/27 24 10 FL
27/28 5 4 FL
Sheffield U 27/28 18 6 FL
28/29 8 1 FL
Fordsons 29/30 LI
Cork 30/31 LI
31/32 LI

BLAIR John Wilson
b. Ballymoney 12.11.1882 d. Morecambe 20.9.1934
Cliftonville Olympic
Cliftonville 04/05 IL
05/06 IL
06/07 IL
Belfast Celtic 07/08 IL
Cliftonville 07/08 IL
Belfast Celtic 08/09 IL
Cliftonville 08/09 IL
Belfast Celtic 09/10 IL
Celtic 10/11 1
Motherwell 10/11 6
Belfast Celtic 10/11 IL
11/12 IL
Linfield 11/12 IL
Shelbourne 12/13 IL
13/14 IL
Distillery 13/14 IL

BLAIR Robert

Morton 23/24 4 2

BLAIR Thomas
b. Glasgow 24.2.1892 d. Dundee 1961
Vale of Clyde
Kilmarnock 11/12 2
12/13 31
13/14 9
14/15 20
15/16 37
16/17 28
17/18 33
18/19 26
19/20 40
Manchester C 21/22 38 FL
Edmonton CNR
Cumberland U
Boston Wonder Workers 25/26 17 ASL
Fall River Marksmen 25/26 12 ASL
26/27 22 ASL
Hartford Americans 27/28 11 ASL
New Bedford Whalers 27/28 29 ASL
28/29 25 ASL
29A 6 ASL
Fall River Marksmen 29/30 1 ASL
Pawtucket Rangers 31S 9 ASL
Ayr U 31/32
Linfield 32/33 IL
Sheppey U 33/34
Sittingbourne
Dundee U 37/38 1 D2

BLAIR William 1 cap
b. Greenock 11.3.1872
Morton
Third Lanark 91/92 17 1
92/93 15 1
93/94 13
94/95 18 1
95/96 16
96/97 12 1

BLAIR William

Falkirk 25/26 5

BLAIR William G

Queen's Park 23/24 20
24/25
25/26 1

BLAKE Andrew
b. West Lothian c1904
Rosslyn Jnrs
Cowdenbeath 25/26 16
Broxburn U 26/27 D2
Crewe A 27/28 5 FL
28/29 8 FL
Chester 29/30 1 CCL
Nantwich T
Stafford R 32/33
Wardle & Barbridge

BLAKE Gardner Wallis
b. Linlithgow 1911
Kingussie Juveniles
St Andrews U
Airdrieonians 30/31
Cowdenbeath 31/32
Airdrieonians 32/33 23
33/34 34
Carlisle U 33/34 3 1 FL
Crewe A 34/35 35 1 FL
35/36 38 1 FL
36/37 30 FL
37/38 35 FL
38/39 38 3 FL

BLAKELEY James

Clydevale
Port Glasgow A 06/07 8 1

BLANCHFLOWER Frederick William
b. Govan 1891
Petershill
St Mirren 12/13 2

BLESSINGTON James 4 caps
b. Linlithgow 28.2.1874 d. Newton Abbot 18.4.1939
Leith Hibernian
Leith A 91/92 20 8
St Bernards L 92/93
Celtic 92/93 15 4
93/94 18 6
94/95 12 5
95/96 16 9
96/97 17 5
97/98 5 1
Preston NE 97/98 5 FL
98/99 10 1 FL
Derby Co 99/00 2 FL
Bristol C 99/00 21 7 SL
Luton T 00/01 27 9 SL
01/02 25 6 SL
02/03 30 5 SL
Leicester F 03/04 34 7 FL
04/05 28 2 FL
05/06 29 7 FL
06/07 7 2 FL
07/08 1 FL
08/09 1 FL

BLOXHAM Albert
b. Solihull 29.11.1905 d. Crawley 29.8.1996
Overton on Dee
Oswestry T
Torquay U
Birmingham 27/28 3 FL
Rhyl
Chesterfield 28/29 7 1 FL
Raith R 28/29 5 1
Yeovil T 29/30
30/31
Millwall 31/32 35 8 FL
32/33 35 3 FL

BLUE Charles

Third Lanark 00/01 4
01/02
Arthurlie 02/03 D2

BLUE James

Broxburn U
Albion R 19/20 15 1
20/21 16 6
Vale of Clyde 21/22
Hamilton A 21/22 1

BLYTH George
b. Motherwell 18.10.1906 d. Nottingham 30.8.1984
Perth Roselea
Perth YMCA
Newburgh WE
Hibernian 29/30 15
30/31 31
31/32 D2
32/33 D2
33/34 33
34/35 8
St Johnstone 34/35 6
Notts Co 35/36 18 FL
36/37 42 FL
37/38 39 FL
Grantham

BLYTH James

Loanhead Mayflower
Hamilton A 16/17 8 2

BLYTH James C

Pollok Jnrs
Dumbarton 12/13
13/14 15 3

BLYTH Robert Fleming
b. Muirkirk 16.10.1869 d. Milton 7.2.1941
Glenbuck A
Middlesbrough I
Rangers 91/92 5 1
92/93
93/94 6 1
Preston NE 94/95 13 1 FL
95/96 30 5 FL
96/97 30 FL
97/98 17 1 FL
98/99 24 FL
Portsmouth 99/00 27 SL
00/01 26 3 SL
01/02 23 1 SL
02/03 18 SL
03/04 27 SL

BLYTH William
b. Lochgelly
Lochgelly Celtic
Dundee 29/30 13
30/31 31 1
31/32 19
32/33 20 1
33/34 31 3
34/35
Dunfermline A 34/35 6
35/36 8

BLYTH William Naismith
b. Dalkeith 17.6.1895 d. Worthing 1.7.1968
Wemyss A
Manchester C
Arsenal 14/15 12 2 FL
Third Lanark L 18/19 1
Arsenal 19/20 29 5 FL
20/21 40 7 FL
21/22 25 1 FL
22/23 31 9 FL
23/24 27 3 FL
24/25 17 1 FL
25/26 40 7 FL
26/27 33 2 FL
27/28 39 7 FL
28/29 21 1 FL
Birmingham 29/30 19 4 FL
30/31 2 FL

BOAG George H

Broxburn A
Heart of Midlothian 16/17 6

BOAG Richard

Lochee Harp
Dunfermline A 34/35 7
Cowdenbeath 35/36 D2
36/37 D2
37/38 D2
38/39 D2

BOARDMAN George
b. Glasgow 20.10.1904
Ashfield
Partick T 26/27 2
27/28 21 3
28/29 8 2
29/30 13 2
30/31 17 5
31/32 15
32/33 17 10
Bradford PA
Nairn Co 35/36

BOLAND Charles
b. Kilmarnock 5.10.1895 d. Scotland 7.2.1969
Lilymount
Kilmarnock 19/20 2
20/21 1
Queen of the South 21/22
Fulham 21/22 2 1 FL
22/23 1 FL
Queen of the South 22/23
Galston 23/24 D3
24/25 D3
Arthurlie 24/25
Galston 24/25 D3
25/26 D3
Beith 26/27

BOLGER William

Clydebank 17/18 4 3

BOLT Robert
b. Lochgelly 29.1.1912
Kelty Our Boys
Rosslyn
Heart of Midlothian 33/34 1
34/35
Dunfermline A 34/35 21
35/36 33
36/37 38 2
Falkirk 37/38 38 5
38/39 36 3
Rangers
Third Lanark 46/47 21
Falkirk 47/48 21 2
Inverness Caledonian

BOLTON Hugh
b. Port Glasgow c1881
Clydeville
Port Glasgow A 02/03 20 4
03/04 21 5
04/05 26 3
Newcastle U 05/06 1 FL
Everton 05/06 13 4 FL
06/07 31 12 FL
07/08 27 9 FL
08/09 4 FL
Bradford PA 08/09 16 3 FL
09/10 13 4 FL
Morton 10/11 24 1
11/12 26
12/13 7
Glentoran 13/14 IL
Johnstone 16/17

BOLTON James McFarlane
b. Clydebank 22.3.1906
Bridgeton Waverley
St Johnstone 26/27 1
27/28 10
28/29 28
29/30 17
Clapton Orient 30/31 29 1 FL
31/32 8 FL
York C 32/33 7 FL
Coleraine 33/34 IL

BOND John
b. Preston
Preston NE 13/14 1 1 FL
Motherwell 14/15 14 3

BOND Thomas

Ardrossan Winton R
Kilmarnock 12/13 1

BONE James M

St Johnstone 36/37 1
37/38 1

BONE John W
b. Motherwell
Motherwell 26/27
27/28
28/29 4 2
29/30 1
St Mirren 30/31 1

BONE Thomas
b. Greenock
Glasgow Perthshire
Hibernian 02/03 3
03/04
Mountpottinger 04/05
Distillery 05/06 IL
06/07 IL
07/08 IL
Glenavon 08/09

BONE William R

Rangers 15/16 2
Vale of Leven

BONNAR J

Abercorn 90/91 17 1
91/92 14 5
92/93 8 3

BONNER William

Morningside R
Third Lanark 06/07 3

BONOMY John
b. Dalziel 1918
Dalziel High School
Royal Albert 35/36
Queen's Park 36/37 8
37/38 4
38/39 27
Motherwell

BONTHRON Robert Pollock
b. Dundee 1883
Raith A
Raith R
Dundee 02/03 1
Manchester U 03/04 33 1 FL
04/05 32 FL
05/06 26 2 FL
06/07 28 FL
Sunderland 07/08 22 1 FL
Northampton T 08/09 31 SL
09/10 28 SL
Birmingham 10/11 11 1 FL
Airdrieonians L 11/12 5
Leith A 12/13 D2

BOOTH Frank
b. Hyde 1882 d. Manchester 22.6.1949
Stockport Co 01/02 6 1 FL
Manchester C 02/03 9 FL
03/04 24 3 FL
04/05 33 8 FL
05/06 28 7 FL
Bury 06/07 13 FL
07/08 34 3 FL
08/09 9 1 FL
Clyde 09/10 24 4
10/11 20 9
Manchester C 11/12 4 FL

BORELAND Henry
b. Rutherglen d. Rutherglen 1962
Rutherglen Glencairn
Clyde 27/28 36 7
28/29 18 3
29/30 29 12
30/31 20 6
Glentoran 31/32 IL
Morton 32/33 23 2

BORLAND John

Shawfield Jnrs
Hibernian 34/35 17 6
35/36 1
East Stirlingshire 36/37 D2

BORLAND John Thompson Mathieson
b. Rutherglen 6.9.1900 d. Rutherglen 8.12.1979
Rutherglen Glencairn
Raith R 22/23 17 1
Kilmarnock 23/24 38 3
24/25 15 5
Cowdenbeath L 24/25
Hamilton A 25/26 38 5
26/27 27 3
Charlton A 27/28 5 1 FL
Merthyr T 28/29 40 2 FL
Southend U 29/30 21 3 FL
Barrow T 29/30
Alloa A 30/31 D2
Rutherglen Glencairn 31/32
Stenhousemuir 32/33 D2

BORTHWICK Andrew J

Gala Fairydean
Hibernian 19/20 1

BORTHWICK John James Blacklaw
b. Leith 15.2.1886
Royal Oak
Edinburgh Clifton
Wemyss Violet
Lochgelly U 06/07
Hibernian 06/07 2
07/08 28
Everton 07/08 1 FL
08/09 1 FL
09/10 19 FL
10/11 4 FL
Millwall 11/12 11 SL

BORTHWICK Martin Caldwell
b. West Calder 31.5.1917
Bonnybridge Rose
Kilmarnock 37/38 2
38/39 9 4
46/47
Stirling A 47/48
Gala Fairydean

BORTHWICK Walter
b. Newington 9.1.1899
Broxburn Shamrock
East Fife
Cowdenbeath
Hibernian 16/17 27
17/18 27 ?
Partick T 18/19 25 1
19/20 19
20/21 13
21/22 3
Bristol C 21/22 1 FL
Cowdenbeath
Hartlepools U 22/23 2 FL
Nithsdale W 23/24 D3

BOURHILL Robert Gray
b. Anderston 1909
Yoker A
Morton 32/33 38
33/34 D2
34/35 D2
Ayr U 34/35 7
35/36 21
36/37 11 D2
Dunfermline A 36/37 20
Babcock & Wilcox
Kings Park

BOVILL John McKeown
b. Rutherglen 21.3.1886 d. Scotland 1954
Strathclyde Jnrs
Rangers 07/08 2
Blackburn R 08/09
Chesterfield T 08/09 18 3 FL
09/10
10/11
Liverpool 11/12 23 7 FL
12/13 1 FL
13/14 3 FL
Linfield 14/15 IL
15/16 IL
16/17 IL

BOW James
b. Lochore 14.12.1910
Lochore
Hearts o'Beath
Hamilton A 29/30
30/31 4
St Cuthberts W L 30/31
Hamilton A 31/32
Leith A 32/33 D2
St Bernards 33/34 D2
Clapton Orient 34/35
35/36
Gateshead 36/37 1 FL

BOW John
Falkirk 18/19 7 ?
19/20 4 1

BOWEN
Third Lanark 94/95 18

BOWER Robert
Dunfermline Jnrs
Dundee 16/17 37

BOWERS Daniel
St Mirren
Hamilton A 19/20 4

BOWIE A
Partick T 21/22 7 1

BOWIE Alexander
b. Newcastle 21.9.1903 d. North Shields 22.9.1978
Rosehill Villa
Wallsend
Newcastle U
Barnsley 23/24 4 FL
24/25 1 FL
Aberdeen 24/25 6 2
Kettering T 25/26
26/27
Guildford C 27/28
Nelson T 28/29
Gainsborough T 28/29
Market Harborough T 28/29
Loughborough Corinthians 29/30
Goole T 29/30
Stamford T 29/30
Waterford Celtic T 29/30
Walker Celtic 30/31
Usworth Colliery 30/31
Biggleswade T 31/32
Evesham T 31/32

BOWIE Alexander
Cowdenbeath 27/28 1
28/29
Dunfermline A 28/29 D2

BOWIE James
Abercorn 90/91 16 1
91/92 22 2
92/93 18 2
93/94 13 ? D2
94/95 7 ? D2
95/96 D2
Johnstone 95/96

BOWIE James M 2 caps
b. Partick 9.7.1888 d. 1969
Rockbank
Maryhill Jnrs
Queen's Park 08/09 29 3
09/10 26 1
10/11 12 1
Rangers 10/11 17 4
11/12 24 5
12/13 22 6
13/14 28 7
14/15 36 6
15/16 26
16/17 20
Airdrieonians L 16/17
Rangers 17/18 33 5
18/19 26 14
Queen's Park L 18/19
Rangers 19/20 39 12
20/21 23 2
21/22 5 1

BOWIE John
b. Govan
St Anthonys
Pembroke Dock
Partick T 15/16 35 13
16/17 36 13
17/18 29 6
18/19 28 18
19/20 36 11
20/21 9
21/22
Dumbarton 21/22 10
Forres Mechanics 22/23
23/24
24/25
25/26
26/27
27/28

BOWIE Nathaniel W
Clackmannan Celtic
Alloa A 20/21
21/22 D2
22/23 3

BOWIE Thomas
Johnstone
Morton 05/06 4

BOWIE Thomas A
b. Alloa
Queen's Park 01/02 11 4
02/03 13 3
Alloa A

BOWIE William 1 cap
Linthouse
Clyde 91/92 19 1
92/93 8
93/94 11 ? D2
94/95 10 1
95/96 9
96/97 17
Linthouse 96/97 D2

BOWMAN George Alexander 1 cap
b. Montrose 27.6.1872
Montrose
Third Lanark 93/94 11 1
94/95
95/96 18 1
96/97 8
97/98 1
98/99 1
99/00
00/01
Montrose 01/02
(Played for both Third Lanark and Montrose throughout 1897 and 1898)

BOYCE Charles
Queen's Park 23/24 3

BOYCE Charles H
Queen's Park 15/16 10
16/17 3

BOYCE Thomas Dodd
b. St Giles, Elbury 2.8.1905
Ardrossan Winton R
St Mirren 26/27 11
Southend U 27/28 7 FL
Clydebank 28/29 D2
Partick T 29/30
Bristol R 30/31 8 FL
Leith A 31/32 14
East Fife 31/32 8 D2
32/33 34 D2
Bo'ness 33/34 D2
34/35 D2
Partick T 35/36 3
Kings Park 36/37 D2

BOYD Alexander P
b. Galston (?)
Cumnock
Ayr U 23/24 5

BOYD David
b. West Greenock * c1870
Abercorn 92/93 4 2
Rangers 93/94 10 5
94/95 13 2
95/96 4 1
Preston NE 96/97 26 12 FL
97/98 11 FL
Abercorn
Linfield 00/01 IL

BOYD David
Third Lanark 99/00 3 2

BOYD H
Third Lanark 92/93 10 6
93/94 15 6

BOYD Hugh
Port Glasgow Clydevale
Morton 08/09 3
Abercorn 09/10

BOYD James
Kilbirnie Ladeside
Benhar Heatherbell
Airdrieonians 07/08 15 4
Kilmarnock 08/09 5 1
Dykehead
Bathgate

BOYD James
b. Shotts 1894 K.I.A., Somme 3.8.1916
Heart of Midlothian 14/15 38
15/16 36

BOYD James Murray 1 cap
b. Glasgow 29.4.1907 d. Bournemouth 22.3.1991
Petershill
St Bernards 24/25 D2
25/26 D2
Newcastle U 26/27 2 FL
27/28 10 3 FL
28/29 27 7 FL
29/30 15 1 FL
30/31 23 9 FL
31/32 37 18 FL
32/33 37 13 FL
33/34 33 2 FL
34/35 14 5 FL
Derby Co 35/36 8 1 FL
36/37 1 FL
Bury 36/37 9 2 FL
Dundee 37/38 26 4
Grimsby T 38/39 37 9 FL
39/40 1 FL

BOYD Robert 2 caps
b. c1867 d. Mossend 1930
Mossend Swifts
Third Lanark
Leith A 94/95 12 4
95/96 14 ? D2
Middlesbrough 96/97
Mossend Swifts 97/98
Leith A 97/98 D2
Mossend Swifts 97/98
Leith A 97/98 D2

BOYD Robert
Dundee 00/01 5 1
Vale of Leven

BOYD William Gillespie 2 caps
b. Cambuslang 27.11.1905 d. Bristol 14.12.1967
Regent Star
Royal Albert
Larkhall Thistle
Clyde 30/31 19 15
31/32 37 30
32/33 37 32
33/34 18 14
Sheffield U 33/34 22 15 FL
34/35 20 15 FL
Manchester U 34/35 6 4 FL
Carlisle U T 35/36
Workington 35/36
Luton T 35/36 13 11 FL
Southampton 36/37 19 7 FL
Weymouth T 37/38
Workington 38/39
Nuneaton B

BOYLE F
Rutherglen Glencairn
Hibernian 03/04 5

BOYLE James
b. Springburn 11.7.1866
Towerhill
Celtic 90/91 7 1
91/92 1
Clyde 92/93 1
Royal Arsenal 93/94 10 1 FL
94/95 28 2 FL
95/96 10 1 FL
96/97 14 1 FL
Dartford

BOYLE John
b. 24.12.1913
Armadale Thistle
Bathgate
Celtic 32/33
33/34
34/35
35/36
36/37 9
37/38 1
Hibernian
Hamilton A

BOYLE Patrick
Cambuslang Hibs
Port Glasgow A 02/03 3
03/04 25
04/05
Aberdeen 05/06 19 2
06/07 33
Bristol R 07/08 29 1 SL

BOYLE Peter
b. Carlingford 26.4.1876 d. Doncaster 24.6.1939
Gaelic Club
Albion R 95/96
96/97
Sunderland 96/97 5 FL
97/98 23 FL
98/99 2 FL
Sheffield U 98/99 16 FL
99/00 28 FL
00/01 29 FL
01/02 28 FL
02/03 26 FL
03/04 24 FL
Motherwell 04/05 14
Clapton Orient 05/06 10 FL
06/07
Wigan T 07/08
Chorley 07/08
Eccles B

BOYLE Peter
Hibernian 00/01 9 4
01/02 10
Broxburn 01/02
Hibernian 02/03
Raith R *

BOYLE Richard H
b. Dumbarton
Dumbarton Episcopalians
Dumbarton Union
Dumbarton 90/91 17 1
91/92 22 1
Everton 92/93 25 FL
93/94 21 1 FL
94/95 30 2 FL
95/96 30 3 FL
96/97 29 FL
97/98 22 FL
98/99 34 1 FL
99/00 29 FL
00/01 2 FL
01/02 9 FL
Dundee 02/03 16
03/04 26 2
04/05 25 1
05/06 5

BOYLE Robert
b. Cowie
Cowie W
Celtic 12/13 8
Alloa A
McKeesport (Pittsburg)

BOYLE William
Dumbarton 94/95 9 3
95/96 3 2
96/97 2 ? D2

BOYNE John
Johnstone
Morton 08/09 2
09/10 1
East Stirlingshire 09/10 D2

BOYTON John
b. Glasgow 1889
Kilsyth Emmet R
Hull C 12/13 10 1 FL
13/14 3 FL
Linfield 14/15 IL
15/16 IL
? 16/17
17/18
18/19
Clyde 19/20 24 1
20/21 3
Arthurlie 21/22
22/23

BRACKENRIDGE John
Stranraer
Rangers 05/06
Clyde 06/07 20 2
Airdrieonians 07/08 17 4

BRACKENRIDGE John
Rutherglen Bridge
Airdrieonians
Clyde 12/13 4

BRADFORD John
Kirkintilloch Harp
Morton 10/11 34
11/12 30
12/13 34
13/14 35
14/15 37
15/16 35
16/17 29
17/18 34
18/19 2
19/20
St Mirren 20/21 10
21/22 41
22/23 32
23/24 38
24/25 33
25/26 36
26/27 25

BRADLEY Eli John
b. Dudley 1883 d. ?.5.1952
Bilston U
Dudley T
WBA 04/05 3 FL
05/06 15 3 FL
06/07 7 2 FL
07/08 3 1 FL
Luton T 08/09 11 6 SL
Coventry C 09/10 37 4 SL
10/11 33 11 SL
11/12 28 4 SL
12/13 7 1 SL
Heart of Midlothian 12/13 8
Dudley T

BRADLEY James M
b. Glasgow
St Mungo's
Brig o'Lea
Neilston V
Cowdenbeath 33/34
Kilmarnock 33/34 1
Galston 34/35
Ayr U 35/36 3
Girvan

BRADLEY John
b. Blantyre
St Rochs
Hibernian 26/27 35 11
27/28 30 11
28/29 35 13
29/30 23 3
30/31 19 3

BRADSHAW Thomas 1 cap
b. Bishopton 7.2.1904 d. Doncaster 22.2.1986
Woodside Juveniles
Hamilton A T
Bury 22/23 3 FL
23/24 31 1 FL
24/25 37 1 FL
25/26 42 2 FL
26/27 40 FL
27/28 40 4 FL
28/29 10 FL
29/30 5 FL
Liverpool 29/30 17 FL
30/31 35 FL
31/32 42 FL
32/33 39 3 FL
33/34 39 FL
34/35 31 FL
35/36 41 FL
36/37 31 FL
37/38 2 FL
Colchester U 38/39 SL
South Liverpool 38/39
Third Lanark 38/39 5
South Liverpool

BRADY
St Bernards 97/98 1 1

BRADY Alexander
b. Cathcart 2.4.1865 d. Renton 19.10.1913
Dundee Harp
Renton Thistle
Partick T
Sunderland
Burnley 88/89 20 7 FL
Sunderland 88/89
89/90
Everton 89/90 13 8 FL
90/91 21 9 FL
Broxburn Shamrock L
Celtic 91/92 19 4
Sheffield W 92/93 26 5 FL
93/94 25 4 FL
94/95 26 5 FL
95/96 24 4 FL
96/97 24 7 FL
97/98 27 8 FL
98/99 6 1 FL
Clydebank
Renton

BRADY Andrew
Third Lanark 08/09 8 1
09/10
Arthurlie 10/11 7 D2

BRADY J
Renton 91/92 13 3

BRADY J
St Bernards 93/94 17 9
94/95 4 2
95/96 1

BRADY Joseph

Glenboig Jnrs
Airdrieonians 28/29 3
29/30
Derry C 30/31 IL

BRADY Joseph M

Dunfermline A 26/27 2

BRADY Thomas

Hamilton A 06/07 6
Girvan

BRADY Thomas

Wishaw Jnrs
Hibernian 35/36 36 18
36/37 25 3
Aberdeen 37/38 14 4
38/39 13 5
St Mirren

BRAE William
b. Kelvin 4.11.1902 d. Cheltenham 22.4.1968
Petershill
Ayr U 23/24 1
24/25 10 1
25/26 29 12 D2
26/27 36 16 D2
27/82 32 21 D2
28/29 37 11
29/30 38 13
30/31 20 5
31/32 31 8
32/33 33 3
33/34 34 11
34/35 26 3
Lille T 35/36
Clyde T 35/36
Swindon T 35/36 6 FL
Cheltenham T 36/37
Evesham T 37/38
38/39

BRAIDFORD Lowingham
b. Wallsend 17.11.1894 d. Wallsend 1926
Wallsend T
Clydebank 18/19 19 ?

BRAND Alexander A
b. Aberdeen
Hall Russells
Arbroath 33/34 34 33 D2
34/35 31 26 D2
35/36 22 9
36/37 38 22
37/38 23 15
38/39 17 7
Forfar A

BRAND Arthur

Dundee 03/04 1
04/05 12 3
Leyton 05/06
06/07
St Johnstone 07/08

BRAND Norman Rodger
b. Dundee 1912
Stobswell
Queen of the South 35/36 2
36/37
Nottingham F 36/37 FL
Brechin C 36/37 D2
Larne 37/38 IL
Ballymena U 37/38 IL
Distillery 38/39 IL
Glenavon 38/39 IL
39/40 IL
Dundee U
Ballymena U
Linfield 42/43 IL

BRAND Robert A
b. Scotland 1888
Argyll & Sutherland Highlanders
Motherwell 09/10 9 1
10/11 16 6
Bristol C 11/12 8 FL
Kings Park 12/13

BRANDER Thomas

Vale of Leven
Rangers 15/16 3
Vale of Leven

BRANDER Thomas

Clydebank 17/18 31 10
18/19 28 ?
19/20 9 1

BRANDON Thomas 1 cap
b. Kilbirnie 26.2.1869
Clippsons
Johnstone
Port Glasgow A
Renfrew A
St Mirren 87/88
88/89
Blackburn R 89/90 22 1 FL
90/91 17 FL
Sheffield W 91/92 19 1 FA
92/93 30 1 FL
Nelson 93/94
Blackburn R 93/94 13 FL
94/95 28 FL
95/96 27 FL
96/97 27 FL
97/98 29 FL
98/99 32 FL
99/00 21 FL
St Mirren 00/01 8

BRANNAN James
b. Smithson *
Dumbarton *
Bo'ness * 30/31 D2
Ayr U 31/32 9 1
32/33 21 5
33/34 28 5
34/35 8 2
Stranraer 34/35

BRANNAN Thomas G

Leith A 31/32 1

BRANNICK James
b. c1885 K.I.A. 10.8.1917
Everton 12/13 3 2 FL
13/14 FL
St Mirren 14/15 36 11
15/16 2

BRANSCOMBE Francis Arthur
b. Dennistoun 1889
Clydebank Jnrs
Partick T 08/09 11 2
09/10 21 4
10/11 26 2
11/12 18 1
12/13 32 15
13/14 25 4
14/15 31 7
Vale of Leven 15/16
Rangers 15/16 7 5
Partick T 16/17 18 2

BRANT Henry
b. Motherwell 11.6.1905 d. 1978
New Stevenston
Cambuslang R
Newarthill Thistle
Albion R 22/23 1
23/24 D2
24/25 D2
25/26 D2
26/27 D2
27/28 D2
28/29 D2
Bury 29/30 23 6 FL
30/31 FL
Dundee U 31/32 33 12
32/33 23 8 D2

BRASH Archibald Theodore
b. Uphall 1873 d. Paisley 1938
St Mirren 92/93 17 6
93/94 15 8
Sheffield W 94/95 26 8 FL
95/96 22 3 FL
96/97 27 4 FL
97/98 18 FL
Crewe A 98/99 17 8 LL
Sheffield W 99/00 25 6 FL
Leicester F 00/01 14 5 FL
Aberdeen 01/02

BREBNER Ronald Gilchrist
b. Darlington 23.9.1881 d. Chiswick 11.11.1914
Darlington
Rangers 05/06
Darlington 06/07
Elgin C 07/08
08/09
Queen's Park 09/10 3
10/11 7

BREBNER William

Aberdeen 04/05 2 D2
05/06 1
Forfar A 05/06
Aberdeen 06/07 7
07/08 1

BREMNER Tom Hutton
b. Cathcart 1912 d. 1969
Queen's Park 29/30 3
30/31 28 6
31/32 29 3
32/33 26 7
33/34 24 7
34/35 32 7
Motherwell 35/36 32 9
36/37 23 4
37/38 31 10
38/39 33 12
Stranraer
Hamilton A 46/47 15 4

BRESLIN Andrew

Carfin Emmet
Hibernian 03/04 2

BRESLIN Bernard 1 cap
b. Carfin c1874 d. Harthill 10.11.1913
Carfin Shamrock
Hibernian 93/94 15 ? D2
94/95 14 ? D2
95/96 18 2
96/97 14 1
97/98 17 1
98/99 18 1
99/00 18 2
00/01 18 1
01/02 16
02/03 19
03/04 21 1
04/05 25
05/06 15
Celtic

BRESLIN John

Motherwell 08/09 3

BRESLIN Joseph

Montrose
Third Lanark 30/31 D2
31/32 36 14
32/33 29 11
33/34 26 8
Margate 34/35

BRESLIN Patrick
b. Maryhill 2.10.1881
Johnstone Hibernian
Johnstone
Celtic T 98/99 1

BREWSTER George 1 cap
b. Culsalmond 7.10.1893 d. Scotland c1963
Mugiemoss
Aberdeen 12/13 7
13/14 11
14/15 25 2
15/16 34 3
16/17 20 1
Ayr U L 17/18 13 ?
Falkirk L 18/19 2
Aberdeen 19/20 22 3
Everton 19/20 5 FL
20/21 29 FL
21/22 25 3 FL
22/23 5 1 FL
Wolverhampton W 22/23 11 FL
Lovells A 22/23
Wallasey U 23/24
Brooklyn Wanderers 23/24 6 ASL
Inverness Caledonians 24/25

BRIDGES George

Dalry
Kilmarnock 05/06 1
Aberdeen 05/06 1

BRIGGS Alfred Ernest
b. Milton 1888 d. Clydebank 1950
Clydebank Jnrs
Heart of Midlothian 12/13 10
13/14 3
14/15 38
15/16 1
16/17
17/18 6

BRIGGS William

Third Lanark 96/97 1
97/98 1

BRISCOE James Edward Rotherham
b. Clockface 23.4.1917 d. Northampton 17.4.1981
St Helens T
Preston NE 36/37 5 FL
Heart of Midlothian 37/38 28 8
38/39 34 9
46/47 2
Northampton T 46/47 13 1 FL
47/48 23 11 FL
48/49 17 5 FL
Nuneaton B
Wolverton T

BRITTON (James?)
d. 1903
Clyde 92/93 2
71st Highlanders *

BRITTON John
b. Campsie 18.3.1900 d. Campsie 8.10.1953
Duntocher Hibs
Albion R 20/21 3
21/22 14
22/23 38
23/24 D2
Dundee 24/25 37
25/26 31
Tottenham H 25/26 9 FL
26/27 18 FL
27/28 13 FL
28/29
29/30
Derry Celtic 30/31
31/32
Kirkintilloch Rob Roy 31/32

BROAD James
b. Stalybridge 10.11.1891 d. Chelmsford 22.5.1963
St Marks (West Gorton)
Stalybridge C
Manchester C 09/10
Manchester U 10/11
Royal Corunna 11/12
Manchester C 12/13
Oldham A 13/14 10 4 FL
14/15 5 1 FL
Morton 17/18 16 9
18/19 23 15
Bacup B
Millwall 19/20 39 32 SL
20/21 9 4 FL
Las Palmas 20/21
Stoke 21/22 41 25 FL
22/23 30 22 FL
23/24 37 14 FL
Barcelona 24/25
Sittingbourne 24/25
Everton 24/25 14 8 FL
25/26 4 FL
New Brighton 26/27 11 3 FL
Watford 26/27 1 1 FL
Caernarfon T 27/28
Taunton U 28/29
Geneva
Fleetwood 31/32
Morecambe 31/32

BROADFOOT W

Airdrieonians 32/33 1

BROADFOOT William Loclie
b. c1909
Dunbeath Corinthians
Heart of Midlothian 27/28 1

BROADHEAD Daniel M

Queen's Park 12/13 1
13/14
14/15 8

BROADLEY Andrew C

Kirkintilloch Rob Roy
Vale of Leven
Third Lanark 24/25 9
25/26
Falkirk 26/27 1
Stenhousemuir 27/28

BROCK Thomas

Strathclyde
Ayr U 17/18 13 ?
18/19 5

BROCKLEY

Hibernian 17/18 1 ?

BRODIE

Abercorn 96/97 2

BRODIE Alexander

Rangers 02/03 1 1

BRODIE Duncan

Partick T 98/99 4
Cumnock

BRODIE John
b. Dumbarton 5.1.1896
Maryhill Jnrs
Dumbarton Harp
Celtic 16/17
Ayr U L 17/18 1 ?
Celtic 17/18 1
Dumbarton L 17/18 1
Celtic 18/19
Dumbarton Harp L 18/19
Chelsea 19/20
Dumbarton Harp

BRODIE John Charles
b. Kilmarnock c1868 d. Dalmellington 9.7.1901
Hurlford
Kilmarnock
Burnley 90/91 2 FL
Kilmarnock 91/92
Third Lanark 92/93 12 6
Kilmarnock 92/93
Nottingham F 93/94 9 5 FL
Kilmarnock

BRODIGAN James
b. Old Monkland 24.4.1873 *
Carfin
Hibernian 98/99 4 2

BROGAN James

Bristol R
Airdrieonians 18/19 15 5

BROOKS

Clyde 91/92 1

BROOKS George

Western U
St Bernards 35/36 D2
36/37 D2
Clyde 36/37 16 2
37/38 6 1
Kings Park 37/38 D2
St Bernards 38/39 D2
East Fife

BROWELL Thomas
b. Walbottle 19.10.1892 d. Blackpool 8.10.1955
Newburn Grange
Hull C 10/11 32 16 FL
11/12 16 16 FL
Everton 11/12 17 12 FL
12/13 26 12 FL
13/14 7 2 FL
Manchester C 13/14 27 13 FL
14/15 10 1 FL
Motherwell L 16/17 3 ?
Manchester C 19/20 30 22 FL
20/21 42 31 FL
21/22 38 21 FL
22/23 15 3 FL
23/24 14 4 FL
24/25 14 6 FL
25/26 32 21 FL
Blackpool 26/27 24 14 FL
27/28 28 9 FL
28/29 14 4 FL
29/30 1 FL
Lytham 30/31
31/32
32/33
33/34
Morecambe

BROWN

Cambuslang 90/91 18 11
91/92 9 1

BROWN

Clyde 92/93 7 1
93/94 1 ? D2

BROWN

Leith A 92/93 1

BROWN

Heart of Midlothian 93/94 3

BROWN Alexander 1 cap
b. Beith 7.4.1879
Glenbuck
Kilsyth W
St Bernards 94/95 1
95/96 15 8
Preston NE 95/96 1 FL
96/97 20 9 FL
97/98 20 12 FL
98/99 23 6 FL
Portsmouth 99/00 23 17 SL
Tottenham H 00/01 20 10 SL
01/02 26 18 SL
Portsmouth 02/03 25 19 SL
Middlesbrough 03/04 33 11 FL
04/05 11 3 FL
Luton T 04/05 2 SL
05/06 31 15 SL
06/07 34 14 SL
Kettering T

BROWN Alexander

Dundee 98/99 1

BROWN Alexander
b. c1908
Wellesley
Hibernian T
St Johnstone 29/30 6 1

BROWN Alfred
b. c1900 d. Largs ?.4.1930
Shawfield Jnrs
Morton 21/22 30 5
22/23 32 3
23/24 28 5
24/25 30 4
25/26 20 1
USA
Newcastle U

BROWN Allan W

Parkhead Jnrs
Clyde 19/20 17 6
20/21 27 15
21/22 32 24
22/23 31 8
23/24 28 11
Hamilton A 24/25 36 15
25/26 7 1
Raith R 26/27 D2
Partick T 26/27 1
Stranraer

BROWN Andrew 2 caps
b. Kilmarnock d. by 1930
Westmarch
St Mirren 90/91 11
91/92 20 2
92/93 16 1
93/94 14 1
94/95 13 1
95/96 7
Abercorn

BROWN Andrew

Larkhall YMCA
Hamilton A 21/22 1

BROWN Andrew H

Rugby XI
Kilmarnock 05/06 21 4
06/07 6 1
Canada
Kilmarnock 10/11
Galston 10/11
Rangers 10/11 3 2
11/12 8 1
12/13 6 4
Dumbarton L 12/13
Rangers 13/14 10
St Mirren 14/15 37 6
15/16 35 5
16/17 30 1
Ayr U 17/18 13 ?
18/19 1 ?

BROWN Andrew O
b. Glasgow
Parkhead Jnrs
Kilsyth R
Kilwinning R
Kilmarnock 25/26 1
26/27 9 1
27/28
Queen of the South 27/28

BROWN Charles
Mossend Swifts
Leith A 94/95 5
95/96 11 ? D2
96/97 12 ? D2
97/98 17 ? D2
Blackburn R 98/99 1 FL
Leith A 98/99 4 ? D2

BROWN Charles
Royal Albert
Hibernian 30/31 16 2
Clydebank 31/32
Falkirk 31/32 8
Babcock & Wilcox

BROWN Colin
Wallyford Bluebell
East Fife 28/29 24 6 D2
29/30 18 4 D2
30/31 12 2
31/32 2 D2
Bo'ness 31/32 D2

BROWN Craig
b. Mainkirk 22.1.1893
Lesmahagow
Carluke Milton R
Leith A
St Bernards
Armadale 12/13
13/14
Bradford C 14/15 3 1 FL
Bathgate L 16/17
Motherwell L 16/17 33 5
Hibernian L 17/18 6 ?
Bradford C 19/20 6 FL
Motherwell 19/20 25 2
20/21 38
21/22 38
22/23 30 2
23/24 17 1
Cowdenbeath 24/25 12
Morton 25/26 2
Peebles R 26/27
27/28
28/29

BROWN D C
St Mirren 95/96 5 6

BROWN David Carre
b. Broughty Ferry 26.11.1892
Dundee St Josephs
Dundee
Morton 11/12
12/13
Peebles R 13/14
Dundee 13/14 1 2
14/15 28 19
15/16 38 27
16/17 36 31
Rangers L 17/18
Peebles R
Dundee 19/20 13 11
Stoke 19/20 31 13 FL
20/21 19 4 FL
Notts Co 21/22 14 7 FL
Kilmarnock 22/23 19 4
Darlington 23/24 40 27 FL
24/25 40 39 FL
25/26 17 8 FL
Crewe A 26/27 37 22 FL
27/28 24 7 FL
Barrow 27/28 24 7 FL

BROWN David Crichton
b. Broughty Ferry 26.7.1889
Forthill A
Tottenham H 09/10 1 FL
Reading T 09/10
Birmingham T 09/10
Merthyr T T 09/10
Morton 09/10 1
10/11 10 5
11/12 23 9
12/13
Northampton T 13/14 13 4 SL

BROWN Edwin
Raith R 22/23 3

BROWN Edwin A
Tranent Jnrs
Heart of Midlothian 20/21 1
21/22 1

BROWN George
St Mirren 97/98 7 2

BROWN George
Stenhousemuir 95/96
96/97
97/98
98/99
Morton 99/00 2 ? D2
Stenhousemuir 99/00
Morton 00/01 20
01/02 18 3
02/03 1

BROWN George Clark Phillips 19 caps
b. Glasgow 7.1.1907
Glasgow Ashfield
Rangers 29/30 17 11
30/31 29 3
31/32 32 1
32/33 38
33/34 35 1
34/35 34 1
35/36 28 2
36/37 35 1
37/38 32
38/39 19 2

BROWN George J
Queen's Park 35/36 4
36/37 10
37/38 3

BROWN George M
Raith R 25/26 18 13

BROWN Henry
Heart of Midlothian 09/10 5
10/11 9 1
Stockport Co 11/12 2 FL

BROWN Henry Summers
b. Kirkcaldy 18.9.1907 d. 1963
Wemyss A
Hibernian 28/29 27 11
29/30 35 6
30/31 31 10
31/32 D2
Darlington 32/33 30 11 FL
33/34 28 6 FL
Chesterfield 33/34 12 1 FL
34/35 42 15 FL
35/36 40 7 FL
36/37 17 4 FL
Plymouth A 36/37 16 6 FL
37/38 24 6 FL
38/39 5 FL
Reading 38/39 26 4 FL

BROWN Hugh Allan
b. Glasgow 11.3.1896 d. Paisley 4.8.1952
Anderston Thornbank
St Anthonys
Celtic 16/17 22
17/18 32 1
18/19 32 2
19/20 10
20/21
Clackmannan L 20/21
Dunfermline A 21/22
Partick T 21/22
Merthyr T 21/22 16 1 FL
Caerphilly T 22/23
23/24
Dunkeld & Birnam

BROWN Hugh J
Glasgow Perthshire
Queen's Park 14/15 1

BROWN J
Third Lanark 94/95 10 2

BROWN J
Queen's Park 13/14 1

BROWN J A McK
Port Glasgow A 06/07 3

BROWN James
Dundee Our Boys
Dundee 93/94 13 1

BROWN James
b. 1870
Galston
Kilmarnock 95/96 18 1
96/97 4 1

BROWN James
b. West Calder d. 1955
Champfleurie
Bo'ness Our Boys
Rangers
Heart of Midlothian 00/01 2
Rangers 00/01
01/02
St Bernards 02/03 D2
03/04 D2
Cowdenbeath 04/05 D2
05/06 D2
06/07 D2
Dunfermline A 07/08
08/09
Lochgelly U 09/10
10/11
11/12
12/13
13/14
14/15 D2

BROWN James
Edinburgh Bainfield
Heart of Midlothian 04/05 16 5
05/06 11
06/07 6 1
St Bernards 07/08 D2

BROWN James
b. Campbelltown
Campbelltown U
Campbelltown A
Rangers 11/12 1
Kilmarnock 12/13 3

BROWN James
Petershill
Airdrieonians 12/13 31
13/14 38
14/15 38
15/16 3
Raith R 15/16 23
16/17 20
17/18
18/19
19/20 14
20/21 19
21/22 41
22/23 38
23/24 26
Clydebank 24/25
Dunfermline A 24/25

BROWN James
Larkhall Thistle
Motherwell 19/20 19 1
20/21 2

BROWN James
b. Springburn
Benburb
Motherwell 37/38 2
38/39 2

BROWN James B
Dumbarton 14/15 5 3

BROWN John
Shettleston
Third Lanark 12/13 31 5
13/14 26 4
14/15 24 10
15/16 9 2

BROWN John
Dumbarton 13/14 11 2

BROWN John

Club		Season	Apps	Gls	Lge
Shawfield					
East Stirlingshire		21/22			
St Johnstone					
Brechin C					
Morton		25/26	6	2	
		26/27	15	5	
Burnley		26/27			
Nelson		26/27	2		FL
Manchester Central					

BROWN John
b. c1920

Club		Season	Apps	Gls	Lge
Union COS Church, Ibrox					
Third Lanark		36/37			
		37/38	6	1	
		38/39	2		

BROWN John Alexander
b. Dysart ?.5.1887 d. 7.12.1943

Club		Season	Apps	Gls	Lge
Clackmannan Jnrs					
Hearts o'Beath					
Alloa A		08/09			
Falkirk		09/10	14	3	
		10/11	29	9	
Celtic		11/12	27	5	
		12/13	13	2	
Chelsea		12/13	11	3	FL
		13/14	3		FL
		14/15	2	1	FL
Falkirk	L	15/16	24	4	
		16/17	2		
Raith R		19/20			
Dunfermline A		20/21			
		21/22			
Falkirk	L				
Clackmannan		22/23			
Falkirk		23/24			
		24/25			
Clackmannan		25/26			
Lochgelly U		26/27			

BROWN John Bell 1 cap
b. Troon 21.2.1915 d. Prestwick 27.8.2005

Club		Season	Apps	Gls	Lge
Glenburn R					
Shawfield Jnrs					
Clyde		35/36	22		
		36/37	31		
		37/38	38		
		38/39	38		
Hibernian		46/47	1		
		47/48	11		
Dundee		47/48	10		
		48/49	4		
		49/50			
Kilmarnock		50/51			

BROWN John Findlay
b. Newtongrange

Club		Season	Apps	Gls	Lge
Newtongrange Star					
Dundee		23/24	27		
		24/25	18	1	
		25/26	32		
		26/27	38	1	
		27/28	30	1	
		28/29	29		
		29/30	36		
		30/31	37		
		31/32	21		
		32/33	2		
		33/34	1		

BROWN John M

Club		Season	Apps	Gls	Lge
Queen's Park		38/39	3		
		46/47			
		47/48	9		
Shrewsbury T					

BROWN Joseph

Club		Season	Apps	Gls	Lge
Larkhall Thistle					
Third Lanark		31/32	6	2	
		32/33	18	4	
		33/34	18	3	
Sheffield W		34/35			FL
Airdrieonians		35/36	6		

BROWN Joseph
b. Troon 10.4.1913

Club		Season	Apps	Gls	Lge
Troon A		32/33			
		33/34			
		34/35			
Shawfield Jnrs		35/36			
Aberdeen		35/36	3		
		36/37			
Watford		37/38	6	2	FL
Frickley Colliery					

BROWN Peter

Club		Season	Apps	Gls	Lge
Renton Glen Albion					
Dumbarton					
Renton		19/20			
Dumbarton		20/21	20		
Renton		20/21			
Bolton W	T	20/21			
Vale of Leven		21/22			D2
Bo'ness		22/23	31	2	D2

BROWN Richard

Club		Season	Apps	Gls	Lge
Kilbirnie Ladeside					
Clyde		13/14			
		14/15			
		15/16			
		16/17	1		

BROWN Robert
b. Kilmarnock 1872 d. Kilmarnock 13.12.1950

Club		Season	Apps	Gls	Lge
Kilmarnock Woodend					
Kilmarnock		95/96	15		D2
		96/97	15	1	D2
		97/98	17		D2
		98/99	17		D2
		99/00	16		
		00/01	5		
Lanemark		01/02			
Kilmarnock		01/02	4		
Nithsdale W		02/03			
		03/04			
Ayr		04/05			
Maxwelltown Volunteers					
Nithsdale W					
Dumfries					
Lanemark					
Nithsdale W					

BROWN Robert
b. Kilwinning 1891

Club		Season	Apps	Gls	Lge
Kilwinning R					
Rangers		10/11	4		
		11/12	5		
		12/13	12		
		13/14	10		
Stevenston U	L	13/14			
Rangers		14/15	15		
Dumbarton	L	14/15			D2
Third Lanark		15/16	33		
		16/17	31		
		17/18	32	?	
		18/19	21	?	
Morton		19/20	39	2	
		20/21	39	1	
		21/22	30		
		22/23	23		
Kilmarnock		23/24	22	1	
		24/25	24	4	
		25/26	3		

BROWN Robert M

Club		Season	Apps	Gls	Lge
Queen's Park Strollers					
Morton		04/05	1		
		05/06	1		

BROWN Samuel
b. Glasgow c1901

Club		Season	Apps	Gls	Lge
Rutherglen Glencairn					
Third Lanark		22/23	14		
Kings Park	L	22/23			D2
Third Lanark		23/24	23	2	
		24/25	10		
		25/26			D2
		26/27			D2
		27/28			D2
Third Lanark		28/29	2		
East Stirlingshire	L	28/29			D2
Bournemouth		29/30	31		FL
		30/31	27		FL
Brighton		31/32	4		FL
Chester		32/33			
Swindon T		32/33	2		FL
Stranraer	T	33/34			

BROWN Thomas
b. Beith 1880

Club		Season	Apps	Gls	Lge
Glenbuck Cherrypickers					
Leicester F		99/00	21	6	FL
		00/01	15	9	FL
		01/02	13	9	FL
Chesterfield T		01/02	9	8	FL
Third Lanark					
Leicester F		02/03	23	14	FL
Portsmouth		03/04	3	3	SL
Dundee		04/05	12	9	

BROWN Thomas

Club		Season	Apps	Gls	Lge
St Bernards		99/00	1		
		00/01			
Cowdenbeath		01/02			
Broxburn U		02/03			

BROWN Thomas

Club		Season	Apps	Gls	Lge
Lanemark					
Kilmarnock		06/07	1		
Lanemark					

BROWN Thomas
b. Sunderland

Club		Season	Apps	Gls	Lge
Sunderland Royal R					
Sunderland		07/08	1		FL
St Mirren		08/09	34	19	
		09/10	7	4	

BROWN Thomas Law
b. Glenbuck 17.4.1921 d. Edinburgh 10.5.1966

Club		Season	Apps	Gls	Lge
Cambuslang R					
Rangers	T	36/37			
Cambuslang R		37/38			
Heart of Midlothian		38/39	29	4	
Millwall		46/47	22	3	FL
		47/48	34	3	FL
		48/49	11	1	FL
Charlton A		48/49	20	1	FL
		49/50	14		FL
Leyton Orient		50/51	29		FL
		51/52	38	3	FL
		52/53	31	2	FL
Dartford					

BROWN William
b. Newmilns 1885

Club		Season	Apps	Gls	Lge
Newmilns					
Partick T		03/04			
		04/05			
		05/06	1		
Ayr Parkhouse		05/06			
Vale of Leven		06/07	?	16	D2
West Ham U		07/08	17	4	SL
		08/09	2		SL

BROWN William
b. Glasgow c1895

Club		Season	Apps	Gls	Lge
Cambuslang R					
Everton		14/15			FL
Parkhead Jnrs					
Celtic		16/17			
		17/18			
Vale of Leven	L	17/18			
Celtic		18/19	2	1	
Dundee		19/20	6		
Kings Park					
Cowdenbeath		20/21			
		21/22			
Lochgelly U		21/22			D2

BROWN William
b. Cambuslang 10.5.1899

Club		Season	Apps	Gls	Lge
Flemington Hearts					
Cambuslang R					
Everton		14/15	4		FL
St Mirren		16/17	36		
		17/18	32		
		18/19	22		
Everton		19/20	20		FL
		20/21	10		FL
		21/22	16		FL
		22/23	8		FL
		23/24	37		FL
		24/25	20		FL
		25/26	28		FL
		26/27	25		FL
		27/28	2		FL
Nottingham F		28/29	4		FL
		29/30	1		FL
Liverpool Cables					

BROWN William
b. Coatbridge 26.4.1914

Club		Season	Apps	Gls	Lge
Bedlay Jnrs					
Kilmarnock		34/35	2		
		35/36	4		
		36/37	7		
		37/38	14		

BROWN William

Club		Season	Apps	Gls	Lge
Dunblane R					
East Stirlingshire					
Falkirk		37/38	11	1	
		38/39	27	3	

BROWN William P

Club		Season	Apps	Gls	Lge
Blantyre BC					
Queen's Park		09/10	4		
		10/11	4		
		11/12			
		12/13	3	2	
Motherwell		13/14	4		

BROWN William P

Club		Season	Apps	Gls	Lge
Heart of Midlothian		18/19	1		

BROWN William Walker
b. Coatbridge 24.6.1912
Strathclyde
Chelsea 33/34 FL
Dunfermline A 34/35 14
Stockport Co 35/36 1 FL
36/37 1 FL
37/38 6 FL
Bradford C 38/39 4 FL
39/40 2 FL

BROWNING Alexander

Tranent Jnrs
Albion R 31/32 D2
32/33 D2
33/34 D2
34/35 33 1
35/36 10 1
Leith A 36/37 D2
Airdrieonians 37/38 12 D2
Leith A L 37/38 D2

BROWNING John 1 cap
b. Dumbarton 29.11.1888 d. c1958
Mossfield Amateurs
Glasgow Perthshire
Bonhill Hibernian 08/09
Dumbarton Harp 08/09
Vale of Leven 09/10 D2
10/11 16 ? D2
Celtic 11/12
Dumbarton Harp L 11/12
Vale of Leven L 12/13 D2
Celtic 12/13 21 8
13/14 37 8
14/15 38 15
15/16 38 9
16/17 35 12
17/18 32 9
18/19 9 1
Chelsea 19/20 5 1 FL
Vale of Leven 20/21
Dumbarton 20/21 33 3
21/22 39 2
Vale of Leven 22/23

BROWNING William

Queen's Park 33/34 32 5
34/35 5 3
35/36
36/37 5
37/38 11 1
38/39 31 12
Cowdenbeath 46/47 D2

BROWNLIE James 16 caps
b. Blantyre 15.5.1885 d. 29.12.1973
Blantyre V
Third Lanark 06/07 33
07/08 34
08/09 30
09/10 31
10/11 33
11/12 30 1
12/13 31
13/14 32
14/15 34 1
15/16 30
16/17 37
17/18 1
Airdrieonians L 18/19 4
Morton L 18/19 21
Third Lanark 19/20 25
20/21 42
21/22 36
22/23 22
Dundee U 23/24
24/25
25/26
Matches for Airdrieonians played under the name of Brown

BROWNLIE John
b. 1880
Levern V
Arthurlie 98/99
99/00
00/01
Third Lanark 01/02 11
02/03 2
Motherwell * 02/03
Arthurlie 03/04 D2

BROWNLIE Thomas

Glasgow Ashfield
Raith R 11/12 17 1
Cowdenbeath 12/13 D2

BROWNLIE Thomas
b. c1918
Benburb
Rangers 33/34
34/35
Raith R L 35/36 D2
Kilmarnock 36/37 2

BROWNLIE William
d. 1943
Hibernian *
Hamilton A 06/07 28
07/08 30
08/09 32
09/10 24
10/11 9
Hamilton (Ontario)

BRUCE

Third Lanark 92/93 3

BRUCE

Leith A 93/94 10 1

BRUCE

Third Lanark 98/99 1

BRUCE Daniel 1 cap
b. Bonhill 20.10.1870 d. Bonhill 6.2.1931
Vale of Leven 90/91 13 5
91/92 18 8
Rangers 92/93 4 4
Notts Co 92/93 25 12 FL
93/94 26 18 FL
94/95 29 15 FL
95/96 9 3 FL
Small Heath 95/96 9 1 FL
Perth

BRUCE David
b. Perth 23.2.1911 d. Bridge of Earn 15.9.1976
Perth Thistle
East Fife 30/31 5 1
Dundee East Craigie
Leicester C 35/36 1 FL
Bristol R 36/37 12 2 FL
St Mirren 37/38 4
38/39 14
Airdrieonians *

BRUCE Duff

Charlton A
Aberdeen 22/23 1
23/24 4
24/25 14
25/26 34
26/27 32
27/28 9
Charlton A 28/29 FL
Brechin C 29/30 D2

BRUCE Henry Moore

Queen's Park 07/08 1

BRUCE James

Parkhead
St Mirren 14/15 1
15/16 28 10

BRUCE Robert (Frederick?)

Cowie W
Kirkintilloch Rob Roy
Raith R 16/17 1
Partick T 16/17 2
17/18 16
18/19
Alloa A 19/20
Kirkintilloch Rob Roy
Nelson 21/22 7 FL
Plean
Stenhousemuir
Broxburn U

BRUCE Robert 1 cap
b. Paisley 29.1.1906
St Anthonys
Aberdeen 24/25 16 2
25/26 17 3
26/27 36 20
27/28 25 11
Middlesbrough 27/28 12 4 FL
28/29 35 11 FL
29/30 36 12 FL
30/31 27 9 FL
31/32 35 12 FL
32/33 35 5 FL
33/34 35 9 FL
34/35 22 3 FL
Sheffield W 35/36 5 FL
Ipswich T 36/37 25 11 SL
37/38 17 5 SL
Mossley

BRUCE W

Vale of Leven 90/91 1
91/92 4

BRUCE Walter

St Mirren 97/98 1
98/99 15 1
99/00 16 1
00/01 18 2
01/02 18 1
02/03 22 2
03/04 22 3
04/05 4
05/06 1

BRUCE William

St Anthonys
Clyde 26/27 1

BRUCE William
b. Airdrie
Lochrin
Airdrieonians
St Mirren 27/28 6
28/29 7
29/30 3
30/31 2
Leith A 31/32 18
Albion R 32/33 D2
33/34 D2
34/35 26 3
35/36 34 8
36/37 37 9
Queen of the South 37/38 29 1
38/39 25

BRUTON Leslie Hector Ronald
b. Foleshill 1.4.1903 d. Coventry 2.4.1989
Bell Green Wesleyans
Foleshill
Coventry C
WBA T
Peterborough U
Southampton 23/24 5 FL
24/25
25/26 2 FL
Peterborough U 26/27
27/28
Raith R 28/29 17 14
Blackburn R 29/30 12 5 FL
30/31 24 18 FL
31/32 2 FL
Liverpool 31/32 1 FL
32/33 6 1 FL
Leamington T
Coventry C T 35/36

BRYAN

Vale of Leven 91/92 3 1

BRYCE Daniel

Morton 02/03 5

BRYCE James

Queen's Park 07/08 9
08/09 2
09/10 7
10/11 3

BRYCE Robert Stewart

b. Grangemouth 17.11.1904 d. Buckrose 1970

Club	Season	Apps	Goals	Lge
Grange R				
Falkirk	23/24	19	5	
	24/25	21	2	
East Stirlingshire	25/26			
Stenhousemuir				
Grange R				
Bournemouth	28/29	29	15	FL
	29/30	35	9	FL
Luton T	30/31	25	3	FL
	31/32	9	5	FL
Kings Park	32/33			
	33/34			
	34/35			
	35/36			
	36/37			
Bo'ness	37/38			

BRYCE Thomas

Club	Season	Apps	Goals	Lge
Partick T	98/99	4		
	99/00	10		D2

BRYCE William

Club	Season	Apps	Goals	Lge
Westmarch				
Morton	01/02	14		

BRYDEN George

b. Walker 1893

Club	Season	Apps	Goals	Lge
Walker Celtic				
Allendale				
Hartlepools U	13/14			
Heart of Midlothian	14/15	6	1	
Hartlepools U	19/20			

BRYDSON James

Club	Season	Apps	Goals	Lge
6th DRV				
Partick T	98/99	1		
Hamilton A				

BRYERS James

Club	Season	Apps	Goals	Lge
St Anthonys				
Motherwell	26/27	3		
	27/28	3		
	28/29	1		

BRYSON Robert Weir

Club	Season	Apps	Goals	Lge
Yoker A				
Dumbarton	13/14	14		
Vale of Leven	14/15			D2
Dumbarton Harp	15/16			

BRYSON William B

Club	Season	Apps	Goals	Lge
Morton Jnrs				
Hibernian	36/37	13		
Morton	37/38	1		

BUCHAN

Club	Season	Apps	Goals	Lge
Dumbarton	91/92	1		

BUCHAN Colin Linwood

b. Bradford 1890

Club	Season	Apps	Goals	Lge
Queen's Park	13/14	20	3	
Brentford				
Dundee	19/20	6	1	
Linfield	20/21			IL
	21/22			IL
Peebles R	22/23			

BUCHAN James

b. Perth 1881

Club	Season	Apps	Goals	Lge
St Johnstone	00/01			
	01/02			
Hibernian	02/03	20	2	
	03/04	23	2	
Woolwich Arsenal	04/05	8		FL
Manchester C	04/05	7		FL
	05/06	29	1	FL
	06/07	27		FL
	07/08	27	3	FL
	08/09	38	4	FL
	09/10	20		FL
	10/11	6		FL
Motherwell	11/12	14		
Kilmarnock	11/12	5		
	12/13	15		
Forfar A	13/14			
St Johnstone	14/15			D2

BUCHAN William Ralston Murray

b. Grangemouth 17.10.1914 d. Grangemouth 6.7.2003

Club	Season	Apps	Goals	Lge
Grange R				
Celtic	32/33	2	1	
	33/34	7	1	
	34/35	28	13	
	35/36	38	11	
	36/37	32	11	
	37/38	16	13	
Blackpool	37/38	26	12	FL
	38/39	34	10	FL
	39/40	3		FL
	46/47	19	9	FL
	47/48	12	4	FL
Hull C	47/48	18	5	FL
	48/49	22	7	FL
Gateshead	49/50	14	3	FL
	50/51	42	9	FL
	51/52	32	4	FL
	52/53			
Coleraine	53/54			IL
	54/55			IL
East Stirlingshire	55/56	10	2	D2

BUCHANAN

Club	Season	Apps	Goals	Lge
Vale of Leven	90/91	5	2	
	91/92	1		

BUCHANAN A

Club	Season	Apps	Goals	Lge
Hibernian	22/23	1		

BUCHANAN Alexander

Club	Season	Apps	Goals	Lge
Kings Park				
Morton	01/02	6		
Kings Park				

BUCHANAN Alexander King

Club	Season	Apps	Goals	Lge
Heart of Midlothian	99/00	1	1	

BUCHANAN Archibald

Club	Season	Apps	Goals	Lge
Dundee U	31/32	10		
	32/33	33	2	D2
Bo'ness	33/34			D2
	34/35			D2

BUCHANAN George

b. Paisley 1888 d. Bishopton 2.2.1934

Club	Season	Apps	Goals	Lge
Levern V				
St Mirren	07/08	3	1	
	08/09	2	2	
	09/10	14	7	
Heart of Midlothian	09/10	11	12	
	10/11	25	6	
Bradford PA	10/11	2	1	FL
	11/12	24	5	FL
	12/13	26	3	FL
Morton	13/14	29	21	
	14/15	31	16	
	15/16	28	19	
	16/17	2	2	
	17/18	1	1	
	18/19	2		
	19/20			
St Mirren	20/21			

BUCHANAN James

Club	Season	Apps	Goals	Lge
Cambuslang	90/91	14	3	
	91/92	8	1	

BUCHANAN James

b. Kirkliston 10.10.1898

Club		Season	Apps	Goals	Lge
Bellstane Birds					
Winchburgh Violet					
Broxburn U					
Aberdeen	T	20/21			
Hibernian		20/21			
		21/22	11	7	
		22/23	13	2	
		23/24	6	1	
Bournemouth		24/25	18	2	FL
		25/26	25	5	FL
Raith R	L	25/26	2		
Bournemouth		26/27	16	3	FL
		27/28	6	1	FL
East Stirlingshire		28/29			D2
Nelson		28/29	32	7	FL
		29/30	34	8	FL
Ashton National	T	30/31			
Clitheroe		30/31			
Bray Unknowns		30/31			LI
		31/32			LI
Shamrock R		32/33			LI
		33/34			LI
Leith A		34/35			D2
Bangor		35/36			

BUCHANAN John 1 cap

Club	Season	Apps	Goals	Lge
Cambuslang	90/91	5		
	91/92	13		

BUCHANAN John 2 caps

b. Paisley 15.3.1899 d. 3.10.1947

Club	Season	Apps	Goals	Lge
Johnstone				
St Mirren	19/20	21	13	
	20/21	27	4	
Morton	21/22	18	4	
	22/23	31	2	
	23/24	36	2	
	24/25	29	2	
	25/26	34	13	
	26/27	37	3	
	27/28			
Rangers	27/28	13	1	
	28/29	32	2	
	29/30	25		
	30/31	26		
Linfield	31/32			IL
East Stirlingshire	32/33	24		

BUCHANAN Peter

Club	Season	Apps	Goals	Lge
St Bernards	97/98	17		
	98/99	7		
	99/00	16	1	
	00/01	14	?	D2

BUCHANAN Richard

b. 1879

Club	Season	Apps	Goals	Lge
Cambuslang Hibernian				
Third Lanark	00/01	18	5	
	01/02			
Arthurlie	02/03			D2

BUCHANAN Robert

Club	Season	Apps	Goals	Lge
Cambuslang R				
Rutherglen Glencairn				
Airdrieonians	09/10	1		
	10/11	3		

BUCHANAN Robert John

b. Johnstone 1868 d. Southwark 1909

Club	Season	Apps	Goals	Lge
Johnstone				
Abercorn	90/91	14	7	
	91/92	8		
Sunderland A				
Burnley	92/93	22	6	FL
	93/94	18	4	FL
Royal Arsenal	94/95	25	9	FL
	95/96	17	8	FL
Southampton	96/97	20	11	SL
	97/98	19	10	SL
	98/99	2		SL
Sheppey U				

BUCHANAN William

Club	Season	Apps	Goals	Lge
Queen's Park	31/32	1		

BUCHANAN William Duncan

Club	Season	Apps	Goals	Lge
Queen's Park	35/36	15	1	
	36/37	21		
	37/38	32	2	
	38/39	23	1	

BUCKTON Walter

Club	Season	Apps	Goals	Lge
Partick T	06/07	1		

BUICK Albert Thorogood 2 caps

b. Arbroath 17.1.1875 d. 25.3.1948

Club	Season	Apps	Goals	Lge
Arbroath				
Heart of Midlothian	96/97	2		
	97/98	5		
Arbroath	97/98			
Heart of Midlothian	98/99	3		
	99/00	9		
	00/01	20		
	01/02	18		
	02/03	19	1	
Portsmouth	03/04	32	1	SL
	04/05	26		SL
	05/06	32	1	SL
	06/07	33	1	SL
	07/08	26	3	SL
	08/09	35		SL
	09/10	23	2	SL
	10/11	20		SL

BUIST Robert W

b. Govan 5.10.1869 d. Plumstead c1944

Club	Season	Apps	Goals	Lge
Fairfield R				
Cowlairs	90/91	12		
Clyde	91/92	5	1	
Royal Arsenal	91/92			
	92/93			
	93/94	17	1	FL
Royal Ordnance				

BULLOCH Hugh Cairns
b. Larkhill 2.6.1908
Royal Albert
Morton 30/31 14
31/32 20 1
32/33 17
Portadown 33/34 IL
34/35 IL
Newcastle U 35/36 5 FL
New Brighton 36/37 30 2 FL
37/38 18 FL
Portadown 37/38 IL
New Brighton 38/39 34 1 FL
39/40 4 1 FL
Portadown 39/40 IL
40/41 IL
Aircraft U 41/42
?
Portadown 47/48 IL

BULLOCH James
b. Craigneuk c1910 d. Lubeck 27.4.1992
Law Scotia
Hamilton A 29/30 23
30/31 33 1
31/32 34 1
32/33 32
33/34 33
34/35 34
35/36 38
36/37 4
Morton
Alloa A

BULLOCH William
b. Larkhall
Royal Albert
Port Glasgow A 06/07 18
Royal Albert L 06/07
Port Glasgow A 07/08 33 2
Tottenham H 08/09 SL
Kilmarnock 08/09 5 2
Royal Albert 09/10
Partick T 10/11 34
11/12 31 1
12/13 31 2
13/14 33 1
14/15 22 2
15/16 32 1
16/17 35
17/18 29
18/19 30
19/20 39
20/21 32
Third Lanark
Partick T 21/22 15
22/23 24
Port Glasgow A 23/24

BUNCE John
Dundee 98/99 4 1

BURDEN Frederick
Stockport Co 08/09 21 FL
09/10 23 1 FL
10/11 14 FL
Heart of Midlothian 10/11 14
11/12 27
St Mirren 12/13 34 1
13/14 22

BURGESS Charles Millar
b. Montrose 20.11.1873 d. Massachusetts 21.5.1960
Montrose
Dundee 95/96 17
Sunderland 95/96 FL
Dundee 96/97 13
97/98 12
Millwall 98/99 24 1 SL
99/00 26 SL
Newcastle U 00/01 30 FL
Portsmouth 01/02 27 SL
02/03 17 SL
Montrose

BURKE James
Third Lanark 90/91 10 4
91/92 8 1
Notts Co 92/93 15 4 FL
Grantham R 93/94
Lincoln C 94/95 18 2 FL
95/96 29 4 FL
96/97 6 FL
Grantham R
Ilkeston

BURKE Joseph
Kirkintilloch Rob Roy
Albion R 37/38 D2
38/39 25 12

BURKE Michael
b. Blythwood 28.6.1904 d. Broomhill 16.10.1984
Dumbarton Harp
Old Kilpatrick
Glasgow Ashfield
Clyde 29/30 14 1
Dunfermline A 30/31 D2
Aberdeen 31/32
Dundalk 32/33 LI
33/34 LI
Lincoln C 34/35 11 FL
35/36 16 2 FL
Southport 36/37 20 2 FL
Rochdale 37/38 8 FL
Morton 38/39 D2
Burton T T

BURKE Nicholas
b. Glasgow 7.11.1907 d. 7.2.1978
Maryhill Hibs
Airdrieonians 28/29 12 10
29/30 21 10
30/31 3 1
Portadown 31/32 IL

BURNETT James J
b. Aberdeen
Victoria U 95/96
96/97
Aberdeen 97/98
98/99
99/00
00/01
01/02
Portsmouth 02/03 5 4 SL
03/04 10 5 SL
Dundee 04/05 7
Grimsby T 05/06 28 6 FL
06/07 23 7 FL
Brighton 07/08 16 3 SL
Leeds C 08/09 18 2 FL
09/10 2 FL

BURNETT John
Kirkcaldy U
Hibernian 08/09 13 3
East Fife

BURNETT Robert G
Hibernian 06/07 1

BURNETT Robert Gemmill
b. Dundonald 24.4.1886 d. Kilmarnock 28.8.1950
Kilmarnock Rugby XI
Queen's Park 08/09 1
09/10 15
10/11 7
Kilmarnock 10/11 1
11/12 8
12/13 3
13/14 1
14/15
15/16 1
16/17 4
17/18
18/19 1

BURNS
Third Lanark 90/91 6 3

BURNS George W
Queen's Park 05/06 3

BURNS Hugh
b. Dumbarton
St Anthonys
Dumbarton Harp
Renton Glencairn
Dumbarton 18/19 9
Renton 19/20
20/21
Rochdale 21/22 15 FL
Oldham A T
East Stirlingshire *

BURNS Hugh
b. Glasgow
Shawfield Jnrs
Morton 26/27 4
27/28 D2
28/29 D2
29/30 9

BURNS John
b. c1895
St Anthonys
Celtic 18/19 13 3
Dumbarton L
Dumbarton Harp L
Hamilton A L 18/19 2
Vale of Leven L
Celtic 19/20
Queen of the South
East Stirlingshire 25/26 D2
Canada

BURNS Oliver Houston
b. Larkhall 16.5.1914
Royal Albert
Queen of the South 35/36 7
36/37 10 5
37/38 8
Airdrieonians 37/38 D2
Glenavon 38/39 IL
Burnley 38/39 FL
Oldham A 46/47 25 5 FL
Halifax T 47/48 27 5 FL
Nelson

BURNS Patrick
Denbeath Star
Dundee 14/15 16
15/16 29
16/17 23
17/18
18/19
Alloa A 19/20

BURNS Peter
6th GRV
Hibernian 98/99 2 1
6th GRV

BURNS Robert
Rangers 95/96 6

BURNS Robert
Abercorn 96/97 11
Lincoln C 97/98 2 FL

BURNS Robert
b. Edinburgh ?.8.1882
Royal Field Artillery
Salisbury C 08/09
Heart of Midlothian 08/09 8 2
09/10 9 8
Fulham 09/10 4 1 FL
10/11 14 6 FL
Broxburn A 11/12

BURNS Thomas
Rutherglen Glencairn
Airdrieonians 17/18 7
18/19 12 2
Dumbarton Harp 19/20
20/21
Vale of Leven 21/22 D2
Derby Co T 21/22 FL
East Stirlingshire 22/23 D2
Royal Albert 23/24 D3
Vale of Leven 24/25 D3
25/26 D3
Bo'ness 26/27 D2

BURNS Thomas
Spencer & Johnstone 20/21
Alton U 21/22
Alloa A 22/23 3
Queens Island 22/23 IL
23/24 IL
24/25 IL
25/26 IL
26/27 IL
Coventry C 26/27
Larne 26/27 IL

BURNSIDE Robert
Leith A 91/92 21
92/93 2
93/94
94/95
Northern

BURRELL
Third Lanark 91/92 1

BURRELL George
b. Kinghorn
Burntisland Shipyard
Crossgates Primrose
Rosslyn
Falkirk 29/30 1
St Mirren 30/31

BURT George R

Grange R
Heart of Midlothian 31/32 1
Queen of the South 32/33 D2
East Stirlingshire 33/34 D2

BURT James

Johnstone
Morton 02/03 1
Johnstone

BURTON Andrew Douglas
b. Lochgelly 1884
Thompsons R
Lochgelly U 03/04
Motherwell 04/05 25 6
Bristol C 05/06 37 9 FL
06/07 34 14 FL
07/08 32 8 FL
08/09 35 8 FL
09/10 33 3 FL
10/11 21 4 FL
Everton 11/12 12 4 FL
Reading 12/13 32 11 SL
13/14 36 5 SL
? 14/15
19/20
East Fife 20/21
21/22 23 3 D2

BURY

Vale of Leven 91/92 1

BUSBY

Vale of Leven 91/92 21

BUSBY Charles
b. Caldercruix
Shotts U
Partick T 35/36 10
36/37 8
37/38 20
38/39 7

BUSBY Thomas
b. Alexandria 6.9.1872
Vale of Leven
Kilmarnock 95/96 16 D2
96/97 16 D2
97/98 18 D2
98/99 17 D2
99/00 17
00/01 16 3
01/02 18
02/03 10

BUTCHART James
b. 1882
Morton 02/03 6 1
West Ham U 03/04 3 SL

BUTLER Hugh

Queen's Park 00/01 2

BUTLER John T
b. Creetown 1889
Creetown Volunteers
Rangers
Morton 07/08 2 2
Rangers
Creetown Volunteers 10/11
Motherwell 10/11 13 6
Bristol C 11/12 28 11 FL
12/13 15 1 FL
Newport Co 13/14 23 3 SL
Third Lanark 14/15 7

BUTLER Matthew

Kelty R
Raith R 15/16 6
East Fife

BUTTAR James

Dundee 94/95 6 1

BUTTERY Archibald

Wishaw
Motherwell 08/09 21
Royal Albert

BYRNE

Third Lanark 98/99 1

CABRELLI Peter
b. Dundee 1909 d. 14.12.1994
Osborne
Aberdeen * 29/30
Dundee
Inter Milan T
Genoa T
Forfar A
Falkirk 34/35 11
35/36 D2
Kings Park 35/36 D2
St Mirren 36/37
Raith R 37/38 34 D2
38/39 37 1

CAFFREY Robert

Larkhall Thistle
Port Glasgow A
Partick T 14/15 14
15/16 10

CAHILL James
b. c1919
Rutherglen Glencairn
Celtic 36/37
37/38
Kilmarnock 38/39 3

CAHILL Richard

St Mirren 06/07 1

CAIE Alexander
b. Nigg 25.6.1877 d. Cowell, Mass ?.11.1914
Victoria U
Woolwich Arsenal 96/97 8 4 FL
Bristol C 97/98 21 18 SL
98/99 18 5 SL
99/00 13 7 SL
Millwall 99/00 7 1 SL
00/01 19 4 SL
Newcastle U 01/02 19 1 FL
02/03 10 1 FL
Brentford 03/04 22 SL
Motherwell 04/05 6
Westmount (Can)
Sons of Scotland (Can)
Rosedale (Can)

CAIL Samuel George
b. Middlesbrough 1888
Army football
Middlesbrough 06/07 1 FL
07/08 16 10 FL
08/09 25 9 FL
09/10 25 8 FL
10/11 26 7 FL
11/12 30 12 FL
12/13 13 3 FL
13/14 FL
Aberdeen 14/15 35 9
15/16 22 4
16/17 31 5
17/18
18/19
19/20 2
Stalybridge C

CAIRD

St Mirren 93/94 1

CAIRNCROSS Archibald
b. Jedburgh 1889
Peebles R
Bradford PA
Third Lanark 13/14 4
Peebles R

CAIRNEY

St Mirren 99/00 17 1
00/01 1
Vale of Leven

CAIRNEY Hugh

Bellshill A
Dumbarton 16/17 24 14
17/18 6 1
Airdrieonians L 17/18 15 7

CAIRNEY James Mougan
b. Calton 29.11.1902
Duntochter Hibernian
St Anthonys
Celtic 22/23 3
Arbroath L 22/23 3 D2
Arthurlie 23/24 D3
Whittalls Carpet Factory 24/25
Boston Wonder Workers

CAIRNEY John

Partick T 98/99 2
Lugar Boswell

CAIRNEY Joseph

Clydebank 20/21 5

CAIRNS Andrew

St Bernards 97/98 7
98/99 13
Kirkcaldy U

CAIRNS David

Raith R 25/26 14
Kettering T 26/27

CAIRNS James Roberts

Heart of Midlothian 88/89
89/90
90/91 1

CAIRNS Thomas 8 caps
b. Merryton 30.10.1890 d. Larkhall ?.12.1967
Burnbank A
Larkhall Thistle
Bristol C 11/12 10 1 FL
Peebles R 12/13
St Johnstone 13/14 11 1 D2
Rangers 13/14 8 2
14/15 36 15
15/16 34 12
16/17 24 12
17/18 34 11
18/19 28 11
Hamilton A L 18/19 1
Rangers 19/20 35 13
20/21 38 12
21/22 40 12
22/23 36 10
23/24 31 10
24/25 31 11
25/26 17 4
26/27 15 3
Bradford C 27/28 41 9 FL
28/29 38 9 FL
29/30 33 7 FL
30/31 16 6 FL
31/32 7 1 FL

CAIRNS William

St Mirren 00/01 2

CALDER

St Mirren 18/19 1 ?

CALDER Charles

Aberdeen 15/16 2
16/17 35

CALDER John
b. Kilbirnie 19.10.1913
Glengarnock YMCA
Dalry Thistle
Leicester C 31/32 1 FL
Falkirk 32/33 13 3
St Johnstone 33/34 17 15
Dunfermline A 34/35 2 1
Alloa A T 35/36 D2
Morton 35/36 D2
Bolton W 36/37 13 4 FL
37/38 14 7 FL
Barnsley 38/39 9 5 FL
Morton 39/40
40/41
Albion R 41/42
Morton

CALDER Thomas
b. Fauldhouse
Fauldhouse U
Airdrieonians 26/27 3
27/28
28/29 5
29/30 3
30/31 2
31/32 5
32/33 16
33/34 32
34/35 36
35/36 29
East Fife 36/37 D2

CALDERHEAD David
b. Dumfries 25.10.1889 d. 1958
Dumfries Primrose
Maxwelltown Volunteers
Lincoln C 06/07
Chelsea 07/08
08/09
09/10
10/11 10 FL
11/12 1 FL
12/13 16 1 FL
13/14 7 1 FL
Motherwell 14/15 1
Clapton Orient 19/20 1 FL

CALDERWOOD D
Queen's Park 20/21 8

CALDERWOOD G
Queen's Park 07/08 1
08/09 1

CALDERWOOD Stewart
b. Linwood 3.12.1905
Rutherglen Glencairn
Partick T 26/27 28
27/28 13
28/29 24
29/30 11
30/31 38
31/32 38
32/33 35
33/34 32
34/35 38
35/36 37 4
36/37 32 5
37/38 18

CALDERWOOD William
Queen's Park 19/20 3
20/21
21/22 23
22/23 2 D2
Brooklyn Wanderers 23/24 25 ASL
24/25 26 ASL

CALDOW
Cowlairs 90/91 1

CALDWELL Charles
St Mirren 08/09 1

CALDWELL Charles
Beith
Queen's Park 10/11 2

CALDWELL James
Johnstone
Abercorn
Partick T 98/99 5
Johnstone

CALDWELL John
b. Shawwood 28.11.1874
Newmilns
Hibernian
Royal Arsenal 94/95 30 1 FL
95/96 29 FL
Third Lanark 96/97 15
Woolwich Arsenal 96/97 15 1 FL
97/98 20 FL
Brighton U 98/99 21 SL
Galston 99/00
00/01
Brighton 01/02 16 5 SL
02/03 10 5 SL
03/04 11 SL

CALDWELL John
Kirkintilloch Rob Roy
Third Lanark 22/23
23/24 11
Clydebank 24/25 D2
25/26 23 1
Fall River Marksmen 26/27 16 1 ASL
Clydebank 27/28 D2
Fall River Marksmen 28/29 42 ASL
29A 19 1 ASL
29/30 8 1 ASL
New Bedford Whalers 30A 5 ASL
Fall River Marksmen 30A 18 1 ASL
New York Yankees 31S 5 ASL
Fall River 31S 6 ASL
New Bedford Whalers 31A 17 1 ASL

CALLACHAN Henry
b. Madras 9.4.1903 d. Leicester 11.2.1990
Kirkintilloch Rob Roy
Parkhead Jnrs
Celtic 25/26 6
Alloa A L 25/26 1 D2
Celtic 26/27 5
Beith L 26/27
Leicester C 27/28 3 FL
28/29 FL
29/30 FL
Tunbridge Wells R 30/31
Burton T 31/32
Wigan A 32/33 40 CCL

CALLAGHAN Bernard
Fauldhouse WE
St Mirren 13/14 22
14/15 26
15/16 29
16/17 33
17/18 24 1
18/19 20 ?

CALLAGHAN John H
Irvine
Third Lanark 07/08 2
08/09
09/10
10/11
Ton Pentre

CALLAGHAN Patrick 1 cap
b. Glasgow 12.8.1879 d. 26.2.1959
Jordanhill
Hibernian 99/00 18 6
00/01 20 6
01/02 18 5
02/03 21 11
03/04 19 3
04/05 25 10
05/06 24 7
06/07 27 2
07/08 27 9
08/09 22 1
09/10 27 4
10/11 28 3
11/12 22 2
12/13 5 2
13/14 6

CALLAGHAN Patrick
Hibernian 21/22 4

CALLAGHAN Thomas machine Gunner
K.I.A ?.3.1917 – reported on 3.3.17
Glossop 04/05 4 FL
05/06 31 4 FL
06/07 38 4 FL
Manchester C 07/08 2 FL
08/09 FL
Partick T 09/10 28 3
10/11 29 5
St Mirren 11/12 18 3
Partick T 12/13 23 1

CALLAGHAN Thomas
b. Govan 1901
St Anthonys
Third Lanark 24/25
Nithsdale W L 24/25 D3
Third Lanark 25/26 D2
26/27 D2
Dunfermline A 26/27 18 4
Middlesbrough 27/28
Third Lanark 28/29 19 2
29/30
Glentoran 30/31 IL
Cork C 31/32 LI
Darlington 32/33 2 FL
Third Lanark T 33/34
Raith R T 33/34 D2
Coleraine IL

CALLAN Andrew
Morton Jnrs
St Mirren 36/37 27 5
37/38 12 1
Dunfermline A 38/39 D2

CALLENDER James
Falkirk 08/09
09/10 1

CALLENDER John
Benburb
Partick T 07/08 17
08/09 10 4

CAMERON
Leith A 94/95 1

CAMERON
Clyde
Airdrieonians 17/18 2 1

CAMERON
Ayr U 17/18 12 ?

CAMERON
Clyde 20/21 1

CAMERON David C
b. Troon
Irvine Meadow
Kilmarnock 10/11 2
Hurlford
Kilmarnock 13/14
Hurlford
Galston
New York Giants 23/24 11 1 ASL
24/25 20 2 ASL
25/26 3 ASL
28/29 1 ASL

CAMERON David F
Queen's Park 14/15 1

CAMERON David Francis
b. Middleton 12.9.1902 d. Scotland 1978
Cameron Highlanders
Akeld
Queen's Park 19/20 33 2
Chelsea 20/21 13 2 FL
21/22 13 FL
22/23 25 FL
23/24 11 FL
24/25 11 FL
Heart of Midlothian 25/26 2
Helensburgh L 26/27
Portsmouth 26/27
Heart of Midlothian 27/28 2
Dunfermline A 27/28 25 2
Nottingham F 28/29 10 FL
29/30 11 1 FL
Colwyn Bay U 30/31

CAMERON Donald Scott
St Bernards 98/99 9 3
99/00 9 7
Rangers 00/01 9 5
Partick T 00/01 2 1
Falkirk 01/02
Camelon
St Bernards 03/04

CAMERON Duncan
Ayr Parkhouse
Beith
Kilmarnock 05/06 1 1
Beith 05/06
St Mirren 05/06 2
Bathgate
Beith L 06/07
Cowdenbeath 06/07

CAMERON Duncan
b. Glasgow c1881
Clyde 02/03
Brighton 03/04 19 SL
Clyde 04/05
Montrose 04/05
05/06
Port Glasgow A 06/07 22
07/08 6

CAMERON Duncan

St Mirren 07/08 1
Ayr Parkhouse

CAMERON J

Motherwell 11/12 1

CAMERON James

St Mirren 87/88
88/89
89/90
90/91 13
91/92 1

CAMERON James

Clyde 11/12 15 9
12/13 1
Abercorn 13/14 D2

CAMERON James
b. Inverness
Cameron Highlanders
Third Lanark
Inverness Clachnacuddin
Mitcham A
Heart of Midlothian 19/20 8
20/21 6
21/22 29
22/23 12
QPR 23/24 24 FL
Indiana Flooring 25/26 19 1 ASL
26/27 17 1 ASL
New York Nationals 27/28 7 ASL
New York Giants 27/28 40 1 ASL
28/29 8 ASL

CAMERON James
b. Dalmuir
Maryhill
Clydebank 18/19 2 ?
19/20 2 1
20/21 18 6

CAMERON James

Shettleston Jnrs
Airdrieonians 20/21 17
Dykehead 21/22
22/23
Albion R 22/23 18
23/24 D2
24/25 D2
25/26 D2
26/27 D2
27/28 D2
28/29 D2
29/30 D2

CAMERON James Scott
b. Lochee 27.5.1906 d. Dundee 16.12.1935
Lochee Central
Dundee Harp
Montrose
Lochee Harp
Dundee U 28/29 16 7 D2
29/30 20 2
30/31 34 8 D2
Chester 30/31
Shelbourne 31/32 LI
Celtic 32/33 4 2
Arbroath 33/34 D2
Forfar A 34/35 D2

CAMERON John 2 caps
b. Kirkwoodin 1880 d. 1945
Kirkwood Thistle
St Mirren 00/01 3
01/02 12
02/03 22
03/04 25
Blackburn R 03/04 2 FL
04/05 34 FL
05/06 7 FL
06/07 19 FL
07/08 2 FL
Chelsea 07/08 32 FL
08/09 35 FL
09/10 26 FL
10/11 34 FL
11/12 36 FL
12/13 16 FL
Port Vale 13/14 32 CL

CAMERON John S
b. Clydebank
Parkhead
Motherwell 26/27 6 3
27/28 34 18
28/29 21 7
29/30 16 10
St Johnstone 29/30 11 2
30/31 37 27 D2
31/32 27 9 D2
Dundee 32/33 12

CAMERON Robert J

Queen's Park 09/10 2 1
10/11 3 1

CAMERON Ronald

Dumbarton Fern
Duntocher Hibs
St Mirren
Kilmarnock
Morton 24/25 5 1
Bethlehem Steel 24/25 2 1 ASL
New Bedford Whalers 24/25 14 5 ASL
Newark Skeeters 24/25 9 3 ASL
Bethlehem Steel 25/26 2 1 ASL
Dumbarton 25/26 D2
Huddersfield T 25/26 FL
New Bedford Whalers 26/27 1 ASL
? 27/28
28/29
29/30
30/31
Ballymena 31/32 IL
Cork 32/33 LI
Cowdenbeath 33/34 11 3
Cork 34/35 LI
Dumbarton 35/36 D2

CAMERON William S

Third Lanark 18/19 6 ?

CAMERON William Smith
b. New Spynie 15.5.1886 d. Bolton 15.10.1958
Burnbank A 02/03
Albion R 03/04 D2
Renton 03/04
Glossop 04/05 19 11 FL
05/06 32 12 FL
Bolton W 06/07 14 3 FL
07/08 12 2 FL
Blackburn R 07/08 3 FL
08/09 17 FL
09/10 17 10 FL
10/11 16 1 FL
11/12 14 1 FL
12/13 6 6 FL
Bury 12/13 16 7 FL
13/14 22 10 FL
Hull C 13/14 13 1 FL
14/15 34 8 FL
Clydebank 15/16
Hamilton A 15/16 6 4
Vale of Leven 16/17
Bury 19/20 2 FL

CAMPBELL

Cowlairs 90/91 1

CAMPBELL

Third Lanark 90/91 1

CAMPBELL

Clyde 91/92 1

CAMPBELL

St Mirren 91/92 2
92/93 1

CAMPBELL

Dumbarton 92/93 4 1
93/94 11 1
94/95 18 6
95/96 4

CAMPBELL

St Bernards 94/95 1

CAMPBELL

Motherwell 03/04 1

CAMPBELL

Morton 17/18 1

CAMPBELL Alexander

Parkhead Jnrs
Albion R 21/22 3
22/23 9 2

CAMPBELL Alexander Ferguson
b. Dalmuir 24.1.1897 d. Blackpool 25.4.1975
Old Kirkpatrick
Glasgow Ashfield
Queen's Park 19/20 4
Oldham A 20/21 25 6 FL
21/22 12 FL
Swansea T 22/23 6 2 FL
Oldham A 23/24 4 2 FL
Mossley

CAMPBELL Andrew
b. Lasswade
Loanhead Mayflower
Heart of Midlothian 23/24 7 5
Kilmarnock L 23/24 5 1
Morton 24/25
Dundee 25/26 21 9
26/27 32 30
27/28 5 1
28/29 15 6
29/30 31 15
30/31 28 14
31/32 37 14
32/33 9 1
Dumbarton 32/33 D2
Raith R 32/33 D2
Lincoln C

CAMPBELL Archibald
d. ?.9.1918
Kirkintilloch Rob Roy
Clyde 06/07 10
Carlisle U 07/08
Albion R
Ayr 09/10 D2
Ayr U 10/11 22 9 D2
11/12 ? ? D2
12/13 ? ? D2
13/14 1
Abercorn

CAMPBELL Archibald
b. Crook ?.8.1904
Leadgate Park
Craghead U
Spennymoor U 21/22
22/23
Aston Villa 22/23 FL
23/24 1 FL
24/25 3 FL
Lincoln C 25/26 35 2 FL
26/27 19 2 FL
Craghead U 27/28
Washington Colliery 27/28
Dundee 28/29 4
Washington Colliery

CAMPBELL Charles

Lochgelly Hearts
Cowdenbeath 15/16
Hibernian 16/17 27 8
17/18 11 ?
18/19 3 ?

CAMPBELL Charles

Third Lanark 19/20 11
20/21 6

CAMPBELL Charles

Strathclyde
Clyde 32/33 9
Dundee U 33/34 30 D2

CAMPBELL Dugald
b. 1879
Abercorn
Third Lanark 00/01 4

CAMPBELL Duncan

Yoker A
Rangers 03/04 4 1
04/05 2
Portsmouth 04/05 5 SL

CAMPBELL Duncan

b. Alloa

Alva Albion R				
Cowdenbeath	28/29	7	3	
	29/30	32	5	
	30/31	36	2	
	31/32	33	3	
	32/33	27	1	
St Johnstone	33/34	33	1	
	34/35	32	3	
	35/36	11		
East Fife	36/37			D2

CAMPBELL George

b. Largs 28.3.1871 * d. Kirkcaldy 4.4.1898

Renton				
Aston Villa	90/91	15	1	FL
	91/92	20		FL
	92/93	15	1	FL
Dundee	93/94	5		
	94/95	12		
Renton	95/96			D2

CAMPBELL George

Edinburgh Myrtle				
Falkirk	04/05			D2
	05/06	14	9	
	06/07	2	1	

CAMPBELL Herbert A

Dunfermline A	24/25			D2
	25/26			D2
	26/27	2		

CAMPBELL Hugh

b. Glasgow

Ruchill Church				
Shawfield Jnrs				
Morton	32/33	7	1	
Rangers	32/33	2	1	
	33/34			
Ballymena U	34/35			IL
Clapton Orient	35/36	8	1	FL
Distillery	36/37			IL
Cardiff C	36/37	1		FL
Distillery	36/37			IL
Stranraer	37/38			
Ballymena U	37/38			IL
Halifax T	37/38	25	1	FL

CAMPBELL Ian George

b. S Africa (?)

Rothesay V				
Partick T	38/39	3		
Albion R				

CAMPBELL J

Hibernian	23/24	2		

CAMPBELL J

Morton	24/25	28	16	

CAMPBELL James 2 caps

b. Kilmarnock 8.8.1868 d. Kilmarnock 20.4.1938

Kilmarnock Thistle				
Kilmarnock	95/96	15	8	D2
	96/97	16	12	D2
	97/98	15	11	D2
	98/99	14	12	D2
	99/00	11	4	
	00/01	4	1	

CAMPBELL James

Third Lanark	38/39	1		

CAMPBELL James S

b. Lochgelly

St Andrews U				
Hearts of Beath				
St Bernards				
Cowdenbeath	34/35			D2
Dunfermline A	35/36	5	2	

CAMPBELL John 12 caps

b. Glasgow 1872 d. 2.12.1947

Possil Hawthorn				
Benburb				
Celtic	90/91	14	5	
	91/92	22	12	
	92/93	17	8	
	93/94	12	8	
	94/95	9	2	
Aston Villa	95/95	26	26	FL
	96/97	29	13	FL
Celtic	97/98	18	9	
	98/99	11	2	
	99/00	16	6	
	00/01	20	10	
	01/02	14	8	
	02/03	15	13	
Third Lanark	03/04	21	6	
	04/05	19	6	

CAMPBELL John 4 caps

b. Govan 1877

Ferntower				
Renton Union				
Linthouse				
Partick T	94/95	17	4	D2
	95/96	18	6	D2
Blackburn R	96/97	28	3	FL
	97/98	27	7	FL
Rangers	98/99	16	12	
	99/00	8	6	
	00/01	17	6	
	01/02	12	4	
West Ham U	02/03	18	1	SL
Hibernian	03/04	23	1	
	04/05	20	6	
	05/06	11	2	
New Brompton	05/06	15	3	SL
Partick T	06/07	23	7	
Dumbarton Harp				

CAMPBELL John

Port Glasgow A	05/06	4		

CAMPBELL John

Queen's Park	14/15	1		

CAMPBELL John

Queen's Park	17/18	5		
	18/19			
	19/20	2		
Renton				

CAMPBELL John

b. Newmilns

Army				
Kilmarnock	18/19	1		

CAMPBELL Kenneth 8 caps

b. Cambuslang 6.9.1892 d. Macclesfield 28.4.1977

Clyde Vale				
Rutherglen Glencairn				
Cambuslang R				
Liverpool	11/12	7		FL
	12/13	37		FL
	13/14	34		FL
	14/15	15		FL
Partick T L	18/19	1		
Liverpool	19/20	32		FL
Partick T	19/20	4		
	20/21	38		
	21/22	34		
New Brighton	22/23			
Stoke	22/23	8		FL
	23/24	11		FL
	24/25	9		FL
	25/26	7		FL
Leicester C	25/26	26		FL
	26/27	39		FL
	27/28	6		FL
	28/29	8		FL
South Shields	29/30			
New Brighton	29/30	26		FL
	30/31	29		FL

CAMPBELL Malcolm

b. Stenhousemuir

Stenhousemuir				
Falkirk	23/24	24	1	
	24/25	18	4	
Dundee U	25/26	30	10	
	26/27	24	3	
	27/28	13	4	D2
East Stirlingshire	28/29			D2
	29/30			D2
	30/31			D2
Ballymena U				

CAMPBELL Neil

Glasgow Ashfield				
St Mirren	18/19	9	?	

CAMPBELL Peter 1 cap

Volunteers				
Glasgow Perthshire				
Burton Swifts	94/95	12		FL
	95/96	28		FL
Morton	96/97	15	?	D2
	97/98	17	?	D2
Burton Swifts	98/99	33		FL
Morton	99/00	7	?	D2
	00/01	17		
	01/02	16		
	02/03	4		

CAMPBELL Robert

b. Lugar 1882 d. Ayr 13.3.1931

Lugar Boswell				
Craigston Strollers				
Partick T	97/98			
	98/99	3		
	99/00	18		D2
	00/01	9	1	
	01/02	22		D2
	02/03	20		
	03/04	18	1	
	04/05	14		
Rangers	04/05	2		
Millwall	05/06	28		SL
Bradford C	06/07	29		FL
	07/08	30		FL
	08/09	25		FL
	09/10	34		FL
	10/11	23	1	FL
	11/12	26		FL
	12/13	16		FL
	13/14	24		FL
	14/15	17		FL

CAMPBELL Robert

Queen's Park	21/22	1		

CAMPBELL Robert

Fauldhouse U				
Third Lanark	31/32			
	32/33	15	2	
	33/34			
Ballymena U	34/35			IL

CAMPBELL Robert Gordon

b. Ellon 27.1.1883 d. Townhead 31.5.1942

Kintore Village				
Crosshill Winton				
Rutherglen Glencairn				
Queen's Park Victoria				
Queen's Park	04/05	18	1	
Celtic	05/06	12		
Rangers	05/06	6		
	06/07	26	12	
	07/08	32	25	
	08/09	22	16	
	09/10	14		
	10/11	23	1	
	11/12	32		
	12/13	22		
	13/14	17		
Kilmarnock	14/15	6	3	
Ayr U	15/16	1		
	16/17	5		

CAMPBELL Robert Stewart

Kelty U				
Rangers	36/37			
	37/38			
Raith R	38/39	7		

CAMPBELL T Fred

Queen's Park	02/03	14		
	03/04	18		
	04/05	13	1	
	05/06			
	06/07			
	07/08	8		

CAMPBELL Thomas Kerr
b. Glasgow
Queen's Park 26/27 10
27/28 23
28/29 11
29/30 23
30/31 35
31/32 16
32/33 36
33/34 29
34/35 19
35/36 36
36/37 28
37/38 10

CAMPBELL Walter
Burnbank A
Celtic T
Clyde 14/15 4
15/16 14 1

CAMPBELL Walter
Armadale
St Mirren 22/23 3
Johnstone 22/23 D2

CAMPBELL William
b. Kilmalcolm
Kilmalcolm
Partick T 08/09 2
09/10 6
10/11 25
11/12 20
Barrow 12/13
Partick T 13/14 31
14/15 36
15/16 19

CAMPBELL William
Hamilton A 17/18 4

CAMPBELL William
Raith R 19/20 2
St Bernards

CAMPBELL William
Third Lanark 28/29 7

CAMPBELL William
Kilwinning R
Morton 29/30 7
Beith 29/30

CAMPBELL William
Queen's Park 29/30 2

CAMPBELL William B
Clyde 97/98 2

CAMPBELL William Cecil
Bootle 88/89
89/90 20 1 FA
Everton 90/91 13 1 FL
91/92 4
Bootle 92/93
93/94
94/95
95/96
Everton 96/97 3 1
Clyde 97/98 17 3
98/99 15 2
99/00 1

CAMPEY John Arthur
b. Glanford Brigg 1892
Falkirk 15/16 1

CANNING John
Morton 08/09 4
Port Glasgow A 09/10 5 1
10/11 D2
11/12 D2

CANNON Thomas
b. Lochgelly
Lochgelly U 19/20
Hibernian 20/21 24

CANT Andrew Fairweather
b. Kirton 6.10.1899
Dunfermline Discharged Soldiers
Raith R 19/20 7 1
Alloa A 20/21
East Fife 21/22 33 25 D2
Bradford C 22/23 13 3 FL
23/24 1 FL
East Fife 23/24 17 14 D2
Dunfermline A 24/25 D2
Dundee U 24/25 8 2 D2
Barnsley T 24/25
Kings Park

CAPPER Thomas
b. Newton le Willows 14.7.1891 d. Tranmere 30.11.1971
South Liverpool
Southport Vulcan
Dundee 19/20 7
Southend U 20/21 39 FL
21/22 39 FL
Wigan B 22/23 5 FL
Wallasey U

CARABINE James 3 caps
b. Blantyre 23.11.1911 d. ?.12.1987
Larkhall Thistle
Third Lanark 31/32 14
32/33 31 1
33/34 27
34/35 D2
35/36 35 1
36/37 37 1
37/38 34 1
38/39 30 5
46/47 8 1

CARGILL David
Dundee 14/15 16 1
15/16
16/17 3

CARGILL Thomas
Perth Roselea
Woodside
Dundee East Craigie
Forfar EE
Arbroath 35/36 14 3
Montrose 36/37 D2
Brechin C 37/38 D2

CARLIN James
b. Kinning Park 8.12.1877
Stevenston Thistle
Paisley Celtic
Celtic 96/97 1
Victoria U
Reading
Clyde
Stevenston Thistle
Glossop 99/00 8 1 FL
Arthurlie
Barnsley 00/01 16 4 FL
01/02 32 5 FL

CARLOW Francis William
b. Renton 1903
Partick T 22/23 2 2
Dumbarton 23/24 D2

CARLYLE Hugh
b. Newmains c1911
Shieldmuir Celtic
Motherwell 33/34 1
Derry C 34/35 IL
35/36 IL
36/37 IL
37/38 IL
38/39 IL
39/40 IL
40/41 IL
41/42 IL
42/43 IL
Glentoran 43/44 IL
Derry C 44/45 IL
45/46 IL
Coleraine 46/47 IL
Derry C 47/48 IL
48/49 IL
49/50 IL
? 50/51
51/52
52/53
Ballymoney U 53/54

CARMICHAEL
Clydebank 18/19 2 ?

CARMICHAEL Hamish
Petershill
Ayr U 32/33 12 1

CARMICHAEL Robert
b. Paisley 1885
Baillieston Thistle
Shettleston
Sunderland 06/07 1 FL
Heart of Midlothian 07/08
St Mirren 08/09 16 3
Oldham A 09/10 5 1 FL
Third Lanark 10/11 29 12
11/12 10 1
Clyde 11/12 17 5
12/13 18 6
Shelbourne 13/14 IL
14/15 IL
15/16 IL
16/17 IL
17/18 IL
Dumbarton 18/19 5 ?

CARNIHAN William
Blantyre V
Partick T 21/22 4
Bethlehem Steel 22/23 18 ASL
23/24 23 ASL
24/25 30 ASL
25/26 34 ASL
26/27 35 1 ASL
27/28 45 1 ASL
28/29 6 ESL
29/30 19 ASL
Newark Americans 30A 14 ASL
31S 9 ASL
New York Americans 31A 1 ASL

CARR Bernard
Blantyre St Josephs
Blantyre
Hamilton A 11/12 10 1

CARR Thomas
St Mirren 06/07 5 2

CARRICK
Dumbarton 92/93 1

CARRICK Alexander
Queen's Park 28/29 2

CARRIGAN
Abercorn 91/92 1

CARRIGAN Michael
Oatlands
Bellshill A
Hibernian 15/16 1
Motherwell 16/17

CARROLL Edward
b. Bessbrook 20.8.1901 d. Bessbrook 26.10.1975
Bessbrook
Newry T
Glenavon 20/21 IL
21/22 IL
Cardiff C 21/22
New Cross 22/23
Newry T 23/24 IL
24/25 IL
Glenavon 24/25 IL
25/26 IL
Aberdeen 25/26 5 1
Dundee U L 26/27 21 11
Brooklyn Wanderers 26/27
New York Nationals 27/28
Dundalk 27/28 LI
28/29 LI
Newry T 29/30 IL
30/31 IL
Dolphin 30/31 LI
Glenavon 31/32 IL
32/33 IL
Dundalk 32/33 LI
33/34 LI
34/35 LI
Dolphin 34/35 LI
35/36 LI
36/37 LI
Dundalk 37/38 LI

CARROLL Francis
b. Bessbrook 12.6.
Bessbrook Strollers
Cliftonville 18/19 IL
Belfast Celtic 19/20 IL
20/21 IL
Manchester C 20/21 12 FL
21/22 4 FL
22/23 FL
23/24 2 FL
24/25 FL
Newry T 25/26 IL
Dundee U T 26/27 3
27/28
Newry T 28/29 IL

CARROLL James
b. Maryhill 31.10.1909 d. Lost at sea ?.3.1944
Strathclyde
Newry T 27/28 IL
Belfast Celtic 27/28 IL
28/29 IL
29/30 IL
30/31 IL
Shelbourne 31/32 LI
32/33 LI
Belfast Celtic 33/34 IL
Clyde 33/34 28 9
34/35 27 10
Leicester C 34/35 12 1 FL
35/36 31 15 FL
36/37 22 6 FL
37/38 29 3 FL
Luton T 38/39 13 FL
39/40 3 FL
Ayr U

CARRUTH John
Rangers
Port Glasgow A 05/06 4
Rangers

CARRUTH Joseph
b. 12.3.1914 d. 26.11.1988
Springburn U
Petershill
Celtic 36/37 7 6
37/38 19 15
38/39 13 6
Stirling A T

CARRUTHERS
Clyde 96/97 1

CARRUTHERS Alexander Neilson
b. Loganlea 12.5.1914 d. Bolton 1977
Heart of Midlothian 34/35 1
Falkirk 35/36
36/37 28 19
Bolton W 36/37 1 FL
37/38 25 4 FL
Falkirk 38/39 29 14
Rochdale 46/47 13 4 FL
Rossendale U

CARRUTHERS Peter
b. Galashiels c1908 d. 6.9.1993
Dunfermline A 27/28 7 1
Heart of Midlothian 28/29 4 3
St Bernards
Leith A 30/31 18 4
Bo'ness
Hibernian 32/33 D2
Edinburgh C
Gorgie Hearts

CARRUTHERS W
Third Lanark 37/38 2

CARSON
Clyde 92/93 1

CARSON
Morton 22/23 1

CARSON Hugh
Lanemark
Kilmarnock 11/12 9 1
Abercorn 12/13 D2
Bathgate

CARSWELL John L
Clyde 29/30 1
East Stirlingshire 30/31 D2

CARSWELL Robert
b. Port Glasgow
Port Glsgow Amateurs
Morton 22/23 2
Hartlepools U 23/24 2 FL

CARTMELL John Range
b. Blackpool 28.8.1890 d. Richmond on Thames 23.2.1979
Huddersfield T
Blackpool
Mardy
Abertillery T
Royal Engineers
Heart of Midlothian 16/17 19 2
Royal Engineers
Brentford 19/20 35 2 SL
20/21 27 FL
Bournemouth
Gillingham 23/24 4 FL
Lytham 24/25

CARVER William
b. Broughty Ferry c1912 d. Hereford ??.8.2003
Forthill A
Arbroath 30/31 2 D2
Forthill A
Arbroath 31/32 1 D2
Forthill A
Arbroath 32/33 1 1 D2
33/34 33 12 D2
34/35 30 15 D2
35/36 22 3
East Fife 36/37 6 4 D2
Forfar A 36/37 D2

CASCIANI Patrick Vincent
b. Dundee 1907
Dundee St Josephs
East Fife 29/30 37 D2
30/31 21
31/32 34 D2
32/33 30 D2
33/34 27 D2
34/35 26 D2
35/36 15 D2

CASKIE James
b. Possilpark 30.1.1914 d. Glasgow 1977
Ashfield
St Johnstone 33/34 3 2
34/35 8
35/36 4
36/37 25 4
37/38 34 5
38/39 33 5
Everton 38/39 5 1 FL
Rangers 46/47 13 3
47/48 12
48/49 1
Forfar A 49/50 9 1 D2
Berwick R

CASSELLS
Clyde 91/92 3

CASSIDY James
b. Dalry 2.12.1869
Kilmarnock A
Kilmarnock
Glasgow Hibernian
Bolton W 89/90 15 13 FL
Carfin Shamrock L
Bolton W 90/91 16 8 FL
91/92 26 18 FL
Celtic L 91/92 1
Bolton W 92/93 27 9 FL
93/94 29 11 FL
94/95 26 9 FL
95/96 22 7 FL
96/97 9 2 FL
97/98 24 7 FL

CASSIDY James
Duntocher Hibs
Hibernian 20/21 3
21/22 1
22/23
Bethlehem Steel 23/24 ASL

CASSIDY John
Kings Park * 36/37 D2
Hamilton A 37/38 1
38/39 1

CASSIDY Joseph
b. Dalziel 30.7.1872
Motherwell A
Blythe
Newton Heath 92/93 4 FL
Celtic L 93/94 18 4
94/95 10 6
Newton Heath 94/95 8 8 FL
95/96 19 16 FL
96/97 28 17 FL
97/98 30 14 FL
98/99 34 18 FL
99/00 29 15 FL
Manchester C 99/00 1 FL
00/01 30 14 FL
Middlesbrough 01/02 32 14 FL
02/03 26 7 FL
03/04 34 12 FL
04/05 28 FL
05/06 6 FL
Workington

CASSIDY Joseph 4 caps
b. Cadder 10.10.1896 d. Glasgow 23.7.1949
Vale of Clyde
Celtic 12/13 3
Vale of Atholl L 13/14
Kilmarnock L 13/14
Abercorn L 13/14 D2
Ayr U L 13/14 19 2
Celtic 13/14 1
14/15
Black Watch
Celtic 15/16 4
Clydebank L 15/16
Scottish Horse
Celtic 16/17 3
17/18 1
18/19 6 3
Clydebank L 18/19 1 ?
Celtic 19/20 28 6
20/21 39 19
21/22 38 18
22/23 33 22
23/24 33 25
Bolton W 24/25 22 7 FL
Cardiff C 25/26 24 6 FL
Dundee 26/27 27 4
27/28 24 5
Clyde 28/29 19 4
Ballymena U 28/29 IL
29/30 IL
30/31 IL
Dundalk 30/31 LI
Morton 31/32 5
Dundalk 31/32 LI

CATTERSON Robert
b. Barrhead
Neilston V
Strathclyde
Dumbarton 16/17 5 1

CAVAN Daniel
Heart of Midlothian 08/09 12 6
09/10 11 2
Johnstone 10/11

CHALK Charles
East Stirlingshire
Maryhill
Rangers 03/04 4 1
Hamilton A 04/05
Plymouth A SL
Dumbarton 08/09 D2

CHALMERS
Clyde 94/95 5

CHALMERS A W
Queen's Park 22/23 13 7 D2
23/24 33 5
24/25 7 1

CHALMERS Alexander
St Mirren 97/98 4 1
98/99 9 4
99/00 2
Wishaw Thistle
Abercorn 01/02
Lanark

CHALMERS Alexander

Club	Season	Apps	Goals	League
Maryhill				
Kirkintilloch Rob Roy				
Airdrieonians	08/09	6	1	
	09/10	1		
	10/11	4		
Third Lanark	10/11	7	3	
	11/12	10	1	
Vale of Leven	12/13			D2

CHALMERS Andrew

b. Girvan 15.2.1897

Club	Season	Apps	Goals	League
Girvan				
Dumbarton	20/21	8	1	
	21/22	27	4	
Bradford C	21/22	15	4	FL
	22/23	19	2	FL
	23/24	32	6	FL
	24/25	25	4	FL
	25/26	27	5	FL
Kettering T				

CHALMERS David

b. Leven 22.7.1891 d. 24.4.1920

Club	Season	Apps	Goals	League
Leven Celtic				
Buckhaven				
Kilmarnock	09/10	13	1	
Arthurlie L	10/11			D2
Third Lanark	10/11			
Raith R	11/12	9	2	
East Fife	12/13			
York C	13/14			
Grimsby T	13/14	2		FL
	14/15	3		FL
East Fife				
Gillingham	19/20	12	1	SL

CHALMERS David

Club	Season	Apps	Goals	League
Cadzow St Annes				
St Anthonys				
Clydebank	21/22	42	7	
	22/23			D2
	23/24	30	5	
	24/25			D2
	25/26	32	8	
	26/27			

CHALMERS J

Club	Season	Apps	Goals	League
Rangers	24/25	12	2	
	25/26	6	3	

CHALMERS James

b. Old Luce 3.12.1877

Club	Season	Apps	Goals	League
Beith				
Morton	96/97	16		D2
Sunderland	97/98	24	4	FL
	98/99	3		FL
Preston NE	98/99	10	1	FL
Notts Co	99/00	25	2	FL
Beith	00/01			
Partick T	00/01	6		
Watford	01/02	30	6	SL
Tottenham H	02/03	4		SL
	03/04	6	1	SL
Swindon T	04/05	31	2	SL
	05/06	31	11	SL
Norwich C	06/07	14	2	SL
Beith	07/08			
Clyde	08/09	22	14	
	09/10	25	8	
	10/11	5	3	
Beith				

CHALMERS James

Club	Season	Apps	Goals	League
Broxburn A				
Port Glasgow A	08/09	10	4	
Broxburn A				

CHALMERS John

b. Beith 1884

Club	Season	Apps	Goals	League
Rutherglen Glencairn				
Rangers	04/05	1		
Beith	05/06			
Stoke	05/06	5	5	FL
	06/07	26	11	FL
	07/08	9	3	FL
Bristol R	08/09	1	1	SL
Clyde	08/09			
	09/10			
Woolwich Arsenal	10/11	29	15	FL
	11/12	19	6	FL
Morton	11/12	7	2	
	12/13	33	15	
West Stanley	13/14			
Clyde	13/14	12	10	
Shelbourne	14/15			IL

CHALMERS John

Club	Season	Apps	Goals	League
Croy Celtic				
Dumbarton	15/16	9		

CHALMERS John

Club	Season	Apps	Goals	League
Camelon Jnrs				
Airdrieonians	32/33	7		
Bo'ness	33/34			D2

CHALMERS Thomas

Club	Season	Apps	Goals	League
Clyde	99/00	1		

CHALMERS William

b. Bellshill 25.7.1904

Club	Season	Apps	Goals	League
Bellshill Academy				
Bellshill				
Queen's Park	22/23	13	7	
	23/24	33	5	
	24/25	7	1	
Rangers	24/25	12	2	
	25/26	6	3	
	26/27			
Newcastle U	27/28	1	1	FL
	28/29	19	8	FL
	29/30	15	4	FL
	30/31	6		FL
Grimsby T	31/32	6	1	FL
Bury	32/33	38	10	FL
	33/34	19	6	FL
	34/35	16	1	FL
	35/36	25	6	FL
Notts Co	36/37	38	8	FL
	37/38	26	8	FL
Aldershot	38/39	37	10	FL
	39/40	3		FL

CHALMERS William G

Club	Season	Apps	Goals	League
St Johnstone	26/27	5	1	

CHALMERS William Stewart 1 cap

b. Glasgow 5.3.1907

Club	Season	Apps	Goals	League
Mount Florida				
Queen's Park	25/26	3		
	26/27	19	4	
	27/28	35	12	
	28/29	28	5	
Heart of Midlothian	29/30	22	3	
	30/31	17	4	
	31/32	16	5	
Cowdenbeath				
Manchester U	32/33	22	1	FL
	33/34	12		FL
Dunfermline A	34/35	30	5	
	35/36	29	2	
	36/37	32	9	

CHAMBERS Hugh

b. Glasgow

Club	Season	Apps	Goals	League
St Anthonys				
Clyde	17/18	18	?	
	18/19	17	?	
	19/20	3	1	
	20/21	17	1	
	21/22	24	1	
	22/23	37		
	23/24	30	1	
Cowdenbeath	24/25	36	1	
	25/26	28	2	
	26/27	29	3	
	27/28	27	2	
	28/29	5		
Hamilton A	28/29	14		

CHAMBERS Thomas 1 cap

Club	Season	Apps	Goals	League
St Bernards				
Heart of Midlothian	92/93	3	3	
Burnley	92/93	16	5	FL
Heart of Midlothian	93/94	16	6	
	94/95	16	8	
	95/96	8	3	
Burnley	96/97	10	6	FL
St Bernards	97/98	11	3	

CHANDLER Albert

b. Carlisle 15.1.1897 d. Carlisle 28.1.1963

Club	Season	Apps	Goals	League
Dalston Beach Reds				
Carlisle U				
Machine Guns Corps				
Derby Co	19/20	11		FL
	20/21	10		FL
	21/22	42		FL
	22/23	37		FL
	23/24	31		FL
	24/25	38		FL
Newcastle U	25/26	29		FL
	26/27	4		FL
Sheffield U	26/27	19		FL
	27/28	32		FL
	28/29	19		FL
Mansfield T	29/30			
Northfleet U	29/30			
Manchester Central	29/30			
Holme Head	30/31			
Queen of the South	31/32			
	32/33			
	33/34	1		

CHAPLIN George Duncan 1 cap

b. Dundee 26.9.1888 d. Coventry 14.5.1963

Club	Season	Apps	Goals	League
Dundee Arnott				
Dundee	07/08	32		
	08/09	6		
Bradford C	08/09	15		FL
	09/10	33		FL
	10/11	22		FL
	11/12	1		FL
	12/13			FL
	13/14	1		FL
	14/15	15		FL
Coventry C	19/20	23		FL
	20/21	32		FL
	21/22	42		FL
	22/23	12		FL

CHAPLIN Jonathan Fowler

b. Dundee 10.10.1882 d. Doncaster 15.4.1952

Club	Season	Apps	Goals	League
Dundee W	02/03			
Dundee	03/04	2		
	04/05	25		
Tottenham H	05/06	2		SL
	06/07	34		SL
	07/08	30		SL
Dundee	08/09	26		
	09/10	26		
	10/11	9		
Manchester C	10/11	15		FL

CHAPMAN George

b. Edinburgh c1901

Club	Season	Apps	Goals	League
Musselburgh Bruntonians				
Bathgate	21/22	2	2	D2
Heart of Midlothian	21/22	1		
	22/23	10		
	23/24	4		
Raith R	24/25	12		

CHAPMAN George R

b. Broxburn 23.10.1886

Club	Season	Apps	Goals	League
Edinburgh Myrtle				
Heart of Midlothian	05/06	3		
	06/07	2		
Raith R	07/08			D2
Blackburn R	08/09	36	1	FL
	09/10	31	4	FL
Rangers	10/11	28	3	
	11/12	2	1	
Blackburn R	11/12	22	9	FL
	12/13	25	10	FL
	13/14	19	9	FL
	14/15	4	2	FL
Accrington S				

CHAPMAN John

Club	Season	Apps	Goals	League
Muirkirk Jnrs				
Kilmarnock	01/02	3		
	02/03			
Nithsdale W	03/04			

CHAPPLE Alexander

Club	Season	Apps	Goals	League
Motherwell	02/03			D2
	03/04	4		
Ayr				

CHAPPLE George

Club	Season	Apps	Goals	League
Renfrew V				
Clyde	06/07	4		
	07/08	9		
	08/09	12		
Reading	09/10			SL
Clyde	10/11	3		

CHATTON James Harold
b. Enniskillen 23.4.1899
Kirkintilloch Rob Roy
Dumbarton 20/21 13
21/22 27
22/23 D2
Partick T 23/24 24 2
24/25 23
25/26 24
Indiana Flooring 26/27 31 1 ASL
Heart of Midlothian 26/27
New York Nationals 27/28 23 ASL
28/29 41 ASL
29A 21 ASL
29/30 29 ASL
Shelbourne 30/31 LI
Dumbarton 31/32 D2
Shelbourne 31/32 LI
Dumbarton 32/33 D2
Cork 33/34 LI
34/35 LI

CHATWIN Charles
Aberdeen 13/14 1
14/15 22 1
15/16 22

CHERRIE
Clyde 91/92 12 3
92/93 10
93/94 1 D2

CHERRY James
b. Kilwinning 20.9.1897
Kilwinning Eglington
Kilmarnock 19/20 3
20/21 5
21/22 4
Clydebank 22/23
Ardrossan winton R
Kilwinning R
Kilwinning Eglington

CHEYNE Alexander George 5 caps
b. Glasgow 28.4.1907 d. Arbroath 6.8.1983
Shettleston Jnrs
Aberdeen 25/26 3
26/27 23 7
27/28 32 9
28/29 35 17
29/30 34 15
Chelsea 30/31 34 9 FL
31/32 19 1 FL
Nimes 32/33
33/34
Chelsea 34/35 3 1 FL
35/36 6 1 FL
Colchester T 36/37
Colchester U 37/38 15 8 SL
38/39 29 14 SL

CHEYNE William Alan
b. Fraserburgh c1913
Fraserburgh
Rangers 33/34 3
34/35 6
35/36 19
36/37 17 1
37/38 9
38/39 2
Motherwell

CHISHOLM
Dumbarton 92/93 1

CHISHOLM George G
Port Glasgow A 09/10 1

CHITTICKS Robert
b. Linwood c1889
Chelsea
St Mirren 10/11 1
11/12
Johnstone * 12/13 D2

CHORLTON James Edward
Falkirk 18/19 1 ?

CHRISTIE
St Mirren 91/92 1
92/93 1

CHRISTIE
St Bernards 94/95 1

CHRISTIE
St Bernards 96/97 2 1

CHRISTIE Alexander Gray
b. Paisley 27.6.1896 d. Reading 22.5.1981
Paisley Central YMCA
Larkhall Thistle
Hamilton A 14/15 13 1
15/16 11 4
Royal Naval Barracks
Reading 19/20 30 2 SL
20/21 37 1 FL
Walsall 21/22 30 1 FL
Southampton 22/23 5 FL
Norwich C 23/24 5 FL
Rochdale 24/25 31 1 FL
25/26 42 4 FL
26/27 33 FL
27/28 33 FL
Exeter C 28/29 4 FL
Aldershot 29/30 20 2 SL
30/31 3 SL
H & G Simonds A

CHRISTIE Alexander Jack 3 caps
b. Dunblane 28.9.1873
Edinburgh University
Queen's Park 97/98
98/99
99/00
00/01 2
St Bernards 01/02 D2
Queen's Park 02/03 14 4
03/04 1
Dunblane

CHRISTIE David
Abercorn 95/96 8 ? D2
96/97 4

CHRISTIE David
Forres Mechanics
Edinburgh University
Queen's Park 37/38 33 6
38/39 30 5
Aberdeen

CHRISTIE David Fiddes
b. Arbroath 1.4.1899
Arbroath 21/22 19 6 D2
Albion R 22/23 10 2
Celtic 22/23
Arbroath A 22/23
Third Lanark 23/24 3
East Stirlingshire 23/24 D3
24/25 D2
Port Vale T 25/26
Barrow 26/27 21 5 FL

CHRISTIE James
Raith R 19/20 5 1

CHRISTIE James
Buckhaven V
Hibernian 33/34
34/35 4

CHRISTIE Robert
b. Thornton
Lochgelly Albert
Cardenden
Partick T 35/36 9
36/37 3
Arbroath 37/38 32 3
38/39 27 7

CLARK
Vale of Leven 91/92 1

CLARK Andrew
b. Leith 1881
Heart of Midlothian 99/00 16
00/01 15
Stoke 01/02 34 FL
02/03 19 FL
Plymouth A 03/04 31 SL
04/05 29 SL
05/06 23 1 SL
Leeds C
East Fife 07/08
Clyde

CLARK Andrew
Rutherglen Glencairn
Clyde 32/33 9
Morton 33/34 D2

CLARK Andrew W K
Parkhead Jnrs
Kilmarnock 35/36 5 1

CLARK D
Rangers 92/93 1 1

CLARK Frank
Falkirk 18/19 11
Raith R 19/20 4

CLARK James
b. Kilmarnock
J & M Craigs
Musselburgh A
Wallyford Violet
Kilmarnock Winton
Kilmarnock 11/12 8 3
12/13 2
Hurlford
Kilmarnock 13/14 6
Arthurlie
Hurlford
Kilmarnock 19/20 4 3

CLARK James
b. Rutherglen 23.4.1903
Rutherglen Glencairn
Kilmarnock 24/25 19 1

CLARK James
Dunfermline A 26/27 26
27/28 25

CLARK James
Lochhead
Hamilton A 30/31 3

CLARK James
b. Tyneside
Newburn
Throckley Welfare
Margate T 34/35
Arsenal 34/35 FL
Hibernian 35/36 3 1
Barnsley 36/37 11 1 FL
Distillery 37/38 IL
Waterford 38/39 LI
Derry C 39/40 IL

CLARK James Ferguson
b. Kilwinning 5.5.1911
Kilwinning Eglington
Partick T 32/33 7
Benburb Star 33/34
Southend U 34/35 FL
Denny Hibs 35/36
Derry C 36/37 IL

CLARK James Robinson
b. Bensham 20.10.1895 d. Gateshead ?.9.1947
Annfield Plain
Jarrow
Newcastle U 22/23 3 1 FL
23/24 8 1 FL
Leeds U 24/25 3 FL
Swindon T 25/26 18 6 FL
Morton 26/27 1
Ashington 26/27 5 FL
Shelbourne 27/28 LI

CLARK John
b. Edinburgh 24.7.1880 d. Belvedere Hospital 16.6.1906
Holytown Thistle
Clyde L
Celtic 02/03 2 1
Clyde

CLARK John
b. Beith
Beith Caledonian
Beith 06/07
07/08
Morton 08/09 11
Ayr Parkhouse
Beith
Galston
Johnstone 12/13

CLARK John

Strathclyde					
Queen's Park		11/12	22	7	
		12/13	7	1	
Motherwell		12/13	1		
Morton		13/14	7	3	
St Mirren		14/15	33	18	
		15/16	3	2	
		16/17	1	1	
Glentoran	L	16/17			IL
Linfield	L	17/18			IL
St Mirren		18/19	11	?	
Clyde	L	18/19	2	?	
St Mirren		19/20	17	4	

CLARK John

Hibernian		14/15	22	5	
Abercorn		15/16			

CLARK John

Dumbarton		19/20	1		

CLARK John
b. Coatbridge 4.3.190C

Black Watch Regiment					
Bo'ness		21/22	31	2	D2
		22/23	27	3	D2
Arsenal		22/23	2		FL
		23/24	2		FL
		24/25	2		FL
		25/26			FL
Luton T		26/27	8	1	FL
Bo'ness		27/28	19		
Third Lanark		27/28			
Bo'ness		28/29			D2

CLARK Joseph
b. Dundee

Dundee		96/97	16	8	
		97/98	11		
Brighton U		98/99	6		SL
Dundee		98/99			
Newton Heath		99/00	8		FL
Lochee U					
Dunfermline A					
East Fife					

CLARK Joseph McGhee
b. Maryhill 4.5.1892

Govan St Anthonys					
Motherwell	T				
Celtic		11/12	2	1	
		12/13			
Cowdenbeath		12/13		7	D2
Abercorn		13/14			D2
Renton		13/14			

CLARK Richard S

Arthurlie					
Motherwell					
Airdrieonians		35/36	3		
Stenhousemuir		36/37			D2

CLARK William
b. Beith 16.9.1900

Beith					
Arthurlie	L	27/28			
Clyde	L	27/28			
Carlisle U	T	27/28	5		
Kilmarnock		28/29	8		
		29/30	1	1	
		30/31	1		
Beith					

CLARK William

Banknock					
St Mirren		27/28	8	2	

CLARK William
b. Brechin 1909 d. Perth 26.9.1991

Brechin V					
Brechin C					
St Johnstone		29/30			
		30/31			D2
		31/32	1		D2
		32/33	38	2	
		33/34	33	1	
		34/35	20		
		35/36	23		
		36/37	19		
		37/38	12		
		38/39	27		
Cowdenbeath					

CLARK William

Bo'ness					
Hibernian		31/32			D2
		32/33			D2
		33/34	5		

CLARK William

Larkhall Thistle					
Ayr U		34/35	4		
		35/36	16		
Kings Park					

CLARK William B
b. Airdrie 1881 d. Bristol 17.3.1937

Port Glasgow A		02/03	21	6	
		03/04	23	4	
Bristol R		04/05	31	9	SL
		05/06	31	6	SL
		06/07	35	10	SL
		07/08	36	9	SL
Sunderland		08/09	11	2	FL
		09/10	29	2	FL
Bristol C		10/11	24	1	FL
Leicester F		11/12	6	1	FL

CLARKE A

Queen's Park		16/17	1		

CLARKE Bruce Mitchell
b. Johannesburg 4.10.1910

Hillside Jnrs					
Montrose		28/29			D2
Third Lanark		28/29			D2
		29/30			D2
		30/31			D2
		31/32	12	2	
		32/33	18		
		33/34	29	7	
Corale A (Paris)		33/34			
Fulham		34/35	40	1	FL
		35/36	26		FL
		36/37	39		FL
		37/38	5		FL
		38/39	2		FL
Worcester C		39/40			

CLARKE James

Tranent Jnrs					
Clyde		34/35			
		35/36	20	2	
		36/37	5		
		37/38	2		

CLARKE John
b. Rosewell 1905

Rosewell Rosedale					
St Mirren					
Hibernian		25/26	7		
		26/27	3		
Dunfermline A		27/28	2		
Third Lanark		28/29	15	2	
		29/30			D2
		30/31			D2
		31/32	26		
		32/33	16	3	
Carlisle U		33/34	28	1	FL
Cowdenbeath		34/35			D2
		35/36			D2
		36/37			D2
		37/38			D2

CLARKSON Alexander

Ardrossan Winton R					
Dumbarton		13/14	8		

CLARKSON Andrew H

Queen's Park		00/01	17	1	
		01/02	3	1	

CLARKSON Robert

Maryhill V					
Third Lanark		07/08	8	1	
		08/09	3		
Renton					

CLARKSON Thomas

Burnbank A					
Morton		01/02	9	1	
Stenhousemuir		01/02			
Morton		02/03	4		

CLARKSON Thomas
b. Glasgow

Troon A					
Kilmarnock		36/37	14	6	
Dundee U		37/38	24	11	D2

CLARKSON W

Clyde		11/12	1		

CLEASBY Harold R

Port Glasgow Jnrs					
Airdrieonians		23/24	2		

CLEGHORN Thomas
b. St Andrew, Edinburgh 13.2.1870

Leith A		92/93	15	1	
		93/94	15		
Blackburn R		94/95	28	3	FL
		95/96	17		FL
Liverpool		95/96	2		FL
		96/97	17		FL
		97/98	30		FL
		98/99	5		FL
Portsmouth		99/00	22		SL
		00/01	21		SL
		01/02	15		SL
		02/03			SL
Plymouth A		03/04	1		SL
		04/05	1		SL

CLELAND James

Minerva					
Third Lanark		93/94	5	1	
		94/95	6	1	
St Bernards		95/96	7	2	
Liverpool					
Abercorn		96/97	5	2	
Partick T		97/98	6	2	

CLELAND John

Galston					
Port Glasgow A		04/05	25		
		05/06	4		
		06/07	10		
		07/08	13		

CLELAND William
b. Gartcosh c1910

Glenboig St Josephs					
Hibernian		29/30			
		30/31	11	1	
		31/32			D2
		32/33			D2
		33/34			
Waterford		34/35			LI

CLELLAND James B

Edinburgh Myrtle					
Falkirk		05/06	2		
Cowdenbeath					

CLELLAND Robert

Queen's Park Strollers					
Shettleston					
Motherwell		34/35	4	2	
		35/36	1		

CLEMENTS Harry
b. West Bromwich 1883
d. West Bromwich ?.2.1939

Worcester C		02/03			
WBA		03/04	10		FL
Worcester C		04/05			
		05/06			
Shrewsbury T					
St Mirren		06/07	11	2	
		07/08	30	5	
		08/09	25	4	
		09/10	21	5	
		10/11	9		
Third Lanark		11/12	4		

CLEMENTS Robert 1 cap

Leith A		91/92	10	3	
		92/93	1		

CLEMIE Samuel Turner
b. Lugar 11.4.1904 d. Ballochmyle 6.1.1970

Lugar Boswell					
Kilmarnock		25/26	9		
		26/27	20		
		27/28	30		
		28/29	32		
		29/30	36		
		30/31	38		
		31/32	18		
East Stirlingshire		32/33	5		

CLIFFORD Hugh
b. Carfin 8.4.1873
Hibernian
Derby Co
Carfin Shamrock
Stoke 90/91 17 1 FA
91/92 13 1 FL
Celtic 91/92 1
92/93 5
Stoke 93/94 1 FL
Carfin Shamrock
Motherwell 94/95 2 ? D2
Liverpool
Manchester C 95/96 4 1 FL
Carfin R

CLIFFORD Samuel
Mossend Hibs
Hamilton A 14/15 4
15/16 1

CLIFFORD Thomas
b. Kilbirnie 1875
Annbank
Newton Heath
Ayr
Glossop 98/99 24 1 FL
99/00 15 FL
Luton T
Celtic
Beith 03/04
Motherwell 04/05 16 1
Nottingham F

CLUNAS Charles
b. Johnstone 1894 K.I.A., Pas de Calais 8.2.1916
Kilbarchan A
Clyde 12/13 4 2
13/14 11 1
14/15 4

CLUNAS William McLean 2 caps
b. Johnstone 29.4.1899 d. Johnstone 1.9.1967
Kilbarchan A
Johnstone
Luton T T
St Mirren 20/21 4
21/22 39 2
22/23 31 7
23/24 15
Sunderland 23/24 21 FL
24/25 41 4 FL
25/26 38 9 FL
26/27 37 6 FL
27/28 35 3 FL
28/29 37 12 FL
29/30 35 8 FL
30/31 12 FL
Morton 31/32 31 2
32/33 32 8
33/34
Inverness Thistle 34/35

CLYNE David Johnstone Robertson
b. Dennistoun 1916 d. Barra ?.5.1944
Queen's Park 37/38 4
38/39 1

COATS Archibald
b. 27.1.1911 d. Bangor 2.11.1993
Portsmouth
Glentoran 32/33 IL
Bangor 32/33 IL
33/34 IL
Dundee 34/35 38 30
35/36 38 28
36/37 38 25
37/38 38 13
38/39 34 26 D2
Third Lanark 46/47
47/48

COBBAN William L
Raith R 15/16 13 2
16/17 5 1

COCHRANE
Clyde 94/95 1

COCHRANE Alexander Fraser
b. Glasgow 8.8.1900
Shawfield Jnrs
Alloa A 22/23 27 8
Middlesbrough 22/23 6 1 FL
23/24 18 4 FL
24/25 23 1 FL
25/26 20 2 FL
Darlington 26/27 41 8 FL
27/28 40 8 FL
28/29 20 8 FL
Bradford C 28/29 16 9 FL
29/30 38 17 FL
30/31 15 1 FL
Chesterfield 31/32 27 1 FL
Llanelly 32/33
Northampton T 33/34 9 1 FL
34/35 33 6 FL
Swindon T 35/36 13 1 FL
Partick T 35/36
East Stirlingshire 36/37 D2
37/38 D2
Dumbarton 37/38 D2
Rothwell
Brigstock

COCHRANE Andrew
Third Lanark 95/96 3

COCHRANE Andrew
b. Vale of Leven
Bonhill Union
Strathclyde
Rangers 05/06 10
Vale of Leven

COCHRANE David S
b. 30.1.
Dunblane R
Denny Hibs
Nelson 27/28 2 2 FL
Bo'ness 27/28 2 1
Armadale 27/28 D2

COCHRANE Thomas H
Queen's Park 00/01 6 1
01/02 3

COCKBURN
Cambuslang 90/91 1

COEN Joseph Leonard
b. Glasgow 4.12.1911 d. Grantham 19.10.1941
Bellahouston Academy
Mosspark Amateurs
Parkview U
Clydeholm Jnrs
Clydebank 30/31
Celtic 30/31
Clydebank L 30/31
Nithsdale W L 30/31
Celtic 31/32 3
Stenhousemuir L 31/32 D2
Guildford C 32/33
Bournemouth 32/33 11 FL
33/34 25 FL
Luton T 34/35 37 FL
35/36 36 FL
36/37 12 FL
37/38 26 FL
38/39 31 FL
39/40 3 FL

COGLAN (or COUGHLAN)
Morton 04/05 9

COHAM John Harding
b. Southampton 12.3.1891 d. Blackpool 4.5.1969
St Pauls A
Eastleigh A
Bishopstoke
Southampton 10/11 6 SL
Partick T 11/12 20 5
12/13 3 1
Dumbarton Harp

COID David
b. Blythswood 13.9.1891 d. Glasgow 7.3.1966
Pollok
Petershill
Kilbarchan A
Clyde 14/15 7
East Stirlingshire
Cowdenbeath 19/20
Armadale T 20/21
Portsmouth 20/21 7 3 FL

COLE Andrew James
Port Glasgow Jnrs
St Mirren 11/12 3 1
12/13 17 2
Dunfermline A 13/14

COLE Philip
Airdrie Jnrs
Third Lanark 04/05 12 2
Clyde
Bradford PA
Heart of Midlothian 08/09 33 8
09/10 27 8
Dunfermline A 10/11
Airdrieonians 11/12 20 2
Dunfermline A 12/13 D2

COLEMAN John
b. Cardross 3.1.1870 d. 4.5.1927
Cathcart
Netherlee
Vale of Leven Hibs
Hibernian
Celtic 88/89
89/90
90/91
91/92 4 1
92/93 1

COLLIER William
b. Kirkcaldy 1895
Raith R 11/12 5
Regina Thistle
Bethlehem Steel
Philadelphia Field Club 21/22 11 1 ASL
Fall River Marksmen 22/23 11 ASL
23/24 12 ASL
24/25
25/26 1 ASL
Newark Skeeters 25/26 2 1 ASL

COLLIER William 1 cap
b. Kirkcaldy 4.6.1891 d. Dunfermline 17.4.1954
Black Watch
Forfar Yeomanry
Inverkeithing Jnrs
Raith R 19/20 4
20/21 35 4
21/22 40 1
22/23 34
23/24 20 2
Sheffield W 24/25 14 FL
Kettering T 25/26

COLLIGAN George
b. Beith
Beith
Abercorn 94/95 4 ? D2
95/96 14 ? D2
96/97 12 1
97/98 3 ? D2
Beith 97/98
Morton 98/99 11 ? D2
99/00 18 ? D2
00/01 19 1
01/02 11
Beith 02/03
Abercorn 02/03

COLLINS
Third Lanark 91/92 1

COLLINS Alan
b. Kilmarnock 24.1.1918 d. Kilmarnock 10.4.2002
Kilmarnock Academicals
Cumnock Jnrs
Kilmarnock 36/37 11 3
37/38 34 14
38/39 16 6
46/47 19 9
47/48 30 24
Raith R 48/49 D2
49/50 25 9
50/51 5 1
Stenhousemuir 51/52 D2
52/53 D2

COLLINS David
b. Dumbarton
Dumbarton Fern
Dumbarton 31/32 D2
Bradford PA 32/33 7 2 FL
33/34 D2
Morton 34/35 D2
35/36 D2
36/37 D2
37/38 35 5

COLLINS David

Royal Albert
Airdrieonians 33/34 18 3
34/35 19 7
Peterborough U

COLLINS Francis J
b. Belfast 16.11.1891
Wanderers (Dublin)
Jacobs 17/18
18/19
19/20
20/21
Celtic 21/22 2
Jacobs 22/23 LI
23/24 LI
24/25 LI
25/26 LI
26/27 LI
27/28 LI
28/29 LI
29/30 LI
30/31 LI
31/32 LI

COLLINS Henry
b. Govan 1863 d. Govan ?.3.1931
Petershill
Glasgow Ashfield
Falkirk 05/06 18 2
06/07 20 1
07/08 34 2
08/09 ? ?
09/10 11
Clyde 10/11 17 1
11/12 31 2
12/13 27 1
13/14 35
14/15 32 1
Motherwell 15/16 25

COLLINS Hugh
b. Craigneuk 1901
Wishaw YMCA
Hamilton A 22/23 24 11
23/24 23 11
Ayr U L 24/25
Partick T 24/25 9 4
Dundee U 24/25 4 1 D2
Queen of the South 25/26 D2
Brooklyn Wanderers 25/26 7 2 ASL
Philadelphia Field Club 25/26 7 1 ASL
Aldershot

COLLINS James

Cambuslang 90/91 16
Everton 91/92 6 FL
92/93 9 FL

COLLINS Patrick

Kirkintilloch Rob Roy
Hibernian 09/10 12

COLLINS Thomas 1 cap
b. Leven 16.4.1882 d. Edmonton 13.7.1929
Leven Thistle
Heart of Midlothian 03/04 18
04/05 4
Bathgate L 04/05
East Fife 05/06
Heart of Midlothian 06/07 32
07/08 29 1
08/09 34
09/10 25
10/11 15
Tottenham H 10/11 25 FL
11/12 33 FL
12/13 28 1 FL
13/14 15 FL
14/15 12 FL

COLLINS Thomas

Cambuslang R
Airdrieonians 03/04 17
04/05 2
05/06
Hamilton A 06/07 5
Albion R

COLMAN Donald Cameron 4 caps
(born Donald Cunningham)
b. Renton 14.8.1878 d. Aberdeen 5.10.1942
Tontine A
Glasgow Perthshire
Tontine A
Renton
Sunderland T
Maryhill Jnrs
Motherwell 05/06 27
06/07 12
Aberdeen 07/08 28
08/09 34
09/10 34
10/11 32
11/12 32
12/13 33
13/14 34
14/15 37
15/16 26
16/17 23 1
17/18
St Mirren 18/19 1 ?
Renton 18/19
Aberdeen 19/20 11
Dumbarton 20/21 17
21/22 24
22/23 7 D2

COLOMBO Bail
b. Leith
Clydebank
Heart of Midlothian 07/08 21 4
Leith A 08/09 D2
Heart of Midlothian 09/10 11 1
Leith A 10/11 D2
Kirkcaldy U 11/12
St Johnstone 11/12 6 1 D2
12/13 D2
13/14 D2
14/15 D2
Bathgate 15/16

COLQUHOUN

Dumbarton 94/95 1
95/96 1

COLQUHOUN David Wilson
b. Motherwell 9.1.1906 d. Motherwell 3.6.1983
Blantyre V
St Mirren 26/27 2
27/28 13 1
28/29 37
29/30 35
30/31 38 2
Tottenham H 31/32 36 1 FL
32/33 29 1 FL
33/34 13 FL
34/35 3 FL
Luton T 34/35 12 FL
35/36 4 FL
Rochdale

COLQUHOUN James

St Mirren 96/97 2

COLQUHOUN John C

Dalnair Juveniles
St Anthonys
Partick T 13/14 7
14/15 2
Vale of Leven L 14/15 D2

COLVILLE George
b. Kingassie 4.3.1874
Annbank
Blackpool 96/97 5 FL
Hibernian 96/97
Annbank 97/98
Glossop NE 98/99 33 1 FL
99/00 32 1 FL
00/01 28 FL
01/02 12 FL
02/03 FL
Fulham 03/04 6 SL
Annbank 04/05
05/06
06/07
07/08
Port Glasgow A 08/09 27
09/10 25
10/11 1 ?

COLVIN Peter S

Queen's Park 13/14 2

COMBE Alex D

View Park
Bellshill A
Airdrieonians 10/11 4 1
Dunfermline A 11/12

COMMON James

Adventurers
Heart of Midlothian
English football 88/89
89/90
Heart of Midlothian 90/91 1

COMRIE Alexander

Armadale
Falkirk 16/17 34 4
17/18 33 ?
18/19 22 ?

COMRIE Alexander

Dunipace Jnrs
Clyde 20/21 3

COMRIE Andrew
b. Denny
Kirkintilloch Rob Roy
Partick T 19/20 14 2
20/21 7 1
Stenhousemuir

COMRIE Daniel

St Johnstone * 13/14 11 7 D2
14/15 25 5 D2
Armadale
Falkirk 16/17 18 5

COMRIE George Smart
b. Denny 31.3.1885
Dunipace Jnrs
Third Lanark
Millwall 05/06 SL
06/07 SL
07/08 SL
08/09 SL
Dundee 09/10 22
10/11 26 2
11/12 28 3
Huddersfield T 12/13 15 FL
Forfar A 13/14

COMRIE James
b. Denny 31.3.1881 K.I.A.,France 9.8.1916
Dunipace (?)
Third Lanark 03/04 4 1
04/05 24 4
05/06 26 11
Reading 06/07 35 SL
Glossop 07/08 35 1 FL
08/09 3 FL
Bradford C 08/09 12 1 FL
09/10 31 2 FL
Lincoln C 10/11 12 1 FL
Grantham
Stenhousemuir
Reading 12/13 36 SL
13/14 22 1 SL
14/15 34 SL

COMRIE John

Dunipace Jnrs
Dundee 10/11 1
Stenhousemuir 11/12

COMRIE John

Armadale
Bradford C
Airdrieonians 15/16 17 1
16/17 26
17/18 8

CONDIE Hugh S

Queen's Park 21/22 2

CONLIN George Fyffe
b. Glasgow
Baillieston
Rangers 29/30
30/31 2
Ayr U 30/31 5 1
31/32
32/33
Hamilton A 33/34 3 1
Ballymena U 34/35 IL

CONLIN James
b. Durham 6.7.1881 d. Flanders 23.6.1917
Capt Colts Rovers
Cambuslang
Hibernian
Falkirk
Albion R
Bradford C 04/05 29 3 FL
05/06 32 2 FL
Manchester C 06/07 35 2 FL
07/08 37 6 FL
08/09 27 4 FL
09/10 35 11 FL
10/11 27 4 FL
Birmingham 11/12 21 2 FL
Airdrieonians 12/13 25 5
Broxburn U

CONNABOY Michael
b. Edinburgh 29.11.1901 d. Edinburgh 18.7.1947
Loanhead Mayflower
Dunfermline A
Alloa A 22/23 23 2
23/24 D2
24/25 D2
25/26 D2
Raith R 26/27 D2
Cowdenbeath 26/27 16 1
27/28 14 1
New York Nationals 28/29 40 1 ASL
Yeovil T
Wolverhampton W 31/32
Exeter C 32/33 4 1 FL
Darlington 33/34 10 FL
Arbroath

CONNABOY Thomas
b. Straiton 10.11.1911 d. Penicuik 22.11.1974
Arniston R
Arbroath 34/35 10 1 D2
35/36 10 1
36/37 7
Leith A
Darlington 37/38 1 FL
Bangor C 37/38 IL
Southampton

CONNACHAN James
b. Glasgow 29.8.1874
Duntochter Hibs
Glasgow Perthshire
Duntochter Hibs
Celtic 96/97 1
97/98
Airdrieonians 98/99 1 D2
Newton Heath 98/99 4 FL
Glossop 98/99 11 4 FL
99/00 17 4 FL
Leicester F 00/01 29 6 FL
Nottingham F 01/02
Morton 01/02 5 1
Renton 02/03
03/04
04/05
05/06
Britannia (Canada) 06/07
Dumbarton Harp

CONNACHER James
Bathgate
Heart of Midlothian 16/17 8 3
17/18 7
18/19 2

CONNELL Archibald
b. Darvel 22.4.1900
Darvel
Motherwell 26/27 2
Queen of the South
Notts Co 27/28 4 1 FL

CONNELL Archibald
b. Glasgow
Hibernian 28/29 1
29/30 3

CONNELL John
b. Scotland
St Mirren 94/95 16 3
95/96 8
Galston 95/96
Newcastle U 96/97 24 3 FL

CONNELL W
Ayr U 13/14 2

CONNELL William
b. Newmilns 17.3.1907 d. 1982
Newmilns
Kilmarnock 27/28 15 1
28/29 37 12
29/30 23 6
30/31 36 8
31/32 37 14
32/33 15 6
33/34 15 2
Galston
Ayr U 34/35 2
Beith 35/36
Stenhousemuir 35/36 D2

CONNELLY James
Parkhead
Falkirk 04/05 D2
05/06 6 2

CONNELLY Peter
Lochee
Dundee 19/20 1

CONNER John Cuthbertson Tippett
b. Kirkmuirhill 26.4.1898 d. Wishaw 27.5.1967
Blantyre Celtic
Celtic 21/22
Alloa A 22/23 2
23/24 D2
Dykehead L 24/25 D3
Plymouth A 25/26 FL
Newport Co 26/27 13 FL
Torquay U 27/28 25 FL
Guildford C

CONNOLLY Bernard
b. Glasgow 27.6.1894
Vale of Clyde
Celtic 13/14 9 3
Dumbarton Harp L 13/14
Vale of Atholl L
Vale of Leven L 13/14 D2
Celtic 14/15
Ayr U L 14/15 14
Celtic 15/16
Wishaw Thistle L 15/16
Clydebank L 15/16
Celtic 16/17 4
Stevenston U L 16/17
Dumbarton Harp L 16/17
Celtic 17/18
18/19
Cambuslang R

CONNOLLY Joseph A
b. c1910
Morningside V
Leith A 31/32 4

CONNOLLY Patrick
b. Hamilton 14.4.1901 d. Hairmyes Hospital 18.2.1969
Kirkintilloch Rob Roy
Celtic 21/22 3
22/23 24
23/24 21 3
Third Lanark L 23/24
Celtic 24/25 38 6
25/26 36 6
26/27 38 7
27/28 38 5
28/29 35 10
29/30 27 5
30/31
Shelbourne L 30/31 LI
Celtic 31/32
Morton L 31/32 12
Armadale L 32/33
Hibernian 32/33 D2
Airdrieonians 32/33
Bo'ness
Played for Airdrieonians reserves under an assumed name during 32/33

CONNON John
b. Aberdeen
Aberdeen Richmond
Aberdeen 19/20 39 14
20/21 25 5
21/22 13 1
22/23 15 2
23/24 1
St Johnstone 24/25

CONNOR James 4 caps
b. Renfrew 1.6.1909 d. Sunderland 8.5.1980
Paisley Celtic
Glasgow Perthshire
St Mirren 26/27 6
27/28 28 3
28/29 29 8
29/30 37 6
Sunderland 30/31 40 11 FL
31/32 36 5 FL
32/33 30 8 FL
33/34 38 4 FL
34/35 37 9 FL
35/36 42 6 FL
36/37 19 3 FL
37/38 1 FL
38/39 11 2 FL

CONNOR James
Shawfield Jnrs
Albion R 36/37 23 4
37/38
Glentoran 38/39
39/40

CONNOR John
b. Garngad 7.9.1911 d. Glasgow 28.5.1994
St Rochs Jnrs
Alloa A L
Celtic 32/33 1
Airdrieonians L 32/33 21 22
Celtic 33/34 3 1
Airdrieonians 34/35 32 14
Albion R L 34/35 6 8
Airdrieonians 35/36 38 33
Plymouth A 36/37 32 17 FL
37/38 10 2 FL
Swansea T 38/39 12 1 FL
Queen of the South
Alloa A 46/47 D2
St Johnstone 46/47 5 2

CONNOR Nathaniel
b. Johnstone 2.7.1882 d. Elderslie 30.5.1952
Johnstone 01/02
02/03
Port Glasgow A 02/03 1
03/04 22 1
04/05 7
Celtic T 04/05
Abercorn 04/05 D2
Johnstone 05/06
Abercorn 05/06 D2
Arthurlie 06/07 D2
Johnstone 07/08
08/09
Clyde 08/09
Brighton 09/10 9 4 SL
Johnstone

CONNOR Robert
Heart of Midlothian 00/01 1
Johnstone

CONNOR Robert
Vale of Clyde
Partick T 02/03 15 7
03/04 2
St Bernards

CONWELL Lawrence Doyle
b. Aberdeen 26.9.1909 d. Coventry 20.12.1972
Arthurlie
Aberdeen 34/35 6 1
Portadown 35/36
West Ham U 35/36 6 1 FL
36/37 2 FL
Coventry C 37/38 2 FL
Hinckley U

COOGAN Edward
Morton 06/07 1

COOK
Dumbarton 17/18 1

COOK Charles
b. Glasgow 3.6.1898
Bellshill A
Queen of the South
Bradford C 20/21 5 FL
21/22 2 FL
Bury 22/23 1 FL
Morton 23/24 10
Wigan B 23/24 3 FL
Coventry C 23/24 3 FL
Philadelphia Field Club 24
Bradford PA 24/25 2 FL
Shawsheen Indians 25/26 20 2 ASL
Fall River Marksmen 25/26 1 ASL
New York Giants 25/26 2 ASL
?
Ayr U T 31/32

COOK George
St Mirren 94/95 17
95/96 3
Galston

COOK Harry L
Renfrew Jnrs
Kilmarnock 34/35 1
Dumbarton 35/36 D2

COOK R
Morton 25/26 2

COOK Robert Coltart
St Johnstone 38/39 22 10

COOK Ronald R
Queen's Park 20/21 4

COOK William
b. Coleraine 20.11.1909 d. Fazackerley ?.4.1993
Port Glasgow A
Celtic 29/30 11
30/31 33
31/32 33
32/33 24
Everton 32/33 20 FL
33/34 35 FL
34/35 29 FL
35/36 25 FL
36/37 41 FL
37/38 35 FL
38/39 40 5 FL
39/40 3 FL
Ellesmere Port T 46/47
Rhyl A

COOK William Lindsay 3 caps
b. Dundee 11.3.1903 d. Dundee ?.6.1981
Dundee NE
Forfar A
Dundee 25/26 36 3
26/27 33 11
27/28 30 4
28/29 18 3
Bolton W 28/29 16 FL
29/30 41 6 FL
30/31 26 7 FL
31/32 34 4 FL
32/33 27 3 FL
33/34 30 2 FL
34/35 29 6 FL
35/36 31 7 FL
Blackpool 36/37 19 1 FL
Reading 37/38 33 3 FL
Dundee 38/39 18 1 D2

COOKE Edward
b. Govan 6.4.1896
St Anthonys
Third Lanark 16/17 10 4
Abercorn L 16/17
Armadale
Renton 18/19
Millwall 19/20 13 1 SL
20/21 1 FL
Dartford 21/22
22/23
23/24

COOPER
Leith A 94/95 7

COOPER Alex
Falkirk
Queen's Park 11/12 1
12/13 9
13/14 1

COOPER John C
Queen's Park 32/33 22
33/34 17
34/35 2
35/36 13

COOPER William
b. Mexborough
Denaby
Barnsley 06/07 2 FL
Portsmouth 07/08 SL
Dundee 08/09 2

COOPER William
b. Aberdeen c1910 d. ?.5.1994
St Machar Juveniles
Mugiemoss
Aberdeen 27/28 2
28/29 3
29/30 14
30/31 20
31/32 37
32/33 34
33/34 38 2
34/35 38
35/36 38
36/37 37
37/38 32
38/39 14
46/47 13
47/48 7
Huntly

CORBETT David John Risk
b. Camelon 1.2.1910 d. Shieldhall 11.1.1995
Old Plean Amateurs
Linlithgow Rose 29/30
Heart of Midlothian 29/30
Camelon 30/31
31/32
Ayr U 32/33 6
Dundee U 33/34 32 2 D2
34/35 33 1 D2
35/36 16 3 D2
West Ham U 36/37 FL
37/38 FL
Southport 38/39 FL

CORBETT Donald
Grange R
Falkirk 20/21 8 4
21/22
22/23
23/24
Linfield 23/24 IL

CORBETT Michael
Heart of Midlothian 04/05 5 1
Third Lanark 05/06

CORCORAN Patrick
b. Milton 16.6.1893
Mossend Hibernian
Clyde 12/13 3
13/14 32 3
14/15 2
Shelbourne L 14/15 IL
Royal Albert L 15/16
Hamilton A L 16/17 23 5
Renton L 16/17
Albion R L 17/18
Celtic L 18/19 3
Royal Albert L 19/20
Hamilton A 19/20 17 3
Bathgate 20/21
Plymouth A 20/21 21 2 FL
21/22 36 6 FL
22/23 36 6 FL
23/24 38 3 FL
24/25 37 FL
25/26 20 6 FL
Luton T 26/27
Bathgate 26/27 D2
East Stirlingshire 26/27 D2

CORDINER William L
b. Coatbridge
Queen's Park 27/28 6 3
28/29 6 3
29/30 2
30/31 14 9
31/32 1

CORNER George
Shettleston
St Mirren 13/14 15
14/15 7
15/16 14 1
Clydebank 16/17
Kilsyth Emmet

CORNOCK
Vale of Leven 90/91 13
91/92 11

CORNOCK John
Ashfield Jnrs
Airdrieonians 21/22 1
Ashfield Jnrs * 22/23
Vale of Leven * 23/24 D2

CORRANCE Robert
Renfrew Jnrs
Margate
East Stirlingshire 36/37 D2
Falkirk 36/37 16
Albion R 37/38 D2

CORRIGAN Edward
b. New Monkland 18.5.1900
St Anthonys
Petershill
Celtic 24/25 4
25/26
Ayr U L 25/26 D2
St Bernards L 25/26 D2
Dundee 26/27
St Bernards 26/27 D2

CORRIGAN Michael
Airdrieonians 17/18 2 1

COSGROVE Michael Docherty
b. Dundee 20.5.1901
Dundee NE
Dundee Hibs 20/21
Tottenham H 21/22
22/23
Celtic 22/23
Brooklyn Wanderers 23/24 23 9 ASL
24/25 1 ASL
Barnsley T 24/25 FL
Aberdeen 24/25 5 2
25/26 33
26/27 18
27/28 9 3
Bristol R 28/29 38 6 FL
29/30 20 FL

COTTERILL E
Dumbarton 20/21 1

COTTINGHAM Thomas McLanaghan
b. Camlachie 1.10.1901
Parkhead Jnrs
Hamilton A 21/22 16
Luton T 22/23 1 FL
Airdrieonians 22/23 1
Dundee Hibernian 23/24 10 D2
Carlisle U 23/24
Weymouth 24/25
Bo'ness 24/25 D2
25/26 D2
26/27 ? 17 D2
27/28 27 5
Queen of the South
Alloa A

COULTER James
Clyde 98/99 13 1
99/00 3

COULTER Walter McFarlane
K.I.A. 20.5.1917
Queen's Park 13/14 1

COUPER George A
Heart of Midlothian 05/06 10 2
06/07 14 5
Everton 06/07 3 1 FL
07/08 1 FL

COUPER James
Dunfermline A
Cowdenbeath 32/33 6

COUPER Robert
Clyde 10/11 12 5
11/12 2
12/13
13/14 4
East Stirlingshire L 13/14 D2
St Bernards 14/15 D2

COURTS John

Club		Season	Apps	Goals	League
Fifeshire Jnrs					
Alloa A		07/08			
Heart of Midlothian		07/08	1		
		08/09	14	3	
		09/10	2		
Cowdenbeath		10/11			D2
Alloa A		11/12			
		12/13			
		13/14			
		14/15			
Lochgelly U		15/16			
Alloa A					
Alva Albion R					

COUTTS John

Club		Season	Apps	Goals	League
Kirkintilloch Rob Roy					
Clydebank		19/20	6		

COUTTS John

Club		Season	Apps	Goals	League
Alloa A					
Dumbarton		21/22	15		
		22/23			D2
		23/24			D2
Helensburgh		24/25			D3

COUTTS William Farquharson

b. Gorgie 26.6.1909 d. Leicester 25.7.1991

Club		Season	Apps	Goals	League
Edinburgh Ashton					
Dunbar U		30/31			
Heart of Midlothian		30/31			
		31/32	2		
Leith A	L	31/32	10	3	
Heart of Midlothian		32/33	20	9	
		33/34	13	5	
Leicester C		34/35	6	1	FL
		35/36	6	1	FL
		36/37	11		FL
		37/38	13	2	FL
		38/39	12		FL
		39/40	2		FL

COVENTRY Thomas

Club		Season	Apps	Goals	League
Rosslyn					
Falkirk		28/29	1		
		29/30	4		
Portadown		30/31			IL
Waterford		31/32			LI
Drumcondra		31/32			LI
Belfast Celtic	T	32/33			IL
		33/34			IL
Portadown		34/35			IL

COVENTRY William

Club		Season	Apps	Goals	League
Dundee		95/96	1		

COWAN

Club		Season	Apps	Goals	League
Renton		91/92	3	1	
		92/93	2		

COWAN

Club		Season	Apps	Goals	League
Leith A		92/93	3		

COWAN

Club		Season	Apps	Goals	League
St Bernards		93/94	3		
		94/95	14		

COWAN Alexander

Club		Season	Apps	Goals	League
Hamilton A		07/08	1		

COWAN Archibald

Club		Season	Apps	Goals	League
Parkhead					
Queen's Park		15/16	31	7	
		16/17			
		17/18	25	4	
		18/19	30	4	
St Mirren		19/20	14	2	
Leith A					
Johnstone					
Clydebank		21/22	3		
Preston NE		22/23			
		23/24			
		24/25			
Helensburgh		25/26			D3

COWAN David

b. West Carron 30.11.1910

Club		Season	Apps	Goals	League
Alva Albion R					
Rochdale		30/31	24	2	FL
Stenhousemuir		31/32			D2
		32/33			D2
		33/34			D2
		34/35			D2
Falkirk		34/35	3	1	
		35/36	26	22	D2
		36/37	5	1	
Arbroath		36/37	9	2	
		38/39	9		
Dumbarton					

COWAN Harry

Club		Season	Apps	Goals	League
Catrine					
Ayr U		19/20	2	1	
		20/21	3	1	

COWAN Henry

b. Cambuslang

Club		Season	Apps	Goals	League
Cambuslang R					
Clyde		16/17	38		
		17/18	34	?	
		18/19	31	?	
		19/20	30		
		20/21	36		
		21/22	39		
		22/23	36		
		23/24	21	1	
New Bedford Whalers		25/26	36	1	ASL
		26/27	40		ASL
Hartford Americans		27/28	9		ASL
New York Nationals		27/28	3		ASL
Fall River Marksmen		27/28	4		ASL
J & P Coats		28/29	5		ASL
New Bedford Whalers		29A	5		ASL
		29/30	2		ASL
		30A	1		ASL

COWAN James

Club		Season	Apps	Goals	League
Clyde		97/98	6		

COWAN John

b. Dumbarton ?.12.1870 d. Scotland ?.5.1937

Club		Season	Apps	Goals	League
Vale of Leven		90/91	17	3	
		91/92	19	2	
Preston NE		92/93	26	2	FL
		93/94	29	7	FL
Rangers		94/95	16	3	
Aston Villa		95/96	22	11	FL
		96/97	15	7	FL
		97/98	21	5	FL
		98/99	6	3	FL
Dundee Harp		99/00			
		00/01			

COWAN John

Club		Season	Apps	Goals	League
Banknock Jnrs *					
Falkirk		20/21	2		
Clackmannan		21/22			D2

COWAN John

b. Auchterarder

Club		Season	Apps	Goals	League
Clyde		26/27	2	1	
Morton		26/27	3		

COWAN Joseph

b. Prestonpans 25.2.1910 d. Windygates 18.4.1991

Club		Season	Apps	Goals	League
Markinch R					
Wellesley Jnrs					
Celtic		29/30			
		30/31	1	1	
Raith R		31/32	34	34	D2
		32/33	27	35	D2
		33/34	?	15	D2
East Fife		34/35	24	28	D2
		35/36	30	31	D2
		36/37	30	13	D2
		37/38	15	10	D2

COWAN Robert

Club		Season	Apps	Goals	League
Motherwell		04/05	16	1	
		05/06	7	4	
Albion R					

COWAN Thomas Shillington

b. Aghalee 9.9.1899

Club		Season	Apps	Goals	League
Willowfield					
Linfield		20/21			
		21/22			
		22/23			
Queens Island		23/24			
		24/25			
Falkirk		25/26	12		
Queens Island		26/27			
Ulster U					
Canada					

COWAN William Duncan 1 cap

b. Edinburgh 9.8.1896

Club		Season	Apps	Goals	League
Dalkeith Thistle					
Tranent Jnrs					
Dundee		19/20	5	1	
		20/21	17	2	
		21/22	16	3	
		22/23	30	6	
Newcastle U		23/24	22	6	FL
		24/25	35	10	FL
		25/26	30	7	FL
Manchester C		26/27	22	11	FL
St Mirren		27/28	10	4	
		28/29			
Peebles R		28/29			
Harrogate T		28/29			
Northfleet	T	29/30			
North Shields		29/30			
Hartlepools U		30/31	3	2	FL
Darlington		30/31	7	1	FL
Bath C		31/32			SL
		32/33			SL
Wolviston St Peters					

COWDEN John William

Club		Season	Apps	Goals	League
St Mirren		00/01	15	4	

COWIE Alexander

Club		Season	Apps	Goals	League
Ashfield					
Raith R		24/25	1		

COWIE Andrew David

b. Motherwell 11.3.1913 d. 19.1.1972

Club		Season	Apps	Goals	League
Dundee		35/36	1		
		36/37	6		
		37/38	36	2	
		38/39	17	1	D2
Aberdeen		38/39	16		
		46/47	18		
		47/48	27		
Swindon T		48/49	35	2	FL
		49/50	35	2	FL
		50/51	19		FL

COWIE Charles

b. Falkirk 23.4.1907 d. Falkirk 25.12.1971

Club		Season	Apps	Goals	League
Carron Welfare					
St Ninians Thistle		27/28			
Heart of Midlothian		27/28	2		
		28/29	2		
		29/30	3		
Barrow		30/31	33		FL
Dunfermline A		31/32			D2
		32/33			D2
Barrow		33/34	38		FL
		34/35	41		FL
		35/36	1		FL
Ipswich T		36/37	27	2	SL
		37/38	7		SL
		38/39	6		FL

COWIE David

Club		Season	Apps	Goals	League
Forfar A					
Dundee		01/02	1	1	
		02/03			
		03/04	1	1	
		04/05	23	10	
		05/06	10		
Clyde		06/07	17	3	
Forfar A		07/08			
Clyde		07/08	13		
Forfar A		08/09			
		09/10			
		10/11			
		11/12			

COWIE Gordon

Club		Season	Apps	Goals	League
Clydebank		19/20	5	2	
		20/21	5		

COWIE James George

b. Keith 8.6.1904 d. 21.4.1966

Club		Season	Apps	Goals	League
Keith Strathlisa					
Raith R		27/28	2	1	
Arbroath	L	27/28	10	4	D2
York C		28/29			
Raith R		29/30			D2
Keith		29/30			
York C		29/30	14	4	FL
		30/31	4	5	FL
Keith					

COWIE John

Club		Season	Apps	Goals	League
Buckie Thistle					
Falkirk		25/26	8		
		26/27	7		
		27/28	16		
Stenhousemuir					
Forres Mechanics					

COWIE John

J & P Coats					ASL
Morton		29/30	6		
		30/31	22		
		31/32	2		

COX

Leith A		91/92	1		
		92/93	9		

COX James

b. Darvel c1907

Darvel U					
Falkirk		25/26	18	9	
		26/27	6	1	
Clyde		27/28	1		

COX John

b. Darvel 9.5.1910 d. Darvel 17.9.1990

Darvel Jnrs					
Hamilton A		31/32	16	1	
		32/33	9		
		33/34	31		
		34/35	35		
		35/36	36		
		36/37	37	1	
		37/38	32		
Preston NE		38/39	5	1	FL
Ayr U					
Stranraer					

COX W

Heart of Midlothian		93/94	2		
		94/95	15		

COX William

b. Falkirk 22.10.1897

Govan YMCA					
Renfrew Jnrs					
Army					
Whiteinch Glenbuck					
Clydebank		18/19	20	?	
Cardiff C		19/20	20	5	SL
Newport Co	L	20/21	6	2	FL
Vale of Leven		21/22			
Workington		21/22			
Nottingham F		22/23	1		FL
Workington					

COX William

St Bernards					
Hamilton A		22/23	24		

COX William

St Rochs					
Falkirk		27/28	13	2	
		28/29	19	1	
Albion R		29/30			D2
		30/31			D2
Ballymena		31/32			IL
Coleraine		32/33			IL
Solway Star		33/34			
		34/35			

COX William James

b. England 1883

Rossendale U					
Bury		02/03			FL
		03/04	4		FL
Plymouth A		04/05	12	1	SL
Leicester F		05/06	3		FL
Accrington S		05/06			
Preston NE		05/06			FL
Dundee		06/07	31	18	
Heart of Midlothian		06/07	1		
		07/08	8	4	
Bradford PA		07/08	15	5	SL

COYLE

Cambuslang		91/92	17		

COYLE Hugh

b. Glasgow 11.6.1905

St Anthonys					
Dundee		22/23	4		
		23/24	33		
		24/25	4		
Motherwell		24/25	21		
Fall River Marksmen		25/26	42	4	ASL
		26/27	38		ASL
		27/28	36	4	ASL
Philadelphia		28/29	10	1	ASL
Fall River Marksmen		28/29	1		ASL
Brooklyn Wanderers		28/29	1		ASL
Bridgeport Bears		29A	2		ASL
Philadelphia		29A	5	1	ASL
Bridgeport Hungaria		29/30	6		ASL
Newark		29/30	2		ASL
Fall River Marksmen		30A	22	4	ASL
Pawtucket Rangers		31S	18		ASL

COYLE Stewart

Beith					
Dykehead					
Clyde		98/99	1		
Abercorn					

COYLE Terrence

b. Broxburn 16.7.1897

Broxburn A					
Broxburn U		21/22			
Heart of Midlothian		21/22			
		22/23	17		
St Johnstone		23/24	24	4	D2
Broxburn U		24/25			D2
Heart of Midlothian		24/25			
St Johnstone		25/26	1		
East Fife		25/26	13		D2
Crystal Palace		25/26	24	2	FL
		26/27	5		FL
Stafford R		27/28			
Bromsgrove R					
Cookley					

CRADDOCK Claude William

b. Grimsby 2.8.1902 d. Gillingham 13.12.1976

Chatham Centrals					
Gillingham		24/25	3	1	FL
Sittingbourne	L	24/25			
Grays T	L	25/26			
Gillingham		25/26	13	2	FL
Brentford		26/27	12	5	FL
		27/28	11	6	FL
Dundee		27/28	2	2	
		28/29	18	5	
Sheppey U		29/30			
Rochdale		30/31	34	10	FL
Darlington		31/32	10	2	FL
Tunbridge Wells R					

CRAIG

St Mirren		91/92	1		

CRAIG

Abercorn		92/93	2		

CRAIG

Dumbarton		94/95	18	6	

CRAIG

Clydebank		18/19	1		

CRAIG Alexander

b. Kilmarnock 1878 d. Toronto 16.2.1948

Kilmarnock Winton					
Kilmarnock		98/99	15		D2
		99/00	18		
		00/01	20		
		01/02	18		
		02/03	21		
		03/04	23		
Southern League Football		04/05			
Ayr Parkhouse		05/06			
Beith	L				
Galston					
Hurlford					

CRAIG Alexander

Morton		08/09	4		

CRAIG Alexander Brackenridge

b. Galway 2.4.1886

Rutherglen Glencairn					
Rangers		04/05	3		
		05/06	25		
		06/07	12		
		07/08	23		
		08/09	28		
		09/10	9		
		10/11	1		
Morton		11/12	28		
		12/13	17	1	
		13/14	36		
Rangers		14/15	37		
		15/16	5		
		16/17			
		17/18			
		18/19			
Johnstone		19/20			

CRAIG Allan 3 caps

b. Paisley 7.2.1904

Paisley Carlisle					
Saltcoats V					
Motherwell		24/25	19		
		25/26	28		
		26/27	37		
		27/28	38	1	
		28/29	38	1	
		29/30	38		
		30/31	37		
		31/32	37	1	
		32/33	12		
Chelsea		32/33	19		FL
		33/34	30		FL
		34/35	42		FL
		35/36	41		FL
		36/37	41		FL
		37/38	7		FL
		38/39	16		FL
Dartford					

CRAIG Charles Thomson

b. Dundee 11.7.1876 d. Bingham 12.1.1933

Dundee Our Boys					
Dundee		93/94			
Dundee W		94/95			
Dundee		95/96	1		
		96/97			
		97/98			
		98/99	7	4	
Silvertown					
Thames Ironworks		99/00	16		SL
West Ham U		00/01	26	1	SL
		01/02	28	1	SL
Nottingham F		02/03	31		FL
		03/04	33	2	FL
		04/05	31		FL
		05/06	33		FL
		06/07	7		FL
Bradford PA		07/08	28		SL
Bradford C		08/09	6		FL
Norwich C		08/09	20	1	SL
		09/10	28		SL
Southend U		10/11	23		SL
		11/12	?		SL
Merthyr T		12/13	34		SL
		13/14	25		SL

CRAIG David

Dundee Our Boys					
Dundee		93/94	13	1	

CRAIG David

Alloa A		22/23	10		
		23/24			D2
East Stirlingshire		23/24			D3

CRAIG David L

Queen's Park		21/22	5	1	
		22/23	2		D2

CRAIG Frederick Glover
b. Larkhall 16.1.1891
Larkhall Thistle
Plymouth A 12/13 4 SL
13/14 10 SL
14/15 24 SL
Hamilton A 15/16 9
16/17 29
17/18 4
Ayr U 17/18 3
Motherwell 18/19 29
Plymouth A 19/20 40 SL
20/21 42 FL
21/22 36 FL
22/23 41 FL
23/24 42 FL
24/25 42 FL
25/26 42 FL
26/27 34 3 FL
27/28 12 1 FL
28/29 40 FL
29/30 30 1 FL
Barrow 30/31 14 FL

CRAIG George
St Anthonys
Albion R 20/21 9 1

CRAIG Harold
Benburb
Clyde 06/07 4 1

CRAIG Harold W
Maryhill
Port Glasgow A 07/08 9 1
Vale of Leven

CRAIG James
Rangers 05/06 1

CRAIG John
Glenafton A
Third Lanark 36/37 5 1

CRAIG John Jackson
Royal Albert
Ayr U 37/38 9
38/39 17 9

CRAIG Robert
b. Beith 2.5.1888 K.I.A., Boulogne 19.4.1918
Vale of Garnock Strollers
Celtic 06/07 9
Stenhousemuir L 06/07
Celtic 07/08 1
08/09 3
Kilmarnock L 08/09
Morton L 08/09
Brighton
Carlisle U
Darlington 10/11
Renton
Bo'ness
Dundee Hibernian 11/12 20 4 D2
Abercorn
Abertillery T

CRAIG Robert A
b. c1913
Abergeldie
St Johnstone 36/37 1

CRAIG Thomas
Middlesbrough 04/05 2 FL
Falkirk 05/06
06/07 3
Stockport Co 06/07 1 FL
07/08 35 FL

CRAIG Thomas
Clydebank 20/21 3
21/22 20
Kings Park 22/23 D2

CRAIG Thomas Breckenridge 8 caps
b. Laurieston 18.7.1895 d. Halifax 30.1.1963
Tullibody
Grange R
Everton T
Celtic 19/20 5 3
Clyde L 19/20
Celtic 20/21 2
21/22 1
Alloa A 22/23 29 7
Rangers 23/24 17 12
24/25 21 2
25/26 31 2
26/27 30 2
27/28 34 3
28/29 34 6
29/30 27 2
30/31 14 1
31/32 8 1
32/33 4
33/34 8
34/35 6 1

CRAIGIE Alexander McCarthur
b. Newington 1907
Burntisland Shipyard
East Stirlingshire 32/33 23 10
Partick T 32/33 10 8
Cowdenbeath 32/33
Partick T 33/34 8 3
Cowdenbeath 34/35 D2
Morton 35/36 D2
Raith R L 35/36 D2
Morton 36/37 D2
Kings Park 37/38 D2

CRAIGIE Claude V
Montrose
Queen's Park 08/09 4 3
09/10 23 1
10/11 24 2
11/12 29
12/13 11

CRAIGIE James
Kings Park
Dundee 31/32 12 7

CRAIK Herbert J
b. Scotland
Morton 00/01 3 1
01/02 4
02/03 19 1
Liverpool 03/04 1 FL
Heart of Midlothian 04/05 2
Paisley Academicals

CRAIK James
Dundee East End
Dundee 93/94 1

CRAINEY Daniel
Motherwell 02/03 D2
03/04 18 1
04/05 15

CRAINEY Peter
b. Whifflet
Blackpool
Airdrieonians 33/34 1

CRANSTON Thomas
b. c1891 K.I.A.,Iraq 13.1.1916
Ardrossan Celtic
Raith R 12/13 33 5
13/14 24 2
Third Lanark 13/14 7
Stevenston U 14/15
Clyde 14/15 22 5

CRAPNELL James Sermagour 9 caps
b. Paisley 4.6.1903 d. Paisley 24.12.1991
Cambuslang R
Airdrieonians 26/27 24
27/28 38
28/29 38
29/30 36
30/31 32
31/32 33 1
32/33 26
Motherwell 32/33 11
33/34 26

CRAVEN Joseph McNae
b. Paisley 15.2.1910
Mosspark Amateurs
Parkhead
Partick T 32/33
33/34
Northampton T 34/35 FL
35/36 1 FL
St Mirren 36/37 25
37/38 34
38/39 36

CRAW William
Paisley Academicals
Port Glasgow A 06/07 1
St Mirren 06/07 4

CRAWFORD
Heart of Midlothian 90/91 1

CRAWFORD Alexander
b. Glasgow 1876 d. 11.6.1937
Crown A
Clyde 95/96 10 3
96/97 2
97/98 3 1
98/99 12 4
Bristol C 99/00 21 1 SL
Clyde 00/01 11 ? D2
Celtic 01/02 6 2
Morton L 01/02 8 1
Celtic 02/03 4 1
Morton L 02/03
Partick T 02/03 5
03/04 18 4

CRAWFORD David 3 caps
b. Paisley 9.3.1873 d. ?.7.1937
Victoria
St Mirren 92/93 16
93/94 16 1
Rangers 94/95 6
95/96 2
96/97 7 1
97/98 6
98/99 17
99/00 8
00/01 4
01/02 8
02/03 4
St Mirren 03/04 4
04/05 19
05/06 20 1
06/07 19

CRAWFORD Evelyn C
Queen's Park 03/04 4 2
04/05 8
05/06
06/07 4

CRAWFORD James 5 caps
b. Glasgow 21.5.1904 d. ?.5.1976
Keppochhill School
Queen's Park 23/24 35 4
24/25 33 8
25/26 34 1
26/27 33 6
27/28 31 3
28/29 33 16
29/30 31 7
30/31 19 8
31/32 32 8
32/33 35 14
33/34 23 4
34/35 28 5
35/36 31 8
36/37 26 7

CRAWFORD James
Millport *
Vale of Leven *
Dumbarton * 27/28 D2
28/29 D2
29/30 D2
Cowdenbeath 30/31 1
St Johnstone 31/32 3 D2

CRAWFORD John
b. Fife
Partick T 21/22 5

CRAWFORD John
b. Edinburgh
Dalkeith Thistle
Newtongrange Star
Dundee 26/27 13
27/28 18
28/29 3
Alloa A 29/30 D2
Leith A 30/31 34 1
31/32 36
Alloa A 32/33 D2

CRAWFORD John

Newtongrange Star
Dumbarton
St Bernards
Hibernian 33/34 18
34/35 4
Dunfermline A 34/35 17
35/36 38
36/37 18
Cowdenbeath 37/38 D2
38/39 D2

CRAWFORD John Chalmers
b. Stirling 11.10.1902 d. Stirling ?.5.1973
Fallin Violet
Stenhousemuir L
Alloa A
Blackburn R 24/25 1 FL
25/26 18 FL
26/27 23 FL
27/28 40 FL
28/29 40 FL
29/30 26 FL
30/31 FL
31/32 7 FL
East Stirlingshire L 32/33 19

CRAWFORD Richard

Partick T 00/01 2 1
Dunfermline A

CRAWFORD Robert

Clyde 92/93 2 1
93/94 4 ? D2
94/95 15 2
95/96 17 6
Bury 95/96 2 FL
Clyde 96/97 10 1

CRAWFORD Robert

Rangers 96/97 7 3
Clydebank 96/97
Abercorn 97/98 D2
Clydebank

CRAWFORD Ronald
b. South Africa
Lochee Central
St Johnstone 28/29 1
Thames 29/30 SL
30/31 4 FL
Rotherham U 31/32 3 FL
St Johnstone 31/32 3 D2
Arbroath 32/33 4 D2

CRAWFORD William

Heart of Midlothian 95/96 1

CRAWFORD William

Kilsyth R
Clydebank
Clyde 25/26
26/27 5
Stenhousemuir 26/27 D2
27/28 D2
28/29 D2
29/30 D2
30/31 D2
Waterford 30/31 LI
31/32 LI
Cork Bohemians 32/33 LI

CRAWLEY Francis

Morton 20/21 1

CRAWLEY Thomas Anthony
b. Blantyre 10.11.1911 d. Coventry 1976
Blantyre V
St Mirren T
Third Lanark T
Hamilton A 32/33 21 17
33/34 25 8
Motherwell 33/34 2 4
34/35 6 5
Preston NE 35/36 2 FL
Coventry C 35/36 2 1 FL
36/37 4 FL
37/38 5 FL
38/39 18 14 FL
39/40 3 2 FL
46/47 13 1 FL

CRAWSHAW Cyril
b. Eccles 2.3.1916 d. Trafford 27.1.2003
Newton Heath Loco
Rossendale U
Rochdale 36/37 2 FL
Fleetwood 37/38
Rossendale U 37/38
Queen of the South 38/39 2
Exeter C
Stockport Co
Hull C 46/47 2 1 FL
Stalybridge C

CREE

Abercorn 90/91 4

CREE Archibald
b. Trabboch 1898
Coylton Jnrs
Kilmarnock 20/21 4
21/22 1

CREE Archibald

Hibernian 22/23 1

CREER William

Recliffe
Army
Dunfermline A
Clyde 06/07 15 7
07/08 3
08/09
09/10 5 2

CREIGHTON Thomas
b. Springburn 29.7.1908
Strathclyde
Bo'ness 27/28 15
Armadale 27/28 D2
South Shields 28/29 1 FL
Merthyr T 29/30 25 FL

CRERAR Daniel

Crieff Morrisonians
Queen's Park 11/12 4 1

CRERAR William
b. Darvel 8.10.1876
Ayr Parkhouse 97/98
98/99
Clyde 99/00
Kilmarnock 00/01 6 4
Rangers 01/02
02/03
03/04
Third Lanark 04/05 7 1
Ayr Parkhouse 05/06
Third Lanark 05/06
Ayr Parkhouse 05/06
Galston
Ayr Parkhouse

CRESSWELL Elijah

Queen's Park 13/14 19 3
14/15 17 2
15/16 34 4
16/17 5
17/18 22 2

CRESSWELL Warneford
b. South Shields 5.11.1897 d. South Shields 20.10.1973
Army
Heart of Midlothian L 15/16 1
Hibernian L 17/18
South Shields 19/20 34 1 FL
20/21 38 FL
21/22 26 FL
Sunderland 21/22 12 FL
22/23 38 FL
23/24 32 FL
24/25 38 FL
25/26 37 FL
26/27 25 FL
Everton 26/27 15 FL
27/28 36 FL
28/29 32 1 FL
29/30 30 FL
30/31 42 FL
31/32 40 FL
32/33 41 FL
33/34 25 FL
34/35 25 FL
35/36 4 FL

CRICHTON Alexander P
b. Leslie
Heart of Midlothian 19/20 1
20/21
Bo'ness 21/22 4 D2

CRICHTON Archibald

Kilmarnock Rugby XI
Kilmarnock 02/03 9 1
Galston L 02/03
Kilmarnock 03/04 17
04/05 20
05/06 18
06/07 16
Barrow 07/08
Kilmarnock 07/08 2 1
08/09 5
Ayr Parkhouse 09/10
Kilmarnock

CRICHTON George

Burnbank A
Motherwell 12/13 1

CRICHTON R

Queen's Park 14/15 3

CRICHTON Thomas
b. Sanquhar
Nithsdale W
Partick T 18/19 3
19/20 16
20/21 34
21/22 29
22/23 35
23/24 33
24/25 32
25/26 6

CRICHTON William

Shettleston
Third Lanark 14/15 7 2
15/16 14 4
Vale of Leven
East Stirlingshire 20/21

CRICHTON William
b. Kirkcaldy
Thornton R
Arbroath 27/28 1 D2
East Stirlingshire 27/28 D2
28/29 D2
29/30 D2
30/31 D2
31/32 D2
32/33 38 1
Raith R 33/34 D2

CRILLEY William

b. Cowdenbeath 1903 d. Brooklyn, NJ 1955

Club		Season	Apps	Goals	League
R & J Dick Ltd Welfare		18/19			
Clyde	T	18/19			
Shawfield Jnrs	T	18/19			
Cambuslang R		19/20			
		20/21			
Alloa A		20/21			
		21/22	?	49	D2
		22/23	12	2	
Celtic		22/23	3	1	
Alloa A		22/23			
New York		22/23	5	5	ASL
		23/24	2		ASL
New York Giants		23/24	2	1	ASL
Indiana Flooring		24/25	11	4	ASL
New York Giants		25/26	28	5	ASL
		26/27	3	1	ASL
J & P Coats		26/27	9	3	ASL
Philadelphia Field Club		26/27	2	1	ASL
New York Nationals		27/28	4		ASL
New York Hispano		27/28			
Alloa A		29/30	?	?	D2
		30/31	?	?	D2
Newark Americans		30A	2	2	ASL
New York SC		30A	1		ASL
Fall River		31S	5		ASL
Brooklyn Wanderers		31S	7	14	ASL
New York Americans		31A	10	9	ASL
Bohemians Queens Club					
Nassau					
Brooklyn Hispanos					
St Marys Celtic					

CRINGAN Robert

Club		Season	Apps	Goals	League
Ayr U		16/17	29	2	
		17/18	3	?	
Hamilton A		17/18	1		

CRINGAN William 5 caps

b. Pontfegh 15.5.1890 d. 12.5.1958

Club		Season	Apps	Goals	League
Douglas Water Thistle					
Sunderland		10/11	1		FL
		11/12	17		FL
		12/13	10		FL
		13/14	26	3	FL
		14/15	24		FL
Wishaw Thistle	L	15/16			
Ayr U		15/16	17		
		16/17	36	2	
		17/18	6		
Celtic		17/18	30	1	
		18/19	29	3	
		19/20	40	3	
		20/21	25	2	
		21/22	37		
		22/23	35		
		23/24	6		
Third Lanark		23/24	30		
Motherwell		24/25	16	1	
Inverness Thistle					
Bathgate		25/26			

CROAL David

Club		Season	Apps	Goals	League
Falkirk		16/17	25	9	
		17/18	27	?	
Petershill		18/19			
		19/20			
Dunfermline A		20/21			

CROAL James Anderson 3 caps

b. Hutchesontown 27.7.1885
d. South Petherton 16.9.1939

Club		Season	Apps	Goals	League
Falkirk High School					
Rangers		05/06	3		
Ayr Parkhouse	L	05/06			
Rangers		06/07			
		07/08			
		08/09			
		09/10			
Alloa A	L	10/11			
Dunfermline A	L	10/11			
Falkirk		10/11	15	3	
		11/12	26	3	
		12/13	28	11	
		13/14	28	14	
Chelsea		14/15	27	6	FL
Falkirk	L	18/19	10	?	
Chelsea		19/20	32	6	FL
		20/21	33	7	FL
		21/22	21	3	FL
Dunfermline A	L	21/22			
Fulham		21/22	11	2	FL
		22/23	19	4	FL
		23/24	6		FL

CROMPTON Joseph J

Club		Season	Apps	Goals	League
Maryhill Jnrs					
Morton		30/31	2	1	

CRONE William

b. Dublin c1892

Club		Season	Apps	Goals	League
Belfast Celtic		11/12			IL
		12/13			IL
		13/14			IL
Celtic		13/14	7	2	
		14/15	5	5	
		15/16	4	2	
		16/17			
Distillery		16/17			IL
		17/18			IL
Glentoran		18/19			IL
Linfield R					

CRONIN John A

Club		Season	Apps	Goals	League
Vale of Leven					
Hamilton A		08/09	1		

CROOK Robert

Club		Season	Apps	Goals	League
Dundee		99/00	1		

CROOKSTON Thomas

Club		Season	Apps	Goals	League
Queen's Park		00/01	1		

CROOT Frederick Richard

b. Rushden 1886 d. Rushden 5.7.1958

Club		Season	Apps	Goals	League
Wellingborough		04/05	33	3	SL
Sheffield U		05/06	1		FL
		06/07	7		FL
Leeds C		07/08	38	9	FL
		08/09	37	2	FL
		09/10	35	7	FL
		10/11	30	8	FL
		11/12	32	7	FL
		12/13	32	5	FL
		13/14	10	1	FL
		14/15	5		FL
Stevenston U		16/17			
Rangers	L	16/17	9	1	
Clydebank		17/18	16	1	
		18/19			
		19/20	7		

CROSBIE

Club		Season	Apps	Goals	League
Clyde		18/19	1	?	

CROSBIE James

Club		Season	Apps	Goals	League
Larkhall Thistle					
Motherwell		20/21	1		
		21/22			
Peebles R		22/23			

CROSBIE James

b. Galston

Club		Season	Apps	Goals	League
Saltcoats V					
Airdrieonians		29/30			
		30/31			
		31/32	1		
		32/33	21		
		33/34	27	2	
		34/35	36	1	
		35/36	2		

CROSBIE John Anderson 2 caps

b. Glenbuck 9.10.1895 d. 1.2.1982

Club		Season	Apps	Goals	League
Glenbuck Cherrypickers					
Muirkirk A					
Saltcoats V					
Ayr U		13/14	7		
		14/15	5	3	
		15/16	16	3	
		16/17	36	6	
		17/18	31	?	
		18/19	22	7	
		19/20	40	17	
Rangers	L				
Birmingham		20/21	42	14	FL
		21/22	34	10	FL
		22/23	32	1	FL
		23/24	31	1	FL
		24/25	40	8	FL
		25/26	40	8	FL
		26/27	39	6	FL
		27/28	28	7	FL
		28/29	38	4	FL
		29/30	39	7	FL
		30/31	31	2	FL
		31/32	15	3	FL
Chesterfield		32/33	3		FL
Stourbridge					

CROSBIE William

b. Beith

Club		Season	Apps	Goals	League
Vale of Clyde					
Ayr U		18/19			
Clyde	L	18/19			
Ayr U		19/20	16	1	
		20/21	23	2	
Royal Albert		21/22			
Barrhead		22/23			

CROSS Alexander

b. Rutherglen c1920 d. Kinnesswood ?.3.1998

Club		Season	Apps	Goals	League
Rutherglen Academy					
Queen's Park		38/39	20	2	
		46/47	1		

CROSS John H 1 cap

b. 1879

Club		Season	Apps	Goals	League
Wishaw Thistle					
Third Lanark		98/99	7	4	
		99/00	15	6	
		00/01	17	1	
		01/02	6		
		02/03	19		
		03/04	25	1	
QPR		04/05	23		SL
Wishaw Thistle					
Third Lanark		05/06	18	4	
		06/07	24	1	
		07/08	24		
		08/09	21	2	
		09/10	15	1	

CROSS Robert M

b. Rutherglen

Club		Season	Apps	Goals	League
Queen's Park		35/36	6		
		36/37			
		37/38	38		
		38/39	13		

CROSS William B

b. 1883

Club		Season	Apps	Goals	League
Wishaw Hearts					
Cambuslang Swifts					
East Stirlingshire					
Third Lanark		01/02	8	4	
		02/03	4	1	
Q P R		03/04	13	2	SL
		04/05	19	2	SL
Brentford		05/06	16		SL

CROSSAN Bernard

b. c1869 d. 24.12.1917

Club		Season	Apps	Goals	League
Benburb					
Celtic		90/91	4	2	
Preston NE		90/91	7	3	FL
Third Lanark		91/92	16	4	
St Bernards		92/93			
		93/94	18	11	
		94/95	14	3	
Celtic		95/96	4	1	
		96/97	1		

CROSSAN Patrick James

b. Addiewell c1893 d. Liberton 28.4.1933

Club		Season	Apps	Goals	League
Arniston R					
Heart of Midlothian		11/12	8		
		12/13	21		
		13/14	38		
		14/15	37		
		15/16	1		
		16/17			
Linfield		16/17			IL
Heart of Midlothian		17/18	2		
		18/19	10	1	
		19/20	36	4	
		20/21	25		
		21/22	39	3	
		22/23	12		
		23/24	32	3	
		24/25	22		
Leith A		25/26			D2

CROSSAN William R

Club		Season	Apps	Goals	League
Kilbirnie Ladeside					
Vale of Gournock					
St Mirren		06/07	2		
		07/08	11		
Huddersfield T					

CROSSKEY Thomas Roland
b. Hastings 1905

Crystal Palace		26/27			FL
Albion R		27/28			D2
		28/29			D2
Heart of Midlothian		28/29	1		
		29/30	4		
		30/31	3		
		31/32	1		
Cowdenbeath		32/33	28		
Albion R		33/34			D2
		34/35	38		
		35/36	9		
Montrose		36/37			D2
		37/38			D2
Morton		37/38	12		
Montrose		38/39			D2

CROZIER James Paterson Lyle
b. Milton 29.10.1906

Ashfield					
Hull C		27/28	3		FL
Celtic		28/29	2		
Forfar A	L	28/29			D2
Ayr U	L	28/29			
Derry C		29/30			IL
Linfield		29/30			IL
Ashfield		30/31			
Brechin C		31/32			D2
		32/33			D2
		33/34			D2
Morton	T	33/34			D2

CRUIKSHANK William

Banks o'Dee					
Aberdeen		16/17	13	1	

CRUM John 2 caps
b. Glasgow 1.1.1912 d. Hyndland 6.7.1969

Argyle Thistle					
Ashfield					
Celtic		32/33	3	2	
		33/34	30	10	
		34/35	10	2	
		35/36	38	9	
		36/37	37	10	
		37/38	38	24	
		38/39	29	14	
Morton					

CRUMLEY Robert W
b. Lochee 1878

Lochee U					
Newcastle U		04/05	1		FL
		05/06	3		FL
Dundee		06/07	2		
		07/08	34		
		08/09	33		
		09/10	31		
		10/11	31		
Darlington		11/12			
Arbroath		12/13			
		13/14			

CRUMP Leslie Victor
b. Wolverhampton 10.10.1902 d. Newcastle 1983

Sunbeam Motors					
Kilmarnock		25/26	13	3	
		26/27	11	1	
Bournemouth		27/28	4		FL

CUGGY

Clydebank		18/19	1	?	

CULBERT William

Bridgeton Waverley					
Clyde		31/32			
Queen of the South		32/33			D2
		33/34	37		
		34/35	26		
		35/36	21		
		36/37	10		
		37/38	1		

CULLEN James
b. c1896

Morton		13/14	2	1	
		14/15			
		15/16	1		
Vale of Clyde					
Hamilton A		20/21	24	6	
		21/22	6	2	
Third Lanark		22/23	19	4	
Armadale					
Dykehead					

CULLEN Joseph
b. Glasgow d. Glasgow 27.10.1905

Stanley Swifts					
Benburb					
Celtic		91/92	12		
		92/93	17		
		93/94	18		
		94/95	3		
		95/96	1		
		96/97	7		
Tottenham H		97/98	21		SL
		98/99	22		SL
Lincoln C					

CULLEN Matthew

Airdrieonians					
Rangers		91/92	5		
Airdrieonians		92/93			
		93/94			
Albion R		94/95			

CULLEN William McKenzie
b. Gorbals 18.12.1896

Petershill					
Glasgow Perthshire					
Third Lanark		20/21	16	9	
Kings Park		21/22			D2
		22/23			D2
Reading		23/24	2		FL
Kings Park					
Bathgate					

CULLEY James
b. Condorrat 20.7.1915 d. Torrance 30.7.1981

Camelon Jnrs					
Hibernian		34/35	2		
		35/36	17		
		36/37	8		
		37/38	6		
Lincoln C		38/39	5		FL
Alloa A					

CULLEY William Neill
b. Kilwinning 26.8.1892 d. Irvine 9.11.1955

Kilwinning Eglington					
Kilwinning R					
Ardrossan Winton R		11/12			
Kilmarnock		11/12	4		
		12/13	27	6	
		13/14	21	7	
		14/15	31	12	
Third Lanark	L	14/15			
Kilmarnock		15/16	36	23	
Renton	L	15/16			
Kilmarnock		16/17	25	16	
		17/18	27	16	
		18/19	24	20	
		19/20	26	14	
		20/21	24	5	
		21/22	40	20	
		22/23	16	10	
Clyde		22/23	9	3	
		23/24	16	2	
Weymouth		24/25			
Bristol R		25/26	8	5	FL
		26/27	31	26	FL
		27/28	18	14	FL
Swindon T		28/29	3	1	FL
Weymouth					
Kilmarnock		29/30			
Galston	L	29/30			
Kilwinning Eglington					

CUMMING Arthur

Raith R		09/10			D2
		10/11	34	3	
		11/12	23		
		12/13	30		
		13/14	9		
Dundee					

CUMMING David

Dundee		21/22	1		

CUMMING David Scott 1 cap
b. Aberdeen 6.5.1910 d. Kirriemuir 18.4.1993

Woodside Thistle					
Hall Russells					
Aberdeen		30/31	7		
		31/32	1		
		32/33			
		33/34	5		
Arbroath		34/35	34		D2
		35/36	36		
		36/37	11		
Middlesbrough		36/37	32		FL
		37/38	28		FL
		38/39	38		FL
		46/47	37		FL
Partick T					

CUMMING James Ferguson
b. Alexandria 9.7.1891

Clydebank Jnrs					
Benburb					
Maryhill					
Manchester C		13/14	23	3	FL
		14/15	12		FL
Aberdeen		15/16	15	3	
		16/17	11	1	
Dumbarton		18/19	2		
West Ham U		19/20	10		FL
		20/21	5		FL

CUMMING Lawrence Stanley Slater
b. Londonderry 10.4.1905

Dunoon U					
Alloa A		26/27			D2
		27/28			D2
Huddersfield T		27/28	1		FL
		28/29	17	6	FL
		29/30	1		FL
Oldham A		29/30	25	11	FL
Southampton		30/31	20	4	FL
Alloa A		31/32			D2
		32/33			D2
Queen of the South		33/34	29	19	
		34/35	26	13	
		35/36	23	9	
		36/37	18	6	
St Mirren		37/38			
Hamilton A		38/39	4	1	

CUMMINGS George Wilfred 9 caps
b. Thornbridge 5.6.1913 d. Birmingham 9.4.1987

Thornbridge Waverley					
Thornbridge Welfare					
Grange R					
Partick T		32/33	30		
		33/34	36	1	
		34/35	34		
		35/36	14		
Aston Villa		35/36	27		FL
		36/37	12		FL
		37/38	36		FL
		38/39	40		FL
		39/40	3	1	FL
		46/47	31		FL
		47/48	30		FL
		48/49	34		FL

CUNNINGHAM

Abercorn		90/91	1		

CUNNINGHAM

Abercorn		96/97	1	1	

CUNNINGHAM Albert

Port Glasgow A		05/06	22	1	
Rangers		06/07	10	3	
		07/08	3		
Clyde		08/09	11	6	
Ayr Parkhouse		09/10			D2

CUNNINGHAM Andrew Nesbit 12 caps
b. Galston 30.1.1890 d. Scotland 8.5.1973

Galston Riverside R					
Newmilns					
Kilmarnock		09/10	24	18	
		10/11	29	14	
		11/12	29	14	
		12/13	31	11	
		13/14	37	9	
		14/15	34	9	
Rangers		14/15	3	2	
		15/16	20	18	
		16/17			
		17/18	4	4	
		18/19	15	4	
		19/20	39	23	
		20/21	40	24	
		21/22	32	14	
		22/23	35	11	
		23/24	30	13	
		24/25	33	7	
		25/26	31	18	
		26/27	29	7	
		27/28	31	14	
		28/29	8	3	
Newcastle U		28/29	10	2	FL
		29/30	2		FL

CUNNINGHAM Finlay

St Mirren		32/33	5	3	
		33/34	5	1	
		34/35	2		
		35/36			D2
		36/37	35	3	
		37/38	27		
		38/39	18		

CUNNINGHAM George Bruce

Club	Season	Apps	Goals	Note
Port Glasgow A *				
Queen's Park	12/13	5		
	13/14	1		

CUNNINGHAM Harry

b. Irvine 8.1.1898 d. 1972

Club	Season	Apps	Goals	Note
Irvine Meadow				
Irvine V				
Cumnock Jnrs				
Ayr U	20/21	14	3	
	21/22	27	7	
	22/23	29	7	
	23/24	36	9	
	24/25	35	7	
Kilmarnock	25/26	22	9	
	26/27	34	19	
	27/28	35	34	
	28/29	35	23	
	29/30	24	14	
	30/31	6	1	
Carlisle U				T

CUNNINGHAM Henry

b. c1908 d. London ?.3.1929

Club	Season	Apps	Goals	Note
Cambuslang R				
Celtic				
Kilmarnock	27/28	4	1	

CUNNINGHAM James

b. Glasgow 1885

Club	Season	Apps	Goals	Note
Cambuslang Hibernian				
St Mirren	04/05	17	2	
	05/06	6	4	
	06/07	24	8	
	07/08	33	6	
	08/09	24	7	
	09/10	26	7	
	10/11	33	18	
Kilmarnock	11/12	25	6	
Galston	12/13			
Cowdenbeath	12/13			D2
	13/14			D2
Airdrieonians	14/15	4		

CUNNINGHAM Joel

b. Lochie 1905

Club	Season	Apps	Goals	Note
Dundee Logie				
Lochie U				
Aberdeen	24/25	1		
Newport Co	25/26	2		FL
QPR	26/27	19		FL
	27/28	36		FL
	28/29	38		FL
	29/30	36		FL
	30/31	31		FL
	31/32	8		FL
Walsall	32/33	42		FL
	33/34	7		FL
York C	34/35	42		FL
Dartford	35/36			
Folkestone T	36/37			
Dartford				

CUNNINGHAM John

b. Glasgow 1879 d. 1910

Club	Season	Apps	Goals	Note
Benburb				
Celtic				T
Burnley				
Glasgow Hibs				
Celtic	90/91	1		
	91/92	5		
Partick T				
Heart of Midlothian	92/93	1		
Rangers				
Glasgow Thistle				
Preston NE	93/94	16	1	FL
	94/95	12	5	FL
	95/96	19	3	FL
	96/97	4		FL
Sheffield U	97/98	24	7	FL
Aston Villa	98/99			
Newton Heath	98/99	15	3	FL
Wigan Co	99/00			
	00/01			
Barrow				

CUNNINGHAM John

b. Alexandria

Club	Season	Apps	Goals	Note
Vale of Leven				
Dundee U	28/29	5		D2
	29/30	4		

CUNNINGHAM Peter

Club	Season	Apps	Goals	Note
Dechmont Hearts				
Blantyre V				
Cambuslang R				
Hibernian	18/19	9		
Blantyre V				

CUNNINGHAM Peter

b. Glasgow 13.7.1906 d. Kirkintilloch 3.9.1934

Club	Season	Apps	Goals	Note
Glasgow Ashfield				
Clyde	27/28	28	20	
	28/29			
	29/30			
Partick T	30/31	7	5	
Cork	31/32			LI
Rangers	31/32			
Barnsley	32/33	14	17	FL
Port Vale	33/34	2		FL
Crewe A	33/34	15	13	FL

CUNNINGHAM Robert

Club	Season	Apps	Goals	Note
Baillieston				
St Mirren	10/11	19	4	
	11/12	7		
Abercorn	12/13			D2
	13/14			D2
St Mirren	13/14	2	1	
Morton	13/14			
Girvan	14/15			
Millwall	19/20	1		SL

CUNNINGHAM Thomas

Club	Season	Apps	Goals	Note
Larkhall Thistle				
Port Glasgow A	07/08	27		
	08/09	6		

CUNNINGHAM W

Club	Season	Apps	Goals	Note
Heart of Midlothian	31/32	3		

CUNNINGHAM William C

b. Galston 1893

Club	Season	Apps	Goals	Note
Galston Hearts				
Galston Riverside R				
Kilmarnock	11/12	6		
	12/13	18		
	13/14	11		
Galston	13/14			L
Kilmarnock	14/15	36		

CURLEY John

Club	Season	Apps	Goals	Note
Raith R	25/26	6		

CURLEY John

b. Ayrshire

Club	Season	Apps	Goals	Note
Armadale				
Alloa A	32/33			D2
	33/34			D2
Queen of the South	34/35	19	1	

CURRAN John

b. Bellshill

Club	Season	Apps	Goals	Note
Glasgow Benburb				
Celtic	92/93	7		
	93/94	12		
	94/95	1		
Liverpool	94/95	12		FL
	95/96	6		FL
Hibernian	95/96	1		
Motherwell	95/96			D2

CURRAN John

Club	Season	Apps	Goals	Note
Celtic				
Hamilton A				
Partick T	04/05	5	2	
Hamilton A				
Abercorn	08/09			D2
	09/10			D2
	10/11	16		D2
	11/12			D2
	12/13			D2
Hamilton A				

CURRAN John

b. c1896

Club	Season	Apps	Goals	Note
Shawfield				
St Mirren	21/22	4		

CURRAN Peter

b. Saltcoats

Club	Season	Apps	Goals	Note
Kilwinning R				
Partick T	37/38	21		
	38/39	27		
	46/47	30		
	47/48	18		
	48/49	8		
Ayr U	49/50	7		D2

CURRIE Alexander

b. c1898

Club	Season	Apps	Goals	Note
Greenfield U				
Rutherglen Glencairn				
Clyde	17/18	20	?	
	18/19	8	?	

CURRIE Alexander Ferguson

b. Stewarton 5.5.1881

Club	Season	Apps	Goals	Note
Stewarton Cunninghame				
Queen's Park	02/03	14	6	
	03/04	7		
Kilmarnock	04/05	14	1	
Airdrieonians	04/05	1		
	05/06	18	2	
	06/07	9	1	
	07/08	1		
Queen's Park	07/08	5	1	

CURRIE David

Club	Season	Apps	Goals	Note
Cambuslang R				
Ayr U	32/33	9		
	33/34	37	1	
	34/35	34		
	35/36	18	1	
	36/37	33		D2
	37/38	38	1	
	38/39	38	1	

CURRIE David S

d. 10.1.1931

Club	Season	Apps	Goals	Note
Kings Park				
Airdrieonians	24/25	2		
	25/26	2		
	26/27	18		
	27/28	30		
	28/29	32		
Connahs Quay				

CURRIE Dominic

Club	Season	Apps	Goals	Note
Denbeath Celtic				
Wellesley				
Heart of Midlothian	19/20	1		
	20/21			
East Fife	20/21			
Broxburn U				
Clackmannan	23/24			

CURRIE Duncan

b. Kilwinning 13.8.1892 K.I.A. Somme 1.7.1916

Club	Season	Apps	Goals	Note
Kilwinning R				
Heart of Midlothian	12/13	3		
	13/14	5		
	14/15	35		
	15/16	1		

CURRIE George

Club	Season	Apps	Goals	Note
Queen's Park	21/22	2		

CURRIE John

Club	Season	Apps	Goals	Note
Salsburgh				
Airdrieonians	17/18	2	?	

CURRIE Patrick

Club	Season	Apps	Goals	Note
Buckhaven				
Dundee	07/08	1	1	

CURRIE Peter

b. Armadale

Club	Season	Apps	Goals	Note
St Bernards				
Armadale				
Bradford C	13/14	5	1	FL
	14/15	12	1	FL
Broxburn U				
Dumbarton	20/21	4		

CURRIE Peter

Club	Season	Apps	Goals	Note
Armadale				
Falkirk	16/17	3		

CURRIE Robert

Club	Season	Apps	Goals	Note
Minerva				
Partick T	94/95	2		D2
	95/96	18	3	D2
	96/97	11	3	D2
	97/98	17		
	98/99	9	2	
East Stirlingshire	98/99			
Partick T	99/00	1		D2

CURRIE Robert
b. Kilwinning 1884

Arthurlie				
Middlesbrough				
Abercorn *	03/04			
Kilwinning R				
Morton	06/07	12	7	
Bury	06/07	8	2	FL
	07/08	21	5	FL
	08/09	15	2	FL
	09/10	24	13	FL
	10/11	37	10	FL
	11/12	11	1	FL
Heart of Midlothian	12/13	17	1	
	13/14	12	3	

CURRIE Walter Robertson
b. Lochgelly 5.10.1895

Denbeath Star				
Cowdenbeath				
East Fife				
Raith R	16/17	18	2	
	17/18			
	18/19			
	19/20	3		
Leicester C	19/20	10	1	FL
	20/21	21		FL
	21/22	1		FL
Bristol R	22/23	42		FL
Lochgelly U				

CURTIS Thomas

Benburb				
Partick T	11/12	6		

CUTHBERT

Cambuslang	90/91	2		

CUTHBERT Clement

Kings Park	T			
Clyde	21/22	26	2	
USA				

CUTHBERT James
b. Edinburgh

Bo'ness				
Aston Villa				
Leith Renton				
Clyde	35/36	11	1	
Dumbarton	36/37			D2
Clyde	36/37	6		

CUTHBERT William

Clyde	31/32	24		

CUTHBERTSON A

Abercorn	90/91	15		
	91/92	21		
	92/93	17		
	93/94	5	?	D2

CUTHBERTSON D

Abercorn	90/91	16		
	91/92	21		
	92/93	18	1	
	93/94	5	?	D2

DAILLY John

Hibernian	95/96	3	1	
Motherwell	95/96			D2
	96/97			D2
Lincoln C	97/98	1		FL

DAINTY Herbert Charles
b. Geddington 2.6.1879 d. Kettering 10.9.1957

Kettering T	97/98			
	98/99			
Leicester F	99/00	30	3	FL
New Brighton Tower	00/01	33	3	FL
Leicester F	01/02	23		FL
Northampton T	02/03	29	1	SL
Notts Co	03/04	20		FL
Southampton	04/05	31	1	SL
Dundee	05/06	30	5	
	06/07	34	6	
	07/08	33	8	
	08/09	30	3	
	09/10	28	1	
	10/11	32	1	
Bradford PA	11/12	22	1	FL
	12/13	34		FL
	13/14	7		FL
Ayr U	13/14	27		
	14/15	33		
Dundee Hibs	14/15			D2

DALGARNO James (Douglas James?)
b. Aberdeen * 1890 *

Aberdeen	08/09	5	2	

DALGLEISH Elphinston M
b. Scotstown 1915

Queen's Park	35/36	3		

DALGLEISH John

St Anthonys				
St Mirren Jnrs				
Hamilton A	18/19	6		

DALGLEISH John George

Queen's Park	12/13	7		
	13/14	1		

DALLAS

Clyde	92/93	2		

DALLAS James
d. Winnipeg ?.4.1911

Beith				
St Mirren	98/99	3	1	
	99/00	1		

DALLAS William

Dundee Forthill				
Stonehaven				
Hibernian	36/37	3	2	
Hull C	36/37			FL
Montrose	37/38			D2

DALRYMPLE George

Glasgow Perthshire				
Hibernian	03/04	17	5	
	04/05	4	2	
	05/06			
	06/07	5	2	
Raith R	06/07			D2
Ayr Parkhouse	07/08			D2

DALRYMPLE Robert Rodie
b. Paisley 2.1.1880 d. Worthing 26.7.1970

Westmarch				
Abercorn	00/01			
	01/02			
Kilbarchan	02/03			
Heart of Midlothian	02/03	6	2	
Plymouth A	03/04	27	7	SL
	04/05	30	3	SL
Rangers	05/06	13	4	
Portsmouth	06/07	31	8	SL
Fulham	07/08	33	19	FL
	08/09	31	12	FL
	09/10	29	6	FL
	10/11	5	2	FL
Clapton Orient	10/11	17	6	FL
	11/12	31	13	FL
	12/13	18	3	FL
	13/14	36	9	FL
	14/15	30	7	FL
	19/20	7		FL
Ton Pentre				

DALTON Bryan J

Clyde	16/17	4		
	17/18	7	?	

DALY James

Shamrock R	31/32			LI
Aberdeen	32/33	4		
Shamrock R	32/33			LI
	33/34			LI

DALY Samuel

Clyde	95/96	10	8	
	96/97	1		
Galston				

DALZIEL Andrew

Edinburgh Emmet				
Hibernian	28/29	12	1	

DAND Colin
b. Kirkcaldy 1899

Abbotshall				
Armadale				
Heart of Midlothian	21/22	10		
	22/23	31	1	
	23/24	27	2	
	24/25	28		
	25/26	24	5	
	26/27	9	3	
Dunfermline A	27/28	30	1	
	28/29			D2
Hamilton A	29/30	6		

DARGE William

Hamilton A	38/39	4	1	

DARGUE James Henderson
b. Blantyre 1882 d. Townhead 3.5.1937

Burnbank A				
Hamilton A				
Glossop NE	05/06	7		FL
Airdrieonians	06/07	30	8	
Heart of Midlothian	07/08	25	5	
Bristol R	08/09	37	2	SL
Royal Albert	09/10			
	10/11			
	11/12			
	12/13			
Hamilton A	13/14	14	1	

DARROCH John
b. Alexandria 1872 d. Dundee 24.11.1949

Dumbarton				
Renton				
Vale of Leven	90/91	2		
	91/92	5		
Sheffield W	91/92	12		FA
	92/93	13		FL
	93/94	3		FL
Dundee	94/95	18		
	95/96	18		
Bury	96/97	28		FL
	97/98	30		FL
	98/99	20	1	FL
	99/00	28		FL
	00/01	32		FL
	01/02	5		FL
Blackburn R	01/02	17		FL
Dundee	02/03	22		
	03/04	8		
	04/05	1		
	05/06	8		
	06/07			
	07/08			
	08/09			
Dundee Hibs	09/10			

DARROCH John

Port Glasgow A	05/06	8		

DARROCH William

Wishaw				
Airdrieonians	03/04	4	3	
Albion R	03/04			

DART James
b. Ladyburn

Morton	04/05	12	1	
	05/06			
Morton	06/07	26	2	
	07/08	29	4	
	08/09	6		
	09/10	15		

DAVID Norman
b. Aberdeen

Mugiemoss				
Aberdeen	29/30			
	30/31	8	5	
	31/32	5	2	

DAVIDSON

Leith A	92/93	3		

DAVIDSON A

Dumbarton Harp				
Motherwell	09/10			
	10/11	14	3	

DAVIDSON Alexander

Third Lanark	T			
Bolton W				
Clyde	06/07	1		

DAVIDSON Alexander

Schools football
Partick T 10/11 1
11/12 1
12/13 8
13/14 4
Dumbarton 14/15 21 1

DAVIDSON Alexander

Castle Douglas
Partick T
Castle Douglas
Kilmarnock 11/12 1

DAVIDSON Alexander Laude
b. Beith 27.9.1878
Beith
Third Lanark 99/00 9 4
New Brompton U 99/00
Glossop NE 99/00 13 1 FL
Manchester C 99/00 5 1 FL
00/01 2 FL
Reading 01/02 21 9 SL
02/03 5 2 SL
West Ham U 02/03 9 3 SL
Luton T 02/03 9 7 SL
Fulham 03/04 1 SL
New Brompton 03/04 3 SL
Kilmarnock 03/04
Aberdeen 04/05
Stockport Co 04/05
Atherton Church House 05/06
Bolton W 06/07
Wigan T 06/07
Nelson 06/07
07/08
Macclesfield T 07/08
Denton 08/09

DAVIDSON Alexander M
b. c1920
St Rochs
Hibernian 37/38 12 2
38/39 3

DAVIDSON Andrew

Duntocher Hibs
Clyde 03/04
Leyton 04/05
Burnley 05/06 35 8 FL
06/07 11 3 FL
Croydon Common 07/08 17 13 SL
Partick T 08/09 1
Belfast Celtic 09/10 IL
10/11 IL
Distillery 10/11 IL
Croydon Common 11/12 22 11 SL

DAVIDSON Andrew
b. c1892
Rutherglen Glencairn
Celtic 13/14 5
Vale of Atholl L 13/14
Wishaw Thistle L 13/14
St Mirren 14/15 31
15/16 19 1
South Shields
Glasgow University
South Shields

DAVIDSON Andrew

Clydebank 20/21 1

DAVIDSON Edward

Motherwell 09/10 17
10/11 6

DAVIDSON George
b. Dunipace
Dunipace
Falkirk 28/29 1
29/30 1
30/31
Albion R 31/32 D2

DAVIDSON James

Motherwell 21/22 6

DAWSON James M

St Bernards
Albion R 20/21 10 1

DAVIDSON James S

Morton 21/22 1

DAVIDSON James Wilkie
b. Edinburgh 25.10.1873
Leith A
Celtic 92/93 14 8
93/94 3
94/95 5 2
Burnley 95/96 18 3 FL
96/97 2 FL
Lincoln C L 96/97 9 1 FL
Tottenham H 97/98 17 8 SL
Brighton U 98/99 14 1 SL
99/00 14 6 SL
Burnley 99/00 2 1 FL
00/01 14 2 FL
01/02 29 3 FL

DAVIDSON John

Dundee 20/21 2

DAVIDSON John Campbell
b. Glenbuck 31.1.1894
Glenbuck A
Solway Star
Coventry C 22/23 4 FL
Kilmarnock 23/24 1
Nithsdale W 23/24
Thornhill

DAVIDSON John M

St Anthonys
Kilmarnock 38/39 1

DAVIDSON Joseph

Petershill
Raith R 13/14 4
Newarthill

DAVIDSON Robert
b. West Calder d. Brisbane ?.5.1935
West Benhar Juveniles
Albion R
Dykehead
Celtic 98/99 6
99/00 8
Belfast Celtic L 99/00 IL
Celtic 00/01 19
Heart of Midlothian L 00/01 3
Airdrieonians L 00/01 1 D2
Celtic 01/02 11
Manchester C 02/03 26 FL
03/04 6 FL
Airdrieonians 04/05 21
05/06 13
06/07 28
07/08 26
08/09 10
09/10 28
Bathgate
Balimba R (Aus)

DAVIDSON Robert

Clydebank 25/26 2

DAVIDSON Robert Trimming
b. Lochgelly 23.4.1913 d. Coventry ?.10.1988
Prinlaws U
Hamilton A T
Bowhill R 30/31
St Bernards 31/32 D2
32/33 D2
St Johnstone 32/33 6 1
33/34 30 18
34/35 22 9
Arsenal 34/35 11 2 FL
35/36 13 FL
36/37 28 9 FL
37/38 5 2 FL
Coventry C 37/38 16 1 FL
38/39 28 8 FL
39/40 1 FL
Kings Park
Hinckley A 48/49
Redditch T

DAVIDSON Robert W
b. c1895
Earnock R
Larkhall U
Armadale
St Mirren 15/16 12

DAVIDSON Stewart 1 cap
b. Aberdeen 1.6.1886 d. East Ham 26.12.1960
Aberdeen Shamrock
Aberdeen 05/06 1
06/07 4
07/08 7 1
08/09 7
09/10 19
10/11 7
11/12 23
12/13 31
Middlesbrough 13/14 30 1 FL
14/15 36 FL
Aberdeen 16/17 3
Middlesbrough 19/20 42 1 FL
20/21 37 FL
21/22 40 2 FL
22/23 22 FL
Aberdeen 23/24 26
24/25 6
25/26
Forres Mechanics 26/27
27/28
28/29
29/30
30/31

DAVIDSON William

Dundee 98/99 14
Heart of Midlothian 98/99
Bo'ness 98/99

DAVIDSON William
b. Glasgow
Queen's Park 03/04 1
04/05 4 1
05/06 16 8
Falkirk 06/07 32 4
07/08 31 2
08/09 28 1
09/10 20 1
Airdrieonians 09/10 28
10/11 14 3
Middlesbrough 10/11 16 FL
Everton 11/12 25 3 FL
12/13 13 FL
St Mirren 13/14 14 3

DAVIDSON William Forrest
b. Hamilton 5.11.1918 d. Netley 26.1.1999
Hamilton A 36/37 8

DAVIE

Rangers 92/93 6

DAVIE George

Renton 91/92 10 2
92/93 1
93/94 13
94/95 10 D2
95/96 D2
96/97 D2

DAVIE John

Rangers 00/01
01/02
02/03
Renfrew V 03/04
04/05
Alloa A 05/06
Hamilton A 06/07 27 1
07/08 7 1
08/09 21 1
09/10 30 8
10/11 29 2
11/12 14 2
Raith R L 11/12 D2
12/13 D2
Dumbarton 13/14 1

DAVIE John
b. Dunfermline 19.2.1913 d. Shrewsbury ?.6.1994
St Bernards
St Johnstone
Dunfermline Wednesday
Hibernian 33/34
Arsenal
Hibernian 34/35 3
Margate 35/36
Brighton 36/37 34 13 FL
37/38 38 17 FL
38/39 27 9 FL
39/40 2 2 FL
Stockton
Barnsley 46/47 6 FL
Kidderminster H
Shrewsbury T

DAVIES Jack

Newarthill					
Heart of Midlothian		19/20	12	5	
		20/21	3		
Broxburn U		21/22			D2

DAVIES Samuel Herbert

b. Wrexham 5.11.1894 d. St Annes on Sea 6.7.1972

Queen's Park		21/22	35	2	
		22/23	2		D2
Morton		22/23	18		
		23/24	5		
Manchester U		24/25			FL
		25/26			FL
		26/27			FL
Crewe A		27/28	3		FL
		28/29	1		FL
Sandbach R					

DAVIN Martin

b. Dumbarton 9.5.1905 d. Romford 9.11.1957

Vale of Clyde					
Dumbarton		26/27			D2
Bury		27/28	7	1	FL
		28/29	8	3	FL
		29/30	23	5	FL
Bolton W		30/31	3		FL
Hull C		30/31	8	1	FL
Yeovil T		31/32			
Airdrieonians		32/33	11		
Clapton Orient		33/34	15	2	FL
Guildford C					
Ashford T					
Briggs Motor Bodies					

DAVIS Robert

Pollok Jnrs					
Falkirk		24/25	4	1	
		25/26	1		
Broxburn U					

DAVITT Michael

b. Bridgeton 22.10.1912 d. 24.2.1973

League Hearts					
Baillieston Jnrs					
St Francis Jnrs					
Celtic		35/36			
		36/37			
		37/38	1		
		38/39			
Renfrew Jnrs					

DAVY R

Heart of Midlothian		91/92	3		

DAVY Walter K

Alloa A					
Hamilton A		06/07	4		
		07/08	1		
Ayr Parkhouse		07/08			D2
Hamilton A					

DAWSON Daniel

b. Larkhall 26.6.1912

Larkhall Thistle					
Celtic		32/33			
		33/34	4		
		34/35	8		
		35/36			
		36/37	6	2	
		37/38			
Queen of the South		38/39	32	9	

DAWSON David

Lochgelly U					
Blackburn R	T				FL
Raith R		21/22	8	6	
Dunfermline A		22/23			D2

DAWSON James

Heart of Midlothian		17/18	17	8	
		18/19	9	1	
Dumbarton		18/19			
Southampton					

DAWSON James 14 caps

b. Falkirk 30.10.1909 d. 19.1.1977

Camelon Jnrs					
Rangers		29/30			
		30/31	1		
		31/32	13		
		32/33	20		
		33/34	30		
		34/35	37		
		35/36	38		
		36/37	38		
		37/38	26		
		38/39	33		
Falkirk		46/47	30		
		47/48	27		
		48/49	21		

DAWSON James Maxwell

Liverpool					
St Bernards		20/21			
Albion R		20/21			
Alloa A		21/22			D2
St Mirren		22/23	1		
Bo'ness					

DAWSON James S

Dunfermline Jnrs					
Clydebank		21/22	3		

DAWSON John

Dundee		98/99	1		

DAWSON Joseph

Inverkeithing					
Cowdenbeath		32/33	2		
Kelty Our Boys					
Inverkeithing					
St Bernards		36/37			D2

DAWSON Kenneth

b. Forres

Forres Thistle					
Nairn Co					
Sheffield U	T	33/34			
Forres Mechanics		34/35			
Falkirk		34/35	4	3	
		35/36	?	39	D2
		36/37	38	26	
		37/38	33	20	
		38/39	23	14	
Blackpool		38/39	12	1	FL
Falkirk		38/39			

DAWSON Percival Hall

b. Cullercoats 4.12.1889 d. Cullercoats 1974

Whitley A					
North Shields A					
Heart of Midlothian		10/11	9	2	
		11/12	18	15	
		12/13	25	24	
		13/14	28	24	
Blackburn R		13/14	8	3	FL
		14/15	28	20	FL
Dumbarton	L	18/19	6	?	
Blackburn R		19/20	23	14	FL
		20/21	33	17	FL
		21/22	27	13	FL
		22/23	21	5	FL
Preston Colliery		23/24			
Barrow					

DEAKIN John

b. c1920

Johnstone Jnrs					
St Mirren		37/38	26	3	
		38/39	13	2	

DEAN Alfred

b. West Bromwich 2.1.1877 d. Wolverhampton 21.1.1959

Tantany R					
West Bromwich Standard					
Walsall Town Swifts		95/96			
WBA		96/97	2	1	FL
		97/98	5	2	FL
Walsall		98/99	30	13	FL
		99/00	12	5	FL
		00/01	23	11	FL
Nottingham F		00/01	7		FL
Grimsby T		01/02	17		FL
Bristol C		02/03	25	10	FL
		03/04	32	15	FL
		04/05	27	12	FL
Swindon T		05/06	34	10	SL
Millwall		06/07	36	7	SL
Dundee		07/08	18	10	
Millwall		08/09	24	8	SL
Wellington T		09/10			
		10/11			
		11/12			
		12/13			
		13/14			

DEANS

St Mirren		90/91	5		

DEANS William Richardson

b. Renfrew 1908 d. Renfrew ?.6.1938

Renfrew					
Yoker A		29/30			
Clydebank Jnrs					
Rangers		31/32	1		
		32/33	1		
		33/34			
Margate		34/35			
Cowdenbeath		35/36			D2
		36/37			D2
Dumbarton					
Kings Park					

DELANEY James 13 caps

b. Cleland 3.9.1914 d. Cleland 26.9.1989

Cleland St Marys					
Wishaw Jnrs	T	32/33			
Stoneyburn Jnrs		32/33			
Celtic		33/34			
		34/35	30	15	
		35/36	30	18	
		36/37	32	14	
		37/38	26	7	
		38/39	25	14	
Manchester U		46/47			FL
		47/48			FL
		48/49			FL
		49/50			FL
		50/51			FL
Aberdeen		50/51	21	4	
		51/52	10	4	
Falkirk		52/53	20	13	
		53/54	7	3	
Derry C		53/54			IL
		54/55			IL
Cork A		55/56			LI
Elgin C		56/57			

DE MEZA John

Heart of Midlothian		08/09	1		

DEMPSEY

Cowlairs		90/91	3	2	

DEMPSEY John

Hamilton A		33/34	1		
		34/35			
		35/36			
St Bernards		36/37			D2

DEMPSEY John

Stenhousemuir *					
Newry T *		37/38			
Albion R		38/39	21	2	

DEMPSTER George

Dundee		30/31	12	7	

DEMPSTER James Barclay

b. Newarthill 30.1.1896

Newarthill Thistle					
Sunderland		19/20	5		FL
		20/21	25		FL
		21/22	10		FL
Airdrieonians		22/23	8		
		23/24	7		
St Johnstone		23/24	13		D2
		24/25	38		
		25/26	11		
Dundee U		26/27	13		
Bo'ness		27/28	24		
Bathgate		28/29			D2
Bo'ness		29/30			D2

DEMPSTER Morton

Dundee		29/30	1		
Keith					

DEMPSTER Morton

Irvine Meadow					
Dundee		36/37			
		37/38			
St Mirren		38/39	2		
Morton					
Cowdenbeath		46/47			D2

DENHOLM John

Cambuslang R					
St Mirren		13/14	3		

DENMARK James

b. Shettleston 13.5.1913

Tollcross Clydesdale					
Parkhead					
Third Lanark		31/32	1		
		32/33	1		
		33/34	28	1	
		34/35			D2
		35/36	35		
		36/37	37		
Newcastle U		37/38	17		FL
		38/39	34		FL
		39/40	4		FL
Queen of the South		46/47	17		
Ashington					

DENOON John

Motherwell		13/14	3		

DENYER Albert Edward Curly

b. Plaistow 9.4.1893 d. Swindon 15.3.1969

Ilford					
West Ham U		12/13	29	11	SL
		13/14	17	5	SL
Swindon T		14/15	17	10	SL
Heart of Midlothian		16/17	13	6	
		17/18	5	1	
Swindon T		19/20			SL
		20/21	24	8	FL
		21/22	20	6	FL
		22/23	32	6	FL
		23/24	37	3	FL
		24/25	40	2	FL
		25/26	39	6	FL
		26/27	34	5	FL
		27/28	39	5	FL
		28/29	24	4	FL
		29/30	35	4	FL
Evesham T		30/31			
West End Sports					

DEUCHAR William Stewart

b. Perth 1903

Raith R		24/25	4	3	
		25/26	33		
		26/27			D2
		27/28	6		
Dundee U		28/29	30		D2
		29/30	21	1	
Forfar A		30/31			D2
?		31/32			
		32/33			
		33/34			
		34/35			
Fair City A		35/36			

DEVAN Charles

b. Girvan 22.4.1901 d. Girvan 20.1.1980

Ashfield					
Glasgow St Anthonys					
Clydebank		23/24	10		
Morton		23/24	8	1	
South Shields		24/25	12		FL
Grimsby T		25/26	32	8	FL
		26/27	18	4	FL
Fulham		27/28	7	2	FL

DEVAN William Gemmell

b. Whitletts 23.2.1909 d. Paddington 12.12.1966

Whitletts					
Ayr U		28/29	2		
Nelson	T	29/30			
Ards	T	29/30			
Mansfield T	T	30/31			
Sanquhar		31/32			
Coleraine		31/32			IL
		32/33			IL
Linfield		32/33			IL
Coleraine Caledonians		32/33			
Watford		33/34	10	1	FL
		34/35	23	6	FL
		35/36	28	14	FL
		36/37	25	11	FL
		37/38	4	1	FL
Ayr U	T	37/38			
Scammells					

DEVERS Tommy

Benburb					
Aberdeen		33/34			
		34/35	4	1	
		35/36	7	4	

DEVINE Archibald 1 cap

b. Lochore 2.4.1887 d. Lochgelly 30.9.1964

Minto R					
Lochgelly U		04/05			
Heart of Midlothian	T	04/05	1		
Lochgelly U		05/06			
		06/07			
Raith R		07/08			D2
Heart of Midlothian		08/09	3	1	
Falkirk		09/10	25	13	
Bradford C		10/11	24	8	FL
		11/12	13		FL
		12/13	11	1	FL
Woolwich Arsenal		12/13	11	2	FL
		13/14	13	3	FL
Shelbourne		14/15			
Bradford C		14/15			FL
Lochgelly U		15/16			
Dunfermline A					
Lochgelly U		20/21			

DEVINE Charles

Hibernian		97/98	2	2	
Manchester C					

DEVINE Daniel

b. Dumbarton 1870

Dumbarton A					
Renton		91/92	22	1	
		92/93	5		
Royal Arsenal		93/94	2		FL
Partick T		94/95	4		D2

DEVINE J

Third Lanark		22/23	5		

DEVINE James

Pollok Jnrs					
Ayr U		16/17	5		
		17/18	21	?	
		18/19	13		

DEVINE John

b. Twechar 10.6.1899 d. Glasgow 8.7.1949

Kilsyth R					
Plymouth A		21/22	3		FL
		22/23	11	2	FL
		23/24			FL
East Stirlingshire		24/25			D2
Kettering T		25/26			
Charlton A		26/27	19		FL
Dundee		26/27	1		
Southport		27/28	33	1	FL
Crewe A					
Kilsyth R					
Croy Celtic					

DEVINE John Steven

b. Aberdeen

St Rochs					
Aberdeen		35/36	1		
		36/37	2		
		37/38	11	3	
QPR		3839	7	3	FL

DEVINE Matthew

b. East Kilbride c1919 d. East Kilbride 5.4.1985

Royal Albert					
Hibernian		36/37	1		
Ayr U		37/38	18	3	
Hamilton A		38/39	7	2	
		46/47	18		
		47/48			D2
		48/49			D2
		49/50			D2
Stranraer					

DEVLIN James

Blackstoun R					
Celtic		90/91			
Abercorn					
Paisley Celtic					
Celtic		94/95	2		
Royal Albert					
Chorley					
Dundee		96/97			
Sunderland					
Woolwich Arsenal		97/98	1		FL
Airdrieonians		97/98			D2
Third Lanark		98/99	3	2	
Albion R					
Army					
Albion R					

DEVLIN James Thomas

b. Mossend 6.10.1903 d. Scotland

Vale of Clyde					
Shawfield Jnrs					
Kilsyth R					
Third Lanark		23/24	2		
Kings Park					
Birmingham		24/25	2	1	FL
Preston NE		25/26	5	1	FL
		26/27	3		FL
Liverpool		27/28			FL
Swindon T		28/29	1		FL
Brooklyn Wanderers		29A	17	6	ASL
		29/30	24	8	ASL
		31S	9		ASL
Aberdeen		31/32			
Walsall		32/33	4		FL
Fall River Marksmen		32/33			ASL
FC Zurich		33/34			
Fleetwood T		33/34			
Oldham A		34/35	2		FL
Racing Club de Roubaix					
Fleetwood T					

DEVLIN John

Mossend Celtic					
Celtic		94/95	2	1	
Airdrieonians		95/96	6	3	D2
Chorley					
Tottenham H		96/97	20	1	SL
Millwall		97/98	6	2	SL
Third Lanark					
Albion R					
Army					
Albion R					
Nithsdale W					
Lanesmark					

DEVLIN John

b. Glasgow

St Anthonys					
Arbroath		36/37	26	4	
		37/38	35	5	
		38/39	7	1	
Cowdenbeath					

DEVLIN Joseph

Dundee		96/97	18	6	
		97/98	8	4	

DEVLIN William Alexander				
b. Bellshill 30.7.1899 d. Glasgow ?.7.1992				
Vale of Clyde				
Kings Park	21/22	12	17	D2
Clyde	21/22	9	2	
	22/23	1		
Cowdenbeath	22/23			D2
	23/24		25	D2
	24/25	38	33	
	25/26	30	40	
Huddersfield T	25/26	4	4	FL
	26/27	28	10	FL
Liverpool	26/27	1	1	FL
	27/28	18	14	FL
Heart of Midlothian	27/28	15	12	
Macclesfield	28/29			
Cowdenbeath	29/30	20	5	
Mansfield T	30/31	21	15	ML
Cowdenbeath	30/31			
Burton T	30/31			
Shelbourne	31/32			LI
Olympique Marseilles	32/33			
Bangor C	32/33			
Boston T	33/34			
Ashton National	34/35			
Olympique Marseilles	35/36			
Zurich				
DEVLIN William J				
St Rochs				
Hibernian	38/39	1		
Arthurlie				
DEWAR				
Dumbarton	17/18	1		
DEWAR James				
Third Lanark	06/07	3		
DEWAR John (John McSeveny?)				
Strathclyde				
Blackburn R				
Hamilton A	34/35	1		
	35/36	9		
Morton	36/37			D2
Larne *	37/38			IL
Chirnside U	37/38			
DEWAR Neil Hamilton 3 caps				
b. Lochgilphead 11.11.1908 d. Lochgilphead 10.1.1982				
Lochgilphead U				
Third Lanark	31/32	37	35	
	32/33	28	23	
Manchester U	32/33	15	6	FL
	33/34	21	8	FL
Sheffield W	33/34	16	8	FL
	34/35	18	6	FL
	35/36	32	19	FL
	36/37	18	10	FL
Third Lanark	37/38	35	18	
	38/39	35	25	
DEWAR William S				
Heart of Midlothian	07/08	3		
DIAMOND George				
Carluke Milton R				
Motherwell	03/04	15		
DIAMOND James				
St Mirren	00/01	3		
DICK				
Third Lanark	93/94	1		
DICK Alexander				
b. Harthill				
Armadale				
Airdrieonians	19/20	10	2	
	20/21	41		
	21/22	37		
	22/23	37		
	23/24	38		
	24/25	35		
	25/26	32		
	26/27	13		
Dykehead				
DICK Alexander				
b. Hamilton				
Ayr U T				
Rangers	24/25	1	1	
St Johnstone	25/26	22	4	
Hamilton A	26/27	24	17	
	27/28	25	12	
Queen of the South	28/29			D2
Bethlehem Steel	29/30	24	10	ASL
Newark Americans	30A	28	6	ASL
	31S	13	3	ASL
	31A	11		ASL
	31/32			
Larne T	32/33			IL
DICK Andrew				
Larkhall Thistle				
Motherwell	20/21	5	2	
DICK Andrew				
b. Aberdeen c1900				
Larkhall Thistle				
Armadale				
Airdrieonians				
Aberdeen	22/23	1		
	23/24	10		
Bristol R	25/26	19		FL
Motherwell				
Ayr U				
Aberdeen				
DICK Douglas C				
b. Scotland				
Morton				
Rangers	92/93	2	1	
Liverpool	93/94	10	3	FL
Third Lanark	93/94	1		
Morton	94/95			D2
	95/96			D2
DICK John				
Vale of Clyde				
Queen's Park	04/05	17		
	05/06	13	1	
	06/07	4		
	07/08	1		
Motherwell	07/08	3		
Hurlford	08/09			
DICK John				
Rangers	16/17	1		
	17/18	1		
DICK Thomas				
Kirkintilloch Rob Roy				
Airdrieonians	24/25	1		
DICK William Russell				
b. Harthill 12.6.1901				
Armadale				
Airdrieonians	25/26	6		
Hibernian	26/27	30		
	27/28	36		
	28/29	37	2	
	29/30	36		
	30/31	26		
Bradford PA	31/32	11		FL
Raith R	32/33			D2
DICKIE				
Falkirk	18/19	2	?	
DICKIE James				
b. Montrose 22.9.1903 d. 25.6.1960				
Buckie Thistle				
Preston NE	25/26	3	1	FL
Forres Mechanics	26/27			
St Johnstone	26/27	5		
New Brighton	27/28	42	11	FL
	28/29	14	4	FL
Bristol C	28/29	25	3	FL
	29/30	23	1	FL
Chester	30/31	40	19	CCL
Macclesfield T	31/32			
Chester	32/33	1		FL
New Brighton	32/33	27	4	FL
DICKIE John				
Strathclyde				
Rangers	06/07	20	3	
	07/08	9		
Clyde	08/09	12	3	
Chesterfield	09/10			
Dumbarton	10/11	4		D2
DICKIE Matthew 3 caps				
b. Rhu 19.8.1873 d. 30.12.1959				
Helensburgh Arthurlie				
Helensburgh V				
Renton	94/95	13	?	D2
	95/96	16	?	D2
Rangers	95/96			
	96/97	18		
	97/98	17		
	98/99	18		
	99/00	17		
	00/01	20		
	01/02	15		
	02/03	21		
	03/04	15		
Clyde	04/05			
DICKIE Percy				
b. Bucksburn 11.12.1907				
Mugiemoss				
Aberdeen	29/30	4	1	
	30/31	19	2	
	31/32	6		
	32/33	4		
St Johnstone	32/33	25	3	
	33/34	15	4	
	34/35	33	6	
	35/36	36	2	
	36/37	34		
Blackburn R	37/38	17	1	FL
	38/39	2		FL
Aberdeen				
Peterhead				
DICKIE William Cunningham				
b. Kilmarnock 2.5.1893 d. Sittingbourne 15.1.1960				
Riccarton				
Kilbirnie Ladeside	10/11			
	11/12			
Kilmarnock	12/13	24	6	
	13/14	15	1	
	14/15	7		
	15/16	26	4	
	16/17			
	17/18	1		
	18/19	14	4	
Chelsea	19/20	28		FL
	20/21	7		FL
Stoke	20/21	2		FL
	21/22	12		FL
Sittingbourne	22/23			
Sheppey U				
DICKSON				
Cowlairs	90/91	4		
DICKSON				
St Mirren	07/08	1		
DICKSON				
Heart of Midlothian	18/19	2	?	
DICKSON				
Falkirk	20/21	1		
DICKSON Donald				
Hibernian	10/11	20	4	
DICKSON Herbert				
Queen's Park	30/31	4		
	31/32	23		
	32/33			
	33/34	23		
	34/35	34		
	35/36	35		
	36/37	35		
	37/38	27		
	38/39	34	2	
DICKSON Hugh M				
Queen's Park	21/22	19	3	
	22/23	38	3	D2
	23/24	30		
	24/25	1		
DICKSON J Allan				
b. Nitshill				
Levern V				
Third Lanark	08/09	12	1	
	09/10	1		
Nottingham F	10/11			FL
Ayr U	11/12			D2
DICKSON James				
Dundee	94/95	5	1	

DICKSON James

Forfar A					
Dundee		02/03	3	4	
		03/04	20	14	
Dunfermline A					

DICKSON James

Heart of Midlothian		04/05	10		

DICKSON James

Heart of Midlothian		04/05	1		
		05/06	26		
		06/07	25		
		07/08	16	1	
		08/09	15	1	
Dykehead		09/10			

DICKSON James

Wellwood Star					
Clyde		15/16	7		
Albion R		16/17			

DICKSON James

Raith R		19/20	7		
		20/21	23		

DICKSON James

Queen's Park		18/19	9		
		19/20	9		
		20/21	27	1	
Hamilton A		21/22	14	5	
		22/23	3		
		23/24			
		24/25	2		
Royal Albert		24/25			D3
Shawsheen Indians		25/26	19	1	ASL
Providence Clamdiggers		25/26	10	1	ASL
J & P Coats		26/27	2		ASL

DICKSON James
b. Ireland

Dunfermline A		26/27	23	2	
		27/28	31	11	

DICKSON James

Leith A		30/31	1		

DICKSON John
b. Larkhall

Burnbank A					
Motherwell		03/04	23		
		04/05	12		
Hamilton A		05/06			

DICKSON Thomas Whitford

Dunfermline A		27/28	28	3	
France					
Fordsons		29/30			LI
		30/31			LI
Portadown		31/32			IL
Cork		31/32			LI
Partick T		32/33	10	2	
Cowdenbeath		33/34	4		
West Ham U	T	34/35			FL

DICKSON William

Downfield A					
Dundee		10/11	4		
Downfield A					
Aberdeen		11/12	1		

DICKSON William P

Rutherglen Glencairn					
Airdrieonians		20/21	27	2	
		21/22	1		

DILLETT J A (possibly Alexander WHITLET?)

Port Glasgow A		04/05	1		

DIMMER Hyam
b. Scotstown c1916

Strathclyde					
Kilsyth R					
Rangers	T	35/36			
Ayr U		35/36	15	1	
		36/37	34	25	D2
		37/38	28	9	
		38/39	13	2	

DINNIE Charles
b. Arbroath 1887

Dundee		09/10	6	2	
		10/11			
Huddersfield T		11/12	16		FL
		12/13	1		FL

DINNING James T

Queen's Park		21/22	1		
		22/23	6	1	D2

DINSMORE Harry R

Queen's Park		01/02	13	1	
		02/03	7	3	
Third Lanark		02/03	1		
Rangers		03/04	1		

DIVERS

Clydebank		18/19	4	?	

DIVERS John 1 cap
b. Glasgow 19.9.1873 d. 1910

Vale of Clyde					
Benburb					
Hibernian					
Celtic		93/94	7	3	
		94/95	10	5	
		95/96	5	1	
		96/97	7	4	
Everton		97/98	26	11	FL
		98/99	4		FL
Celtic		98/99	9	5	
		99/00	8	5	
		00/01	16	5	
Hibernian		01/02	9	6	
		02/03	2		
		03/04	14	2	

DIVERS John 1 cap
b. Clydebank 6.8.1911 d. Glasgow 8.6.1984

Clydebank BG					
Linwood St Convals					
Rothesay Royal Victoria					
Renfrew Jnrs					
Celtic		32/33			
		33/34	8	2	
		34/35			
		35/36	2		
		36/37	5	4	
		37/38	20	19	
		38/39	35	17	
Oldham A	T				
Morton		46/47	24	4	
Oldham A		47/48	1		FL
Morton		47/48	15	7	
		48/49	7	1	
		49/50			
Portadown		50/51			IL

DIVET

Hibernian		06/07	1		

DIXON Arthur
b. Chadderton 1892 d. Shaw 25.12.1965

Washbrook Primitives					
Woodhouse					
Tonge					
Oldham A		13/14	20		FL
		14/15	9		FL
St Mirren	L	15/16	11		
	L	16/17	37	2	
Rangers		17/18	32		
		18/19	34	2	
St Mirren	L	18/19	1	?	
Rangers		19/20	30		
		20/21	41	2	
		21/22	42		
		22/23	34	2	
		23/24	37		
		24/25	36		
		25/26	37		
		26/27	3		
Cowdenbeath		27/28	29		
		28/29	37	3	

DIXON David

Queen's Park		08/09	15	7	
Hibernian		08/09			

DIXON Donald M

Hibernian		08/09	6	2	
		09/10	28	2	
		10/11			
		11/12	3		
Motherwell		11/12	6		
		12/13	4		
		13/14	5		
Wishaw Thistle					

DOBBIE

St Bernards		93/94	1		

DOBBS Arthur
b. c1913

Yoker A					
St Rochs					
Derby Co		33/34	3	1	FL
		34/35			FL
Larne		35/36			IL
Third Lanark		35/36	1		
Stranraer		35/36			
Workington					

DOBIE Robert
b. 1875

St Bernards		96/97	2		
Bury		97/98	10		FL
Reading		98/99	3	1	SL

DOBIE Robert

Morton		04/05	9		
Kilbirnie Ladeside					

DOBIE Robert T

Leith A		94/95	4	1	
		95/96	14	?	D2

DOBSON James

Tranent Jnrs					
Hibernian		29/30	21	12	
		30/31	8	3	
		31/32			D2

DOBSON James

Leith A	T				
Dunfermline A		32/33			D2
		33/34			D2
		34/35	30	10	
		35/36	33	11	
		36/37	12	2	

DOCHERTY James

Cambuslang Hibs					
Partick T		06/07	2		
Dundee Hibs					

DOCHERTY James
b. Rutherglen c1907

Cambuslang R					
Rangers		27/28			
		28/29			
Ayr U		29/30	7		
		30/31			
Clyde		31/32	7		

DOCHERTY John

Glasgow W					
Vale of Leven					
Dumbarton		95/96	15		
Celtic		95/96			
		96/97			
		97/98	1		
Dumbarton	L	97/98	13		D2
Celtic		98/99	3		
		99/00	7		
Vale of Leven					
Renton					

DOCHERTY John

St Mirren		04/05	1		

DOCHERTY John

Bellshill A					
Hibernian		07/08	12	1	
		08/09	6	1	

DOCHERTY Patrick
b. c1913

St Rochs					
Croy Celtic					
Falkirk		34/35	3		
		35/36			
Leith A		36/37			D2

DOCHERTY William
b. Maybole

Irvine Meadow					
Partick T		32/33	4		
Larne		33/34			IL

DOCKERY George

Third Lanark		92/93	7		
Derby Co		93/94	4		FL

DODDS A

Third Lanark		93/94	1		

DODDS James G

Peebles R					
Heart of Midlothian		32/33	7	4	
Dunfermline A	T	33/34			D2
Third Lanark	T	33/34			
Larne		34/35			IL
		35/36			IL
Peebles R		36/37			
Penicuik A		37/38			

DODDS John

Queen's Park		03/04	1		

DODDS John McD
b. Glasgow

Queen's Park		28/29	4		
		29/30	22	3	
		30/31	8	2	
		31/32	18	12	
		32/33	24	27	
		33/34	26	20	
		34/35	31	27	
		35/36	27	17	
		36/37	31	12	

DODDS Joseph

Heart of Midlothian		98/99	1		
Airdrieonians					

DODDS Joseph 3 caps
b. Carluke 14.7.1887 d. 14.10.1965

Braidwood U					
Carluke Milton R					
Celtic		08/09	16	1	
Kilmarnock	L	08/09			
Celtic		09/10	12		
		10/11	25		
		11/12	33	2	
		12/13	34	1	
		13/14	36	2	
		14/15	36	3	
		15/16	38	6	
		16/17	38	6	
		17/18	27	1	
Ayr U	L	17/18	1	?	
Queen of the South	L	17/18			
Celtic		18/19	12	2	
		19/20	14		
Cowdenbeath		20/21			
Celtic		21/22	30	4	
Queen of the South		22/23			
		23/24			D3
		24/25			D3

DODDS Robert J

Queen's Park		33/34	1		

DODDS William

Duntocher Hibs					
St Mirren		21/22			
		22/23	2		

DOHERTY

Vale of Leven		90/91	8		

DOHERTY John
b. 1917

St Eugenes (Derry)					
Derry C		34/35			IL
		35/36			IL
		36/37			IL
Celtic		37/38			
		38/39	2		
Derry C		39/40			IL
Coleraine		39/40			IL
Portadown		40/41			IL
?		41/42			
Derry C		42/43			IL
Coleraine		43/44			IL

DOLAN Francis
b. Old Monkland 24.4.1870 d. Old Monkland 12.2.1933

Celtic		90/91	2		
		91/92			
		92/93			
		93/94			
Coatdyke Gaelic					

DOLAN Michael
b. Uddingston 30.9.1868 d. Uddingston 27.7.1910

Drumpellier					
Celtic		88/89			
		89/90			
Uddingston					
Celtic		90/91	3		
		91/92			
		92/93			
		93/94			
Coatdyke Gaelic					

DOLLAR Andrew

Grange R					
Port Glasgow A		09/10	11		

DONAGHER Michael
b. Kilmarnock

Cronberry					
Barnsley		04/05	31		FL
		05/06	34	1	FL
Raith R		06/07			D2
		07/08			D2
		08/09			D2
		09/10			D2
		10/11	7		
Lochgelly U		11/12			

DONAGHY Bernard
b. Londonderry 23.12.1882 K.I.A., Somme 1.7.1916

Derry Celtic		00/01			IL
Ulster		00/01			
Derry Celtic		01/02			IL
Belfast Celtic		02/03			IL
		03/04			IL
Glentoran		03/04			IL
Hibernian		04/05	15	7	
Derry Celtic		05/06			IL
Manchester U		05/06	3		FL
Derry Celtic		06/07			IL
Burnley		07/08	5	2	FL
Derry Celtic		08/09			IL
		09/10			IL
		10/11			IL
		11/12			IL
		12/13			IL

DONAGHY Charles
b. Meerut, India 1883 d. London 1949

Rangers		03/04	5	2	
		04/05	1		
Chelsea		05/06	1	1	FL
		06/07	1		FL
Royal Albert		07/08			
Rochdale		08/09	12	4	LC
USA					

DONALD Adam

Airdrieonians		15/16	13		

DONALD Alexander
b. Kirkintilloch 29.5.1900

Kirkintilloch Harp					
Partick T		22/23	4		
		23/24	11	3	
		24/25	22		
		25/26	30		
Indiana Flooring		26/27	39	3	ASL
Heart of Midlothian		27/28			
New York Nationals		27/28	21		ASL
		28/29	48		ASL
		29A	21	1	ASL
		29/30	29	1	ASL
Chelsea		30/31	12	1	FL
		31/32	12		FL
Bristol R		32/33	39		FL
		33/34	38		FL
		34/35	38		FL
		35/36	21		FL
Dunfermline A					

DONALD David Morgan
b. Coatbridge 21.7.1885 d. Derby 19.1.1932

Albion R		05/06			D2
		06/07			D2
		07/08			D2
Bradford PA		08/09	14	2	FL
		09/10	13		FL
Derby Co		09/10	11		FL
		10/11	27	1	FL
		11/12	7	1	FL
Chesterfield T		12/13			
Watford		13/14	22	3	SL
QPR		14/15	35	4	SL
		19/20	40	5	SL
		20/21	22		FL
Ilkeston U		21/22			
Hamilton A		22/23	13	3	

DONALD Richard
b. Aberdeen 20.2.1911 d. Aberdeen 31.12.1993

Aberdeen		30/31	5		
		31/32	6	6	
		32/33	1		
		33/34	1		
		34/35	3		
Dunfermline A		35/36	15	1	
		36/37	6		
Aberdeen		37/38			
		38/39	2		

DONALDSON Alexander

Alva Albion R					
Falkirk		07/08	2		

DONALDSON Andrew
b. Airdrie (or Motherwell?) 5.6.1884

Ashfield					
Motherwell		06/07	32	4	
		07/08	31	11	
Airdrieonians		08/09	30	6	
		09/10	28	7	
		10/11	34	9	
Celtic		10/11			
		11/12	17	6	
Airdrieonians		11/12	8	4	
		12/13	34	13	
		13/14	36	17	
		14/15	37	14	
		15/16	35	5	
		16/17	32	4	
		17/18	33	4	
Third Lanark		18/19	33		
		19/20	11	2	
Airdrieonians		19/20	15	5	
St Johnstone		20/21			
		21/22			D2
Dykehead					

DONALDSON John

Wallyford					
Leith A		10/11	21		D2
		11/12			D2
Falkirk		11/12	6		
		12/13	33		
		13/14	29		
		14/15	1		
		15/16	28		
		16/17	20		

DONALDSON John

Forfar Celtic					
Clyde		34/35	9	4	

DONALDSON John

Heart of Midlothian		38/39	2		

DONALDSON John W

Queen's Park		19/20	25		
		20/21	8	2	
Tottenham H		21/22			FL

DONLEVY Patrick

Kilsyth Emmet					
Duntochter Hibernian					
Glasgow Perthshire					
Celtic		98/99	1		
Airdrieonians		98/99	1		D2
Thornliebank					
Arthurlie					
Thornliebank					

DONNACHIE Alexander
b. c1895

Royal Albert					
Hamilton A		20/21	12	6	
		21/22			
St Bernards		22/23			D2
Clydebank		22/23			D2
Carlisle U		23/24			

DONNACHIE Joseph 3 caps
b. Kilwinning 1885
Rutherglen Glencairn
Albion R 03/04 D2
04/05 D2
Morton 04/05 2
Newcastle U 05/06 2 FL
Everton 05/06 8 FL
06/07 13 FL
07/08 16 FL
08/09 4 FL
Oldham A 08/09 31 3 FL
09/10 18 3 FL
10/11 38 2 FL
11/12 34 2 FL
12/13 32 2 FL
13/14 36 3 FL
14/15 28 3 FL
Rangers 18/19 5
Everton 19/20 16 FL
Blackpool 20/21 19 1 FL
Chester 21/22 37 4 CCL
22/23 28 4 CCL

DONNELLY John A
Queen's Park 30/31 6 2
31/32 2

DONNELLY John F
b. c1912
Armadale
Leith A 32/33 D2
Albion R 33/34 D2
34/35 25
Hibernian 35/36
Dundee U 36/37 D2
37/38 D2
Bo'ness 38/39

DONNELLY Robert
Kilwinning R
Kilmarnock 19/20 3 1

DONNELLY Robert
b. Craigneuk 1908
Wishaw Jnrs
Partick T 31/32 17
32/33 11
33/34 14
34/35 32
Manchester C 35/36 30 FL
36/37 7 1 FL
Morton 37/38 7
Stranraer

DONNELLY Samuel
b. Ayr
Irvine Meadow
Partick T 32/33 7
Rochdale T 33/34 FL

DONNELLY William
b. Magherafelt 1872 d. Provan 1.8.1948
St Mungo Jnrs
Vale of Clyde
Hibernian 93/94 9
94/95 12
Clyde 95/96 17
Liverpool 96/97 6 FL
97/98
Clyde 98/99 18
99/00 2
Celtic 00/01 3
Belfast Celtic 00/01 IL
01/02 IL
02/03 IL

DONOGHUE John
b. New York 22.1.1903 d. Glasgow 11.7.1971
St Francis Jnrs
Shawfield Jnrs
Celtic 26/27 17 1
Third Lanark L 26/27 D2
Cowdenbeath L 27/28
Celtic 27/28 7
28/29 14
29/30 4
Belfast Celtic L 29/30 IL
Wrexham 30/31 31 1 FL
31/32 36 1 FL
Celtic 32/33
Excelsior de Roubaix 32/33

DONOGHUE Patrick
Musselburgh Bruntonians
Hibernian 34/35
Tranent Jnrs 35/36
36/37
Heart of Midlothian 37/38 8 4
Leith A 38/39 D2

DOOLAN Alexander
b. Tarbolton 7.8.1889 d. Goodmayes 19.4.1937
Annbank
Kilmarnock 07/08 2
Beith L 08/09
Kilmarnock 09/10 3
10/11 1
11/12
12/13
Beith L 12/13
Bradford C 12/13 2 FL
13/14 FL
14/15 FL
19/20 20 FL
Preston NE 20/21 31 FL
21/22 30 FL
22/23 16 FL
Mold

DOOLAN James
Pollok
St Mirren 17/18 14
Ayr U L 17/18 1

DOOLAN Patrick
b. Shotts 1906 d. Bridgeton ?.7.1926
Cleland Jnrs
Aberdeen 25/26 3 1

DOONIN William
Mossend Hibs
Cleland
Third Lanark 10/11 2
11/12 8
Dykehead 12/13
Pontypridd

DORAN Isaac
Celtic
Clyde L 99/00 1
Celtic 99/00
Abercorn

DORANS James
Neilston V *
St Mirren *
Abercorn * 05/06 D2
06/07 D2
Partick T 07/08 1
08/09 2

DORANS William McEwan
b. Kinning Park 1902
Partick T 19/20 1

DORBIE
Kilmarnock 16/17 1

DORN John
Falkirk 29/30 1 1

DORNAN William
b. Pumpherston
Pumpherston Violet
Broxburn St Andrews
Leith A
Hibernian L 13/14 1
L 14/15 5
Leith A 15/16
Hibernian 15/16 18
16/17 34
17/18 31 ?
18/19 25 ?
19/20 19
20/21 21
21/22 40
22/23 36
23/24 31
24/25 31
25/26 35
26/27 27
27/28 3
Queen of the South 28/29 D2
29/30 D2
30/31 D2

DORRAN Owen
b. Kilwinning 12.12.1897 d. Scotland 25.4.1972
Saltcoats V
Cowdenbeath 23/24 D2
24/25 3 1
Raith R 25/26 21 4
26/27 D2
27/28 20 4
28/29 22 4
Morton 29/30 31 4
Connahs Quay 30/31
Wigan B 30/31 17 4 FL
Falkirk
Stevenston U
New Brighton 31/32 3 FL
East Stirlingshire 32/33 1
Shelbourne 33/34 LI

DORWARD David
b. Dundee
Dundee NE
Dundee U 28/29 24 D2
29/30 21 1
Charlton A 30/31 FL
31/32 FL
Bray Unknowns 32/33

DORWARD Thomas
Dundee Harp
Dundee 07/08
08/09
09/10 1
Arbroath

DORWARD William
St Mirren Jnrs
St Mirren 17/18 23 4
Ayr U L 18/19 4
Third Lanark 18/19 2 ?
Renton 19/20
20/21
USA

DOUGAL George
Hibernian 96/97 17 5
97/98 16 1
Manchester C 97/98 8 2 FL
98/99 31 7 FL
99/00 23 2 FL
00/01 13 1 FL
Glossop 01/02 10 FL

DOUGAL James 1 cap
b. Denny 3.10.1913 d. Walton on Thames 17.10.1999
Kilsyth R
Falkirk 32/33 27 13
33/34 11 2
Preston NE 33/34 11 2 FL
34/35 21 3 FL
35/36 32 9 FL
36/37 30 3 FL
37/38 32 14 FL
38/39 40 19 FL
46/47 5 1 FL
Carlisle U 46/47 21 3 FL
47/48 39 10 FL
48/49 10 2 FL
Halifax T 48/49 22 2 FL
Chorley

DOUGAL Peter
b. Denny 21.3.1909 d. Denny 12.6.1974
Dunipace Thistle
Falkirk
Burnley 26/27 FL
27/28 6 2 FL
Clyde 28/29 11 2
29/30 1
Southampton 29/30 12 1 FL
30/31 14 4 FL
31/32 3 FL
Stade Francais 32/33
Chesterfield T 33/34 FL
Arsenal 33/34 5 FL
34/35 8 1 FL
35/36 8 3 FL
Everton 37/38 11 2 FL
Bury 38/39 16 2 FL

DOUGALL Neil
Morton 30/31 1

DOUGALL Robert

b. Falkirk 1908
Forth R
Bo'ness L 28/29 D2
Hamilton A 29/30 17 1
30/31 36
31/32 29 1
32/33 37 3
33/34 7
Blackpool 33/34 34 1 FL
34/35 21 1 FL
35/36 19 FL
Reading 37/38 38 1 FL
38/39 36 6 FL
39/40 3 FL

DOUGALL William

b. Denny 25.10.1895 d. Burnley 15.11.1966
Denny Hibs
Falkirk 20/21 23
21/22 38 1
22/23 37
23/24 32
24/25 37 2
25/26 28 15
Burnley 25/26 11 FL
26/27 37 FL
27/28 12 1 FL
Clyde 28/29

DOUGAN Hugh

Clyde 99/00 18 1

DOUGAN Patrick

Heart of Midlothian 09/10 2

DOUGLAS

St Mirren 90/91 10 4
91/92 19 5
92/93 16
93/94 12

DOUGLAS Alex

Queen's Park 13/14 1
14/15 9 1
15/16 6 1

DOUGLAS Alick W

Coupar Angus
Kilmarnock 08/09 25 12
09/10 4 1
Lanemark 10/11
Lochgelly U 10/11
Aberdeen 11/12 3

DOUGLAS Arthur

Larkhall Thistle
Clyde 34/35 32 2
35/36 10 2
Hamilton A L 35/36 4 1
Clyde 36/37 5 1
Albion R 37/38 D2
Glentoran 38/39 IL
39/40 IL
40/41 IL
41/42 IL
42/43 IL
43/44 IL
Derry C 44/45 IL
Dundela 44/45
Dundalk 45/46 LI
46/47 LI
Ards 46/47 IL
47/48 IL
48/49 IL
Ballymoney U 49/50

DOUGLAS James

Falkirk 27/28 3
28/29 5
Alloa A 29/30 D2

DOUGLAS James

b. Torpichen
Standburn R
Partick T 37/38 14 3
38/39 26 3
Stenhousemuir

DOUGLAS James H

Third Lanark 01/02 3 1

DOUGLAS Peter

Hibernian 99/00 7 1

DOUGLAS Peter

Lochgelly U
Dunfermline A
Heart of Midlothian 06/07 5 1

DOUGLAS Thomas Alexander

b. Whitletts 11.9.1910 K.I.A., Middle East ?.3.1943
Kilwinning A
Motherwell 27/28 1 1
28/29 2 1
29/30
30/31 4 2
Blackpool 31/32 25 10 FL
32/33 33 5 FL
33/34 2 FL
Burnley 33/34 36 7 FL
34/35 19 6 FL
35/36 8 FL
Witton A 36/37
37/38
Rochdale 38/39 8 FL

DOUGLAS W R V

Queen's Park 08/09 5

DOUGLAS William

b. Dundee
Dundee Our Boys
Ardwick 91/92 22 FA
92/93 20 FL
93/94 16 FL
Newton Heath 93/94 7 FL
94/95 30 FL
95/96 18 FL
Derby Co
Blackpool 96/97 30 FL
97/98 30 FL
Warmley 98/99 14 SL
Dundee 99/00 2

DOUGLAS William R

Leith Amateurs
Hibernian 34/35 2 1

DOW David

Dundee 93/94 2

DOWALL William

b. Thornliebank
Thornliebank Spiersbridge Church
Kilbirnie Ladeside
Motherwell 29/30 21 24
30/31 25 14
31/32 32 4
32/33 25
33/34 9 1
34/35 6
St Mirren L 34/35 15 1
Bury 35/36 10 2 FL
Lincoln C 36/37 5 FL
Red Star Paris 37/38
Ballymena U 38/39 IL
Notts Co 38/39 6 FL

DOWDS John

Rutherglen Glencairn
Strathclyde
Third Lanark 16/17 2
Albion R 17/18
Clyde L 17/18
Albion R 18/19
19/20
Renton 19/20

DOWDS Peter 1 cap

b. Johnstone 12.12.1867 d. Johnstone 3.9.1895
Broxburn Shamrock
Celtic 89/90
90/91 18 15
91/92 18 1
Aston Villa 92/93 20 3 FL
Stoke 93/94 17 FL
Celtic 94/95 3

DOWELL Leonard

Portobello Thistle
Partick T 24/25 1
25/26
26/27
Gillingham

DOWIE Samuel

Hibernian 10/11 1

DOWLING Michael

b. Jarrow 30.3.1890 d. Rotherham 1969
Jarrow Croft
St Mirren 09/10 16
Sheffield W 10/11 7 FL
Portsmouth 11/12 22 4 SL
12/13 20 4 SL
Jarrow 13/14
Lincoln C 14/15 14 1 FL
19/20 14 3 FL
Ebbw Vale

DOWNIE Alexander

Queen's Park Strollers
Third Lanark 01/02 1

DOWNIE Alexander Leck Brown

b. St Rollox 1876 d. Withington 9.12.1953
Glasgow Perthshire
Third Lanark 98/99 4
Bristol C 99/00 21 2 SL
Swindon T 00/01 26 1 SL
01/02 29 1 SL
Manchester U 02/03 22 5 FL
03/04 29 4 FL
04/05 32 1 FL
05/06 34 FL
06/07 19 2 FL
07/08 10 FL
08/09 23 FL
09/10 3 FL
Oldham A 09/10 29 FL
10/11 15 FL
Crewe A 11/12 12 CL

DOWNIE Edwin

Heart of Midlothian 97/98 1
Tottenham H 97/98 7 SL
98/99 4 SL
Chesterfield T 99/00 21 FL
Stockport Co 00/01 6 FL

DOWNIE James

Kilbarchan A
Dundee 19/20 3 3

DOWNIE R

b. USA
Fifeshire (USA)
Third Lanark 13/14 1

DOWNIE Robert 1 cap

b. Anderston 19.3.1867 d. Old Kilpatrick 27.7.1893
Thornliebank
Third Lanark 90/91 17
91/92 22
92/93 9

DOWNIE William

Bellshill A
Motherwell 09/10 7
10/11 7

DOYLE Daniel 8 caps

b. Paisley 16.9.1864 d. Glasgow 8.4.1918
Rawyard Jnrs
Darngavil
Slamannan Barnsmuir
Broxburn Shamrock
Hibernian
Broxburn Shamrock
East Stirlingshire
Sunderland
Hibernian
Heart of Midlothian L
Newcastle EE
Grimsby T
Bolton W
Everton 89/90 22 FL
90/91 20 FL
Celtic 91/92 21
92/93 15
93/94 13 1
94/95 15
Dykehead 94/95
Celtic 95/96 12 1
96/97 16 1
97/98 16
98/99 5

DOYLE Francis
b. Hutchesontown 20.11.1901 d. Glasgow 19.5.1965
Benburb
Rutherglen Glencairn
Vale of Clyde 20/21
Airdrieonians 20/21 5 2
21/22 13 4
22/23 20 7
23/24 2
Fulham 23/24 25 9 FL
24/25 5 FL
Celtic 26/27 8 2
27/28 9
28/29
Ayr U 29/30

DOYLE Thomas
b. Motherwell 15.1.1916
New Stevenston A
Blantyre Celtic 35/36
Celtic 35/36
Arbroath L 36/37 8
Celtic 36/37 3
37/38 2
Rochdale 38/39 29 FL
Stockport Co

DRAIN Thomas
b. Pollokshaws 1880
Drongan
Ayr 01/02 ? ? D2
02/03 ? ? D2
Maybole
Bradford C 03/04 22 9 FL
04/05 10 3 FL
Leeds C 05/06 9 3 FL
Kilmarnock 05/06 2
06/07 15 3
Aberdeen 07/08 7
Vale of Leven 08/09
Carlisle U
Exeter C 08/09 14 1 SL
Woolwich Arsenal 09/10 2 FL
Nithsdale W
Galston

DRAPER Colin
Third Lanark 95/96 14

DRUMMOND Daniel G
Bellahouston Academy
Queen's Park 10/11 10 1
11/12 32 4
12/13 27 1
Motherwell 13/14 10 1

DRUMMOND George
Partick T 98/99 2
Falkirk
Albion R 02/03

DRUMMOND James
b. Bellshill 24.4.1881
Bellshill A
Celtic 01/02 4 1
Manchester C 01/02 13 2 FL
02/03 14 3 FL
03/04 1 FL
Partick T 03/04
04/05 3

DRUMMOND James
Larkhall Thistle
Hamilton A 35/36
36/37 5
37/38
East Stirlingshire 38/39 D2

DRUMMOND John 14 caps
b. Alva 13.4.1870 d. Falkirk 24.1.1935
Falkirk 86/87
87/88
88/89
89/90
90/91
91/92
Rangers 91/92 4
92/93 17 1
93/94 17
94/95 16
95/96 16
96/97 16
97/98 16
98/99 5
99/00 15
00/01 18
01/02 12
02/03 19
03/04 14 1
Falkirk 04/05 D2

DRUMMOND R
Rangers 93/94 1

DRUMMOND Robert
Heart of Midlothian 17/18 11 3

DRYDEN Joseph B
Aberdeen 30/31 1

DRYSDALE John
b. Dunfermline 2.12.1913
Tranent Jnrs
Queen's Park 33/34
Rangers 34/35
35/36 9 5
36/37 7
37/38 2
Kilmarnock 38/39 36 3
Dumbarton
Raith R
Kilmarnock
St Cuthberts W
Newton Stewart
St Cuthberts W

DUCEY Joseph
Hamilton A 33/34 4 2
Arthurlie

DUCKWORTH Evelyn P
Queen's Park 12/13 12 4
13/14 1
Morton

DUDGEON John F
b. c1912
Tynecastle R
Hibernian 30/31 7
Portsmouth 31/32
32/33
Bo'ness T 33/34
Cowdenbeath 33/34 13
Bo'ness 34/35
Chirnside U

DUDLEY George
b. Gartcosh 26.2.1916 d. Halesowen 23.12.1979
Twechar U
Albion R 34/35 3
35/36 19 5
36/37 16 3
Kings Park
Vono Sports
WBA 38/39 6 2 FL
Banbury Spencer
Cradley T
Netherton
Cradley Heath
Accles & Pollock

DUFF Alexander
Cowlairs
Abercorn 90/91 1
91/92 20
Northern 92/93
Cowlairs 93/94 D2
94/95 D2
Old Castle Swifts 94/95
95/96
96/97
Thames Ironworks 96/97
97/98

DUFF Alexander
Kilsyth R
St Mirren 20/21 20 1
21/22 18
22/23 9
Johnstone 23/24 D2
Armadale
Bo'ness 26/27 D2
27/28 25

DUFF David
b. Belfast 1900
Belfast Celtic
Glentoran 14/15 IL
15/16 IL
16/17 IL
17/18 IL
Linfield 18/19 IL
Airdrieonians 18/19 1
19/20 11 3
Wallsend 20/21
Belfast U 20/21
21/22
Queens Island 21/22 IL
Dundela 22/23
Glentoran 23/24 IL
Fall River Marksmen 24/25 1 ASL
Brooklyn Wanderers 24/25 3 ASL
Queens Island 25/26 IL
Glentoran 26/27 IL

DUFF Henry A
b. Stevenston 1886 d. WW1
Crosshill Winton
Kilmaurs Jnrs
Arthurlie
Nithsdale W
St Mirren 06/07
Clyde 07/08 6
Manchester C 07/08 FL
QPR 08/09 20 SL
Motherwell 09/10 16
Airdrieonians 10/11 26 1
St Mirren 11/12 28 3
Kilmarnock 12/13 26 5
13/14 6 1

DUFF James
Renton Thistle
Celtic 30/31
Renton Thistle 31/32
East Stirlingshire 32/33 5

DUFF John
b. Perth
St Johnstone YMCA
Arbroath 30/31 10 2 D2
31/32 30 D2
32/33 34 2 D2
33/34 32 D2
34/35 34 7 D2
35/36 36 1
36/37 31 1
37/38 7 1

DUFF Robert
Falkirk 15/16 1

DUFF Thomas
b. Ayr 18.5.1867
Cartvale
Morton
Cowlairs 90/91 18
Celtic 91/92 8
Cowlairs 92/93
93/94 D2
94/95 D2
Northern

DUFF Thomas
Banks o'Dee
Aberdeen 16/17 3

DUFFUS John Murison
b. Aberdeen 10.5.1901 d. Stockport 18.9.1975
Aberdeen Richmond
Dundee
Dumbarton 19/20 5 2
Bo'ness L 19/20
Scunthorpe U
Llanelly 21/22
Caerau
Clapton Orient 22/23 6 FL
Tottenham H
Norwich C 24/25 19 FL
25/26 31 2 FL
26/27 27 2 FL
Stockport Co 27/28 6 3 FL
Hyde U 28/29
Hurst
Congleton T

DUFFUS Robert Morrice Duncan
b. Aberdeen 28.2.1891 d. Aberdeen 19.3.1949
Aberdeen East End
Aberdeen Richmond
Aberdeen 12/13
13/14
14/15
Dundee 15/16 25 2
16/17 26
17/18
18/19
Dumbarton 19/20 34
20/21
Millwall 21/22 5 FL
Scunthorpe U 21/22
Clapton Orient 22/23 5 FL
Accrington S 23/24 29 FL
Bangor C

DUFFY Charles

East Stirlingshire
Liverpool
Raith R 16/17 4

DUFFY James

Lochgelly Celtic
Hamilton A 28/29 5
Kings Park

DUFFY Richard
b. Dumbarton 24.9.1914
Yoker A
Millwall 33/34 5 FL
34/35 FL
Alloa A 35/36 D2
36/37 D2
Falkirk 36/37 10 1
37/38 16
38/39 12

DUFFY Robert McFarlane Davidson
b. Dundee 19.4.1913
Dundee St Josephs
Lochee Harp
Celtic 35/36
36/37 1
37/38 1
38/39 2
46/47

DUFFY William

Kings Park
Airdrieonians 33/34 5 1
Alloa A 33/34 D2

DUGGINS Alfred Edward
b. Aston 2.11.1897 d. Lichfield 14.5.1969
Kingsbury Colliery
Redditch T
Aberdeen 22/23 2
Heart of Midlothian 23/24
Preston NE 23/24 2 FL
Walsall 24/25 12 FL
New Brighton 25/26 13 3 FL
Redditch T 26/27
Gresley R
Harlaston U

DUGUID John M

Queen's Park 25/26 1 1
26/27 7 6
27/28 1

DUGUID William
b. Wishaw
Heart of Midlothian 05/06 1
Albion R 05/06 D2
Hibernian 06/07 29 2
07/08 32 2
08/09 31
09/10 28
Wishaw Thistle 10/11
Middlesbrough 10/11 10 FL
11/12 6 FL
12/13 8 FL

DUNBAR

St Mirren 90/91 3 1

DUNBAR Henry

Glasgow St Anthonys
Raith R
Dumbarton Harp 15/16
Raith R 16/17 2

DUNBAR Michael
b. Cathcart 30.10.1863 d. Glasgow 6.9.1921
Busby Linwood
Busby Cartvale
Netherlee L
Cowlairs
Hibernian
Celtic 88/89
89/90
90/91 11 3
91/92
92/93 2

DUNBAR Thomas
b. Busby 18.8.1868 d. 28.4.1908
Rutherglen
Hibernian
Busby Cartvale
Celtic 90/91 4
St Mirren L 90/91
Rangers 91/92 11
Celtic 92/93 16
93/94 8
94/95 13 1
95/96 6 2
96/97 4
Busby Cartvale

DUNCAN Adam Scott Mathewson
b. Dumbarton 2.11.1888 d. Helensburgh 3.10.1976
Dumbarton Oakvale
Dumbarton Corinthians
Clydebank Jnrs
Shettleston
Dumbarton 06/07 D2
Newcastle U 07/08 4 FL
08/09 14 2 FL
09/10 13 2 FL
10/11 22 5 FL
11/12 12 1 FL
12/13 7 FL
Rangers 13/14 21 5
14/15 19 2
15/16 32 10
16/17 28 9
17/18
18/19
Celtic L 18/19 2
Partick T L 18/19
Dumbarton 18/19 1 ?
19/20 27 2
Cowdenbeath 20/21
21/22
Dumbarton 22/23 D2

DUNCAN Alexander

East Fife 27/28 20 D2
28/29 31 1 D2
29/30 36 D2
30/31 17
31/32 8 D2
32/33 3 D2
East Stirlingshire 33/34 D2

DUNCAN Andrew
b. Kilmarnock 15.10.1883
Shettleston Jnrs
Kilmarnock 05/06 13
Dumfries
Beith
Bradford PA 09/10 FL
Galston
Dumfries

DUNCAN Andrew P

Rutherglen Glencairn
St Johnstone 34/35 12
35/36 2
36/37 3
37/38 1
East Fife

DUNCAN Charles Stanley
b. Kinross 1889
Kelty R
Dunfermline A 12/13 D2
Birmingham 12/13 6 4 FL
13/14 12 1 FL
14/15 4 1 FL
East Fife 15/16
Rangers 16/17 25 15
Third Lanark 17/18 18 ?
St Mirren 18/19 24 ?
Clyde 19/20 35 8
20/21 33 13
21/22 41 15
22/23 33 3
Dundee 23/24 30 7
24/25 27 9
25/26 11 1
Arbroath 26/27 10 2 D2

DUNCAN David
b. Glasgow ?.4.1892
Glasgow St Anthonys
Bellshill A
Albion R 10/11 19 ? D2
Fulham 11/12 9 FL
Woolwich Arsenal 12/13 3 1 FL
Albion R 13/14 D2
14/15 D2
15/16
16/17
17/18
18/19
19/20 31
20/21 30 2
Bathgate 21/22 D2
Heart of Midlothian 21/22 4
Dundee Hibs 21/22 11 D2
Peebles R 22/23

DUNCAN David

Hibernian 21/22 12 4
22/23 5 2
23/24 11 1

DUNCAN David R

Falkirk 18/19 6 ?
19/20 2

DUNCAN Hector
b. Aberdeen
Aberdeen Hawthorn
Clydebank Jnrs
Queen's Park 16/17 4
17/18 18

DUNCAN James

Dundee East Craigie
Dundee 11/12 1
St Johnstone L 12/13 1 D2
Dumbarton T 12/13

DUNCAN James
b. Paisley
Hurlford U
Auchinleck Talbot
Kilmarnock 30/31 21 2
31/32 29 4
32/33 4 1
Glentoran 33/34 IL
34/35 IL
Coleraine 35/36 IL
Glentoran 35/36 IL
Sligo R 36/37 LI
Glentoran 36/37 IL

DUNCAN John 1 cap
b. Lochgelly 14.2.1896 d. Leicester 14.3.1966
Denbeath Star
Kirkcaldy U
Lochgelly U 15/16
Raith R 16/17
17/18
18/19
19/20 2
20/21 40 9
21/22 39 9
Leicester C 22/23 41 20 FL
23/24 34 13 FL
24/25 40 30 FL
25/26 34 12 FL
26/27 42 5 FL
27/28 21 3 FL
28/29 27 2 FL
29/30 40 3 FL

DUNCAN Peter

Hibernian 10/11 1

DUNCAN Peter

Queensferry A
Heart of Midlothian 16/17 1

DUNCAN Robert
b. Cardross 13.5.1874, or Bonhill 4.10.1874
d. Renton ?.5.1933
Renton 91/92 18 5
92/93 4
93/94 14 1
94/95 17 ? D2
95/96 14 ? D2
96/97 16 ? D2

DUNCAN Robert

Partick T 97/98 17
98/99 16 2
99/00 1 D2

DUNCAN Stanley Smart

Queen's Park 36/37 3
37/38 22 1
38/39 12

DUNCAN Thomas

Lochgelly U
Raith R L 15/16 2

DUNCAN Thomas Grossett
b. Lochgelly 1.9.1901 d. Leicester 9.2.1940
Lochgelly U
Raith R 19/20 40 5
20/21 9
21/22 38 7
Leicester C 22/23 29 5 FL
23/24 12 1 FL
Halifax T 24/25 26 5 FL
25/26 6 FL
Bristol R 26/27 13 2 FL
Kettering T

DUNCAN William
b. Kilsyth 14.3.1880
Condorrat Hearts
Strathclyde
Airdrieonians 03/04 26
04/05 24
05/06 30
06/07 34
07/08 34
08/09 31
09/10 17
Clyde L 09/10
Celtic L 09/10 9
St Mirren 10/11 18
11/12 27
Airdrieonians
Bethlehem Steel 18/19
19/20
20/21
21/22
Fall River Marksmen 22/23 3 ASL

DUNCAN William T

Glenboig St Josephs
Arbroath 29/30 4 1 D2
30/31 30 D2
31/32 10 1 D2
Whifflet Emerald 32/33
Airdrieonians 32/33 16
East Stirlingshire 33/34 D2

DUNCANSON David

Arbroath 38/39 1

DUNCANSON Matthew

Duntocher Hibs
Partick T 02/03 5 1
Abercorn

DUNCANSON William L
b. Kilmarnock 3.12.1876
Kilmarnock Shawbank
Sunderland
Kilmarnock 99/00 1
Lanemark
Galston

DUNDAS James

Dundee East End
Dundee 93/94 17 12
94/95 16 1
95/96 18 4
96/97 9

DUNLOP

Abercorn 90/91 1

DUNLOP Allan

Port Glasgow A 10/11 14 ? D2
Kilmarnock 10/11 2 1
11/12 2
Beith
Morton 12/13 11
13/14 6
Aberdare A
Morton 14/15 5
15/16 1
16/17 1
17/18
18/19
Abercorn 19/20

DUNLOP Andrew

Benburb
St Mirren 07/08
08/09
09/10 1

DUNLOP Archibald

Annbank
Ayr U 20/21 3

DUNLOP Francis
b. Glasgow
Benburb
Aberdeen 36/37 25
37/38 16
38/39 30
46/47 27
47/48 14

DUNLOP G

St Mirren 90/91 1

DUNLOP Harry

Duntocher Hibs
Morton 25/26 11 2
26/27 5 2
Third Lanark 27/28
Coleraine 27/28 IL
28/29 IL
29/30 IL
Belfast Celtic 29/30 IL
Coleraine 30/31 IL

DUNLOP James 1 cap
b. Paisley 17.5.1870 d. Paisley 11.1.1892
Sandyford
Underwood Strollers
St Mirren 90/91 18 8
91/92 15 2

DUNLOP James

St Mirren 02/03 3

DUNLOP James Murdoch

Glasgow Ashfield
Heart of Midlothian 35/36 5 2
St Mirren 36/37 7 1
37/38
Glenavon 37/38 IL

DUNLOP John

Third Lanark 94/95 2 1
95/96 16 10
96/97 17 4

DUNLOP John

Queen's Park 03/04 7 2
04/05
05/06 1

DUNLOP John
b. Irvine 18.12.1900 d. 3.3.1982
Irvine V
Kilmarnock 22/23 21 3
23/24 8 1
24/25 18 3
25/26 26 3
26/27 4
27/28
Arthurlie 28/29 D2
Kilmarnock 28/29 25 3
29/30 23

DUNLOP John J

Levern V *
Rangers
Port Glasgow A 07/08 7
Morton 08/09 2
Beith
Preston NE 12/13 FL

DUNLOP John W

Vale Ocuba
Hamilton A 35/36 1
Albion R 35/36 1

DUNLOP Robert

Clyde 99/00 4 2

DUNLOP William
b. Annbank
Annbank
Sunderland 92/93 5 FL
93/94 26 1 FL
94/95 18 1 FL
95/96 23 1 FL
96/97 26 1 FL
97/98 26 3 FL
98/99 13 2 FL
Rangers 99/00 6
Partick T 00/01 1
Annbank

DUNN Alexander McLachlan
b. c1893 d. Port Bannatyne ?.1.1925
Glasgow Perthshire
Ashfield
Partick T 14/15 1
Abercorn 15/16

DUNN Bertie
b. Montrose 15.8.1893
Blantyre V
Alloa A 21/22 D2
22/23 20 1
23/24 D2
Clapton Orient 24/25 3 FL
25/26 1 FL
Carlisle U

DUNN James

Glasgow Perthshire
Third Lanark 11/12 2
Motherwell 12/13
13/14 2

DUNN James 6 caps
b. Glasgow 25.11.1900 d. Liverpool 20.8.1963
St Anthonys
Hibernian 20/21 31 9
21/22 40 6
22/23 35 6
23/24 31 9
24/25 35 23
25/26 36 17
26/27 34 11
27/28 27 9
Everton 28/29 24 4 FL
29/30 12 FL
30/31 28 14 FL
31/32 22 10 FL
32/33 25 10 FL
33/34 23 4 FL
34/35 6 FL
Exeter C 35/36 22 4 FL
Runcorn

DUNN James

Maryhill
Clyde 38/39 1

DUNN John

Benburb
Raith R 19/20 21 2
20/21 9 3

DUNN William Marshall
b. Lambhill 9.10.1910 d. Glasgow 7.9.1980
Newton Villa
Glasgow Ashfield
Celtic 33/34 5 1
34/35 3 1
Brentford 35/36 2 FL
36/37 1 FL
Southampton 37/38 14 3 FL
Bo'ness L 38/39
Raith R 38/39

DUNSIRE Andrew
b. Buckhaven 11.10.1902 d. Buckhaven 6.10.1980
Abbotshill Jnrs
Kinghorn A
Raith R 19/20 1
Abbotshill Jnrs 20/21
Dunniker
Third Lanark 24/25 3
Anstruther R
Raith R
Broxburn U
Kettering T 26/27
27/28
Crystal Palace 28/29 3 1 FL
29/30 2 FL
Dartford 30/31
31/32
Raith R
Forfar A

DUNSMORE

St Mirren 92/93 3 2

DUNSMORE Thomas

Lanemark
Partick T 10/11 3
11/12 6
12/13 10
13/14 3
Dunfermline A 14/15 D2
15/16
Albion R 16/17

DUNSMORE Thomas Hamilton
b. Motherwell 23.5.1914
Motherwell MW
Bellshill A
Royal Albert
Hibernian 35/36 3
36/37 20
37/38 16
Luton T 38/39 40 FL
Albion R

DUNSMUIR Robert

Motherwell 16/17 9
17/18 5

DUNSMUIR Robert

Blantyre V
Armadale
Heart of Midlothian 20/21
21/22 5

DURNAN James
b. Campbelltown 10.11.1894
Campbelltown A
Plymouth A 14/15 24 SL
Partick T 16/17 23
Vale of Leven 17/18
Dumbarton 17/18 21 2
18/19 21 ?
Swansea T 19/20 34 1 SL
20/21 13
21/22 12
22/23
Llandrindod Wells 23/24
Northampton T T 24/25 FL

DURNIAN Patrick

Hibernian 10/11 5

DUTHIE

Hibernian 18/19 2 ?

DYER James

Glasgow Perthshire
Rangers T 32/33
Glasgow Perthshire 33/34
34/35
Ayr U 35/36 33
36/37 4 D2
37/38 27 1
38/39 37

DYER Kenneth M
b. Govan
Govan High School
St Mirren 27/28 9 1
28/29 22 4
29/30 2
Queen of the South *
Edinburgh C * 34/35

DYER Peter

Denny Jnrs
Dundee 22/23 2

DYET James
b. Dalry 14.6.1908 d. Falkirk 21.7.2005
Smith & Wellstood
Cowie Juveniles
Kings Park 29/30 16 25 D2
Falkirk 30/31 34 24
31/32 2 1
Middlesbrough T 31/32 FL
Dundee U 31/32 15 5
32/33 21 9 D2
Kings Park 33/34 20 16 D2

DYKES James 2 caps
b. Law 12.10.1916
Wishaw High School
Law Thistle
Carluke R T
Parkhead T
Heart of Midlothian 33/34
34/35
35/36 1
36/37 25 1
37/38 38
38/39 35
Dundela
Portadown
Glentoran 42/43 IL
43/44 IL
44/45 IL
Newry T
Ross Co
Dundalk 46/47 LI
Portadown 47/48 IL
48/49 IL
49/50 IL
Banbridge T 50/51

EADIE A William

Queen's Park 02/03 2
03/04
04/05 8
05/06 2
06/07
07/08
Partick T 08/09 5

EADIE James

St Bernards 98/99 1
Dunblane 98/99
99/00
Queen's Park 00/01 7
01/02 15
02/03 1
Dunblane 02/03
Queen's Park 03/04 22
04/05 21
05/06 4

EADIE William

Johnstone
St Mirren 01/02
02/03
03/04
04/05
05/06
06/07 1

EADIE William Philip
b. Greenock
Greenock Overton
Morton 02/03 6
03/04 15 1
04/05 25
05/06 25
Manchester C 06/07 31 FL
07/08 29 3 FL
08/09 10 1 FL
09/10 23 2 FL
10/11 29 FL
11/12 26 FL
12/13 31 FL
13/14 6 FL
Derby Co 14/15 31 FL

EADON

Dumbarton 18/19 1

EADON John

Morton 20/21 1

EADON John Polloc
b. Glasgow 3.9.1889 d. 14.1.1961
Maryhill
Tottenham H 13/14 5 FL
14/15 FL
Ayr U 18/19 14 ?

EAGLESHAM

Abercorn 90/91 2
91/92 1

EAGLESHAM John

Clydebank Jnrs
Queen's Park 23/24 2 1
Helensburgh 24/25 D3
Clydebank 25/26

EARLEY Arthur

Dumbarton 20/21 10 1

EASTON

St Mirren 90/91 1 1
91/92 3 2

EASTON Andrew
b. Armadale 14.3.1877
Leith A
Airdrieonians 99/00 D2
Leith A 00/01 D2
Heart of Midlothian 01/02 3
Millwall 02/03 29 SL
03/04 22 SL
Rangers 04/05 10
Bradford C 05/06 14 FL

EDGAR

Clyde 97/98 1

EDGAR David James
b. Edinburgh 5.2.1902 d. South Shields
Raith R
Burnley
East Fife 21/22 10 D2
22/23 30 2 D2
23/24 30 6 D2
24/25 9 1 D2
Heart of Midlothian 24/25 15 1
Airdrieonians L 24/25 7
Heart of Midlothian 25/26 7 3
East Fife L 26/27 D2
Heart of Midlothian 26/27 5 1
27/28 3 1
28/29 5
USA
Aldershot 32/33 4 FL
Darlington 33/34 36 6 FL
34/35 42 13 FL
35/36 10 1 FL
Cannock T
Hexham
Workington

EDGAR John

b. Scotland

Parkhead					
Woolwich Arsenal		01/02	10	1	FL
		02/03			
Airdrieonians		03/04	12		
Aberdeen		04/05	14	3	
		05/06	23	4	
		06/07	15	2	
		07/08			
		08/09			
Hibernian	T	09/10	4		
Aberdeen		10/11	1		
		11/12	2		

EDGAR John

Port Glasgow A		06/07	30	3	
		07/08	19		

EDMONDS Hugh

b. Chryston 1884

Smithson					
Hamilton A		06/07	30		
Distillery		07/08			IL
		08/09			IL
Linfield		09/10			IL
Bolton W		09/10	2		FL
		10/11	6		FL
Manchester U		10/11	12		FL
		11/12	29		FL
Glenavon		12/13			IL
Distillery		13/14			IL
Jarrow		14/15			
		15/16			
		16/17			
		17/18			
Distillery		18/19			IL
Whitehall		19/20			

EDWARD Jock

Aberdeen		24/25	25	2	
		25/26	17		
		26/27	37	1	
		27/28	8		
Southampton *		28/29			FL
Huntly		29/30			

EDWARDS David Maxwell

b. Partick 1900 d. Cowdenbeath 17.6.1946

Rutherglen Glencairn					
Morton		19/20	42		
		20/21	38		
		21/22	39		
		22/23	37		
		23/24	38		
		24/25	2		
		25/26	5	2	
Bethlehem Steel		26/27	39		ASL
		27/28	31		ASL
		28/29	5		ESL
New Bedford Whalers		28/29	9		ASL
Holley Carburetors					
Morton		30/31	13		
Cowdenbeath		30/31	10		
		31/32	38		
Dundee		32/33	15		
Arbroath		33/34	32		D2

EDWARDS James

Morton		25/26	7	2	
		26/27			
Arbroath		26/27	14	10	D2

EDWARDS William

Falkirk		06/07	2		

EGAN Thomas

b. c1911

Wishaw Jnrs					
Hibernian		33/34	7		
		34/35	37		
		35/36	35	3	
		36/37	34	1	
		37/38	19	5	

EGERTON William F

Queen's Park		36/37	1		
		37/38			
Raith R		38/39			

EGGO Robert Mollison

b. Brechin 22.11.1895 d. Sheffield 23.5.1977

Brechin NE					
Heart of Midlothian		18/19	1		
		19/20	2		
Dunfermline A		19/20			
Sheffield W		19/20	4		FL
		20/21	19		FL
Reading		21/22	42	1	FL
		22/23	36	1	FL
		23/24	39		FL
		24/25	42		FL
		25/26	41		FL
		26/27	40		FL
		27/28	41		FL
		28/29	8		FL

EGLINGTON Matthew

b. Motherwell

Larkhall Thistle					
Hamilton A		10/11	30		
		11/12	22		
		12/13	28		
		13/14	27		
Motherwell		14/15	9		

EGLINTON Dugald

Abercorn		96/97	2		
		97/98			D2
Hamilton A					

ELDER

Falkirk		18/19	2		

ELLIOTT

Cowlairs		90/91	12		

ELLIOTT Alexander Cooper

b. Maryhill 10.1.1905

Glasgow Perthshire					
Partick T		27/28	32	2	
		28/29	28	5	
		29/30	35		
		30/31	38	3	
		31/32	29	1	
		32/33	33	2	
		33/34	33	2	
		34/35	26		
		35/36	34		
		36/37	23	1	
		37/38	25		
		38/39	33		

ELLIOTT George Washington

b. Middlesbrough 7.1.1889 d. Middlesbrough 27.11.1948

Redcar Crusaders					
South Bank					
Grangetown					
Middlesbrough		09/10	15	4	FL
		10/11	25	10	FL
		11/12	35	17	FL
		12/13	33	22	FL
		13/14	32	32	FL
		14/15	29	14	FL
Celtic	L	18/19	1		
Middlesbrough		19/20	38	31	FL
		20/21	36	26	FL
		21/22	26	13	FL
		22/23	33	23	FL
		23/24	24	7	FL
		24/25	17	5	FL

ELLIOTT Samuel

Kilwinning Eglington					
Kilwinning R					
Irvine V					
Cumnock Jnrs					
Kilmarnock		19/20	1		
Dykehead					

ELLIS Benjamin

b. Aberbargoed 11.4.1906 d. Motherwell 11.1.1966

Aberbargoed					
Bargoed					
New Tredegar					
Bargoed A					
Bangor					
Motherwell		31/32	38		
		32/33	33	1	
		33/34	29		
		34/35	38		
		35/36	36	2	
		36/37	37	1	
		37/38	32	3	
		38/39	36	6	

ELLIS David

b. Blackfriars, Glasgow 2.3.1900

Cameron Highlanders					
Glasgow Ashfield		19/20			
Airdrieonians		19/20	14	1	
		20/21	28	1	
		21/22	22	2	
Maidstone U		22/23			
Manchester U		23/24	11		FL
St Johnstone		24/25	23		
		25/26	9	1	
		26/27			
Bradford C		27/28			FL
Brighton	T	28/29			FL
Arthurlie					

ELLIS James 1 cap

b. c1867 d. Alberta 1939

Mossend Swifts					
Heart of Midlothian		91/92	3	3	
		92/93	11	1	
Leith A		92/93			
Third Lanark		92/93	12	3	

ELLIS Robert

Port Glasgow A		04/05	2		

ELMORE George V

b. Wednesbury 1884 d. 1952 X KIA 1.7.16 L/Cpl 15th Bn R Scots [illegible]

Wednesbury YMCA					
Broadheath					
WBA		02/03	4	1	FL
Bristol R		03/04	22	7	SL
Witton A					
Altrincham					
Glossop		07/08	24	8	FL
		08/09	11	8	FL
Blackpool		09/10	34	7	FL
Partick T		10/11	32	12	
		11/12	20	6	
St Mirren		12/13	34	9	
		13/14	28	8	
Witton A		14/15			
St Bernards		15/16			

EMERSON Charles

Shotts U					
Albion R		19/20	3		
Shotts U		20/21			
		21/22			
		22/23			
		23/24			
		24/25			
		25/26			
New Bedford Whalers		26/27	2	1	ASL
Philadelphia Field Club		26/27	3		ASL
J & P Coats		26/27	4	1	ASL

ENGLISH Samuel

b. Coleraine 18.8.1908 d. Yoker ?.4.1967

Port Glasgow Jnrs					
Old Kilpatrick					
Yoker A		28/29			
		29/30			
		30/31			
Rangers		31/32	35	44	
		32/33	25	10	
Liverpool		33/34	28	19	FL
		34/35	19	6	FL
Queen of the South		35/36	24	8	
Hartlepools U		36/37	34	18	FL
		37/38	36	9	FL
Duntochter Hibs					

ERENTZ Henry

b. Dundee 17.9.1874 d. Dundee 19.7.1947

Dundee		94/95	1		
		95/96			
Oldham Co		96/97			
Newton Heath		97/98	5		FL
Tottenham H		98/99	22		SL
		99/00	16		SL
		00/01	21		SL
		01/02	30		SL
		02/03	25		SL
		03/04	16		SL
Swindon T		04/05	16		SL

ERSKINE David

Dundee		16/17	4		

ERSKINE George Rowlands

b. Aberdeen 22.10.1914

Hall Russells					
Aberdeen		37/38	3		
Carlisle U		37/38	1		FL
Forfar A		38/39			D2

ESPIE Alexander (or John?)

Dundee 96/97 2
Chatham

EVANS John

Ardeer Rec
Dundee 35/36 29
36/37 36
37/38 20
Motherwell 38/39 2
Arbroath
Dundee U

EVANS Samuel
b. Glasgow 8.2.1904
Clydebank Jnrs
St Mirren 23/24 22 1
24/25 20 1
Clydebank 25/26 37 7
26/27
Reading 27/28 FL
28/29 2 FL
Ballymena 28/29 IL
York C 29/30 37 7 FL
30/31 29 5 FL
Scarborough 31/32 FL
Darlington 32/33 2 FL

EWART John 1 cap
b. Oakbank 14.2.1891 d. Bellshill 22.6.1943
Douglas Park
Bellshill R
Bellshill A
Larkhall Thistle
Airdrieonians 08/09 3
09/10 13
10/11 34
11/12 34
Bradford C 12/13 33 FL
13/14 32 FL
14/15 37 FL
19/20 40 FL
20/21 37 FL
21/22 35 FL
22/23 41 FL
Airdrieonians 23/24 30
24/25 36
25/26 36
26/27 20
Bradford C 27/28 28 FL
Preston NE 28/29 31 FL
29/30 4 FL

EWART Thomas

Cambuslang R
Motherwell 10/11 2

EWING Alexander

Irvine Meadow
Kilmarnock 09/10 2
Hurlford 10/11

EWING George

Clydebank Jnrs
Partick T 32/33 1 1

EWING James

Newtongrange Star
Raith R 08/09 D2
09/10 D2
10/11 32
11/12 1
Third Lanark 11/12 3

EWING James

Kilsyth R
Partick T 38/39 21
Cowdenbeath

FAGAN William
b. Musselburgh 20.2.1917 d. Wellingborough 29.2.1992
Balgonia Scotia
Wellesley Jnrs
Celtic 34/35 1
35/36 5 3
36/37 6 6
Preston NE 36/37 29 6 FL
37/38 6 FL
Liverpool 37/38 31 8 FL
38/39 39 14 FL
39/40 3 FL
46/47 18 7 FL
47/48 15 5 FL
48/49 13 2 FL
49/50 35 11 FL
50/51 4 FL
51/52 3 FL
Distillery 51/52 IL
Weymouth 52/53
53/54
54/55

FAIRBAIRN David

Celtic 95/96
96/97
97/98
98/99
Partick T 99/00 9 5 D2
00/01 1
Raith R 00/01
Partick T 01/02

FAIRBAIRN John

Heart of Midlothian 90/91 13
91/92 22
92/93 14
93/94 16
94/95 3
95/96 17
96/97 18
97/98 17

FAIRBAIRN John Jnr

Heart of Midlothian 91/92 13 9

FAIRFOUL Thomas
b. West Calder 16.1.1881 d. 1952
Lanark A
Patna
Kilmarnock 04/05 16 1
05/06 26 4
Third Lanark 06/07 32 19
07/08 28 2
08/09 34
09/10 32 2
10/11 33 2
11/12 33
12/13 13 1
Liverpool 13/14 38 FL
14/15 24 FL

FAIRGRAY Norman Murray
b. Dumfries 28.10.1880 d. Dumfries c1956
Dumfries Primrose
Maxwelltown Volunteers 01/02
02/03
Kilmarnock 03/04 1
Maxwelltown Volunteers 04/05
Lincoln C 05/06 21 4 FL
06/07 38 3 FL
07/08 1 FL
Chelsea 07/08 28 1 FL
08/09 18 FL
09/10 6 2 FL
10/11 2 FL
11/12 10 FL
12/13 9 2 FL
13/14 6 FL
Motherwell 14/15 32 3
Queen of the South 19/20
20/21

FAIRGRIEVE Walter Robert
b. Edinburgh 30.8.1874 d. Buckhaven 15.10.1923
Dalry Primrose
Glasgow Perthshire
Everton T FL
Southampton 98/99 1 SL
Luton T 99/00 13 5 FL
Hibernian 99/00
Partick T 00/01 5 1
Heart of Midlothian 00/01 2 1
Dunfermline A

FAIRLIE John

Tranent Jnrs
Airdrieonians 27/28 2
Middlesbrough
Bathgate 28/29 D2
Dumbarton 29/30 D2

FAIRWEATHER Alexander

Dundee 06/07 2

FALCONER James
b. Tarbolton 6.7.1910
Kilmarnock Academicals
Kilmarnock 30/31 1
31/32 7
32/33 1
Ayr U T 33/34 4
Galston T 33/34
Ayr U

FALCONER John Stevenson
b. Govan 14.11.1898
Plantation Hearts
Ibrox Waverley
Gower Thistle
St Anthonys
Cowdenbeath 21/22 D2
22/23 D2
23/24 D2
24/25 14
25/26 36
26/27 37
27/28 35
28/29 9
29/30
30/31
Celtic 31/32 7
32/33
East Stirlingshire T 33/34 D2
Creetown
Stranraer 35/36

FALLOON Edward
b. Larne 20.12.1903 d. Larne 4.7.1963
Newington R
Crusaders 22/23
23/24
24/25
25/26
26/27
Aberdeen 27/28 2
28/29 1 1
29/30 6
30/31 13
31/32 21 3
32/33 33 1
33/34 31
34/35 32 1
35/36 34
36/37 34
37/38 16
Clyde 37/38 12
38/39 32
Larne 39/40 IL
Crusaders 40/41

FALLOW Alexander J

Third Lanark 97/98 9
98/99 7

FARMER Andrew Richmond
b. Paisley 11.7.1915
Paisley Mossvale YMCA
Glasgow Benburb
Rangers T 34/35
Sunderland T 34/35 FL
Motherwell 35/36 1
Aldershot 36/37 17 1 FL
Portadown 37/38 IL
Kings Park 37/38 D2
Dunfermline A 38/39 D2

FARMER Joseph

Neilston V
St Mirren 31/32 8
32/33 6
Kings Park 33/34 D2

FARQUHARSON Alexander

Partick T 98/99 4
Clydebank

FARQUHARSON Hugh Hamilton
b. Paisley 27.9.1910 d. Paisley 6.11.1940
Renfrew Jnrs
Hull C 34/35 4 FL
35/36 3 FL
Dunfermline A 36/37 33

FARR Andrew Martin
b. Larkhall 7.8.1911
Larkhall Thistle
Clyde 31/32 20 3
Yoker A
Margate 35/36
36/37
37/38
Arsenal 37/38 FL
38/39 2 1 FL
Airdrieonians
Heart of Midlothian

FARR Robert
Albion R
Bathgate
Heart of Midlothian 10/11 3
Cowdenbeath 11/12 D2
12/13 D2
Bathgate
Tranent

FARRELL Patrick
b. Athlone 2.2.1912 d. Hull 19.3.1987
Home Farm
Bohemians 32/33 LI
33/34 LI
34/35 LI
Hibernian 35/36 1
36/37 14 4
37/38 13 2
38/39 5 1
Alloa A

FARRELL Peter
b. Glasgow
Cumbernauld Thistle
Bellshill A
Clyde 11/12 1
12/13 28
13/14 15
Renton L 13/14
Clyde 14/15 38
Partick T L 14/15
Clyde 15/16 34
16/17 34
Stevenston U L 16/17
Clyde 17/18 9
Kilmarnock L 17/18 1
Clyde 18/19
19/20 9
20/21 42
21/22 29
22/23 10
23/24 28
Nairn Co 24/25

FARRELL Robert
Morton 02/03 1

FARRELL Robert
b. Larne 1.1.1906 d. Hove 17.1.1971
Dundee NE
Dundee 26/27 4
27/28 12
Portsmouth T 28/29 FL
Brighton 28/29 32 4 FL
29/30 37 6 FL
30/31 38 5 FL
31/32 38 8 FL
32/33 41 10 FL
33/34 41 6 FL
34/35 36 5 FL
35/36 35 6 FL
36/37 35 7 FL
37/38 39 3 FL
38/39 10 6 FL

FARRELL Thomas
b. Earlstown
Woolwich Arsenal
Manchester C 06/07 3 FL
Airdrieonians 07/08 9 1
08/09 6

FARRELL William
Dumbarton 15/16 21 1
Stevenston U 15/16
Clyde

FARRINGTON Thomas
Montrose
Rangers 11/12 1
12/13 7
Thornhill

FAUGHNAN John
b. Shotts * 1883 *
Mossend Hibs
Third Lanark 10/11 8 1
Ayr U L 10/11 D2
Third Lanark 11/12 1 1
Dykehead 12/13
Vale of Leven 13/14 D2

FAULDS
Third Lanark 90/91 4 1

FAULDS Daniel
Bellshill A
Hamilton A 17/18 13 2

FAULDS Thomas G
b. Hurlford
Hurlford
Ayr U 30/31 2
Albion R 31/32 D2

FAULTLESS Charles Edward
b. Bridgeton 5.3.1908 d. Clydebank 27.11.1998
Glasgow Churches League
Morton 27/28 D2
28/29 D2
29/30
30/31
31/32
32/33
St Mirren 33/34 1
Motherwell
Beith

FEATHERSTONE Henry Wilson
b. Wallsend 20.6.1888 d. 1956
Wallsend Park Villa
St Mirren 09/10 17
10/11 20 6
Cardiff C 11/12 SL
12/13 SL
13/14
Ashington U 14/15
19/20
Belfast U 20/21
Ashington 20/21
21/22 31 2 FL
22/23 35 1 FL
Halifax T 23/24 21 2 FL
Stanley U

FEENEY Owen
b. c1912
Kinglasie
Denbeath
Dundee 29/30 5 3
East Fife
Bishopshire Swifts
Cowdenbeath 33/34 30 5
St Mirren 34/35 7 1
35/36 D2
Cowdenbeath 36/37 D2

FERGUSON Albert James
b. Gourock
Port Glasgow Jnrs
Partick T 22/23 18
23/24
Dumbarton 24/25 D2

FERGUSON Alexander
b. Montfieth
Lochee Harp
St Johnstone 34/35 28 4
35/36 20 8
Heart of Midlothian 36/37 14 2
37/38 1 1

FERGUSON Alexander
Hibernian 35/36 8 1

FERGUSON Archibald
b. Lochore 9.12.1918 d. Dunfermline 19.3.1998
Crossgates Primrose
St Andrews U
Raith R 37/38
38/39 14
Doncaster R 46/47 39 FL
47/48 22 FL
Wrexham 48/49 35 FL
49/50 42 FL
50/51 32 FL
51/52 6 FL
52/53 11 FL
Dunfermline A 53/54 1 D2

FERGUSON Daniel
Cleland R
Hibernian 08/09 13 2
Queen's Park
Royal Albert
Blackpool T
Pontypridd 13/14

FERGUSON David
Heart of Midlothian 09/10 1

FERGUSON Ernest
Dundee 15/16 31
16/17 15

FERGUSON George
Dundee 97/98 1

FERGUSON George
Battlefield Jnrs
Lochgelly U T 21/22 D2
Third Lanark 21/22 17 9
22/23
Arthurlie 23/24 D3

FERGUSON H H P
Queen's Park 10/11 6

FERGUSON Harry
b. Clackmannan c1908
Alva Albion R
St Johnstone 25/26 1
26/27 9
27/28 5
28/29 13
29/30 32 1
30/31 32 9 D2
31/32 30 6 D2
32/33 24 8
33/34 36 12
34/35 25 11
35/36 30 9
36/37 21 5
37/38
Kings Park T 38/39 D2

FERGUSON Hugh
b. Craigneuk 2.3.1897 d. Dundee 9.1.1930
Motherwell Hearts
Parkhead 14/15
Helensea 15/16
Vale of Leven 15/16
Motherwell 16/17 29 24
Third Lanark L 17/18 1
Mid Annandale L 17/18
St Mirren L 17/18
Motherwell 17/18 30 35
18/19 25 19
19/20 35 33
20/21 36 42
21/22 33 35
22/23 29 29
23/24 33 27
24/25 37 28
25/26 12 12
Cardiff C 25/26 26 19 FL
26/27 39 25 FL
27/28 32 18 FL
28/29 20 14 FL
Dundee 29/30 17 2

FERGUSON James
b. Glasgow 1885
Strathclyde
Airdrieonians 04/05 16
05/06 27 3
06/07 26
Blackburn R 07/08 9 1 FL
08/09 17 FL
09/10 4 FL
10/11 2 FL
11/12 FL
12/13 FL
St Johnstone 12/13 1 D2

FERGUSON James
Cambuslang Hibs
Woolwich Arsenal 06/07 1 FL
Partick T 07/08 29 2

FERGUSON James

b. Glasgow
Shettleston

Rangers	12/13			
	13/14	1		
	14/15			
Clydebank	17/18	30		
	18/19	28	?	
	19/20	39		
	20/21	41		
	21/22	31		

FERGUSON James

Aberdeen	15/16	1		

FERGUSON James

b. Halbert
Renton

Dumbarton	13/14	35	2	
	14/15	21	1	
Cowdenbeath				
Albion R	19/20	4	1	
Renton *	20/21			

FERGUSON James Stirling

b. Longriggend 30.8.1896 d. Caldercruix 21.9.1952
Airdriehill Shamrock

Partick T	16/17	26		
	17/18	18		
	18/19	1		
St Rochs				
Brentford	26/27	38		FL
	27/28	27		FL
Notts Co	27/28	10		FL
	28/29	42		FL
	29/30	41		FL
	30/31	35		FL
	31/32	30		FL
Ayr U	32/33	3		

FERGUSON John

Jordanhill Jnrs				
Celtic T	94/95	1	1	
Blackburn R	94/95			FL
Hibernian	95/96	8	3	
Third Lanark	95/96			
	96/97			
Partick T	96/97	13	3	D2
	97/98	8	6	
	98/99	8	1	

FERGUSON John

Glenbuck Cherrypickers				
Hamilton A	07/08	27		
	08/09	10		
Nithsdale W	09/10			
Cowdenbeath				

FERGUSON John

b. Dundee 1887 d. Bethlehem, USA 19.9.1973

Arbroath				
St Johnstone	10/11			
Dundee	11/12	21		
Leeds C	12/13	17		FL
Gateshead				
Clydebank	14/15			
Bethlehem Steel				
Philadelphia Field Club	21/22	22		ASL
J & P Coats	22/23	24		ASL
Bethlehem Steel	23/24	15		ASL
	24/25	14		ASL
	25/26	5		ASL
	26/27	9		ASL
	27/28	2		ASL

FERGUSON John

b. Lochanside c1891 K.I.A., Somme 23.10.1916
Edinburgh University
Aberfoyle

St Bernards	10/11	22		D2
	11/12			D2
	12/13			D2
Third Lanark	13/14	23	6	
	14/15	8		
	15/16	10		

FERGUSON John

b. c1915
Shettleston

Albion R	36/37	15		

FERGUSON Pearson

b. Coalburn 28.8.1909 d. Gourock 17.3.1985
Queen of the South
Kello R

Ayr U	29/30	31	14	
	30/31	23	6	
Cork	31/32			LI
Ayr U	32/33	18	5	
Queen of the South	32/33	?	?	D2
Carlisle U	33/34	29	8	FL
	34/35	38	11	FL
?	35/36			
	36/37			
	37/38			
East Stirlingshire	38/39			D2

FERGUSON Pearson

Montrose				
Morton	37/38	1		

FERGUSON Robert

b. Cleland
Cleland R

Third Lanark	05/06	4		
	06/07	19		
	07/08	29	1	
	08/09	33	4	
	09/10	34	2	
	10/11	34		
	11/12	33		
Liverpool	12/13	38	2	FL
	13/14	36		FL
	14/15	18		FL
Wishaw Thistle	15/16			

FERGUSON Robert

b. c1916
Yoker A
Heart of Midlothian

St Mirren	36/37	37	10	
	37/38	28	8	
	38/39	34	5	

FERGUSON Robert C

St Mirren	06/07	4		

FERGUSON Thomas

b. Denny
Bedlay Jnrs

Falkirk	19/20	40		
	20/21	35		
	21/22	41		
	22/23	38		
	23/24	38		
	24/25	38		
	25/26	38		
	26/27	37		
	27/28	38		
	28/29	38		
	29/30	37		
	30/31	26		
	31/32	5		

FERGUSON Thomas E

Yoker A				
Motherwell	36/37	13	1	

FERGUSON Thomas W F

Motherwell	38/39	1		

FERGUSON William

Jordanhill				
Maryhill				
Celtic	94/95	4	4	
	95/96	13	4	
	96/97	8	5	
Burnley	96/97	4	1	FL
	97/98	9	3	FL
	98/99	15	4	FL
	99/00	5		FL
Manchester C				

FERGUSON William

Lanemark				
Kilmarnock	99/00	6	2	
	00/01	6	1	
Lanemark				
Nithsdale W	02/03			
Maxwelltown Volunteers				
Partick T	03/04	1		
	04/05	3	1	
Nithsdale W				
Lanemark				
Thornhill				

FERGUSON William

Falkirk	17/18	2	?	

FERGUSON William

Falkirk	19/20	11	4	

FERGUSON William

Rosyth Dockyard				
Fauldhouse U				
Falkirk	34/35	5	1	

FERGUSON William Copeland

b. Muirkirk 13.2.1901 d. Dumfries 31.8.1960
Kellsbank Juveniles
Kello R

Queen of the South W	19/20			
	20/21			
Chelsea	21/22			FL
	22/23	9		FL
	23/24	27	1	FL
	24/25	30	2	FL
	25/26	27		FL
	26/27	42	3	FL
	27/28	41	1	FL
	28/29	22		FL
	29/30	11	2	FL
	30/31	25		FL
	31/32	21	2	FL
	32/33	17		FL
Queen of the South	33/34	29	2	
	34/35	29	1	
	35/36	16		
	36/37	5		

FERNIE

Morton	16/17	1	?	

FERRIER Frank

Dundee	95/96	1		
	96/97			
	97/98			
	98/99	4		

FERRIER George

Yoker A				
Morton	13/14	32	1	
	14/15	35		
	15/16			
	16/17			
	17/18			
	18/19	1	?	
	19/20	31		
	20/21	1		
Stevenston U	21/22			
Johnstone	21/22			D2
	22/23			D2
Paterson Silk Sox	22/23	3		ASL
New York National Giants	23/24	26		ASL
Indiana Flooring	24/25	28		ASL
New york Giants	25/26	2		ASL
Newark Skeeters	27/28	1		ASL

FERRIER J

Dumbarton	92/93	5		

FERRIER Robert

b. Dumbarton ?.7.1874 d. Motherwell 11.12.1947

Dumbarton	93/94	15	4	
Sheffield W	94/95	23	4	FL
	95/96	23	1	FL
	96/97	20	6	FL
	97/98	28	2	FL
	98/99	32		FL
	99/00	32	2	FL
	00/01	34		FL
	01/02	30		FL
	02/03	33		FL
	03/04	31		FL
	04/05	21		FL

FERRIER Robert
b. Sheffield c1900 d. Dumbarton ?.4.1971
Petershill
Motherwell 18/19 16 4
19/20 39 9
20/21 38 10
21/22 40 5
22/23 37 8
23/24 36 11
24/25 37 7
25/26 38 12
26/27 35 19
27/28 38 27
28/29 36 29
29/30 37 32
30/31 35 12
31/32 36 13
32/33 37 26
33/34 29 8
34/35 28 7
35/36 25 14
36/37 9 6

FERRIER William

Dundee East End
Dundee 93/94 17
94/95 5
95/96
96/97
Linfield 97/98 IL

FERRIS

St Mirren 95/96 2

FERRIS Robert

Falkirk 11/12 2 1

FIDDES James
b. Grangemouth c1917
Grange R
Rangers 34/35 3
35/36 17 6
36/37 4 1
37/38 14
38/39 19 6
Falkirk 46/47 19 3
47/48 29 4
48/49 30 3
49/50 27 4
50/51 25 2
Ross Co
Stenhousemuir 51/52 D2
52/53 28 3 D2

FIELD Richard
b. Sunderland 2.8.1891 d. Sunderland 15.7.1965
Kings Hall Wesleyan Club
Lambton Star
Willington
Sunderland 14/15
Barry T 19/20
20/21
Dumbarton 21/22 7
Aberdare A 22/23 24 FL
Norwich C 23/24 28 FL
Grimsby T 24/25 32 FL
Accrington S 25/26 42 FL
26/27 10 1 FL
Boston T 27/28
West Stanley

FINDLAY Alexander

Thornliebank
Third Lanark 03/04 1
Vale of Leven

FINDLAY Andrew
b. Newburn on Tyne 6.11.1896 d. Tiverton 1969
Newburn
Tottenham H 19/20
20/21
21/22
Wigan B 22/23 22 FL
23/24 8 1 FL
Darlington T
Dundee 25/26 24 3
Portsmouth

FINDLAY Andrew
b. Hooley Hill (Lancs)
Roslyn Jnrs
St Mirren 21/22 8
22/23 36
23/24 33
24/25 30
25/26 35
26/27 32
27/28 31
28/29 15
Dundee U 29/30 9
Cork C 30/31 LI

FINDLAY Hugh

Hamilton A 37/38 3

FINDLAY James

Hamilton A 06/07 10 1

FINDLAY John
b. Riccarton 19.10.1892 d. Newcastle 31.3.1933
Kilmarnock Shawbank
Celtic T
Rangers 03/04 1
Airdrieonians 04/05 25 1
05/06 30 1
06/07 33 2
07/08 31 4
08/09 32 1
Newcastle U 09/10 11 1 FL
10/11 18 FL
11/12 7 3 FL
12/13 17 FL
13/14 20 FL
14/15 11 1 FL
19/20 36 FL
20/21 25 1 FL
21/22 5 1 FL
22/23 FL
23/24 3 FL

FINDLAY Richard V
b. Glasgow
London Caledonians
Queen's Park 06/07 14 2
07/08 8 1

FINDLAY Robert 1 cap
b. Galston 29.3.1877 d. Bayonne 13.8.1926
Kilmarnock Rugby XI
Kilmarnock 96/97 6 2 D2
97/98 15 8 D2
98/99 18 11 D2
99/00 12 4
Celtic 00/01 12 6
01/02 2 1
Kilmarnock 01/02 1
02/03 17 5
03/04 9 3
Dundee T 04/05 7 1
Motherwell 05/06 20 10
06/07 2
Hamilton A 06/07 2 1
07/08 5 1
Port Glasgow A 08/09 27 6
09/10 26
St Bernards 09/10 D2
10/11 D2

FINDLAY Thomas
b. Galston 10.8.1881
Kilmarnock Rugby XI
Kilmarnock 01/02 7 1
02/03 16 4
03/04 3
Morton 03/04 1
Motherwell 04/05 7 1
05/06 30 14
Hibernian 06/07 27 9
07/08 13
Kilmarnock L 07/08 3 1
Port Glasgow A 08/09 26 5
09/10 31 7
10/11 18 ? D2
Nithsdale W 11/12
Albion R L 11/12 D2

FINDLAY Thomas
b. Port Glasgow 26.2.190C
Port Glasgow A
Derby Co 22/23 3 FL
23/24 1 FL
24/25 FL
Merthyr T 25/26 24 FL
Morton 26/27 2
Brechin C 26/27

FINDLAY William

Kilmarnock A
Clyde 97/98 2

FINDLAY William
b. Musselburgh 15.1.1904
Musselburgh Bruntonians
Third Lanark 20/21 3
21/22 34 1
22/23 10
23/24 23
24/25 23 5
New York Nationals 28/29 8 2 ASL
Brooklyn Wanderers 30A 3 ASL

FINDLAY William

Bathgate 23/24 D2
Motherwell 23/24 4

FINLAY Andrew
b. Hutchesontown 10.2.1901
Shawfield Jnrs
Port Vale 21/22 1 FL
St Rochs
Airdrieonians 22/23 3
Manchester C 23/24 FL
Crewe A 23/24 12 3 FL
Third Lanark 24/25
Dundee U 25/26 13 1
Hibernian 26/27 9
27/28 19 3
28/29 32 4
Portadown 29/30 IL
Cork C 30/31 LI
Shawfield Jnrs 31/32
Coleraine 31/32 IL

FINLAY John
K.I.A. 20.9.1916
Vale of Leven 07/08 D2
08/09 D2
Airdrieonians 09/10 20

FINLAY William

St Mirren 96/97 4

FINLAYSON A

Queen's Park 08/09 1

FINLAYSON David

Queen's Park 10/11 1

FINLAYSON Duncan
b. Aldershot 19.4.1894 d. Auckland 11.5 1964
Glasgow University
Motherwell 12/13 10 5
13/14 21 4
14/15 37 1
15/16 36 8
16/17 21 2
17/18 17 1
18/19 5
19/20
20/21 10 1
Clydebank 21/22 5

FINLAYSON James B

Larkhall Thistle
Third Lanark 20/21 3
21/22 13 3

FINLAYSON John
b. Thornliebank 14.6.1912
Thornliebank
Motherwell 30/31
31/32
East Stirlingshire 32/33 7 1
Cowdenbeath 32/33 13 2
Clapton Orient 33/34 1 FL
34/35 10 FL
Ashford T 34/35
Luton T 35/36 33 3 FL
36/37 40 2 FL
37/38 39 3 FL
38/39 42 1 FL
39/40 3 FL

FINLAYSON Robert

Thornliebank
Third Lanark 24/25 5
East Stirlingshire * 25/26 D2
Vale of Leven * 26/27

FINNIGAN, William Jordan
b. Edinburgh 24.11.1912 d. Oxford 23.4.2006
Bo'ness Cadora
Hibernian 37/38 24 6
38/39 20 1
46/47 18 1
47/48 15
48/49 8
49/50
Dunfermline A 50/51 D2
51/52 D2

FINNIE David

Cambuslang R
Dumbarton 17/18 30 4
Clyde 17/18 2 ?
Dumbarton 18/19 6 ?

FISHER Albert James
b. Denny 23.12.1876 d. Edinburgh 8.2.1921
Vale of Forth
Kings Park 91/92
92/93
93/94
94/95
East Stirlingshire 95/96
St Bernards 96/97 14 7
Aston Villa 97/98 18 5 FL
Celtic 98/99 10 3
Preston NE L 98/99 FL
Celtic 99/00
East Stirlingshire L 99/00
Newton Heath 00/01 25 2 FL
01/02 17 1 FL
Kings Park 01/02
02/03
Vale of Leithen 02/03
Fulham 03/04 1 SL
Woodville U 04/05
Grays U

FISHER Alexander

Rankinston Seaview
Ayr U
Galston L 32/33
Ayr U 32/33 7 4
33/34 7 2
Stranraer L 33/34
Ayr U 34/35 13 4
35/36 8 5
36/37 6 2 D2
Cork 36/37 LI
Sligo R 36/37 LI
Dartford 37/38

FISHER Peter

Aberdeen
Dundee Hibs T
Dundee Forthill
Aberdeen 20/21 21 14
21/22 2
Dundee Hibs 22/23

FISHER Peter
b. Glasgow
St Francis
St Anthonys 32/33
33/34
Clyde 34/35 21 5
Stenhousemuir 35/36 D2
Watford 36/37 3 1 FL
Burnley 36/37 5 FL
37/38 14 2 FL
38/39 4 FL
Dunfermline A

FISHER William

Crossgates Thistle
Kirkcaldy U
Dundee 14/15 16 2
15/16 29 3
16/17 16 3

FITCHIE Thomas Tindal
b. Edinburgh 11.12.1881 d. Streatham 17.10.1947
West Norwood
Woolwich Arsenal 01/02 3 4 FL
Tottenham H 01/02 1 SL
Woolwich Arsenal 02/03 1 FL
Queen's Park 03/04
Fulham 04/05 9 6 FL
05/06 22 9 FL
05/06
London Caledonians
West Norwood 06/07
Queen's Park 06/07 20 6
Norwich C 06/07 SL
Queen's Park 07/08 23 14
Brighton 07/08 SL
Woolwich Arsenal 08/09 21 8 FL
Glossop 09/10 14 3 FL
10/11 21 6 FL
11/12 7 FL
Fulham 12/13 8 2 FL
London Caledonians
Pilgrims

FITTON Robert

Bellshill A
Airdrieonians 11/12 3

FITZGERALD Leslie
b. Glasgow
Queen's Park 29/30 11 3
30/31 6 1
31/32 10
32/33 5
33/34 13 4
Ayr U 34/35 22 3
35/36 8 2

FITZPATRICK Patrick

Blantyre V
Hibernian 06/07 19 2

FITZPATRICK Samuel

Morton 13/14 1

FITZSIMONS John Thomas
b. Glasgow 3.3.1915
Dumfries St Josephs
St Rochs
Celtic 34/35
35/36 2
36/37 2
37/38 1
Alloa A
Clyde
Falkirk 46/47 15 6
Hamilton A 46/47 12 3
Clyde 47/48 21 7
48/49

FITZSIMMONS Charles Campbell
b. St Ninians 1910
Alva Albion R
Partick T 30/31 3
31/32 8
St Bernards 32/33 D2
33/34 D2
34/35 D2
35/36 D2
36/37 D2
Alloa A 37/38 D2

FITZSIMMONS Patrick J
b. c1916
Preston NE 37/38 FL
Queen of the South 38/39 37 3

FITZSIMMONS Thomas
b. Annbank 21.10.1870
Annbank
Celtic T 92/93 1
Newton Heath 92/93 18 5 FL
93/94 9 1 FL
Annbank
St Mirren 94/95 3 1
Annbank 95/96
Fairfield 95/96
Glossop NE
Fairfield
Oldham Co
Chorley
Wigan Co
Annbank

FLANAGAN William
b. Birmingham c1876
Smethwick Carriage Works
Oldbury T
Aston Villa 95/96
Burton W 96/97 9 1 FL
Leicester F 97/98 4 FL
Glentoran 98/99 IL
99/00 IL
00/01 IL
Morton 00/01 1
Port Glasgow A 00/01 4 ? D2
Distillery 01/02 IL

FLANAGHAN Henry Nixon
b. Nottingham 1896
Bedlay Jnrs
Third Lanark 19/20 35 5
20/21 12
Aberdeen 20/21 25 5
21/22 4
Maidstone U 22/23
Grimsby T 23/24 3 FL
Scunthorpe U T 23/24
Adams A 23/24
York C T 23/24
Denaby U

FLANNAGAN Matthew (or Michael) Joseph
b. Govan ? 1872
Benburb
Celtic 92/93 1 1

FLANNIGAN Patrick

Hibernian 97/98 1

FLANNIGAN Patrick
b. Kelty 19.5.1909
Rosyth Dockyard
Kelty R
Cowdenbeath 26/27 6
Lochgelly U L 26/27
Cowdenbeath 27/28 11 1
28/29 4
Liverpool 28/29 FL
Bradford C 29/30 1 FL
New York Giants 30A 28 1 ASL
31S 15 1 ASL
31A 20 ASL
Glenavon 32/33
Rosyth Rec

FLANNIGAN Thomas
b. Edinburgh 27.5.1908 d. Darlington 23.5.1981
Edinburgh Emmet
Dundee 26/27 1
27/28
Stoke 28/29 5 FL
Hull C 29/30 2 FL
Loughborough Corinthians
Darlington T 31/32 FL
Rochdale 31/32 2 FL
Stafford R
Buxton 32/33
St Etienne
Shrewsbury T 33/34
34/35

FLEMING

Abercorn 90/91 17

FLEMING

Heart of Midlothian 90/91 1

FLEMING

Rangers 91/92 1

FLEMING

St Mirren 91/92 20
92/93 1

FLEMING

Vale of Leven 91/92 3 1

FLEMING

Clyde 92/93 2
93/94 4 D2

FLEMING Alexander

Armadale
Arthurlie
Clydebank 22/23 D2
23/24 31 1
24/25 D2
25/26 19 1

FLEMING Daniel

Vale of Clyde
Hibernian 14/15 21 5
Abercorn 15/16
16/17
17/18
18/19
Armadale 19/20

FLEMING James

Morton 02/03 8
03/04 1

FLEMING James

Linlithgow Rose
Hibernian 26/27 2
Bathgate 27/28 D2

FLEMING James W

Forth W
Hibernian 38/39 2

FLEMING James William 3 caps

b. Glasgow 5.12.1901 d. ?.5.1969
Shettleston Jnrs
St Johnstone 23/24 29 23 D2
24/25 35 19
25/26 8 2
Rangers 25/26 21 17
26/27 26 16
27/28 34 33
28/29 35 33
29/30 34 27
30/31 13 5
31/32 24 16
32/33 21 12
33/34 13 16
34/35 4 1
Ayr U 34/35 22 12
35/36 20 5

FLEMING John

Renton 93/94 18 4
94/95 D2
East Stirlingshire

FLEMING John

Bellshill A
Clyde 12/13 15 5
13/14 10 1
14/15 22 5

FLEMING John

K.I.A., Langemarck 21.3.1916
Armadale
Bonnyrigg Rose A
St Bernards 09/10
Newcastle U FL
Tottenham H FL
Rangers 15/16 4 1

FLEMING Joseph

Dundee 93/94
94/95 14 3

FLEMING Joseph

Dundee 97/98 3

FLEMING Samuel

b. Tollcross
Vale of Clyde
Hibernian 11/12 16 1
12/13 30 6
13/14 26 11
14/15 8 3
15/16 38 10
16/17 21 4
17/18
18/19 3 ?
St Mirren 18/19 1 ?
Clyde 18/19 4 ?
19/20 17 7
20/21 21 6
21/22 19 3
22/23 3
Albion R 22/23 30 10

FLEMING Thomas

b. Beith 1890 d. Quincey, USA 1965
Beith 06/07
Fore River Shipyard (USA)
Morton 08/09 13 1
Ayr Parkhouse 09/10 D2
Beith 10/11
11/12
12/13
13/14
Bethlehem Steel 14
15
16
17
18
19
20
Philadelphia 20/21
J & P Coats 21/22
22/23
23/24
Boston Wonder Workers 24/25 ASL
25/26
26/27

FLEMING Thomas N

b. Glasgow 15.11.1901 d. Quincy, Mass ?.3.1965
Shettleston
Dundee 19/20 2
20/21 10
21/22 2
Fulham 21/22 17 FL
22/23 37 FL
23/24 23 FL
24/25 32 FL
25/26 2 FL
Wigan B 25/26 17 FL
26/27 5 FL
Dundee U 26/27 5
27/28 16 D2

FLEMING William

b. Alexandria 30.4.1901
Duntochter Hibernian
Vale of Leven
Celtic 24/25 19 10
Ayr U 25/26 31 21 D2
26/27 33 3 D2
27/28 37 D2
28/29 35 1
29/30 31
30/31 28
31/32 30
32/33 35
33/34 25
Dundee U 34/35 31 D2

FLEMING William

b. c1918
Scottish Dyes
Falkirk 36/37 2
37/38
38/39 4 1

FLEMMING Daniel

Morton 00/01 3

FLETCHER Brough

b. Mealsgate 9.3.1893 d. Bristol 12.5.1972
Chilton Colliery
Shildon A
Barnsley 14/15 32 7 FL
Partick T L 16/17 6
17/18 4
18/19
Barnsley 19/20 37 9 FL
20/21 39 1 FL
21/22 39 18 FL
22/23 39 4 FL
23/24 23 2 FL
24/25 19 2 FL
25/26 20 9 FL
Sheffield W 25/26 2 FL
Barnsley 26/27 25 9 FL
27/28 32 11 FL
28/29 9 1 FL

FLETCHER Daniel

Greenock Volunteers
Partick T 99/00 D2
00/01 3
Morton 01/02
Motherwell 01/02 D2

FLETCHER Eli

b. Tunstall 15.12.1887 d. Longsight 6.8.1954
Earlestown 05/06
Crewe A 05/06
Northwich V 06/07
Goldenhill W
Hanley Swifts
Crewe A 09/10 20 BDL
10/11 32 4 BDL
Manchester C 11/12 35 1 FL
12/13 33 FL
13/14 36 FL
14/15 37 FL
Clydebank L 18/19 1
Manchester C 19/20 34 1 FL
20/21 35 FL
21/22 38 FL
22/23 5 FL
23/24 20 FL
24/25 27 FL
25/26 1 FL
Watford 26/27 23 FL
Sandbach R 27/28
Ards 28/29 IL

FLETCHER H M

Queen's Park 02/03 4

FLETCHER Harry M

Queen's Park 06/07 7
07/08 6
08/09 2
09/10 1

FLUCKER Peter Hogg

b. North Leith 1907
Musselburgh Bruntonians
Heart of Midlothian 28/29 1
29/30 2 2
Queen of the South 30/31 D2
31/32 D2
Hibernian 32/33 D2
33/34 23 11
34/35 9 5
Arbroath 35/36 22 7
St Bernards 36/37 D2
37/38 D2
38/39 D2

FOLEY James

b. Cork 19.3.1914 d. Cork 14.10.1952
Cork Celtic
Cork 31/32 LI
32/33 LI
Belfast Celtic 33/34 IL
Cork 33/34 LI
Celtic 34/35
35/36 5
36/37 1
Plymouth A 36/37 18 FL
37/38 21 FL
Cork C 38/39 LI
39/40 LI
40/41 LI
Cork U 40/41 LI
41/42 LI
42/43 LI
43/44 LI
St Josephs 44/45
Cork U 44/45 LI
45/46 LI
46/47 LI

FOLLET Arthur V

Carluke Milton R
St Mirren 21/22 2

FOLLEY William

Falkirk 06/07 5
East Fife L 07/08

FORAN Joseph W

b. Paisley
Greenlaw Strollers
Celtic
St Mirren L 90/91 2
Celtic 91/92 1 1
92/93 1
Johnstone 93/94
94/95
Paisley Celtic 94/95

FORBES

Albion R 19/20 1

FORBES Charles

Crieff Academy
Aberdeen 23/24 3
24/25 1
25/26 2

FORBES Frederick James
b. Leith 5.8.1894
Leith Benburb
Heart of Midlothian 20/21 34 23
21/22 26 11
Everton 22/23 10 4 FL
23/24 3 FL
24/25 1 FL
Plymouth A 24/25 11 4 FL
25/26 41 13 FL
26/27 42 15 FL
27/28 33 14 FL
28/29 31 6 FL
Bristol R 29/30 24 4 FL
30/31 39 6 FL
Leith A 31/32 9 1
Workington
Northampton T 32/33 35 3 FL
Airdrieonians

FORBES George Alexander

Tranent Jnrs
Queen's Park 38/39 1

FORD

Leith A 31/32 1

FORD Andrew D
b. Coatbridge
Queen's Park 15/16 13
16/17 26 1
17/18 28 2
18/19 15 1
Kilmarnock 18/19 1
Albion R 19/20 33 1
20/21 36 3
21/22 18 1
Alloa A 22/23 16

FORD Charles Joseph
b. Edinburgh 20.9.1905 d. Leith ?.4.1951
Rosewell Rosedale
Newcastle U 31/32 1 FL
32/33 FL
Partick T 33/34 2
Leith A 34/35 D2
Penicuik A 35/36
Benford

FORD John

Aberdeen 06/07 6

FORD Joseph

Morningside
Hamilton A 17/18 11
18/19 2

FORD Richard J

Irvine Meadow
Ayr U 22/23 3
23/24 14
Beith 23/24 D3
St Bernards 23/24 D2

FORD William
b. 1881
The Rovers
Arbroath
Heart of Midlothian 03/04
Motherwell L 03/04 15 1
Heart of Midlothian 04/05
Portsmouth 04/05 6 SL
West Ham U 05/06 7 1 SL
Arbroath 06/07

FORD William Gracey
b. Dundee 1872 d. 1948
Dundee 95/96 2
WBA 96/97 12 1 FL
Hurlford Thistle
New Brompton 97/98 22 10 SL
Luton T 98/99 23 8 FL
Gravesend U 99/00 18 2 SL

FORDYCE Robert

Broxburn U
Airdrieonians 23/24 1
St Bernards 24/25 D2

FORDYCE William
b. Perth
St Johnstone YMCA
Arbroath 30/31 36 D2
31/32 35 D2
32/33 34 D2
33/34 34 D2
34/35 34 D2
35/36 35
36/37 33
37/38 38
38/39 38

FORREST Charles

Hibernian 06/07 2

FORREST George A
b. Wallyford
Heart of Midlothian 19/20 3
20/21 3
21/22 14
Alloa A 22/23 27 1
Toronto Ulster
Bethlehem Steel 24/25 19 5 ASL
25/26 24 8 ASL
26/27 29 12 ASL
? 27/28
York C 28/29
Heart of Midlothian 29/30
Raith R 30/31 D2
31/32 D2
32/33 D2
Plymouth A 33/34 FL
34/35 FL
Mansfield T

FORREST J S

Dumbarton 21/22 1

FORREST James
b. Lanarkshire 1878
Wishaw U
Motherwell
Stoke 02/03 6 3 FL
Bradford C 03/04 27 5 FL
04/05 23 13 FL
05/06 3 FL
Hamilton A 06/07 21 4
Ayr

FORREST James
b. Lesmagahow 1.1.1894
Nethanvale Thistle
Maryhill
Clyde 14/15
15/16 31 1
16/17 22
17/18 6 ?
18/19 1 ?
19/20 22
20/21 28
21/22 42
22/23 38
Preston NE 23/24 2 FL
24/25 31 FL
25/26 18 FL
Bethlehem Steel 25/26 ASL
Cowdenbeath 26/27 24 1
Providence Clamdiggers 27/28 2 2 ASL

FORREST Samuel
b. Paisley 29.12.1890 d. Paisley 9.9.1967
Westmarch
Petershill
Fulham 12/13 6 FL
13/14 1 FL
Reading 13/14 21 SL
Fulham 14/15 1 FL
Raith R 16/17 29 1
Clydebank 17/18 15
18/19 8

FORREST William
b. c1903
Wallyford Bluebell
Heart of Midlothian 25/26
26/27 12
27/28 8
St Bernards

FORREST William M
b. Musselburgh
St Johnstone 28/29 17
29/30 27

FORREST William M

Leith A 30/31 34 2
31/32 14
Forres Mechanics 32/33

FORRESTER Thomas

Harthill
Hamilton A 23/24 2
Royal Albert
Helensburgh 25/26 D3

FORSYTH

Dumbarton 94/95 3

FORSYTH

Third Lanark 22/23 1

FORSYTH David

Co-operative U
Partick A
Partick T 02/03 2
Arthurlie 02/03

FORSYTH John B

Wemyss Jnrs
Hamilton A 24/25 3

FORSYTH John F

Heart of Midlothian 99/00 1

FORSYTH Matthew
b. Glasgow
Shotts Battlefield
Glasgow Perthshire
Aberdeen 20/21 23
21/22 35
22/23 37
23/24 31
24/25 33
25/26 2
Forres Mechanics 26/27
27/28
Keith 28/29

FORSYTH Thomas E

Airdrieonians 10/11 1
Queen's Park 11/12 2
12/13 28 5
13/14 6 1
Airdrieonians L 13/14 3

FORTUNE John
b. Tradeston 1867 d. Gorbals ?.6.1935
Clyde 91/92 8
Third Lanark

FOSTER Alex

Denbeath Star
Montrave U
Raith R 15/16 24

FOSTER David

Cowdenbeath 02/03
Hearts of Beath
Dundee 03/04 3
Dunfermline A

FOTHERINGHAM William
b. Larkhall
Larkhall Thistle
Airdrieonians 19/20 42
20/21 39
Dundee 21/22 42
22/23 38
23/24 35
Morton 24/25 34
25/26 33
26/27 38
St Mirren 27/28 32
28/29 13
29/30 36
30/31 37
31/32 38
32/33 7
Queen of the South 33/34 31
34/35 38
35/36 34
36/37 13

FOWLER

Cowlairs 90/91 3

FOWLER William

Motherwell 23/24 2

FOX

St Mirren 91/92 1

FOX Bernard

Bellshill A
Airdrieonians 03/04 7 2
04/05 4

FOYERS Robert 2 caps
b. Hamilton 22.6.1868 d. Glasgow 16.8.1942
Burnbank Swifts
St Bernards 89/90
Heart of Midlothian 90/91 1
91/92
92/93
St Bernards 93/94 17 1
94/95 16
Newcastle U 95/96 25 FL
96/97 9 FL
St Bernards 96/97
Clyde 97/98 4
Hamilton A 98/99 2 D2

FRAME David

Rutherglen Glencairn
Ashfield
Airdrieonians 20/21 11
Alloa A L 20/21
Dykehead 21/22
Clydebank 21/22 18
22/23 D2
23/24 35
Third Lanark 24/25
Raith R 25/26 35

FRAME James
b. Blantyre c1915
Stoneburn
Hamilton A 34/35
35/36 2

FRAME Thomas
b. Burnbank 5.9.1902 d. Paisley 17.1.1988
Burnbank A
Cowdenbeath 26/27 1
Lochgelly U L 26/27
Cowdenbeath 27/28 10
28/29 24 2
29/30 37
30/31 38 1
31/32 33 4
32/33 9 1
Manchester U 32/33 33 2 FL
33/34 18 2 FL
34/35 FL
35/36 FL
Southport 36/37 38 FL
Rhyl 37/38
Bridgnorth T

FRAME W

Third Lanark 24/25 32

FRAME William G
b. Larkhall
Larkhall Thistle
Clyde 18/19 25
19/20 42
St Bernards 20/21
Clyde 20/21 17
21/22 33
22/23 30
23/24 37
Motherwell 24/25 26
25/26 38
26/27 36
27/28 17
28/29 35
29/30 21
St Mirren T 29/30
Dunfermline A 30/31 D2
Gateshead 31/32 6 FL
Bray Unknowns 32/33 LI
33/34 LI
Linfield 34/35 IL
35/36 IL
36/37 IL
Motherwell 37/38
38/39 10

FRASER

Rangers 91/92 4 4

FRASER

St Mirren 91/92 1

FRASER

Dumbarton 16/17 1

FRASER Alexander

Clydebank Jnrs
Rangers 02/03 15 1
03/04 14
04/05 13
05/06 2

FRASER Alexander

Queen's Park 17/18 1

FRASER Alexander C

Hamilton A 32/33 1

FRASER Andrew

Dundee 12/13 1

FRASER D

Rutherglen Glencairn
Partick T 95/96 1 D2
96/97
97/98 1

FRASER David

St Bernards
Leith A 94/95 17 1
95/96 14 ? D2
Lincoln C 96/97 1 FL

FRASER James
b. c1887
Inverness Clachnacuddin
Morton 08/09 4
St Mirren

FRASER James

Clyde 09/10 1

FRASER John

Clyde 95/96 1
Morton 95/96 D2

FRASER John 1 cap
b. Dumbarton 10.11.1876 d. Stoke Newington 1.10.1952
Dumbarton 96/97 7 ? D2
Motherwell 97/98 14 ? D2
Notts Co 97/98 10 2 FL
98/99 31 3 FL
Newcastle U 99/00 30 8 FL
00/01 19 1 FL
St Mirren 01/02 18 6
Southampton 02/03 26 15 SL
03/04 22 2 SL
04/05 25 8 SL
Dundee 05/06 28 5
06/07 30 6
07/08 33 2
08/09 32 4
09/10 29 4
10/11 18 4
11/12 18 2

FRASER John

Thornliebank Jnrs
Clyde 22/23 5
Wolverhampton W T
Willenhall 23/24
Wellington St George 23/24

FRASER Joseph

Dundee 15/16 20

FRASER Robert
b. Motherwell d. S Africa c1986
Law Scotia
Albion R 28/29 D2
29/30 D2
30/31 D2
Aberdeen 31/32 21
32/33 25 1
33/34 29
34/35 36 1
35/36 37
36/37 18 1
37/38 28 1

FRASER Robert
b. Glasgow 23.1.1917
Dunoon A
Ashfield
Hibernian 37/38
38/39 34
46/47 5
Newcastle U 46/47 3 FL
47/48 20 FL
48/49 3 FL

FRASER Thomas
b. Galston
Newcastle U
Dundee
Clyde 25/26
26/27 38
27/28 38
28/29 37
Bethlehem Steel 29/30 19 ASL
Newark Americans 31S 1 ASL

FRASER William

Dumbarton 20/21 9 3

FRASER William
b. Glasgow 5.3.1905
Glasgow Ashfield
Partick T 26/27 19 6
27/28 1 1
28/29 27 7
29/30
30/31 5 2

FRASER William Clark
b. Perth 9.12.1906
Kirkcaldy
Dunipace
East Stirlingshire T
Raith R T
Northampton T 26/27 10 FL
27/28 7 4 FL
St Johnstone 28/29 1
29/30
East Stirlingshire 30/31 D2
31/32 D2
32/33 27 3

FREEBAIRN

Rangers 92/93 2

FREEBAIRN William
b. Glasgow c1875
Partick T 92/93 1 SA
93/94 18 12 D2
94/95 16 4 D2
Abercorn 95/96 14 ? D2
Leicester F 96/97 30 9 FL
97/98 14 5 FL
East Stirlingshire 98/99
Partick T 99/00 18 17 D2
00/01 9 2

FREEMAN Joseph

Shrewsbury T
Glossop 02/03 2 FL
Chester
Hamilton A 09/10 21 11
10/11
Walsall 11/12

FRENCH George
b. Lanarkshire
Shawfield Jnrs
Morton 19/20 36 27
20/21 35 25
21/22 36 28
22/23 18 15
23/24 8 2
24/25 16 1
25/26 28 12
26/27 5 2
Arthurlie 26/27 D2

FRENCH John D

Heart of Midlothian 10/11 1

FREW Archibald

Glasgow Ashfield
Liverpool T FL
Dumbarton 13/14 10

FREW James
- b. Ballochmyle 16.3.1900
- Lugar Boswell
- Lanemark 19/20
- Hurlford 20/21
- Nithsdale W 20/21
- Kilmarnock 20/21 1
- Nithsdale W L 20/21
- Kilmarnock 21/22 18 1
- Nithsdale W L 21/22
- Chelsea 22/23 14 FL
- 23/24 8 FL
- 24/25 18 FL
- 25/26 2 FL
- 26/27 FL
- Southend U 27/28 33 FL
- 28/29 23 FL
- Carlisle U 29/30 24 2 FL

FREW James Hearty
- b. Kinghorn 21.5.1892 d. Leeds 27.4.1967
- Kilsyth Emmet *
- Alloa A * 12/13
- Newcastle C
- Heart of Midlothian 14/15 5
- 15/16 12
- 16/17
- 17/18
- 18/19 1
- 19/20 2
- Leeds U 20/21 36 FL
- 21/22 23 FL
- 22/23 33 FL
- 23/24 4 FL
- Bradford C 24/25 13 FL
- 25/26 18 FL
- 26/27 17 FL

FREW John
- Hibernian 28/29 19 1

FREW John
- Newmilns
- Ayr U 29/30 2

FREW Thomas
- b. Dunfermline 1878 d. Dunfermline ?.9.1921
- Hearts of Beath
- Heart of Midlothian 98/99 2
- Hearts of Beath 98/99
- Heart of Midlothian 99/00 3
- 00/01 2
- Falkirk 01/02
- Cowdenbeath 01/02
- Hearts of Beath 02/03

FRIEL Daniel
- d. by 1911
- Vale of Leven *
- Accrington *
- Burnley * 88/89 22 FL
- 89/90 5 1 FL
- 90/91 FL
- Vale of Leven 91/92 6 1

FRIZZELL James
- Overton A
- Morton 25/26 6 1
- 26/27 13 2

FROST
- St Bernards 93/94 1

FULLARTON Alexander Sutherland
- b. Stevenston 6.6.1895
- Saltcoats V
- Celtic 16/17 1
- Stevenston U L 16/17
- Clydebank 17/18 13
- Stevenston U
- Kilmarnock 20/21 1
- Stevenston U 21/22
- Kilwinning R
- Ardeer Recreation

FULLARTON George
- Kilmarnock Rugby XI
- Kilmarnock 05/06 12
- 06/07 6
- Galston

FULLARTON William Millwright
- b. Tradeston 1882
- Vale of Leven 01/02
- Queen's Park 01/02 14
- 02/03 11
- 03/04 12
- Sunderland 03/04 2 FL
- 04/05 24 FL
- 05/06 5 FL
- Nottingham F 05/06 20 FL
- Plymouth A 06/07 34 SL
- New Brompton 07/08 SL
- 08/09 22 SL
- 09/10 4 SL

FULLER William
- Ayr U 31/32 2
- Mosspark Amateurs

FULLERTON William
- Dundee 97/98 2

FULTON (possibly William - Scottish intl)
- Abercorn 91/92 1

FULTON David
- b. Gorbals 16.10.1895
- St Marks
- Pollok A 12/13
- Kilmarnock 13/14 25
- 14/15 2
- 15/16 34 2
- 16/17 29 7
- Dumbarton Harp L 16/17
- Kilmarnock 17/18 23 9
- 18/19 7 3
- St Mirren 18/19 1 ?
- Clydebank 19/20 31 9
- 20/21 23 2
- Bo'ness 21/22 D2
- Dunfermline A 21/22 D2
- Tranmere R 21/22 9 3 FL

FULTON G
- Queen's Park 17/18 3 1

FULTON George
- Petershill
- St Johnstone 32/33 24 20
- 33/34 21 10
- 34/35 1 1
- Raith R 34/35 D2
- 35/36 D2
- 36/37 D2
- St Johnstone 37/38 2 1

FULTON James
- Vale of Bannock
- Falkirk 21/22 5

FULTON John Connell
- b. Paisley 1890 d. Paisley 8.11.1926
- Paisley Thistle
- Neilston V
- Abercorn
- Morton 10/11 29 1
- 11/12 31
- 12/13 31
- Rangers 13/14 14 1
- Morton 14/15 3
- 15/16
- 16/17
- 17/18
- 18/19
- 19/20 5
- Johnstone 20/21

FYFE
- St Mirren 92/93 3
- 93/94 10 3

FYFE Andrew
- Queen's Park 19/20 13 10
- 20/21 24 11
- 21/22 23 10
- 22/23 10 2 D2
- 23/24 12 6
- 24/25 3 1

FYFE Andrew
- b. Cambusnethan 24.10.1913
- Parkhead Jnrs
- Kilmarnock 34/35 1
- 35/36 6
- 36/37 2
- 37/38 21
- 38/39 18
- Morton 46/47 28 3
- 47/48 14
- 48/49 5
- 49/50 D2
- Newton Stewart

FYFE George
- b. Govan
- Neilston V
- Hibernian 04/05 18 2
- Watford 05/06 9 1 SL
- 06/07 29 1 SL
- 07/08 27 3 SL
- 08/09 30 SL
- 09/10 24 2 SL
- Dundee Hibs 10/11 D2
- Dumbarton 11/12 D2
- Dundee Hibs 11/12 D2
- Halifax T 11/12
- Abercorn

FYFE James
- St Anthonys
- Partick T
- Alloa A 22/23 13
- 23/24 D2
- Partick T 23/24

FYFE James
- Arthurlie
- Clydebank 23/24 3

FYFE John H 1 cap
- South Western
- Third Lanark 94/95 15 5
- 95/96 9 5
- Rangers 95/96

FYFE R
- Clyde 96/97 4

GABRIEL James
- b. c1906 d. Perth ?.6.1987
- East Fife 28/29 31 D2
- 29/30 34 1 D2
- 30/31 12 1
- Forfar A 30/31 D2
- Chelsea * 30/31 FL
- Charlton A 30/31 FL

GAFFNEY Peter
- b. Kirknewton 9.11.1897
- Loanhead Mayflower
- Bo'ness 19/20
- Hamilton A 19/20 1
- 20/21 6
- Alloa A 21/22 D2
- 22/23 1
- Dunfermline A 22/23 D2
- Doncaster R 23/24 2 FL
- Denaby U 23/24
- Barrow 24/25 17 FL
- New Brighton 24/25 7 FL
- 25/26 12 3 FL
- Coventry C 26/27 2 FL
- Ashington 27/28 FL
- Torquay U 27/28 FL
- Aldershot 27/28 7 1 SL
- 28/29 5 SL

GAILEY James
- Ayr
- Partick T 02/03 17 1
- 03/04 1
- Ayr

GALBRAITH Alexander
- St Bernards 97/98 2
- Vale of Leven 97/98
- St Bernards 98/99 15 1
- 99/00 16
- Vale of Leven

GALBRAITH Alexander

Port Glasgow A 98/99 6 ? D2
99/00 6 ? D2
00/01 14 ? D2
01/02 ? ? D2
02/03 15 7
03/04 18 8
04/05 4
Motherwell 05/06 24 10
Morton 06/07 22 6
07/08 4

GALBRAITH Alexander

St Mirren 04/05 1

GALBRAITH David

Bellshill A
Preston NE 09/10 3 FL
10/11 1 FL
11/12 FL
12/13 FL
Albion R 13/14 D2
14/15 D2
15/16
16/17
Airdrieonians 17/18 17 1

GALBRAITH H

Dumbarton 90/91 17 5
91/92 7 1

GALBRAITH Joseph S

Kilsyth Emmet
Third Lanark 28/29 3

GALL Thomas William George
b. Dennistoun 5.5.1906
Bridgetown Waverley
Clyde
Kings Park 26/27 D2
Falkirk 27/28 16 2
28/29 36 8
29/30 36 5
30/31 38 13
31/32 34 5
32/33 31 4
Aberdeen 33/34 22 3
West Ham U 34/35 1 FL
St Mirren 35/36
36/37 23 5

GALLACHER

Vale of Leven 90/91 3 1

GALLACHER Private

Aberdeen 15/16 9

GALLACHER Bernard
b. West Greenock 1894 K.I.A. ?.6.1916
Morton 06/07 1
07/08 11
Dumbarton Harp

GALLACHER Hans
b. Inverkeithing c1910
Anstruther R
Rangers T
Arbroath 28/29 15 6 D2
29/30 37 8 D2
Dunfermline A 30/31 D2
Leith A 30/31 12
31/32 5
Shelbourne
Rosyth Dockyard Rec

GALLACHER Hugh
b. Galston 11.5.1870 d. Girvan 20.5.1941
Maybole
Celtic 89/90
90/91 1
Preston NE 90/91 16 6 FL
91/92 26 3 FL
92/93 12 2 FL
Lanemark
Sheffield U 92/93 9 4 FL
93/94 29 4 FL
Leicester F 94/95 25 6 FL
95/96 22 5 FL
Rossendale
Nelson
New Brompton 97/98 22 2 SL
98/99 6 1 SL

GALLACHER Hugh Kilpatrick 20 caps
b. Bellshill 2.2.1903 d. Gateshead 11.6.1957
Tannockside A
Hatton Rigg Thistle
Bellshill Academy
Bellshill A
Queen of the South T 20/21
Airdrieonians 21/22 11 7
22/23 18 9
23/24 34 33
24/25 32 32
25/26 16 10
Newcastle U 25/26 19 23 FL
26/27 38 36 FL
27/28 32 21 FL
28/29 33 24 FL
29/30 38 29 FL
Chelsea 30/31 30 14 FL
31/32 36 24 FL
32/33 36 19 FL
33/34 23 13 FL
34/35 7 2 FL
Derby Co 34/35 27 23 FL
35/36 24 15 FL
Notts Co 36/37 32 25 FL
37/38 13 7 FL
Grimsby T 37/38 12 3 FL
Gateshead 38/39 31 18 FL
39/40 3 FL

GALLACHER James
b. Paisley
Johnstone U
Clydebank 24/25 D2
25/26 38
26/27 D2
Ayr U 27/28 D2
28/29
Canada
St Mirren 29/30 2

GALLACHER Patrick

Tottenham H 03/04 SL
04/05 SL
Luton T 05/06 SL
06/07 SL
Partick T 07/08 26

GALLACHER Patrick
b. Springburn 9.1.1913 d. Hastings ?.6.1983
St Agnes Welfare
Dunoon A
Millwall 33/34 FL
34/35 FL
Third Lanark 35/36 37 9
36/37 2
Blackburn R 36/37 25 FL
37/38 1 FL
Bournemouth 38/39 14 1 FL
39/40 3 2 FL
46/47 18 FL
47/48 3 2 FL
Weymouth
Dundalk 50/51 LI

GALLACHER Robert Linton
b. Stevenston 22.10.1917
Ardeer Recreation
Kilmarnock 35/36 2
36/37 5
37/38 10 2
38/39 3
Alloa A L 38/39 D2

GALLACHER William

Renton
Vale of Leven
Dumbarton 17/18 3
Renton
Helensburgh
Vale of Leven 25/26 D3

GALLAGHER Hugh Samuel
b. Clydebank 1901
St Anthonys
Clyde 23/24 31 2
24/25 D2
25/26 D2
Crystal Palace 26/27 24 FL
27/28 11 FL
Clydebank
Leith A

GALLAGHER James
b. Coatbridge 3.10.1910
Coatbridge Emerald
Shettleston Celtic
Celtic 29/30 2
30/31
Belfast Celtic L 30/31 IL
Clydebank L 30/31
Celtic 31/32
Hamilton A L 31/32
Nithsdale W 32/33
Bo'ness 33/34 D2
Waterford 33/34 LI

GALLAGHER Patrick
b. Johnstone 25.4.1865 d. Glasgow 7.6.1899
Johnstone R
Cowlairs
Hibernian
Celtic 88/89
89/90
90/91 15 1
91/92 12
92/93 4

GALLAGHER Patrick
b. Johnstone 15.5.1871
Johnstone
Celtic 92/93 2 1
Johnstone

GALLAGHER Patrick
b. Ramelton 16.4.1893 d. Scotstoun 17.6.1953
Renfrew St James
Clydebank
Celtic 11/12 9 2
12/13 33 10
13/14 37 21
14/15 33 15
15/16 37 27
16/17 28 22
17/18 33 17
18/19 29 14
19/20 22 11
20/21 39 10
21/22 39 17
Rangers L 21/22
Celtic 22/23 31 8
23/24 35 5
24/25 28 7
New Bedford Whalers 25/26
Celtic 25/26 1
Falkirk 26/27 26 5
27/28 26 3
28/29 14 2
Derry C 29/30 IL
Falkirk 29/30 12 2
30/31 31 6
31/32 20 2

GALLOGLEY Thomas
b. Larkhall 4.4.1891 d. Coatbridge 26.8.1976
Bedlay Jnrs
Plymouth A 13/14 2 1 SL
14/15 34 8 SL
Royal Albert 15/16
Motherwell 16/17 5
Albion R
Airdrieonians 18/19 8 ?
Vale of Leven * 18/19
Plymouth A 19/20 27 3 SL
20/21 22 2 FL
21/22 31 7 FL
22/23 9 FL
Exeter C 23/24 21 1 FL
Queen of the South

GALLOWAY David Wilson
b. Kirkcaldy 6.5.1905
Wellesley Jnrs
Raith R 27/28 11 3
28/29 28 5
29/30 D2
30/31 D2
Aberdeen 31/32 14 1
Preston NE 32/33 21 FL
33/34 10 1 FL
Port Vale 34/35 12 FL
Carlisle U 35/36 38 4 FL
36/37 42 5 FL
37/38 29 2 FL
Clapton Orient 38/39 2 FL
Tunbridge Wells R

GALLOWAY James B

Haywood Jnrs
Third Lanark 13/14 6 1
14/15
15/16
16/17
17/18 1 ?

GALLOWAY John

Dumbarton Harp
Hibernian 18/19 5 ?

GALLOWAY John A
b. Grangemouth 29.10.1918
Grange R
Rangers 34/35
35/36
36/37
37/38 2
38/39 2
Chelsea

GALLOWAY Thomas
b. Kilmarnock 1887
Juvenile A
Kilmarnock A
Kilmarnock 05/06 8 3
Hurlford L 05/06
Arthurlie L 05/06 D2
Ayr 06/07 D2
Stockport Co 07/08 11 FL
08/09 21 FL
09/10 22 FL
10/11 22 FL
Preston NE 11/12 15 FL
12/13 9 FL
Portsmouth 12/13 3 SL
13/14 ? SL

GALLOWAY W

Queen's Park 21/22 1

GALT Alexander
b. c1916
Arthurlie 36/37
Partick T 37/38 1
Arthurlie 38/39

GALT James

Ardeer Thistle
Beith
St Mirren 06/07 1
Beith

GALT James Hill 2 caps
b. Saltcoats 11.8.1885 d. 17.11.1935
Stevenston
Ardrossan Winton R
Ardeer Thistle
Rangers 06/07 21
07/08 27 2
08/09 24
09/10 25
10/11 18 1
11/12 26 2
12/13 27
13/14 17
Everton 14/15 32 2 FL
15/16
Partick T 16/17 3

GANE George Herbert
b. Kingswood ?.2.1886 d. Kingswood 19.6.1967
Workington
Bradford C 10/11 1 FL
11/12 18 FL
12/13 4 FL
13/14 12 FL
Airdrieonians 13/14 11
14/15 26
Bristol C * 19/20 1 FL
Douglas *
Bristol R * 20/21 1 FL

GANSON

Abercorn 91/92 2 1

GARDEN William Brownie
b. Kilsyth 20.9.1904
Kilsyth R
Arbroath 24/25 2 D2
Celtic 24/25 1
Alloa A L 25/26 D2
Nithsdale W L 25/26 D3
Kilsyth R 26/27
Kings Park 27/28 D2
Kilsyth R

GARDINER Andrew

Milnathorn
Cowdenbeath 33/34 1

GARDINER Archibald
b. Penicuik 17.3.1913
Penicuik A
Burnbank A
Clapton Orient T FL
Heart of Midlothian 31/32 13 8
32/33 9 6
33/34 2
Leicester C 33/34 15 10 FL
34/35 3 1 FL
Wrexham 34/35 24 10 FL
35/36 21 2 FL
Hamilton A 36/37 11 4
Olympique Lille T 36/37
Brideville 37/38 LI
Morton T 37/38
Inverness Thistle

GARDINER George
b. Edinburgh
Blantyre Celtic
Clydebank 26/27 D2
27/28
28/29 D2
Dundee U 29/30 38
30/31 33 4 D2
31/32 33 1
32/33 30 1 D2
Leith A 33/34 D2

GARDINER Graham

Queen's Park 21/22 1

GARDINER Henry
b. Kilmarnock 1868 d. Hamilton 24.6.1922
Renton
Bolton W 90/91 12 1 FL
91/92 26 1 FL
92/93 24 2 FL
93/94 18 1 FL
Rangers 94/95 2

GARDINER James

Airdriehill Shamrock
Partick T 16/17 10
17/18 5

GARDINER John
b. Glasgow
Queen's Park 31/32 24
32/33 33
33/34 26
34/35 25
35/36 33
36/37 29

GARDINER John Graham
b. Hamilton 14.11.1904
Blantyre V
Motherwell 25/26 6
Coventry C 26/27 36 FL
27/28 15 FL
Wolverhampton W 28/29 3 FL
Norwich C 28/29 1 FL
Kettering T 29/30
Workington 30/31
31/32
Barrow 32/33 2 FL
Lancaster T

GARDINER Leslie Lickley
b. Dundee 10.8.1918
Broughty Ferry Ex-Servicemen
Hibernian 36/37 15 5
Torquay U 37/38 14 5 FL
Clapton Orient

GARDINER Peter

Falkirk 19/20 1
20/21 11
St Johnstone 21/22 27 D2
22/23
23/24
24/25
Forfar A 25/26 D2
St Johnstone 26/27 2

GARDINER Robert
b. Motherwell 1895
Blantyre V
Motherwell 17/18 24 7
18/19 31 4
19/20 33 4
20/21 24
Reading 21/22 30 4 FL
22/23 41 13 FL
23/24 28 6 FL
Kings Park 24/25 D2
East Stirlingshire 25/26 D2

GARDINER Thomas

Heart of Midlothian 95/96 1
96/97

GARDINER Thomas L

Falkirk 19/20 2 1

GARDINER William
b. Earnock
Hamilton A 12/13 7 1
St Johnstone 13/14 18 7 D2

GARDINER William A

Parkhead
Partick T 09/10 27 11
10/11 30 13
11/12 23 5
12/13 15 4
13/14 17 2
14/15 17 1

GARDINER William S

Queen's Park 21/22 9

GARDNER

Abercorn 96/97 3

GARDNER Andrew
b. Oban 26.9.1877
Kilbarchan V
Kilbarchan
Clyde 95/96 6
96/97 17 4
97/98 10
98/99 4
99/00 12
00/01 18
Grimsby T 01/02 31 4 FL
Newcastle U 02/03 18 3 FL
Bolton W 03/04 8 1 FL
Brighton 04/05 22 9 SL
QPR 05/06 5 SL
06/07 SL
Carlisle U 07/08
Johnstone 08/09
Carlisle U

GARDNER David Richmond 1 cap
b. Glasgow 31.3.1873 d. Longcliffe 5.11.1931
Third Lanark 95/96
96/97 17
97/98 16 1
98/99 15
Newcastle U 99/00 34 1 FL
00/01 29 1 FL
01/02 14 FL
Grimsby T 02/03 27 FL
03/04 22 FL
West Ham U 04/05 29 SL
05/06 34 SL
06/07 14 SL
Croydon Common 07/08 9 SL
08/09 SL
09/10 2 SL

GARLAND Charles

Dunfermline A 32/33 D2
Falkirk T 32/33
Dunfermline A 33/34 D2
34/35 5
Cowdenbeath 34/35 D2

GARRETT Archibald
b. Douglas 16.3.1886 d. 18.11.1959
Glenbuck Cherrypickers
Hamilton A 06/07 11 1
07/08 8
08/09 6
Millwall 09/10 40 4 SL
10/11 21 SL
Hamilton A 11/12 29
12/13 26
Millwall 13/14 22 SL
14/15 23 SL
Hamilton A 15/16 17 1
Vale of Leven 16/17
Heart of Midlothian 17/18 11
18/19 6

GARRETT Archibald Campbell

b. Lesmagahow 17.6.1919 d. Bristol 10.4.1994

Burnbank A					
Lesmagahow Jnrs					
Larkhall Saints					
Airdrieonians		35/36			
		36/37			D2
Preston NE		37/38	2	2	FL
Heart of Midlothian		38/39	18	17	
		46/47	4	3	
Northampton T		46/47	35	26	FL
		47/48	16	9	FL
Birmingham C		47/48	8	1	FL
		48/49	10	4	FL
Northampton T		48/49	21	8	FL
		49/50	11	7	FL
		50/51	11	1	FL
Wisbech T					
Holbeach U					

GARRETT Charles

Cadzow Oak					
Airdrieonians		04/05	6		
Albion R		05/06			D2
		06/07			D2
Royal Albert		07/08			

GARRITY John

b. Kirkintilloch 1897

Pollok Jnrs					
Kilmarnock		19/20	2		
		20/21	9		
		21/22	6		
Queen of the South	L	21/22			
Pollok Jnrs		22/23			
Vale of Leven		23/24			D2

GARRY Edward

b. Renton 7.3.1885 d. Derby 28.5.1955

Dumbarton Harp					
Celtic		04/05			
Ayr	L	05/06			D2
Celtic		05/06	2		
		06/07	3	1	
Stenhousemuir	L	06/07			
Derby Co		07/08	30	8	FL
		08/09	23	4	FL
		09/10	7	3	FL
		10/11	35	2	FL
		11/12	22		FL
		12/13	3		FL
Bradford PA		13/14	36		FL
		14/15	8		FL
Dumbarton		15/16	17		
		16/17	21	3	

GARSIDE William

Third Lanark		94/95	11	3	
		95/96	16	4	
		96/97			
Bury		97/98	5		FL

GARVIE Edwin S

d. Germany 15.10.1915

Queen's Park		11/12	9		
		12/13	33	1	
		13/14	37	6	
		14/15	6		

GAULT James

Victoria Thistle					
Abergeldie					
Aberdeen		05/06	28		
		06/07	22		
West Ham U		07/08	35		SL
		08/09	14		SL

GAVIGAN Peter

b. Gorbals 11.12.1897 d. Dundee 2.3.1977

Vale of Clyde					
Fulham		20/21	10		FL
		21/22	22	1	FL
		22/23	7		FL
		23/24	25		FL
		24/25	7		FL
Clapton Orient		25/26	34	1	FL
		26/27	16	9	FL
Bilston U		27/28			
St Johnstone		27/28	31	5	
		28/29	37	2	
		29/30	9		
Dundee		30/31	29		
		31/32	19	1	
		31/32			
Montrose		32/33			D2
Dundee U		32/33	13		D2

GAVIN

Heart of Midlothian		29/30	1		

GAVIN Charles

b. Coatbridge

Glasgow Ashfield					
Aberdeen		33/34	3		
		34/35	6		
		35/36	5		
Arbroath		36/37	19		
		37/38	38		
		38/39	37		

GAY John O

St Rochs					
St Johnstone		23/24	16		D2
		24/25	3		

GEATONS Charles

b. Lochgelly 16.7.1907 d. Lochgelly 20.6.1970

Lochgelly Celtic					
Celtic		27/28			
		28/29	2		
		29/30	23		
		30/31	29	1	
		31/32	26		
		32/33	34	2	
		33/34	14	2	
		34/35	31		
		35/36	34	1	
		36/37	35	1	
		37/38	20	2	
		38/39	30	3	

GEBBIE Alexander Allan

b. Muirkirk 11.11.1901

Muirkirk Ex-Service					
Kilmarnock	T	21/22			
Muirkirk A					
St Mirren		24/25	17	4	
		25/26	14	8	
		26/27	17	5	
		27/28	14	3	
		28/29	27	11	
		29/30	29	5	
		30/31	25	5	
		31/32	38	4	
		32/33	37	1	
		33/34	28	1	
		34/35	33		
		35/36			D2
Aldershot		36/37	12		FL

GEDDES James

b. Stane Shotts 1902 d. ?.10.1937

East Benhar					
Shotts U					
Dykehead					
Beith					
St Mirren		20/21	3		
Albion R		20/21	1		
		21/22	6	1	
		22/23	30		
		23/24			D2
		24/25			D2
		25/26			D2
Bristol C		26/27	3		FL
		27/28	2	1	FL
		28/29			FL
Morton		29/30	12	1	
Brechin C		30/31			D2

GEDDES John

b. Glencraig 11.4.1908 d. 1937

Lochgelly Celtic					
Celtic		27/28	2		
		28/29			
Gillingham		29/30	10	1	FL
Rhyl		29/30			
		30/31			
		31/32			
Tunbridge Wells R		32/33			
Bolton W	T	33/34			FL
Rotherham U	T	33/34			FL
East Stirlingshire		33/34			D2
		34/35			D2
Newry T		35/36			IL

GEDDES T

Falkirk		12/13	1		

GEDDES William G D

Queen's Park		35/36	1		

GEEHRIN Patrick

b. Musselburgh c1889

Bonnyrigg Thistle					
Celtic		10/11	1		
Alloa A	L	10/11			
Bristol C					
Alloa A					
Armadale					

GEEKIE James

Busby Cartvale					
Morton		23/24	5	1	

GEMMELL

Third Lanark		92/93	3		

GEMMELL David

Glasgow Perthshire					
Ayr U		36/37	30	16	D2
		37/38	31	4	
		38/39	31	8	

GEMMELL James

b. Glasgow 17.11.1880

Duntochter Hibs					
Clyde		00/01	9		D2
Sunderland		00/01	3		FL
		01/02	31	8	FL
		02/03	22	8	FL
		03/04	29	10	FL
		04/05	32	6	FL
		05/06	29	6	FL
		06/07	30	1	FL
Stoke		07/08	11	2	FL
Leeds C		07/08	16	3	FL
		08/09	28	8	FL
		09/10	23	3	FL
Sunderland		10/11	21	1	FL
		11/12	16	2	FL
Third Lanark		11/12	1	1	
		12/13	14		
West Stanley					

GEMMELL Robert

Prestwick Glenburn R					
Glasgow Ashfield					
Ayr U		31/32	5		

GEMMELL Thomas

Hibernian		98/99	7	4	

GEOGHAN John J

Queen's Park		26/27	1		

GEORGE Frank

Dundee		93/94	1	1	

GERRAND Wastel C

b. Ayr

Ayr Fort					
Motherwell		26/27			
		27/28	3		
		28/29	1		
Montrose		29/30			D2
		30/31			D2
		31/32			D2
		32/33			D2
		33/34			D2
		34/35			D2
Arbroath		35/36	2		

GERRARD John

Dundee		98/99	9	1	
Forfar A					

GETGOOD George

b. Coylton 15.11.1892 d. Kidderminster 22.7.1970

Ayr Seaside					
Ayr U		12/13			D2
		13/14			
Reading		14/15			SL
Ayr U		15/16	13	1	
Reading		19/20			SL
		20/21	37	1	FL
Willenhall Swifts		21/22			
Birmingham		21/22	10		FL
Southampton		21/22	11		FL
		22/23	24	1	FL
Wolverhampton W		22/23	17		FL
		23/24	36	1	FL
		24/25	2		FL
Kidderminster H		24/25			
		25/26			
Aberdare A		26/27	5		FL
Shrewsbury T		26/27			
Gala Fairydean		27/28			
Bathgate		27/28			D2
Bo'ness		28/29			D2
Nuneaton T					
Midland Red Sports					

GHEE Thomas
b. Kilmarnock 1873
Kilmarnock
Darwen 93/94 8 FL
94/95 11 FL
Kilmarnock 94/95
95/96
St Mirren 95/96 2
96/97 17 1
Newcastle U 97/98 28 FL
98/99 32 FL
99/00 28 1 FL
00/01 32 2 FL
01/02 9 FL

GIBB George
b. Cambusnethan c1891 K.I.A., France 7.6.1917
Cambuslang R
Third Lanark 14/15 28
15/16 9

GIBB Henry

Rangers
Morton 99/00 14 ? D2
00/01 3
Stenhousemuir

GIBB Robert

Clyde 95/96 1
96/97

GIBB William

Heart of Midlothian 16/17 5
17/18 1

GIBB William

Dundee Stobswell
Arbroath 27/28 1 2 D2
Dundee 28/29 8 3
Arbroath L 28/29 28 35 D2
Dundee 29/30
Arbroath 29/30 D2
30/31 6 4 D2
31/32 D2
32/33 D2
Montrose 33/34 D2

GIBB William Watson

Clyde 97/98 3

GIBBON James

Ayr U 17/18 12 ?

GIBBON Thomas
b. West Hartlepool 24.3.1891 d. Wolverhampton 12.4.1975
Hartlepool St Josephs
Houghton R
Glossop 13/14 4 FL
Merthyr T 14/15 ? ? SL
19/20 36 SL
Dundee 20/21 41
21/22
Luton T 22/23 39 FL
23/24 30 FL
QPR
Mid Rhondda
Torquay U

GIBBONS Michael

Lumphinnans Swifts
Falkirk 10/11
11/12 4
12/13 10 1
13/14 30 6
14/15 26 6
15/16 36 5
16/17 17 4
17/18 1 ?
Cowdenbeath 17/18
Falkirk 18/19 6 ?
East Fife

GIBBONS Thomas

Third Lanark 96/97 1
97/98 4
98/99 16 5
99/00 15 5
Partick T 00/01 13 1

GIBBS Thomas Smith
b. Dennistoun 1902 d. Springburn 26.8.1932
Sighthill
Glasgow Ashfield
Queen's Park 23/24 18
24/25 38
25/26 17
Dunfermline A 25/26 D2
Partick T 26/27 2

GIBSON

Clyde 96/97 1

GIBSON A

Musselburgh A
Rangers 12/13 3

GIBSON Adam Paton
b. Kilmarnock 3.6.1890
Cronberry Eglinton
Rangers 10/11 6 5
11/12
Portsmouth 12/13 1 SL
13/14 1 SL
St Mirren 13/14 26 6
York C 14/15
Chesterfield Municipal 19/20
Rotherham T 20/21
Chesterfield 21/22 1 FL

GIBSON Andrew
b. Camlachie 1.7.1890
Kelvinhaugh
Strathclyde
Southampton 11/12 18 4 SL
Celtic T 11/12 2
Leeds C 12/13 5 FL

GIBSON David
b. Kilmarnock 29.9.1895 d. Kilmarnock 26.9.1964
Shawfield Jnrs
Kilmarnock 19/20 42 1
20/21 42
21/22 40 1
22/23 35
23/24 38
24/25 29
25/26 10
Preston NE 25/26 13 FL
Springfield Babes 26/27 13 ASL
Fall River Marksmen 27/28 13 ASL
Providence Clamdiggers 27/28 27 ASL
28/29 48 ASL
29A 15 ASL
30A 27 ASL
Fall River 31S 11 ASL
Queen of the South
Galston

GIBSON Frederick Thomas Bertrand
b. Pilgrims Rest (SA) 8.12.1888 d. Nuneaton 15.3.1952
Bablake School
Lichfield GS
Iona Star
Bedworth T
Sunderland Royal R
Sunderland 09/10 2 FL
Raith R 10/11 25 ? D2
Dunfermline A 11/12
Raith R 12/13 30 10
13/14 33 8
14/15 37 11
15/16 14 3
16/17 24 6
Heart of Midlothian 17/18 27 3
Coventry C 19/20 28 2 FL
20/21 21 2 FL
21/22 5 1 FL
Nuneaton T
Atherstone T
Collycroft U

GIBSON George Bennett
b. Hamilton 29.9.1903 d. London 1990
Dundee 22/23 2 1
23/24
St Johnstone L 23/24 9 2 D2
Dundee 24/25 3
Hamilton A 24/25 9 4
25/26 37 8
26/27 27 4
Bolton W 26/27 14 9 FL
27/28 38 6 FL
28/29 40 17 FL
29/30 42 13 FL
30/31 35 12 FL
31/32 27 8 FL
Chelsea 32/33 13 5 FL
33/34 32 9 FL
34/35 23 1 FL
35/36 33 4 FL
36/37 19 3 FL
37/38 9 1 FL

GIBSON Harry
b. Port Glasgow 2.6.1905 d. Larkhall 12.6.2001
Port Glasgow Jnrs
Partick T 27/28 24 21
28/29 21 10
Mansfield T 29/30 34 29 ML
Morton 30/31
East Fife 31/32 D2

GIBSON James Burton
b. Kirkcaldy 24.6.1889 K.I.A., Gallipoli 5.9.1915
St Andrews University
Raith R 11/12 D2
12/13 17 2

GIBSON James Davidson 8 caps
b. Larkhall 12.6.1901 d. Erdington 1.1.1978
Kirkintilloch Rob Roy
Glasgow Ashfield
Larkhall Thistle
Partick T 21/22 24 3
22/23 22 9
23/24 30 9
24/25 29 6
25/26 34 6
26/27 29 11
Aston Villa 26/27 1 FL
27/28 24 1 FL
28/29 5 2 FL
29/30 26 1 FL
30/31 39 2 FL
31/32 34 1 FL
32/33 38 3 FL
33/34 27 FL
34/35 9 FL
35/36 10 FL

GIBSON Neil 14 caps
b. Larkhall 23.2.1873
Larkhall Thistle
Larkhall Jnrs
Royal Albert
Rangers 94/95 8
95/96 17 1
96/97 17 2
97/98 15 1
98/99 18 3
99/00 16 1
00/01 19 1
01/02 13 1
02/03 17 1
03/04 17 1
Partick T 04/05 20 1
05/06 18 3
06/07 27 1
07/08 23
08/09 14 1
Wishaw Thistle 09/10
Royal Albert 10/11

GIBSON Neil
b. Larkhall
Clyde 23/24 22
24/25 D2
25/26 D2
26/27 36 5
27/28 33 2
28/29 27 4
29/30 34 2
30/31 30
31/32 26 1
32/33 5

GIBSON Robert

Alloa A 06/07
East Stirlingshire L 06/07
Falkirk 07/08 32
08/09
Morton 09/10 24
Falkirk 10/11 8

GIBSON Robert J
b. Glasgow
Vale of Clyde
Clydebank 19/20 2
Vale of Leven 20/21
21/22 D2

GIBSON Robert James
b. Scotswood 1887
Scotswood
Bury 08/09 14 1 FL
Crystal Palace 09/10 2 1 SL
Middlesbrough 10/11 28 4 FL
Newcastle U 11/12 2 FL
Lincoln C 12/13 1 FL
Chesterfield T 13/14
Third Lanark 14/15 9 2

GIBSON Thomas
Morton 06/07 3

GIBSON Thomas
Heart of Midlothian 16/17 9 4

GIBSON William
b. Flemington 1868 d. Lincoln 15.9.1911
Flemington Thistle
Cambuslang 87/88
Sunderland 88/89
89/90
90/91 8 FL
91/92 21 FL
92/93 30 4 FL
93/94 18 2 FL
Rangers 94/95 17 1
Sunderland 95/96 16 1 FL
Notts Co 96/97 29 FL
97/98 12 FL
Lincoln C 98/99 25 FL
99/00 30 FL
00/01 30 FL
01/02 29 FL
02/03 17 1 FL

GIBSON William
Langlands Thistle
Kilmarnock Rugby XI
Kilmarnock 02/03 12 2
03/04 17 4
04/05 4 1
Luton T 05/06 SL
Hurlford 05/06
Kilmarnock 05/06 2
06/07
Ayr Parkhouse 07/08 D2
Barrow 07/08
Hurlford
Lanemark

GIBSON William
Port Glasgow A
Morton 20/21 39
21/22 15
22/23 2
Dumbarton 23/24 D2
24/25 D2
25/26 D2
Fall River Marksmen 26/27 28 ASL
Boston Wonder Workers 27/28 37 ASL
28/29 33 ASL
Bethlehem Steel 29/30 16 ASL
Glentoran 30/31 IL
31/32 IL
32/33 IL
33/34 IL

GIBSON William Alexander
b. Edinburgh 1864 d. Edinburgh ?.10.1936
Heart of Midlothian 85/86
86/87
87/88
88/89
89/90
90/91 3

GIBSON William Muir
b. Larkhall 21.7.1896
Larkhall Thistle
Cadzow St Annes
St Anthonys
Ayr U 19/20 9
20/21 31 2
21/22 40 2
22/23 38
Newcastle U 23/24 20 1 FL
24/25 34 FL
25/26 22 1 FL
26/27 32 FL
27/28 10 FL
28/29 6 FL
Inverness Clachnacuddin

GIFFORD James
Bedlay Jnrs
Partick T 14/15 9
Airdrieonians 15/16 2
Albion R

GILBERT James
Valleyfield A
Edinburgh Civil Service
Heart of Midlothian 16/17 4 3

GILBERT James
Queen's Park 23/24 1
24/25
25/26 10

GILCHRIST George B
Clyde
Rangers 04/05 1
Partick T 04/05 14
05/06 21
06/07 18 1
Clyde 07/08 9
Partick T 08/09 1

GILCHRIST John Wotherspoon 1 cap
b. Tollcross 30.3.1899 d. ?.2.1950
Strathclyde
St Anthonys
Celtic 19/20 31 2
20/21 32
21/22 41 2
22/23 23 2
Preston NE 22/23 17 FL
23/24 2 FL
Carlisle U L 23/24
Third Lanark 24/25 8
Dunfermline A L 24/25 D2
Bathgate L 24/25 D2
Brooklyn Wanderers 25/26 6 ASL
Chicago Bricklayers
J & P Coats 26/27 3 ASL

GILCHRIST Thomas
b. Larkhall 29.12.1885
Ashgill R
Shettleston T
Third Lanark 05/06 5
06/07 16 5
07/08 19 3
Heart of Midlothian 07/08 8 2
Rangers 08/09 2
09/10 13 4
Kilmarnock 10/11 26 5
Motherwell 11/12 29 9
12/13 28 5
13/14 29 10
Rangers 14/15
Dumbarton 15/16 19 2
Celtic 19/20
East Stirlingshire 19/20
Kings Park 20/21
Bo'ness 21/22 3 1 D2
Clackmannan 21/22 D2

GILCHRIST William S
Rothesay Royal V
Morton 03/04 8 5
Queen's Park 04/05 4 1
05/06
06/07 1

GILDEA Harry
b. Falkirk 1890 K.I.A. 9.4.1917
Lochgelly St Patricks
Hibernian 08/09 6 3
Grimsby T 09/10 3 FL
Bristol C 10/11 1 FL
Lochgelly U 11/12
East Fife 12/13
Lochgelly U 13/14
Dumbarton 13/14 27 4
14/15
Lochgelly U 15/16

GILDEA Peter
b. 1884 d. New Monkland 5.11.1940
Lochgelly R
Lochgelly U 02/03
03/04
Cowdenbeath 04/05
Airdrieonians 04/05 7 1
05/06 15 2
06/07 10 5
Bury 06/07 20 1 FL
07/08 24 3 FL
08/09 FL
Lochgelly U 09/10

GILDEA William Franklyn
b. Broxburn ?.11.1884 d. Scotland
Lochgelly St Patricks
Falkirk 09/10 1
Bradford C 10/11 7 FL
Birmingham 11/12 18 1 FL
Belfast Celtic 11/12 IL

GILFEATHER Edward
b. Auchterderan 2.6.1903
Glencraig Celtic
Cowdenbeath 22/23 D2
Celtic 22/23
Ayr U L 22/23
Celtic 23/24
Dundee Hibernian L 23/24 24 3 D2
L 24/25 34 1 D2
Celtic 25/26 3 1
Alloa A L 25/26 D2
Hibernian 26/27 22
27/28 32 3
28/29 38 1
29/30 17
30/31 15
Clydebank 31/32
32/33
Leith A 33/34 D2

GILFILLAN David
Renton 93/94 3 1
94/95 8 ? D2
95/96 13 ? D2

GILFILLAN John
b. Townhill 29.9.1897 d. Portsmouth 2.1.1976
Woodend Juveniles
Musselburgh Bruntonians
Inverkeithing U
Heart of Midlothian 20/21
21/22 15
22/23 8
23/24 1
East Stirlingshire L 23/24 D3
Heart of Midlothian 24/25 1
25/26 3
26/27 20
East Fife L 26/27 D2
Heart of Midlothian 27/28 35
28/29 1
Portsmouth 28/29 24 FL
29/30 42 FL
30/31 42 FL
31/32 42 FL
32/33 36 FL
33/34 42 FL
34/35 40 FL
35/36 42 FL
36/37 21 FL
QPR 37/38 21 FL
Portsmouth Electricity

GILGUN Patrick
b. West Shotts 30.12.1901 d. Carfin 26.9.1981
Newmains
Law Scotia
Celtic 23/24 3 1
Vale of Leven L 23/24 D2
Celtic 24/25
East Stirlingshire L 24/25 D2
Brighton 25/26 3 3 FL
Norwich C 26/27 12 4 FL
Sittingbourne
Lloyds

GILHOOLEY

Motherwell		16/17	2		

GILHOOLY Michael 1 cap

b. Glencraig 26.11.1895

Glencraig Celtic					
Celtic	T	13/14			
Abercorn		13/14			D2
Vale of Leven					
Clydebank		18/19	26		
		19/20	31	1	
Hull C		20/21	38		FL
		21/22	27	1	FL
Sunderland		21/22	4		FL
		22/23	6		FL
		23/24	10		FL
Retired		24/25			
Bradford C		25/26	30		FL
		26/27	22		FL
QPR		27/28	9		FL
Troon A					

GILHOOLY Patrick

b. Draffan 6.7.1876 d. Cleland 20.2.1907

Vale of Avon					
Larkhall Thistle					
Cambuslang Hibs					
Celtic		96/97	4	1	
		97/98	15	8	
		98/99	11	1	
		99/00	15	9	
		00/01	1		
Sheffield U		00/01	15	4	FL
Tottenham H		01/02	10		SL
		02/03	7	2	SL
		03/04	1		SL
Brighton		04/05	15	5	SL

GILLAN J

Dumbarton		92/93	5		

GILLAN John

Dumbarton		95/96	9		
		96/97	12	?	D2

GILLAN John

b. Ardrossan 22.10.1917

Ardrossan Winton R					
Kilmarnock		37/38	1		
Ardeer Recreation					
Irvine Meadow					

GILLESPIE

St Mirren		92/93	2		

GILLESPIE A

Queen's Park		01/02	1		

GILLESPIE Alexander T

b. Denny

Denny A					
Alloa A		10/11			
		11/12			
Cowdenbeath		12/13			D2
		13/14			D2
		14/15			D2
		15/16			
		16/17			
		17/18			
Ayr U		18/19	28		
		19/20	40	2	
		20/21	26		
Ton Pentre		21/22			
Aberdare A		22/23	32		FL
Ayr U					
Ashton National					

GILLESPIE Frank E

Battlefield					
Clydebank		21/22	7		
Queen's Park		22/23	10		D2
		23/24	1		
		24/25	15		
		25/26	6		
		26/27	4		
		27/28	8		

GILLESPIE James 1 cap

b. Scotland d. Bearsden ?.8.1932

Morton					
Sunderland		90/91	2	3	FL
Sunderland A		91/92			
Sunderland		92/93	23	10	FL
		93/94	24	10	FL
		94/95	26	12	FL
		95/96	25	5	FL
		96/97	29	8	FL
Third Lanark		97/98	14	7	
		98/99	17	3	
		99/00	1		
Ayr					

GILLESPIE James

b. 1886

Buckhaven Jnrs					
Third Lanark		07/08	2		
QPR		08/09	1		SL
Motherwell		09/10	17		
Distillery		10/11			IL

GILLESPIE John

Queen's Park					
Dunblane		01/02			
Partick T		01/02			
		02/03			
		03/04	3		

GILLESPIE John

b. Annick Lodge

Irvine Meadow					
Kilmarnock		36/37	3		
		37/38	6	4	
		38/39			
Alloa A	L	38/39			D2
Hurlford		46/47			
Coleraine		46/47			

GILLESPIE Matthew

b. Strathclyde 24.12.1869

Glasgow Thistle					
Blackburn R		92/93	6	1	FL
Accrington					
Strathclyde					
Leith A		94/95	14	4	
Lincoln C		95/96	23	8	FL
		96/97	8	1	FL
Newton Heath		96/97	15	2	FL
		97/98	20	3	FL
		98/99	28	8	FL
		99/00	10	5	FL

GILLESPIE Robert 4 caps

b. Kilsyth 28.4.1901 d. 11.6.1960

Battlefield					
Queen's Park Strollers					
Queen's Park		19/20	7		
		20/21	38	3	
		21/22	41	3	
		22/23	36	6	D2
		23/24	37	2	
		24/25	35	17	
		25/26	34	4	
		26/27	34	10	
		27/28	27	4	
		28/29	35	10	
		29/30	31	3	
		30/31	29	2	
		31/32	33	8	
		32/33	11	2	

GILLESPIE Thomas Bennet

b. Girvan 28.2.1901

Hurlford					
Queen of the South		22/23			
Hamilton A		23/24	20	1	
Queen of the South		24/25			D3
Preston NE		25/26			FL
Bethlehem Steel		26/27	32	33	ASL
		27/28	43	28	ASL
		28/29	6	2	ESL
		29/30	23	4	ASL
Newark Americans		30A	21	3	ASL
		31S	11	4	ASL
Preston NE		31/32			FL
Queen of the South	T	32/33			D2

GILLESPIE Thomas L

St Mirren		33/34	1		

GILLESPIE William Blyth

b. Buckhaven 29.10.1903

Leven R					
Buckhaven V					
East Fife		21/22	13		D2
		22/23	35		D2
		23/24	38	1	D2
		24/25	27		D2
		25/26	36	3	D2
		26/27	34		D2
Newcastle U		27/28	7		FL
		28/29	2		FL
Bristol R		29/30	2		FL
St Mirren		30/31	4		
East Fife		30/31	19		
		31/32	36		D2
Distillery		32/33			IL
		33/34			IL
		34/35			IL
Bangor		35/36			IL
		36/37			IL
East Fife		36/37	3		D2

GILLICK Torrance 5 caps

b. Airdrie 19.5.1915 d. Airdrie 16.12.1971

Petershill		31/32			
		32/33			
Rangers		33/34	2		
		34/35	27	17	
Everton		35/36	23	9	FL
		36/37	42	14	FL
		37/38	16	3	FL
		38/39	40	14	FL
		39/40	3		FL
Rangers		46/47	27	12	
		47/48	21	9	
		48/49	8	4	
		49/50	2		
		50/51			
Partick T		51/52	7	1	

GILLIES

Vale of Leven		91/92	1	1	

GILLIES Alexander

b. Cowdenbeath 1874 d. Lohgelly 1921

Lochgelly U					
Bolton W		95/96	6		FL
Manchester C		95/96	3		FL
Lochgelly U		96/97			
Heart of Midlothian		96/97	6	3	
Sheffield W		96/97	2		FL
Leicester F		97/98	4		FL
Lochgelly U		98/99			
Dumbarton					

GILLIES Andrew

Clydebank Jnrs					
Morton		06/07	21	5	
		07/08	1		
		08/09	17	3	

GILLIES Andrew

Port Glasgow A		09/10	4	1	
		10/11	1	?	D2
Queen's Park		10/11	10	1	

GILLIES Archibald

Duntocher Hibs					
St Mirren		21/22	26	1	
		22/23	37	6	
		23/24	18	6	
		24/25	31	7	
		25/26	26	3	
		26/27	9	2	
Dumbarton		27/28			D2
		28/29			D2

GILLIES G

Queen's Park		10/11	3		

GILLIES John Crawford

b. Glasgow 22.10.1918

Shawfield Jnrs					
Ayr U		36/37			D2
Clyde		36/37	12	3	
		37/38	35	8	
		38/39	35	8	
St Mirren					
Brentford		46/47	5		FL
Morton		46/47	2	2	
		47/48	2		

GILLIGAN Alexander

Dundee East End
Dundee 93/94 17 6
94/95 12 5
95/96 12 3
Bolton W 96/97 22 6 FL
97/98 28 2 FL
98/99 28 6 FL
99/00 20 3 FL

GILLIGAN John Ross
b. Dundee c1884 d. Dundee 11.6.1946
Dundee W
Partick T 04/05 1
05/06
Clyde 06/07 31
07/08 28
08/09 12
09/10 26
10/11 15
11/12 27
12/13 17
13/14 34
14/15 32
15/16 3
16/17
17/18
18/19 3

GILLIGAN Samuel

Dundee 97/98 2

GILLIGAN Samuel Anderson
b. Dundee 18.1.1882
Belmont A
Dundee Violet
Dundee 02/03 8 3
03/04 1
Celtic 03/04 13 10
Bristol C 04/05 30 15 FL
05/06 36 19 FL
06/07 37 13 FL
07/08 33 19 FL
08/09 29 9 FL
09/10 23 3 FL
Liverpool 10/11 15 5 FL
11/12 23 10 FL
12/13 2 FL
Gillingham 13/14 33 7 SL
14/15 32 8 SL
Dundee Hibs
Forfar A

GILLOW Wilfred Bernard
b. Preston 8.7.1892 d. Middlesbrough 12.3.1944
Lancaster T
Preston NE
Fleetwood
Blackpool 12/13 24 3 FL
13/14 2 1 FL
Preston NE 14/15 3 1 FL
Partick T L 18/19 4
Preston NE 19/20 4 FL
Grimsby T 19/20 14 FL
20/21 35 FL
21/22 31 2 FL
Lancaster T
Grimsby T 23/24 17 3 FL
24/25 6 FL

GILMARTIN Sean

Johnstone A
Hibernian 38/39 1

GILMOUR Alexander

Rosslyn
Raith R 22/23 17 5
Dundee Hibs 23/24 36 6 D2
24/25 32 5 D2
St Bernards 25/26 D2
26/27 D2
? 27/28
28/29
29/30
30/31
Markinch Amateurs 31/32

GILMOUR Campbell Hamilton
b. Kilmarnock 28.5.1906 d. Kilmarnock 7.11.1966
Troon A
Kilmarnock 31/32 9 3
32/33 13
33/34 2
Galston L 33/34
Kilmarnock 34/35 1
Belfast Celtic 34/35 IL
Hamilton A 34/35
Distillery 35/36 IL

GILMOUR F

Queen's Park 15/16 2 1

GILMOUR Frank

Shettleston
Alloa A 22/23 7
23/24 D2
24/25 D2

GILMOUR George

Heart of Midlothian 07/08 8 3
08/09 15 3
09/10 18 2
10/11 7
Raith R 10/11 19
11/12 17

GILMOUR George
b. Hurlford
Arniston R
Hamilton A 27/28 17
28/29 4
29/30 18
30/31 32
31/32 3
Tunbridge Wells R 32/33
33/34

GILMOUR George

Hamilton A 34/35 8 6
35/36 12
36/37 18 3
37/38 19 4
Falkirk 38/39 3

GILMOUR H Robert

Queen's Park 09/10 11 1
10/11 3 1
Falkirk 10/11 1

GILMOUR John Rooney 1 cap
b. Bellshill 15.6.1901 d. 26.2.1963
Bathgate
Dundee 23/24 16
24/25 13 1
25/26 11
26/27 17 2
27/28 34 3
28/29 35 3
29/30 36
30/31 29
31/32 32 1
32/33 36 3
33/34 33
34/35 35
35/36 6
Yeovil T 36/37
Dundee U 37/38 8 D2

GILMOUR Robert
b. Paisley
St Mirren Jnrs
Hibernian 18/19 20 ?
19/20 6 1
20/21 1
Dunfermline A 21/22
USA

GILMOUR Thomas

Albion R 34/35 9 2
35/36 8
Raith R 36/37 D2
37/38 34 35 D2
38/39 15 3
Rangers 38/39 2
Dunfermline A

GILROY Thomas
b. Coatbridge c1906
Fauldhouse U
Dundee U 25/26 18
26/27 26
Falkirk 27/28 29
28/29
29/30 22
30/31
Albion R 31/32 D2

GIRDWOOD Neil
b. Law
Law Volunteers
Hibernian 10/11 18
11/12 32
12/13 31 1
13/14 35 3
14/15 29
15/16 30
Wishaw Thistle 16/17
17/18
18/19
Hibernian 19/20 2

GITTINS Alfred
b. Manchester ?.7.1886
Atherton Church House
Adlington
Bolton W
Blackpool 04/05 1 FL
05/06 FL
Luton T 06/07 23 5 SL
QPR 07/08 36 16 SL
08/09 6 1 SL
Aston Villa 08/09 1 FL
Croydon Common 09/10 27 8 SL
Fulham 10/11 FL
Portsmouth 10/11 4 SL
11/12 SL
Partick T 12/13 19 5
13/14 12
Dumbarton 13/14 5 1
14/15 30 8
15/16 16 1

GLANCY Lawrence
b. Cowdenbeath 29.7.1902
Cowdenbeath St Brides
Hearts o' Beath
Cowdenbeath T
Hibernian T
Celtic 21/22 1
Clackmannan L 21/22
Cowdenbeath L 21/22
Celtic 22/23
Bo'ness 23/24 D2

GLANCY Thomas

Inverkeithing U
Falkirk 14/15 38 3

GLANCY Thomas
b. Glencraig 1894 d. Glencraig ?.2.1949
Glencraig Celtic
Falkirk 18/19 10 ?
19/20 33 3
20/21 31 10
21/22 38 8
22/23 29 7
23/24 26 2
St Johnstone 24/25 30 6
Cowdenbeath 25/26 26 3
26/27 25 1
27/28 28 1
28/29 20 2
29/30 30 1
30/31 35 2
31/32 33
32/33 34 2
33/34 29

GLASGOW John

Dykehead
Hamilton A 07/08 20 7
08/09 17 1
09/10 1
Dykehead

GLASGOW Samuel Little
b. Leadhills 15.4.1897
Leadhills
Nithsdale W
Celtic 20/21 3
Nithsdale W L 20/21
Celtic 21/22
21/22
Dykehead L 22/23
St Johnstone 22/23 20 D2
23/24 D2
Dykehead 23/24 D3

GLASS

Rangers 91/92 1

GLASS John F

Inverness Caledonian
Kilmarnock 08/09 25 1
09/10 9
Inverness Caledonian

GLASS John Shaw
b. Govan 5.11.1908
Benburb
Kilmarnock 32/33 36
33/34 19 1
34/35 1
Rosewell Rosedale
Dumbarton 36/37 D2

GLEGG Charles

Morton 00/01 2

GLEGG Thomas

Falkirk
Stenhousemuir 99/00
Morton 00/01 16 6

GLEN Alexander
b. Dundee d. Dundee 29.4.1991
Forthill Jnrs
Lochee Harp
Raith R 36/37 D2
37/38 34 5 D2
38/39 24 2
Dundee U

GLEN David

Brechin C
Dundee 06/07 4
07/08
Brechin C 08/09

GLEN James

Falkirk 32/33 1

GLEN Robert 3 caps
b. Renton 16.1.1875
Renton 91/92 1
92/93 11 1
93/94 3
Sheffield W 93/94 1 FL
Renton 94/95 8 ? D2
95/96 15 ? D2
96/97 11 ? D2
Rangers 96/97 1
97/98 5
Hibernian 98/99 17
99/00 18
00/01 18
01/02 18
02/03 3
03/04 25
04/05 18
05/06 17
06/07 5
Renton

GLENN John

Rangers 13/14 4

GLOVER Edmund J
b. c1912
Lochee Harp
Dundee U 31/32 5

GLOVER John
b. 1880 d. 1958
Wishaw Thistle 01/02
Albion R 02/03
03/04 D2
Royal Albert 03/04
04/05
05/06
Albion R L 05/06 D2
Wishaw Thistle 06/07
07/08
08/09
09/10
Kilmarnock 09/10 12
10/11 1
Wishaw Thistle
Albion R

GLOVER William

Morton 08/09 13
Celtic

GODFREY Edward John
b. West Ham 17.9.1903 d. Woolwich 5.3.1977
UGB
Erith & Belvedere
Charlton A 25/26 12 3 FL
26/27 19 4 FL
Dundee 27/28 21 1
Peterborough U 28/29
29/30
30/31
Folkestone 31/32
32/33
Bexleyheath & Welling

GODFREY Robert

Falkirk 13/14 2
14/15 3
Bathgate
Ayr U 20/21 17
Alloa A 20/21
Dumbarton 21/22 16
East Stirlingshire 22/23 D2
Vale of Leven 22/23 D2

GODFREY Thomas
b. Stenhousemuir 15.1.1904 d. Redditch 16.12.1983
Dunipace Jnrs
Stenhousemuir T
Falkirk Amateurs
East Stirlingshire
Falkirk 22/23 2
23/24 2
Bo'ness
Clackmannan
Forfar A
Stenhousemuir
Stoke C 27/28 6 FL
28/29 2 FL
29/30 1 FL
Walsall 30/31 38 2 FL
Swindon T 31/32 41 FL
32/33 8 FL
Folkestone 33/34
Worcester C 34/35
35/36

GODFREY William Paterson
b. Stenhousemuir 29.4.1910 d. 1978
Alva Albion R T
Aberdeen 31/32
32/33 15
Plymouth A 33/34 4 FL
34/35 10 FL
35/36 1 FL
Luton T 35/36 5 FL
36/37 1 FL
Vauxhall Motors

GOLD Andrew
b. Douglas Water
Clydebank 19/20 3

GOLD John

Hurlford
Heart of Midlothian 10/11 2
Third Lanark 11/12 1

GOLDIE

Third Lanark 96/97 1

GOLDIE Alexander

Stevenston U
Third Lanark 15/16 13 1

GOLDIE Alexander
b. Hurlford 15.11.1896 d. Kilmarnock 6.11.1918
Saltcoats V
Hurlford
Kilmarnock 17/18 23 9
18/19 11 7

GOLDIE Archibald
b. Hurlford 5.1.1874 d. Bordesley Green 2.4.1953
Clyde 94/95 18
Liverpool 95/96 22 FL
96/97 29 1 FL
97/98 28 FL
98/99 26 FL
99/00 21 FL
New Brighton Tower 00/01 34 FL
Small Heath 01/02 33 FL
02/03 34 FL
03/04 10 FL
Crewe A 04/05 27 BDL
05/06 34 1 BDL
06/07 34 2 BDL
07/08 34 BDL

GOLDIE George C

Lanemark
Kilmarnock 13/14 19 1
14/15 14 1
15/16 22 4
16/17 9 1
17/18
18/19
Stevenston U

GOLDIE Hugh
b. Dalry 10.2.1874
Hurlford Thistle
St Mirren 94/95 16 2
Everton 95/96 15 1 FL
96/97 3 FL
Celtic 97/98 13
98/99 12
Dundee 98/99
Barry T 99/00
Dundee 00/01 15
01/02 14
New Brompton 02/03 30 1 SL
03/04 11 1 SL

GOLDIE John Wyllie
b. Hurlford 10.11.1889
Hurlford Thistle
Fulham 08/09 8 FL
09/10 10 FL
10/11 13 FL
Glossop 11/12 33 FL
Bury 12/13 35 1 FL
13/14 38 1 FL
14/15 31 2 FL
Kilmarnock L 15/16 15
L 16/17 37 1
L 17/18 17 1
Dundee L 17/18
Kilmarnock L 18/19 11
Bury 19/20 39 1 FL
Kilmarnock 20/21 29 2
21/22 32
22/23 31 1
Clyde L 22/23 23

GOLDIE Malcolm

Clyde 12/13 11
St Bernards 13/14 D2
Clydebank 14/15 D2
15/16
16/17
17/18 19 4
18/19 31 ?
19/20 27 7
20/21 30 6
21/22 38 3
Bethlehem Steel 22/23 27 4 ASL
23/24 27 9 ASL
24/25 34 9 ASL
25/26 31 11 ASL
26/27 37 10 ASL
27/28 43 9 ASL
Fall River Marksmen 28/29 42 5 ASL
29A 18 4 ASL
29/30 2 ASL
Pawtucket Rangers 29/30 15 2 ASL
New Bedford Whalers 29/30 1 ASL

GOOD Hugh Jardine
b. Motherwell 2.7.1901 d. Cathcart 2.12.1958
Wishaw YMCA
Kilmarnock 21/22 4
Wishaw YMCA 22/23
23/24
Middlesbrough 24/25 8 FL
25/26 2 FL
Exeter C 26/27 4 FL
Bristol C 27/28 FL
Torquay U 27/28 16 FL
Raith R 28/29 14
Bo'ness L 28/29 D2
Raith R 29/30 D2
Lovells A 29/30
Glentoran 30/31 IL
Larne 31/32 IL
Montrose

GOODFELLOW George
b. Leith 10.12.1869 d. South Leith 1912
Heart of Midlothian 90/91 14
91/92 21
92/93 8

GOODWIN Alexander Hill

Ayr Fort
Ayr U 10/11 2 D2
11/12 D2
12/13 D2
13/14 15 2
14/15 6
15/16
16/17
17/18
18/19 1

GOODWIN John A

Ardrossan Winton R
Kilmarnock 12/13 21
13/14 11 2
Barrow 14/15
Kilmarnock 15/16 2

GOODWIN John L

Ayr Fort
Ayr Parkhouse
Ayr U 10/11 10 ? D2
Rangers 10/11 10 4
11/12 17 8
12/13 19 7
13/14 1
Ayr U 14/15 31 4
Kilmarnock L 14/15 1

GORDON

Clyde 06/07 2

GORDON Allister Edward

Rockbank
Queen's Park 06/07 10 1
Port Glasgow A 06/07 4
07/08 4
Morton 07/08 1
Queen's Park 07/08 1
08/09 1
09/10
Dumbarton 10/11 D2

GORDON Andrew

Queen's Park 18/19 1

GORDON Charles
b. Dumbarton
Rutherglen Glencairn
Dumbarton 19/20 24 3
20/21 5 1
Johnstone 20/21
Renton 20/21
Dumbarton 21/22 6

GORDON Daniel
b. West Calder 7.1.1881 d. Romford 1958
Broxburn 01/02
Heart of Midlothian 01/02
Broxburn 02/03
Everton 03/04 FL
Southampton 04/05 6 SL
Falkirk 05/06 24
06/07 32
St Mirren 07/08 25
Middlesbrough 08/09 1 FL
Bradford PA 08/09 27 FL
09/10 23 FL
Hull C 09/10 5 FL
10/11 6 FL
Southampton 11/12 12 SL

GORDON David
b. Edinburgh
Shaftesbury
Heart of Midlothian 18/19 1
19/20 3
Armadale L 19/20
Hamilton A 20/21 10 1

GORDON David

Arniston Jnrs
Airdrieonians 23/24 5
24/25 7 1
25/26 4
26/27 1
Morton L 26/27
Airdrieonians 27/28 4 1
28/29 4
29/30
Leith A 29/30 D2

GORDON David Smith
b. Leith 29.12.1882
Leith A
Hull C 05/06 38 12 FL
06/07 37 1 FL
07/08 23 FL
08/09 36 3 FL
09/10 36 FL
10/11 32 2 FL
11/12 31 FL
12/13 29 FL
13/14 14 FL
Leith A 14/15 D2
15/16
Hibernian 16/17 35
Kilmarnock 16/17 1
Hibernian 17/18 27 ?
18/19 16 ?

GORDON Francis

Cambuslang R
Dundee 23/24 1

GORDON James

Arbroath
Hibernian 06/07 14
07/08 16
Leith A 08/09 D2
09/10 D2
Coventry C 10/11 SL
Bathgate 11/12

GORDON James Eadie 10 caps
b. Saltcoats 23.7.1888 d. 22.11.1954
Thornwood A
Renfrew V
Rangers 06/07 1
07/08 22 1
08/09 25 6
09/10 19 2
10/11 28 5
11/12 29 2
12/13 28 1
13/14 31 4
14/15 30 8
15/16 31 8
16/17 6 1
Heart of Midlothian L 16/17 1
Rangers 17/18 16 11
18/19 16 5
19/20 33 10
Dunfermline A

GORDON John
b. Kirkcudbright 11.4.1899
Bellshill Jnrs
Queen's Park 20/21 5 1
Port Vale 22/23 22 3 FL
Morton 23/24 37 2
24/25 15 2
25/26 19 3
Luton T 26/27 10 FL
27/28 3 FL
Dunfermline A 27/28 1

GORDON John

Loanhead Mayflower
Bonnyrigg Rose
Hibernian 20/21 4 1
21/22 1
St Bernards 22/23 D2
Leeds U 22/23 FL

GORDON John George
b. South Shields 20.12.1908 d. South Shields 28.1.1982
Havelock Jnrs
Boldon CW
Leeds U 31/32 FL
Rochdale 32/33 32 FL
33/34 34 1 FL
Queen of the South 34/35 13
35/36 4
36/37 19
South Shields 37/38
Jarrow 38/39
Blyth Spartans

GORDON Louis

Glasgow Ashfield
St Mirren 16/17 11

GORDON R

Morton 26/27 11

GORDON Robert
b. Leith 1873 d. 1938
Leith R
Leith A
Heart of Midlothian 90/91
Middlesbrough I 91/92
92/93
Heart of Midlothian 93/94 2
Aston Villa 94/95 4 4 FL
Leicester F 94/95 21 12 FL
Woolwich Arsenal 95/96 20 6 FL
Reading 96/97 13 7 SL
Forfar A
St Bernards

GORDON Robert George D

Edinburgh University
Queen's Park 37/38 28
Northampton T

GOSSLAND

Leith A 94/95 4

GOSSMAN James

Yoker A
Queen's Park 21/22 25 4
22/23 10 5 D2
Kilmarnock 23/24 9 1
Peebles R 24/25 D3
Queen of the South 24/25 D3
25/26 D2
Raith R

GOUDIE David W

Rangers 01/02 1

GOUDIE James Ramsey

Benburb
Plymouth A
Clyde 38/39 8 2

GOUDIE William B

Rangers
Partick T 00/01 18
Falkirk 01/02
Rangers 01/02
Falkirk

GOUGH Harold
b. Chesterfield 31.12.1890 d. Castleford 1970
Spital Olympic
Castleford T
Bradford PA 10/11 3 FL
Castleford T 11/12
12/13
Sheffield U 13/14 37 FL
14/15 37 FL
Hibernian L 17/18 4
L 18/19 17
Sheffield U 19/20 39 FL
20/21 27 FL
21/22 36 FL
22/23 28 FL
23/24 38 FL
Castleford T 24/25
25/26
Harrogate 26/27
Oldham A 26/27 4 FL
Bolton W 27/28 4 FL
Torquay U 28/29 39 FL
29/30 17 FL

GOULD John Daniel
b. 16.12.1919
Neilston V
Third Lanark T
Arbroath 38/39 38 7
46/47 D2
Ayr U 47/48 D2
Stenhousemuir

GOULD William Ross
b. Ayr ?.9.1899 d. Ayr 1955
Irvine Meadow
Queen's Park 19/20 2
20/21 39
Ayr U 21/22
Rangers 21/22
22/23
23/24
Kilmarnock 24/25 37
25/26 29
26/27 18
Retirement
Galston 28/29

GOULDEN John Thomas
b. Sunderland 26.12.1903 d. Hull 1981
Needlers
Hull C 24/25 2 FL
25/26 FL
26/27 FL
Raith R 27/28 3

GOURLAY Adam
Rangers 04/05 3
05/06 6
Morton 06/07 5
Cowdenbeath 07/08

GOURLAY Adam
St Mirren 08/09 16 1

GOURLAY Archibald Jamieson
b. Stirling 1910
Alva Albion R
Kings Park
Dunipace Jnrs
Partick T 33/34 5
34/35 7
Albion R L 35/36 12
Hibernian 36/37 30
37/38 32
38/39 4

GOURLAY David
Queen's Park 00/01 1
Clyde

GOURLAY H
Cambuslang 90/91 18 8
91/92 12 1

GOURLAY James
Partick T 98/99 1
Annbank

GOURLAY James
Raith R 09/10 D2
10/11 30 6
11/12 26 9
12/13 21 3
13/14 2
Kirkcaldy U 13/14
Raith R 14/15 3

GOURLAY James
Falkirk 23/24 1

GOURLAY James McCrorie 2 caps
b. Kilmaurs 1.11.1860 d. Annbank 10.3.1939
Abercorn
Cambuslang 87/88
88/89
89/90
90/91 1
91/92 2

GOURLAY James Walter
b. Annbank
Annbank Juveniles
Cambuslang R
Port Glasgow A 08/09 22 6
Everton 09/10 4 2 FL
10/11 28 4 FL
11/12 16 2 FL
12/13 7 FL
Morton 13/14 29 15
14/15 37 23
15/16 30 17
16/17 34 14
17/18 26 6
18/19 25 5
19/20 33 5
20/21 31 9
21/22 23 2
22/23 28 5
23/24 35 6
24/25 36 2
25/26 22 4
Third Lanark 26/27 D2

GOURLAY S
Cambuslang 91/92 10

GOURLAY Thomas
b. Greenock
Kilbarchan
Third Lanark 19/20 9 3
Beith

GOURLAY Thomas
b. Kirkcaldy c1915
West Calder U
Dunfermline A 36/37 13 2

GOURLEY James
b. Maryhill 1862 d. Cambuslang 8.6.1926
Cambuslang 87/88
88/89
89/90
90/91
91/92 3

GOVAN Alexander
Heart of Midlothian 04/05 6
Albion R 05/06 D2

GOVAN John
b. Paisley
Johnstone R
St Johnstone 26/27 3
East Fife 27/28 D2

GOW Donald Robertson 1 cap
b. Blair Atholl 8.2.1868 d. Middlesbrough 1945
Cessnock Bank
Rangers 85/86
86/87
87/88
88/89
89/90
90/91 16 1
Sunderland 91/92 16 FL
Rangers 92/93 10
Sunderland 93/94 18 1 FL
94/95 7 FL
95/96 30 FL
96/97 27 FL
New Brighton Tower 97/98
Millwall 98/99 6 SL
Girvan

GOW J
Clyde 91/92 1

GOWANS David
Dundee W
Dundee 02/03 4
03/04
04/05
05/06
06/07
07/08
08/09
09/10 3
10/11
Forfar A 11/12
Dundee Hibs 12/13 11 D2

GOWDY Joseph
b. Belfast
Glentoran 19/20 IL
20/21 IL
Falkirk 20/21 9 2
21/22 17
Queens Island 22/23 IL
23/24 IL
Falkirk 24/25 26 1
25/26 30 5
26/27 20
27/28 12 2
East Fife 28/29 27 2 D2
29/30 37 6 D2
30/31 10 1

GOWDY William Alexander
b. Belfast 24.12.1903 d. Larne 16.3.1958
Duncairn O
Cliftonville Olympic
Highfield
Duncairn OB
Cliftonville Olympic 26/27
Dundalk 26/27 LI
Ards 27/28 IL
Brantwood 27/28
Ards 28/29 IL
Hull C 29/30 25 FL
30/31 33 1 FL
31/32 7 FL
Sheffield W 31/32 1 FL
31/32 FL
Gateshead 32/33 4 FL
Linfield 33/34 IL
34/35 IL
Hibernian 35/36 10 1
Goole T 36/37
Altrincham 37/38
Aldershot 38/39 3 FL

GRACIE James
Dumbarton 94/95 10
95/96 4 1
96/97 4 ? D2

GRACIE Thomas
b. Glasgow 12.6.1889 d. Glasgow 23.10.1915
Wellwood Star
Strathclyde
Airdrieonians 06/07 5 2
07/08 7 1
Hamilton A 08/09 5 1
Arthurlie 09/10 D2
Morton 10/11 28 22
Everton 10/11 7 1 FL
11/12 6 FL
Liverpool 11/12 6 1 FL
12/13 13 1 FL
13/14 15 3 FL
Heart of Midlothian 14/15 37 29

GRAHAM
Vale of Leven 91/92 1

GRAHAM
Hibernian 03/04 1

GRAHAM
Motherwell 15/16 1

GRAHAM
Albion R 19/20 1

GRAHAM
Raith R 19/20 1

GRAHAM A
Vale of Leven 90/91 1

GRAHAM Alexander
Hamilton A
Third Lanark 18/19 26 ?

GRAHAM Alexander Cameron
b. Kirkintilloch 25.8.1881
Clydebank Jnrs
Kilmarnock 04/05 5 3
05/06 21 9
Kirkintilloch Rob Roy
Airdrieonians 06/07 19 7
Clyde 07/08 25 13

GRAHAM Alexander Cameron
b. Coatbridge 26.8.1912
Burnbank Amateurs
Vale of Clyde 33/34
West Ham U 34/35 FL
Albion R 35/36 8
Cowdenbeath 35/36 D2
Stenhousemuir
Morton 36/37 D2
Rochdale 37/38 11 4 FL
Bradford PA 37/38 7 FL
Halifax T 38/39 14 3 FL

GRAHAM Alexander J
Queen's Park 23/24 6
24/25 34
25/26 3
26/27 16

GRAHAM Archibald
St Mirren 99/00 4

GRAHAM David
Armadale
Heart of Midlothian 15/16 8
16/17
Stevenston U 17/18

GRAHAM David B
Third Lanark 24/25 2

GRAHAM Francis
Dunipace
Port Glasgow A 05/06 22 6

GRAHAM George Kretchen

b. Glasgow					
Vale of Clyde					
Shettleston					
Morton		25/26			
		26/27			
		27/28			D2
		28/29			D2
Bournemouth		28/29	17	2	FL
Caernarvon T		29/30			
Boston T		30/31			
Waterford		30/31			LI
Morton		31/32	23	6	
East Stirlingshire		31/32			D2
Ards		32/33			IL
A Welsh club					
Ards		33/34			IL
Jarrow					

GRAHAM Harry Nicol

b. Edinburgh 16.12.1887 d. Canongate 1.3.1940					
Granton Oakvale					
St Bernards		08/09			D2
		09/10			D2
Bradford C		09/10	1		FL
		10/11	10		FL
Birmingham		11/12	12	4	FL
Raith R		12/13	31	6	
Heart of Midlothian		13/14	35	12	
		14/15	37	18	
		15/16	32	12	
		16/17	15	1	
		17/18			
		18/19			
		19/20	15	1	
		20/21	9	2	
Leicester C		20/21	22		FL
		21/22	31	4	FL
		22/23	39	6	FL
		23/24	18	4	FL
St Bernards		24/25			D2
Reading		25/26	9		FL
		26/27	4		FL

GRAHAM James

Vale of Clyde					
Morton		25/26	9	2	
		26/27	31	3	

GRAHAM James

b. c1913					
Glasgow St Anthonys					
Motherwell		35/36	2		
		36/37	9	3	
		37/38	2		
Glenavon		38/39			IL

GRAHAM John

b. Alloa					
Woodburn					
Alva Albion R					
Rangers		99/00	13	3	
		00/01	5	2	
Heart of Midlothian	L	00/01	6	1	
Rangers		01/02	3		
		02/03	2		
Kilmarnock		03/04	8	2	
Alloa A		03/04			
		04/05			
		05/06			
Brighton		05/06	1		SL
Kilwinning Eglington					

GRAHAM John Alexander 1 cap

b. Hurlford 11.7.1890 d. Islington 1943					
Hurlford					
Hamilton A					
Larkhall U					
Woolwich Arsenal		12/13	12	2	FL
		13/14	13		FL
		14/15	26		FL
Vale of Leven					
Hamilton A		16/17	14	7	
		17/18	30	15	
		18/19	1		
Arsenal		19/20	22	4	FL
		20/21	30	5	FL
		21/22	21	3	FL
		22/23	17	1	FL
		23/24	25	1	FL
Brentford		24/25	25	4	FL
		25/26	25	9	FL
Folkestone T					

GRAHAM John Lang

b. Dalry 7.8.1881 d. Saltcoats 15.5.1965					
Kilmarnock Rugby XI					
Kilmarnock		00/01	15	6	
		01/02	17	5	
Bristol R		02/03	17	4	SL
Celtic		03/04	4		
Millwall		04/05	1		SL
Accrington S		04/05			
Brighton	T	05/06			SL
Kilwinning Eglington		05/06			
Hamilton A		06/07			
Clyde					

GRAHAM Joseph W

b. Hebburn					
Wallsend					
Heart of Midlothian		09/10	2		
		10/11			
Stockport Co		11/12	1		FL
		12/13			FL
		13/14	14	1	FL
		14/15	26	2	FL
		19/20	36		FL
		20/21	9		FL
Exeter C		21/22	12		FL
New Brighton					
Ashton					

GRAHAM Robert

b. Glasgow 1882					
Cartha					
Queen's Park Strollers					
Third Lanark		01/02	1	1	
		02/03	14	3	
		03/04	23	10	
Fulham		04/05	23		SL
Third Lanark		05/06	23	6	
Everton		06/07	2		FL
Bolton W		07/08			FL
Third Lanark		07/08			
Partick T		09/10	15		
St Johnstone		10/11			

GRAHAM Robert

Falkirk Jnrs					
Falkirk		05/06	3		
Cowdenbeath					

GRAHAM Robert

Parkhead Jnrs					
Aberdeen		37/38			
		38/39	10		

GRAHAM Samuel

b. Galston 7.4.1878					
Galston					
Shankhouse					
Newcastle U		02/03	2		FL
		03/04			FL
		04/05	3		FL
Norwich C		05/06	24	6	SL
Kilmarnock		05/06	2		
		06/07	17	3	
Galston		07/08			
Ayr		08/09			D2
		09/10			D2
Ayr Parkhouse	L	09/10			D2
Ayr U		10/11	19	?	D2
Galston					

GRAHAM T

Vale of Leven		90/91	14	7	

GRAHAM W

Vale of Leven		90/91	3		

GRAHAM Walter

b. Coalburn c1907					
Douglas Water Thistle					
Ayr U		28/29			
		29/30	5		
		30/31			
Coalburn		31/32			

GRAHAM William

Dundee		93/94	1		

GRAHAM William A

Anstruther R					
Raith R		27/28	8		

GRAINGER John

St Mirren		18/19	27	?	
		19/20	11	5	
Alloa A		20/21			
Dumbarton		21/22	4		
Bethlehem Steel		22/23	13	1	ASL
		23/24	11	8	ASL
		24/25	33	8	ASL
		25/26	16	4	ASL
		26/27	22	6	ASL
		27/28	31	6	ASL
Fall River Marksmen		28/29	36	5	ASL
New Bedford Whalers		29A	3		ASL
		29/30	24	5	ASL

GRAINGER William

Vale of Clyde					
Clyde		26/27	2		
Kings Park		27/28			D2

GRANGER John

b, Dumbarton 16.7.1899					
Vale of Leven Jnrs					
Dumbarton		21/22			D2
Vale of Leven		21/22			D2
Celtic		21/22			
		22/23	4		
		23/24	8		
Armadale	L	23/24			D2
Celtic		24/25	1		
Forfar A	L	24/25			
Vale of Leven		25/26			D3
Dumbarton		26/27			D2
Melbourne Caledonian					
Ards		30/31			IL
Vale Ocoba					

GRANT

Leith A		91/92	1		

GRANT David M

b. Dundee					
Heart of Midlothian		35/36	1		
		36/37	1		

GRANT Donald

Dundee Fairfield					
Heart of Midlothian					
Aberdeen		38/39	4		

GRANT Duncan C

Forres Mechanics					
Partick T		12/13	2		

GRANT George

b. Bonnyrigg					
Stoneyburn					
Tranent Jnrs					
Falkirk		33/34	27	8	
Workington		34/35			
Tranent Jnrs		34/35			
Albion R		35/36	35	6	
		36/37	4		
St Bernards		36/37			D2
		37/38			D2
Clapton Orient		38/39	19	4	FL
Ballymena U		39/40			

GRANT Hugh

Dunaskin Lads					
Kilmarnock		05/06	3		
Hurlford					
Maybole					

GRANT James S

Vale of Carron					
St Mirren		06/07	9		
		07/08	34		
		08/09	33		
		09/10	16		
		10/11	16		
Clyde		10/11	8		
		11/12	21		
		12/13	28		
Kilmarnock		13/14	28		
Clyde					

GRANT John

Ayr U		18/19	3	?	

GRANT Peter G

Hamilton A					
Scottish Amateurs					
Queen's Park		02/03	2		

GRANT Robert
Falkirk 18/19 2

GRANT Robert
b. Glasgow
Queen's Park 27/28 2
28/29 18
29/30 33
30/31 35 2
31/32 35 2
32/33 33
33/34 32
34/35 29
35/36 6

GRANT Thomas
Giffnock
Clydebank 20/21 2
21/22 5

GRANT Walter A
b. Aberdeen c1890 d. Swanley 1940
Balnagask
Banks o'Dee
Aberdeen 15/16 15 1
16/17
17/18
18/19
19/20 6
20/21 2 1
21/22 5 1
22/23 19 1
23/24 37 3
24/25 7
Raith R 25/26 20 2
Crystal Palace 26/27 17 5 FL
27/28 4 FL
28/29 FL
Bedford T 29/30
Walthamstow Grange 30/31
Bexleyheath & Welling 31/32
32/33
33/34
Swanley

GRANT William
Bo'ness
Petershill
Armadale
Morton 15/16 12 4
16/17 10
17/18 23 1
18/19 10 6
St Mirren L 18/19 2 ?
Morton 19/20 13
20/21 1

GRANT William
Queen's Park 17/18 11 3

GRANT William
Carluke R
Airdrieonians 33/34 20 9

GRANT William Middleton
b. Bo'ness 14.11.1904
Vale of Grange
Bo'ness 25/26 D2
East Stirlingshire 26/27 D2
27/28 D2
Blackpool 27/28 18 FL
28/29 27 FL
29/30 40 FL
30/31 42 FL
31/32 42 FL
32/33 18 FL
33/34 5 FL
34/35 28 FL
Motherwell 35/36 38
36/37 30 1
37/38 26
38/39 6

GRASSAM William
b. Larbert 20.11.1878
Redcliffe Thistle 96/97
Maryhill 97/98
98/99
Burslem Port Vale 99/00 31 5 FL
West Ham U 00/01 20 9 SL
01/02 29 10 SL
02/03 29 18 SL
Celtic 02/03
03/04 2
Manchester U 03/04 23 9 FL
04/05 6 2 FL
Leyton 05/06
West Ham U 05/06 14 3 SL
06/07 37 9 SL
07/08 32 9 SL
08/09 8 2 SL
Brentford 09/10 4 SL

GRAY
Heart of Midlothian 90/91 2 1
91/92 2

GRAY
Third Lanark 91/92 1

GRAY
St Mirren 93/94 1

GRAY
Morton 10/11 1

GRAY A
Heart of Midlothian 95/96 1
96/97 3 1
97/98 2

GRAY Alexander
b. Bainsford 11.9.1892
East Plean U
Stenhousemuir
Celtic 12/13 12 4
Alloa A L 12/13
Ayr U L 12/13 D2
Celtic 13/14
Ayr U L 13/14 31 12
Celtic 14/15 1
Ayr U L 14/15 19 1
Celtic 15/16
Ayr U L 15/16 31 2
Celtic 16/17
Ayr U L 16/17 3
Falkirk L 16/17 5
Celtic 17/18
Kilmarnock 18/19 22 3
Ayr U 18/19 10 ?
19/20 13 2
Stenhousemuir
Johnstone
Vale of Leven
Arthurlie
Stenhousemuir

GRAY Alexander A
Morton 07/08 2

GRAY Alexander Duncan
b. Glasgow 4.5.1901
Glasgow Perthshire
Johnstone
Vale of Leven
Kilmarnock 23/24 30 19
24/25 28 8
25/26 14 4
Bristol C 26/27 8 3 FL
Queen of the South 27/28 D2
Morton 28/29 D2
Queen of the South 28/29 D2

GRAY Allan
Kilbirnie Ladeside
Partick T 07/08 15 2
Abercorn

GRAY Archibald 1 cap
b. Govan 24.8.1878
Govan Columbia
Glasgow Ashfield
Hibernian 99/00 2
00/01 6
01/02 3
02/03 18 2
03/04 18
Woolwich Arsenal 04/05 26 FL
05/06 28 FL
06/07 23 FL
07/08 30 FL
08/09 32 FL
09/10 13 FL
10/11 26 FL
11/12 5 FL
Fulham 11/12 7 FL
12/13 13 FL
14/15 4 FL

GRAY David H
b. Dumfries
5th KOSB (Dumfries)
Queen of the South W 19/20
Ayr U L 19/20
Queen of the South W 20/21
Kilmarnock L 20/21
Huddersfield T T 20/21
Kilmarnock 21/22 11 2
Queen of the South 22/23
23/24 D3
24/25 D3
25/26 D2
26/27 D2
Mid Annandale

GRAY Douglas Herbert 10 caps
b. Alford 4.4.1905 d. 1972
Aberdeen Mugiemoss
Rangers 25/26 21
26/27 30
27/28 38
28/29 35
29/30 34
30/31 38 2
31/32 35
32/33 37
33/34 37
34/35 36
35/36 38
36/37 36
37/38 35
38/39 35

GRAY Fred
Rangers 16/17 2 1

GRAY Frederick B
Clyde 09/10 9
East Stirlingshire 10/11 10 ? D2
Clyde 11/12
St Mirren 12/13 17
13/14 34 1
14/15 9
15/16 25 3
16/17
17/18 4
18/19
19/20 6

GRAY H
Clyde 95/96 1 2
96/97 11 6

GRAY James
Abercorn 96/97 13

GRAY James
Clyde 99/00 5 2
Royal Albert
Clyde 02/03

GRAY James
Clydebank Jnrs
Kilmarnock 08/09 6
Partick T L 08/09
Kilmarnock 09/10 1
10/11 2 1
11/12 2
Dumbarton Harp 12/13
Arthurlie 13/14 D2
Kilmarnock

GRAY James

Renfrew
Partick T 17/18 15 1
18/19 11 1

GRAY James A
b. Bristol 1878 d. 1937
Royal Albert
Bristol R 03/04 32 3 SL
Aston Villa 04/05 7 FL
Rangers 05/06 26
06/07 20
Tottenham H 07/08 15 SL
Leyton 08/09 24 SL
09/10 SL
10/11 34 2 SL
11/12 29 1 SL

GRAY James N D

Abercorn
Queen's Park 04/05 5 1
St Mirren 05/06 15 5
06/07 6 1

GRAY John
b. Glasgow
Albion R 92/93
Rangers 93/94 18 9
94/95 7 4
Clyde 95/96 15 6
Hamilton A

GRAY John

Clyde 98/99 3

GRAY John

Kilwinning Eglinton
Morton 02/03 11 1

GRAY John

Kirkcaldy U
Airdrieonians 07/08 6
Raith R 08/09 D2
Motherwell 09/10 33 5
10/11 23 1
11/12 26 4
12/13 34 7
13/14 37 4
14/15 36 7
15/16 30 1
16/17 34 2
17/18 13 2
Vale of Leven 18/19
Albion R 19/20 18 1

GRAY John Lyon
b. Stenhousemuir 4.5.1881
Elder Park
Celtic 00/01 2 1
01/02
Cape Town Caledonians

GRAY Josiah

Aston Villa
Rangers 03/04 1

GRAY Robert

Lenzie
Meadowside
Partick T 96/97 2 D2
97/98 10 6
98/99 15 1
Everton 99/00 15 1 FL
00/01 5 FL
01/02 FL
Partick T 02/03 19 3
03/04 14 5
04/05 20 3
05/06 27 7
06/07 22 2

GRAY Robert

St Bernards 99/00 10 1
00/01 8 ? D2

GRAY Robert
b. Whifflet
Bellshill A
Glasgow Ashfield
Airdrieonians 18/19 10
19/20 17
Albion R 20/21 4
21/22
Queens Island 22/23 IL

GRAY Samuel

Port Glasgow A 05/06 6 1
06/07 2 1
Arthurlie

GRAY William
b. Partick 6.2.1881 d. Egypt 18.8.1915
Inverness Thistle
Partick T 02/03 3
03/04 11 1
04/05 3
05/06 22 2
Southampton 06/07 28 SL
Partick T 07/08 21 3
08/09 26 1
Raith R 09/10 D2

GRAY William

Parkhead
Ayr U 13/14 3

GRAY William
b. Maryhill 30.5.1907
Wyndford Star
Maryhill Hibernian
Celtic 27/28
28/29 26 12
Hamilton A 29/30 28 15
Colwyn Bay U 30/31
Dolphin 30/31 LI
Hamilton A 31/32 4 5
Maryhill Jnrs

GRAY William

Glentoran * 35/36 IL
Inverness Thistle * 36/37
Partick T 36/37 19 3

GRAY William James S

St Mirren 99/00 7 1

GRAYDON

Third Lanark 91/92 4 1

GRAYDON

Clyde 92/93 2

GRAYDON John

Queen's Park FP
Parkhead
Dundee 09/10 8
10/11 2 1
11/12 1

GREECHAN James
b. Glasgow (?)
Petershill
Hibernian 03/04 3
04/05
Bo'ness 05/06
Brentford 06/07 12 2 SL
Clapton Orient 07/08 30 8 FL
Glossop 07/08 2 FL
08/09 17 3 FL
Stockport Co 09/10 15 4 FL

GREEN Thomas
b. Liverpool 25.11.1893 d. Liverpool 1975
Southport Vulcan
West Ham U 19/20 3 FL
Southport 19/20
South Liverpool
Accrington S 21/22 30 23 FL
Stockport Co 22/23 32 17 FL
Clapton Orient 23/24 24 10 FL
Heart of Midlothian 23/24 6 3
24/25 15 16
Third Lanark 25/26 D2
Flint T U 25/26
Wavertree A
Milners Safe Works

GREEN William

Clyde 06/07 1
07/08
Dumbarton 08/09 D2

GREEN William

Aberdeen 13/14 6

GREENHORN William

Maryhill *
Glasgow Perthshire *
Petershill *
Clydebank Jnrs * 15/16
Bellshill A 16/17
Hamilton A 17/18 28 3
Renton 18/19
Ayr U 18/19 2
Johnstone
Renton

GREENLEES Donald
b. Glasgow 14.1.1875 d. Atherton 5.2.1955
St Mirren 96/97 1
97/98 17 1
98/99 18
Southampton 99/00 8 SL
St Mirren 00/01 13
01/02 18
02/03 21 1
03/04 23
04/05 18 1
05/06 24
06/07 28 1
Morton 07/08 30 1
Eastleigh Junction
Shirley Warren
White Star Lines

GREENSHIELDS George

Plean
Albion R 20/21 34 2
21/22 32 3
Dundee 22/23 11
Motherwell 22/23 14 1
23/24 3
Newcastle U T 23/24 FL
Airdrieonians T 23/24 1
Motherwell 24/25 19 1
25/26
Dumbarton 26/27 D2

GREENWOOD Adam
b. Larne 1889 d. Larne 1951
Larne 07/08 IL
08/09 IL
09/10 IL
Airdrieonians 09/10 2
Belfast Celtic 10/11 IL
11/12 IL
Linfield 12/13 IL

GREGG

Abercorn 92/93 1

GREIG Andrew John Smith
b. Aberdeen 19.10.1893
Mugiemoss
Aberdeen 11/12 22
12/13 10
13/14 32
14/15 9
15/16 5
16/17 2
Raith R L 16/17 1
Darlington 21/22 20 FL
22/23 36 FL
23/24 39 FL
Shildon 24/25
25/26
Montrose 26/27

GREIG Robert

Irvine Meadow
Hurlford 21/22
22/23
Kilmarnock 23/24 1
Galston 24/25 D3
Nithsdale W 25/26 D2
Galston

GRIBB

Clyde 96/97 1

GRIBBIN James

Pollok
St Anthonys
Bo'ness 27/28 4
Clyde 27/28 4
Bathgate 28/29 D2

GRIERSON Archibald

Raith R 10/11 13
Kirkcaldy U

GRIEVE John
b. Scotland c1885
Distillery 03/04 IL
04/05 IL
Hibernian 05/06 24
06/07 27 2
07/08 29 3
08/09 11
Watford 09/10 34 1 SL
10/11 28 SL
Stoke 11/12 23 1 SL

GRIEVE Robert B
b. Greenock 28.3.1884
Greenock Volunteers
Morton 02/03 2
03/04 16 4
04/05 21 3
05/06 22 10
Manchester C 06/07 19 6 FL
07/08 17 10 FL
08/09 8 2 FL
Accrington S 09/10
Leicester F 10/11 4 2 FL
Southport Central 11/12
Accrington S 11/12

GRIEVE William
St Mirren 07/08 4

GRIEVE William
St Mirren 19/20 2
20/21 10 1

GRIEVE William G
Queen's Park 05/06 2
06/07 4
Port Glasgow A 07/08 3

GRIFFIN Ronald George
b. Camberwell Green 18.10.1919 d. Surrey ?.2.1987
Larkhall Thistle
St Mirren 37/38 5
Lincoln C 38/39 1 FL
Brentford 38/39 FL
Watford

GRIFFITHS Thomas
b. Coatbridge
Renfrew V
Petershill
Blantyre V
Third Lanark 07/08 21 14
Bolton W 08/09 4 FL

GRONBACH Charles John
b. Bowhill 1909 d. ?.4.2002
Cowdenbeath Excelsior
Cowdenbeath Bruntonians
Cowdenbeath Wednesday
Cowdenbeath 33/34 8
East Fife L 33/34 6 D2
Cowdenbeath 34/35 9 D2

GROSERT Alexander Ramsay
b. South Leith 1889
Newtongrange Star
Leith Amateurs
Hibernian 11/12 2
12/13 29 4
13/14 25
14/15 25
Leith A L 14/15 D2
Hibernian 15/16 1
16/17
17/18 2 ?
18/19 7 ?
19/20 15
Aberdeen 20/21 29
21/22 17
22/23 21
Dunfermline A 23/24

GROVE Robert
b. Shettleston 10.11.1902
Vale of Clyde
Partick T 23/24 22 7
24/25 29 8
25/26 35 10
26/27 36 41
27/28 34 11
28/29 5
29/30 26 2
30/31 14 3
31/32 21
32/33 8 1

GROVE William
Queen's Park 21/22 2
22/23
23/24
24/25
25/26
26/27
Armadale 27/28 D2
Arbroath 28/29 16 5 D2

GROVES
Leith A 92/93 5

GROVES William 3 caps
b. Leith 9.11.1869 d. Edinburgh 13.2.1908
Stella Maris CYMS
Hibernian
Thistle L
Leith Harp L
Hibernian
Celtic 88/89
89/90
Everton
Celtic 90/91 2 2
WBA 90/91 8 2 FL
91/92 20 4 FL
92/93 30 1 FL
Aston Villa 93/94 22 4 FL
94/95 FL
Hibernian 95/96 5 1
Celtic 96/97 2 1
Rushden T

GUNN Alexander
Carluke R
Airdrieonians 33/34 7 1

GUNN Felix
Parkhead Jnrs
Dumbarton 15/16 33
16/17 13
17/18 12 1
18/19
Dumbarton Harp 19/20

GUNN John
Bolton W 95/96 6 5 FL
Manchester C 96/97 21 4 FL
Clyde 97/98 1

GUNN John C
b. Largs
Largs Thistle
Kilmarnock 21/22 4

GUNZEON James
Maxwelltown Volunteers
Heart of Midlothian T 02/03 2
Kilmarnock 03/04 26
Maxwelltown Volunteers 04/05
05/06
Carlisle U 05/06

GURNER
St Bernards 99/00 1

GUTHRIE James Alexander Thomson
b. Perth 13.6.1918 d. 10.9.1981
Luncarty
Scone Thistle
Dundee 32/33 17 3
33/34 20 4
34/35 36 5
35/36 38 3
36/37 32 2
Portsmouth 37/38 38 1 FL
38/39 38 FL
Guildford C
Crystal Palace 46/47 5 FL

GUTHRIE John
Rosslyn Jnrs
Alloa A T
Partick T T
Heart of Midlothian 32/33 1
33/34
Alloa A 34/35 D2
Cowdenbeath 35/36 D2

GUTHRIE William
Kilmarnock 18/19 5 1
19/20
Nithsdale W 20/21
Douglas W 21/22
22/23

GUY
Cambuslang 90/91 4

HADDEN Joseph
Shettleston
Ardrossan Celtic
Rangers 07/08 2

HADDOW Andrew Sorbie
b. Glasgow 8.4.1903
Strathclyde Jnrs
Morton 26/27 38 18
Burnley 27/28 1 FL
New York Nationals 28/29 11 3 ASL
Clyde 28/29 11 6
Dundee U L 29/30 14 10
30/31 8 8 D2
Clyde 30/31 5 3
31/32 2
Ballymena 31/32 IL
Etoile Rouge (Switz) 32/33

HADDOW David 1 cap
b. Dalserf 12.6.1869
Albion R 88/89
89/90
Derby Co 90/91 16 FL
Albion R 90/91
Rangers 91/92 22
92/93 18
93/94 15
94/95 11
Motherwell 95/96 5 D2
Burnley 95/96 4 FL
96/97 9 FL
97/98 24 FL
New Brighton Tower 98/99 34 FL
Tottenham H 99/00 20 SL
00/01 3 SL

HADDOW George
Renfrew V
Heart of Midlothian 07/08 8

HADDOW John
b. Plean
Linlithgow Rose
Rangers 27/28 1
Dumbarton 28/29 D2
29/30 D2
Bo'ness 30/31 D2
Kings Park 31/32 D2
32/33 D2
33/34 D2
34/34 D2
34/35 D2
Falkirk 35/36 8 11 D2
Leith A 36/37 D2

HAFEKOST Charles Henry
b. Sunderland 22.3.1890 d. South Shields 1967
Sunderland Royal R
Gillingham 12/13 21 4 SL
13/14 29 10 SL
Liverpool 14/15 1 FL
Hamilton A 19/20 3
Hartlepool U 19/20

HAGAN John
Dumbarton A
Renfrew
Dumbarton 19/20 2
20/21 1
Dumbarton Harp 20/21

HAGAN Patrick
d. K.I.A, Thiepval 14.7.1916
Belfast Celtic
Hibernian 05/06 25 5
Brentford 06/07 33 7 SL
07/08 16 4 SL
Hibernian 07/08 9 3
Port Glasgow A 08/09 30 9
09/10 27 2

HAGGART William
b. Edinburgh ?.8.1874 d. 1934
Dalry Primrose
Edinburgh Royal
Aston Villa 98/99 1 FL
99/00 1 FL
Partick T 00/01 13
Edinburgh Thistle

HAGGARTY Alexander					
b. Kirkcaldy c1917					
Burntisland Shipyard					
Cowdenbeath		29/30	6		
		30/31	1		
Alloa A		30/31			D2
		31/32			D2
Rosyth Rec					

HAGGARTY Matthew					
Maryhill					
Vale of Leven		10/11			D2
Dumbarton		11/12			D2
Third Lanark		12/13	1		
Vale of Leven		13/14			
Abercorn					

HAGGO Douglas Cameron					
b. Kilmarnock 1896					
Kirkintilloch Rob Roy					
Dumbarton		21/22	7		

HAIG					
Renton		92/93	3		

HAIG Robert S					
St Mirren		94/95	6		
		95/96	14		
		96/97	12		

HAIG Robert T					
Clyde		97/98	11		
		98/99			
		99/00	3		

HAIR Alexander					
b. Glasgow 9.3.1902					
Strathclyde					
Partick T		23/24	30	16	
		24/25	6	2	
Queen of the South	L	24/25			D3
Partick T		25/26	1	1	
Third Lanark	L	25/26			
Partick T		26/27	36	41	
		27/28	11	6	
		28/29	7	12	
Alloa A	L	28/29			D2
Preston NE		28/29	31	19	FL
		29/30	13	3	FL
Shelbourne		30/31			LI
Bray Unknowns		30/31			LI
Colwyn Bay U		31/32			
Worcester C		32/33			
		33/34			
Burton T					

HAIR William					
b. Edinburgh 1904					
Newtongrange Star					
Broxburn U		25/26			D2
Bo'ness		25/26			D2
		26/27	?	11	D2
Rangers		26/27	2	2	
		27/28			
Grimsby T		28/29	6	2	FL
Peebles R					
Rhyl A		29/30			
Flint T U		29/30			
Leith A		30/31	3		

HALCROW Ronald John					
b. Maryhill 1914					
Pointhouse Amateurs					
Maryhill					
Morton Jnrs					
Pollok					
Ayr U		37/38			
		38/39	2		

HALDANE Edward					
Pollok					
Third Lanark		11/12	2		
		12/13	1		
Vale of Leven					

HALKET James					
Croy Celtic					
Hibernian		18/19	11	?	

HALKETT Alexander L					
K.I.A. 21.2.1917					
Dundee		01/02	1		
		02/03	2		
		03/04	13		
Aberdeen		04/05	16	1	D2
		05/06	22		
		06/07	30		
		07/08	29	1	
		08/09	19		
Portsmouth		09/10			
		10/11			
St Johnstone		11/12	16		D2
		12/13	19	3	D2

HALKETT John					
Dundee		99/00	1		
		00/01			
		01/02	6		

HALL Alexander Noble					
b. Peterhead 26.4.1886					
Toronto Scots					
Galt (Canada)					
Peterhill					
St Bernards		05/06			D2
		06/07			D2
Newcastle U		07/08	6	1	FL
Dundee		07/08	3		
		08/09	3		
		09/10	20	8	
Portsmouth		10/11	11	1	SL
Motherwell		11/12	11		D2
Dunfermline A		12/13			D2

HALL Alexander Richmond					
b. Kirkcaldy 1865 d. Dunfermline 1938					
Raith R					
Sheffield W		92/93	17	2	FL
		93/94			FL
Heart of Midlothian		94/95	12	1	
		95/96	2		
Dundee		96/97	18		
Tottenham H		97/98	21		SL
		98/99	3		SL
Aberdour					

HALL Coomb					
b. North Leith 1871 d. Port Elizabeth ?.3.1932					
St Bernards					
Blackburn R		90/91	14	4	FL
		91/92	15	6	FL
		92/93	13	6	FL
		93/94	26	3	FL
		94/95	12	7	FL
St Bernards		94/95	4		
		95/96	11	2	
Wanderers (SA)					
Port Elizabeth					

HALL Ellis					
b. Ecclesfield 22.6.1889 d. Sheffield 17.3.1947					
Ecclesfield Bible Class					
Hull C		05/06	3		FL
		06/07	5		FL
Hastings & St Leonards U		07/08			
		08/09			
Stoke		09/10	8		SL
Huddersfield T		10/11	24	1	FL
		11/12	15	1	FL
South Shields		12/13			
		13/14			
		14/15			
Hamilton A		19/20	40		
		20/21	41	2	
		21/22	37		
Millwall	T	22/23			FL
Halifax T		22/23	38	1	FL
		23/24	40		FL
		24/25	37	1	FL
Rochdale		25/26			FL
		26/27			FL
Consett					

HALL Frederick					
Clyde		97/98	3	1	
		98/99	2	1	
		99/00	4		

HALL James					
Queen's Park		35/36	3		
		36/37	6	2	
Aberdeen		37/38			

HALL James					
Kirk Lane Mission					
Neilston V					
Rutherglen Glencairn					
Third Lanark		36/37	8		
Ayr U		37/38	18		
		38/39	37		

HALL Matthew					
b. Renfrew 1884					
St Mirren		04/05	20	3	
		05/06	17	3	
Sunderland		06/07	8	1	FL
Clyde		07/08	31	3	
		08/09	9	1	
		09/10			
Alloa A		10/11			
Third Lanark		10/11	1		

HALL Robert					
Heart of Midlothian		12/13	1	1	

HALL Stuart					
Dundee		96/97	17		

HALL William					
St Mirren		01/02	12		

HALLERON Peter					
Dumbarton		21/22	10	4	
		22/23			D2
Alloa A		23/24			D2
Dumbarton Harp					
Royal Albert					
Vale of Leven		25/26			D3

HALLEY Alexander					
b. c1889					
Law					
Hibernian		09/10	10	1	

HALLEY George					
b. Lanark 29.10.1887					
Glenbuck Cherrypickers					
Kilmarnock		07/08	11		
		08/09	28	2	
		09/10	29	3	
		10/11	24	1	
Bradford PA		11/12	37	1	FL
		12/13	25	7	FL
Burnley		12/13	8		FL
		13/14	33	2	FL
		14/15	11		FL
		19/20	26		FL
		20/21	26		FL
		21/22	34	1	FL
Southend U		22/23	21	2	FL
Bacup B					

HALLIDAY David					
b. Dumfries 11.12.1897 d. Banchory 5.1.1970					
Tayleurians					
Queen of the South W					
St Mirren		20/21	13	2	
Albion R	L	20/21			
Dundee		21/22	28	23	
		22/23	26	10	
		23/24	36	38	
		24/25	36	19	
Sunderland		25/26	42	38	FL
		26/27	33	36	FL
		27/28	38	36	FL
		28/29	42	43	FL
		29/30	11	4	FL
Arsenal		29/30	15	8	FL
Manchester C		30/31	24	14	FL
		31/32	40	28	FL
		32/33	8	3	FL
		33/34	4	2	FL
Folkestone					
Clapton Orient		33/34	21	19	FL
		34/35	32	14	FL
Yeovil T		35/36			SL
		36/37			SL
		37/38			SL

HALLIDAY William
b. Dumfries 14.11.1906 d. Dumfries
Noblehill
Queen of the South
Newcastle U 27/28 1 FL
Third Lanark 28/29 29 9
Connahs Quay 29/30
Boston T 29/30
Exeter C 30/31 6 1 FL
31/32 5 FL
Gainsborough T 32/33
Queen of the South 33/34
Hyde U

HALLIGAN John
b. Glasgow c1899
Shawfield
Hibernian 20/21 16 3
21/22 42 3
22/23 35 3
23/24 31 10
24/25 38 9
25/26 33 8
26/27 34 10
27/28 29 3
28/29 37 4
29/30 33 2
30/31 7
31/32 D2
32/33 D2
33/34 12 2

HALLWOOD Charles
b. Wales
Heart of Midlothian 12/13 2
13/14 2
Lochgelly U 14/15 D2

HAMILL Alexander
b. Dumbarton 1912
Renton Thistle
Cowdenbeath 30/31 34 3
31/32 25 2
32/33 33 10
33/34 28 8
34/35 D2
Blackburn R 35/36 16 4 FL
36/37 5 FL
Barnsley 36/37 17 4 FL
37/38 7 FL
Carlisle U 38/39 25 2 FL

HAMILL Hugh
b. Dumbarton
Third Lanark 27/28 D2
28/29 37 15
Falkirk 29/30 37 14
30/31 38 3
31/32 37 11
32/33 38 5
33/34 33
34/35 37
35/36 D2
36/37 20
Alloa A T 37/38 D2

HAMILL Michael
b. Belfast 19.1.1885 d. Belfast 19.7.1943
St Pauls Swifts
Belfast R
Red Hand
Belfast Celtic 07/08 IL
08/09 IL
09/10 IL
10/11 IL
Celtic L 10/11
Manchester U 11/12 16 1 FL
12/13 15 1 FL
13/14 26 FL
Belfast Celtic 14/15 IL
15/16 IL
Distillery 16/17 IL
Celtic L 16/17 7
17/18
Belfast Celtic 18/19 IL
Celtic 18/19
Belfast Celtic 19/20 IL
Manchester C 20/21 28 FL
21/22 24 FL
22/23 41 FL
23/24 25 1 FL
Boston Wonder Workers 24/25 38 1 ASL
25/26 28 ASL
New York Giants 26/27 1 ASL
Belfast Celtic 26/27 IL
27/28 IL
28/29 IL
29/30 IL

HAMILTON
St Mirren 91/92 8 3

HAMILTON
Third Lanark 91/92 1

HAMILTON
Heart of Midlothian 92/93 4

HAMILTON
St Mirren 93/94 1

HAMILTON
Clyde 17/18 1

HAMILTON Alexander
Denny A
Clyde 06/07 4

HAMILTON Alexander C
Queen's Park 24/25 10
Hamilton A 25/26 3
Cowdenbeath

HAMILTON Carrick
Queen's Park 02/03 12
03/04 1
04/05
Partick T 05/06 20 5
Queen's Park 06/07 12 2
Stevenston U

HAMILTON David
b. Glasgow 21.10.1882 d. Glasgow 23.1.1950
Cambuslang Hibernian
Celtic 01/02
Clyde L 01/02 D2
Ayr L 01/02
Celtic 02/03 17 2
03/04 13 6
04/05 24 7
05/06 26 6
06/07 23 7
07/08 21 10
08/09 31 9
09/10 33 4
10/11 22
11/12 12 2
Dundee 12/13 14 1
Bathgate 13/14
Broxburn U 14/15

HAMILTON David
b. c1879 d. Dennistoun ?.9.1911
St Mirren 01/02 16 9
02/03 15 9
03/04 3 2
Ayr

HAMILTON Gavin
b. Motherwell
Queen of the South
Motherwell 21/22 6
22/23
23/24 3
Arbroath 23/24 23 D2
24/25 35 3 D2
25/26 37 2 D2
26/27 31 5 D2
27/28 20 2 D2
28/29 20 1 D2
29/30 4 D2
Montrose 29/30 D2
30/31 D2
31/32 D2

HAMILTON George
Lanemark 11/12
12/13
Arthurlie 12/13 D2
13/14 D2
14/15 D2
Heart of Midlothian 15/16 12 1
16/17
Kilmarnock 17/18 17 2
18/19
Clydebank 19/20

HAMILTON George 5 caps
b. Irvine 7.12.1917 d. Aberdeen 23.5.2001
Irvine Meadow
Queen of the South 37/38 31 9
Aberdeen 38/39 37 17
46/47 26 17
47/48 8 2
Heart of Midlothian 47/48 13 6
Aberdeen 48/49 20 10
49/50 26 9
50/51 28 17
51/52 19 13
52/53 18 15
53/54 15
54/55 4 2
Hamilton A 55/56 D2

HAMILTON Gladstone 1 cap
b. Glasgow 23.7.1879
Ayr
Port Glasgow A 02/03 17 3
03/04 4
04/05 23 6
05/06 16
St Mirren 06/07 8 2
Port Glasgow A 07/08 29 3
Brentford 08/09 3 SL
Port Glasgow A 08/09
09/10 17

HAMILTON Gordon D
Queen's Park 38/39 3

HAMILTON J
Abercorn 96/97 16 5

HAMILTON J
Queen's Park 03/04 1

HAMILTON James 3 caps
b. Glasgow
Queen's Park 85/86
86/87
87/88
88/89
89/90
90/91
91/92
92/93
93/94
Rangers 94/95 2 1
Queen's Park 95/96
96/97
97/98
Airdrieonians 98/99 15 4 D2
99/00 1 D2

HAMILTON James
Dundee 96/97 8

HAMILTON James
Queen's Park 08/09 2
09/10 26 6
10/11 19 3
Clyde 11/12 28 10
12/13 21 2
Partick T 13/14 25 2

HAMILTON James 1 cap
b. Bargeddie 16.6.1901 d. Glasgow 1975
Vale of Clyde
St Mirren 21/22 3
22/23 30
23/24 34
24/25 13
Rangers 25/26 29 2
26/27 6
27/28
Blackpool 28/29 25 FL
29/30 3 FL
Barrow 29/30 28 2 FL
30/31 15 FL
Armadale 30/31 D2
Galston 31/32
32/33

HAMILTON James
East Stirlingshire 32/33 3

HAMILTON James R
Heart of Midlothian 00/01 3 1

HAMILTON James R
Rangers 00/01
01/02 1

HAMILTON James R

Motherwell 03/04 5 2

HAMILTON James R

Rangers 06/07 2 1

HAMILTON James S

Leith A 31/32 9

HAMILTON James S

Cowdenbeath 32/33 4

HAMILTON James Stevenson
b. New Cumnock 16.8.1906
Girvan Jnrs
Hamilton A
Ayr U 30/31 1
Rochdale 31/32 39 FL
32/33 38 FL
Wrexham 33/34 37 FL
34/35 42 1 FL
35/36 41 FL
36/37 42 FL
37/38 1 FL
Carlisle U 38/39 28 FL
Chester

HAMILTON James W

Arthurlie 35/36
36/37
Clyde 37/38 11 1

HAMILTON John

Royal Albert
Third Lanark 97/98 2

HAMILTON Robert

Dunfermline A
Partick T 11/12 11
Australia

HAMILTON Robert

Lanemark
Partick T 13/14
14/15
Lanemark
Kilmarnock 16/17 1

HAMILTON Robert Cumming 11 caps
b. Elgin 13.5.1877 d. Elgin 2.5.1948
Elgin C
Queen's Park 96/97
Rangers 97/98 15 18
98/99 18 21
99/00 16 17
00/01 19 20
01/02 16 9
02/03 19 13
03/04 24 28
04/05 17 19
05/06 20 9
Fulham 06/07 28 11 SL
Rangers 07/08 11 3
Heart of Midlothian 07/08 5 1
Elgin C 08/09
Morton 08/09 26 13
09/10 31 12
Dundee 10/11 31 17
11/12 30 14
12/13 28 4
13/14 4 2
Elgin C 13/14
Buckie Thistle 13/14

HAMILTON Robert Templeton
b. Newry 11.11.1903 d. Cardiff 7.2.1964
Damolly R
Portadown
Newry T 24/25 IL
25/26 IL
26/27 IL
Rangers 26/27 1
27/28 21
28/29 34
29/30 29
30/31 27
31/32 5
32/33 4
Bradford C 33/34 7 FL
34/35 16 FL
Third Lanark 35/36 23 1
36/37 18
37/38 6
Morton 37/38 9
Bangor 38/39 IL

HAMILTON Samuel

Queen's Park 02/03 4

HAMILTON T

Leith A 94/95 5 3

HAMILTON Thomas

Clyde 94/95 7
95/96 7

HAMILTON Thomas

Albion R
Clyde 96/97
97/98 3
Lanemark

HAMILTON Thomas
b. New Cumnock 10.2.1893 d. Preston 25.12.1959
New Cumnock Afton Lily
Cronberry Eglington
Kilmarnock 13/14 1
14/15 30 2
15/16 36
16/17 33 4
17/18 32 3
18/19 30
19/20 41
20/21 29 3
Preston NE 20/21 14 FL
21/22 37 FL
22/23 38 FL
23/24 36 FL
Dick, Kerrs L 24/25
Preston NE 24/25 18 FL
25/26 27 FL
26/27 28 FL
27/28 42 FL
28/29 29 FL
Manchester Central 29/30
Great Harwood
Leyland Motors

HAMILTON Thomas

Larkhall Thistle
Hamilton A 13/14 2
Dumbarton 14/15 38
15/16 38
16/17 10
Renton
Hamilton A 16/17 9
Renton

HAMILTON Thomas
b. Stevenston
Ardrossan Winton R
Kilmarnock
Clydebank 18/19 9
Stevenston U
Falkirk 20/21 28 4
21/22 32 1
Llanelly 22/23
Hull C T 23/24 2 FL

HAMILTON Thomas 1 cap
b. Renfrew 1906 d. Saltcoats ?.7.1964
Kirkintilloch Rob Roy
Rangers 23/24
24/25
25/26 16
26/27 37
27/28 33
28/29 38
29/30 38
30/31 37
31/32 25
32/33 18
33/34 1
Falkirk 34/35 25

HAMILTON W

Leith A 94/95 2

HAMILTON William

Cleland Amateurs
Partick T 03/04 1

HAMILTON William
b. Cowdenbeath c1890 d. Dunfermline ?.8.1921
Dunfermline A
Partick T 11/12 27 3
12/13 9
13/14 13
14/15 28 1
15/16 31 2
16/17 16
17/18 27
18/19 32 3
19/20 32 1
20/21 30 2

HAMILTON William

Clyde 14/15 1
15/16 1
Rangers 16/17 1

HAMILTON William

Clyde 17/18 2

HAMILTON William G

Queen's Park 21/22 2

HAMPTON Colin McKenzie
b. Brechin 1.9.1888
Brechin R
Brechin C
Motherwell 09/10 4
10/11 32
11/12 32
12/13 31
13/14 35
Chelsea 13/14 1 FL
14/15 1 FL
19/20 15 FL
20/21 6 FL
21/22 9 FL
22/23 25 FL
23/24 22 FL
Brechin C 24/25 D2
25/26 D2
Crystal Palace 25/26 3 FL

HANDLING Hamilton
d. c1956
St Cuthberts W
Hibernian 98/99 11 3
99/00 2
00/01 18 7
01/02 11 7
02/03 1

HANLIN Alexander W

Burnbank A
St Mirren 36/37 11 2
37/38 12 2
38/39 4 1

HANLON John
d. 1976
Fauldhouse WE
Hamilton A 12/13 3
13/14 12
Peebles R 13/14
Hamilton A 14/15 36 5
15/16 37 6
16/17
Heart of Midlothian L 16/17 1
Hamilton A 17/18
18/19
19/20 21 4
20/21 37 6
21/22 38 6
Heart of Midlothian 22/23 18 2
Bathgate
Peebles R
Alloa A 25/26 D2

HANNAH

Dumbarton 90/91 5

HANNAH A B

Clyde 96/97 9

HANNAH Andrew Boyd					1 cap
b. Renton 17.9.1864 d. Clydebank ?.6.1940					
Renton		83/84			
		84/85			
		85/86			
		86/87			
		87/88			
WBA		88/89			
Renton		88/89			
Everton		89/90	22		FL
		90/91	20		FL
Renton		91/92	18		
Liverpool		92/93	22	1	LL
		93/94	24	1	FL
		94/95	18		FL
Rob Roy		95/96			
		96/97			

HANNAH George					
b. Loanhead					
Loanhead Mayflower					
Hamilton A		19/20	20		
		20/21	35	2	
Cowdenbeath		21/22			D2
Broxburn U		22/23			D2
Dundee Hibs		23/24	10		D2
		24/25			
New Brighton		25/26	6		FL
Loanhead Mayflower					

HANNAH George L					
Falkirk		21/22	6	1	
East Stirlingshire		22/23			D2

HANNAH J					
Renton		92/93	1		

HANNAH James					1 cap
b. Glasgow c1868					
Third Lanark		88/89			
		89/90			
Sunderland A		90/91			
Sunderland		91/92	22	17	FL
		92/93	28	19	FL
		93/94	20	6	FL
		94/95	28	9	FL
		95/96	26	9	FL
		96/97	28	8	FL
Third Lanark		97/98	11		
		98/99	12	3	
QPR		99/00	17	3	SL
Dykehead		00/01			
Sunderland Royal R					

HANNAH James					
Dundee		97/98	2		

HANNAH John					
Clydebank Jnrs					
Third Lanark		11/12	1	1	
		12/13	28	1	
		13/14	34		
		14/15	31	2	
		15/16	18		
		16/17	37	1	
		17/18	16	?	
		18/19	16	?	
Dumbarton		18/19			

HANNAH John					
Clydebank		20/21	1		

HANNAH John					
Arthurlie					
St Mirren		22/23	1		
		23/24	1		

HANNAH Robert					
b. Aberdeen					
Aberdeen		10/11	2		
		11/12	2		
		12/13	20	1	
		13/14	26		
		14/15	1		
		15/16			
		16/17			
		17/18			
		18/19			
		19/20	36		
		20/21	25		
		21/22	3		
Peterhead					

HANNAH Robert					
Renfrew					
St Mirren		15/16	8	1	
Johnstone		15/16			
Renton		16/17			

HANNAH Robert					
Clyde		16/17	1		

HANNIGAN Patrick					
d. 15.3.1945					
Galston					
Kilmarnock	T	11/12	1		
Galston					
Beith					
Hurlford					
Dumbarton Harp					
Arthurlie					
Dumbarton Harp		19/20			
Hibernian		20/21	32	5	
		21/22			
St Johnstone		21/22	13	3	D2
		22/23			D2
Arthurlie		22/23			
Peebles R	L	22/23			
Millwall					

HANSEN Carl					
b. Denmark					
Copenhagen					
Rangers		21/22	11	8	
		22/23	10	6	
		23/24	2		

HANSON H C (Hjalmar?)					
Clydebank Jnrs					
Motherwell		10/11	12	1	
Renton		11/12			

HARDIE					
Heart of Midlothian		10/11	1		

HARDIE					
Armadale					
Ayr U		17/18	3	?	

HARDIE Alexander Shaw					
b. Kilsyth 8.7.1898					
Kilsyth R					
Third Lanark		22/23	6		
		23/24			
		24/25	3		
Charlton A		25/26	28	3	FL
Plymouth A		25/26	11		FL
		26/27	40	1	FL
		27/28	42		FL
		28/29	31	2	FL
		29/30	35		FL
		30/31	39	1	FL
		31/32	17		FL
		32/33	17		FL
Exeter C		33/34	18	1	FL
Truro C					

HARDIE George					
b. Renton					
Blantyre Celtic					
Third Lanark		21/22	2		
		22/23	5		
Arbroath		23/24	38	4	D2
		24/25	34	4	D2
		25/26	29	7	D2
		26/27	34	7	D2
		27/28	34	6	D2
		28/29	23	2	D2
Montrose	L	28/29			D2
Arbroath		29/30	32	3	D2
		30/31	4		D2
		31/32			D2

HARDIE James					
Burnbank A					
Alloa A					
Queen of the South		29/30			D2
Airdrieonians		30/31	1		

HARDIE W					
Morton		12/13	1	1	

HARDY William					
b. Bedlington 18.4.1892 d. Newton Abbot 1981					
Bedlington U					
Heart of Midlothian		09/10	4		
Stockport Co		10/11	1		FL
Cardiff C		11/12	23		SL
		12/13	21	1	SL
		13/14	38		SL
		14/15	37		SL
		19/20	22	1	SL
		20/21	42	1	FL
		21/22	32	1	FL
		22/23	35		FL
		23/24	39	4	FL
		24/25	35		FL
		25/26	37	1	FL
		26/27	40		FL
		27/28	41		FL
		28/29	24	1	FL
		29/30	6		FL
		30/31	12		FL
		31/32	8		FL

HARE Andrew					
Ashfield					
Airdrieonians		20/21	2		

HARKER Richard					
b. Wardley Colliery					
Newcastle U					
Crystal Palace		05/06	?	?	SL
		06/07	35	8	SL
Hibernian		07/08	32	20	
		08/09	31	8	
Heart of Midlothian		09/10	28	8	
		10/11	31	9	
Crystal Palace		11/12	15	7	SL
Darlington					

HARKINS James					
b. Paisley 1905					
Dalbeattie Star					
Petershill					
Third Lanark		24/25	1		
Solway Star					
Luton T		27/28	4	3	FL
Port Vale		27/28			FL
Bo'ness		27/28	3		
		28/29			D2
		29/30			D2
		30/31			D2
Solway Star					

HARKINS John					
b. Bathgate 21.2.1909					
St Marys Guild					
Dalkeith Thistle					
Albion R		28/29			D2
		29/30			D2
Millwall		30/31	3	1	FL
		31/32			FL
		32/33	5		FL
		33/34	9		FL
		34/35	9		FL
Albion R		35/36	20	4	

HARKNESS Henry					
Sunderland					
Heart of Midlothian		10/11	1	1	

HARKNESS John Diamond					11 caps
b. Govanhill 27.9.1907 d. 6.10.1985					
Mount Florida					
Queen's Park		25/26	20		
		26/27	38		
		27/28	35		
Heart of Midlothian		28/29	36		
		29/30	34		
		30/31	35		
		31/32	37		
		32/33	36		
		33/34	36		
		34/35	38		
		35/36	38		
		36/37	2		

HARKNESS William					
Queen of the South		38/39	13	2	
		46/47			
Cowdenebeath	T	47/48			D2
Carlisle U					
Workington					

HARLEY Alexander John
b. Edinburgh 17.7.1898 d. Cardiff 9.2.1984
Bonnyrigg Rose A
Bathgate
Heart of Midlothian 25/26 24
26/27 7
Caernarvon T 26/27
New Brighton 27/28 27 14 FL
Millwall 28/29 7 4 FL
Rhyl A 29/30
Connahs Quay 29/30
Norwich C 30/31 1 FL

HARLEY Bruce
b. c1904
Musselburgh Bruntonians
Heart of Midlothian 24/25
25/26
26/27
27/28
28/29
Dundee U 29/30 11
30/31 13 1 D2

HARNETT Charles
b. c1901
Inverkip R
Morton 22/23 1
Helensburgh 23/24 D3
24/25 D3

HARPER
St Mirren 90/91 1

HARPER Archibald
b. St Ninians 1887 d. Millhall Colliery 18.2.1913
Dundee 07/08 3
Fulham 08/09 FL
Aberdeen 09/10 2
10/11 2
11/12 2

HARPER Harry
Battlefield
Partick T 20/21 3
21/22
Bo'ness 22/23 D2

HARPER William 11 caps
b. Winchburgh 19.1.1897 d. Plymouth 25.4.1989
Winchburgh Thistle
Winchburgh Violet
Broxburn St Andrews
Edinburgh Emmet
Hibernian 20/21 35
21/22 42
22/23 35
23/24 28
24/25 31
25/26 7
Arsenal 25/26 19 FL
26/27 23 FL
Fall River Marksmen 27/28 29 ASL
28/29 50 ASL
Boston Wonder Workers 28/29 4 ASL
29A 20 ASL
29/30 1 ASL
New Bedford Whalers 29/30 31 ASL
Arsenal 30/31 19 FL
31/32 2 FL
Plymouth A 31/32 20 FL
32/33 37 FL
33/34 14 FL
34/35 4 FL

HARRIS
Third Lanark 96/97 1

HARRIS Cecil Norman
b. Shropshire
Hibernian 27/28 1
28/29 6
Darlington 29/30 17 FL
30/31 4 FL

HARRIS Charles
Shawfield Jnrs *
Bo'ness * 22/23 D2
23/24 D2
Falkirk 24/25 32
25/26 22

HARRIS George D
Glasgow Perthshire
Third Lanark 20/21 11
21/22 3

HARRIS James Somerville
b. Gorbals 17.5.1906
Shawfield
Hamilton A 26/27 15
Dunfermline A 27/28 29
28/29
Manchester C 29/30 FL
Rotherham U 30/31 10 FL
Waterford 30/31 LI
31/32 LI
Cork Bohemians 32/33 LI
Glentoran 32/33 IL
33/34 IL
Bangor 34/35 IL

HARRIS Joseph 2 caps
b. Glasgow 19.3.1896 d. Glasgow 29.10.1933
Strathclyde
Partick T 13/14 18 1
14/15 25 1
15/16 11
16/17 22
17/18 17
18/19 4
19/20 27
20/21 33
21/22 28 3
22/23 21
Middlesbrough 22/23 8 FL
23/24 32 FL
24/25 16 FL
Third Lanark
Newcastle U 25/26 16 FL
26/27 9 FL
27/28 41 1 FL
28/29 39 1 FL
29/30 38 FL
30/31 6 FL
York C 31/32 25 FL
32/33 37 FL

HARRIS Joshua
b. Glasgow 5.12.1891 d. Leeds 1966
Vale of Clyde
Glasgow Ashfield
Burnley 10/11 24 FL
11/12 33 5 FL
Bristol C 12/13 32 2 FL
13/14 31 5 FL
14/15 35 8 FL
Partick T L 15/16 2
Clydebank L 18/19 8 ?
Bristol C 19/20 35 5 FL
20/21 42 2 FL
21/22 30 3 FL
Leeds U 22/23 39 5 FL
23/24 41 5 FL
24/25 42 3 FL
25/26 4 1 FL
Fulham 25/26 27 1 FL
26/27 15 1 FL

HARRIS Neill 1 cap
b. Shettleston 30.10.1894 d. Swindon 3.12.1941
Vale of Clyde
Partick T 13/14 16 5
14/15 18 10
15/16 22 16
16/17 27 12
Kilmarnock L 16/17 1
Rangers L 16/17 1 1
Partick T 17/18 23 16
St Mirren L 17/18 5 7
Partick T 18/19
19/20 34 23
Newcastle U 20/21 33 16 FL
21/22 34 22 FL
22/23 37 13 FL
23/24 33 15 FL
24/25 33 19 FL
25/26 4 2 FL
Notts Co 25/26 22 8 FL
26/27 26 16 FL
Shelbourne 27/28 LI
Oldham A 27/28 31 14 FL
28/29 8 2 FL
Third Lanark 28/29 7 6
29/30
Burton T 30/31
31/32
Distillery 32/33 IL
33/34 IL

HARRIS William
Armadale
Airdrieonians 12/13 3

HARRISON
St Mirren 91/92 5 1
92/93 3 1

HARRISON George
Dunfermline A 35/36 9
36/37 4
Leith A 37/38 D2
38/39 D2
Kings Park

HARRISON James
b. Bolton c1914
Army
Hibernian 36/37 15 4
37/38 5 1
Cardiff C 37/38 1 FL
Rochdale T 37/38 FL
Chorley

HARRISON Robert G
b. Greenock 1911
Port Glasgow Jnrs
Airdrieonians 30/31 11 2
31/32 6 2
32/33 22 6
33/34 26 7
Hamilton A 34/35 36 17
35/36 37 21
36/37 32 16
37/38 19 16
Rangers 37/38 10 2
38/39 4 3
Hamilton A

HARROWER
Third Lanark 99/00 1

HARROWER James
b. Clackmannan c1878
Clackmannan
Hibernian 99/00 13
00/01 16
01/02 17
02/03 12
03/04 26 2
04/05 25 1
05/06 22
06/07 27
07/08 2
Clackmannan 07/08
Kings Park 07/08
Clackmannan

HARROWER William J
Shettleston
Third Lanark 14/15 1
Vale of Leven

HART
Dumbarton 18/19 1

HART
Motherwell 18/19 1 2

HART
St Mirren 18/19 1 ?

HART Alexander
b. 1883 d. Camlachie 6.11.1940
Glasgow Ashfield
St Mirren 16/17
17/18
18/19 5
Vale of Clyde 19/20

HART Archibald
b. Glasgow
Rutherglen Glencairn
Third Lanark 36/37 19 3
37/38 20 4
38/39 15 3

HART Hunter
b. Glasgow 11.3.1897 d. West Cheshire 1954
Parkhead White Rose
Parkhead
Airdrieonians 17/18 32
18/19 33
19/20 41 1
20/21 39 3
21/22 25
Everton 21/22 17 FL
22/23 40 1 FL
23/24 42 2 FL
24/25 24 FL
25/26 26 FL
26/27 39 1 FL
27/28 41 1 FL
28/29 40 FL
29/30 20 FL

HART John
b. Motherwell c1897 d. 29.6.1963
Larkhall Thistle
Rangers 18/19
Hamilton A L 18/19 4 1
Albion R 19/20 25 10
St Johnstone 20/21
Motherwell 21/22 19 3
22/23 5 2
23/24
St Johnstone 24/25 25 8
25/26 20 9
Ross Co
Dundee U 26/27 27 1
27/28 35 10 D2
28/29 32 9 D2
29/30 20 3

HART John
Troon A
Shettleston
Bo'ness 27/28 18 5

HART Joseph
b. Larkhall
Larkhall Thistle
Rangers 17/18 3 2
18/19 3 3
Kilmarnock L 18/19 1
Renton 18/19

HART Robert
Queen's Park 00/01 1
01/02 1
02/03 3
03/04 3
04/05 2
05/06 4
06/07 1

HART Robert McKenzie
b. Melrose c1909
Cowie Juveniles
Ayr U 29/30 17 8
30/31 7 2

HART Thomas
Queen of the South 37/38 2

HARTE Patrick
b. Dalziel 1915
Clydesdale Corinthians
St Rochs
Wishaw Jnrs
Preston NE 34/35 FL
35/36 FL
36/37 FL
Torquay U 37/38 5 1 FL
Hibernian 38/39 1 2

HARTLEY Abraham
b. Dumbarton 8.2.1872 d. Southampton 9.10.1909
Artizan Thistle
Dumbarton 92/93 8 5
Everton 92/93 1 1 FL
93/94 6 2 FL
94/95 11 5 FL
95/96 15 8 FL
96/97 14 5 FL
97/98 3 3 FL
Liverpool 97/98 7 FL
Southampton 98/99 22 15 SL
Woolwich Arsenal 99/00 5 1 FL
Burnley 99/00 13 5 FL

HARTLEY James Milburn
b. Dumbarton 29.10.1876
Dumbarton 94/95 7 1
95/96 7 5
Sunderland 95/96 5 FL
96/97 6 1 FL
Burnley 96/97 1 FL
Lincoln C 96/97 9 5 FL
Tottenham H 97/98 15 7 SL
98/99 2 1 SL
Lincoln C 99/00 33 15 FL
00/01 34 10 FL
01/02 28 9 FL
02/03 34 13 FL
Rangers 03/04 4
Port Glasgow A 04/05 23 11
Brentford 05/06 19 3 SL
New Brompton 06/07 18 10 SL
07/08 14 3 SL
Port Glasgow A 08/09
09/10

HARVEY Harry
Wallsend Park Villa
St Mirren 09/10 11
10/11 5

HARVEY James
b. Stevenston
Kilwinning Segton
Kilwinning R
Stevenston U
Kilwinning R
Kilmarnock 22/23 6

HARVEY James
Third Lanark 31/32 7
32/33 2
33/34 7
34/35 D2
35/36 20
36/37 18
37/38 1
East Stirlingshire 38/39 D2

HARVEY John
b. Scotland
Renton
Sunderland 90/91 15 3 FL
Clyde 91/92 21 3
92/93 5 3
Sunderland 92/93 21 5 FL
93/94 24 2 FL
94/95 7 FL
95/96 16 4 FL
96/97 13 FL
Newcastle U 97/98 24 4 FL
98/99 3 1 FL

HARVEY John
Abercorn 95/96 7 ? D2
96/97 3

HARVEY John
Partick T 97/98 1
Derby Co

HARVEY John
Aberdeen 04/05 7 2 D2
05/06 1

HARVEY John
b. Wallyford d. 1980
Ormiston Primrose
Heart of Midlothian 32/33
Bo'ness 33/34 D2
Heart of Midlothian 33/34 1
34/35 2
35/36 27 2
36/37 16
37/38 9
East Fife L 37/38 D2
Kilmarnock 38/39 34 2
45/46 9

HARVEY John Arthur H
Partick T
Derby Co 94/95 5 FL
Ilkeston T
Abercorn 95/96 7 D2
96/97 3

HARVEY Thomas H
Partick T 00/01 19
01/02 19 D2
02/03 21
03/04 23 2
04/05 23 1
05/06 13
06/07 16

HARVEY Thomas McK
Queen's Park 29/30 2
30/31 1
31/32 8

HARVIE
Third Lanark 93/94 2

HARVIE John
b. Duntocher
Benburb
Falkirk 15/16 18 4
16/17 38 4
17/18 30 ?
18/19 25 ?
19/20 27 3
Clydebank 20/21 21 3
21/22 D2
22/23 D2
23/24 D2
24/25 D2
Johnstone 25/26 D3
Dumbarton 25/26 D2

HASSON Herbert B
b. c1913
Bute A
Third Lanark 32/33 3
33/34 4

HASSON William Craig
b. Glasgow 12.6.1905 d. Kensington 1976
Shettleston
Clyde 26/27 30 2
27/28 17 1
Oldham A 28/29 16 FL
29/30 40 10 FL
30/31 38 4 FL
31/32 19 4 FL
32/33 10 3 FL
33/34 11 1 FL
Millwall 34/35 13 2 FL
Chesterfield 35/36 2 FL

HASTIE
Heart of Midlothian 90/91 6

HASTIE
Vale of Leven 91/92 2

HASTIE Archibald
b. Shotts 1913
Douglas Water Thistle
Partick T 33/34 3
34/35 22 11
35/36 30 7
36/37 3 1
Huddersfield T 36/37 9 1 FL
37/38 4 FL
Motherwell 37/38 8 2
38/39 1 1
Bradford C 38/39 31 9 FL

HASTIE George
b. Glasgow
Govan Glentoran
Glasgow Ashfield 06/07
07/08
08/09
Kilmarnock 09/10 23 3
Bristol R 10/11 21 6 SL
Bath C 11/12
Kilmarnock 11/12 11
St Johnstone 12/13 3 1 D2
Abercorn 12/13 D2
13/14 D2
Leicester F 14/15 17 1 FL
Belfast U 15/16 IL
Arthurlie 15/16
16/17
17/18
18/19
Belfast Celtic 19/20 IL
Abercorn 19/20
Johnstone 20/21

HASTIE Isaac
Birmingham C
Airdrieonians 18/19 7 1

HASTIE John
Carluke Milton R
Partick T 02/03 4 2
03/04 3 1
04/05 1
Bathgate 04/05
Dykehead
Heart of Midlothian
Hamilton A 09/10 3
10/11 27 3
11/12 10
Dykehead 12/13

HASTIE John

Glenbuck Cherrypickers
Nithsdale W
Glenbuck Cherrypickers
Celtic 10/11 16 3
11/12
Raith R L 11/12 16 4
Nithsdale W

HASTIE John

Eastwood Jnrs
St Mirren 18/19 12 ?
Reading 19/20 15 6 SL
Plymouth A 19/20 2 SL
Middlesbrough 20/21 1 FL
Dundee

HASTINGS

Dumbarton 95/96 2

HASTINGS George

St Mirren 99/00 17 1

HAUGH Albert

Glasgow Perthshire
Maryhill
St Anthonys
Partick T 18/19 5 1
19/20 6
Maryhill Jnrs

HAUGH John

Third Lanark 97/98 1

HAWTHORN James

Queen's Park 05/06 2

HAWTHORN William
b. Glasgow 1908
Maryhill Hibernian
Kilsyth R
Alloa A 31/32 D2
32/33 D2
Bradford PA 32/33 11 FL
33/34 21 FL
Airdrieonians 34/35 23
35/36 36
New Brighton 36/37 42 FL
37/38 42 FL
38/39 24 FL
39/40 3 FL

HAXTON James

Lochgelly R
Lochgelly U 02/03
Motherwell 03/04
04/05 25 9
Bristol R 05/06 SL
Aberdeen 06/07 7
Lochgelly U

HAY Andrew H

Queen's Park 25/26 1
26/27 12
27/28 3
28/29
Arthurlie Amateurs 29/30

HAY George

Newtongrange Star
Third Lanark 33/34 4 4
34/35 D2
35/36 35 21
36/37 29 16
Queen of the South 37/38 29 11
38/39 36 16

HAY James 11 caps
b. Beith 12.12.1880 d. Ayr 4.4.1940
Woodside Annbank Jnrs
Celtic T
Annbank
Ayr 01/02 ? ? D2
Annbank
Celtic 02/03
Annbank L 02/03
Celtic 03/04 24 2
04/05 26 3
05/06 30 4
06/07 24 1
07/08 22 3
08/09 32
09/10 29 2
10/11 30
Newcastle U 11/12 35 7 FL
12/13 31 FL
13/14 33 FL
14/15 33 FL
Ayr U 15/16 24
16/17 38
17/18 23 ?
Heart of Midlothian
Clydebank 18/19 1
Ayr U

HAY Norman W

Queen's Park 00/01 10 1
St Mirren 00/01

HAY Walter

Rangers 34/35 1

HAY Walter M
b. Glasgow
Petershill
St Mirren 24/25 6
25/26 2
26/27 10
27/28 16
28/29 32
29/30 38
30/31 30
31/32 37
32/33 36
33/34 27

HAY William
b. Maryhill 1871
Maryhill
Queen's Park
Partick T 86/87
87/88
88/89
Rangers 89/90
90/91
91/92 1
Millwall 92/93
London Caledonians 92/93
93/94
Clapton
Tottenham H 94/95
Queen's Park 94/95
London Caledonians 95/96
Rangers 96/97 1

HAYDOCK Thomas
d. ?.9.1917
Queen's Park 13/14 1
14/15 16
15/16 9

HAYMAN

Third Lanark 91/92 1

HAYWOOD Norman Scott Carmichael
b. Portobello 7.9.1910 d. Kirkcaldy 30.7.1979
Peebles R
Watford 33/34 1 FL
Peebles R 34/35
Queen of the South 35/36 16 2
36/37 5
Leith A 36/37 D2
Raith R 37/38 34 47 D2
38/39 22 10
Leith A
Peebles R

HAZELDEAN James William
b. c1885
Heart of Midlothian 15/16 5
Portobello Thistle
Alloa A 19/20

HEADRICK James
b. Alva 1898 d. Gleneagles ?.6.1925
Stirling Emmet
Dundee Hibs 21/22 30 2 D2
Alloa A 22/23 21 1

HEALEY John

Dunfermline A 26/27 5

HEALY James
b. Craigneuk 14.9.1901 d. Craigneuk 5.12.1969
Shieldmuir Celtic
Celtic 24/25 2
Montrose L 24/25 D3
Stenhousemuir L 24/25 D2
Motherwell L 24/25 2
Plymouth A 25/26 10 3 FL
26/27 FL
27/28 5 FL
28/29 10 1 FL
29/30 3 FL
Bristol C

HEARD Richard

Clyde 17/18 2 ?
18/19 11 ?

HEARTY Hugh
b. Lesmahagow 22.3.1913 d. St Albans ?.4.1992
Royal Albert
Heart of Midlothian 32/33 4
33/34 11
34/35 6
Clyde
Cardiff C 35/36 18 FL
Clapton Orient 36/37 35 1 FL
37/38 37 1 FL
38/39 26 FL
Rochester City Police

HEATLIE Thomas

Duns
Heart of Midlothian 11/12 3

HEDLEY George Thomas
b. Lanchester 1882 d. Hartlepool ?.6.1937
West Stanley
Middlesbrough 05/06 3 FL
Chester 05/06
Heart of Midlothian T 05/06 2
Hull C 05/06 11 1 FL
06/07 38 1 FL
07/08 29 FL
Leicester F 07/08 3 FL
08/09 32 1 FL
Luton T 09/10 21 4 SL
Hartlepool U 10/11
11/12
Crook T 12/13
Jarrow Caledonians
Brandesburton

HEEPS Alexander

Falkirk 25/26 4
26/27 3 1
Bo'ness 27/28 16 6
Falkirk 28/29 1
Stenhousemuir

HEEPS Andrew
b. Muiravonside 15.12.1899
Banknock Jnrs
Dunfermline A 24/25 D2
Airdrieonians 24/25 1
25/26 3
26/27 5
27/28 7
Brentford 28/29 2 FL
Camelon 29/30
Bo'ness 30/31 D2
31/32 D2
32/33 D2
Dumbarton 32/33 D2

HEEPS James
b. Falkirk 14.11.1899
Banknock Jnrs
Plymouth A 20/21 16 1 FL
21/22 FL
Hamilton A 22/23 10
New York Giants 23/24 6 4 ASL
24/25
Bathgate 25/26 D2

HEGAN John A S

Morton 13/14 1

HEGARTY Thomas
b. Hartlepool 1882
West Hartlepool Perseverance
West Hartlepool 03/04
04/05
Stockport Co 05/06 3 2 FL
Sunderland Royal R 06/07
07/08
West Hartlepool 08/09
09/10
Heart of Midlothian 10/11 19
11/12 20 3
12/13 6

HEGGERTY Thomas
Whitrigg U
Hibernian 26/27 4 2
27/28 10 7

HEGGIE William
Churches League football
Clyde 12/13 1
St Johnstone 13/14 3 D2
Abercorn 14/15 D2

HEMPHILL Alexander Y
b. 1885 d. Drowned ?.12.1926
Maryhill
Workington
Albion R 10/11 17 ? D2
Hamilton A 11/12 8 1
Dunfermline A

HEMPSEY John
b. c1889 d. Tradeston 2.8.1938
Port Glasgow A
Morton 11/12 3
Rangers 12/13 17
Morton L 12/13
Rangers 13/14 22
14/15 12
15/16 21
16/17 21
Kilmarnock L 16/17 1
Rangers 17/18 25
18/19 29
19/20
Kings Park 20/21
Morton 21/22 3

HENDERSON
Leith A 91/92 5

HENDERSON
Vale of Leven 91/92 3

HENDERSON
Renton 92/93 6

HENDERSON
Third Lanark 92/93 1 1
93/94 13 2

HENDERSON
St Bernards 96/97 1

HENDERSON
Hibernian 07/08 4

HENDERSON
Dumbarton 18/19 1 ?

HENDERSON Adam
b. Darlington 16.6.1873
Airdrie Fruitfield
Airdrieonians
Preston NE 93/94 2 FL
94/95 26 10 FL
95/96 23 4 FL
96/97 26 11 FL
Celtic 97/98 9 4
Bristol St Georges 98/99
Preston NE 99/00 25 11 FL
00/01 15 1 FL

HENDERSON Albert
Penicuik A
Falkirk 14/15 35
15/16 1
16/17 13
17/18 1 ?
18/19 15 ?

HENDERSON Alex
Falkirk 13/14 10

HENDERSON Alexander
Falkirk 19/20 3
20/21
Dumbarton 21/22 36

HENDERSON Alexander
b. c1903
Murrayfield Amateurs
Cowdenbeath 25/26 1

HENDERSON Alexander
Dundee NE
Dundee U 26/27 5 1
27/28 2 D2
East Fife 28/29

HENDERSON Andrew
Penicuik A
Heart of Midlothian
Falkirk 14/15 9
15/16
16/17
17/18
18/19 12

HENDERSON Charles
Montrose
Hibernian 04/05 5 1
Aberdeen 05/06 8
Hibernian
Montrose
Arbroath
Brechin C 08/09

HENDERSON Charles John
b. Durham ?.4.1870
South Bank
Grimsby T 92/93 11 1 FL
Leith A 93/94 13 3
Bolton W 94/95 28 14 FL
Wolverhampton W 95/96 30 9 FL
Sheffield U 96/97 14 3 FL
South Bank

HENDERSON David
Larkhall Thistle
Motherwell 20/21 12
21/22 6
Royal Albert 22/23
Mid Annandale 23/24 D3

HENDERSON Douglas
Queen's Park 18/19 6
19/20
Albion R 20/21

HENDERSON George
Cowlairs 89/90
90/91 15 2

HENDERSON George
Dundee 05/06 25 1
06/07 20

HENDERSON George
b. High Blantyre 15.12.1873
Coatbridge St Patricks
Burnbank Swifts
Motherwell 93/94 3 ? D2
94/95 2 ? D2
Airdrieonians 95/96 14 ? D2
96/97 15 ? D2
Preston NE 97/98 2 FL
Swindon T 98/99 23 4 SL
99/00 28 6 SL
Millwall 00/01 26 9 SL
Nottingham F 01/02 23 2 FL
02/03 23 FL
03/04 15 1 FL
04/05 21 1 FL
05/06 21 1 FL
Hamilton A 06/07 5
Girvan

HENDERSON George Donald
b. Forfar 15.4.1897 d. Dundee 14.6.1953
Forfar Celtic
Forfar A
Dundee 19/20 7
Rangers 19/20 6 2
20/21 23 21
21/22 28 21
22/23 28 23
23/24 31 19
24/25 37 27
25/26 13 7
26/27 4 3
Darlington 26/27 14 6 FL
New York Nationals 27/28 32 11 ASL
Dundee U 28/29 33 10 D2
29/30 36 12
Rhyl

HENDERSON George Turnbull 1 cap
b. Ladhope 2.5.1880 d. Birmingham 27.1.1930
Queen's Park
Dundee 01/02 2
02/03 12
Rangers 02/03 2
03/04 18
04/05 14
Middlesbrough 05/06 10 FL
Chelsea 05/06 3 FL
06/07 37 FL
07/08 14 1 FL
08/09 6 FL
Glossop 09/10 6 FL

HENDERSON Hugh
Falkirk 12/13 1

HENDERSON J
Leith A 92/93 18 8
93/94 12 6

HENDERSON J
Broxburn A
Cowdenbeath 21/22 D2
Heart of Midlothian 22/23 18 2
Cowdenbeath 23/24 D2
Broxburn U
Edinburgh C

HENDERSON James
b. Thornhill 1867
5th Kirkcudbright RV
Rangers 89/90
90/91 13 6
91/92 7
92/93
Royal Arsenal 93/94 22 10 FL
94/95 15 7 FL

HENDERSON James
Annbank
Partick T 00/01 3

HENDERSON John
b. Scotland d. ?.7.1932
Clyde 94/95 18
Newcastle U 95/96 30 FL
Clyde 96/97 4
Burnbank Swifts

HENDERSON John
Clyde 06/07 ?

HENDERSON John
St Anthonys
Partick T 18/19 16 5

HENDERSON John
Kelty R
Manchester U
St Mirren 18/19 3 ?

HENDERSON John Neil

b. Dumfries c1874 d. Maxwelltown 30.8.1930

5th KRV				
Dumfries				
Celtic	95/96			
	96/97	3		
Victoria U	97/98			
Lincoln C	98/99	33	4	FL
	99/00	31	2	FL
	00/01	12	2	FL
Leicester F	00/01	13		FL
Small Heath	00/01	4		FL
Maxwelltown Volunteers				
Carlisle U				
Maxwelltown Volunteers				
KOSB				
Annan U				
Nithsdale W				

HENDERSON Joseph

b. 1872

Leith A	92/93	18	8	
	93/94	12	6	
Bury	94/95	16	9	FL
	95/96	27	8	FL
	96/97	30	6	FL
	97/98	14	4	FL

HENDERSON Peter

Windygates R				
Raith R	15/16	13		
East Fife	16/17			
	17/18			
	18/19			
Lochgelly U	19/20			

HENDERSON R

Clydebank	20/21	6		

HENDERSON Richard

Port Glasgow Jnrs				
Morton	11/12	3		
Johnstone *	12/13			D2

HENDERSON Robert H

b. Maryhill d. ?.5.2006

Ruchil Church				
Glasgow Perthshire				
Partick T	37/38	2		
	38/39	7		
	46/47			
	47/48	25		
	48/49	20		
	49/50	14		
Dundee	50/51	14		
	51/52	22		
	52/53	10		
	53/54	2		
	54/55	4		
Dundee U	55/56	1		D2

HENDERSON Robert M

Petershill Jnrs				
Kilmarnock	16/17	35	1	
	17/18	30		
	18/19	1		
Clackmannan	19/20			
Alloa A	19/20			
Port Vale	19/20			
Morton				

HENDERSON Roger

Carluke Milton R				
Clyde	12/13	6		
	13/14	9		
	14/15	7		
Bathgate *				

HENDERSON T

Leith A	92/93	4		

HENDERSON W

Dumbarton	90/91	1		

HENDERSON W

Hibernian	11/12	1		

HENDERSON William

Thornliebank				
Third Lanark	03/04			
Airdrieonians	04/05	13	4	

HENDERSON William

b. Edinburgh 1898 d. Rosyth 1964

Edinburgh Waverley				
St Bernards	19/20			
Airdrieonians	20/21	39	36	
	21/22	11	3	
Manchester U	21/22	21		FL
	22/23	2	1	FL
	23/24			FL
	24/25	22	14	FL
Preston NE	24/25	9	1	FL
Clapton Orient	25/26	29	7	FL
Heart of Midlothian	26/27	13	9	
Morton	27/28			D2
Torquay U	28/29	15	10	FL
Exeter C	29/30	5		FL

HENDERSON William P

b. Dundee 1883

Norwood				
Dundee	04/05			
	05/06	26	1	
	06/07	21		
Heart of Midlothian	06/07	5	2	
	07/08	16		
New Brompton	08/09	25		SL
Bradford C	09/10	4		FL
Grimsby T	10/11	23	2	ML
	11/12	4		FL
Scunthorpe U	12/13			
Dundee Hibs	13/14	19	1	D2

HENDREN James

b. Annbank c1887 d. Edinburgh 19.6.1915

Carson Thistle				
Kilmarnock	04/05	4		
USA				
Maybole				
Annbank				
Nithsdale W	09/10			
Cowdenbeath	10/11	15		D2
Hibernian	11/12	22	3	
	12/13	32	18	
	13/14	32	18	
	14/15	36	14	

HENDRIE Richard

b. Airdrie 25.11.1895 d. Maidstone 15.4.1964

Royal Navy				
Petershill				
Heart of Midlothian	14/15			
Queen's Park	15/16			
	16/17	2		
	17/18			
Airdrieonians	18/19	1		
Maidstone U	19/20			
	20/21			
	21/22			
	22/23			
Gillingham	23/24	40		FL
	24/25	25		FL
	25/26	6		FL
Margate	26/27			
Grays Thurrock	26/27			
Brentford	27/28			FL

HENDRY

Abercorn	91/92	1		

HENDRY

Dumbarton	93/94	2	1	

HENDRY

Morton	17/18	1		

HENDRY John

Port Glasgow A	03/04	3		

HENDRY Joseph

b. Greenock

Maryhill				
Morton	07/08	16		
	08/09	29		
	09/10	28		
Rangers	09/10	2		
	10/11	31	1	
	11/12	32	1	
	12/13	13		
	13/14	29	2	
	14/15	17	1	
	15/16	18	1	
	16/17	6		
	17/18			
Dumbarton	18/19	24	?	
Third Lanark	19/20	20	1	
St Johnstone	20/21			
	21/22			D2
Distillery	22/23			IL

HENDRY Robert

b. Dumbarton 1876

Dumbarton	95/96	16		
	96/97	13		
Rangers	96/97			
Everton	97/98			FL
Notts Co	97/98	7		FL
Morton	98/99	4		
Dumbarton	98/99			
Renton				

HENDRY William Harold

b. Newport on Tay ?.6.1864 d. Shrewsbury 4.5.1901

Dunblane Thistle				
Dundee W				
WBA	88/89	16	3	FL
Kidderminster H				
Stoke	88/89	2		FL
	89/90	14	1	FL
Preston NE	89/90	1		FL
	90/91	13		FL
Sheffield U	90/91	7		ML
	91/92	15		NL
	92/93	20	2	FL
	93/94	29	1	FL
	94/95	20	1	FL
Dundee	95/96	16		
Bury	96/97	8		FL
West Herts	97/98	5		SL
Brighton U	98/99	20		SL
Shrewsbury T				

HENNESSEY

Third Lanark				
Ayr U	17/18	1	?	

HENRY Hamilton Stillic

b. Troon 7.7.1916 d. 1957

Troon A	34/35			
	35/36			
Glenafton A	35/36			
Kilmarnock	36/37	3	2	
	37/38	4	2	
	38/39	5	3	
	45/46	1	1	
	46/47	8	4	
Arbroath	47/48			D2

HENRY William Armstrong

b. Glasgow 6.9.1884

Blantyre V				
Rangers	06/07	19		
	07/08	12		
Falkirk	08/09			
Leicester F	09/10	38		FL
	10/11	37		FL
	11/12	14		FL
Manchester C	11/12	25		FL
	12/13	37	1	FL
	13/14	33		FL
	14/15	34		FL
	19/20	13		FL
St Bernards				

HEPBURN Robert 1 cap

b. Cambusnethan 29.9.1903

Dykehead				
Ayr U	25/26	7		D2
	26/27	36		D2
	27/28	38		D2
	28/29	38		
	29/30	33		
	30/31	38		
	31/32	37		
	32/33	35		
	33/34	17		
	34/35	35		
	35/36	17		
Stranraer	36/37			

HEPBURN Robert Stanley

Queen's Park	24/25	1		
	25/26	2		
Alloa A	25/26			D2

HEPPENSTALL Frank

b. South Hindley 1885

Denaby U				
Barnsley	04/05	9	1	FL
Denaby U				
Swindon T	07/08	9		SL
	08/09	23	3	SL
Woolwich Arsenal	09/10	18		FL
	10/11	5		FL
Stalybridge C	11/12			
	12/13			
Hamilton A	13/14	31	1	

HERBERT John

East Fife	29/30	5	3	D2
	30/31	19	4	
	31/32	35	19	D2
	32/33	25	14	D2
	33/34	3	1	D2
Raith R	33/34			D2
Dundee U	33/34	4		D2

HERBERTSON Samuel

b. c1889 K.I.A.,Dardanelles 12.7.1915

Irvine V				
Fulham				
Glentoran				
Beith				
Linfield	11/12			IL
Beith	12/13			
Ayr U	13/14	13		

HERD Alec

b. Bowhill 8.11.1911 d. Dumfries 21.8.1982

Hearts of Beath				
Hamilton A	28/29	1	1	
	29/30	8		
	30/31	22	5	
	31/32	27	10	
	32/33	27	25	
Manchester C	32/33	16	7	FL
	33/34	37	17	FL
	34/35	37	14	FL
	35/36	33	10	FL
	36/37	32	15	FL
	37/38	35	12	FL
	38/39	35	20	FL
	39/40	3		FL
	46/47	28	11	FL
	47/48	4	1	FL
Stockport Co	47/48	10	4	FL
	48/49	39	7	FL
	49/50	32	15	FL
	50/51	23	5	FL
	51/52	6	4	FL

HERD Andrew Clark 1 cap

b. Cardenden 28.6.1902 d. Australia 1.12.1984

Bowhill Star				
Hearts of Beath				
Dundee	21/22	15		
	22/23			
	23/24	1		
East Fife	24/25	?	?	D2
Bowhill Star				
Dunfermline A	25/26	?	?	D2
	26/27	32	1	
Heart of Midlothian	27/28	35		
	28/29	31		
	29/30	21		
	30/31	27		
	31/32	16		
	32/33	32	4	
	33/34	35	2	
	34/35	29		
	35/36	27		
	36/37	14		
East Fife	37/38	24	1	D2
	38/39	20	2	D2

HERD Richard

Hibernian	18/19	1	?	

HERNON Daniel

b. Uddingston c1913

Duntocher Hibs				
Maryhill Jnrs				
Ayr U	35/36	7		
	36/37	2		D2

HERRON Andrew

b. Glasgow

Benburb				
Kilmarnock	21/22	12		
	22/23	15		

HERRON James

Arbroath				
Dundee	16/17	26	2	
	17/18			
	18/19			
Dundee Hibernian	19/20			
	20/21			
Arbroath	21/22	33	4	D2
	22/23			D2
	23/24			D2
Forfar A	24/25			D2

HEWITT Robert Wallace

Kilmarnock Winton				
Kilmarnock	98/99	2		D2
	99/00	3		
	00/01	8		
Hurlford				
Galston	03/04			
	04/05			
	05/06			
Maxwelltown Volunteers	05/06			
Abercorn	06/07			D2
Westmount (Canada)				
Galston				

HICKIE James

Leith A				
Falkirk	17/18	10	?	
	18/19	19	?	
	19/20	20	2	
	20/21			
	21/22			
Musselburgh Bruntonians	22/23			

HICKIE James

b. c1914

Larkhall Thistle				
Clyde	37/38	25		
	38/39	38		

HICKIE William

b. Larkhall 9.12.1902 d. Lancaster 27.4.1957

Waterloo R				
Larkhall Thistle	24/25			
Aberdare A	24/25	12		FL
	25/26	2		FL
Aberaman	25/26			
	26/27			
Ebbw Vale	26/27			
	27/28			
Peebles R	28/29			
Aberdeen	29/30	14	1	
Newport Co	30/31	24	2	FL
Fulham	31/32	9		FL
Aldershot	32/33	3		FL
Guildford C	33/34			
	34/35			
	35/36			
Basingstoke T				

HIDDLESTONE James

Govan Hearts				
Benburb				
St Johnstone	38/39	3		

HIGGINBOTHAM Harry B

b. Ashfield, NSW 27.7.1894 d. Springburn 3.6.1950

Kilsyth R				
Petershill				
Third Lanark	16/17			
St Mirren	16/17	29	1	
	17/18	27	7	
	18/19			
South Shields	19/20	7		FL
Luton T	19/20	11	5	SL
	20/21	28	4	FL
	21/22	30	12	FL
	22/23	23	10	FL
Clapton Orient	22/23	14	1	FL
	23/24	5		FL
Nelson	23/24	4		FL
Reading	24/25	24	3	FL
Mid Rhondda				

HIGGINS

Clydebank	18/19	7	?	

HIGGINS Alexander 4 caps

b. Kilmarnock 4.11.1885 d. Newcastle 15.3.1939

Belle Vue Jnrs				
Kilmarnock	04/05			
Newcastle U	05/06	3	1	FL
	06/07	1		FL
	07/08	11	2	FL
	08/09	26	5	FL
	09/10	16	5	FL
	10/11	26	8	FL
	11/12	15	4	FL
	12/13	18	8	FL
	13/14	1		FL
	14/15	9	3	FL
Kilmarnock	19/20	26	4	
Nottingham F	20/21	33	7	FL
Jarrow	21/22			
Norwich C	21/22	7	2	FL
Wallsend	22/23			
Workington				
Preston Colliery				

HIGGINS Andrew Kincade

b. Gartsherrie 29.4.1909 d. Newport 9.11.1966

Gartsherrie A				
Stoneyburn Jnrs				
Dunblane R				
Cowdenbeath	29/30	25	6	
	30/31	19	4	
Gartsherrie A L				
WBA	30/31			FL
Millwall	31/32	5		FL
Exeter C	32/33	22	9	FL
Newport Co	33/34	34	10	FL
	34/35	6	2	FL
Notts Co	34/35	10	2	FL
Olympique Lillois	35/36			
Racing Club d'Arras	36/37			
	37/38			
Newport Co	38/39	2		FL

HIGGINS George

Queen's Park	05/06	19		

HIGGINS George

Dreghorn				
Third Lanark	23/24	13	2	

HIGGINS Hugh

Beith Amateurs				
St Mirren	04/05	2		
Beith Amateurs				

HIGGINS John

b. Waterloo 20.5.1902 d. Newmains 31.12.1961

Wishaw Jnrs				
Third Lanark	24/25	15		
Queen of the South	25/26			D2
Bathgate				

HIGGINS Thomas

b. Glasgow

Baillieston Jnrs				
Heart of Midlothian	29/30	10		
	30/31	7		
	31/32			
	32/33	1		
	33/34	1		
Northampton T	34/35	3		FL
Scarborough				

HIGHET Alexander Galt

Queen's Park	37/38	1		

HIGHET J J

Queen's Park	06/07	1		

HIGHET Thomas

Queen's Park	06/07	4	1	

HILL

Clyde	92/93	2		

HILL Alexander

St Johnstone	10/11			
Queen's Park	11/12	5	1	
	12/13	10	2	

HILL Alexander

Third Lanark	13/14	2		

HILL Cumberland

St Mirren	06/07	7		
Port Glasgow A	07/08	5		
Beith				

HILL D

Queen's Park	11/12	2		

HILL David Alexander 1 cap

b. St Quivox 16.12.1881 d. Vancouver 21.5.1928

Underwood Strollers				
Ayr Parkhouse	04/05			D2
Third Lanark	04/05	2		
	05/06	18		
	06/07	11		
	07/08	25		
	08/09	20		

HILL David Fairbairn
b. Prestwick 2.6.1904 d. Ivybridge 12.8.1989
Barr & Stroud
Anniesland YM
Yoker A 25/26
26/27
Alloa A 27/28 D2
28/29 D2
Hamilton A 29/30 23
30/31 6
31/32 30
32/33 38
33/34 38
34/35 4
Plymouth A 34/35 12 FL
35/36 1 FL
36/37 1 FL
Southport 37/38 34 FL
38/39 39 1 FL
39/40 1 FL

HILL Frank Robert 3 caps
b. Forfar 21.5.1906 d. Lafayette, Cal 26.8.1993
Forfar WE
Forfar A 24/25 D2
25/26 D2
26/27 D2
27/28 D2
Aberdeen 28/29 14 1
29/30 37 1
30/31 30 3
31/32 17 4
Arsenal 32/33 26 1 FL
33/34 25 FL
34/35 15 3 FL
35/36 10 FL
Blackpool 36/37 42 8 FL
37/38 3 FL
Southampton 37/38 32 1 FL
38/39 19 2 FL
Preston NE
Crewe A 46/47 15 FL
47/48 5 FL

HILL John
b. Plains
Glengowan
Plains Bluebell
Airdrieonians
Queen's Park
Heart of Midlothian 90/91 8 1
91/92 18 1
92/93 6

HILL John
b. Dumbarton 17.1.1884
Clydebank Jnrs
Dumbarton 06/07 D2
07/08 D2
08/09 D2
09/10 D2
10/11 16 D2
11/12 D2
Dumbarton Harp 12/13
Celtic 13/14 2
Vale of Leven 13/14 D2
Renton
Vale of Leven 17/18

HILL John
Queen's Park 06/07 1

HILL John
b. Paisley
Yoker A
Hibernian 31/32 D2
32/33 D2
33/34 5
34/35 27
35/36 11
Stenhousemuir 36/37 D2
Cowdenbeath 37/38 D2
38/39 D2

HILL Percy
b. Hampshire
Southampton
Everton 05/06 13 FL
06/07 1 FL
Manchester C 06/07 21 FL
07/08 18 FL
08/09 FL
09/10 FL
Airdrieonians 09/10 15 1
10/11 28
Swindon T 11/12 8 SL

HILL Samuel
b. Belfast c1886
Mountpottinger
Linfield 06/07 IL
07/08 IL
Motherwell 08/09 20 10
09/10 7 1
10/11 5
Belfast Celtic 11/12 IL

HILL William
Partick T 98/99 3
Clyde 99/00 4

HILL William
Rothesay Royal V
Stenhousemuir
Rangers 35/36 1
Airdrieonians L 36/37 D2
Stenhousemuir 37/38 D2

HILL William
b. c1919
Dundee Stobswell
Arbroath 38/39 9 1

HILLCOAT Daniel
St Mirren 11/12 5
12/13
13/14
14/15 1
15/16 38
16/17 37
17/18 9
18/19
19/20 5
Kilmarnock 20/21 37
Johnstone 21/22
East Stirlingshire 22/23 D2
Bathgate 23/24 D2
24/25 D2
Leith A 25/26 D2
26/27 D2
Johnstone

HILLCOAT Daniel
Johnstone U
Morton 20/21 14 4
21/22 2

HILLEY Cornelius
b. Dennistoun 29.9.1902 d. New Addington 18.2.1959
St Anthonys
Raith R 23/24 12 1
24/25 20
Third Lanark 25/26 D2
Crystal Palace 26/27 33 2 FL
27/28 10 2 FL
Thames 28/29 SL
Derry C 29/30 IL
30/31 IL
Rochdale 31/32 3 FL
Coleraine 31/32 IL
Ruskin (Croydon)

HILLEY Hugh
b. Garngad 19.3.1899 d. Paisley 14.9.1987
St Anthonys
Celtic 21/22 1
22/23 25
Armadale L 22/23 D2
Dundee L 22/23
Celtic 23/24 33
24/25 37
25/26 37
26/27 37
27/28 3
28/29
29/30

HILLHOUSE Hugh H
Clydebank Jnrs
Queen's Park 17/18 6 3
18/19 10 2
19/20 6
Arthurlie

HILLHOUSE Ivie Campbell
b. Glasgow 1906
St Anthonys
Clyde 26/27 9
27/28 1
Bathgate 27/28 D2
? 28/29
29/30
Pollok 30/31

HILLHOUSE William
b. Hurlford
Stevenston
Motherwell 13/14 15 1
14/15 7
15/16
16/17
17/18
18/19
Albion R 19/20 19 7
20/21 31 8
Clyde 21/22
Third Lanark 21/22 34 8
22/23 31 5
23/24 14

HILLIGAN Samuel Henry
b. Maryhill 13.10.1892
Glasgow Perthshire
St Mirren 22/23 5
Bo'ness 22/23 D2
23/24 D2
24/25 D2
25/26 D2
Reading 26/27 2 FL
Arthurlie 27/28 D2
St Bernards 27/28 D2
28/29 D2

HILLMAN John
b. Tavistock 30.6.1871 d. Burnley 1.8.1955
Burnley 91/92 26 FL
92/93 28 FL
93/94 27 FL
94/95 19 FL
Everton 94/95 6 FL
95/96 29 FL
Dundee 96/97 18
97/98 18
Burnley 97/98 5 FL
98/99 19 FL
99/00 31 FL
00/01 FL
01/02 20 FL
Manchester C 01/02 14 FL
02/03 31 FL
03/04 28 FL
04/05 32 FL
05/06 10 FL
Millwall 06/07 1 SL

HILSDON George Richard
b. Bromley by Bow 10.8.1885 d. London 7.9.1941
South West Ham
Castle Swifts
Clapton Orient
Luton T 02/03 8 SL
West Ham U 03/04 1 SL
04/05 7 4 SL
05/06 9 3 SL
Chelsea 06/07 32 27 FL
07/08 33 24 FL
08/09 34 25 FL
09/10 15 3 FL
10/11 26 18 FL
11/12 10 1 FL
West Ham U 12/13 32 13 SL
13/14 17 6 SL
14/15 20 5 SL
Heart of Midlothian L 16/17 8 4
Chatham 19/20
20/21
Gillingham 21/22 FL

HILTON Sidney
Aberdeen 05/06 1

HINCHCLIFFE Fred
b. Tillicoultry c1915
Alva Albion R
Partick T 34/35
35/36 4 1
36/37
Dunfermline A 37/38

HINSHELWOOD
Cowlairs 90/91 1

HIRD Thomas
b. Crook 31.12.1912 d. Newcastle ?.3.1989
Roddymoor Jnrs
Stanley U 30/31
Bolton W T 30/31 FL
Stanley U 31/32
West Stanley 32/33
Spennymoor U 32/33
Hartlepools U 33/34 42 9 FL
34/35 42 13 FL
Portsmouth 35/36 1 FL
36/37 FL
Selsey 37/38
St Johnstone 38/39 6 2

HIRST

St Mirren 92/93 1

HIRST James

Arthurlie
Partick T 96/97 4 D2
97/98 2
Arthurlie

HISLOP D

Leith A 92/93 4 1
93/94 3 1

HISLOP David

Partick Westburn
Partick T 88/89
89/90
Rangers 90/91 18 9
Aston Villa 91/92 FL

HOARE Gordon Rahere
b. Greenwich 18.4.1884 d. Putney 27.10.1973
West Norwood
Bromley
Woolwich Arsenal 07/08 1 FL
08/09 11 5 FL
09/10 1 FL
Glossop 09/10 10 3 FL
10/11 1 FL
Bromley 10/11
Woolwich Arsenal 10/11 14 6 FL
11/12 3 1 FL
Glossop 11/12 10 3 FL
12/13 23 9 FL
13/14 4 2 FL
West Norwood
Bromley
Queen's Park 13/14 11 3
Arsenal 14/15 FL
Northfleet 14/15
Fulham 19/20 2 FL
Bromley

HODGE

Dumbarton 91/92 1

HODGE John

Kilsyth Emmet
Hamilton A 06/07 2
07/08
Dumbarton Harp 08/09
Lochgelly U 09/10

HODGE John McGeachie
b. Greenock 5.5.1879
Overbon A
Newborn Thistle
Port Glasgow Jnrs
Port Glasgow A
Celtic 98/99
99/00 13 6
00/01 13 6
01/02 8 6
Morton L 01/02
Portsmouth 02/03 SL
Morton
Thornliebank

HODGE Robert

Kirkintilloch Rob Roy
Clyde 23/24 2

HODGE W

Rangers 90/91 9
91/92 15

HODGE William
b. Twechar
Baillieston
Rangers 25/26 2
Brentford

HODGES Frank Charles
b. Nechells Green 20.1.1891 d. Southport 5.6.1985
Alum Rock All Souls
Birmingham City Gas
Birmingham 13/14 10 1 FL
14/15 17 3 FL
St Mirren L 18/19 4
Manchester U 19/20 18 4 FL
20/21 2 FL
Wigan B 21/22 33 6 FL
Crewe A 22/23 7 1 FL
23/24 15 FL
Stalybridge C
Winsford U

HODGKINSON John

Newton Stewart
Clyde 11/12 2

HOGG Alexander S
b. Airdrie
Glenboig Cameronians
Kilmarnock 27/28 6
28/29 10
29/30 10
Albion R 30/31 D2
Partick T 31/32 1
Montrose 32/33 D2
33/34 D2
Bo'ness * 34/35

HOGG George 2 caps
b. West Calder 2.12.1869 d. Bulawayo 1939
West Calder
Mossend Swifts
Heart of Midlothian 93/94 18
94/95 15
95/96 16 2
96/97 16
97/98 15 1
98/99 18
99/00
00/01 12 2
01/02 11 1
02/03 18
03/04 16
Bathgate 04/05

HOGG George

Heart of Midlothian 17/18 1

HOGG James
b. West Calder
West Calder
Hibernian 99/00 18
00/01 19
01/02 15
02/03 15
Portsmouth 03/04 26 SL

HOGG James

Hibernian 04/05 20
05/06 19
06/07 8

HOGG James 1 cap
b. Coylton
Vale of Clyde
Ayr U 18/19 32 2
19/20 35 1
20/21 39 1
21/22 39
22/23 32 1
23/24 30 1
24/25 17 1
Clydebank 25/26 37 1
26/27 D2
Prestwick Glenburn R 27/28

HOGG James B

Dunfermline A 36/37 13

HOGG John
b. West Calder 25.8.1879
West Calder Swifts
Heart of Midlothian 99/00 16
00/01 1
01/02 15
Middlesbrough 02/03 28 FL
03/04 32 FL
04/05 9 FL
05/06 23 FL
Luton T 06/07 24 SL
07/08 22 SL

HOGG Robert 1 cap
b. Larkhall 10.5.1914 d. Paisley 15.4.1975
Royal Albert
Celtic 31/32
32/33 18
33/34 38
34/35 36
35/36 38
36/37 35
37/38 38
38/39 38
46/47 26
47/48 5
Alloa A 48/49 D2

HOGG Robert

Partick T
Bo'ness 32/33 D2
Cork 33/34 LI
Dundee 34/35 1
Dundee U 35/36 2 D2
Brideville 35/36 LI
Dumbarton 35/36 D2

HOGG Robert

Arbroath V
Airdrieonians 34/35 14 4
35/36 18 5
36/37 25 11 D2
37/38 28 31 D2

HOGG W

Heart of Midlothian 92/93 5
93/94 16

HOGG William
b. Newcastle 25.5.1879 d. Sunderland 30.1.1937
Willington A
Sunderland 99/00 19 9 FL
00/01 34 8 FL
01/02 28 10 FL
02/03 31 4 FL
03/04 33 11 FL
04/05 32 9 FL
05/06 27 7 FL
06/07 30 8 FL
07/08 27 9 FL
08/09 21 10 FL
Rangers 09/10 26 6
10/11 30 14
11/12 30 18
12/13 16 5
Dundee 13/14 34 17
14/15 28 2
Raith R
Montrose
Dundee 20/21 2
Dundee U 21/22 9 2 D2
Brooklyn Wanderers 22/23 1 1 ASL
23/24 23 12 ASL
24/25 40 14 ASL
25/26 7 ASL
Providence Clamdiggers 25/26 23 14 ASL
Philadelphia Field Club 26/27 28 9 ASL
Newark Skeeters 27/28 24 17 ASL
New York Giants 27/28 15 2 ASL
28/29 1 1 ESL
Brooklyn Wanderers 28/29 1 1 ASL

HOGGAN Matthew
b. Standford
Grange R
Raith R 27/28 13
28/29 28
29/30 D2
30/31 D2
31/32 D2
32/33 D2
33/34 D2
34/35 D2
New Brighton 35/36 38 FL

HOLBEM Walter
b. Sheffield ?.11.1884 d. Ascot 18.6.1930
Heeley Friends
Sheffield W 06/07 6 FL
07/08 8 FL
08/09 26 FL
09/10 26 FL
10/11 20 FL
Everton 11/12 11 FL
12/13 7 FL
St Mirren 13/14 14
Preston NE 13/14 8 FL
14/15 29 FL
Southport Central

HOLLAND Gilbert
b. England

Tranent Jnrs				
Queen's Park	35/36	11	3	
Albion R	36/37	6	4	
Dundee	37/38	3	1	

HOLLAND John C

Blackpool				
Ayr U	33/34	37	4	
	34/35	34	3	
	35/36	30		
Galston	36/37			
Kings Park	37/38			D2
	38/39			D2
Dumbarton				

HOLLEY

Clydebank	17/18	1		

HOLLINGWORTH J
b. c1887

Sheffield district				
Heart of Midlothian	09/10	2	1	

HOLMES J Albert
b. Mansfield 1886

Hucknall Constitutional				
Nottingham F	05/06	5		FL
Mansfield Wesley				
Chesterfield T	07/08	14	3	FL
	08/09	37	6	FL
Nelson	09/10			
Mansfield Mechanics	10/11			
Coventry C	11/12	30	3	SL
	12/13	38	8	SL
	13/14	26	6	SL
Heart of Midlothian	13/14	3		
Coventry C	14/15	8		SL
Portsmouth				

HOLMES William

Third Lanark	13/14	1		

HOLT Arnold Andrew
b. Sheffield c1891

Kidderminster H				
Denaby U				
Sheffield U	11/12			FL
Newport Co	12/13			SL
Cardiff C	12/13	3		SL
Merthyr T	13/14	3		SL
Linfield	13/14			IL
Belfast Celtic	14/15			IL
Clyde	17/18	1		
Distillery	18/19			IL
Linfield	18/19			IL
Chesterfield Municipal	19/20	17	1	ML
Gillingham	20/21	6		FL
Mansfield T	20/21	21	2	ML
Sutton T	21/22			
Wath A				

HOLT James P

Thorntree U				
Armadale Thistle				
Dunfermline A	36/37	6		

HOLTON W S

Queen's Park	15/16	3		

HONEYMAN John William
b. Middlesbrough 29.12.1893 d. Maidstone 1972

Cargo Fleet & Cochrane Works				
Middlesbrough	19/20	1		FL
Dundee	20/21	12	1	
Maidstone U	21/22			
	22/23			
Grimsby T	23/24	21	1	FL
Chatham	24/25			
	25/26			
Margate	26/27			
New Bedford Whalers	26/27			ASL
J & P Coats	26/27	3		ASL
Maidstone U	26/27			
	27/28			
Folkestone T	28/29			
Kreemy Works				

HONEYMAN Muir

Glasgow Ashfield				
Partick T	15/16	37	5	
	16/17	14		
Heart of Midlothian	17/18	5		

HOOD Alexander Robertson

Leith A	99/00			D2
St Bernards	99/00	6		
Heart of Midlothian	00/01	3		
St Bernards	00/01	8	?	D2
Cowdenbeath				

HOOD James
b. Dalry 1900

Kilwinning Eglington				
Kilmarnock	21/22	9		
	22/23	34		
	23/24	26		
	24/25	38	2	
	25/26	37	2	
	26/27	30		
	27/28	14		
Kilwinning R				
Kilwinning Eglington				
Dalry Thistle	30/31			

HOOD William

Kilbirnie Ladeside				
Clyde	24/25			
	25/26			
	26/27	31	5	
	27/28	30	10	
	28/29	13	4	

HOPE James

Balgonia Scotia				
Raith R	12/13	15	3	
East Fife	13/14			
	14/15			
	15/16			
Raith R	16/17	3		

HOPE John
b. Bishop Auckland 15.6.1905 d. Bishop Auckland 1982

Crook T				
Derby Co	26/27	3		FL
	27/28	5	1	FL
	28/29			FL
	29/30	1	1	FL
Bury	29/30	12		FL
	30/31	23		FL
Spennymoor U	31/32			
Washington Colliery	32/33			
Falkirk	32/33	13		
	33/34	21	4	

HOPE John D

Queen's Park	05/06	11	2	

HOPE Thomas

Army				
St Ninians Thistle				
Falkirk	13/14	4		

HOPE Thomas

Newton Villa				
Clyde	34/35	16	7	
	35/36	19	7	
	36/37	15	3	
	37/38	18	3	
Ayr U	38/39	12	3	

HOPECRAFT Allan C F

Hull C				
Kilmarnock L	17/18	1		

HOPEWELL David

Rutherglen Glencairn				
Armadale				
East Stirlingshire	20/21			
	21/22			D2
Arthurlie	22/23			
	23/24			D3
Cowdenbeath	24/25	38		
	25/26	38		
	26/27	23		
	27/28	6		
Raith R	27/28	19		
	28/29	38		
Dundee	29/30	1		
Bangor	30/31			IL
Pollok Jnrs	30/31			

HOPKINS David

Motherwell	04/05	5	1	
Galston				

HORN John

Kilbirnie				
Hibernian	04/05	4		

HORNE Alexander

Blantyre V				
Hamilton A	08/09	10	5	
Royal Albert				
Wishaw Thistle				

HORNE Andrew

Buckhaven U				
Cowdenbeath	01/02			
	02/03			
Dundee	03/04	11	2	
Cowdenbeath	04/05			
East Fife				

HORNE John N

Third Lanark	09/10	1		
Abercorn	10/11	22		D2
	11/12			D2
Vale of Leven	12/13			D2

HORSBURGH Balfour

Kings Park				
Dumbarton	20/21			
Clydebank	21/22	5	1	

HOSIE Andrew

Queen's Park	29/30	9	1	
	30/31	4		
	31/32	1		
	32/33	11	3	
	33/34	21		
	34/35	15		
	35/36	36	1	
	36/37	35		
	37/38	20		
	38/39	23		

HOSIE Robert
b. c1891

Clydebank Jnrs				
Vale of Leven				
Third Lanark	08/09	23	4	
	09/10	13	6	
	10/11	25	6	
	11/12	25	4	
	12/13	10	1	
St Bernards	13/14			D2
Clydebank	14/15			D2
	15/16			
	16/17			
	17/18			
	18/19			
	19/20			
	20/21			
Todd Shipyards	21/22	12	1	ASL
Paterson Silk Sox	22/23	1		ASL
New York Field Club	23/24	10	2	ASL
Brooklyn Wanderers	24/25	30	3	ASL
	25/26	8	2	ASL
New York Giants	25/26	6		ASL

HOTCHKISS John

Falkirk Jnrs *				
East Stirlingshire *				
Falkirk	06/07	10		
Leith A				
East Stirlingshire				
Alloa A	09/10			

HOTSON Walter

Armadale				
Falkirk	30/31	7		
	31/32			
Dundee U	32/33	4		D2

HOUSTON Alexander

Maryhill				
Clydebank	24/25			D2
	25/26	17	2	

HOUSTON Alexander

Bathgate				
Falkirk	27/28	21	8	
	28/29	17	3	

HOUSTON Harry

St Mirren 00/01 2
Kilbarchan A 01/02
Port Glasgow A 02/03
Kilbarchan A 03/04
Morton 03/04
Kilbarchan A 03/04

HOUSTON James
b. 1899
Nithsdale W
Kilmarnock 19/20 2
20/21 8
Nithsdale W 21/22
Queen of the South 22/23
23/24 D3
Nithsdale W 24/25 D3

HOUSTON John
b. Ahoghill 17.9.1889
Linfield 11/12 IL
12/13 IL
Everton 12/13 7 FL
13/14 18 2 FL
14/15 1 FL
Linfield 15/16 IL
16/17 IL
17/18 IL
18/19 IL
Ulster R 19/20
Partick T 19/20 17 1
20/21
21/22
Belfast Bohemians 21/22
22/23

HOUSTON Matthew B

Queen's Park 04/05 3
05/06 17
06/07 1
Morton 06/07 14 1
07/08 10 1
Dumbarton 07/08
Rangers

HOUSTON Robert
b. Leven 9.1.1877 d. Edmonton 29.11.1954
Leven
St Bernards 97/98 7 4
98/99
99/00 11 4
00/01 2 ? D2
Heart of Midlothian 00/01 8 3
01/02 15 6
Tottenham H 02/03 9 SL
East Fife 03/04

HOUSTON Robert Gardner
b. Kilbarchan 1888 K.I.A. 9.5.1915
Kilbarchan A
Partick T 11/12 3
12/13 5
Abercorn 13/14 D2
Johnstone 14/15 D2

HOWARD Frederick
b. Walkden 1891
Walkden Wednesday
Manchester C 12/13 16 11 FL
13/14 29 11 FL
14/15 33 18 FL
19/20 1 FL
Mid Rhondda U 20/21
Pontypridd 21/22
Gillingham 21/22 FL
Ayr U 22/23 6 3
Clyde 22/23 13 6
Dundee Hibs L
Port Vale 23/24 12 2 FL
New Brighton 23/24 10 4 FL
Wrexham 24/25 1 FL
Sittingbourne T 25/26
Welshpool 25/26
Holyhead T 25/26

HOWAT Robert W
b. Dreghorn
Irvine Royal Academy
Dreghorn Jnrs
Kilmarnock 21/22 2
22/23
Galston L 22/23
Kilmarnock 23/24 4
Nithsdale W
Clydebank L 24/25 D2
Galston
Kilmarnock L 25/26
Royal Albert
Galston
Ayr U L 29/30

HOWAT Thomas

Blantyre V
Airdrieonians 10/11 6
11/12 6
Dumbarton 12/13 D2

HOWDEN William H 1 cap

Benburb
Rutherglen Glencairn
Rangers 99/00 1
00/01
Partick T 01/02 10 D2
02/03 9
03/04 17
04/05 19
05/06 30
06/07 24
07/08 16
Abercorn 08/09 D2
Partick T 09/10 28
10/11 9
Abercorn 11/12 D2
12/13 D2
Beith 13/14
14/15
Arthurlie 15/16

HOWE Robert 2 caps
b. Dumbarton 3.8.1903 d. 20.6.1979
Shotts U
Petershill
Hamilton A 27/28 37 8
28/29 38 15
29/30 35 15
30/31 31 4
31/32 18 2
Heart of Midlothian 32/33 11 3
33/34 5 1
Third Lanark 33/34 10 2
34/35 D2
35/36 32 5
36/37 14 3
Queen of the South 36/37 13 1
St Johnstone 37/38 14 3
Dundee U 38/39 17 2 D2

HOWES Arthur
b. Leicester 1876
Leicester Waverley
Leicester F 96/97 10 FL
97/98 2 FL
Reading 97/98 1 SL
Lincoln C T 97/98
Leicester F 98/99 9 FL
99/00 FL
Dumbarton 00/01
Dundee 01/02 17
Brighton 02/03 2 SL
03/04 33 SL
QPR 04/05 11 SL
05/06 12 SL
06/07 26 SL

HOWIE Andrew

St Johnstone 38/39 12 2

HOWIE Alexander

Hibernian 93/94 16 ? D2
94/95 5 ? D2
95/96 5 1
96/97 1 1

HOWIE David
b. Galston 15.7.1886 d. Bradford 1.7.1930
Galston
Kilmarnock 06/07 20 4
07/08 33 4
08/09 32 5
09/10 29 11
10/11 27 8
Bradford PA 11/12 31 3 FL
12/13 35 8 FL
13/14 28 2 FL
14/15 34 FL
19/20 41 1 FL
20/21 39 1 FL
21/22 29 2 FL
22/23 32 4 FL
23/24 33 FL
24/25 4 2 FL

HOWIE James 3 caps
b. Galston 19.3.1878 d. London ?.1.1963
Galston A
Kilmarnock 98/99 10
99/00 14 6
00/01 9 2
Galston T 00/01
Kilmarnock 01/02 17 2
Bristol R 02/03 26 10 SL
Newcastle U 03/04 29 14 FL
04/05 31 12 FL
05/06 29 11 FL
06/07 31 8 FL
07/08 24 10 FL
08/09 26 6 FL
09/10 25 6 FL
10/11 3 FL
Huddersfield T 10/11 26 3 FL
11/12 32 7 FL
12/13 24 8 FL
13/14 2 FL

HOWIE Matthew

St Mirren Jnrs
Kilmarnock 18/19 14 2
Hamilton A L 18/19 2
Neilston V 19/20
Paisley Vulcan 20/21
Saltcoats V 21/22

HOWIE Robert Fisher
b. Crosshouse
Crosshouse Castle R
Cumnock Jnrs
Kilmarnock 37/38 2
Kilmarnock Jnrs

HOWIE Robert M

Annbank
Clyde 13/14 16 2
Galston
Kilmarnock 14/15 1 1
Clyde
Abercorn
Stevenston U 17/18
Clyde 17/18 7 ?
Stevenston U

HOWIESON James 1 cap
b. Rutherglen 7.6.1900 d. 1974
Rutherglen Glencairn
Airdrieonians 21/22 18 5
22/23 21 8
23/24 27 6
St Johnstone 24/25 19
Dundee U 25/26 10 5
St Mirren 25/26 17 4
26/27 37 10
Hull C 26/27 12 3 FL
27/28 27 4 FL
New Bedford Whalers 28/29 35 9 ASL
Hull C 29/30 28 5 FL
Shelbourne 30/31 LI
31/32 LI
Clyde 32/33 21 4
33/34 16 2
Alloa A 34/35 D2
Glenavon 34/35 IL
Belfast Celtic 34/35 IL

HOWIESON James
b. Dunfermline
Kelty R
Falkirk 27/28 2
28/29 9 ?
29/30 3
Dunfermline A 29/30 D2
30/31 D2
31/32 D2
32/33 D2
Leith A 33/34 D2

HUBBARD

Abercorn 91/92 8
92/93 2

HUDSON J M

Maryhill
Falkirk 07/08 8 3

HUDSON Joseph W
b. Airdrie
Queen's Park 14/15 2
15/16 6
Albion R 16/17
17/18
Airdrieonians 18/19 2

HUGALL James Cockburn

b. Whitburn 26.4.1889 d. Sunderland 23.9.1927

Sunderland Co-op Wednesday					
Sunderland Royal R					
Whitburn					
Clapton Orient		10/11	1		FL
		11/12	18		FL
		12/13	4		FL
		14/15	31		FL
		19/20	35		FL
		20/21	35		FL
		21/22	2		FL
Hamilton A		22/23	17		
Durham C		23/24	35		FL
Sunderland Co-op Wednesday					

HUGHES

Cowlairs		90/91	2		

HUGHES John

b. Barrhead 4.8.1901

Neilston A					
Parkhead Jnrs					
Celtic		22/23	5		
		23/24			
Hibernian	L	23/24	7		
Clydebank	L	23/24	9		
Celtic		24/25			
Alloa A	L	24/25			D2
Ayr U	L	24/25	17		
Alloa A		25/26			D2
Vale of Leven					
St Anthonys					

HUGHES William

b. Winchburgh c1909 d. Keith 1.1.1996

Bellstane Birds					
Bathgate		26/27			D2
		27/28			D2
Celtic		28/29	8	3	
		29/30	11	1	
Ayr U	L	29/30			
Celtic		30/31	8	3	
		31/32	11	3	
Hibernian	L	31/32			D2
Celtic		32/33	6		
		33/34	35	1	
		34/35	11	1	
		35/36	4	2	
Clyde		36/37	26		
		37/38	31	3	
Bo'ness	L	37/38			
Arbroath		38/39	19	4	

HULLOCK James

b. Newcastle

Crystal Palace		08/09	5		SL
		09/10	3		SL
		10/11			SL
		11/12			SL
		12/13			SL
Third Lanark		13/14	24		
Stockport Co		14/15			
Croydon Common					

HUME John

b. Newhaven d. Aberdeen 24.10.1961

Broxburn A					
Aberdeen		07/08	33		
		08/09	30		
		09/10	31	1	
		10/11	32		
		11/12	32	1	
		12/13	21	1	
Airdrieonians		12/13			
Aberdeen		13/14	16		
		14/15	24		
		15/16	30		
		16/17	3		
Hibernian		16/17	15		
Aberdeen		17/18			
		18/19			
		19/20	30		
Darwen		20/21			
		21/22			
Arbroath		22/23	5		D2
Peterhead		23/24			
Brooklyn Wanderers		24/25	9		ASL
Newark Skeeters		25/26	3		ASL

HUME William

b. Bo'ness

Bo'ness		27/28	28		
Falkirk		28/29	29		
		29/30	38		
		30/31	19		
St Bernards		31/32			D2
Bo'ness	T	32/33			

HUME William

Aberdeen		38/39	3		
		46/47	4	1	
		47/48	2		

HUME William Charles S

b. c1917

Bonnyridd Rose A					
Heart of Midlothian		36/37			
		37/38	4		

HUMPHREYS Lawson

Renfrew					
Partick T		16/17	7	1	

HUNT Patrick

b. Darlington

Shawfield Jnrs					
Hamilton A		23/24	10	1	
		24/25	35	4	
		25/26	31	1	
		26/27	34	2	
		27/28	23		
		28/29	14	2	
Burnley		28/29	8		FL
		29/30			FL
Belfast Celtic		30/31			IL
		31/32			IL
Alloa A					

HUNTER

Third Lanark		90/91	1		

HUNTER A W

Queen's Park		06/07	3		

HUNTER Alexander

b. Lochwinnoch *

Morton		98/99	17	?	D2
		99/00	10	?	D2
		00/01	4		
		01/02	1		
Kilbirnie Ladeside		02/03			
		03/04			
Port Glasgow A		04/05	3		
Johnstone		05/06			

HUNTER Alexander

b. Hamilton

Larkhall Thistle					
Hamilton A		20/21	7		
		21/22	25		
		22/23	32		
		23/24	35		
		24/25	17		
		25/26	9		
Dumbarton	L	25/26			D2
Hamilton A		26/27	25		
		27/28	31		
Motherwell		28/29	15		
		29/30	32		
		30/31	33		
		31/32	1		
Bo'ness		31/32			D2
Hamilton A		32/33	5		
		33/34	5		

HUNTER Alexander Campbell

b. Renfrew 27.9.1895

Renfrew					
Queen's Park		18/19	21		
		19/20	39		
Tottenham H		20/21	11		FL
		21/22	12		FL
Wigan B		22/23	23		FL
		23/24	16		FL
Armadale		24/25			D2
New Bedford Whalers		25/26	2		ASL

HUNTER Daniel

Clyde		96/97	6		

HUNTER Edward

Ardrossan Winton R					
Hurlford					
Saltcoats V					
Ayr U		20/21	9		

HUNTER George

b. Glasgow

Benburb					
Morton		25/26	33		
		26/27	38	1	
		27/28			D2
		28/29			D2
		29/30	18		
		30/31	31		
		31/32	19		
		32/33	35		

HUNTER George

b. Methil 14.11.1903

Denbeath Star					
Partick T		27/28	8		
		28/29	6		
		29/30	11	1	
		30/31	6	2	
St Johnstone		31/32	19	2	D2

HUNTER Henry

Raith R		10/11	2		
		11/12	5	2	

HUNTER Humphrey G

Queen's Park		37/38	7		
		38/39	26	2	

HUNTER James

Falkirk		19/20	15		

HUNTER James

Tranent Jnrs					
Dundee		24/25	18	2	
		25/26	11	1	
		26/27	18	4	
		27/28	6	1	

HUNTER James Aiton

b. Balfron 5.7.1898

Newcastle U					
Motherwell		19/20	3		
Falkirk		20/21	36		
		21/22	31		
		22/23	34	1	
		23/24	20		
Newcastle U		23/24	6		FL
		24/25	4		FL
Heart of Midlothian	T	25/26			
New Bedford Whalers		25/26	40		ASL
		26/27	20		ASL
		27/28	45		ASL
		28/29	16		ASL
		29A	19		ASL
		29/30	30		ASL

HUNTER John

b. c1881 d. Preston 13.3.1928

St Mirren		95/96	2		
		96/97	8	1	
Preston NE		97/98	15		FL
		98/99			FL
Portsmouth		99/00	9		SL
		00/01	15	2	SL
		01/02			SL
Preston NE		02/03	33	1	FL
		03/04	31		FL
		04/05	31	1	FL
		05/06	37	1	FL
		06/07	37	1	FL
		07/08	17	1	FL

HUNTER John 1 cap

b. Johnstone 6.4.1878 d. 12.1.1966

Abercorn		97/98	4	?	D2
		98/99	16	?	D2
Liverpool		99/00	20	6	FL
		00/01	8	3	FL
		01/02	9	1	FL
Heart of Midlothian		02/03	22	10	
		03/04	21	4	
Woolwich Arsenal		04/05	22	4	FL
Portsmouth		05/06	16	6	SL
		06/07	22	5	SL
Dundee		07/08	30	18	
		08/09	31	28	
		09/10	26	6	
		10/11	2		
Clyde		10/11	17	4	

HUNTER John

Raith R		12/13	3		
East Fife					

HUNTER John
b. Stenhousemuir 11.4.1905
Burnhead Hearts
Falkirk 21/22 15 1
22/23 34 5
23/24 36 5
24/25 31 8
25/26 26 3
26/27 37 11
27/28 23 8
Reading 28/29 42 4 FL
29/30 31 2 FL
30/31 15 1 FL
Brideville 31/32 LI
Guildford C 31/32

HUNTER John
b. Coatbridge 13.4.1916
Coatbridge St Augustines
Lochryn Amateurs
Shettleston Jnrs
Kilsyth Emmet
Kilmarnock 37/38 15
38/39 38
46/47 2
47/48 24
Stenhousemuir 48/49 D2

HUNTER R 1 cap

Yoker
St Mirren 90/91 7
91/92 6

HUNTER Robert

St Mirren 01/02 2 1

HUNTER Robert

Tillicoultry R
Third Lanark 02/03 10 4

HUNTER Robert
b. Stevenston c1907
Saltcoats V
Clyde 29/30 2
Portadown 29/30 IL
30/31 IL
31/32 IL

HUNTER William

St Bernards 94/95 1
95/96 3
96/97 1

HUNTER William
b. Springside
St Bernards
Airdrieonians 05/06 23 6
06/07 21 4
07/08 23 15
Kilmarnock L 07/08 4 4
Airdrieonians 08/09 28 26
Rangers 09/10 17 19
Hamilton A 10/11 5
Airdrieonians 11/12 17 6
Motherwell 12/13 12 3
Lochgelly U
Cowdenbeath 13/14 D2
Motherwell 14/15 1

HUNTER William

St Johnstone 38/39 13

HURRY George Farquhar

Clyde 93/94 14 ? D2
94/95 3 3
Linthouse 94/95
St Mirren 95/96 2 2
Linthouse 95/96 D2
96/97 D2

HUSBAND John
b. Dunfermline 28.5.1918 d. 30.4.1992
Yoker A
Partick T 38/39 5
46/47 28
47/48 25
48/49 3
49/50 11

HUSBAND William
b. Kilmarnock
Kilmarnock Celtic
St Mirren 08/09 10 1
09/10 23
10/11 26 5
11/12 21 4
Burnley 12/13 28 7 FL
13/14 10 FL
Hamilton A 14/15 35 6
15/16 10 4
Vale of Leven

HUSHIE John
b. c1914
Plean
Bo'ness Cadora
Musselburgh A
Falkirk 36/37
37/38 13 4
38/39 12 2

HUSSON Robert

Dundee 13/14 1
14/15
15/16 1
Dundee Hibs L 16/17

HUTCHESON

Dumbarton 90/91 6 2

HUTCHESON

Vale of Leven 91/92 5

HUTCHESON David High
b. Dundee c1894
Dundee NE
Dundee Stobswell
Dundee 14/15 37 2
15/16
16/17
17/18
18/19
19/20 22
20/21 16
South Shields 21/22 38 1 FL
22/23 33 FL
23/24 31 FL
24/25 40 FL
25/26 35 3 FL
26/27 8 FL
27/28 4 FL

HUTCHESON James

Cadzow St Anns
Hibernian 26/27 1

HUTCHESON John Hughes McGreavy
b. Larbert 31.3.1909 d. Braintree 7.1.1979
Preston A
Falkirk 27/28 9 2
28/29 17
29/30 32 2
30/31 34 3
31/32 31 2
32/33 32 1
33/34 30 1
Chelsea 33/34 6 FL
34/35 11 1 FL
35/36 5 FL
36/37 FL
37/38 FL
Ipswich T 38/39 FL
Crittall A

HUTCHINSON

Falkirk 32/33 5
Belfast Celtic T
Distillery 34/35 IL

HUTCHINSON Harold Bonthron
b. Carstairs 25.3.1883
Blantyre V
Everton 04/05 FL
Morton 05/06 22
Bristol R 06/07 30 1 SL
Norwich C 07/08 28 SL
Morton 08/09 1

HUTCHINSON Robert
b. Gosforth 22.12.1894 d. Gosforth 1971
Gosforth
St Mirren 14/15 2
Palmers (Jarrow)
Newcastle U 19/20 FL
20/21 FL
Ashington 21/22 22 4 FL
Nelson 22/23 38 2 FL
23/24 22 FL
Stockport Co 23/24 4 1 FL
Chesterfield 24/25 13 1 FL
Barrow 25/26 37 4 FL
New Bedford Whalers 26/27 10 ASL
Springfield Babes 26/27 2 ASL
Fall River Marksmen 26/27 5 2 ASL
Newark Skeeters 26/27 2 ASL
Hartford Americans 27/28 11 ASL
Darlington 27/28 3 FL
West Stanley

HUTCHINSON Thomas
b. Glasgow 1871 d. 1933
Govan
Stockton
Govan Whitefield
Darlington
Nelson
WBA 94/95 30 13 FL
95/96 14 3 FL
Celtic 96/97 2
Abercorn 96/97 3
Stockport Co

HUTCHINSON William

Shettleston
Partick T 19/20 2
20/21

HUTCHISON Alexander

Leith A 31/32 3 1

HUTCHISON David Campbell
b. Shotts 29.10.1908
Dykehead
Albion R 25/26 D2
Motherwell 26/27 28 4
27/28 5 1
Carlisle U 28/29 32 4 FL
29/30 40 25 FL
30/31 39 19 FL
31/32 37 13 FL
Luton T 32/33 26 9 FL
33/34 27 13 FL
34/35 2 FL
Airdrieonians 35/36 18 3
Stenhousemuir
Bournemouth 36/37 2 1 FL

HUTCHISON Duncan
b. Kelty 3.3.1904 d. Dundee 12.1.1973
Leathens Heatherbell
Rosewell Rosedale
Dunfermline A 26/27 17 1
Dundee U 27/28 35 27 D2
28/29 35 34 D2
29/30 3 3
Newcastle U 29/30 14 5 FL
30/31 25 10 FL
31/32 1 1 FL
Derby Co 31/32 2 1 FL
32/33 21 1 FL
33/34 6 2 FL
Hull C 34/35 38 8 FL
Dundee U 35/36 31 14 D2
36/37 34 16 D2
37/38 31 19 D2
38/39 28 6 D2

HUTCHISON George

Queen's Park 08/09 2

HUTCHISON Harry

Rangers 15/16
Falkirk 15/16 8 1
Hibernian 15/16 17 9
16/17
17/18
18/19
Rangers 19/20

HUTCHISON Jack
b. c1905
Swansea T
Chelsea
Peterborough U
Raith R 28/29 14 2

HUTCHISON Robert

Denbeath Star
Raith R 15/16 36 2
16/17 11
Dunfermline A *

HUTTON John 10 caps
b. Dalziel 29.10.1898
Motherwell
Heart of Midlothian
Larkhall Thistle
Bellshill A
Hall Russells
Aberdeen 19/20 38 5
20/21 29 1
21/22 29
22/23 35
23/24 33
24/25 32
25/26 35 2
26/27 10 5
Blackburn R 26/27 17 FL
27/28 37 FL
28/29 14 FL
29/30 18 3 FL
30/31 21 FL
31/32 20 1 FL
32/33 FL

HUTTON Robert

Raith R 28/29 2

HYNDS James

Pollok Jnrs *
Partick T 13/14 16 3
14/15 4
15/16 1
Vale of Leven

HYNDS Samuel

Clydebank Jnrs
Motherwell 35/36 2
36/37 10
37/38 12
Dunfermline A 38/39 D2

HYNDS Thomas
b. Hurlford 1880
Hurlford Thistle
Celtic 97/98
98/99 11 2
Bolton W L 98/99 8 FL
Celtic 99/00 2
Clyde L 99/00 4
Celtic 00/01 13
Bolton W L
Manchester C 01/02 29 2 FL
02/03 31 1 FL
03/04 32 4 FL
04/05 33 2 FL
05/06 33 FL
Arsenal 06/07 13 FL
Leeds C 07/08 37 FL
Heart of Midlothian 08/09 32 4
09/10 3
Dumbarton 10/11 2
Ladysmith
Musselburgh 12/13

HYSLOP

Ayr U 17/18 1 ?

HYSLOP Alexander
b. c1914
Dalry Thistle
Portadown 34/35 IL
Huddersfield T 35/36 FL
Albion R 36/37 15
Heart of Midlothian 37/38 9

HYSLOP Thomas 2 caps
b. Mauchline 22.9.1874 d. Elderslie ?.4.1936
Elderslie
Army
Millwall 92/93
93/94
Sunderland 93/94 6 3 FL
94/95 12 7 FL
Stoke 94/95 6 8 FL
95/96 25 18 FL
Rangers 96/97 17 10
Third Lanark 97/98
Rangers 97/98 13 12
Stoke 98/99 12 FL
Rangers 99/00 5 3
Partick T 00/01 14 6
01/02
Dundee W 02/03
Johnstone 03/04
Abercorn
Philadelphia Thistle 06
Tacony

HYSLOP William

Morton 24/25 32
25/26 34 2
Fall River Marksmen 26/27 13 ASL
Indiana Flooring 26/27 13 1 ASL
Morton
New York Giants 29/30 19 1 ASL
Bridgeport/Newark 29/30 3 ASL
Newark Americans 30A 19 2 ASL
31S 5 ASL
31A 11 1 ASL

IGOE John
b. Bonhill 1907
Lochgelly Celtic
Airdrieonians 28/29 5
Charlton A 29/30 FL
Thames 30/31 20 FL
31/32
Cork T 32/33 LI
Cork Bohemians 32/33 LI
Larne 33/34 IL
Lochgelly Amateurs
St Bernards 34/35 D2

IMRIE William Noble 2 caps
b. Buckhaven 4.3.1908 d. Windygates 26.12.1944
Kirkcaldy Jnrs
East Fife Jnrs
Dunniker Jnrs
St Johnstone 27/28 29 1
28/29 35 4
29/30 8 2
Blackburn R 29/30 35 6 FL
30/31 39 4 FL
31/32 33 5 FL
32/33 26 2 FL
33/34 32 6 FL
Newcastle U 33/34 10 4 FL
34/35 23 1 FL
35/36 25 5 FL
36/37 30 5 FL
37/38 37 9 FL
Swansea T 38/39 27 1 FL
Swindon T 39/40 2 FL

INGLIS Anderson

Raith R 09/10 D2
10/11 2
11/12 1

INGLIS David M

Queen's Park 16/17 9
17/18 23
18/19 12
19/20 1
20/21 4

INGLIS Ian
b. Kelty
St Andrews University
Cowdenbeath 33/34 7 2

INGLIS James

Morton 00/01 1

INGLIS John

Kilbarchan A
St Mirren 16/17 3
Abercorn 16/17

INGLIS William White
b. Kirkcaldy 2.3.1897 d. Sale 20.1.1968
Inverkeithing U
Kirkcaldy U 13/14
Raith R 14/15 1
15/16 34
16/17 15 1
19/20 38
20/21 42
21/22 39 2
22/23 11 1
23/24 23 3
Sheffield W 24/25 29 FL
Manchester U 25/26 7 1 FL
26/27 6 FL
27/28 FL
28/29 1 FL
29/30 FL
Northampton T 30/31 36 FL
31/32 24 FL

INGRAM Alexander C

Pollok Jnrs
Queen's Park 29/30 2

INGRAM Cameron
b. Girvan
Girvan
Ayr U 15/16 23 6
16/17 19 3

INNES James

Bellshill A
Hibernian 12/13 3
13/14 8 2
Abercorn 14/15 D2
Dykehead 14/15

INNES James

Raith R 24/25 3
Forfar A
Partick T 28/29

INNES Matthew

Thorntree U
Dundee 35/36 13
36/37 3

INNES Walter
b. Kirkcaldy c1906
Bowhill Star
Cowdenbeath T
Partick T T
Dunfermline A 25/26 D2
26/27
27/28 21 3
Heart of Midlothian 27/28 3
Rhyl 29/29
29/30
Dunfermline A 30/31
Newcastle U T 30/31
Bowhill R

IRELAND James K L

Dundee 98/99 7

IRELAND Robert Johnstone
b. Darvel 22.7.1900 d. Perth 12.7.1962
Darvel
Rangers 24/25 5
25/26 2
26/27 3
27/28
28/29 7
29/30 1
Peebles R L
Liverpool 30/31 1 FL
St Johnstone 31/32 35 3 D2
32/33 31 1
33/34 6
Brechin C L 33/34 D2
Workington 34/35
35/36
Airdrieonians 36/37 1 D2

IRONS James Hay 1 cap
b. Scoonie 30.10.1874
Queen's Park Strollers
Abercorn 98/99 D2
99/00 D2
Queen's Park 00/01 6

IRONSIDE James

Renfrew Jnrs
Albion R 38/39 7 1

IRVINE John
b. Kilbirnie
Dalry Thistle
Kilmarnock 29/30 4
30/31 11 1
31/32 4
Queen of the South 32/33 D2
33/34 14
Alloa A 34/35 D2
35/36 D2
36/37 D2
Dumbarton 37/38 D2

IRVINE Joseph

Distillery
Port Glasgow A
Johnstone 01/02
Abercorn 01/02 D2
02/03 D2
03/04 D2
Thornliebank 04/05
Glossop 04/05 25 4 FL
05/06 23 4 FL
06/07
07/08
08/09
Hamilton A 09/10 25 5
Morton 10/11 5 1
11/12 4
Johnstone 12/13 D2

IRVINE Thomas

Queen's Park 12/13 1

IRVINE Thomas Bennett
b. Springside 6.7.1898 d. Wolverhampton 1955
Springside
Dreghorn
Luton T 22/23 8 FL
Dreghorn 23/24
Ayr U 23/24 5 1

IRVING Samuel Johnstone
b. Belfast 28.8.1894 d. Dundee 17.1.1969
Shildon A
Newcastle U T 10/11 FL
Galashiels U 11/12
Esh Winning 12/13
Bristol C 13/14 13 3 FL
14/15 4 1 FL
Blyth Spartans
Shildon A 19/20
Dundee 20/21 35 1
21/22 24
22/23 29
23/24 12 1
24/25 28 1
25/26 31 2
26/27 1
Cardiff C 26/27 26 5 FL
27/28 21 FL
Chelsea 27/28 11 1 FL
28/29 32 1 FL
29/30 17 1 FL
30/31 20 2 FL
31/32 9 FL
Bristol R 32/33 21 1 FL
Brechin C 33/34 D2

JAAP John
b. Bellshill 1900 d. Pittsburgh ?.5.1974
Philadelphia Field Club 21/22 7 1 ASL
22/23
23/24
24/25
Bethlehem Steel 25/26 17 4 ASL
26/27 35 14 ASL
27/28 40 13 ASL
28/29 4 3 ESL
29/30 19 9 ASL
Heart of Midlothian 30/31 10 2
Newark Americans 31A 10 4 ASL

JACK

Leith A 92/93 4 1

JACK

Leith A 94/95 1

JACK

St Mirren 16/17 1

JACK Archibald
b. Grangemouth 15.8.1889
Forth R
Falkirk 13/14 8 1
Royal Field Artillery
South Shields 19/20 7 1 FL

JACK Edward

St Bernards 96/97 2
Heart of Midlothian

JACK Francis
b. Falkirk
Third Lanark 28/29 12 1
29/30 D2
30/31 D2
31/32 31 12
32/33 33 1
East Stirlingshire 33/34 D2

JACK James

Scottish Dyes
Burnbank A
Stenhousemuir 32/33 D2
33/34 D2
34/35 D2
35/36 D2
Hamilton A 36/37 8

JACK John
b. Kirkintilloch
Kilsyth R
Arbroath 27/28 2 D2
Hamilton A 28/29 21 1
29/30 3

JACK Peter

Newton Thistle
Celtic T 94/95 1
Vale of Clyde
Airdrieonians 95/96 12 4 D2
96/97 D2

JACK Thomas
b. Glasgow
Larbert
Stenhousemuir 23/24 D2
24/25 D2
25/26 D2
Dunfermline A 26/27 36 2
27/28 10

JACKSON

Dumbarton 94/95 2

JACKSON Sergeant

Aberdeen 16/17 10 2

JACKSON

Morton 19/20 1

JACKSON Alexander Skinner 17 caps
b. Renton 12.5.1905 d. Cairo 15.11.1946
Renton Victoria
Shawfield Jnrs
Dumbarton 22/23 27 2 D2
Bethlehem Steel 23/24 28 14 ASL
Aberdeen 24/25 34 8
Huddersfield T 25/26 39 16 FL
26/27 32 6 FL
27/28 39 19 FL
28/29 35 14 FL
29/30 30 8 FL
30/31 4 7 FL
Chelsea 30/31 29 10 FL
31/32 36 15 FL
Ashton National 32/33
Margate 32/33
Nice 33/34
Le Torquet Olympique

JACKSON Andrew
b. Cambuslang c1856 d. Paisley ?.12.1930
Excelsior
Cambuslang 90/91 13 1
91/92 6

JACKSON Andrew

Middlesbrough
St Mirren L 15/16 2

JACKSON Andrew E

Dundee NE
Dundee U 31/32 26 5

JACKSON Archibald

Third Lanark 24/25 1

JACKSON Ernest
b. Glasgow
Maryhill Hibs
Clyde 28/29 3 1
29/30 16 2
30/31 9 1

JACKSON James
b. Cambuslang 15.9.1875
Hamilton A
Elmstown Rosebuds (Aus)
Newton Thistle
Cambuslang 95/96
Rangers 96/97 1
Newcastle U 97/98 27 FL
98/99 30 FL
Woolwich Arsenal 99/00 28 FL
00/01 32 FL
01/02 33 FL
02/03 28 FL
03/04 33 FL
04/05 29 FL
Leyton 05/06 SL
West Ham U 05/06 24 SL
Rangers 06/07 16
07/08 14

JACKSON James
b. Dundee
Dundee 07/08 7
Rangers 08/09 1
09/10 1
Dundee 09/10 2

JACKSON James

St Mirren
Port Glasgow A 08/09 31 1
09/10 22
Hamilton A 09/10 8
Morton 10/11 22
Abercorn 11/12 D2

JACKSON James
b. Newcastle 4.12.1900
Queen's Park Strollers
Queen's Park 18/19 27
Motherwell 19/20 36 1
20/21 18
21/22 22
22/23 21
Aberdeen 23/24 33 1
24/25 34 1
Liverpool 25/26 12 FL
26/27 19 FL
27/28 40 1 FL
28/29 42 FL
29/30 40 FL
30/31 28 FL
31/32 17 FL
32/33 14 1 FL

JACKSON James

Queen's Park 20/21 1

JACKSON James

Shawfield Jnrs
Airdrieonians 23/24 2

JACKSON John 8 caps
b. Possilpark 29.11.1905 d. Nova Scotia 12.6.1965
Kirkintilloch Rob Roy
Partick T 26/27 36
27/28 38
28/29 38
29/30 38
30/31 38
31/32 38
32/33 38
Chelsea 33/34 6 FL
34/35 27 FL
35/36 10 FL
36/37 1 FL
37/38 2 FL
38/39 3 FL
Guildford C 45/46

JACKSON John Bertram
b. Dalry 21.6.1893
Ardeer Thistle

Clyde		08/09			
Celtic	L	08/09			
Clyde		09/10	17	4	
		10/11	22	1	
		11/12	30	7	
		12/13	27	2	
Celtic	L	12/13			
Clyde		13/14	15	2	
Leeds C		13/14	22	3	FL
		14/15	32	6	FL
Ayr U	L	15/16	19	12	
Clyde	L	16/17	25	4	
Rangers	L	16/17			
Celtic		17/18	21	3	
		18/19	6	1	
Clydebank	L	18/19	11	?	
Motherwell		19/20	6		
Dundee		19/20	20	1	
Stevenston U	L	19/20			
Dundee		20/21	37	1	
		21/22	20		

JACKSON Thomas

Queen's Park		08/09	3		

JACKSON Thomas
b. Sunderland 1896
Sunderland WE

Burnley		19/20	1		FL
		20/21			FL
Dundee		20/21	3	2	
West Ham U		21/22	3	1	FL
Jarrow					

JACKSON Thomas Alexander 6 caps
b. Thornliebank 12.11.1878 K.I.A. 9.10.1916
Summerlee Juveniles
Thornliebank

St Mirren		98/99	8		
		99/00	17		
		00/01	16		
		01/02	18		
		02/03	22		
		03/04	23		
		04/05	22	1	
		05/06	23		
		06/07	32	1	
		07/08	19	1	
		08/09			
Bathgate		09/10			
St Johnstone		10/11			
		11/12	9		D2

JACKSON Walter
b. Renton 19.1.1903
Yoker A

Kilmarnock		20/21	3	1	
		21/22	27	9	
		22/23	38	15	
Bethlehem Steel		23/24	23	13	ASL
Aberdeen		24/25	36	13	
		25/26	11	5	
Preston NE		25/26	24	10	FL
		26/27	21	3	FL
Bethlehem Steel		27/28	13	6	ASL
		28/29			
Philadelphia Centennials	L	28/29			

JACKSON William Kennedy
b. Renton 24.12.1899 d. Aberdeen 9.2.1986
Vale of Leven

Duntochter Hibs		21/22			
Everton		21/22			FL
		22/23			FL
Wrexham		22/23	25	8	FL
		23/24	27	2	FL
Vale of Leven		24/25			D3
Aberdeen		24/25	6		
		25/26	35	6	
		26/27	21		
		27/28	38		
		28/29	36		
		29/30	5		
		30/31	29		
		31/32	13	1	
Vale of Leven		31/32			

JACKSON William P
b. Cumnock
Cumnock Townend Thistle

Ayr U		28/29			
		29/30	1	1	

JAMES Alexander Wilson 8 caps
b. Mossend 14.9.1901 d. Islington 1.6.1953
Brandon Amateurs
Orbiston Celtic
Bellshill A
Glasgow Ashfield

Motherwell	T				
Raith R		22/23	25	5	
		23/24	34	11	
		24/25	37	11	
		25/26	4		
Preston NE		25/26	34	14	FL
		26/27	39	11	FL
		27/28	38	18	FL
		28/29	36	10	FL
Arsenal		29/30	31	6	FL
		30/31	40	5	FL
		31/32	32	2	FL
		32/33	40	3	FL
		33/34	22	3	FL
		34/35	30	4	FL
		35/36	17	2	FL
		36/37	19	1	FL

JAMIESON

Cambuslang		90/91	14		
		91/92	21		

JAMIESON

Third Lanark		91/92	1		

JAMIESON

Abercorn		92/93	8		

JAMIESON

Rangers		97/98	1		

JAMIESON Andrew

Broxburn A					
Broxburn U		21/22			D2
Heart of Midlothian		21/22			
		22/23	4		
		23/24			
		24/25	13		
		25/26	24		
		26/27	6		
Kettering T		27/28			
Third Lanark		28/29	33	1	

JAMIESON Andrew (Alex?)
b. c1910 d. Glasgow 5.3.2004
Clydebank Jnrs
Duntocher Hibs

Arbroath		34/35	1	1	D2
		35/36	7		
Montrose		36/37			D2
Alloa A		37/38			D2
Dunfermline A	T	38/39			D2

JAMIESON Forbes

Montrose					
Keith					
Dunfermline A		36/37	10	2	

JAMIESON J William

Maryhill					
Queen's Park		06/07	6		
		07/08	20	2	

JAMIESON James
b. c1888 d. Renfrew ?.12.1919
Longcroft Thistle

St Mirren		11/12	7	1	
Johnstone					
Kilsyth R					

JAMIESON James

Aberdeen		15/16	6	2	
Heart of Midlothian		16/17	2		

JAMIESON John

St Mirren		28/29	1		

JAMIESON John A

Queen's Park		31/32	3		

JAMIESON John J
b. Edinburgh
Tranent Jnrs

Cowdenbeath		20/21			
Rangers		21/22	6		
		22/23	13		
		23/24	1		
		24/25	7		
		25/26	5		
St Johnstone		25/26	25		
		26/27	32		
		27/28	27		
		28/29	10		
		29/30			
Leith A		30/31			
		31/32	3		

JAMIESON William J

Queen's Park		30/31	1		
		31/32			
		32/33	4		

JANES James Town

Clyde		98/99	1		

JARVIE Alexander

St Bernards		97/98	2		

JARVIE Gavin
b. Newton 1879
Cambuslang R

Airdrieonians		01/02	15	2	D2
		02/03	20	1	D2
		03/04	26	2	
Bristol R		04/05	28		SL
		05/06	28		SL
		06/07	34	1	SL
Sunderland		07/08	25	1	FL
		08/09	23	1	FL
		09/10	32		FL
		10/11	11		FL
		11/12	3		FL
Hamilton A		12/13	27		

JARVIE John
b. Old Monkland 19.10.1900 d. Leicester 30.1.1985
Tannochside U
Bellshill A

Third Lanark		23/24	33		
		24/25	23		
Leicester C		25/26	5		FL
Portsmouth		26/27	3		FL
		27/28	1		FL
Southend U		27/28	13		FL
		28/29			FL
Watford	T	29/30			FL
Norwich C		29/30	42		FL
Chester		30/31	26		CCL
Shrewsbury T		31/32			
		32/33			
Solus		33/34			

JARVIE Thomas

Douglas Water Thistle					
Hamilton A		35/36	3		
		36/37	20		
		37/38	13	1	
		38/39	36	2	
Third Lanark					

JARVIS Henry George
b. Hutchesontown 3.12.1889
Benburb
Cambuslang R

Celtic		12/13	6		
		13/14			
Motherwell	L	13/14			
Vale of Leven	L	13/14			D2
Ayr U	L	13/14	6		
Celtic		14/15	1		
Ayr U	L	14/15			
Clyde	L	14/15			
St Mirren	L	14/15	1		
Celtic		15/16			
Falkirk	L	15/16	5		
Celtic		16/17			
		17/18			
Clydebank	L	17/18	6	6	
Celtic		18/19			
Stevenston U	L	18/19			
Stoke		19/20	30	10	FL
		20/21	2		FL
Clydebank		21/22	8	1	
Dunfermline A					
Ayr U					
Ayr Fort		27/28			

JARVIS Sidney
b. Sheffield 1905 d. Perth, Aus 24.6.1994
Eccleshall Church
Nether Edge Amateurs
Hull C 25/26 FL
Darlington 26/27 FL
Kettering T 26/27
Raith R 26/27 D2
27/28 11 1
Middlesbrough 27/28 5 FL
28/29 22 FL
29/30 2 FL
30/31 11 FL
31/32 14 FL
32/33 23 1 FL
33/34 5 FL
34/35 4 FL
Dunkerque 35/36
Darlington 36/37 1 FL

JEFFREY James
Clyde 94/95 6
95/96 10
Galston 95/96

JEFFREY James McKay
b. Rattray 3.11.1874 d. Kennington 8.2.1958
Blairgowrie OB
Fair City A 98/99
Dundee 98/99 1
Fair City A 98/99
Dundee 99/00
00/01
01/02 1
02/03
03/04 25
04/05 22 1
05/06 26
06/07 31 2
07/08 25 1
Millwall 08/09 32 1 SL
09/10 39 SL
10/11 37 SL
11/12 37 SL
12/13 38 SL

JENKINS Alexander
Queen of the South 33/34 6

JENKINS George Edward
b. Leeds
Montreal CPR
Montreal Maroons
Indiana Flooring 26/27 9 5 ASL
Montreal Carsteel
Rangers 27/28
28/29
29/30
30/31
31/32
32/33
33/34 7
34/35 1
35/36
36/37
37/38 12
38/39 5
Kilmarnock 45/46
Hamilton A 46/47 2

JENKINS Robert
b. Springburn 29.12.1909
Dunblane R
Partick T 29/30 4 3
30/31
31/32
Brechin C 32/33 D2

JENKINSON Thomas James 1 cap
b. Edinburgh 21.4.1865 d. Australia
Heart of Midlothian 84/85
85/86
86/87
87/88
88/89
89/90
90/91 2
Liverpool

JENNETT William J
Park U
Petershill
St Johnstone 38/39 8

JENNINGS Edward R
b. Hamilton
Cadzow St Annes
Hamilton A 11/12 5 1

JENNINGS Thomas Hamilton Oliver
b. Strathaven 8.3.1902 d. Johnstone 2.7.1973
Strathaven Academy
Earnock R
Ashfield
Cadzow St Annes
Tottenham H T
Raith R 20/21 15 3
21/22 35 22
22/23 32 8
23/24 31 27
24/25 21 13
Leeds U 24/25 10 3 FL
25/26 42 26 FL
26/27 41 35 FL
27/28 26 21 FL
28/29 17 9 FL
29/30 23 14 FL
30/31 8 4 FL
Chester 31/32 39 31 FL
32/33 9 9 FL
Bangor C 33/34

JESSIMAN George Thomas Russell
b. Gorbals 1900
Morton 22/23 29 1
Arthurlie 23/24 D3
24/25 D2
25/26 D2
26/27 D2
Clyde 27/28 30 2
28/29 36 6
29/30 16 3
30/31
Albion R 31/32 D2
Alloa A 32/33 D2

JESSIMAN James
Langside
Raith R 19/20 13 3

JESSIMAN James T
Arthurlie 24/25
Morton 25/26 30 2
26/27 35 3
27/28 D2
28/29 D2
Middlesbrough T 28/29 FL
Morton 29/30
30/31
Stenhousemuir 30/31 D2

JOBEY George
b. Heddon on the Wall 13.7.1885 d. Chaddesden 9.3.1962
Morpeth Harriers
Newcastle U 06/07 1 FL
07/08 4 1 FL
08/09 10 1 FL
09/10 11 FL
10/11 7 FL
11/12 3 FL
12/13 11 FL
Woolwich Arsenal 13/14 28 3 FL
Bradford PA 14/15 14 4 FL
Hamilton A 15/16 6 1
Hartlepools U 19/20
Leicester C 19/20 30 FL
Northampton T 20/21 42 2 FL
21/22 35 FL

JOHNMAN John
b. Cambusnethan
Carluke Milton R
Motherwell 23/24 31
24/25 26
25/26 27
26/27 37
27/28 35
28/29 38 1
29/30 21
30/31 34
31/32
Stockport Co 32/33 1 FL
Halifax T 33/34 36 FL
Dunfermline A 34/35 37
35/36 30

JOHNSTON
Third Lanark 94/95 3

JOHNSTON
Airdrieonians 14/15 1 1
15/16
16/17
17/18 2

JOHNSTON Angus
b. Govan
Govan High School
Airdrieonians 30/31 15 1
31/32 9 1
32/33 21 1
33/34 10

JOHNSTON Anthony C M
b. c1918
Jordanhill Training College
Queen's Park 35/36 3
36/37
37/38 1
38/39 25
Partick T
Raith R

JOHNSTON Charles
b. Larkhall 26.11.1911
Blantyre V
Motherwell 32/33
33/34 4 1
34/35 2
Doncaster R 35/36 14 3 FL
36/37 22 FL
Mansfield T 37/38 36 4 FL
Dunfermline A 38/39 D2
Rangers
Queen of the South 46/47 27 3
47/48 23 3
48/49 27 5
49/50 22 6
50/51 D2
51/52 14
52/53 22 4

JOHNSTON G
Leith A 30/31 27 6

JOHNSTON Henry Wallace
b. Glasgow 1871 d. Cathcart 10.12.1936
Airdrieonians
Clyde 92/93 8 1
93/94 12
Sunderland 94/95 29 2 FL
95/96 26 2 FL
96/97 5 FL
Aston Villa
Grimsby T 97/98 8 FL
Gravesend U
Third Lanark

JOHNSTON Herbert
b. Dundee 3.4.1912
Dundee Violet
Aberdeen 32/33 5 1
33/34 3
34/35 7 1
Fulham 35/36 4 1 FL
London Paper Mills

JOHNSTON Ian A
b. Oban
Leith Emmet
Arniston R
Partick T 34/35
35/36 8
36/37 10
Third Lanark 37/38 30
38/39 21

JOHNSTON James
Abercorn 94/95 2 ? D2
95/96 4 ? D2
96/97 16

JOHNSTON James
Third Lanark 01/02 17 4
02/03 19 8
03/04 17 8
04/05 21 8
05/06 23 11
06/07 22 7
Swindon T 07/08 37 6 SL
Third Lanark 08/09 29 6
09/10 18 6

JOHNSTON James
Tranent Jnrs
Motherwell 32/33 2
33/34
34/35 4
Arbroath 35/36 19 3
St Bernards 36/37 D2
37/38 D2
38/39 D2

JOHNSTON James G

Heart of Midlothian *
Broxburn U * 26/27
27/28
28/29
29/30
30/31
Leith A 31/32 26 3

JOHNSTON John
b. Riccarton 23.1.1869 d. 5.2.1953
Riccarton V
Rangers 93/94
Riccarton V
Kilmarnock 95/96 19 D2
96/97 10 D2
97/98 16 1 D2
98/99 16 1 D2
99/00 16 1
00/01 6

JOHNSTON John

Dalziel R
Cambuslang R
Sunderland 08/09 1 FL
Motherwell 09/10 13

JOHNSTON Ronald
b. c1921
Victoria Park Amateurs
Albion R 38/39 6 2

JOHNSTON Thomas

St Mirren 97/98 1

JOHNSTON W

Third Lanark 20/21 1

JOHNSTON William

Morton 07/08 2

JOHNSTON William Angus

Queen's Park 38/39 4

JOHNSTONE

Clyde 91/92 14 3

JOHNSTONE

Dumbarton 92/93 6 4
93/94 15 12
94/95 6 1

JOHNSTONE

Rangers 93/94 1

JOHNSTONE

St Bernards 93/94 3

JOHNSTONE

Clyde 95/96 1

JOHNSTONE

Port Glasgow A 02/03 1

JOHNSTONE

Ayr U 16/17 1
17/18
18/19 1 ?

JOHNSTONE Alexander
b. Cullen
Rangers 19/20 1
20/21 3
21/22
Third Lanark L 21/22 30
Rangers 22/23 9 1
23/24 12
Heart of Midlothian 24/25 19
25/26 10
26/27 20
27/28 36
Fall River Marksmen 28/29 18 ASL

JOHNSTONE Alexander

Queen of the South 33/34 1

JOHNSTONE Alexander S

Queen's Park 33/34 1
34/35

JOHNSTONE Archibald M
b. Carluke
Pollok
Hamilton A 23/24 37
24/25 33
25/26 34
26/27 23
27/28 18
East Stirlingshire 28/29 D2
Cowdenbeath 29/30 33
30/31 38
31/32 25
32/33 14
Hamilton A 33/34 1

JOHNSTONE Benjamin

Port Glasgow A
Morton 30/31 7

JOHNSTONE D B

Third Lanark 23/24 5 1

JOHNSTONE David
b. Edinburgh
Heart of Midlothian 38/39 1

JOHNSTONE David B

Prestwick Glenburn R
Partick T 20/21 19 2
21/22 26 1
22/23 3
Arthurlie 23/24 D3

JOHNSTONE George
b. Caldercruix 15.12.1914 d. Kirkcaldy 11.9.1974
Bothwellhaugh A
Benburb
Aberdeen 36/37 10
37/38 38
38/39 34
46/47 26
47/48 28
48/49 15
Dunfermline A 49/50 4 D2
Raith R 49/50 11
Raith R 50/51 28
51/52 27
52/53 21
53/54 14
54/55 9
Dumbarton 55/56 D2
Morton 55/56 D2
Cowdenbeath 56/57 D2
57/58 D2
58/59 1 D2

JOHNSTONE James 1 cap

Abercorn 86/87
87/88
88/89
89/90
90/91 13

JOHNSTONE James
d. Troon ?.11.1924
Motherwell 07/08 11 2
08/09 31 6
09/10 28 4
10/11 24 3
Barrow

JOHNSTONE John

Clyde 97/98 1

JOHNSTONE John

Motherwell 10/11 24

JOHNSTONE John
b. Dalserf
Parkhead Jnrs
Kilmarnock 16/17 11
17/18 16
18/19 8
Hamilton A 18/19 2
19/20 26
20/21 25
Armadale L 20/21
Hamilton A 21/22 5
22/23 10
Royal Albert

JOHNSTONE John Ainslie 3 caps
b. Stevenston 17.11.1902
Stevenston U
Ardeer Thistle
Heart of Midlothian 22/23 5
23/24 8
24/25 9
25/26 4
Cowdenbeath L 25/26 D2
Heart of Midlothian 26/27 32
27/28 37 1
28/29 27 1
29/30 29
30/31 27 1
31/32 35
32/33 36 3
33/34 26 3
34/35 5
Arbroath 35/36 8

JOHNSTONE Joseph

Dundee Violet
Dundee 11/12 1
12/13 23 1
13/14 3
14/15
15/16 1

JOHNSTONE Joseph

Dundee 20/21 6 1
21/22 4 1

JOHNSTONE Joseph

Motherwell Boys Brigade
Renfrew Jnrs
Motherwell 36/37 6 2
37/38 9 1
38/39
46/47 32 7
47/48
48/49
49/50
50/51
51/52
Albion R 52/53 D2

JOHNSTONE Peter
b. Collessie 6.7.1888 K.I.A.,France ?.5.1917
Buckhaven
Kelty R
Glencraig Celtic
Celtic 07/08
08/09 1
09/10 29 11
10/11 19 3
11/12 27 2
12/13 28 2
13/14 36 2
14/15 32 1
15/16 36 2
16/17 2

JOHNSTONE Robert
b. Renton
Renton 94/95 2 ? D2
95/96 11 ? D2
Sunderland 96/97 12 FL
Third Lanark 97/98 18 10
98/99 7 2
Dunfermline A

JOHNSTONE Robert

Morton 25/26 1

JOHNSTONE Robert
b. Coldstream 18.9.1908
Coldstream
Heart of Midlothian 29/30 26 5
30/31 20 5
31/32 33 8
32/33 31 5
33/34 32 4
34/35 27 3
Bradford PA 35/36 16 1 FL
36/37 40 FL
37/38 37 FL
38/39 27 FL
39/40 1 FL

JOHNSTONE Robert

Wishaw
Blantyre Celtic
Partick T 33/34 33
34/35 31
35/36 35
36/37 38
37/38 36
38/39 31
Motherwell

JOHNSTONE W

Cowdenbeath 25/26 20

JOHNSTONE Walter Campbell
b. Govanhill 29.1.1908
Shawfield
Falkirk T 26/27
Coventry C 27/28 23 7 FL
28/29 6 5 FL
Walsall 28/29 FL
Morton 29/30 31 10
30/31 8 1

JOHNSTONE William 3 caps
b. Glasgow ?.11.1864 d. 11.12.1950
Govanhill
Third Lanark 84/85
85/86
86/87
87/88
88/89
89/90
90/91
91/92 15 5
92/93 10 3
93/94 16 6

JOHNSTONE William

Partick T 97/98 1 1

JOHNSTONE William

Dundee 99/00 15 1
00/01 6
01/02 12

JOHNSTONE William
b. Kilmarnock
Kilmarnock Rugby XI
Darvel Jnrs
Kilmarnock 04/05 18
Ayr Parkhouse 05/06
Hurlford 05/06
Lanemark 05/06
Kilmarnock 06/07 3
07/08 1
08/09
09/10
10/11 6
Hurlford 10/11
Kilmarnock 11/12 8

JOHNSTONE William
b. Markinch 18.5.1901
Rosslyn Jnrs
Kings Park 21/22 D2
22/23 D2
Clyde 22/23 2
23/24 14 4
24/25 D2
25/26 D2
26/27 8 5
Reading 26/27 19 8 FL
27/28 30 7 FL
28/29 29 19 FL
Arsenal 29/30 7 3 FL
30/31 2 1 FL
Oldham A 30/31 16 13 FL
31/32 35 11 FL
32/33 17 4 FL
Clyde 33/34 25 8
34/35 30 14
35/36 1
Northwich V

JONES

St Mirren 90/91 5 1
91/92 3
92/93 1

JONES

Abercorn 91/92 1

JONES Alexander
b. Hamilton 15.9.1886 d. 6.2.1958
Rutherglen Glencairn
Motherwell 08/09 17
09/10
10/11
Linfield 11/12 IL
Shelbourne 12/13 IL
13/14 IL

JONES George Benjamin
b. Newtown 29.1.1907 d. Bolton 1982
Newtown
Bolton W 27/28 FL
Hamilton A 28/29 4 1
29/30
Swindon T 30/31 4 1 FL
Rochdale 31/32 19 3 FL
Oldham A 31/32 2 FL
Wigan A 32/33 31 CCL
Nelson 33/34
Southend U 34/35 3 FL
35/36 FL
Crusaders 36/37 IL
Portadown 36/37 IL
Bangor 37/38 IL
Crusaders 37/38 IL

JONES Jack
b. Lurgan 3.4.1907 d. Lurgan 20.3.1986
Wellington
Sunnyside
KOSB
Linfield 28/29 IL
29/30 IL
30/31 IL
31/32 IL
32/33 IL
33/34 IL
34/35 IL
35/36 IL
Hibernian 35/36 19 1
36/37 31 3
Glenavon 37/38 IL
38/39 IL
Bath C

JONES John
b. Gourock c1916 d. Inverclyde 11.3.1999
Army
Morton Jnrs
Third Lanark 36/37 5 1
37/38 25 7
38/39 36 22
46/47 1
Bradford C T 46/47 2 FL
Morton 46/47 3
Stranraer

JONES P Forbes
b. Larbert
Queen's Park 01/02 10 2
02/03 11 3
03/04 20 5
04/05 10 2
Falkirk RUFC

JORDAN Hugh McNaughton
b. Musselburgh 24.7.1908
Falkirk 29/30 7
Norwich C 30/31 18 3 FL
Niddrie Thistle *
Queen of the South * T
Leith A * 33/34 D2
Margate 34/35
Stade de Reims 35/36
36/37
37/38
Olympique Dunkerque 37/38
Stade de Reims 38/39

JORDAN Robert

Forth R
Partick T 32/33 2 1
East Stirlingshire 33/34 D2

JOYCE William
b. Prestonpans 8.4.1877
Morton 93/94 18 ?
94/95 12 ?
Bolton W 94/95 5 3 FL
95/96 20 12 FL
96/97 5 1 FL
Tottenham H 97/98 19 16 SL
98/99 19 10 SL
Thames Ironworks 99/00 27 8 SL
Portsmouth 00/01 21 16 SL
Burton U 01/02 22 8 FL
02/03 29 9 FL
Morton 03/04 15 7
Motherwell 04/05 9 3

KANE Alexander
b. Aberdeen 17.10.1897
KOSB
Broxburn U
Heart of Midlothian 19/20 40
20/21 39
21/22 27
Reading 22/23 42 FL
Portsmouth 23/24 42 FL
242/5 42 FL
25/26 12 FL
West Ham U 25/26 1 FL
26/27 1 FL
Congasco (Toronto)
Bredins Bread (Toronto)

KANE Edward

Denny Hibs
Falkirk 19/20 2
20/21 34 9
21/22 25 6
Cowdenbeath 22/23 D2
23/24 D2
St Bernards 23/24 D2
24/25 D2
Arbroath 25/26 20 6 D2
Lochgelly U 26/27

KAVANAGH Peter Joseph
b. Dublin 11.9.1909 d. Glasgow 15.2.1993
Munster Boys
Melrose Celtic of Fairview
Drumcondra
Bohemians 26/27 LI
27/28 LI
28/29 LI
Celtic 29/30 17 2
30/31 4
31/32 11 3
Northampton T 32/33 1 FL
Guildford C 33/34
Hibernian 33/34 10 3
34/35
Stranraer 35/36
Waterford 35/36 LI
Witton A 36/37
37/38
38/39
Babcock & Wilcox

KAY Alexander

St Bernards 98/99 13
99/00 13
Partick T 00/01 19
Sheffield U 01/02 6 FL

KAY George
b. Dalmuir
Vale of Leven
Abercorn
Hibernian 18/19 7 ?

KAY John C
b. Dunipace 1899 d. 1979
Third Lanark 21/22 1
Kings Park 22/23 D2
Dundee U 23/24 38 D2
24/25 33 1 D2
25/26 38
26/27 34 2
27/28 34 1 D2
Stenhousemuir 28/29 D2
29/30 D2
30/31 D2

KAY John Sharp
b. Dalmellington 1908 d. ?.8.1963
Motherwell Jnrs
Dundee U 27/28 36 11 D2
28/29 36 17 D2
29/30 33 12
30/31 38 24 D2
31/32 29 4
32/33 31 5 D2
Blackpool T 33/34 FL
Crystal Palace T 33/34 FL
Dundee U 33/34 D2
34/35 15 3 D2
35/36 11 6 D2
Brechin C 36/37 D2
Alloa A 37/38 D2

KAYE

Leith A 94/95 14

KEAN

Dumbarton 19/20 1

KEAN Samuel
b. Dumbarton c1918 d. Edinburgh 17.4.2003
Kirkintilloch Rob Roy
Hibernian 37/38 4
38/39 31 8
46/47 24
47/48 13
48/49 21

KEANE John
b. Clydebank 1910
Clydebank Corinthians
Yoker A
Kilmarnock 33/34 37 13
34/35 37 12
35/36 9 1
Falkirk 36/37
Exeter C 36/37 13 1 FL
Gateshead 37/38 3 FL
38/39 2 FL
Hartlepools U
Yoker A

KEARNEY Robert
b. Ashton in Makerfield 6.3.1903 d. Portsmouth 24.2.1931
Burnbank A
Kirkintilloch Rob Roy
Dundee 27/28 1
Portsmouth 28/29 FL
29/30 32 FL
30/31 28 FL

KEATT Richard Hawkins
b. Hamilton 1915
Queen of the South 36/37
37/38 2
Morton 38/39 D2
Dundee U T

KEDDIE Joseph
Hamilton A 36/37 1
37/38 27 10
38/39 22 6
Glentoran 40/41 IL
41/42 IL

KEENAN Henry
b. c1918
Cambuslang R
Clyde 37/38 4 1
Celtic 38/39
Shelbourne 39/40 LI
40/41 LI
Derry C 41/42 IL

KEENAN James
b. Edinburgh c1907
Clydebank Jnrs
Motherwell 26/27 4
27/28 27 8
28/29 2
Airdrieonians 28/29 8
Clydebank Intermediate 29/30
30/31
Bedlay Jnrs 31/32

KEENAN James
b. South Leith 1889 d. Edinburgh ?.8.1937
Cameron Highlanders
Hibernian 27/28 1
Duns
St Bernards

KEENAN James
St Anthonys
West Ham U 33/34 FL
Queen of the South 34/35 2
Clyde T 35/36
Larne 35/36 IL
Partick T 35/36 5 2
Larne 36/37 IL
Red Star de Paris 37/38
Kings Park 38/39 D2

KEENLYSIDE George
b. Jarrow 4.8.1889 d. Jarrow 18.4.1967
Jarrow Royal Oak
Jarrow Park Villa
Jarrow Croft
Sunderland
Jarrow
Dinnington Colliery
Partick T 10/11 8 3
Jarrow Croft
South Shields 19/20 7 FL
20/21 22 3 FL
21/22 31 5 FL
22/23 38 6 FL
Hartlepools U 23/24 24 1 FL
Jarrow 23/24

KEGGINS John
St Mirren 08/09 3
Beith

KEILLOR Alexander Lowson 6 caps
b. Dundee 20.10.1869 d. 16.6.1960
Montrose Academy
Montrose 84/85
85/86
86/87
87/88
88/89
89/90
90/91
91/92
92/93
Dundee 93/94 18 9
94/95 18 2
95/96 16 2
96/97 17
97/98 16 3
98/99 17
99/00 15 1
00/01 20
01/02 2
Montrose 02/03
03/04
04/05
05/06

KEIR Charles
Dumbarton 13/14 19
Armadale 14/15

KEIR James
Third Lanark 24/25 1

KEIR Leitch 5 caps
b. Alloa 22.6.1861 d. 29.6.1922
Dumbarton 82/83
83/84
84/85
85/86
86/87
87/88
88/89
89/90
90/91 15
91/92 19
92/93 14 2
93/94
94/95 18

KEIR Thomas
Heart of Midlothian 95/96 1
96/97 2

KEITH Fred M
St Mirren 09/10 6
Helensburgh 10/11
Vale of Leven 10/11 D2

KEITH Ronald J
Petershill
Motherwell 12/13 2

KEITH William
Queen's Park 14/15 2
15/16 4 3

KELLOCK John
Heart of Midlothian 99/00 2
00/01 1
Cowdenbeath 00/01
Falkirk 01/02

KELLY Charles
b. c1867 d. Airdrie 20.9.1898
Broxburn Shamrock 88/89
Glasgow Hibernian 89/90
Hibernian 89/90
90/91
Celtic L 91/92 2
Busby Cartvale

KELLY D
Hibernian 18/19 1 ?

KELLY Daniel
b. Coatbridge
Bedlay Jnrs
Hamilton A 13/14 12 4
14/15 37 16
15/16 38 15
16/17 32 14
17/18 20 8
18/19 20 7
Motherwell 18/19 4 2
19/20 9 1
Bathgate 20/21
Bo'ness 20/21
21/22 D2
22/23 21 5 D2

KELLY Daniel
Clyde 17/18 3 ?

KELLY Daniel
b. Blantyre 25.6.1904 d. Glasgow ?.8.1941
Blantyre V
Hamilton A 24/25 25 2
25/26 20 12
26/27 5 1
Derby Co 26/27 4 FL
27/28 1 FL
Torquay U 28/29 34 9 FL
29/30 19 4 FL
York C 30/31 22 7 FL
31/32 26 5 FL
Doncaster R 32/33 10 4 FL
33/34 3 FL
34/35
Dundalk 35/36 LI
Clapton Orient 35/36 FL

KELLY Daniel
b. Musselburgh
Musselburgh Bruntonians
Clyde 27/28 2
28/29 7

KELLY Daniel
b. Blantyre c1910
Burnbank A
Hibernian 28/29 2
29/30 4 1

KELLY Francis David
b. Glasgow 8.12.1892 d. Montagris 5.5.1919
Blantyre St Josephs 11/12
Blantyre V 12/13
Celtic T 12/13
Blantyre V 13/14
14/15
Motherwell 15/16 35 8
Hamilton A L 15/16
Motherwell 16/17 35 7
17/18 12 1
Celtic L 17/18 1
Motherwell 18/19 1

KELLY Hugh
Cadzow Oak
Motherwell Celtic
Cambuslang R
Motherwell 11/12 9 1
12/13 26 9
13/14 17 2
Preston NE 14/15 4 1 FL
Clyde 18/19 2 ?
Armadale 19/20
20/21

KELLY James 8 caps
b. Renton 15.10.1865 d. Blantyre 20.2.1932
Renton W
Renton 83/84
84/85
85/86
Hibernian L 86/87
Renton 87/88
Celtic 88/89
89/90
90/91 12
91/92 21
92/93 17 3
93/94 18 1
94/95 12
95/96 17
96/97 10

KELLY James
Overton R
Airdrieonians T
Wishaw U
Blackpool 26/27 1 1 FL
Airdrieonians 27/28 5 2

KELLY James

Armadale					
Bo'ness		27/28	7		
Armadale		27/28			D2

KELLY James G

b. Blantyre

Blantyre Celtic					
Queen's Park		20/21	5		
Hamilton A		21/22	11	2	

KELLY James Steen

b. Belfast 1902

Mountpottinger					
Dundela					
Castlereagh					
Willowfield		22/23			
Bangor		22/23			
Barn		23/24			IL
		24/25			IL
St Johnstone		25/26	10	2	
Fall River Marksmen		26/27	10	3	ASL
		27/28	30	9	ASL
		28/29	27	3	ASL
Bangor		29/30			IL
Barrow		29/30	2		FL
Glentoran		29/30			IL
Portadown		30/31			IL
Ards		31/32			IL
Fall River Marksmen					
Trocadero					

KELLY Jeremiah

b. Hamilton 1900

Uddingston St Johns					
Blantyre V					
Ayr U		24/25	11		
		25/26	31		D2
		26/27	26		D2
Everton		26/27	14		FL
		27/28	40	1	FL
		28/29	21		FL
		29/30	6		FL
Carlisle U		30/31	32		FL
Rennes Universite		31/32			
Dolphin		31/32			LI
Stranraer		32/33			
		33/34			
Glentoran		34/35			IL
Dunfermline A	T	34/35	1		

KELLY John

b. Wishaw 4.5.1903

Wishaw YMCA					
Vale of Fleet		22/23			
Preston NE		22/23			FL
Motherwell		23/24			
		24/25			
Peebles R		25/26			D3
Brighton		25/26	2		FL
Gillingham		26/27	16		FL
Crystal Palace		27/28	22		FL
Thames		28/29			SL
Celtic		29/30	9		
Nithsdale W	L	29/30			
Carlisle U		30/31	35		FL
		31/32	12		FL
		32/33	30		FL
Coleraine		32/33			IL
Motherwell		32/33			
Beith		33/34			

KELLY Patrick

Dumbarton Harp					
Motherwell		09/10	1		
		10/11			
		11/12	33		
		12/13	33		
		13/14	37		
		14/15	33		
		15/16	28		
Dumbarton Harp					
Stevenston U		16/17			

KELLY Patrick

b. S Africa 9.4.1918 d. 1985

Bloemfontein Pirates					
Aberdeen		37/38			
		38/39	4		
Hamilton A					
Barnsley		46/47			FL
		47/48			FL
		48/49			FL
		49/50			FL
		50/51			FL
Crewe A		51/52			FL
		52/53			FL

KELLY S

Motherwell		18/19	2	?	

KELLY T

Motherwell		37/38	1		

KELLY William

b. c1915

Maryhill Jnrs					
St Mirren		34/35	6		
		35/36			D2
		36/37	33	1	
		37/38	31		
		38/39	38		

KELSO

Renton		91/92	7		

KELSO James Scott

b. c1918

Dalry Thistle					
Hibernian		36/37	3		
		37/38	5		
Derry C		38/39			IL
		39/40			IL
		40/41			IL
		41/42			IL
Distlllery		41/42			IL
		42/43			IL
Derry C		42/43			IL
		43/44			IL
		44/45			IL
		45/46			IL

KELSO John

b. Dumbarton c1904

Dumbarton Harp					
Morton		25/26	24		
		26/27	30	1	
		27/28			
		28/29			
Derry C		29/30			IL
Glenavon		30/31			IL
		31/32			IL
		32/33			IL
Cork		33/34			LI

KELSO Robert Robinson 8 caps

b. Cardross 2.10.1865 d. 10.8.1942

Renton					
Newcastle WE		88/89			
Everton		88/89	1		FL
Preston NE		89/90	20		FL
		90/91	18		FL
Everton		91/92	23	2	FL
		92/93	14	1	FL
		93/94	26	1	FL
		94/95	19	1	FL
		95/96	6		FL
Dundee		96/97	16	1	
		97/98	18		
Bedminster		98/99	18	1	SL

KELSO Thomas 1 cap

b. Renton 5.6.1882 d. 29.1.1974

Rangers	T				
Third Lanark		04/05	2		
		05/06	19		
Manchester C		06/07	25		FL
		07/08	25		FL
		08/09	21		FL
		09/10	28		FL
		10/11	31		FL
		11/12	9	3	FL
Dundee		12/13	4		
		13/14	33	5	
Rangers		14/15	22		
Dumbarton		15/16	10		
Aberdare A					
Dumbarton		18/19	2	?	
Abercorn		19/20			

KELVIN Andrew Wallace

b. Kilmarnock c1914 d. Kilmarnock 8.9.1935

Lugar Boswell		30/31			
Auchinleck Talbot		31/32			
Kilmarnock		31/32	4		
		32/33	5	1	
		33/34	20	1	
		34/35	38		

KEMP Frederick

b. Tottenham 1887

Ethelburgas					
Barking St Andrews					
Newportonians					
Barking V					
Woolwich Arsenal		05/06	2		FL
West Ham U		06/07	8		SL
		07/08	3		SL
Dundee		08/09	1		
Falkirk		09/10	2		

KEMP Robert

East Stirlingshire		32/33	33	10	
		33/34			D2
		34/35			D2
		35/36			D2
		36/37			D2
		37/38			D2

KENMUIR Michael

b. Crosshouse d. Kilmarnock

Galston					
Kilmarnock		30/31	1		
Kilwinning R		31/32			
Kilmarnock		32/33	4		
		33/34	2		
		34/35	9	1	
		35/36	4	1	
Ayr U		36/37	1		D2
		37/38			
Kings Park		37/38			D2
Kilmarnock Jnrs					

KENNAWAY James 2 caps

b. Montreal 25.1.1905 d. Johnston, RI 7.3.1969

Rosemount Jnrs					
Montreal Star					
Gurney					
Montreal CPR					
Providence Clamdiggers		27/28	26		ASL
		28/29	50		ASL
		29A	18		ASL
		29/30	22		ASL
		30A	22		ASL
Fall River		31S	17		ASL
New Bedford Whalers		31A	3		ASL
Celtic		31/32	20		
		32/33	28		
		33/34	33		
		34/35	38		
		35/36	33		
		36/37	34		
		37/38	36		
		38/39	36		
SA Healey					
Montreal Vickers					

KENNEDY

Cowlairs		90/91	2		

KENNEDY

Hibernian		17/18	2	?	

KENNEDY Alexander

Benburb					
Clyde		14/15	6	1	
		15/16	1		
Ayr U	L	15/16			

KENNEDY James

Rutherglen Melrose					
Pollok Jnrs					
Clyde		09/10	1		

KENNEDY James

Pollok Jnrs					
Morton		13/14	3		
		14/15	1		

KENNEDY James

b. Grangemouth c1904

Banknock Jnrs					
Falkirk		25/26			
		26/27	32	2	
		27/28	31		
		28/29	27		
		29/30	29		
		30/31	38	2	
		31/32	37		
Rangers		32/33	10		
		33/34	7		
		34/35	13		
		35/36	10		
		36/37	21		
Morton		37/38	26		

KENNEDY James J

St Bernards					
Airdrieonians		16/17	33	5	
		17/18	26	3	
Motherwell		18/19	1		

KENNEDY John 1 cap
b. Edinburgh 1873
Hibernian 93/94 17 ? D2
94/95 16 ? D2
95/96 18 11
96/97 18 7
97/98 16 7
Stoke 97/98 3 FL
98/99 27 5 FL
99/00 29 4 FL
Glossop 00/01 34 6 FL
01/02 3 1 FL
02/03 2 FL

KENNEDY John
Glasgow Perthshire
Queen's Park
Airdrieonians
South Africa 03/04
Airdrieonians 04/05 2

KENNEDY Robert
Broxburn Shamrock
Hibernian 03/04 1

KENNEDY Robert
b. Glasgow
Kirkintilloch Rob Roy
Petershill
Shettleston
Falkirk 26/27 25 17
27/28 22 15
Raith R L 27/28 4
South Shields 28/29 28 11 FL
29/30 42 14 FL
Gateshead 30/31 40 13 FL
31/32 38 16 FL
32/33 35 14 FL
33/34 21 10 FL
Third Lanark 34/35 D2
35/36 31 8
36/37 27 16
37/38 27 15
38/39 2

KENNEDY Samuel
Parkhead Jnrs
Airdrieonians 18/19 18
19/20 3

KENNEDY Samuel
b. Glasgow 1899
Cambuslang R 21/22
Queens Island 21/22
22/23
23/24
24/25
Falkirk 24/25 7 4
25/26 4 1
Clyde 25/26 D2
Fall River Marksmen 26/27 25 12 ASL
Clyde 26/27
Fall River Marksmen 27/28 1 ASL
J & P Coats 27/28 33 3 ASL
28/29 15 13 ASL
New Bedford Whalers 28/29 12 10 ASL
Pawtucket Rangers 29A 18 5 ASL
29/30 3 ASL
30A 14 1 ASL
31S 8 1 ASL

KENNEDY Samuel Watson 1 cap
b. Girvan 8.4.1881 d. 1950
Ayr
Partick T 02/03 18 11
03/04 24 7
04/05 23 13
05/06 27 13
06/07 29 10
07/08 28 11
08/09 23 7
09/10 2
Girvan A 10/11

KENNEDY Thomas
Queen's Park 04/05 2
Albion R

KENNEDY Thomas A
Queen's Park 00/01 15 5
Hamilton A

KENNEDY William
b. Saltcoats 2.2.1912 d. Southampton 12.12.1989
Royal Albert
Portsmouth 31/32 1 FL
32/33 FL
Carlisle U 33/34 8 FL
Portadown 34/35 IL
Crewe A 35/36 8 FL
Southampton 36/37 33 FL
37/38 10 FL
Colchester U L 38/39
Hamilton A 38/39 29 8

KENNEDY William C
b. Glasgow 1912
Moorpark Amateurs
Kilbirnie Ladeside 32/33
Arthurlie 33/34
Kilmarnock 33/34 23 4
34/35 4
Southampton

KENNY William
Burnbank A
Partick T
St Mirren 31/32
32/33 31
33/34 14
Larne 34/35 IL
East Stirlingshire 34/35 D2
35/36 D2
Hamilton A 36/37 2

KERR
Dumbarton 90/91 1 2

KERR
Vale of Leven 91/92 5

KERR Abraham
St Mirren 04/05 1

KERR Alexander
West Calder
Heart of Midlothian 00/01 2
Mossend Swifts

KERR Alick
b. Bowling
Clydebank
Third Lanark 99/00 1

KERR Andrew
b. Ardrossan c1900
Ardrossan Winton R
Partick T 20/21 17 8
21/22
22/23
Luton T 23/24 39 20 FL
24/25 29 5 FL
Reading 25/26 3 1 FL
QPR 25/26 2 FL

KERR Angus H
Third Lanark 32/33 2
33/34 2

KERR David
b. Wishaw (?) c1913
Wishaw Thistle
Stonehouse Violet
Clyde 32/33 4 2
Glentoran 33/34 IL
34/35 IL
Bangor C 34/35
Drumcondra 35/36 LI
Bangor 36/37 IL
Lincoln C 37/38 5 FL
Newark T

KERR Gordon
b. Helensburgh
Cambuslang R
Kirkintilloch Harp
St Ninians Thistle
Queen's Park 12/13 5
13/14 36
14/15 36
Ayr U 15/16 38
16/17 19
17/18
18/19 11
19/20 25
Albion R 20/21 39
21/22 27

KERR James
b. Ormiston 1919 d. Edinburgh 27.5.2001
Ormiston Primrose
Hibernian 38/39 34
46/47 29
47/48 12
48/49 26
49/50 1
50/51
51/52 4
Queen of the South

KERR James W
Leith A
Raith R 38/39 11 2

KERR John
b. Sanquhar 4.11.1894
Queen's Park 14/15 8
Army
Blackburn R 19/20 15 FL
20/21 1 FL
Brentford 21/22 21 1 FL
22/23 42 FL
23/24 22 FL
24/25 FL
Solway Star 25/26 D3

KERR John
b. Hamilton
Parkhead Jnrs
Hamilton A 17/18 18
18/19 21
19/20 25
20/21 22
21/22 27
22/23 26
Preston NE 23/24 FL

KERR John B
Queen's Park 14/15 16

KERR Neil
b. Bowling 13.4.1871 d. 1901
Cowlairs
Rangers 90/91 18 8
91/92 21 7
92/93 13 4
93/94 6 1
Liverpool 94/95 13 3 FL
Nottingham F 95/96 1 FL
Falkirk 96/97
Rangers 97/98 1

KERR Peter 1 cap
b. Musselburgh 20.6.1891 d. 24.4.1969
Prestonpans
Wallyford Bluebell
Wemyss A
Hibernian 10/11 16
11/12 30 3
12/13 31 5
13/14 29
14/15 35
15/16 31 3
16/17 26 1
17/18 21 ?
18/19 3 ?
19/20 26
20/21 29 1
21/22 36
22/23 20 2
23/24 30
24/25 34 1
25/26 35 1
Heart of Midlothian 26/27 29
27/28 26 1
28/29 30 1
29/30 19 2
30/31 1
Leith A 31/32 2
Inverness Caledonian 32/33

KERR Robert C
b. Larkhall
Netherton R
Wishaw YMCA
Third Lanark 21/22 2 1
Larkhall Thistle
Wishaw YMCA
Heart of Midlothian 23/24 2
24/25 1
Wolverhampton W 25/26 13 5 FL
26/27 5 2 FL
Clapton Orient 27/28 23 8 FL
28/29 8 FL
Worcester C

KERR Thomas
b. Midallen
Falkirk 20/21 4
21/22 1
22/23 5
23/24 2

KERR Thomas McDonald
b. New Cumnock 5.1.1909
Kello R 30/31
31/32
32/33
Partick T T 33/34
Notts Co T 33/34 FL
Queen of the South 33/34
34/35 14
Carlisle U 35/36 42 FL
36/37 36 FL
37/38 32 FL
38/39 26 FL
Kello R

KERR Walter

Leith A
Falkirk 18/19 7 ?

KERR William

Queen's Park 14/15 1
Arthurlie

KEY George Brown 1 cap
b. Dennistoun 11.2.1882 d. Glasgow ?.11.1958
Parkhead Jnrs
Heart of Midlothian 99/00 2
00/01 6
01/02 16 1
02/03 16 1
03/04 20 4
04/05 20 1
Chelsea 05/06 33 1 FL
06/07 4 1 FL
07/08 13 FL
08/09 4 FL
Baillieston R

KEY William 1 cap
b. Glasgow
Vale of Clyde
Queen's Park 06/07 31 2
St Mirren 07/08 28
08/09 27 1
09/10 24
Beith 10/11

KEYES Robert

Larkhall Thistle
Morton 32/33 36 13
33/34 D2
Falkirk 34/35 10 5
35/36 D2
36/37 33 24
37/38 38 31
38/39 34 11

KIDD

Motherwell 06/07 1

KIDD John W
b. Glasgow 1884 d. Birmingham 9.8.1927
Maryhill
Third Lanark 04/05 11 5
05/06 10 1
Swindon T 06/07 12 1 SL
07/08 32 7 SL
Third Lanark 08/09 24 5
09/10 26
St Johnstone 10/11
Birmingham 10/11 26 2 FL
11/12 16 6 FL
Brierley Hill A

KIDSTON Robert

Dunipace Jnrs
Falkirk 13/14 2
14/15
15/16
16/17
17/18
18/19
Dunipace Jnrs 19/20

KIERNAN Michael
b. Glenboig
Heart of Midlothian 15/16 2
16/17 37 2
17/18 30
18/19 1 ?
Airdrieonians 18/19 18
Albion R 19/20 11
20/21 14 1
? 21/22
22/23
23/24
Montrose 24/25

KIERNAN Thomas
b. Coatbridge 20.10.1918 d. Coatbridge 26.6.1991
Viewpark Celtic 35/36
Clydebank Jnrs 36/37
Albion R 37/38 D2
38/39 29 13
Celtic 46/47 22 11
Stoke C 47/48 FL
Luton T 48/49 FL
Gillingham
St Mirren 50/51
Barry T 51/52
Albion R 52/53 D2
53/54 D2
Alloa A 54/55 D2
Barry T

KILDAY Hugh

Hamilton A 06/07 23 1
Bathgate
Distillery

KILPATRICK James S

Renfrew Jnrs
Rangers 22/23 1
23/24 2
Morton 24/25 10
Arthurlie 25/26 D2

KILPATRICK Thomas
b. Uddingston
Benburb
Kilsyth St Patricks
Glasgow Ashfield
Hibernian 15/16 12 1
16/17 26 12
17/18 17 ?
18/19 23 ?
19/20 17 5
Cowdenbeath 20/21
Dundee 20/21 22 1
21/22 11
Ayr U 21/22 20 2
22/23 36
23/24 27
24/25 31 1
25/26 36 6 D2
26/27 16 D2
27/28 33 3 D2
28/29 D2
Ballymena 29/30 IL
30/31 IL

KILPATRICK William

Dalziel R
Port Glasgow A 03/04 1

KING

Clyde 95/96 1

KING

Abercorn 96/97 4

KING Alexander 6 caps
b. Dykehead 27.7.1871 d. Shotts 12.12.1957
Dykehead
Airdrieonians 92/93
Albion R 92/93
Wishaw Thistle 93/94
Darwen 94/95 21 10 FL
Dykehead 94/95
Rangers T 94/95
Heart of Midlothian 95/96 16 12
Celtic 96/97 17 5
97/98 16 4
98/99 13 1
99/00 11 1
Dykehead 00/01
St Bernards 00/01 9 ? D2
Dykehead 01/02
02/03
Airdrieonians 03/04 24
Dykehead 04/05

KING Alexander (Allan?)
b. c1911
St Andews U
Cowdenbeath St Leonards
Clyde 29/30 15 1
30/31 38 10
31/32 25 8
32/33
Worcester C 33/34
Dundee U 34/35 33 15 D2
Alloa A 35/36 D2
Brechin C 36/37 D2
Dundee U 36/37 14 5 D2

KING Arthur
b. Kentore 6.8.1887
Aberdeen East End
Aberdeen 08/09 1
09/10
10/11 34
11/12 12
12/13 24
Tottenham H 13/14 19 FL
Belfast Celtic 14/15 IL
Dunfermline A
Dumbarton 21/22 19
Forres Mechanics
Inverness Caledonians

KING George

Dykehead
Leicester Fosse
Hamilton A 09/10 4
10/11 12
Dykehead 11/12

KING James Brown
b. Greenock
Port Glasgow A
Armadale 26/27 D2
27/28 D2
Airdrieonians 28/29 6
29/30
30/31 1
Ballymena 31/32 IL
32/33 IL
33/34 IL
34/35 IL
Summerfield * 35/36
Glentoran * 35/36 IL
36/37 IL

KING James Munro 2 caps
b. Craigneuk 16.4.1906 d. Law 18.7.1985
Carluke R
Hamilton A 29/30 4 1
30/31 14 4
31/32 21 14
32/33 34 11
33/34 38 11
34/35 36 14
35/36 33 10
36/37 37 9
37/38 37 9
38/39 11 2
Alloa A

KING John
b. Shotts 19.1.1874
Cleland Thistle
Dykehead
Wishaw Thistle 93/94
Airdrieonians 93/94
Dykehead 94/95
Darwen 94/95 5 1 FL
Dykehead 95/96
Celtic 95/96
96/97 9
East Stirlingshire 97/98
Dykehead 97/98
98/99
99/00
00/01
Albion R 00/01
Scots Guards

KING John
b. Dykehead

Club		Season	Apps	Goals	
Renfrew					
Shotts U					
Partick T		09/10	3		
		10/11	21	3	
		11/12	22	6	
		12/13	32	2	
Newcastle U		13/14	15	1	FL
		14/15	18	5	FL
Third Lanark		15/16	14	2	
Motherwell		16/17	29	3	
Partick T	L	17/18	28	4	
Newcastle U		19/20	9		FL
Dykehead	L	19/20			
Newcastle U		20/21	12	2	FL
Dykehead		21/22			
Clydebank		21/22	22	4	

KING John

Club		Season	Apps	Goals	
Hibernian		18/19	11	?	

KING John

Club		Season	Apps	Goals	
Fauldhouse U					
Clyde		33/34	4		

KING Robert
b. Dalkeith

Club		Season	Apps	Goals	
Heart of Midlothian		23/24	23	1	
		24/25	18		
		25/26	3		
Raith R	L	25/26	6		
Heart of Midlothian		26/27	25		
		27/28	35		
		28/29	36		
		29/30	30		
		30/31	2		
		31/32	15		
Bo'ness *		32/33			D2
		33/34			D2
East Fife *		34/35			D2
Red Arts		35/36			

KING William S 1 cap
b. Glasgow c1900

Club		Season	Apps	Goals	
Queen's Park		19/20	2		
		20/21			
		21/22			
		22/23	6		D2
		23/24	8		
		24/25	6		
		25/26	12	1	
		26/27	34	3	
		27/28	22		
		28/29	30	1	
		29/30	29	2	
		30/31	37		
		31/32	1		

KINGHORN Alexander
b. Grangemouth

Club		Season	Apps	Goals	
St Bernards		97/98	8	3	
Kings Park					
London Caledonians					
Queen's Park		01/02			
Falkirk					

KINGHORN William John Darroch
b. Strathblane 27.2.1912

Club		Season	Apps	Goals	
Kirkintilloch Rob Roy					
Pollok		34/35			
		35/36			
Queen's Park		36/37	13	4	
		37/38	38	9	
Liverpool		38/39	19	4	FL

KINLOCH

Club		Season	Apps	Goals	
St Mirren		91/92	6	1	

KINLOCH James 1 cap
b. Govan 14.4.1898 d. ?.11.1962

Club		Season	Apps	Goals	
Parkhead Jnrs					
Queen's Park		18/19	28	12	
		19/20	32	7	
Partick T		20/21	35	11	
		21/22	35	12	
		22/23	32	10	
		23/24	16	3	
		24/25	28	7	
		25/26	31	10	
		26/27	13	2	
		27/28	4	1	

KINNAIRD Alexander

Club		Season	Apps	Goals	
Inverness Caledonians					
Celtic	T	32/33			
Elgin C		33/34			
		34/35			
Third Lanark		35/36	20	9	
		36/37	25	9	
		37/38	32	8	
		38/39	4	2	
St Mirren		38/39	8	1	

KINNEAR David 1 cap
b. Kirkcaldy 22.2.1917 d. Crewe ?.5.2001

Club		Season	Apps	Goals	
Burntisland U					
Raith R		33/34			D2
Rangers		34/35	4		
		35/36	12	3	
		36/37	37	8	
		37/38	26	12	
		38/39	26	9	
Third Lanark		46/47	4		
Dunfermline A		47/48			D2
		48/49			D2
Stirling A		49/50	3		

KINROSS John

Club		Season	Apps	Goals	
St Bernards		95/96	8	1	
		96/97	8		
		97/98	2		

KIRBY Herbert Hely
b. Barry 22.3.1903

Club		Season	Apps	Goals	
Barry T					
Bristol C		24/25	5		FL
Charlton A		25/26	7		FL
St Johnstone		26/27	21	3	
Sittingbourne		27/28			
		28/29			
Cardiff C		28/29			FL
Derry C		29/30			IL
Dartford		30/31			
Folkestone T					

KIRBY Norman J Rufus
b. Cockfield 24.6.1908 d. Blackpool ?.1.1977

Club		Season	Apps	Goals	
Shildon A					
Cockfield					
Doncaster R	T	26/27			FL
Cockfield		27/28			
Stockport Co	T	27/28			FL
Manchester U	T	27/28			FL
Crook T		28/29			
Bury		28/29	5		FL
Crook T		29/30			
Swindon T		30/31	42	5	FL
		31/32	24	4	FL
Distillery		32/33			IL
		33/34			IL
Dundee		33/34	23	5	
		34/35	26	3	
		35/36	36	4	
		36/37	25	6	
		37/38	23	5	
		38/39	19	1	D2

KIRK James
b. Motherwell c1915

Club		Season	Apps	Goals	
Blantyre V					
Clyde		33/34	1		
		34/35	10		
		35/36	29		
		36/37	30		
		37/38	20		
		38/39	33	2	

KIRK Joseph

Club		Season	Apps	Goals	
St Ninians Thistle					
Falkirk		31/32	1		

KIRK Joseph

Club		Season	Apps	Goals	
Partick T					
Middlesbrough					
Albion R		32/33			D2
		33/34			D2
		34/35	10	2	
Leith A		35/36			D2

KIRK Robert Hastings
b. Clydebank 22.2.1899

Club		Season	Apps	Goals	
Clydebank Jnrs					
Albion R		21/22	42	4	
		22/23	21	1	
		23/24			D2
Bristol C		24/25	22	1	FL
		25/26	30	4	FL
		26/27	2		FL
Exeter C		27/28	8		FL
		28/29	2		FL
Blackpool		28/29			FL

KIRKBRIDE

Club		Season	Apps	Goals	
Armadale					
Airdrieonians		19/20	2		

KIRKCALDY James William
b. Newcastle 8.11.1885

Club		Season	Apps	Goals	
Northern Temperance					
Newcastle U		05/06	8		FL
		06/07	3	1	FL
		07/08			FL
Kilmarnock	T	08/09	2		
Huddersfield T					

KIRKLAND James

Club		Season	Apps	Goals	
Partick T		98/99	11	4	

KIRKLAND Mungo

Club		Season	Apps	Goals	
Kirkmuirhill					
Ayr U		38/39	2		

KIRKLAND William
b. Carluke 21.6.1914

Club		Season	Apps	Goals	
Stonehouse Violet					
Carluke R		35/36			
Birmingham	T	36/37			FL
Partick T	T	36/37			
Third Lanark		36/37	1		
		37/38	11		
Lincoln C		38/39	3		FL
Third Lanark					

KIRKPATRICK Alexander

Club		Season	Apps	Goals	
St Mirren		30/31	2		

KIRKPATRICK Samuel

Club		Season	Apps	Goals	
Raith R		16/17	7	1	

KIRKWOOD

Club		Season	Apps	Goals	
St Bernards		94/95	2		

KIRKWOOD

Club		Season	Apps	Goals	
Airdrieonians		04/05	1		

KIRKWOOD Andrew
b. Dalserf

Club		Season	Apps	Goals	
Netherburn Jnrs					
Rangers					
Hamilton A	L	22/23	19	2	
Rangers		23/24	3		
		24/25	5		
Third Lanark		24/25	1		
Rangers		25/26	1		
St Johnstone		25/26	18	1	
		26/27	4		
Stenhousemuir		27/28			D2
		28/29			D2
Montrose		29/30			D2
Royal Albert		30/31			
Stonehouse Violet		31/32			

KIRKWOOD Daniel
b. Dalserf 24.12.1900 d. Stonehouse 20.10.1977

Club		Season	Apps	Goals	
Ashgill YMCA					
Airdrieonians		22/23	3	2	
		23/24	1		
Rangers		24/25			
		25/26			
St Johnstone	L	25/26	19	5	
Rangers		26/27	1		
Sheffield W		26/27	17	1	FL
		27/28	1		FL
Brighton		28/29	40	20	FL
		29/30	40	28	FL
		30/31	36	13	FL
		31/32	41	12	FL
		32/33	11	1	FL
Luton T		33/34	2	1	FL
Swindon T		33/34	7		FL

KIRKWOOD David
b. Possilpark

Club		Season	Apps	Goals	
Ashfield					
Kilmarnock		09/10	23		
		10/11	34		
		11/12	28	1	
		12/13	11		
East Stirlingshire		13/14			D2
		14/15			D2
		15/16			

KIRKWOOD James

Club		Season	Apps	Goals	
Kilmarnock					
Abercorn		92/93	15		
Third Lanark		93/94	15	1	

KIRSOP William Smeaton
b. Wallsend 1892
Rome Hill Villa
Wallsend Park Villa
New Hartley R
Kilmarnock 12/13 9 1
Gateshead A 13/14
Barnsley 14/15 5 FL

KIRWAN John Henry
b. Waterford 25.4.1872 d. Hendon 9.1.1959
Kirkdale
Southport Central 95/96
96/97
97/98
Everton 98/99 24 6 FL
Tottenham H 99/00 26 10 SL
00/01 20 5 SL
01/02 28 10 SL
02/03 26 7 SL
03/04 28 4 SL
04/05 26 3 SL
Chelsea 05/06 35 9 FL
06/07 35 8 FL
07/08 2 FL
Clyde 08/09 31 8
Leyton 09/10 37 6 SL

KIVLICHAN William Fulton
b. Galashiels 11.3.1890 d. Glasgow 5.4.1937
Dumfries St Josephs
Maxwelltown Jnrs
Dumfries 04/05
05/06
Rangers 05/06 9 4
06/07 11 3
Celtic 07/08 11 6
08/09 17 3
09/10 24 6
10/11 25 5
Bradford PA 11/12 31 4 FL
12/13 18 FL
13/14 33 2 FL
14/15 6 FL

KNIGHT John

Heart of Midlothian 00/01 1
Leith A

KNOWLES Douglas

Aberdeen Mugiemoss
Motherwell 13/14 2

KNOX Hugh

Morton 01/02 1

KNOX James Philips
b. Ibrox 8.8.1910
Bellahouston Academy
Queen's Park Strollers
Portsmouth 28/29 FL
29/30 FL
Charlton A 30/31 1 FL
St Mirren 31/32 37 24
32/33 32 16
33/34 20 9
34/35 31 11
35/36 D2
36/37 29 19
37/38 30 14
38/39 34 15
Notts Co 39/40 1 FL

KNOX Peter Nellies
b. Douglas Water
Coalburn
Clyde 28/29 17 1
29/30 22
30/31 33 5
31/32 4

KNOX Robert
b. Rutherglen
Kirkintilloch Rob Roy
Airdrieonians 15/16 7
16/17 35
17/18 31 1
18/19 27
19/20 39 1
20/21 19 2
21/22 21
Third Lanark 22/23 7 1
Dundee Hibs 23/24 13 D2

KNOX William
b. Old Cumnock 2.5.1904
Kilbarchan A
Kilbirnie Ladeside
Dundee 22/23 23 1
23/24 24 2
24/25 16
St Mirren 25/26 10 1
26/27
Third Lanark 26/27 D2
Reading 27/28 4 FL
28/29 FL
Norwich C 29/30 3 FL
Carlisle U 30/31 FL
31/32 FL
32/33 FL
Stenhousemuir 33/34 D2

KYLE Archibald
b. Kinning Park (?) 13.7.1883
Parkhead
Rangers 04/05 23 14
05/06 22 8
06/07 27 13
07/08 27 12
Blackburn R 07/08 3 FL
08/09 33 8 FL
Bradford PA 09/10
Bo'ness 09/10
Linfield 09/10 IL
Clyde 10/11 27 6
St Mirren 11/12 34 3
12/13 23 5
13/14 24 4
Hamilton A 13/14 12 6
14/15 32 6
15/16 37 10
16/17 26 9
17/18 22 2

KYLE George Alexander
b. Dunfermline 6.11.1908 d. 17.2.1898
Lethans Heatherbell
Kelty R 27/28
East Stirlingshire 28/29 D2
29/30 D2
Cowdenbeath 30/31 7
Ballymena 31/32 IL
Dunfermline A L 31/32 D2
Bangor C 32/33
33/34
34/35
East Stirlingshire 35/36 D2
36/37 D2
37/38 D2
38/39 D2

KYLE James
b. Glasgow 22.9.1870
Benburb 88/89
89/90
Celtic 90/91 1
91/92

KYLE Joseph Reid

Queen's Park 33/34 3
34/35 27 3
35/36 35 11
36/37 33 15
37/38 37 10
38/39 31 18

KYLE Peter
b. Cadder 21.12.1878 d. Glasgow 19.1.1957
Parkhead
Clyde T 98/99 9 ?
West Ham U T
Heart of Midlothian T
Larkhall Thistle
Liverpool 99/00 4 FL
Leicester F 00/01 31 3 FL
Wellingborough T 01/02 1 SL
West Ham U 01/02 1 SL
Kettering T 01/02 17 6 SL
Wellingborough T
Aberdeen 02/03
Cowdenbeath 03/04
Port Glasgow A 03/04
Royal Albert 04/05
Partick T 04/05
Tottenham H 05/06 25 8 SL
Woolwich Arsenal 06/07 29 13 FL
07/08 23 8 FL
Aston Villa 07/08 4 FL
08/09 1 1 FL
Sheffield U 08/09 10 4 FL
Royal Albert 09/10
Watford 09/10 12 4 SL
Royal Albert 09/10

LAFFERTY

St Bernards 94/95 4

LAFFERTY Hugh
b. Rutherglen 16.11.1901 d. Lenzie 24.12.1971
Bellshill A
Fulham 23/24 1 FL
24/25 3 FL
Arsenal 25/26 FL
St Johnstone 26/27 25
27/28 26
28/29 13 1
29/30 4
New York Giants 30
31
Aberdeen T 31/32
Kings Park 32/33 D2

LAIDLAW James

Newtongrange Star
Heart of Midlothian 16/17 7
17/18 5

LAIDLAW James T

Leith A 30/31 26 17
31/32 30 5
Dunfermline A 32/33 D2

LAIDMAN Christopher

Queen's Park 14/15 11 1

LAING

Dumbarton 90/91 5

LAING

Dumbarton 93/94 2

LAING

Motherwell 20/21 1

LAING James

Strathclyde
Clydebank
Bathgate
Third Lanark 24/25 5
Falkirk 25/26
Vale of Leven 26/27
Dumbarton 27/28 D2

LAING R P

Leith A 91/92 20 6
92/93 14 5

LAING R R

St Bernards 93/94 10 6
94/95 15 3
95/96 13 4

LAING Thomas

St Ninians Thistle
Slamannan
Airdrieonians 07/08 20 7
Bathgate 08/09
Airdrieonians 09/10 4
Armadale

LAING Thomas

Falkirk 11/12 7

LAIRD Alexander

Falkirk 18/19 14 ?

LAIRD Alexander
b. Dennybrook 21.10.1901
Longcroft Thistle
Rangers 21/22 2
Preston NE 22/23 17 2 FL
23/24 11 2 FL
Falkirk 24/25 16 2
25/26 2
Armadale

LAIRD James
b. c1919
Shettleston
St Mirren 37/38 1

LAIRD James H

Albion R 38/39 3 1

LAIRD Joseph
b. c1896 d. Bothwell 1935

Club		Season	Apps	Goals	League
Burnbank A					
Hamilton A		17/18	3		
Vale of Leven		18/19			

LAMB Albert Crossan
b. Auchtermuchty 26.10.1908

Club		Season	Apps	Goals	League
East Craigie					
Brechin C	T				
Dundee Violet					
Dundee U		33/34			
Dundee		34/35	7		
Portadown		35/36			IL
Chesterfield		36/37	8		FL

LAMB James

Club		Season	Apps	Goals	League
Jordanhill					
Partick T		96/97	10	2	D2
Falkirk		97/98			
Partick T		98/99	1	2	
Linthouse					

LAMB John
b. Co Armagh

Club		Season	Apps	Goals	League
Kirkintilloch Rob Roy					
Hibernian		09/10	17	1	
		10/11	22	2	
		11/12	32	1	
		12/13	16		
		13/14	18		
Broxburn U		14/15			
Third Lanark		14/15	9		
		15/16	15	2	
Abercorn		16/17			

LAMB Sidney

Club		Season	Apps	Goals	League
Dundee		15/16	11		

LAMBERT Edward

Club		Season	Apps	Goals	League
Highland Light Infantry					
Third Lanark		07/08	2	2	
		08/09	3		

LAMBIE Alexander
b. Troon 15.4.1897

Club		Season	Apps	Goals	League
Dreghorn Jnrs					
Prestwick Glenburn R					
Kilmarnock		19/20	1		
Troon A		20/21			
Ayr U	T	20/21			
Partick T		21/22	20		
		22/23	32	5	
		23/24	35	5	
		24/25	26	1	
		25/26	32	1	
		26/27	3		
		27/28	33	2	
		28/29	36	1	
		29/30	28		
		30/31	19		
Chester		31/32	1		FL
Swindon T		31/32	25		FL
		32/33	36	1	FL
		33/34	22		FL
Newport Co	T	34/35			FL
Lovells A		34/35			
Distillery	T	34/35			IL

LAMBIE Claude
b. Glasgow 1868 d. Kings Norton ?.7.1921

Club		Season	Apps	Goals	League
Glasgow Thistle					
Burnley		89/90	7	8	FL
		90/91	18	17	FL
Clyde		91/92	7	5	
Cowlairs		91/92			
Highland Light Infantry					
Burnley		92/93	4		FL
Auchterarder Thistle					

LAMBIE James
b. 1879

Club		Season	Apps	Goals	League
Third Lanark		00/01	8	1	

LAMBIE Robert

Club		Season	Apps	Goals	League
Heart of Midlothian					
Third Lanark		34/35			
		35/36	1		
Derry C		36/37			IL
		37/38			IL
		38/39			IL

LAMBIE Thomas
b. Carmunnock (?)

Club		Season	Apps	Goals	League
Glasgow Ashfield					
Third Lanark		10/11	14	2	
		11/12	9	3	
Galston		12/13			
Stevenston U					

LAMBIE Wallace

Club		Season	Apps	Goals	League
Pollok Jnrs					
Queen's Park		18/19	5		

LAMONT James

Club		Season	Apps	Goals	League
Partick T		95/96	13	2	D2
		96/97	17	3	D2
		97/98	7	1	
		98/99			
		99/00			
		00/01	4		

LANDELLS

Club		Season	Apps	Goals	League
Third Lanark		18/19	1	?	

LANDELLS James

Club		Season	Apps	Goals	League
Renfrew					
Motherwell		18/19	3		
Kilmarnock	L	18/19	1		
Abercorn	L	18/19			
Motherwell		19/20			
		20/21			
		21/22	1		

LANDSBOROUGH David
b. Annbank

Club		Season	Apps	Goals	League
Glenburn R					
Kilmarnock		32/33	2		
		33/34	13	2	
		34/35	3	1	
Larne		35/36			IL
Galston					

LANG

Club		Season	Apps	Goals	League
Dumbarton		91/92	1		

LANG John
b. Dumbarton 9.6.1908

Club		Season	Apps	Goals	League
Maryhill					
Dumbarton		31/32			D2
Forthbank		32/33			
Kings Park		33/34			D2
		34/35			D2
Aberdeen		35/36	26	10	
		36/37	9	2	
		37/38	12	4	
Barnsley		37/38	11		FL
		38/39	31	10	FL
		39/40	3		FL
Dumbarton					

LANG Thomas
b. Larkhall 3.4.1905 d. Cleland 12.5.1988

Club		Season	Apps	Goals	League
Larkhall Thistle					
Newcastle U		27/28	1		FL
		28/29	38	10	FL
		29/30	39	4	FL
		30/31	12	4	FL
		31/32	42	11	FL
		32/33	38	9	FL
		33/34	38	9	FL
		34/35	17	6	FL
Huddersfield T		34/35	13	3	FL
		35/36	11	2	FL
Manchester U		35/36	4	1	FL
		36/37	8		FL
Swansea T		37/38	33	1	FL
Queen of the South		38/39	36	16	
Ipswich T		46/47	5	1	FL

LANGLANDS George
b. c1887

Club		Season	Apps	Goals	League
Forfar A					
Dundee		07/08	7	2	
		08/09	29	8	
		09/10	25	6	
		10/11	16	2	
		11/12	28	6	
		12/13	8		
		13/14			
		14/15			
Forfar A		18/19			

LANGMUIR James F

Club		Season	Apps	Goals	League
Queen's Park		25/26	2		
		26/27	11	1	
		27/28	6		

LANGTON Michael
b. Pumpherston

Club		Season	Apps	Goals	League
Heart of Midlothian		28/29	2		
		29/30	9		
East Fife		30/31	29		
Hibernian		31/32			D2
		32/33			D2
		33/34	35		
		34/35	1		
St Bernards		35/36			D2
		36/37			D2

LAPSLEY

Club		Season	Apps	Goals	League
Third Lanark		90/91	17	2	
		91/92	1		

LATIF Mohammed
b. Egypt

Club		Season	Apps	Goals	League
Zamalek					
Jordanhill College					
Rangers		34/35			
		35/36	1		

LATIMER John
b. Hill o'Beath 3.2.1906 d. Newcastle 1979

Club		Season	Apps	Goals	League
Hearts o'Beath					
Portsmouth		28/29	1		FL
		29/30	7		FL
Derry C		30/31			IL
East Stirlingshire		30/31			D2
		31/32			D2
		32/33	28	2	
St Mirren		33/34	27	3	
		34/35	27	5	
		35/36			D2
Dundee		36/37	37	3	
Queen of the South		37/38	19	1	
Rochdale	T	38/39	1		FL
Leith A		38/39			D2

LATTER Samuel

Club		Season	Apps	Goals	League
Third Lanark		28/29	2		

LAUCHLAND John

Club		Season	Apps	Goals	League
Wishaw Thistle					
Motherwell		06/07	1		
Hibernian		06/07	3	1	
Hamilton A		07/08	3		
Wishaw Thistle					

LAUDER

Club		Season	Apps	Goals	League
Abercorn		92/93	1		

LAUDER Alexander
b. Glasgow

Club		Season	Apps	Goals	League
Glasgow Ashfield					
Partick T		18/19	19	3	
		19/20	21	3	
		20/21	16	1	
Port Vale		21/22	21	3	FL

LAUDER Thomas

Club		Season	Apps	Goals	League
Glasgow Ashfield					
Hibernian		29/30	13	3	
		30/31	14	1	
		31/32			D2
		32/33			D2
Arbroath		32/33	22	7	D2
Halifax T	T	33/34			FL

LAUDER William

Club		Season	Apps	Goals	League
Glasgow Ashfield					
Hibernian		29/30	2		
		30/31	7		
Bo'ness		31/32			D2
Montrose		31/32			D2

LAUGHLAND James

Club		Season	Apps	Goals	League
Queen's Park		10/11	8		
		11/12	15	1	
London Caledonians		12/13			
		13/14			
		14/15			
		19/20			

LAURENCE

Club		Season	Apps	Goals	League
Abercorn		90/91	1		

LAURIE

Club		Season	Apps	Goals	League
Third Lanark		91/92	1		

LAURIE John

Newarthill
Dundee 36/37 4
37/38 33
38/39 18 4 D2

LAURIE Thomas

Shettleston
Rangers 12/13
Morton 12/13 3
Pontypridd

LAURIE Thomas

Dumbarton 13/14 3 1

LAVERICK

St Bernards 93/94 3 1

LAVERTY Henry

Pollok Jnrs
Partick T 18/19 5

LAVERY William
b. Thornton c1887
Fylde
Preston NE 06/07 14 FL
Leicester F T 07/08 FL
Preston NE 08/09 8 FL
West Ham U 09/10 2 SL
10/11 15 SL
Belfast Celtic 11/12 IL
12/13 IL
Middlesbrough 13/14 FL
Raith R 13/14 5 1
14/15 37
15/16 13
16/17 3
Heart of Midlothian 16/17 1
Belfast Celtic L 18/19 IL
St Mirren 19/20 35
20/21 28 1
Johnstone T 21/22 D2
Port Vale 21/22 5 FL
United Alkali Works

LAVITY William

Vale of Clyde
Heart of Midlothian 04/05 10 3
Bathgate L 04/05
Falkirk 05/06 2

LAW George 3 caps
b. Arbroath 13.12.1885
Arbroath
Rangers 06/07 6 1
07/08 13
08/09 20
09/10 22
10/11 24
11/12 11
Leeds C 12/13 35 FL
13/14 35 1 FL
14/15 35 FL
15/16
Rangers 16/17 4
Partick T 16/17 4
17/18
18/19
19/20
20/21
Arbroath 21/22 32 D2

LAW J

Rangers 91/92 5 4

LAW James

Vulcan R
Cowdenbeath 09/10 D2
Dundee 10/11 2

LAW John
b. Dumfries c1887
Maxwelltown Volunteers
Rangers 06/07 2 1
Lincoln C 07/08 19 FL
Gainsborough T 08/09 9 1 FL
Carlisle U 09/10
Rangers
5th KOSB (Dumfries)
Kilmarnock 12/13 2
Falkirk 12/13 4 1
Abercorn

LAW John

Tranent Jnrs
Airdrieonians 31/32 29 4
32/33 33 4
33/34 25 7
34/35 27 5
35/36 38 9
Queen of the South 36/37 34 8
37/38 37 16
38/39 29 11
46/47 37 4
47/48
48/49

LAW Robert

Abercorn 96/97 7
Kilmarnock A

LAWLEY George Harry
b. Wolverhampton 10.4.1903 d. Stourbridge 7.4.1987
Bloxwich All Saints
Talbot Stead Works
Darlaston
Bloxwich Strollers 23/24
24/25
Walsall 25/26 26 3 FL
Burton T 26/27
Merthyr T 27/28 18 2 FL
Dundee 27/28 12 1
28/29 22 2
Sunderland 29/30 9 1 FL
30/31 1 FL
Swindon T 31/32 27 3 FL
Worcester C 32/33
Shrewsbury T 33/34
Brierley Hill A
Dudley T
Hednesford T
Cannock T 36/37
Nuneaton T

LAWNS Thomas

Bourock Thistle
Clyde 14/15 5
15/16 4

LAWRENCE Valentine
b. Arbroath 5.5.1889 d. Camberwell 1961
Dundee Violet
Newcastle U T
Forfar A
Manchester C 11/12 19 FL
12/13 1 FL
Arbroath 12/13
Oldham A 13/14 1 FL
Leeds C 14/15 6 FL
Morton 17/18 4
18/19 3
Dumbarton 18/19 9 ?
Darlington
Shildon
Hartlepool U 20/21
Southend U 21/22 18 FL
Abertillery T 22/23
Tunbridge Wells R

LAWRENCE William

Broxburn U
Third Lanark 15/16 11

LAWRIE

Clydebank 20/21 1

LAWRIE Allan

Aberdeen 06/07 1

LAWRIE George

Heart of Midlothian 06/07 2 1
Leith A

LAWRIE George

Rutherglen Glencairn
Hamilton A 20/21 11 2
Bo'ness 21/22 D2

LAWRIE James F
b. c1911
Douglas Water Thistle
Queen's Park 36/37 4

LAWRIE John
b. Knightsbridge
Clydebank Jnrs
Partick T 04/05 2
05/06 9 1
Workington 06/07
07/08
Blackburn R 08/09 2 FL
Workington 08/09
Bristol R 09/10 42 3 SL

LAWRIE Joseph

Airdrieonians 07/08 2
08/09 2

LAWRIE Robert

Glasgow Ashfield
Hibernian 04/05 2 1
05/06 19 2
06/07 25 1
07/08 7 2
Glentoran * 08/09 IL
09/10 IL

LAWRIE William
b. Dumfries 4.8.1899
Clydebank Jnrs
Celtic 19/20 3
20/21
Aberdeen 21/22
22/23
23/24
Peterhead 24/25

LAWS Thomas
b. Summerstown 28.1.1890 d. Wandsworth 10.3.1980
De Nevers Rubber Mills
Summerstown
Fulham 13/14 6 FL
14/15 FL
Morton 16/17 2
17/18 3
Clydebank 17/18 16
18/19 10

LAWSON

Third Lanark 94/95 1

LAWSON

Port Glasgow A 07/08 1

LAWSON Alfred
b. c1913
Forfar EE
Dundee 31/32
32/33
33/34 3

LAWSON Denis 1 cap
b. Campsie 11.12.1897
Kilsyth Emmet
Kilsyth R
St Mirren 19/20 27 5
20/21 35 1
21/22 42 1
22/23 37 4
23/24 13
Cardiff C 23/24 18 FL
24/25 26 1 FL
25/26 20 1 FL
Springfield Babes 26/27 23 2 ASL
Providence Clamdiggers 26/27 16 1 ASL
Wigan B 27/28 28 2 FL
Clyde 28/29 7 1
29/30
Brechin C 30/31 D2

LAWSON Hector Stewart Ramsay
b. Shettleston 21.5.1896 d. Dundee 3.5.1971
Cambuslang R
Shettleston
Rangers 16/17 24 1
17/18 5 1
Third Lanark L 17/18 2 ?
Hamilton A T 17/18
Rangers 18/19 9 2
Clyde L 18/19 2 ?
Rangers 19/20
Vale of Leven L 19/20
Rangers 20/21 2
21/22 2
Third Lanark L 21/22
Rangers 22/23 3
Clyde L 22/23 7
Liverpool 23/24 10 FL
24/25 2 FL
Airdrieonians 25/26
Aberdeen 26/27 6
27/28 18
Brighton 28/29 7 FL
Newport Co 29/30 28 1 FL
30/31 27 FL
Shamrock R

LAWSON James
b. Carnoustie
Neilston V
Dundee 07/08 1
08/09 25
09/10 21
10/11 19
11/12 22
12/13 29
Linfield 12/13 IL
Airdrieonians 13/14 17
Dundee 13/14 7

LAWSON James
Newmilns
Airdrieonians 21/22 2

LAWSON Robert Wilson
b. Darvel
Benburb
Cambuslang R
Clydebank 19/20 1
20/21 28
Johnstone 21/22 D2
Kings Park 22/23 D2
23/24 D2
24/25 D2
25/26 D2
26/27 D2
27/28 D2
Morton 28/29
29/30 30
Dunfermline A 30/31 D2
Larne 30/31 IL
Coleraine 30/31 IL
Glenavon 31/32 IL

LAWSON Thomas
Clyde 17/18 8 ?

LAWSON William
Partick T 95/96 9 4 D2
96/97 18 5 D2
97/98 3
Motherwell 97/98 D2

LAWSON William
Reading
Motherwell 09/10 8 2

LAYCOCK Arnold
Hibernian 11/12 1

LEAN Lewis
Third Lanark 02/03 13 3
Swindon T 03/04 22 5 SL
04/05 30 6 SL
Third Lanark 05/06 3
Swindon T 06/07 15 SL
Liverpool 07/08 FL
08/09 FL
09/10 FL
10/11 FL
11/12 FL
Newport Co 12/13 22 2 SL
Caerphilly T

LEARMOUTH
St Bernards 94/95 1

LECKIE Charles Thomas
Dundee 98/99 10 1

LECKIE Henry
Ardeer Rec
Morton 37/38 31 6

LECKIE Henry G
d. At sea ?.11.1913
Queen's Park 09/10 3
Hamilton A 10/11 16 7
Abercorn 10/11 4 D2
11/12 D2
Bellahouston FP 12/13

LECKIE John S
Queen's Park 07/08 4 1
08/09 14 4
09/10 11 5
10/11 3 1

LECKIE John Thompson
b. Alva 3.3.1906
Alva Albion R
St Johnstone
Alloa A 27/28 D2
Raith R 27/28 10
28/29 36
Bray Unknowns 29/30 LI
30/31 LI
Port Vale 31/32 2 FL
32/33 22 FL
Stockport Co 33/34 5 FL
Cardiff C 34/35 28 FL
35/36 18 FL
Walsall 36/37 26 FL
Carlisle U 37/38 8 FL

LEDDY Henry Christopher
b. Dublin 1888
Belfast Celtic
Distillery
Glenavon 10/11
11/12 IL
Shelbourne 12/13 IL
13/14 IL
Clyde 14/15 2
Shelbourne 15/16 IL
16/17 IL
Belfast U 17/18 IL
Distillery 18/19 IL
Glenavon 19/20 IL
Tranmere R 20/21
Everton 21/22 FL
Chesterfield 21/22 9 1 FL
22/23 36 6 FL
Grimsby T 23/24 13 FL
Shamrock R
Frankfort

LEE
Clydebank 18/19 3 ?

LEE Alexander
St Bernards 97/98 1
98/99 17 6
99/00 11 4
00/01 8 ? D2
01/02
Broxburn 02/03

LEE Bernard James
b. Alloa 5.3.1873
Leith A 94/95 2 1
Bury 94/95 22 12 FL
95/96 2 FL
Newcastle U
Nelson
Bo'ness
Kings Park 00/01
01/02
Brighton 02/03 8 2 SL
Broxburn

LEE Ernest Albert
b. Bridport ?.8.1879 d. Southampton 14.1.1958
Brewery R
Hamworthy St Michaels
Poole
Southampton 00/01 21 2 SL
01/02 27 SL
02/03 29 1 SL
03/04 33 1 SL
04/05 33 1 SL
05/06 31 3 SL
Dundee 06/07 28
07/08 28 2
08/09 33 4
09/10 27 3
10/11 22 1
Southampton 11/12 25 1 SL
12/13 30 3 SL
13/14 19 1 SL
14/15 3 SL

LEE Patrick Francis
b. Uddingston 20.1.1903 d. Stonehouse 1.3.1981
Udingston Rep
Vale of Clyde
Hull C 25/26 18 3 FL
26/27 7 3 FL
Accrington S 27/28 33 1 FL
28/29 41 1 FL
29/30 38 2 FL
Southport T 30/31 2 FL
Ballymena 30/31 IL
Dolphin 30/31 LI
Albion R 31/32 D2
Ballymena 32/33 IL
Dundee 33/34 25 10
Hamilton A 33/34
St Mirren 34/35 3 1
Inverness Caledonian T
Babcock & Wilcox 35/36

LEE R
Leith A 92/93 1
93/94 13 3

LEES Andrew Anderson
b. Holytown 30.4.1896
Renfrew Jnrs
Motherwell 17/18 7
18/19 4 1
Kilmarnock L 18/19 1
Motherwell 19/20 3
Aberdeen 20/21 3
21/22
Swindon T 22/23 1 FL
St Bernards 22/23 D2
Alloa A 23/24 D2
Lochgelly U 23/24 D2
Queen of the South 24/25 D3
Dykehead 24/25 D3
25/26 D3
Broxburn U 26/27 D2

LEES Walter Donald
b. Cronberry 1873
Cronberry Eglington
Celtic 92/93 1
Lincoln C 93/94 28 18 FL
Celtic 94/95 3 2
Lincoln C 94/95 24 7 FL
Barnsley St Peters 95/96 23 6 ML
Darwen 96/97 20 8 FL
Barnsley 97/98 18 9 ML
98/99 31 8 FL
99/00 34 7 FL
00/01 28 4 FL
01/02 32 10 FL
02/03 29 8 FL
03/04 33 4 FL
Watford 04/05 6 2 SL
Barnsley 04/05 1 FL
Denaby U

LEGGATT Charles
Dunfermline A 35/36 1

LEGGE Edward Daniel
b. Bridge of Dee 3.12.1907 d. Aberdeen 14.12.1947

Club		Season	Apps	Goals	League
Balmoral Thistle					
Aberdeen Park Vale					
Arbroath		28/29	1		D2
Aberdeen		28/29	1		
		29/30	21		
		30/31	20		
		31/32	4		
Carlisle U		32/33	31	1	FL
		33/34	41		FL
		34/35	30		FL
York C		35/36	26		FL
		36/37	36	2	FL
		37/38	20		FL
Burton T					
Aberdeen Park Vale					

LEGGE George

Club		Season	Apps	Goals	League
Queen's Park		10/11	2		
		11/12			
		12/13	1		

LEGGETT C

Club		Season	Apps	Goals	League
Kirkintilloch Rob Roy					
Falkirk		34/35	3		
Kings Park		34/35			D2

LEIGHTON John

Club		Season	Apps	Goals	League
Hibernian		95/96	1		
Leicester Fosse		96/97	14		FL

LEIPER J

Club		Season	Apps	Goals	League
Third Lanark		90/91	2		

LEIPER James A

Club		Season	Apps	Goals	League
Queen's Park		09/10	1		

LEIPER Joseph
b. Govan 15.3.1873

Club		Season	Apps	Goals	League
Minerva					
Partick T		91/92	1		SA
Derby Co		92/93	18		FL
		93/94	25		FL
		94/95	28		FL
		95/96	26		FL
		96/97	25		FL
		97/98	22		FL
		98/99	3		FL
		99/00	11		FL
Grimsby T		00/01	31		FL
		01/02	14		FL
Chesterfield T		02/03	25		FL
Partick T		03/04	1		
Motherwell		03/04	17		
Hull C		04/05			
Aberdare		04/05			
Belper T					

LEISHMAN William

Club		Season	Apps	Goals	League
Camelon		00/01			
		01/02			
		02/03			
Falkirk		03/04			
		04/05			
		05/06	29		
		06/07	19		
		07/08	28		
		08/09	15		
		09/10	11		
		10/11	19		
		11/12	20		
		12/13	1		
St Johnstone		13/14	17		D2
		14/15	26		D2
Armadale					

LEITCH Allan

Club		Season	Apps	Goals	League
Clydebank Jnrs					
Partick T		06/07	9	1	

LEITCH Angus

Club		Season	Apps	Goals	League
Neilston V					
St Mirren		17/18	3		
		18/19			
Neilston V					

LEITCH William
b. Cullybackey 1895

Club		Season	Apps	Goals	League
Greenock Overton U					
Port Glasgow A					
Partick T		15/16	35	8	
		16/17	19	2	
Distillery	L	17/18			IL
Partick T		19/20	6		
Coventry C		20/21	20	2	FL
		21/22	4		FL
		22/23	3		FL
Bournemouth		23/24	33		FL
		24/25	40	1	FL
		25/26	8		FL
		26/27			
Helensburgh		27/28			

LEITCH William Smith
b. Saltcoats 14.2.1901

Club		Season	Apps	Goals	League
Irvine Meadow					
Saltcoats V					
Celtic		23/24			
St Bernards	L	23/24			D2
Celtic		24/25	2		
Armadale	L	24/25			D2
Celtic		25/26	3	1	
Ayr U	L	25/26			D2
Kilmarnock		26/27	18	2	
Saltcoats V					
Irvine Meadow					
Saltcoats V					
Ardeer Recreation					
Saltcoats V					

LEITH T

Club		Season	Apps	Goals	League
Heart of Midlothian		13/14	1		

LENATHAN Timothy

Club		Season	Apps	Goals	League
Denny Hibs					
Falkirk		21/22	1		
Dumbarton		22/23			D2
		23/24			D2
Helensburgh		23/24			D3

LENNIE Robert
b. Shotts

Club		Season	Apps	Goals	League
Hibernian		14/15	37	12	
		15/16	33	7	
		16/17	18	5	
Motherwell		17/18	19	2	
		18/19	30	6	
		19/20	37	3	
		20/21	36	7	
		21/22	20	3	
		22/23	26	2	

LENNIE Stewart
b. c1908

Club		Season	Apps	Goals	League
Vale of Leven Amateurs					
Queen's Park		28/29			
Dumbarton		29/30			D2
		30/31			D2
		31/32			D2
Third Lanark		32/33	1		
		33/34	9		

LENNIE William 2 caps
b. Kelvin 26.1.1882 d. Bridge of Don 24.8.1954

Club		Season	Apps	Goals	League
Mossvale					
Queen's Park		01/02	6		
Rangers		02/03	5	2	
Dundee		03/04	16	7	
Royal Albert		04/05			
Fulham		04/05	18	3	SL
Aberdeen		05/06	29	6	
		06/07	31	9	
		07/08	30	10	
		08/09	29	12	
		09/10	31	8	
		10/11	27	8	
		11/12	28	7	
		12/13	22	2	
Falkirk		13/14	16	2	
		14/15			
		15/16			
		16/17			
J M Hendersons FC		17/18			

LENNON George Ferguson
b. Kilwinning 24.5.1895 d. Kilwinning ?.9.1984

Club		Season	Apps	Goals	League
Kilwinning R					
Third Lanark		12/13	1		
Abercorn		12/13			
Third Lanark		13/14	25		
		14/15	34		
		15/16	13		
Ayr U	L	15/16			
Third Lanark		16/17			
		17/18	1	?	
		18/19	5	?	
		19/20	14		
St Mirren		19/20	15		
Luton T		20/21	37		FL
		21/22	39		FL
		22/23	31		FL
Stoke		22/23	2		FL
		23/24	1		FL
Weymouth		24/25			
Bristol R		25/26	4		FL
Airdrieonians		26/27			
Llandudno	T	26/27			
Colwyn Bay U					

LENNON Martin

Club		Season	Apps	Goals	League
Blantyre Celtic *					
Kings Park *		26/27			D2
		27/28			D2
Third Lanark		28/29	19	1	

LENNOX Stuart

Club		Season	Apps	Goals	League
QPR		00/01	10		SL
		01/02	1		SL
Morton		02/03	1		

LEONARD James
b. Paisley 7.10.1904 d. ?.9.1959

Club		Season	Apps	Goals	League
Saltcoats V					
Cowdenbeath		24/25	21	9	
		25/26	38	23	
		26/27	11	5	
Indiana Flooring		26/27	15	8	ASL
Cowdenbeath		27/28	27	15	
New York Nationals		28/29	50	31	ASL
		29A	18	16	ASL
		29/30	6	2	ASL
Cowdenbeath		30/31	8	6	
Sunderland		30/31	26	17	FL
		31/32	9	2	FL
Rhyl A		31/32			
Colwyn Bay U		31/32			
Sunderland		31/32			FL
Morton		32/33	7	1	
Shelbourne		33/34			LI
Shamrock R		34/35			LI
Dolphin		35/36			LI
Fearons A					
Brideville		38/39			Li
Shelbourne		39/40			Li

LEONARD John

Club		Season	Apps	Goals	League
St Mirren		96/97	10	2	
Derby Co		97/98	1	1	FL
Notts Co		97/98	1	1	FL
Eastville R					

LEONARD John
b. Renfrew 1911

Club		Season	Apps	Goals	League
Renfrew					
Lanark U					
Partick T	T	34/35			
Hibernian		35/36	1		
Southport	T	36/37			FL
New Brighton		36/37	8	2	FL

LESLIE

Club		Season	Apps	Goals	League
Leith A		94/95	4		

LESLIE Alfred James
b. Arbroath 11.7.1896 d. Greenock 1974

Club		Season	Apps	Goals	League
Greenock Wayfarers					
Port Glasgow Jnrs					
St Mirren		19/20	21		
		20/21	19		
Houghton le Spring		20/21			
		21/22			
St Mirren		22/23	5	1	
Morton		23/24	20	2	
Torquay U		24/25			
		25/26			
Birmingham		26/27	7		FL
		27/28	42		FL
		28/29	38		FL
		29/30	18		FL
		30/31	24		FL
		31/32	3		FL

LESLIE Andrew R

Queen's Park		14/15	3		
		15/16	4		
		16/17			
		17/18	1		
		18/19	2		

LESLIE James

b. Barrhead c1873 d. Sunderland ?.9.1920

Neilston					
Clyde		94/95			
Bolton W		94/95			FL
Clyde		95/96	14	7	
		96/97	18	6	
Sunderland		97/98	29	7	FL
		98/99	28	7	FL
		99/00	29	6	FL
		00/01	6	2	FL
Middlesbrough		01/02	7	3	FL
Clyde		02/03			
Arthurlie					

LESLIE James Walker

b. Galston 12.7.1908

Newmilns					
Kilmarnock		26/27	2		
		27/28	4		
		28/29	3		
		29/30	1		
		30/31	12		
		31/32	36	1	
		32/33	37		
		33/34	3		
		34/35	24	1	
		35/36	38		
		36/37	28		
		37/38	14	1	
Queen of the South					

LESLIE Thomas Scott

b. Tollcross 26.2.1885 d. Hackney 1948

Vale of Clyde					
Tottenham H		08/09	2		FL
		09/10	7		FL
		10/11	1		FL
Leyton		11/12	20		SL
Gillingham		12/13	31	1	SL
		13/14	38	2	SL
		14/15	38	5	SL
Clyde		15/16	3		
Bathgate		16/17			
Gillingham		19/20	35		SL
Caerphilly T					

LESLIE William

Raith R		10/11	1		
Leith A		11/12			

LETHAM Crawford

b. Prestonpans 9.5.1894 d. Newtongrange ?.11.1930

Newtongrange Star					
Dalkeith Thistle					
Dundee		22/23	19		
		23/24	10		
		24/25	4		
Cowdenbeath		24/25	33		
		25/26	22		
		26/27	2		
Hamilton A		26/27	23		
Barrow		27/28	31		FL
Sittingbourne	T	28/29			
Montrose		28/29			D2
		29/30			D2

LEYDEN

Clyde		97/98	1		

LIDDELL Charles

Bo'ness					
Airdrieonians		03/04	3		

LIDDELL James

b. Baillieston c1905

Clyde		26/27	27	2	
		27/28	24		
		28/29	21		
Connahs Quay		29/30			
Clyde		30/31	4		
Albion R		30/31			D2
Dumbarton		31/32			D2
Albion R		32/33			D2
		33/34			D2
		34/35	37	1	
		35/36	3		
		36/37			
		37/38			D2
		38/39	14		

LIDDELL John

Sherwood V					
Renfrew Jnrs					
St Mirren		14/15	1		

LIDDELL William

b. Hamilton d. 1966

Carluke R					
Ashfield					
Carluke R					
Kilmarnock		32/33	16	2	
		33/34	27	7	
		34/35	6		

LIDDLE Daniel Hamilton Seddon

b. Bo'ness 19.2.1912 d. Wigston 9.6.1982

Bo'ness					
Wallyford Bluebell					
East Fife		29/30	37	9	D2
		30/31	36	2	
		31/32	28	13	D2
Leicester C		32/33	27	8	FL
		33/34	42	13	FL
		34/35	40	14	FL
		35/36	38	5	FL
		36/37	40	9	FL
		37/38	39	10	FL
		38/39	29	5	FL
		39/40	3		Ex
Mansfield T		46/47	1		FL
Stamford T					
Hinckley A					
South Wigston					

LILLEY Thomas

b. New Herrington 1900 d. New Herrington 1964

Methley Perseverance					
Huddersfield T		22/23	3		FL
Nelson		23/24	14		FL
Hartlepools U		24/25	18		FL
		25/26	42		FL
Sunderland		27/28	1		FL
St Mirren		28/29	25	3	
		29/30	37	4	
Fulham		30/31	7		FL
Annfield Plain		31/32			
New Herrington Welfare		31/32			
Shiney Row Swifts					
Sunderland District Omnibus C		33/34			

LILLY Robert

Bellshill A					
Airdrieonians		05/06	6	2	

LINDLEY Frank

b. Sheffield

Dundee					
Motherwell		10/11			
		11/12	23	3	
Sheffield U		12/13	1		FL
Newport Co		13/14	25	4	SL
Luton T		14/15	5		SL

LINDLEY Thomas

Dundee		10/11	13	5	

LINDSAY

Queen's Park		02/03	1		

LINDSAY

Cowdenbeath		32/33	1		

LINDSAY Alexander Findlay

b. Dundee 8.11.1891 d. Dundee 9.12.1971

Dundee Violet					
Raith R		16/17	28	8	
Tottenham H		19/20	3		FL
		20/21	5		FL
		21/22	16	3	FL
		22/23	34	11	FL
		23/24	39	20	FL
		24/25	18	2	FL
		25/26	24	2	FL
		26/27	37		FL
		27/28	19	4	FL
		28/29	6		FL
		29/30	10		FL
Thames		30/31	26	1	FL
Dundee		31/32	2		
Elgin C	T	32/33			

LINDSAY Archibald

b. Rosneath 1882

Rutherglen Glencairn					
Parkhead					
Renton		03/04			
		04/05			
Reading		05/06	25	1	SL
		06/07			
Fulham		07/08	30		FL
		08/09	29		FL
		09/10	8	1	FL
		10/11	11		FL
Dundee		10/11	9	1	
		11/12	23		
St Johnstone		12/13			D2
Third Lanark		13/14			
Lochgelly U		14/15			D2

LINDSAY David 1 cap

St Mirren		99/00	1		
		00/01	20	7	
		01/02	14	3	
		02/03	17	8	
		03/04	22	13	
		04/05	22	7	
Heart of Midlothian		05/06	16	3	
		06/07	5		
West Ham U		06/07	37	4	SL
		07/08	13		SL
Leith A		08/09			D2

LINDSAY Duncan Morton

b. Cambuslang 21.3.1903 d. Ashton ?.11.1972

Cambuslang R					
East Fife		25/26	10	3	D2
Cowdenbeath		26/27	10	6	
		27/28	38	31	
		28/29	38	21	
		29/30	36	23	
Newcastle U		30/31	19	12	FL
Bury		31/32	39	16	FL
Ashton National	L	31/32			
Newcastle U		32/33			FL
Bury		33/34	6	1	FL
Northampton T		33/34	1		FL
Hartlepools U		34/35	37	21	FL
Barrow		35/36	8	3	FL
York C		35/36	25	8	FL
Ashton National					

LINDSAY Fred T

b. St Monance

Raith R		22/23	1		
		23/24			
East Fife		23/24			D2

LINDSAY George

Glasgow Ashfield					
Chryston					
Glenboig					
Coatbridge Rob Roy					
Sheffield W					FL
Airdrieonians		09/10	1		
Albion R		10/11	2	?	D2
		11/12			D2
		12/13			D2

LINDSAY George

Falkirk		11/12	1		

LINDSAY James

b. Johnstone 16.10.1890 d. Glasgow 6.1.1959

Strathclyde					
Clyde		11/12	9	2	
Glentoran		12/13			IL
		13/14			IL
Burnley		14/15	12	4	FL
St Mirren		16/17	31	7	
		17/18	28	6	
Linfield		18/19			
Burnley		19/20	32	6	FL
		20/21	8	2	FL
		21/22	13	3	FL
		22/23	8	3	FL
Llanelly		23/24			
Larne		23/24			IL
		24/25			IL
Accrington S		25/26	5		FL

LINDSAY James

Pollok Jnrs					
Petershill					
Clyde		16/17	9	4	
Abercorn		17/18			
Clyde		18/19	15		

LINDSAY John 3 caps
b. Renton 1862 d. 16.10.1932
Renton
Accrington
Renton 91/92 22
92/93 15
St Bernards 93/94 17

LINDSAY John
b. Dreghorn
Dreghorn
Ayr U 20/21
21/22
22/23
23/24 2
24/25
25/26 D2
St Johnstone 26/27

LINDSAY John
b. Cardenden
Bowhill Jnrs
Inverkeithing Jnrs
Clyde T
Partick T 24/25 9 1
25/26
26/27 6 2
Rhyl A 27/28
Liverpool 28/29 10 1 FL
29/30 4 1 FL
Swansea T 29/30 8 2 FL
30/31 8 1 FL
Rhyl A 31/32
32/33
Bangor C
Lochgelly Amateurs

LINDSAY Joseph

Renton 91/92 7 2
92/93 4

LINDSAY Joseph
b. c1914
Albion R 34/35 5
Portadown 35/36 IL
Dundee 35/36 1
St James Gate 36/37

LINDSAY Thomas
b. Laighpark 11.3.1903 d. Leyland 25.1.1979
Babcock & Wilcox 20/21
21/22
Renfrew Jnrs 22/23
Ardeer Thistle
Pollok 23/24
Kilmarnock 24/25 22 2
25/26 25 8
Alloa A 26/27
Reading 27/28 10 3 FL
Wigan B 28/29 22 4 FL
Rochdale 29/30 7 FL
Watford 30/31 7 FL
New Brighton T 31/32 7 FL
Southport T 31/32 2 FL
Chester T 31/32 FL
Prescot Cables 31/32
32/33
Wrexham 33/34 FL
Leyland Motors 34/35
35/36

LINDSAY Walter

Ayr
Partick T 97/98 5 2
98/99 11 1
Third Lanark

LINDSAY William

Strathclyde
Morton 06/07 18 4
07/08 34 6
08/09 14 1
09/10 31 9
10/11 32 8
11/12 31 5
12/13 26 8
Glentoran 13/14 IL
14/15 IL

LINDSAY William

Port Glasgow Jnrs
Morton Jnrs
St Mirren 38/39 4

LINTON David H

Denbeath Star
Hamilton A T 34/35
Dundee 35/36 2
36/37 12
Partick T 37/38 11 1
38/39 23 1

LINTON J W

Falkirk 05/06 2

LINWARD William Henry
b. Hull 8.2.1877 d. West Ham 1940
Grimsby All Saints
Grimsby T
Doncaster R 00/01
West Ham U 01/02 30 3 SL
02/03 10 SL
Woolwich Arsenal 02/03 13 5 FL
03/04 27 4 FL
04/05 6 FL
Norwich C 05/06 3 SL
Kilmarnock 06/07 19 2
Maidstone U 07/08
08/09
Dartford

LINWOOD Alexander Bryce
b. Drumsmudden 13.3.1920 d. Renfrew 13.3.1920
Muirkirk A
St Mirren 38/39 4
Middlesbrough 46/47 14 3 FL
Heart of Midlothian 47/48 24 15
48/49 12 8
Clyde 48/49 14 6
49/50 29 12
50/51 13 2
Morton 51/52 24 19
52/53 24 17 D2
53/54 28 22 D2
54/55 D2

LISTER Edward

Dundee 98/99 2

LISTER James S
b. Glasgow 1895
Glasgow Perthshire
Kilmarnock * 14/15
Rangers 15/16 5 1
Renton L 15/16
Armadale L 15/16
Dumbarton 16/17 24 13
Morton 17/18 15 8
Bury 19/20 14 6 FL
Hartlepools U 21/22 8 2 FL
Llanelly 22/23
Bournemouth 23/24 28 7 FL
Aberdare A 24/25 16 7 FL
Ebbw Vale

LISTER Robert S
b. Glasgow
Kirkintilloch Rob Roy
Heart of Midlothian 21/22 12 1
22/23 3 1
Queen of the South 23/24 D3
Hamilton A 24/25 24 7
Queen of the South 25/26 D2
Dunfermline A 26/27 10 2
Stoke C 27/28 1 FL
West Ham U
Exeter C 30/31 8 1 FL
Rhyl A

LITHGOW

Leith A 94/95 2

LITTLE Adam
b. Blantyre c1919
Blantyre V
Queen's Park
Rangers 35/36
36/37
37/38
38/39 4
46/47
47/48 1
48/49
49/50
50/51 1
Morton 51/52 30
52/53 27
53/54 28 1 D2

LITTLE Richard
b. Ryton 30.5.1895
Clara Vale Jnrs
Jarrow Croft
Newcastle U 12/13 2 FL
13/14 FL
14/15 1 FL
Hamilton A 19/20 41 4
20/21 39 2
Cowdenbeath 21/22 D2
Motherwell 22/23 35 1
23/24 28 2
24/25 26 1
25/26 36 4
26/27 11 2
27/28 21 1
28/29 1
Morton 29/30 34 5
Dunfermline A 30/31 D2
31/32 D2
Glentoran 32/33 IL
Newry T 33/34 IL

LITTLE William

Baillieston
Shelbourne
Morton 30/31
31/32 1
Leith A 32/33 D2
Newry T 33/34 IL
34/35 IL

LITTLEJOHN James

St Anthonys
St Johnstone 34/35 21
35/36 20
36/37 2
37/38 8
38/39 1
Cowdenbeath
Dundee U

LIVINGSTON Andrew Bowie
b. Dennistoun 6.2.1893
Strathclyde
Rangers 16/17 5 3
Stevenston U L
Dumbarton Harp L
Vale of Leven 19/20
Bathgate
Port Vale 20/21 1 FL
Vale of Leven

LIVINGSTONE

Dumbarton 18/19 1 ?

LIVINGSTONE Alan McKenzie
b. Alexandria 2.12.1899 d. Colwyn Bay 11.4.1970
Vale U
Everton T
Dumbarton Harp 21/22
Hull C 22/23 1 FL
Scunthorpe U 23/24
Hartlepools U T 24/25 3 1 FL
Crewe A T 25/26 FL
New Brighton 25/26 6 FL
Clapton Orient 26/27 1 FL
Merthyr T 27/28 25 3 FL
Swansea T 28/29 FL
Ayr U 29/30 7 2
Chelsea 30/31 FL
Armadale 30/31 D2
East Fife 30/31 2
Walsall T 31/32 1 FL
Oswestry T T 31/32
Colwyn Bay U 31/32
Chester 31/32 FL
Colwyn Bay U 32/33
Dumbarton T 32/33 D2
Ayr U T 32/33
Mansfield T 33/34 33 1 FL
34/35 10 FL
Stockport Co 34/35 FL

LIVINGSTONE Andrew

Strathclyde Jnrs
Kilmarnock 06/07 5 1
07/08 3 2

LIVINGSTONE Dugald
b. Alexandria 25.2.1898 d. Marlow 15.1.1981
Parkhead 15/16
Ashfield 16/17
Celtic 16/17
Dumbarton Harp L 16/17
Celtic 17/18 6
Dumbarton Harp L 17/18
Celtic 18/19 13
Dumbarton Harp L 18/19
Clydebank L 18/19 14
Celtic 19/20 14
20/21 12
Dumbarton Harp L 20/21
Everton 21/22 24 FL
22/23 8 FL
23/24 38 FL
24/25 20 FL
25/26 5 FL
Plymouth A 25/26 10 FL
26/27 12 FL
Aberdeen 27/28 19
28/29 34
29/30 23
Tranmere R 30/31 42 FL
31/32 39 FL
32/33 7 FL

LIVINGSTONE George

Heart of Midlothian 03/04 2 1
04/05 1

LIVINGSTONE George Turner 2 caps
b. Dumbarton 5.5.1876 d. Helensburgh 15.1.1950
Sinclair Swifts
Artizan Thistle
Parkhead
Dumbarton 95/96
Heart of Midlothian 96/97 3 2
97/98 13 3
98/99 18 13
99/00 16 8
Sunderland 00/01 30 11 FL
Celtic 01/02 17 5
Liverpool 02/03 31 4 FL
Manchester C 03/04 29 5 FL
04/05 26 7 FL
05/06 26 7 FL
Rangers 06/07 10 4
07/08 24 10
Manchester U 08/09 11 3 FL
09/10 16 FL
10/11 10 FL
11/12 1 FL
12/13 2 1 FL
13/14 3 FL

LIVINGSTONE John

Third Lanark 02/03 2

LIVINGSTONE John

Newmilns
St Mirren 10/11 2

LIVINGSTONE William

Barclay Curle's
Kings Park T 25/26 D2
Motherwell 25/26 2
? 26/27
27/28
28/29
Dumbarton 29/30 D2

LLOYD Frank
b. London 18.9.1876 d. 1945
Finsbury Park
Wednesbury OA
Woolwich Arsenal 99/00 16 3 FL
Aston Villa 00/01 2 1 FL
01/02 3 FL
Dundee 01/02 5 1
Dudley T
Rangers

LOCHHEAD Alexander 1 cap
b. Johnstone 12.5.1866
Arthurlie
Third Lanark 90/91 4
Morton 90/91
Everton 90/91 1 FL
91/92 5 FL
92/93 9 FL
Third Lanark
Clyde 96/97

LOCHHEAD Arthur William
b. Busby 8.12.1897 d. Edinburgh 30.12.1966
Army
Heart of Midlothian 17/18 16 2
18/19 17
Clyde L 18/19 7 ?
Heart of Midlothian 19/20 18 8
20/21 6 9
Manchester U 21/22 31 8 FL
22/23 34 13 FL
23/24 40 14 FL
24/25 37 13 FL
25/26 5 2 FL
Leicester C 25/26 32 15 FL
26/27 29 13 FL
27/28 41 17 FL
28/29 36 13 FL
29/30 33 10 FL
30/31 35 11 FL
31/32 31 9 FL
32/33 37 12 FL
33/34 25 4 FL
34/35 4 2 FL

LOCHHEAD Dougald
b. Partick 16.12.1904 d. Leeds 29.8.1968
Eaglesham
Maryhill Jnrs
St Anthonys
St Johnstone 25/26 12 1
26/27 3
27/28 3
Walsall 28/29 42 FL
Norwich C 29/30 35 2 FL
30/31 34 FL
31/32 40 1 FL
32/33 34 FL
33/34 31 1 FL
34/35 32 FL
35/36 5 1 FL

LOCHHEAD Matthew
b. Anderston 19.8.1884 d. Swindon 5.4.1964
Beith Hibernians
Beith
St Mirren 06/07 9
07/08 3
Swindon T 08/09 9 SL
Leicester C 08/09 FL
Manchester C 09/10 FL
Beith 10/11
Swindon T 11/12 9 SL
12/13 10 SL
13/14 15 SL
14/15 SL
19/20 16 1 SL
Bath C 20/21
Reading 21/22 1 FL
22/23 5 FL
Bath C 23/24 SL

LOCK Herbert
b. Southampton 21.1.1886 d. Southampton 16.3.1957
St Marys Guild
Southampton 07/08 23 SL
08/09 32 SL
Rangers 09/10 32
10/11 34
11/12 33
12/13 6
13/14 12
14/15 26
15/16 16
16/17 16
Kilmarnock L 16/17 1
Rangers 17/18 7
Ayr U L 17/18 24
Kilmarnock L 18/19 7
St Mirren L 18/19 1
Rangers 18/19 4
Partick T L 18/19 3
Rangers 19/20 35
20/21
Q P R 21/22 6 FL
Southampton 22/23 11 FL
Bournemouth 23/24 13 FL

LOCKIE Thomas
b. Duns 13.1.1906 d. New Earswick 27.7.1977
Duns A
Rangers 27/28
28/29
29/30 2
30/31
Leith A 31/32 12
Barnsley 32/33 14 1 FL
York C 33/34 29 1 FL
Accrington S 34/35 36 FL
Mansfield T 35/36 14 1 FL

LOGAN

Vale of Leven 91/92 13 2

LOGAN

Third Lanark 97/98 1

LOGAN Alexander

Lochgelly Harp
Hibernian 09/10 20 6

LOGAN Alexander T
b. Glasgow ?.2.1880 d. Scotland 1938
Barrhead Ferense
Hibernian 02/03 2
Airdrieonians 03/04
04/05
Arthurlie 05/06 D2
Falkirk 06/07 25 14
Aston Villa 06/07 3 FL
07/08 15 7 FL
08/09 6 2 FL
Falkirk 09/10 30 17
10/11 15 5
Bristol C 10/11 20 7 FL
11/12 17 2 FL
Kilmarnock 11/12 9 5
12/13 14 1

LOGAN Charles

East Stirlingshire
Hibernian 17/18 2 ?
18/19
19/20
Johnstone 20/21

LOGAN David

Irvine Meadow *
Clyde * 33/34
Glenafton A 34/35
Hibernian 34/35
35/36 14
36/37 16
37/38 37
38/39 37

LOGAN Hugh

Glasgow Perthshire
Queen's Park 02/03 5 1
03/04
04/05 7 1
05/06 10 1
06/07
07/08 3

LOGAN Hugh

Blantyre V
St Mirren 11/12 9
12/13 1

LOGAN James 1 cap
b. Dundonald 24.6.1870
d. Loughborough 25.5.1896
Ayr
Sunderland 91/92 2 FL
Ayr 91/92
Aston Villa 92/93 10 7 FL
93/94 4 1 FL
Notts Co 93/94 21 21 FL
94/95 20 10 FL
Ayr 94/95
Dundee 94/95 2
Newcastle U 95/96 7 5 FL
Loughborough 95/96 11 5 FL

LOGAN James Henry
b. West Barnes 17.10.1885
St Bernards
Bradford C 05/06 5 1 FL
Chesterfield T 06/07 26 7 FL
07/08 33 1 FL
08/09 35 1 FL
Bradford PA 09/10 21 1 FL
10/11 32 1 FL
11/12 6 1 FL
Raith R 12/13 31 2
13/14 25 1
14/15 25
15/16 1

LOGAN James Lochhead					
b. Barrhead 8.8.1885 d. Worcester 1958					
Barrhead Ferense					
Queen's Park		03/04	23	3	
		04/05	21	4	
Aston Villa		05/06	8		FL
		06/07	27		FL
		07/08	37		FL
		08/09	28	3	FL
		09/10	16		FL
		10/11	14	2	FL
		11/12	15		FL
Rangers		12/13	24	1	
		13/14	31	5	
		14/15	20	1	
		15/16	26		
		16/17	12	1	
Partick T		16/17	1	1	
St Mirren		17/18	15	1	
Arthurlie		18/19			

LOGAN Thomas					1 cap
b. Barrhead 17.8.1888 d. 1960					
Arthurlie		08/09			D2
		09/10			D2
Falkirk		10/11	32	15	
		11/12	32	10	
		12/13	31	4	
Chelsea		13/14	35	2	FL
		14/15	35	4	FL
Partick T	L	15/16			
Dunfermline A	L	15/16			
Falkirk	L	17/18	4	?	
Chelsea		19/20	22	1	FL
		20/21	15		FL
		21/22			FL
Arthurlie		22/23			

LOGAN William G					
Queen's Park		07/08	2	1	

LOGAN William J					
Queen's Park		11/12	6		

LOGIE William M					
b. c1910					
Dundee Violet					
Portsmouth		30/31			FL
Dundee U		31/32	20	2	

LOGUE John					
b. Glasgow					
Clydebank Jnrs					
Kilmarnock		21/22	1		
Pollok Jnrs					

LONE Henry					
Queen's Park		12/13	8	2	

LONEY Henry					
Denny Hibs					
Falkirk		19/20	25		
Alloa A		20/21			
Dumbarton		21/22	40		
		22/23			D2
		23/24			D2
Alloa A		24/25			D2

LONEY James					
Dunipace					
Clyde		07/08	10		
		08/09	5		
Dundee Hibs		09/10			

LONEY William					2 caps
b. Denny 31.5.1879 d. Glasgow 6.3.1956					
Denny A					
Celtic		00/01	5	1	
		01/02	11		
		02/03	19	1	
		03/04	14		
		04/05	26	6	
		05/06	28	2	
		06/07	10	1	
		07/08	26	3	
Belfast Celtic	L	07/08			IL
Celtic		08/09	22	4	
		09/10	26	3	
		10/11	22	3	
		11/12	22	1	
		12/13	21	1	
		13/14	2		
Motherwell		13/14	13	1	
Partick T		14/15	15	2	
Clydebank		15/16			
		16/17			

LONG Archibald					
Renton					
Clyde		07/08	1		
Vale of Leven		08/09			D2
		09/10			D2
		10/11	19		D2

LONG James					
b. Scotland					
Clyde		98/99	8	5	
		99/00			
		00/01	11	?	D2
Grimsby T		01/02	13	4	FL
		02/03	15	3	FL
		03/04	30	7	FL
Reading		04/05	27	16	SL
		05/06	30	6	SL
Derby Co		06/07	32	8	FL
		07/08	29	10	FL

LONGAIR William					1 cap
b. Dundee 19.7.1870 d. Dundee 28.11.1926					
Rockwell		87/88			
Dundee East End		88/89			
		89/90			
		90/91			
		91/92			
		92/93			
Dundee		93/94	17	1	
		94/95	17		
Newton Heath		94/95	1		FL
Dundee		95/96	16	1	
Sunderland		96/97	2		FL
Burnley		96/97	12	1	FL
Dundee		97/98	10		
Brighton U		98/99	22	2	SL
Dundee		99/00	18	1	
		00/01	20		
		01/02	16		

LONGMIRE Fred					
Dalziel R					
Hamilton A		06/07	5	1	

LONGMUIR Archibald MacDonald					
b. Saltcoats 17.4.1897					
Hall Russells					
Aberdeen					
Ardrossan Winton R					
Celtic		20/21	2	2	
		21/22	8	4	
Blackburn R		21/22	17		FL
		22/23	7	2	FL
Oldham A		23/24	22	4	FL
Wrexham		24/25	40	2	FL
Cowdenbeath	L	25/26			
Wrexham		25/26	40	6	FL
		26/27	35	3	FL
		27/28	38	8	FL
		28/29	41	12	FL
		29/30	29	3	FL

LONIE Thomas					
b. Dundee c1872					
Dundee Harp					
Notts Co					
Darwen		94/95	8	2	FL
Dundee W		94/95	6	?	D2
Dundee		94/95	3	2	
		95/96	7	4	
Stoke		95/96	9	3	FL
Leicester F		96/97	7	2	FL

LORIMER Herbert W					
b. Catrine					
Catrine Thistle					
Kilmarnock		20/21	1		
		21/22			
		22/23			

LORIMER Hugh Harper					
b. Paisley 11.11.1896 d. Pittsburgh c1925					
St Mirren Jnrs					
Tottenham H		19/20	4		FL
		20/21			FL
		21/22	1		FL
Dundee		21/22	8		
Dalbeattie Star					
Carlisle U		22/23			
		23/24			
Boston Wonder Workers		24/25	7		ASL
		25/26	3		ASL
J & P Coats		25/26	15	3	ASL

LORIMER John					
Port Glasgow A		04/05	8		
Albion R					

LORIMER Peter					
St Johnstone		36/37	12	10	
		37/38	21	10	
		38/39	18	10	

LORNE Thomas					
Clackmannan					
Heart of Midlothian		01/02	9	4	

LOUDEN Lewis W					
Queen's Park		29/30	3		

LOUDON Andrew					
Glenboig St Josephs					
St Bernards					
Stranraer					
Albion R		38/39	14		

LOUDON George					
b. c1916					
Airdrie Jnrs					
Partick T	T				
Albion R		37/38			D2
		38/39	34	6	

LOVE Alexander					
b. Armadale c1905					
Blackburn R (W Lothian)					
Hibernian		24/25			
		25/26	2	1	
Kings Park		26/27			D2
Olympic (California)					

LOVE Andrew Robb					3 caps
b. Renfrew 26.3.1905 d. West Petercutter 3.11.1962					
Kirkintilloch Rob Roy					
Aberdeen		25/26	3		
		26/27	7	2	
		27/28	30	10	
		28/29	30	14	
		29/30	33	17	
		30/31	37	8	
		31/32	34	12	
		32/33	25	13	
		33/34	16	3	
		34/35			
Aldershot		35/36	11	2	FL
Montrose		36/37			D2

LOVE George					
b. c1898					
Paisley Vulcan					
St Mirren		20/21	13	8	

LOVE James					
b. Wishaw					
Vale of Clyde					
Third Lanark		17/18	15	?	
		18/19	1	?	
		19/20	7	1	

LOVE William					
b. Thornliebank					
Third Lanark		90/91	12	2	
		91/92	5		
		92/93	8		
Thornliebank *					

LOVE William					
b. c1915					
Burnbank					
Renfrew Jnrs					
Albion R		37/38			D2
		38/39	19	7	

LOVE William Y					
b. Burnbank					
Burnbank A					
Morton		29/30	3		
		30/31	5	1	
Montrose		31/32			D2

LOW Alexander					
Baillieston					
Airdrieonians		05/06	1		
Albion R		06/07			D2
		07/08			D2
		08/09			D2

LOW Alexander 1 cap

b. Greenhill c1910

Club		Season	Apps	Goals	
Bonnybridge Juveniles					
Banknock Jnrs					
Falkirk		29/30	8		
		30/31	15		
		31/32	20	3	
		32/33	36	1	
		33/34	26		
		34/35	25	2	
Workington		35/36			
Tunbridge Wells R		36/37			
		37/38			
Raith R		38/39	24		

LOW Archibald B

Club		Season	Apps	Goals	
Glasgow Ashfield					
Woolwich Arsenal		06/07	3		FL
		07/08			FL
Partick T		08/09	17		
Johnstone		09/10			

LOW George

Club		Season	Apps	Goals	
Clyde		12/13	1		
		13/14	5	1	

LOW George J

Club		Season	Apps	Goals	
Queen's Park		10/11	2		

LOW Henry Forbes

b. Old Machar 1882 d. Sunderland 29.9.1920

Club		Season	Apps	Goals	
Orion					
Aberdeen		03/04	17	5	D2
		04/05	21	2	D2
		05/06	27	4	
		06/07	30	8	
Sunderland		07/08	30	2	FL
		08/09	32	2	FL
		09/10	24	14	FL
		10/11	36	7	FL
		11/12	8		FL
		12/13	37	4	FL
		13/14	22	1	FL
		14/15	14		FL

LOW James 1 cap

Club		Season	Apps	Goals	
Cambuslang		87/88			
		88/89			
		89/90			
		90/91	16	2	
		91/92	15		

LOW James

b. Kilbirnie 9.3.1894 d. 1960

Club		Season	Apps	Goals	
Bishopmill U					
Elgin C					
Edinburgh University					
Heart of Midlothian		12/13	15	5	
		13/14	30	6	
		14/15	35	7	
		15/16	2		
Elgin C					
Rangers		19/20	1		
		20/21	3		
Newcastle U		21/22	24	2	FL
		22/23	37	2	FL
		23/24	20	1	FL
		24/25	17	2	FL
		25/26	4		FL
		26/27	2	1	FL
		27/28			FL
Buckie Thistle		28/29			

LOW John

Club		Season	Apps	Goals	
Dundee		95/96	1		
Arbroath					

LOW John

b. Newtongrange

Club		Season	Apps	Goals	
Denbeath Star					
Heart of Midlothian		18/19	2		
		19/20	13	4	
Dunfermline A		20/21			
Ayr U		21/22	25	1	
Mid Rhondda					
Ayr U		22/23	5		
Manchester U					
Dunfermline A					
Halifax T *		25/26	5	1	FL

LOW Ronald McK

Club		Season	Apps	Goals	
Third Lanark		23/24	1		
		24/25			
		25/26			D2
		26/27			D2
		27/28			D2
Nithsdale W		27/28			

LOW Sam M

Club		Season	Apps	Goals	
Queen's Park		14/15	1		

LOW Thomas

Club		Season	Apps	Goals	
Cowdenbeath					
Airdrieonians		09/10	1		

LOW Thomas Pollock 1 cap

b. Cambuslang 3.10.1874

Club		Season	Apps	Goals	
Parkhead					
Rangers		96/97	9	4	
Blackburn R	T				
Rangers		97/98	12	1	
Dundee		99/00	17	4	
Woolwich Arsenal		00/01	24	1	FL
Abercorn		01/02			D2
		02/03			D2
		03/04			D2
		04/05			D2
Rangers		04/05	1	1	
		05/06	2	1	
Dunfermline A		05/06			
Morton		06/07	10	1	

LOW Wilfred Lawson 5 caps

b. Aberdeen 8.12.1884 d. Newcastle 30.4.1933

Club		Season	Apps	Goals	
Abergeldie					
Montrose	T				
Aberdeen		04/05	4		D2
		05/06	13		
		06/07	29		
		07/08	29	1	
		08/09	32	2	
Newcastle U		09/10	23		FL
		10/11	31	1	FL
		11/12	35	2	FL
		12/13	31	2	FL
		13/14	34	2	FL
		14/15	35		FL
		19/20	38		FL
		20/21	34		FL
		21/22	29	1	FL
		22/23	23		FL
		23/24	10		FL

LOW Wiliam Ross

b. Aberdeen 21.9.1889 d. Redruth 1970

Club		Season	Apps	Goals	
Aberdeen Shamrock					
Aberdeen		09/10	1		
		10/11			
		11/12	4		
		12/13	4		
		13/14	35		
South Shields		14/15			
		15/16			
Aberdeen		16/17	1		
Grimsby T	?				
Gainsborough T		19/20			
Barnsley		20/21	33		FL
		21/22	8		FL
		22/23			FL
Wombwell					
Truro C					
Mabe					

LOWE

Club		Season	Apps	Goals	
Third Lanark		91/92	3	2	

LOWE David B

Club		Season	Apps	Goals	
Queen's Park		20/21	1		

LOWE G D L

Club		Season	Apps	Goals	
Queen's Park		10/11	1		

LOWE Harry

b. Fife

Club		Season	Apps	Goals	
Falkirk		28/29	4	1	
		29/30	2		
Buckie Thistle		30/31			

LOWE John

Club		Season	Apps	Goals	
Heart of Midlothian		09/10	2	1	
		10/11	4		
Merthyr T		11/12			SL

LOWE John

b. Arbroath

Club		Season	Apps	Goals	
Woodside					
Ardenlea					
Arbroath		26/27	17	2	D2
		27/28	15	6	D2
		28/29	31	6	D2
Clyde		29/30	10	1	
		30/31	28	3	
		31/32			
Arbroath		31/32	26	8	D2
		32/33	31	16	D2
		33/34	28	6	D2
		34/35	27	7	D2
		35/36	37	9	
		36/37	35	12	
		37/38	30	8	

LOWE John

d. Lochranza 16.8.1995

Club		Season	Apps	Goals	
Royal Albert					
Clyde		33/34	6	2	
		34/35	10	3	
Hamilton A		35/36	2	1	
		36/37			
		37/38	28		
		38/39	38		

LOWERY Edward

b. Walker 24.10.1907 d. Walker 16.9.2000

Club		Season	Apps	Goals	
Walker Park					
Usworth Colliery					
East Fife		30/31	18	2	
		31/32	37	13	D2
Leicester C		32/33	10	1	FL
		33/34	4		FL
Yeovil T	L	33/34			
Torquay U		34/35	18	4	FL
		35/36	19	8	FL
Darlington		36/37	11	3	FL
Frickley Colliery					
Burton T					

LOWRIE George

Club		Season	Apps	Goals	
Heart of Midlothian		05/06	1		

LOWRY Charles H

b. c1892

Club		Season	Apps	Goals	
Glasgow Perthshire					
Partick T		09/10	5	2	
		10/11	2	2	
		11/12	4	2	
		12/13	7	1	
Girvan	L	12/13			
Abercorn		13/14			D2
		14/15			D2
		15/16			

LUMSDEN

Club		Season	Apps	Goals	
Heart of Midlothian		90/91	1		

LYALL

Club		Season	Apps	Goals	
Cowlairs		90/91	13	2	

LYALL John 1 cap

b. Dundee 16.4.1881 d. Detroit 17.2.1944

Club		Season	Apps	Goals	
Jarrow					
Sheffield W		01/02	31		FL
		02/03	33		FL
		03/04	33		FL
		04/05	29		FL
		05/06	38		FL
		06/07	37		FL
		07/08	35		FL
		08/09	27		FL
Manchester C		09/10	33		FL
		10/11	7		FL
Dundee		10/11	1		
		11/12	34		
		12/13	26		
		13/14	22		
Ayr U		13/14	15		
		14/15	33		
South Shields		15/16			

LYLE Charles Hunter

b. Rothesay 1907

Club		Season	Apps	Goals	
Morton		29/30	30	18	
		30/31	27	14	
		31/32	33	17	
		32/33	32	8	
		33/34			D2
Partick T		34/35	6	6	
St Johnstone		35/36	13	7	

LYLE Robert C

Club		Season	Apps	Goals	
Maryhill					
Glasgow Perthshire					
Partick T		08/09	30	2	
		09/10	19		
Derby Co		10/11	7		FL

LYLE Thomas

Club		Season	Apps	Goals	
Kilmarnock		87/88			
		88/89			
		89/90			
Cowlairs		90/91			
Third Lanark		91/92	7	1	

LYNAS John
b. Blantyre 18.1.1907 d. Blackpool 18.12.1988

Club		Season	Apps	Goals	
Linlithgow Port					
Shettleston					
Rutherglen Glencairn					
Bo'ness		27/28	27	4	
Sunderland		28/29	10	1	FL
Third Lanark		29/30			D2
		30/31			D2
		31/32	29	12	
		32/33	12	2	
		33/34	20	4	

LYNCH Allan
b. Portobello 6.3.1879

Club		Season	Apps	Goals	
Scottish Rifles					
Celtic		97/98	1		
		98/99	1		
Clyde					

LYNCH James

Club		Season	Apps	Goals	
Port Glasgow A		06/07	20	2	
		07/08	11	1	
		08/09	28		
		09/10	31		
Heart of Midlothian		09/10	2		
		10/11			
Middlesbrough					
Kilmarnock		11/12	3		
Stevenston U					

LYNCH John
b. c1916

Club		Season	Apps	Goals	
Cambuslang R					
Dundee		35/36	5		
		36/37	12		
		37/38	22		
		38/39	33		D2

LYNCH Matthew
b. 29.11.1916

Club		Season	Apps	Goals	
Linwood St Convals					
St Anthonys					
Celtic		34/35			
		35/36			
		36/37			
		37/38	14	1	
		38/39	16	1	
		46/47	14		
		47/48			
Dumbarton		48/49			

LYNCH Michael

Club		Season	Apps	Goals	
Greenhead Thistle					
Glasgow Perthshire					
Arbroath		36/37	19	2	
		37/38	10	2	
Derry C		38/39			IL

LYNCH Robert

Club		Season	Apps	Goals	
Vale of Garnock					
St Mirren		05/06	11		
		06/07	3		
Ayr Parkhouse		07/08			D2
		08/09			D2
		09/10			D2

LYNCH Thomas Tracey
b. Dundee c1909

Club		Season	Apps	Goals	
Dundee		28/29	3		
		29/30	15		
		30/31	4	1	
		31/32	13	4	
Larne		32/33			IL
Belfast Celtic		32/33			IL

LYNER David (born LYNAR)
b. Belfast 9.1.1893 d. Belfast 5.12.1973

Club		Season	Apps	Goals	
Owen o'Cork					
Glentoran					
Dundela					
Distillery		10/11			IL
		11/12			IL
Glentoran		12/13			IL
		13/14			IL
		14/15			IL
		15/16			IL
		16/17			IL
		17/18			IL
		18/19			IL
		19/20			IL
		20/21			IL
		21/22			IL
Manchester U		22/23	3		FL
Kilmarnock		22/23	18	5	
		23/24	27	1	
Queens Island		24/25			IL
Dundela		24/25			
Clydebank		24/25			D2
Dundela		25/26			
Clydebank		25/26			
Mid Rhondda		25/26			
New Brighton		26/27	21	1	FL
Glentoran		27/28			IL
Queens Island		28/29			IL
Dundela		29/30			

LYNESS Albert
b. Lisburn 8.6.1912 d. Lisburn 7.7.1990

Club		Season	Apps	Goals	
Rangers		37/38	2	1	
		38/39	4	2	
Linfield		39/40			IL
Distillery		40/41			IL
		41/42			IL
		42/43			IL
		43/44			IL
		44/45			IL
Crusaders		44/45			

LYNN Andrew
b. 1875

Club		Season	Apps	Goals	
Moston					
Third Lanark		00/01	20	6	
		01/02	12	1	
Albion R					

LYNN James

Club		Season	Apps	Goals	
Rutherglen Glencairn					
Ayr U		33/34	2		
		34/35	3		

LYON George H

Club		Season	Apps	Goals	
Whiteinch Glenburn					
Partick T		21/22	1		
Mid Rhondda		22/23			
		23/24			

LYON J F

Club		Season	Apps	Goals	
Aberdeen		08/09	2		

LYON James

Club		Season	Apps	Goals	
Third Lanark		95/96	4		
		96/97	1		

LYON James

Club		Season	Apps	Goals	
Brechin C					
Dundee		05/06	1		
		06/07			
		07/08			
Brechin C		08/09			

LYON John

Club		Season	Apps	Goals	
Clydebank					
Partick T		05/06	17		
		06/07	28		
		07/08	18		
Distillery					

LYON Thomas King
b. Clydebank 17.3.1915

Club		Season	Apps	Goals	
Clydebank Jnrs					
Motherwell	T	33/34			
Yoker A		34/35			
Albion R		34/35	24	14	
		35/36	26	11	
Airdrieonians	L	35/36	10	6	
Albion R		36/37	25	4	
Blackpool		36/37	4		FL
		37/38	2		FL
Chesterfield		38/39	36	22	FL
		39/40	2	1	FL
		47/48	5		FL
New Brighton		48/49	36	7	FL
Prescot Cables		49/50			
Oswestry T		49/50			

LYON William John

Club		Season	Apps	Goals	
Dundee		98/99	7		

LYON William King
b. Birkenhead 7.3.1912 d. Salford 5.12.1962

Club		Season	Apps	Goals	
Clydebank High School FP					
Cowdenbeath		30/31			
Kirkintilloch Rob Roy		31/32			
		32/33			
Queen's Park		33/34	19	1	
		34/35	37	2	
Celtic		35/36	38	6	
		36/37	35	1	
		37/38	36	3	
		38/39	33	5	

LYONS

Club		Season	Apps	Goals	
Cowlairs		90/91	1		

MABBERLEY Ivor
b. Newport 24.5.1889 d. 1951

Club		Season	Apps	Goals	
Swindon V					
Swindon T		10/11	2		SL
Yoker A					
Sheffield U					
Clyde		13/14	17	6	

MACKRELL James
b. New Monkland 13.2.1906 d. Plains 3.1.1977

Club		Season	Apps	Goals	
Longriggend Rob Roy					
Falkirk		27/28	6		
		28/29	9		
		29/30	10		
		30/31	20		
Motherwell		31/32	2		
		32/33	8		
Portsmouth		33/34	2		FL
		34/35	1		FL
Norwich C		36/37	9		FL
		37/38	20		FL
		38/39	9		FL

MADDEN John 2 caps
b. Dumbarton 11.6.1863 d. Prague 17.4.1948

Club		Season	Apps	Goals	
Dumbarton A					
Dumbarton Hibernian					
Dumbarton		86/87			
Gainsborough T		87/88			
Grimsby T					
Celtic		88/89			
Dumbarton					
Celtic		89/90			
		90/91	17	4	
		91/92	11	7	
Sheffield W					
Celtic		92/93	14	5	
		93/94	15	5	
		94/95	14	9	
		95/96	12	3	
		96/97	8		
Dundee		97/98	4		
Tottenham H		97/98	2		SL

MAGINNES John

Club		Season	Apps	Goals	
Kilbarchan					
Morton		05/06	11		
		06/07	7	3	
		07/08	1		

MAGNER Edward
b. Newcastle 1.1.1891 d. Derby ?.7.1948

Club		Season	Apps	Goals	
Stainton Celtic					
West Hartlepool Expansion					
Gainsborough T		09/10	5	1	FL
Everton		10/11	6	2	FL
St Mirren		11/12	8	4	
		12/13	22	18	
		13/14	17	3	
South Liverpool		14/15			
Shelbourne		19/20			IL

MAIDEN Robert

Kelty Jnrs
Dundee 22/23 2

MAILER Andrew

Third Lanark 96/97 4 1
Partick T 96/97 7 4 D2
Cameronians 97/98

MAIN Alexander
b. West Calder
West Calder
Rangers 98/99
West Calder Swifts 98/99
Hibernian 99/00
Woolwich Arsenal 99/00 8 3 FL
00/01 21 6 FL
01/02 28 5 FL
02/03 7 FL
West Calder Swifts
Motherwell 03/04 14 3
Watford 04/05 27 1 SL
05/06 27 SL
06/07 13 SL

MAIN Andrew
b. Glasgow
Maryhill
Bridgeton Waverley
Airdrieonians 26/27 4 2
St Johnstone 26/27 16 4
27/28 27 10
28/29 21 17
29/30 17 4
Hibernian 30/31 23 15
31/32 D2
32/33 D2
Bangor C T 32/33
Bo'ness 32/33 D2

MAIN David
b. Falkirk 1888
Falkirk 09/10 6 2
10/11 3
Sunderland 10/11 2 1 FL
Aberdeen 11/12 23 11
12/13 24 10
13/14 30 9
14/15 24 5
15/16 32 15
16/17 17 4
Falkirk 17/18 21 ?
18/19 17 ?
19/20 16 6

MAIN James

Hibernian 99/00 1

MAIN James 1 cap
b. West Calder 29.5.1886 d. Edinburgh 29.11.1909
Motherwell
Hibernian 04/05 5
05/06 25
06/07 28
07/08 30 2
08/09 29 1
09/10 16 1

MAIN James
b. Motherwell c1916 d. Wishaw 20.4.2006
Parkhead Jnrs
Hibernian
Motherwell 36/37 6 2
37/38 5 1
38/39 3

MAIN John

Royal Albert
Queen's Park 08/09 12 1
09/10 5
Royal Albert 09/10
Motherwell 10/11 7 1
11/12 1

MAIN Robert
b. c1904
Aberdeen 24/25 2
St Bernards 25/26 D2
Dumbarton 26/27 D2

MAIN Robert Frame 1 cap
b. Airdrie 10.2.1909 d. 30.3.1985
Baillieston Jnrs
Rangers 29/30 1
30/31 2
31/32 1
32/33 3
33/34 25 4
34/35 27 5
35/36 20 7
36/37 23 6
37/38 29 6
38/39 8 3
New Brighton 39/40 3 1 FL

MAIN William

Albion R
Hamilton A 08/09 28 8
09/10 18 9
10/11 2

MAINDS Colin
b. Dundee 1884
Renfrew V
Port Glasgow A 05/06 29 3
Rangers 06/07 13 1
Reading 07/08 SL
08/09 SL
Third Lanark 09/10 30 2
10/11 31 1
11/12 29 2
12/13 33
Abercorn

MAIR

Dumbarton 90/91 8 5

MAIR

Dumbarton 92/93 2 1

MAIR Andrew

Dumbarton 21/22 5

MAIR Archibald

Ayr U
Galston L
Ayr U 33/34 5 1
34/35 15 2

MAIR Charles

Newmilns
St Mirren 10/11 8

MAIR David
b. Dumbarton
Renfrew V
Bradford
Glossop 05/06 FL
06/07 37 FL
07/08 37 FL
Dundee 08/09 16 1
09/10 14
10/11 19 3
11/12 2
Motherwell 11/12 24 1
12/13 32
13/14 26 1
14/15 9 1

MAIR G

Queen's Park 16/17 8

MAIR George A

Edinburgh University
Peterhead
Leith A 34/35 D2
35/36 D2
Dunfermline A 36/37 5
Queen of the South 37/38 7

MAIR John

Newmilns
Airdrieonians 05/06 1
Galston

MAIR Matthew
b. Dunlop 3.10.1880
Newmilns
Celtic 01/02 1
Kilmarnock 02/03 5 1

MAIR Peter

Burnbank A
Airdrieonians 15/16 18 4

MAITLAND David J
b. Kilmarnock 1879
Kilmarnock Winton
Kilmarnock 97/98 11 10 D2
98/99 14 11 D2
99/00 14 2
00/01 9 3
Galston L 00/01
Kilmarnock 01/02 7
Galston 02/03
03/04
04/05
Nithsdale W

MAITLAND James
b. Kilmarnock
Kilmarnock 19/20 10

MALCOLM Alexander

Alloa A
Heart of Midlothian 06/07 1

MALCOLM James Gordon
b. Tillicoultry *
Cowdenbeath *
Montrose *
Queen's Park 38/39 1

MALCOLM Robert
b. Loanhead d. 1979
Heart of Midlothian 12/13 1
13/14 4
14/15 6 1
15/16
16/17 4
17/18 1 ?
Loanhead Mayflower
Airdrieonians 20/21 3
Leith A 21/22 D2
22/23 D2
23/24 D2
24/25 D2

MALCOLM Robert

Falkirk 15/16 19 5

MALEY Matthew

Neilston V
Morton Jnrs
Morton 35/36 D2
36/37 D2
37/38 38

MALEY Thomas Edward
b. Portsmouth 8.11.1864 d. 24.8.1935
Cathcart
London Caledonian
Partick T
Third Lanark
Hibernian
Third Lanark
Clydesdale Harriers
Celtic 88/89
89/90
90/91 1
91/92 2
St Mirren L 91/92
Preston NE

MALEY William 2 caps
b. Newry 25.4.1868 d. Glasgow 2.4.1958
Cathcart Hazlebank Jnrs
Third Lanark
Celtic 88/89
89/90
Ardwick L 89/90
Celtic 90/91 14
91/92 13
92/93 10
93/94 13
94/95 13 1
95/96 5
Manchester C L 95/96 1 FL
Celtic 96/97 1
Everton L 96/97 2 FL

MALLOCH John Napier
b. Lochee 2.11.1877 d. Moorthorpe ?.12.1935
East Craigie
Dundee 97/98 12 2
Brighton U 98/99 19 1 SL
99/00 19 2 SL
Sheffield W 00/01 22 4 FL
01/02 19 3 FL
02/03 33 FL
03/04 24 2 FL
04/05 21 FL
05/06 11 1 FL
06/07 12 FL
Barnsley
Frickley Colliery

MALLOY James

Club		Season	Apps	Goals	League
Largs Thistle					
Arthurlie		33/34			
Hibernian		33/34	13	3	
Brechin C		34/35			D2
Montrose		35/36			D2
Cowdenbeath		36/37			D2
		37/38			D2

MALONE Thomas

Club		Season	Apps	Goals	League
Liverpool					
Clyde					
Rangers		25/26	15	2	
Clyde		26/27	27	2	
Boston					

MANDERSON Robert
b. Belfast 9.5.1893 d. Glasgow 27.4.1946

Club		Season	Apps	Goals	League
Clifton					
Dunedin					
Macrory Memorial					
Cliftonville Olympic					
Derry Celtic		11/12			IL
		12/13			IL
		13/14			
Belfast Celtic		13/14			IL
Glenavon		14/15			
Rangers		14/15	1		
		15/16	32		
		16/17	38	2	
		17/18	29		
		18/19	30	2	
		19/20	40		
		20/21	41		
		21/22	38	1	
		22/23	28		
		23/24	32		
		24/25	34		
		25/26	15		
		26/27	12		
Bradford PA		27/28	40		FL

MANN

Club		Season	Apps	Goals	League
Leith A		93/94	17		

MANNION Thomas

Club		Season	Apps	Goals	League
Duntocher Hibs					
Dumbarton		20/21	18	3	
Kings Park		21/22			D2

MANSFIELD Eversley

Club		Season	Apps	Goals	League
Northern Nomads					
Preston NE					
Manchester C *		08/09	1		FL
Queen's Park		08/09			
		09/10	3	1	

MANSON Andrew

Club		Season	Apps	Goals	League
Parkhead *					
Celtic *		21/22			
Clydebank		21/22	14	1	

MANSOUR Mostafa Kamel
b. Egypt c1915 d. Cairo 23.7.2002

Club		Season	Apps	Goals	League
Al Ahly					
Queen's Park		36/37	3		
		37/38			
		38/39	34		

MANTLE Joseph
b. Hetton le Hole 9.5.1908 d. Southport 10.5.1977

Club		Season	Apps	Goals	League
Spennymoor Jnrs					
Hetton Jnrs					
Burnley		27/28	1	1	FL
		28/29	4	1	FL
		29/30	27	14	FL
		30/31	18	6	FL
Plymouth A		30/31	6	1	FL
		31/32	9	6	FL
Chester		32/33	33	34	FL
		33/34	24	18	FL
		34/35	17	11	FL
Carlisle U		35/36	33	22	FL
		36/37	22	16	FL
Stockport Co		36/37	10	7	FL
		37/38	12	4	FL
Heart of Midlothian		37/38	3		
		38/39	1		
Hartlepools U		39/40	2	1	FL

MARCHBANK Walter
b. Glasgow

Club		Season	Apps	Goals	League
Clydebank		19/20	6		
		20/21	32	3	
		21/22	10		
		22/23			D2
		23/24	20		
		24/25			D2
Raith R		24/25	6		
		25/26	14	1	

MARKEY Sergeant

Club		Season	Apps	Goals	League
Aberdeen		13/14	4		

MARSDEN Bertram

Club		Season	Apps	Goals	League
Third Lanark		24/25	2		

MARSH Wilson
b. Hunslet ?.3.1894 d. Scotland ?.9.1989

Club		Season	Apps	Goals	League
Normanton Springs					
Eckington Works					
Chelsea		21/22	1		FL
		22/23			FL
		23/24	9		FL
Dundee		24/25	1		
		25/26	7		
		26/27	38		
		27/28	35		
		28/29	33		
		29/30	33		
		30/31	36		
		31/32	37		
		32/33	23		
		33/34	37		
		34/35	31		
		35/36	33		
		36/37	26		
		37/38	16		
Kilmarnock		37/38	7		

MARSHALL

Club		Season	Apps	Goals	League
Abercorn		96/97	16		

MARSHALL

Club		Season	Apps	Goals	League
St Mirren		30/31	1		

MARSHALL Alex

Club		Season	Apps	Goals	League
Falkirk		12/13	1		

MARSHALL Alex

Club		Season	Apps	Goals	League
Falkirk		15/16	6		

MARSHALL Alexander
b. Dumbarton

Club		Season	Apps	Goals	League
Glasgow Ashfield					
Dumbarton		17/18	23		
		18/19	10	?	
		19/20	5		
		20/21	5	1	

MARSHALL Alexander

Club		Season	Apps	Goals	League
Longcroft Thistle					
St Mirren		19/20	5		

MARSHALL George

Club		Season	Apps	Goals	League
Calderbank					
Airdrieonians		02/03	6	3	D2
		03/04	15	1	
		04/05	13		

MARSHALL Henry James Hall 2 caps
b. Portobello 24.11.1872 d. Leith 16.9.1936

Club		Season	Apps	Goals	League
Portobello Thistle					
St Bernards					
Heart of Midlothian		92/93	7	1	
Blackburn R		92/93	20		FL
		93/94	29	2	FL
		94/95	2		FL
		95/96			FL
Heart of Midlothian		96/97	10		
		97/98	13		
Blackburn R		97/98	2		FL
Heart of Midlothian		98/99	17	2	
Celtic		99/00	8	2	
		00/01			
Alloa	L	00/01			
Raith R	L	00/01			
Celtic		01/02	16	1	
		02/03	5	1	
Clyde		03/04			D2
		04/05			D2
Broxburn A					

MARSHALL James

Club		Season	Apps	Goals	League
Queen's Park		15/16	25	1	
		16/17	1		

MARSHALL James

Club		Season	Apps	Goals	League
Falkirk		23/24	15	4	

MARSHALL James

Club		Season	Apps	Goals	League
Grange R					
Ayr U		38/39	13	3	

MARSHALL James 3 caps
b. Avonbridge 3.1.1908 d. Ashford 27.12.1977

Club		Season	Apps	Goals	League
Shettleston Jnrs					
Rangers		25/26	4	7	
		26/27	25	20	
		27/28	6	6	
		28/29	18	6	
		29/30	26	14	
		30/31	32	20	
		31/32	34	15	
		32/33	34	16	
		33/34	21	7	
Arsenal		34/35	4		FL
West Ham U		34/35	10	2	FL
		35/36	36	10	FL
		36/37	11	2	FL
Ashford					

MARSHALL James Hynd
b. Peterhead 9.6.1890 d. Cathcart 8.7.1958

Club		Season	Apps	Goals	League
Winchburgh					
Vale of Grange					
Bo'ness					
Partick T		11/12	14	9	
		12/13	5	1	
		13/14	27	10	
Bradford C		14/15	12	3	FL
		15/16			
Ayr U	L	16/17	28	20	
Partick T		17/18	26	12	
		18/19	13	10	
Bradford C		19/20	17	7	FL
		20/21	10	2	FL
Oldham A		20/21	31	5	FL
		21/22	29	6	FL
		22/23	20	6	FL
Bangor		23/24			
Southport		23/24	10	1	FL
Rotherham Co		24/25	1		FL
Lincoln C		24/25	3	1	FL
Queen of the South					
Stranraer					

MARSHALL John

Club		Season	Apps	Goals	League
Leith A		94/95	6	1	
		95/96	8	?	D2
		96/97	12	?	D2
Dunfermline A		96/97			

MARSHALL John
b. Stenhousemuir (or Falkirk) 1892

Club		Season	Apps	Goals	League
Bedlington U					
Preston NE		12/13	16	2	FL
		13/14	10	1	FL
Barnsley		13/14	5		FL
		14/15	7	1	FL
Clyde		18/19	4	?	
		19/20	35		
		20/21	38	4	
		21/22	26		
		22/23	23		

MARSHALL John 7 caps
b. Shettleston 1902

Club		Season	Apps	Goals	League
Saltcoats V					
Shettleston					
St Mirren		14/15	13		
		15/16	31	6	
		16/17	37	14	
Stevenston U		16/17			
St Mirren		17/18	27	7	
		18/19	22	?	
Third Lanark		18/19	1	?	
St Mirren		19/20	16	1	
Middlesbrough		19/20	24		FL
		20/21	36		FL
		21/22	33		FL
		22/23	23		FL
Llanelly		23/24			
Brooklyn Wanderers		24/25	33	1	ASL
		25/26	2		ASL
Newark Skeeters		25/26	27	3	ASL
		26/27	37	2	ASL
		27/28	4	1	ASL
Brooklyn Wanderers		27/28	33	2	ASL
Bethlehem Steel		28/29	4		ESL

MARSHALL Robert
b. Dalry 13.3.1900
Dalry Thistle

West Ham U	T	22/23			
Kilmarnock		22/23	1		
Reading		23/24	1		FL

MARSHALL Robert
b. c1911
Renfrew Jnrs

Hibernian		31/32			D2
		32/33			D2
		33/34	11		
		34/35	8	2	
St Mirren		34/35	6		
Clyde		35/36	2		
Glentoran		35/36			IL
Stenhousemuir		35/36			D2
Rhyl		36/37			

MARSHALL Robert C
b. Portobello
Edinburgh Shaftesbury

Heart of Midlothian		25/26	1		
		26/27	6	1	
		27/28	10	3	
Leith A		28/29			D2
		29/30			D2
		30/31	20	3	
		31/32	8	3	

MARSHALL Robert G
b. 1876

Leith A		94/95	4	2	
		95/96	10	?	D2
		96/97	12	?	D2
Liverpool		97/98	17	2	FL
		98/99	3		FL
Portsmouth		99/00	27	7	SL
		00/01	28	4	SL
		01/02	30	6	SL
		02/03	29	2	SL
		03/04	17		SL
Brighton					

MARSHALL Robert W 2 caps

Glasgow St Andrews
Partick

Partick T		84/85			
		85/86			
		86/87			
		87/88			
Rangers		88/89			
		89/90			
		90/91	16	2	
		91/92	20	1	
		92/93	18		
		93/94	18	1	
		94/95	15		
		95/96	12	1	
Abercorn					

MARSHALL Thomas

St Mirren		98/99	6	2	
Bolton W		98/99	1		FL

MARSHALL Thomas D
b. Saltcoats
New Cumnock U

Kilmarnock		25/26	2		
		26/27	2		
Newark Skeeters		27/28	4		ASL

MARSHALL William

Townhill

Raith R		24/25	7	2	

MARSHALSEY William Hendry Gray
b. Lochgelly 18.4.1910 d. Edinburgh 1977
Denbeath Star

St Bernards		30/31			D2
Heart of Midlothian		30/31	1		
		31/32			
St Bernards	L	31/32			D2
Heart of Midlothian		32/33			
Cardiff C		33/34	8	1	FL
Brechin C		34/35			D2
Peebles R					

MARTIN

St Bernards		94/95	1		

MARTIN

Clyde		17/18	1	?	

MARTIN Allan
b. 1873 d. Springburn 12.5.1906

Northern		91/92			
Rangers		92/93	2		
Hibernian		93/94	16	?	D2
		94/95	16	?	D2
Celtic		95/96	17	15	
Hibernian		96/97	17	3	
		97/98	14	9	
		98/99	8	7	

MARTIN Angus
b. Greenock
Rangers

Falkirk		18/19	28	?	
		19/20	3		
		20/21	3		

MARTIN Angus

Partick T		22/23	1		

MARTIN Christopher
b. Co Athlone
St Anthonys

Bo'ness		24/25		34	D2
		25/26			D2
		26/27		29	D2
		27/28	37	7	
		28/29			D2
Falkirk		28/29			
Brooklyn Wanderers		29/30	1		ASL
		30/31			
Bo'ness		31/32			D2

MARTIN David Anderson
b. Dundee 1891 K.I.A. 25.4.1917

Dundee		10/11	1		
		11/12	7	3	
Brechin C		12/13			
Dundee Hibs		13/14	22	18	D2
		14/15	25	29	D2

MARTIN Frederick
b. Clay Cross 1889 d. ?.1.1932
South Kirkby

Barnsley		09/10	3		FL
		10/11	2	1	FL
		11/12	7	1	FL
Sunderland		12/13			FL
Raith R		12/13	9	3	
		13/14	24	13	
		14/15	27	7	
		15/16			
		16/17			
		17/18			
		18/19			
		19/20	4		

MARTIN George F

Queen's Park		17/18	1		

MARTIN George Scott
b. Bothwell 14.7.1899 d. Luton 6.11.1972
Cadzow St Annes

Hamilton A		20/21	19	6	
		21/22	4	1	
Bathgate	L	21/22			D2
Bo'ness		21/22	12	11	D2
		22/23	7	8	D2
Hull C		22/23	27	12	FL
		23/24	39	9	FL
		24/25	35	7	FL
		25/26	32	7	FL
		26/27	41	12	FL
		27/28	30	8	FL
Everton		27/28	10	3	FL
		28/29	18	6	FL
		29/30	40	15	FL
		30/31	15	7	FL
		31/32	2		FL
Middlesbrough		32/33	6		FL
Luton T		33/34	38	12	FL
		34/35	28	7	FL
		35/36	31	8	FL
		36/37	3		FL

MARTIN Hugh Innes
b. St Ninians 10.6.1903 d. Kirkcaldy 1956

Kings Park		25/26			D2
Falkirk		26/27	24	3	
		27/28	27	5	
		28/29	2		
Doncaster R		29/30	2		FL
Kings Park		29/30			D2
		30/31			D2

MARTIN J

Queen's Park		14/15	1		

MARTIN James
b. Bo'ness 21.8.1893 d. Bo'ness 9.2.1940
Bo'ness

Heart of Midlothian		15/16	32		
		16/17	1		
Rangers		16/17	21	4	
		17/18	18	1	
Airdrieonians	L	17/18	2	1	
Morton		17/18	5	1	
Bo'ness		19/20			
Dumbarton		19/20	16	1	
Portsmouth		20/21	17	1	FL
		21/22	40	5	FL
		22/23	39	4	FL
		23/24	41	11	FL
		24/25	40	1	FL
		25/26	35	5	FL
		26/27	1		FL
Aldershot		27/28	16	1	SL

MARTIN James D

Paisley Academicals

Port Glasgow A		07/08	4		
		08/09	11	1	
		09/10	7		
Queen's Park					

MARTIN John

Strathclyde
Glasgow Perthshire
Bellshill A

Clydebank		16/17			
		17/18	4		

MARTIN John

Clydebank		21/22	6	1	
Lochgelly U					

MARTIN Neil

Morton		20/21	9	1	

MARTIN Thomas
b. Glengarnock 28.2.1899
Vale of Clyde

Motherwell		21/22	8		
		22/23	18		
		23/24	11		
		24/25	11		
Fall River Marksmen		25/26	31		ASL
		26/27	15		ASL
Providence Clamdiggers		26/27	4		ASL
J & P Coats		27/28	51		ASL
		28/29	50		ASL
Pawtucket Rangers		29A	19		ASL
		29/30	24	1	ASL
		30A	24	1	ASL
		31S	2		ASL

MARTIN Thomas
b. Buckhaven c1907
Rosslay

Cowdenbeath		29/30	12	2	
		30/31	6		
		31/32	1		

MARTIN William

Wigtownshire
Stranraer

Clyde		10/11	2	1	

MARTIN William

Falkirk		13/14	1		

MARTIN William

Queen's Park		33/34	9	3	
		34/35	29	6	
		35/36	31	9	
		36/37	32	4	
		37/38	37	30	

MARTIN William

Clyde		38/39	33	20	

MARTIN William R
b. c1914

Yoker A		35/36			
		36/37			
		36/37			
Motherwell		37/38	2		
		38/39	2		

MASON Charles

Camelon

Rangers		32/33	2		
		33/34	1		

MASON George

Alloa A
St Mirren 25/26 9 1
Falkirk 26/27 13
East Stirlingshire 27/28 D2
28/29 D2
29/30 D2
30/31 D2
31/32 D2
St Johnstone 32/33 35 3
33/34 36 1
34/35 32 3
35/36 6
36/37 34 1
37/38 28 5
38/39 31 2

MASON James
b. Glasgow 18.6.1919 d. ?.12.1971
Mossvale YMCA
Third Lanark 36/37 18 3
37/38 19 4
38/39 32 4
46/47 17 3
47/48 28 7
49/50 26 5
50/51 25 5
51/52 27 2
52/53 12 1
53/54 3

MASON James R

Queen's Park
Queen of the South 37/38 19

MASON Robert
b. Burnbank
Burnbank A
Clyde 06/07 33
07/08 26
Hamilton A 08/09 25
09/10 10
Bradford PA 09/10 22 FL
10/11 35 FL
11/12 13 FL
12/13 33 FL
13/14 15 FL
Stalybridge C
Burnbank A
Hamilton A 17/18 25
18/19 20
19/20 11

MASON William
b. Wishaw
Heart of Midlothian 89/90
90/91 14 1

MASON William

St Bernards
Hibernian 23/24 2
Bathgate * 24/25 D2
Royal Albert * 25/26 D3

MASSEY Lee

Petershill
Partick T 06/07 2
07/08 18
08/09 27
Ayr Parkhouse 09/10 D2
Ayr U 10/11 21 D2
11/12 D2

MASSIE Alexander 18 caps
b. Possilpark 13.3.1906 d. Welwyn Garden City 20.9.1977
Blockairn Jnrs
Shawfield Jnrs
Petershill
Glasgow Perthshire
Glasgow Benburb
Glasgow Ashfield
Partick T
Ayr U 25/26 10 3 D2
26/27 14 1 D2
Bury 26/27 11 4 FL
27/28 6 FL
Bethlehem Steel 28/29 7 5 ESL
29/30 25 7 ASL
Dolphin 30/31 LI
Heart of Midlothian 30/31 23 4
31/32 33 2
32/33 35 2
33/34 36 10
34/35 35 2
35/36 17
Aston Villa 35/36 24 2 FL
36/37 35 1 FL
37/38 40 2 FL
38/39 42 FL

MASSIE James
b. c1898
Aberdeen East End
Aberdeen 19/20 4

MASSIE William S

Partick T 97/98 13
Ayr 98/99 D2
99/00 D2
00/01 D2
Partick T 01/02 19 5 D2
02/03 18 3
03/04 18 7
04/05 13 4
Morton 05/06 6

MASTERTON

Heart of Midlothian 91/92 12

MASTERTON D

Cowlairs 90/91 14

MASTERTON William

Dundee 14/15 24

MATHER

Buckhaven Thistle
Motherwell 06/07 1

MATHERS John

Rutherglen Glencairn
St Johnstone 38/39 25 1
Dumbarton

MATHIE Alexander

Rangers 95/96 1
96/97

MATHIE David

Parkhead
Hamilton A 18/19 27 ?

MATHIE David
b. Motherwell 15.8.1919 d. Law Hospital 3.1.1954
Larkhall Thistle
Motherwell 38/39 30 20
Derry C 40/41 IL
41/42 IL
Linfield 41/42 IL
Derry C 42/43 IL
Linfield 42/43 IL
Clyde 46/47 5 2
Partick T 46/47 17 18
47/48 21 9
Motherwell 47/48 2 1
48/49 26 14
49/50 2
Llanelly 50/51
Kilmarnock 51/52
52/53 7 4 D2
53/54
Workington 53/54 FL

MATHIESON

Cowlairs 90/91 2

MATHIESON

Leith A 91/92 14 6

MATHIESON

Renton 91/92 14 5
92/93 18 1
93/94 5

MATHIESON James Adamson
b. Methil 10.5.1905 d. Methil 13.4.1950
Dubbleside Hearts
Colinsburgh U
Partick T
Raith R 23/24 17
24/25 37
25/26 38
Middlesbrough 26/27 42 FL
27/28 42 FL
28/29 40 FL
29/30 41 FL
30/31 38 FL
31/32 30 FL
32/33 12 FL
33/34 FL
Brentford 34/35 42 FL
35/36 42 FL
36/37 35 FL
37/38 7 FL
Queen of the South 38/39 38

MATHIESON John Alexander
b. Stevenston 9.12.1904
Saltcoats V
Kilmarnock 25/26 4
26/27 5 1
27/28 4 1
28/29 3
Barrow 29/30 11 1 FL
Distillery 29/30 IL
Saltcoats V 30/31

MATTHEW Henry Moram
b. Dundee 16.4.1870 d. Lochee 19.2.1956
Darlington
Bolton W 92/93 8 FL
Dundee 93/94 8 2
Millwall 94/95 16 2 SL
95/96 17 SL
96/97 17 2 SL
Preston NE 97/98 18 FL
Gravesend U 98/99
Distillery 99/00 IL
00/01 IL
01/02 IL
Watford 02/03 10 SL

MATTHEWS

Clyde 14/15 1

MATTHEWS William

Heart of Midlothian 06/07 1

MAUCHLINE Robert Duff
b. Falkirk 15.12.1913
East Stirlingshire
Grange R
Falkirk 35/36 6 D2
Bo'ness Cadora 36/37
Heart of Midlothian 36/37
37/38 4 1
Blackpool 38/39 4 FL
Barrow 38/39 14 3 FL
Accrington S 39/40 3 FL

MAXWELL

Clyde 91/92 15 1

MAXWELL

Third Lanark 91/92 5

MAXWELL

St Mirren 16/17 1
Abercorn 16/17

MAXWELL Alan
b. Glasgow 1870
Cambuslang 90/91 13 5
Everton 91/92 16 4 FL
92/93 23 7 FL
93/94 4 2 FL
Darwen 93/94 16 3 FL
94/95 27 12 FL
95/96 17 1 FL
Stoke 95/96 8 1 FL
96/97 23 1 FL
St Bernards 97/98 4 1

MAXWELL Alex

St Mirren 12/13 2

MAXWELL Gavin

Club	Season	Apps	Goals	
Burnbank A				
St Mirren	00/01	1		
	01/02			
Royal Albert				
Airdrieonians	04/05	1		
Royal Albert				

MAXWELL James Morton
b. New Cumnock 1882 K.I.A., ?.5.1917

Club	Season	Apps	Goals	
Kilmarnock Shawbank				
Petershill				
Kilmarnock	04/05	9	5	
	05/06	17	3	
	06/07	24	5	
Sheffield W	06/07	7	2	FL
	07/08	20	4	FL
Woolwich Arsenal	08/09	2		FL
Hurlford	09/10			
Galston	09/10			
Carlisle U	10/11			
Lanemark	11/12			
Kilmarnock	12/13	5	1	
Nithsdale W	13/14			

MAXWELL James Morton
b. Kilmarnock 15.1.1913 d. Poole 22.4.1990

Club	Season	Apps	Goals	
Loanhead School				
Kilmarnock	30/31	27	18	
	31/32	31	20	
	32/33	33	32	
	33/34	35	33	
Preston NE	34/35	41	23	FL
	35/36	37	17	FL
	36/37	26	12	FL
	37/38	24	8	FL
	38/39	1		FL
Barnsley	39/40	3	4	FL
Kilmarnock				
Shrewsbury T				

MAXWELL Patrick
b. Stewarton

Club	Season	Apps	Goals	
3rd KOSB				
Cumnock				
Hibernian	18/19	5	?	
Stewarton Jnrs				
Hibernian	20/21	16		
	21/22	1		
Dundee Hibs	21/22	5		D2

MAXWELL Robert James
b. Kirkcudbright

Club	Season	Apps	Goals	
Falkirk	19/20	11		
	20/21	6		

MAXWELL Thomas

Club	Season	Apps	Goals	
Motherwell	10/11	2		

MAXWELL Thomas
b. Cambuslang

Club	Season	Apps	Goals	
Cambuslang R				
Clyde	17/18	10	?	
	18/19	19	?	
Dumbarton Harp	19/20			
Dumbarton	20/21	7		
Dunfermline A	20/21			
Arsenal	21/22	1		FL
Bethlehem Steel	22/23	14	3	ASL
	23/24	23	3	ASL
	24/25	25	1	ASL
New Bedford Whalers	25/26	34	3	ASL
	26/27	36	14	ASL
	27/28	34	2	ASL
	28/29	11		ASL
St Marys Barn				
Dulwich Hamlet				
Mansfield T				

MAXWELL William

Club	Season	Apps	Goals	
St Bernards	99/00	8		
	00/01	10	?	D2

MAXWELL William Sturrock 1 cap
b. Arbroath 21.9.1876 d. Bristol 14.7.1940

Club	Season	Apps	Goals	
Hearts Strollers				
Arbroath	93/94			
Heart of Midlothian	94/95	1		
Dundee	94/95			
Stoke	95/96	25	8	FL
	96/97	29	12	FL
	97/98	21	9	FL
	98/99	31	17	FL
	99/00	22	10	FL
	00/01	28	15	FL
Third Lanark	01/02	16	10	
Sunderland	02/03	7	3	FL
Millwall	03/04	29	23	SL
	04/05	25	11	SL
Bristol C	05/06	38	26	FL
	06/07	37	17	FL
	07/08	34	12	FL
	08/09	11	3	FL

MAY James
b. Cambusnethan

Club	Season	Apps	Goals	
St Mirren	97/98	8	2	
Preston NE	97/98	3		FL

MAY John 5 caps
b. Dykehead 15.4.1878 d. Glasgow 25.7.1933

Club	Season	Apps	Goals	
Bo'ness				
Paisley				
Wishaw Thistle	96/97			
Abercorn	97/98	18		
Derby Co	98/99	31		FL
	99/00	34	1	FL
	00/01	29	4	FL
	01/02	26	3	FL
	02/03	27	4	FL
	03/04	32	4	FL
Rangers	04/05	21	2	
	05/06	21	3	
	06/07	17		
	07/08	26	5	
	08/09	21	2	
	09/10	23	1	
Morton	10/11	34	2	
	11/12	27		
	12/13	33	2	
	13/14	30	2	
	14/15	18	1	

MAYES John
b. Craignuek c1907

Club	Season	Apps	Goals	
Sheildmuir Celtic				
Clyde	31/32	32	1	
	32/33	37	5	
	33/34	19		
	34/35	23		
	35/36	20		
	36/37	7		
Ayr U	36/37	22		D2
	37/38	38	1	
	38/39	37		

MEAGHER James
b. Edinburgh

Club		Season	Apps	Goals	
Newtongrange Star					
Dundee		25/26	10	4	
		26/27	15	5	
Dundee U	L	26/27	9	3	
Dundee		27/28	3		
Fall River Marksmen		28/29	2		ASL
Raith R		28/29	2		
Newtongrange Star		28/29			
St Bernards		28/29			D2
Ayr U		29/30	4		
Dundalk	T	29/30			LI

MEAGHER John W

Club	Season	Apps	Goals	
Musselburgh A				
Hibernian	15/16	7	1	
Musselburgh A	15/16			
Leith A	15/16			

MEAKIN

Club	Season	Apps	Goals	
Clydebank	20/21	1		

MEANEY John

Club	Season	Apps	Goals	
Leith A				
Falkirk	12/13	5	5	
	13/14	8		
Leith A	13/14			D2
Clydebank	14/15			D2
	15/16			
Hibernian	16/17	7	2	
	17/18	29	?	
	18/19	3	?	

MEECHAN John Stewart
b. Falkirk 4.5.1910

Club	Season	Apps	Goals	
Grangemouth Sacred Heart				
Maryhill Hibernian				
St Mirren	28/29	1		
	29/30	14	2	
	30/31	28	1	
	31/32	22	19	
	32/33	13	3	
Burnley	33/34	2		FL
Falkirk	33/34	19	7	
	34/35	12	2	
Kilmarnock	34/35	1		
East Stirlingshire	35/36			D2
	36/37			D2
	37/38			D2
St Johnstone	37/38	8	5	
East Stirlingshire	37/38			D2
Morton	38/39			
Bo'ness				
Forth Jnrs				
Polkemmet Jnrs				
East Stirlingshire				

MEEHAN Peter 1 cap
b. Broxburn 28.2.1872 d. Nova Scotia ?.7.1915

Club	Season	Apps	Goals	
Broxburn Shamrock				
Hibernian	91/92			
	92/93			
Sunderland	93/94	23		FL
	94/95	19	1	FL
Celtic	95/96	15		
	96/97	10		
Everton	96/97	7		FL
	97/98	17		FL
Southampton	98/99	14		SL
	99/00	21	1	SL
Manchester C	00/01	6		FL
Barrow	01/02			
Broxburn A	01/02			
	02/03			
Clyde	03/04			D2
Broxburn Shamrock				

MEIKLE Angus McLaren
b. Dalserf 7.2.1900

Club	Season	Apps	Goals	
Larkhall U				
Royal Albert				
Heart of Midlothian	18/19	1		
Royal Albert	19/20			
Heart of Midlothian	20/21	20	2	
	21/22	26	3	
Portsmouth	22/23	40	5	FL
	23/24	42	5	FL
	24/25	40	3	FL
	25/26	30	8	FL
	26/27	2	1	FL
Grimsby T	27/28	13	2	FL
Bangor C	28/29			
	29/30			
	30/31			
Coalburn Jnrs	31/32			

MEIKLEHAM Archibald C Douglas
b. South Leith 1889

Club	Season	Apps	Goals	
Queen's Park	14/15	3		

MEIKLEJOHN David Ditchburn 15 caps
b. Govan 12.12.1900 d. 22.8.1959

Club	Season	Apps	Goals	
Bellahouston Academy				
Maryhill Jnrs				
Rangers	19/20	10	2	
	20/21	35	4	
	21/22	32	3	
	22/23	34	1	
	23/24	35	6	
	24/25	35	3	
	25/26	12		
	26/27	30	2	
	27/28	34	1	
	28/29	30	5	
	29/30	31		
	30/31	31	1	
	31/32	34	5	
	32/33	31	2	
	33/34	29	2	
	34/35	22	3	
	35/36	25	2	

MELDRUM George
b. Falkirk

Club	Season	Apps	Goals	
Forth R				
Falkirk	19/20	6		
	20/21	22	5	
East Stirlingshire	21/22			

MELDRUM John

Club	Season	Apps	Goals	
Partick T	21/22	1		
	22/23			
Arthurlie	23/24			D3

MELLON James
b. Kelvinside 22.12.1901
Uddingston Jnrs
Wishaw YMCA
Hibernian 24/25 1
25/26 13 3
Brighton 26/27 1 FL
Accrington S 27/28 FL
Distillery 28/29 IL
Shelbourne 28/29 LI
Rhyl

MELLORS Richard Dugdale
b. Mansfield 17.3.1902 d. Sydney 2.10.1960
Mansfield Woodhouse
Chesterfield 20/21
Mansfield T 21/22 2 ML
22/23
23/24
24/25
25/26
Sheffield W 26/27 3 FL
27/28 9 FL
28/29 FL
29/30 1 FL
30/31 1 FL
Reading 31/32 35 FL
32/33 39 FL
33/34 11 FL
Bournemouth 34/35 29 FL
35/36 40 FL
36/37 42 FL
37/38 6 FL
Queen of the South 37/38 12

MELROSE Leonard
Coldstream
Heart of Midlothian 10/11 3 2
Coldstream 11/12

MELVILLE Alexander
Dunoon A
Millhurst Amareurs (Can)
Queen's Park 11/12 4

MELVILLE Daniel
b. Glasgow
Arthurlie 10/11 16 D2
11/12 D2
12/13 D2
13/14 D2
Hull C 13/14 5 FL
East Fife 14/15
Clyde 14/15 8 1
15/16
16/17
17/18 9 ?
Renton 18/19
Albion R 19/20 18
Vale of Leven 20/21

MELVILLE David
b. Tayport 1884
Buckhaven Jnrs
East Fife 03/04
Partick T 03/04
04/05 22
05/06 25 2
06/07 16
Bradford C 07/08 2 FL
08/09 5 FL
Stockport Co 09/10 26 1 FL
10/11 25 1 FL
11/12 22 FL
Southport Central

MELVILLE James
Dundee 12/13 1
13/14 1

MELVILLE James
b. Dykehead
Vale of Clyde
Clyde 18/19 23 ?
19/20
20/21
Cardiff C 21/22 1 FL
East Stirlingshire 21/22 D2
Beith 22/23
23/24 D3
24/25 D3
25/26 D3
26/27

MENZIES
Hibernian 17/18 1 ?

MENZIES Alexander William 1 cap
b. Blantyre 25.11.1882
Blantyre V
Heart of Midlothian 02/03 2 1
Motherwell 03/04 5 3
Arthurlie 04/05 D2
Heart of Midlothian 05/06 27 18
06/07 11 3
Manchester U 06/07 17 4 FL
07/08 6 FL
Luton T 08/09 33 7 SL
Dundee 09/10 2 2
Hamilton A 09/10 6 2
Port Glasgow A 10/11 8 D2
Dumbarton 10/11 5 D2
11/12 D2

MENZIES Donald B
b. Glasgow
Glasgow Ashfield
Cowdenbeath 29/30 9
30/31 34 1
31/32 31
32/33 5
Morton 32/33 3
St Mirren 33/34

MENZIES Henry
Port Glasgow A 02/03 11
Albion R 03/04
Arthurlie 04/05

MENZIES James
Rangers 06/07 1

MENZIES James
Albion R
Hamilton A 08/09 17

MENZIES Malcolm
Ayr Parkhouse
Queen's Park 04/05 2
05/06 5

MERCER Alex R
Dunipace
Queen's Park 15/16 7

MERCER Charles
Distillery 06/07 IL
07/08 IL
08/09 IL
Morton 09/10 29 1
10/11 3

MERCER John
Hibernian 15/16 2

MERCER Robert 2 caps
b. Avonbridge 21.9.1889 d. Selkirk 23.4.1926
Gala Hailes Villa
Selkirk
Leith A
Heart of Midlothian 09/10 28 2
10/11
11/12 27 2
12/13 28 6
13/14 34 6
14/15 6
15/16 31 2
16/17 29 2
17/18 7
18/19 7
19/20 12 2
20/21 15 1
Dunfermline A 21/22 D2
22/23 D2

MERCER William
b. Cowdenbeath 8.11.1874 d. Donibristle 1932
Cowdenbeath 94/95
95/96
96/97
97/98
Hibernian 98/99 8 1
Glossop NE 98/99 2 1 FL
Cowdenbeath 99/00
00/01
01/02
02/03
03/04
04/05
05/06 D2
06/07 D2
07/08 D2
08/09 D2

MERRIE Alexander Breckinridge
b. Saltcoats 20.5.1905
Saltcoats V
Nithsdale W
St Mirren 23/24 9 6
St Johnstone L
Alloa A L 24/25 D2
Portsmouth 25/26 7 2 FL
26/27 FL
27/28 FL
Nithsdale W 27/28
Aberdeen 27/28 7 2
28/29 14 11
29/30 1
30/31 10 13
Ayr U 30/31 9 3
31/32 38 27
32/33 33 18
33/34 1
Hull C 33/34 FL
Clyde 33/34 5 2
Crewe A 34/35 30 11 FL
Brechin C 35/36 D2
France 35/36
Aldershot 35/36 4 2 FL
Ross Co 35/36
Exeter C 35/36 4 2 FL
Workington 35/36
Cork C 36/37 LI
Leith A 36/37 D2
Gloucester C 36/37
Evesham T 37/38

MESS James
Heart of Midlothian 37/38 3
38/39 1
Morton

METHVEN Stewart
Dundee 98/99 14 3

MICHAEL William
b. Wishaw 1874 d. Wishaw 26.7.1938
Wishaw Thistle
Heart of Midlothian 93/94 15 9
94/95 17 9
95/96 12 4
Liverpool 96/97 19 5 FL
Wishaw Thistle 96/97
Heart of Midlothian 97/98 7 4
98/99 17 11
99/00 17 15
Bristol C 00/01 15 12 SL
Falkirk
Wishaw U
Motherwell 03/04

MICHIE Harry
b. Tillicoultry
Alva Albion R
Dundee U 27/28 7 D2
28/29 19 12 D2
29/30 6 1

MIDDLETON A C
Queen's Park 14/15 1

MIDDLETON Alexander
b. Port Gordon 2.6.1902
Buckie Wednesday
Buckie Thistle
Heart of Midlothian 25/26
Charlton A 26/27 5 FL
Heart of Midlothian 26/27
Bo'ness 27/28 16 1
Clyde 28/29 3
29/30
Buckie Thistle 30/31

MIDDLETON Robert
St Bernards 94/95 1
95/96
96/97

MIDDLETON Robert Connan 1 cap
b. Brechin 15.1.1904 d. Kirkcaldy 1996
Brechin V
Brechin C
Cowdenbeath 28/29 21
29/30 37
30/31 14
Sunderland 30/31 23 FL
31/32 27 FL
32/33 9 FL
Burton T 33/34
Chester 33/34 13 FL
34/35 30 FL
35/36 7 FL
37/38 6 FL
Congleton T

MIDDLETON William
b. Hetton le Hole 1893
Boldon Colliery
Newcastle C
Brighton 12/13 1 SL
Ayr U 13/14 38 5
14/15 32 5
15/16 15
16/17 15 4
17/18 23 ?
18/19 27 5
19/20 23 3
Aberdeen 20/21 39 3
21/22 40 1
22/23 31 3
Southend U 23/24 30 FL
Ayr U 24/25

MILL Andrew G
Third Lanark 28/29 21

MILL Arthur
b. Kelty
Third Lanark
East Fife 29/30 33 1 D2
30/31 10
Montrose 31/32 D2

MILL David
Clackmannan
Airdrieonians 19/20 2

MILL Thomas
Falkirk R
Falkirk 19/20 4

MILLAR Alexander
Larkhall Thistle
Kilmarnock 14/15 18

MILLAR Alexander
b. Mossend 21.10.1911 d. 28.1.1978
Mossend Celtic
Parkhead Jnrs 33/34
Shawfield Jnrs 34/35
Celtic 35/36 1
36/37 3
37/38 5
Preston NE 38/39 2 FL
Motherwell 45/46
Dundee U 46/47 20
47/48 3
Morton 48/49
Inverness Caledonian T
Stranraer

MILLAR Henry
b. Paisley ?.6.1874 d. 1930
Abercorn 91/92 8 4
St Mirren 91/92 1 1
92/93 2 1
Preston NE
Bury 94/95 28 16 FL
95/96 25 5 FL
96/97 29 11 FL
97/98 27 6 FL
Reading 98/99 20 6 SL
Sheffield W 99/00 28 14 FL
00/01 4 2 FL
QPR 01/02 24 7 SL

MILLAR James
b. Elgin 1877 d. Michigan 4.1.1932
Elgin C
Rangers 98/99 5
99/00
Middlesbrough 00/01 19 FL
01/02 FL
02/03 1 FL
Bradford C 03/04 24 FL
04/05 24 FL
05/06 36 FL
06/07 31 FL
07/08 3 FL
08/09 FL
Aberdeen 09/10 34 1
10/11 30 1
11/12 13

MILLAR James 3 caps
b. Annbank 2.3.1870 d. Chelsea 5.2.1907
Annbank
Sunderland 90/91 17 9 FL
91/92 24 11 FL
92/93 22 12 FL
93/94 27 20 FL
94/95 29 12 FL
95/96 21 8 FL
Rangers 96/97 15 8
97/98 15 10
98/99 16 11
99/00 7 1
Sunderland 00/01 30 10 FL
01/02 32 9 FL
02/03 31 8 FL
03/04 5 3 FL
WBA 04/05 1 FL

MILLAR John
Port Glasgow A 09/10 16
10/11 16 ? D2

MILLAR John
Hamilton A 14/15 33 2
15/16 8 4

MILLAR John McVey
b. Coatbridge 31.12.1906 d. Rochdale ?.2.1997
Bridgetown Waverley
Saltcoats V
Kilmarnock 27/28 9 2
Barnsley 28/29 17 5 FL
Hartlepools U 29/30 17 5 FL
Burton T T 30/31
Bo'ness T 30/31 D2
Workington 31/32
32/33
33/34
Lancaster T 33/34
34/35
35/36
Glentoran 36/37 IL
Lancaster T 37/38
New Brighton 37/38 1 FL
Rochdale 37/38 26 8 FL
Glasgow Benburb
Exeter C 38/39 9 3 FL
Astley Bridge 38/39
Hyde U

MILLAR Robert
Springbank
St Mirren 09/10 12
10/11 11

MILLAR William
Renton
Heart of Midlothian 09/10 1

MILLAR William
Falkirk 13/14 17 3

MILLAR William Mills
b. Carronshore 20.3.1901 d. York 19.7.1966
Dunipace Jnrs
Bo'ness 23/24 D2
Heart of Midlothian T 24/25
Ayr U 24/25 30 3
25/26 9 1 D2
Rhyl A 26/27
Middlesbrough 27/28 8 2 FL
28/29 8 4 FL
York C 29/30 37 9 FL
30/31 21 3 FL
Glentoran 31/32 IL
Crewe A 31/32 FL
Drumcondra 32/33 LI
York Wednesday

MILLER
Abercorn 92/93 16 5
93/94 14 ? D2

MILLER
St Mirren 94/95 18 8

MILLER
Dumbarton 95/96 2

MILLER Adam
b. Berwick K.I.A. ?.1.1918
Berwick R
Hibernian 05/06 2

MILLER Adam
b. Motherwell
Larkhall U
Hamilton A 10/11 22
11/12 27
12/13 31
13/14 33
14/15 30
15/16 23
16/17 26
17/18 28
18/19 27
19/20 9
St Mirren 19/20
20/21 10
Johnstone 21/22 D2

MILLER Alexander
Dumbarton 90/91 15 1
91/92 19 13
92/93 9
93/94 12
94/95 18
95/96 14
Rangers 96/97
Dumbarton 96/97 D2
Clyde 97/98 1

MILLER Alexander
Leith A 31/32 4

MILLER Andrew
b. Bo'ness 27.2.1899
Vale of Grange
Croy Celtic
Celtic 20/21 3 1
21/22 3
22/23
Dumbarton Harp L 22/23
Celtic 23/24
Dumbarton L 23/24 D2
Nottingham F 24/25 FL
Bo'ness 25/26 D2
26/27 D2
Camelon Jnrs 27/28
28/29
29/30
Montrose 29/30 D2

MILLER Andrew B
b. Larkhall
Larkhall Thistle
Dundee U 26/27 18 1
Heart of Midlothian 27/28
28/29 24 10
29/30 13
30/31 1
31/32
Dundee 32/33 26 6
Raith R

MILLER Archibald 1 cap
b. Larkhall 5.9.1913
Royal Albert
Heart of Midlothian 31/32 2 1
32/33 3 2
33/34 5 2
34/35 12 1
35/36 9
36/37 16 1
37/38 36 2
38/39 19 1
46/47 20 1
Blackburn R 47/48 6 FL
Kilmarnock 48/49 16 D2
49/50
Carlisle U 50/51 1 FL
Heart of Midlothian 51/52
Workington 51/52 FL

MILLER David
b. Paisley c1911 d. ?.9.1992
Paisley YMCA
Yoker A
Clydebank Jnrs
Falkirk 31/32
32/33 11 6
Albion R 33/34 D2
St Mirren
Kings Park
East Fife 37/38 16 2 D2
38/39 25 8 D2

MILLER George
Queen's Park 03/04 3

MILLER George Paterson
b. Edinburgh 1894 d. Edinburgh 17.2.1939
Tranent Jnrs
Shaftesbury
Heart of Midlothian 21/22 24 3
Raith R 22/23 25 3
23/24 35 7
24/25 22 11
Heart of Midlothian 24/25 11 2
25/26 28 3
26/27 19 2
27/28 25 8
28/29 19 3
29/30 16 7
30/31 1
Edinburgh C 31/32 D2
Dunfermline A 31/32 D2

MILLER Hugh B
b. Strathaven c1911
Larkhall Thistle
Hamilton A 30/31
31/32
32/33 3
33/34 7
34/35 7
Albion R 35/36 19 2
36/37 15 1
37/38 D2
38/39 5 1

MILLER James

Dumbarton
Bolton W
Dumbarton 90/91 1
91/92 21

MILLER James

Rangers 96/97 2

MILLER James
b. Glasgow c1891 d. Sheffield 26.6.1935
Maryhill
Sheffield W 12/13 8 FL
13/14 22 FL
Airdrieonians 14/15 33
15/16 36 1
16/17
17/18
18/19 12
19/20 10 1

MILLER James

Peebles R
Heart of Midlothian 15/16 13 7
16/17 5 2
17/18 18 4
18/19 16 6
19/20 32 4
20/21 23 4
21/22 1
Lochgelly U 21/22 D2
22/23 D2
Peebles R 23/24 D3
24/25 D3

MILLER James
b. Greenock
Blantyre V
Hamilton A 14/15
15/16
16/17
17/18
18/19 7 3
St Mirren 19/20
Morton 20/21 10 3
St Mirren 21/22 19
Grimsby T 21/22 29 13 FL
22/23 37 11 FL
23/24 23 8 FL
Manchester U 23/24 4 1 FL
York C 24/25
Boston T 25/26
26/27
Shirebrook 27/28
28/29
29/30

MILLER James

Vale of Leven
QPR
St Mirren 17/18 10
Belfast Celtic 18/19 IL

MILLER James

Kilsyth R
Falkirk 19/20 8

MILLER James

Raith R 19/20 5 1

MILLER James
b. Glasgow 29.1.1904
Maryhill Jnrs
Raith R 24/25 10
25/26 30 1
Preston NE T 25/26
East Fife 26/27 5 D2
Dumbarton 27/28 D2
28/29 D2
29/30 D2
Swansea T 30/31 35 FL
31/32 42 1 FL
32/33 37 1 FL
33/34 25 FL
Millwall 34/35 33 3 FL
Hibernian 34/35 6 1
35/36 13
36/37 29 2
37/38 35
38/39 29
Albion R
Cowdenbeath

MILLER James William Guyett
b. Scotstoun 31.3.1911
Hamiltonhill Social
Glasgow Perthshire 32/33
Brechin C 32/33 D2
Liverpool 32/33 FL
Kilmarnock 33/34 37
34/35 36
35/36 33
36/37 31
Exeter C 37/38 1 FL
Galston 37/38
Alloa A 38/39 D2
Allander U

MILLER John
b. Dumbarton
Clyde 94/95 17 12
Derby Co 95/96 30 11 FL
96/97 28 8 FL
97/98 4 1 FL
Bolton W 97/98 8 FL

MILLER John

Hamilton A
Manchester C 02/03 9 2 FL
03/04 FL
04/05 FL
Airdrieonians 05/06 5 3
Motherwell 05/06 5
06/07 20 9
Hamilton A 07/08 6 2
08/09 27 4

MILLER John
b. Dalziel 12.3.1897
Larkhall Thistle
Blantyre V
Hamilton A 15/16 9
16/17 12
17/18 1
18/19 1 1
Liverpool 19/20 8 FL
Heart of Midlothian 20/21
Aberdeen 21/22 36 23
22/23 12 8
23/24 35 13
24/25 8 2
Partick T 24/25 25 15
25/26 28 15
Aberdeen 26/27 18 8
Clyde 26/27 8 4
Dundee 27/28
Dunfermline A 28/29 D2
Prescot Cables 29/30
Barrow 30/31 13 2 FL
Carlisle U

MILLER John

St Johnstone 24/25 1
Johnstone

MILLER John 5 caps
b. Possilpark c1903
Renfrew
Yoker A
Petershill
St Mirren 24/25 5
25/26 5
26/27 3
27/28 4
28/29 13 1
29/30 35 1
30/31 38
31/32 36 1
32/33 37
33/34 35
34/35 36 2
35/36 D2
36/37 38 2
37/38 37
38/39 2

MILLER John
b. Carmuirs
Camelon
Falkirk 29/30 6
30/31 1
31/32 19 6
Brideville 31/32 LI

MILLER John

Glenafton A
Hibernian 35/36 5
36/37
Cowdenbeath 37/38 D2
Dunfermline A 38/39 D2

MILLER John Blackstock
b. Dumbarton c1890 d. Glasgow 24.11.1932
Dumbarton 13/14 13
Renton L 14/15
Dumbarton 15/16 3 1
Airdrieonians L 15/16 4
Dumbarton 16/17 28
17/18 34
18/19 31
Rangers L 18/19 1
St Mirren 18/19 3
Dumbarton 19/20 40
20/21 27

MILLER Joseph
b. Coleraine 27.4.1899
Largs Thistle
Port Glasgow A
Morton 20/21 10 3
21/22
22/23 2
Arthurlie L
Johnstone 23/24 D3
24/25 D3
Aberdare A 25/26 37 3 FL
Middlesbrough 26/27 40 FL
27/28 40 FL
28/29 40 FL
29/30 20 FL
Dolphin 30/31 LI
Hibernian 30/31 18
Ards
Bournemouth 31/32 3 FL
32/33 40 FL
33/34 32 FL
Ballymena U 34/35 IL
Ross Co

MILLER Kenneth
b. c1917
Rothesay Royal V
St Mirren 36/37 3
37/38 7 3
Airdrieonians 38/39 D2
Arthurlie

MILLER Peter Steedman
b. Bo'ness 15.4.1908 d. Bo'ness 19.5.1979
Bo'ness U
Grange R 27/28
28/29
Falkirk 29/30 17 7
Watford 30/31 14 1 FL
New Brighton 31/32 34 1 FL
32/33 35 13 FL
33/34 33 4 FL
34/35 38 4 FL
Le Havre 35/36
Rotherham U 35/36 11 2 FL
Port Vale 36/37 13 1 FL
Kings Park

MILLER Robert
b. Glasgow
Glasgow Ashfield
Partick T 20/21 1

MILLER Robert
b. c1913
Celtic
Morton 32/33 27

MILLER Thomas

Rangers 94/95
95/96 8 4

MILLER Thomas
b. Elbury c1884 d. 1966
Edinburgh Myrtle
Falkirk 02/03 D2
03/04 D2
04/05 D2
Chelsea 05/06 24 FL
06/07 38 FL
07/08 30 FL
08/09 20 FL
Falkirk 09/10 22
Dundee U 10/11 15 1 D2

MILLER Thomas 3 caps
b. Motherwell 29.6.1890 d. Girvan 3.9.1958
Larkhall Hearts
Glenview
Third Lanark
Larkhall U
Hamilton A 10/11 5 1
11/12 22 8
Liverpool 11/12 8 1 FL
12/13 30 11 FL
13/14 32 16 FL
14/15 33 11 FL
Hamilton A L 14/15
Royal Albert L 15/16
Liverpool 19/20 20 11 FL
20/21 4 3 FL
Manchester U 20/21 25 7 FL
Heart of Midlothian 21/22 27 7
Torquay U 22/23
Hamilton A 23/24 31 2
24/25 29 7
25/26 27 6
26/27 12 3
Raith R

MILLER Thomas

Queen's Park 13/14 1
14/15 2
Vale of Leven

MILLER Thomas N

Barrhead Ferenze
Queen's Park 04/05 23 3
05/06 11 2
Rangers 05/06 1
06/07
Arthurlie 07/08 D2

MILLER Walter
b. Newcastle ?.6.1882 d. Dundee 1928
Wallsend Park Villa
Third Lanark
Sheffield W 07/08 3 FL
West Ham U 08/09 11 5 SL
Blackpool 09/10 31 15 FL
10/11 6 1 FL
Lincoln C 11/12 27 20 ML
12/13 30 8 FL
13/14 6 1 FL
Merthyr T 13/14 9 2 SL
Dundee 14/15 2

MILLER Ward

Dundee 98/99 1

MILLER William

Cowdenbeath
Hibernian 98/99 2
Glossop NE 98/99 3 1 FL

MILLER William

East Stirlingshire
Rangers 08/09 1
09/10 9 1
Morton 09/10 1
10/11 2
Liverpool 11/12 FL
12/13 FL
Falkrik 13/14

MILLER William

Larkhall U
Hamilton A 10/11 4
11/12 3
Royal Albert

MILLER William
b. c1919
Bo'ness Academy
Tranent Jnrs
Queen's Park 35/36
36/37 1

MILLER William H
b. Cambuslang
Cambuslang R
Hibernian 16/17 20 7
17/18 28 ?
18/19
19/20 25 2
20/21 26 3
21/22 17 1
22/23 38
23/24 36 1
24/25 38 1
25/26 35
26/27 23

MILLER William Rennie
b. Camelon 19.1.1910
Alva Albion R
Partick T 29/30 24 4
30/31 11 5
31/32 5
32/33 15 1
33/34 30 8
34/35 38 11
Everton 35/36 15 1 FL
36/37 1 1 FL
Burnley 36/37 23 3 FL
37/38 40 13 FL
38/39 11 2 FL
Tranmere R 38/39 11 1 FL
Falkirk 38/39 10

MILLIGAN Alexander
b. Lochwinnoch 1877
1st Scots Guards
Bristol C 97/98 16 SL
98/99 1 SL
99/00 1 SL
00/01 SL
01/02 SL
Third Lanark 02/03 3
Swindon T 03/04 SL
04/05 SL
Beith

MILLIGAN Dudley
b. Johannesburg 7.11.1916
Fordsbury Rangers (SA)
Dundee T
Clyde 37/38 10 9
Chesterfield 38/39 28 12 FL
39/40 2 1 FL
Linfield 41/42 IL
Distillery 42/43 IL
43/44 IL
Dundalk 43/44 LI
Larne T 45/46
Chesterfield 46/47 19 6 FL
Bournemouth 47/48 37 26 FL
48/49 8 FL
Walsall 48/49 5 1 FL
Ballymena U 49/50 IL

MILLIGAN George Ferguson

Carluke Milton R
Port Glasgow A 08/09 11

MILLIGAN Robert
K.I.A. 1915
Newton Villa
Clyde T 12/13 1
Pontypridd

MILLIKEN Alexander McKinlay
b. Kilmarnock 1914
Lesmahagow 32/33
Irvine Meadow 33/34
34/35
Kilmarnock 35/36 23
36/37 3
37/38 2
Morton 38/39 D2
Kilmarnock Jnrs

MILLIKEN Archibald Twaddle
b. Dennistoun 1909
Rutherglen Glencairn
Kilmarnock 32/33 28
East Fife T 33/34 D2
Dundee U 33/34 4 D2
Dumbarton 34/35 D2

MILLIKEN James

Third Lanark 93/94 1
Leicester F 94/95 FL
St Mirren 95/96 13 5
Tottenham H 96/97 19 6 SL
Clyde 97/98 6 2

MILLIKEN James D
b. Thurso c1884
Yoker A
St Mirren 06/07 2

MILLIKEN William

St Mirren 38/39 2

MILLOY Frederick Walker
b. Kilmarnock 1913 d. Kilmarnock 1979
Portland U
Kilmarnock Winton
Parkhead Jnrs
Kilmarnock 32/33 37
33/34 38
34/35 37
35/36 32 2
36/37 23
37/38 36
38/39 33 1
45/46 23
46/47 3
47/48 D2
St Cuthberts W

MILLS

Vale of Leven 90/91 10 3

MILLS

Renton 92/93 2

MILLS Hugh McMillan
b. Bonhill 9.3.1909 d. Carlisle 1.12.1949
Vale Oakdale
Renton Thistle
Vale of Leven Academy
St Anthonys 27/28
28/29
St Rochs 29/30
Bridgetown Waverley 30/31
Portsmouth T 31/32 FL
West Ham U 32/33 7 3 FL
Cannes L
West Ham U 33/34 4 1 FL
34/35 10 11 FL
Celtic 35/36 1
Luton T 36/37 2 FL
Carlisle U 36/37 11 5 FL
37/38 30 18 FL
38/39 13 5 FL
39/40 2 FL
Stranraer T 46/47

MILLS William 3 caps
b. Alexandria 28.1.1915
Bridgetown Waverley
Aberdeen 32/33 31 18
33/34 35 28
34/35 33 11
35/36 33 17
36/37 31 15
37/38 19 13
Huddersfield T 37/38 4 1 FL
38/39 23 6 FL
39/40 3 FL
Dumbarton
Clyde
Lossiemouth
Huntly

MILLSIP David

Hibernian 25/26 10

MILNE

St Mirren 92/93 5 2

MILNE

Third Lanark 92/93 3

MILNE

St Bernards 95/96 3 1

MILNE Alexander Auld
b. Edinburgh 1872 d. Ayr ?.10.1921
Third Lanark 96/97 5
97/98 10
98/99 17
99/00 2
Ayr Parkhouse

MILNE Alexander Simpson
b. Anderston 24.3.1915
Dunoon A
Third Lanark 35/36 5
36/37 18 9
Lille
Bournemouth 37/38 3 FL
Cowdenbeath 37/38 D2
38/39 D2
East Fife L 38/39 D2

MILNE Arthur
b. Brechin 1915 d. Edinburgh ?.5.1997
Brechin V
Dundee U 34/35 18 23 D2
35/36 27 32 D2
36/37 28 22 D2
Liverpool L
Hibernian 37/38 31 17
38/39 35 20
46/47 3 1
St Mirren 46/47 19 6
47/48 18 6
48/49 23 10
49/50 11 2
Coleraine 50/51 IL
51/52 IL
52/53 IL

MILNE Douglas
Broughty Ex-Servicemen
Arbroath 37/38 6 1
38/39 2 2

MILNE James
Hibernian 13/14 1

MILNE James Low
b. Newtyle 24.1.1911 d. Hinckley 13.12.1997
Lochee West Station
Dundee Arnot T
Dundee Violet T
Dundee U 30/31 36 5 D2
31/32 35 2
Preston NE 32/33 20 FL
33/34 38 FL
34/35 25 FL
35/36 39 1 FL
36/37 35 2 FL
37/38 36 2 FL
38/39 38 3 FL
39/40 3 FL
Wigan A 46/47 36 1 CCL
Morecambe 47/48

MILNE Thomas Aiken
b. Hebburn on Tyne
Hebburn A
St Mirren 06/07 1
07/08 23 8
08/09 27 6
09/10 26 12
10/11 29 3
11/12 24 1
Distillery 12/13 IL
13/14 IL
14/15 IL
15/16 IL
16/17 IL
17/18 IL
18/19 IL
Willowfield 18/19
? 19/20
Queens Island 20/21
Holyoke Falco 21/22

MILNE Victor Edmond
b. Aberdeen 22.6.1897 d. Birmingham 22.9.1971
Medical Corps
Aberdeen University
Aberdeen 19/20 6
20/21 31 1
21/22 37
22/23 36 2
Aston Villa 23/24 24 FL
24/25 21 FL
25/26 24 1 FL
26/27 35 FL
27/28 37 FL
28/29 16 FL

MILNE William
Hibernian 09/10 2
10/11 2

MILNE William
b. Montrose
Montrose
Glossop 10/11 4 1 FL
Blackpool 11/12 25 5 FL
Aberdeen 12/13 18 9
Third Lanark 13/14 16 8
Dundee 14/15 1

MILNE William
Dundee 29/30 11 3
30/31 3
31/32 3

MILTON James J
b. c1910
Vale of Earn
Kings Park 32/33 D2
33/34 D2
Falkirk 34/35 7
Kings Park 34/35 D2
35/36 D2
Dundee U 36/37

MIRK J
Clyde 97/98 3

MIRK James
St Mirren 92/93 16
93/94 16
Heart of Midlothian 94/95 16
95/96 17
96/97 11 1

MITCHELL
Dumbarton 95/96 1
96/97 4 ? D2

MITCHELL
Falkirk 17/18 1 ?

MITCHELL Alexander
Dundee 05/06 5
06/07 8 1
Clyde 06/07 3
07/08 5
Beith

MITCHELL Alexander
b. Kinghorn
Broxburn U
Dunfermline A 26/27 3
27/28 3
Leith A 28/29 D2
29/30 D2
30/31 26
31/32 2

MITCHELL Andrew
b. Airth 30.9.1878
Airth Castle R
East Stirlingshire
Kings Park
Falkirk 05/06 23 11
06/07 16 8
07/08 28 15
08/09
09/10 5 1
10/11
11/12
12/13 1
13/14 1

MITCHELL David 5 caps
b. Kilmarnock 29.4.1866
Kilmarnock Britannia
Kilmarnock A
Kilmarnock Britannia
Kilmarnock 86/87
87/88
88/89
Rangers 89/90
90/91 18
91/92 17
92/93 16 1
93/94 15 1
94/95 11 1
95/96 12 1
96/97 17 1
97/98 11 1
98/99 13
99/00 2

MITCHELL David
Falkirk 05/06 3
East Stirlingshire

MITCHELL Francis William
b. Elgin 25.5.1890
Foundry OB
Milngarvie Allander
Maryhill
Motherwell 11/12 2
12/13 3
Celtic L 12/13
Everton 13/14 13 FL
14/15 2 FL
19/20 8 FL
Liverpool 20/21 15 FL
21/22 3 FL
22/23 FL
Tranmere R 23/34 41 FL
24/25 14 FL
Bangor C
Blue Circle Cement

MITCHELL Gavin
Cowdenbeath 33/34 14

MITCHELL George
Pathhead Jnrs
Raith R 07/08 D2
08/09 D2
09/10 D2
10/11 3
Albion R 11/12 D2

MITCHELL George Henry
Queen's Park 38/39 3 1

MITCHELL Henry G K
Raith R
Heart of Midlothian 07/08 6

MITCHELL James 3 caps
b. Cumnock 1879 d. 1.4.1958
Crosshouse
Kilmarnock 00/01 3
01/02 18
02/03 19
03/04 10
Hurlford 04/05
05/06
Kilmarnock 06/07 27
07/08 33
08/09 30 4
09/10 32
10/11 33 2
11/12 28
12/13 26
13/14 34
14/15 24
15/16 35
16/17 21 1
17/18 30
18/19 6
19/20 1
20/21

MITCHELL J
b. Motherwell
Third Lanark 28/29 18
29/30
Glentoran 30/31 IL

MITCHELL John
b. Paisley 1.2.1885 d. Belfast 3.9.1937
Baillieston Thistle
Celtic 06/07 12
07/08 17
08/09 5
09/10 14
10/11 11
Forfar A L 10/11
Celtic 11/12 5
12/13 25
Cowdenbeath 13/14 D2
14/15 D2
15/16

MITCHELL John A
Aberdeen 16/17 1

MITCHELL Robert
Kilsyth R
Airdrieonians 30/31 1

MITCHELL Thomas
b. Govan 29.5.1904 d. Edinburgh 26.1.1973
Pollok Hawthorn
Petershill
East Fife 27/28 34 7 D2
Bethlehem Steel 28/29 ASL
East Fife 29/30 13 9 D2
30/31 9
31/32 8 3 D2

MITCHELL William
Glasgow Perthshire
Renfrew V
Heart of Midlothian 02/03 2
Abercorn 02/03
Falkirk 03/04

MITCHELL William
Port Glasgow A 07/08 4

MITCHELL William
b. Govan
St Anthonys
Celtic 18/19 5
Hamilton A L 18/19 1
Clydebank L 18/19 2 ?
Dumbarton L 18/19 4 ?
Partick T 19/20 16 1
Alloa A 20/21

MITCHELL William P
Auchinleck Talbot
Ayr U 37/38
38/39 5 1

MOFFAT A
East Kilbride Thistle
Albion R 22/23 2

MOFFAT Andrew Naysmith
b. Rosewell 5.9.1900 d. Dunfermline 27.1.1990
Glencraig R
Kinglassie U 16/17
Glencraig Celtic 17/18
Lochgelly U 19/20
East Fife 20/21
Everton 20/21 1 FL
21/22 FL
Wrexham 22/23 8 FL
East Fife 23/24 2 D2
Lochgelly U 24/25 D3
25/26 D3
26/27
Dunfermline A 27/28 1

MOFFAT W Alexander C
Queen's Park 01/02 13
02/03 7
Ayr

MOFFAT Joseph
b. Paisley 1875
Bo'ness
Abercorn 96/97 2 2
Bo'ness 96/97
Wishaw Thistle 96/97
St Mirren 97/98
Chatham 98/99 6 2 SL
Gravesend U 98/99 1 1 SL
Walsall 99/00 27 13 FL
Tottenham H 00/01 6 3 SL
St Mirren 01/02 15 4
02/03 20 9
Manchester C 03/04 4 2 FL
04/05 13 1 FL
05/06 3 1 FL
Kilmarnock 05/06 2
06/07 9 2
Nelson 07/08
Heart of Midlothian 08/09
Watford 08/09 18 1 SL
Aberdeen 09/10 14

MOFFAT William
b. Blackridge c1902
Harthill A
Hamilton A 22/23 26 7
23/24 32 9
24/25 30 3
25/26 31 13
26/27 31 10
27/28 28 13
28/29 35 5
29/30 38 14
30/31 31 15
31/32 19 6
Motherwell 31/32 11 8
32/33 16 6
Hibernian 33/34 24 8
34/35 25 8
Keith
Airdrieonians 36/37 D2

MOIR Alexander
b. Aberdeen
Mugiemoss
Aberdeen 21/22 3
22/23 7
23/24 21 2

MOIR Andrew
Yoker A
Hibernian 17/18 24 ?
Partick T 17/18

MOIR David
Abercorn 00/01 D2
01/02 D2
02/03 D2
Morton 02/03 1
Abercorn

MOIR James
Banks o'Dee
Aberdeen 16/17 16
Discharged Soldiers XI

MOIR James
Polmadie Hawthorn
Dunoon A
Cowdenbeath 33/34 1

MOIR James Galbraith
b. Bonhill 11.11.1879
Bonhill A
Vale of Leven
Celtic 98/99 1
99/00
Vale of Leven L 99/00
Blackburn R 00/01 32 FL
Celtic 00/01
01/02 8
02/03 19
03/04 6
Blackburn R 03/04 14 FL
04/05 18 FL
05/06 13 FL
Clyde

MOIR Robert Marshall
b. Maryhill 10.5.1904 d. Provan 1955
Vale of Clyde
Morton 24/25 14
25/26 8
St Johnstone
Luton T 26/27 1 FL

MOLLOY William Henry B
b. Barrow 1904
Dumbarton Harp 23/24 D3
24/25 D3
Celtic 25/26 5 2
Arthurlie L 25/26 D2
Celtic 26/27 2
Ayr U L 27/28 D2
Arthurlie L 27/28 D2
Dumbarton 28/29 D2
29/30 D2
30/31 D2
Yeovil T 31/32
Swansea T 32/33 10 2 FL
Bristol C 33/34 7 2 FL
Falkirk 33/34
Dumbarton T 34/35 D2

MONAGHAN Patsy
Maryhill
Raith R 15/16 27 3
16/17 5
Distillery 17/18 IL

MONTEITH Hugh
b. New Cumnock 14.8.1874
Wellington Thistle
Parkhead Jnrs
Celtic
Loughborough 95/96 30 FL
96/97 28 FL
Bristol C 97/98 22 SL
98/99 22 SL
99/00 26 SL
West Ham U 00/01 24 SL
01/02 29 SL
Bury 02/03 30 FL
03/04 13 FL
04/05 11 FL
05/06 23 FL
Kilmarnock 06/07 10
Beith 07/08
Morton
Dundee Hibs

MONTEITH John B
Queen's Park 11/12 3

MONTEITH William Arthur
Glasgow Perthshire
Queen's Park 03/04
Kilmarnock 04/05 21
05/06 19
Beith 06/07
07/08
Dumbarton 08/09 D2
Beith 09/10
Airdrieonians 09/10 4
Dundee U 10/11 17 D2
Albion R 11/12 D2
12/13 D2
13/14 D2
Abercorn

MONTGOMERY Archibald
b. Chryston 27.1.1873 d. ?.1.1922
Chryston A
Rangers 93/94 1
94/95 7
Bury 94/95 2 FL
95/96 29 FL
96/97 29 FL
97/98 24 FL
98/99 27 FL
99/00 16 FL
00/01 7 FL
01/02 29 FL
02/03 4 FL
03/04 21 FL
04/05 23 FL
Manchester U 05/06 3 FL
Bury

MONTGOMERY John
Motherwell 04/05 14
05/06 30
06/07 11
07/08
Port Glasgow A 08/09 10
09/10 20
Hamilton A 09/10 8
10/11 18
Stevenston U *

MONTGOMERY William
b. Gourock 1885 d. Oakland, USA 21.11.1953
Kilwinning R
Rutherglen Glencairn
Bradford C 05/06 15 3 FL
06/07 2 FL
Sunderland 07/08 2 FL
08/09 8 2 FL
Oldham A 09/10 28 16 FL
10/11 17 4 FL
11/12 25 6 FL
Rangers 12/13 7 2
Dundee 12/13 4
13/14 28 4
14/15 9
Stevenston U 15/16
16/17
Ayr U 16/17 13 1

MOODIE John
b. Dunfermline (?) 1919 d. 1.1.1994
Lochore Welfare
Heart of Midlothian 37/38 3
Raith R
Dunfermline A
East Fife
Cowdenbeath
Airdrieonians 46/47 24 D2
47/48 9
Cowdenbeath

MOONEY Angus

Club		Season	Apps	Gls	Lge
Baillieston *					
Clydebank *		26/27			D2
Alloa A *		27/28			D2
Glasgow Perthshire					
Morton		32/33	16		
		33/34			D2
		34/35			D2
		35/36			D2
		36/37			D2
		37/38	24	2	
East Stirlingshire		38/39			D2

MOONEY Hugh

b. Belfast 23.5.1907 d. Brandon ?.3.1975

Club		Season	Apps	Gls	Lge
Kilsyth Emmet					
Belfast Celtic		29/30			IL
Nottingham F		30/31			FL
Stenhousemuir		31/32			D2
Aberdeen		31/32	6		
		32/33	9		
Gillingham		33/34	4		FL
London Paper Mills					

MOONEY Patrick

Club		Season	Apps	Gls	Lge
Hibernian		16/17	12	1	
Vale of Leven		17/18			

MOONEY Thomas

b. Tollcross 31.10.1910 d. Carluke 15.12.1981

Club		Season	Apps	Gls	Lge
Kirkmuirhill					
Stonehouse Violet					
Royal Albert					
Larkhall Thistle					
Celtic					
Airdrieonians		31/32	2		
		32/33	35	7	
		33/34	34	11	
		34/35	37	13	
		35/36	37	6	
		36/37	9	5	D2
Newcastle U		36/37	20	2	FL
		37/38	17	5	FL
		38/39	38	10	FL
		39/40	1		FL
Morton					

MOORE James

Club		Season	Apps	Gls	Lge
Cadzow St Annes					
Hamilton A		21/22	3	1	
Dykehead					

MOORE John

b. Inkerman

Club		Season	Apps	Gls	Lge
Kirkintilloch Rob Roy					
USA					
Saltcoats V					
Aberdeen		25/26	5		
Crystal Palace		25/26	1		FL
Hamilton A		25/26	6		
		26/27	2		
Dundee U	L	26/27	1		
Arthurlie		26/27			D2

MOORE Patrick

b. Ballybough 4.8.1909 d. Dublin 24.7.1951

Club		Season	Apps	Gls	Lge
Clonliffe Celtic					
Bendigo		26/27			
		27/28			
Richmond R		28/29			
Shamrock R		28/29			LI
Cardiff C		29/30	1		FL
Tranmere R		30/31	4		FL
Shamrock R		30/31			LI
Brideville		31/32			LI
Aberdeen		32/33	29	27	
		33/34	29	17	
		34/35	8	1	
Shamrock R		35/36			LI
		36/37			LI
		37/38			LI
Shelbourne		37/38			LI
Brideville		38/39			LI
Shamrock R					

MOORE William

b. 1879

Club		Season	Apps	Gls	Lge
Strathclyde					
Third Lanark		00/01	2		
		01/02			
Arthurlie		02/03			D2

MOORE William

Club		Season	Apps	Gls	Lge
Benburb					
Airdrieonians		33/34	14	7	

MOORE William John

b. Ballyclare 2.8.1895 d. Ballyclare 16.8.1932

Club		Season	Apps	Gls	Lge
Ollardale					
Brantwood					
Glentoran		14/15			IL
		15/16			IL
		16/17			IL
		17/18			IL
		18/19			IL
		19/20			IL
		20/21			IL
Falkirk		20/21	16	1	
		21/22	34		
		22/23	35	4	
		23/24	32		
Lincoln C		23/24	1		FL
		24/25	32	2	FL
Ards		25/26			IL
Glentoran		26/27			IL
		27/28			IL
		28/29			IL

MORAN Hugh

Club		Season	Apps	Gls	Lge
Hearts of Beath					
Cowdenbeath		33/34	12		
Dumbarton		34/35			D2

MORAN Martin

b. Bannockburn 19.12.1879 d. c1950

Club		Season	Apps	Gls	Lge
Benburb					
Celtic		98/99	1		
Clyde		98/99	10	1	
Sheffield U		99/00	7		FL
Middlesbrough		00/01	33	5	FL
		01/02	3		FL
Millwall		02/03	27	5	SL
		03/04	30		SL
Heart of Midlothian		04/05	24	1	
Chelsea		05/06	33	5	FL
		06/07	19	2	FL
		07/08	10		FL
Celtic		08/09	2		
Hamilton A		09/10	20	1	
Albion R		10/11	2	?	D2

MORELAND A

Club		Season	Apps	Gls	Lge
Third Lanark		28/29	21		

MORELAND Andrew

Club		Season	Apps	Gls	Lge
Kirkintilloch Rob Roy					
Albion R		22/23	18	5	
Dykehead		23/24			D3

MORELAND Neil

b. Tarbrax

Club		Season	Apps	Gls	Lge
Pumpherston R					
Heart of Midlothian		13/14	3	1	
		14/15			
		15/16	2		

MORELAND Russell E

b. Glasgow

Club		Season	Apps	Gls	Lge
Queen's Park		22/23	20	17	D2
		23/24	25	3	
		24/25	27	3	
		25/26	37	1	
		26/27	5		
Heart of Midlothian		26/27	3		
Hamilton A		27/28	31	1	
Third Lanark		28/29			D2
		29/30			D2
		30/31			D2
		31/32	21		
		32/33	5		
Clyde		33/34			
		34/35			

MORGAN F (or Charles?)

Club		Season	Apps	Gls	Lge
Rutherglen Glencairn					
Clyde		99/00	9	3	

MORGAN F

Club		Season	Apps	Gls	Lge
Falkirk		30/31	25	13	

MORGAN Hugh

b. Shettleston 7.8.1874

Club		Season	Apps	Gls	Lge
Harthill Thistle					
Airdrieonians		94/95	1		D2
		95/96	1		D2
		96/97	12		D2
Sunderland		96/97	13	6	FL
		97/98	27	5	FL
		98/99	13	4	FL
Bolton W		98/99	12	6	FL
		99/00	30	10	FL
		00/01	4		FL
Newton Heath		00/01	20	5	FL
Manchester C		01/02	12	2	FL
Accrington S		02/03			
		03/04			
Blackpool		04/05	24	5	FL
Nrth Wingfield St Lawrence		05/06			
Hamilton A		06/07	22	11	

MORGAN Hugh 2 caps

b. Longriggend 20.9.1869

Club		Season	Apps	Gls	Lge
Longriggend W					
St Mirren		95/96	1		
		96/97	16	4	
		97/98	18	1	
Liverpool		97/98	4	2	FL
		98/99	32	8	FL
		99/00	23	4	FL
Blackburn R		00/01	29	8	FL
		01/02	29	7	FL
		02/03	21	4	FL
Dundee		03/04	18	4	

MORGAN Hugh

Club		Season	Apps	Gls	Lge
St Mirren		04/05	4		
Kings Park					

MORGAN James

b. Dunaskin d. ?.8.1944

Club		Season	Apps	Gls	Lge
Hamilton A		32/33	9		
		33/34	9		
		34/35	1		
		35/36	35		
		36/37	23		
		37/38	38		
		38/39	38		

MORGAN James

b. Freuchie c1915

Club		Season	Apps	Gls	Lge
Bowhill R					
Dundee		37/38	18		
		38/39	9		D2

MORGAN John

Club		Season	Apps	Gls	Lge
Edinburgh Emmet					
Third Lanark	T	22/23	1		
Clyde	T	23/24			
Ayr U		23/24			

MORGAN Lewis

b. Cowdenbeath 30.4.1911 d. Portsmouth 22.9.1988

Club		Season	Apps	Gls	Lge
Crossgates Primrose					
Lochgelly Celtic					
Bowhill R					
Dundee		31/32	28		
		32/33	38		
		33/34	37	2	
		34/35	37		
		35/36	3		
Portsmouth		35/36	15		FL
		36/37	25		FL
		37/38	42		FL
		38/39	41		FL
		39/40	3		FL
Watford		46/47	42		FL
		47/48	0		FL
Chelmsford C					

MORGAN Matthew Black Biggar

b. Glasgow 24.1.1900 d. Stockport 7.7.1985

Club		Season	Apps	Gls	Lge
Renfrew Jnrs					
St Mirren		24/25	12	2	
		25/26	26	2	
		26/27	20	3	
		27/28	26	3	
		28/29	16	1	
		29/30	11		
Bournemouth		30/31	7		FL
Ayr U		30/31	11	2	
Hibernian		30/31	2		
Glentoran		31/32			IL
Linfield	T	31/32			IL
Coleraine		32/33			IL
Shelbourne		33/34			LI

MORGAN Patrick

Club		Season	Apps	Gls	Lge
Partick T		16/17	4	1	

MORGAN Thomas

Morton 06/07 1
Abercorn

MORGAN Timothy
b. Airdrie
Armadale
Heart of Midlothian 26/27 9 5
27/28 22 17
28/29 11 4
29/30 8
Falkirk 31/32 30 26
32/33 16 6
Morton 32/33 8 8

MORGAN William Albert L
b. Old Hill 3.11.1891
Cradley Heath St Lukes
Birmingham 12/13 5 FL
13/14 13 3 FL
14/15 8 2 FL
Motherwell 16/17 25 6
Third Lanark L 16/17
Motherwell 17/18 30 6
18/19 8 1
Birmingham 19/20 28 6 FL
20/21 5 FL
Coventry C 20/21 29 7 FL
21/22 24 8 FL
Crystal Palace 22/23 29 7 FL
23/24 39 7 FL
24/25 8 FL
Cradley Heath St Lukes
Shrewsbury T

MORICE James

Third Lanark 99/00 1

MORRIS

Clyde 92/93 1

MORRIS

Leith A 92/93 7 2

MORRIS

Hibernian 30/31 1

MORRIS Archibald
b. Leith
Raith R 21/22 8
22/23 2
Alloa A 23/24 D2

MORRIS Charles

Parkmore
Dundee 02/03
03/04 1

MORRIS David Main Liston 6 caps
b. Leith 21.8.1899
Newtongrange Star
Arniston R
Raith R 19/20 1
20/21 18
21/22 42 1
22/23 36
23/24 25 1
24/25 34 3
25/26 19 1
Preston NE 25/26 20 1 FL
26/27 41 2 FL
27/28 42 4 FL
28/29 38 FL
29/30 5 FL
Chester 30/31 38 9 CCL
Dundee U 31/32 12
32/33 D2
Leith A 33/34 D2

MORRIS Hugh
b. Giffnock 19.11.1900
Rutherglen Glencairn
Clyde 15/16 31 4
16/17 29
17/18 17 ?
18/19 30 ?
19/20 41 9
20/21 24
21/22 15
Manchester C 22/23 26 FL
23/24 31 FL
Nottingham F 24/25 22 1 FL
Southend U 25/26 20 6 FL
26/27 33 1 FL
27/28 23 6 FL
28/29 41 1 FL
Newport Co 29/30 22 5 FL

MORRIS Peter
b. c1915
Alva Albion R
Dunfermline A 36/37 10

MORRIS William

Ardeer Thistle
Hurlford
Kilmarnock 22/23 2
Beith 23/24 D3
Brooklyn Wanderers 24/25 38 ASL
25/26 18 2 ASL
26/27 34 ASL
27/28 38 1 ASL
28/29 39 ASL
29A 14 ASL
Bridgeport Hungaria 29/30 3 ASL
New York Americans 31A 20 ASL

MORRISON

St Mirren 90/91 17 9
91/92 14 4

MORRISON

Third Lanark 90/91 4

MORRISON

Heart of Midlothian 92/93 3 1

MORRISON

Third Lanark 92/93 2
93/94 2 1

MORRISON

Dumbarton 95/96 1

MORRISON

St Mirren 96/97 2
97/98 1

MORRISON

Heart of Midlothian 03/04 1 1

MORRISON

Dumbarton 14/15 1

MORRISON Alexander
b. Campsie 5.9.1887
Kilsyth Emmet
Kirkintilloch Rob Roy
Ayr 06/07 D2
Celtic 06/07 1
Clyde 07/08 25 2
Ayr 08/09 D2
09/10 D2
Ayr Parkhouse 10/11 D2

MORRISON Allan S
b. c1921
Alva Albion R
Clyde 38/39 1

MORRISON Dugald M

Dumbarton Harp
Partick T 12/13 8 2
13/14 5
14/15 30
15/16 34 1
16/17 4
Vale of Leven 17/18

MORRISON Evelyn S
b. Wishaw
Hamilton Academy
Moorpark Amateurs
Motherwell T
Stenhousemuir 27/28 23 30 D2
Falkirk 27/28 12 15
28/29 33 43
29/30 13 13
Sunderland 29/30 11 5 FL
30/31 4 2 FL
Partick T 31/32 15 15
Falkirk T 32/33

MORRISON Frank
b. Falkirk 1874
Clyde 92/93 8
93/94 16 D2
94/95 14
95/96 8
96/97 5
Darwen 96/97 27 FL
Millwall 97/98 13 2 SL
98/99 5 SL
Luton T 99/00 13 FL
Barnsley 99/00 15 FL
00/01 32 FL
01/02 1 FL

MORRISON Harold
b. c1913
Queen's Park 32/33 1

MORRISON Herbert

Partick T 94/95 2 D2
95/96 11 1 D2
96/97 10 D2
Linthouse 97/98 D2
Partick T 98/99 1
Third Lanark 99/00 4

MORRISON James
b. Markinch
St Andrews U
Airdrieonians 29/30 7
30/31 35
31/32 12
32/33 19
East Fife 33/34 D2
34/35 D2
35/36 D2
Raith R 36/37 D2
37/38 34 D2
38/39 14

MORRISON James Orr

St Mirren 11/12 2 1
12/13
13/14 12
Falkirk

MORRISON John

Falkirk 07/08 4 1
08/09 11
09/10 3 1
10/11 28 6
11/12 19 2
12/13 22 2
13/14 12
14/15 20 6
15/16 3

MORRISON John
b. Kilsyth 9.11.1909 d. Croy 25.5.1992
Croy Celtic
Celtic 29/30
30/31 5
31/32 11
32/33 3
33/34 4
34/35 13 1
35/36 27
36/37 30
37/38 31
38/39 34

MORRISON John

Dunfermline A 35/36 9 7
36/37 13 6
Heart of Midlothian 37/38

MORRISON Malcolm M
b. c1918
Morriston Church
Third Lanark 35/36 7 3
36/37 3 1
37/38 7 3
East Stirlingshire 38/39 32 36 D2
Ayr U 46/47 D2
47/48 D2
48/49 D2
49/50 D2
Newton Stewart 50/51

MORRISON Robert Graham
b. Glasgow 15.1.1905 d. 19.12.1981

Club		Season	Apps	Gls	Lge
St Rochs					
Airdrieonians		32/33	38		
		33/34	26		
Southport		34/35	19		FL
Forfar A	T	35/36			D2
Falkirk	T	35/36			
Gateshead	T	35/36			FL
Dundee U		35/36	33		D2
Workington		35/36			
Albion R		36/37	23		
Workington					
Forfar A		37/38			D2
Glenavon		38/39			IL

MORRISON Thomas
b. Belfast 1874 d. Belfast 26.3.1940

Club	Season	Apps	Gls	Lge
Stormont				
Glentoran	90/91			IL
	91/92			IL
	92/93			IL
	93/94			IL
Burnley	93/94	4	1	FL
	94/95	3		FL
Glentoran	94/95			IL
Celtic	94/95	2		
	95/96	6	1	
	96/97	8	2	
Burnley	96/97	6	1	FL
	97/98	29	8	FL
	98/99	29	3	FL
	99/00	33	3	FL
	00/01	29	5	FL
	01/02	32	7	FL
	02/03	14	1	FL
Manchester U	02/03	20	6	FL
	03/04	9		FL
Colne	04/05			
Burnley	06/07	1		FL
Glentoran	07/08			IL

MORRISON Thomas Kelly 1 cap
b. Kilmarnock 21.7.1904

Club	Season	Apps	Gls	Lge
Troon A				
St Mirren	25/26	37	2	
	26/27	36	7	
	27/28	25	2	
Liverpool	27/28	15		FL
	28/29	42		FL
	29/30	36		FL
	30/31	39	1	FL
	31/32	35	1	FL
	32/33	32	1	FL
	33/34	33	1	FL
	34/35	8		FL
Sunderland	35/36	21		FL
Gamlingay				
Ayr U	37/38			
	38/39			
Drumcondra				

MORRISON William
b. West Benbar 25.6.1879 d. 19.2.1937

Club	Season	Apps	Gls	Lge
East Lanarkshire				
West Calder	01/02			
St Bernards	02/03			
	03/04			
Fulham	04/05	20	2	SL
	05/06	33	3	SL
	06/07	38	2	SL
	07/08	31	1	FL
	08/09	1		FL
Glossop	08/09	32		FL
	09/10	37	2	FL
Clyde	10/11	24	3	
	11/12	11	2	
Raith R	12/13	20	4	
	13/14	28		
	14/15	18		
Morton	15/16	36		
	16/17	31		
	17/18	31	2	
	18/19	5		

MORRISON William

Club	Season	Apps	Gls	Lge
Newton Villa				
Blantyre V				
Hamilton A	11/12	14		
	12/13	3		

MORRISON William

Club	Season	Apps	Gls	Lge
St Mirren				
Clydebank	23/24	2		

MORRISON William Cockburn
b. Musselburgh 3.7.1904 d. Stockport 1977

Club	Season	Apps	Gls	Lge
Musselburgh Bruntonians				
St Mirren	24/25	34		
Pembroke Dock				
Caernarvon T				
Stockport Co	28/29	2		FL
Stockport Borough Police				

MORTIMER Peter
b. Glasgow 17.8.1875 d. 1951

Club	Season	Apps	Gls	Lge
Elm Park				
Cowlairs				
Elm Park				
Northern				
Leith A	93/94	1		
Royal Arsenal	94/95	23	11	FL
	95/96	27	9	FL
Chatham	96/97	19	6	SL
	97/98	19	11	SL

MORTON

Club	Season	Apps	Gls	Lge
St Mirren	91/92	1		

MORTON

Club	Season	Apps	Gls	Lge
Ayr U	17/18	6	?	

MORTON Alan Lauder 31 caps
b. Partick 24.4.1893 d. 15.12.1971

Club	Season	Apps	Gls	Lge
Airdrie Academy				
Queen's Park	13/14	22	4	
	14/15	37	4	
	15/16	38	8	
	16/17	38	6	
	17/18	33	14	
	18/19	24	3	
	19/20	26	7	
Rangers	20/21	39	6	
	21/22	31	4	
	22/23	35	3	
	23/24	34	6	
	24/25	36	8	
	25/26	29	5	
	26/27	31	10	
	27/28	34	12	
	28/29	37	14	
	29/30	24	5	
	30/31	32	7	
	31/32	14		
	32/33	6	3	

MORTON Alexander

Club	Season	Apps	Gls	Lge
Cambuslang R				
Partick T	01/02	6	1	D2
	02/03	16		
Airdrieonians	03/04	6	2	

MORTON Archibald G
b. Glasgow

Club	Season	Apps	Gls	Lge
Queen's Park	23/24	10	1	
Rangers	24/25	1		
Hamilton A	25/26	6	1	
Morton				

MORTON Hugh

Club		Season	Apps	Gls	Lge
Galston					
Kilmarnock		99/00	4	1	
		00/01	5		
Galston	L	00/01			
Kilmarnock		01/02	15	5	
		02/03	20	1	
		03/04	17	3	
		04/05	18	1	
		05/06	14	1	
		06/07	19	2	
		07/08	14	1	
Morton		07/08	8	2	

MORTON Hugh

Club	Season	Apps	Gls	Lge
Darvel Jnrs				
Rangers	01/02	2		
Kilmarnock	02/03	20		
	03/04	20		
Galston	04/05			
Ayr Parkhouse				

MORTON Hugh Auld 2 caps
b. Newmilns 25.11.1902

Club	Season	Apps	Gls	Lge
Darvel Jnrs				
Kilmarnock	22/23	21	1	
	23/24	19		
	24/25	28		
	25/26	36	2	
	26/27	33	1	
	27/28	35	3	
	28/29	35	5	
	29/30	29	2	
	30/31	35	2	
	31/32	33		
Galston	32/33			
Morton	32/33	13	1	
Kilmarnock	33/34	22		
	34/35	3		
	35/36	10		
	36/37	1		

MORTON James
b. Leith 22.8.1885 d. Edinburgh 29.7.1926

Club	Season	Apps	Gls	Lge
Newtongrange Star				
Hibernian	06/07	13	6	
	07/08	12	3	
Bradford C	07/08			
Stoke	07/08			
Tottenham H	08/09	2		FL
Bo'ness	09/10			
St Bernards	10/11	20	?	D2

MORTON James
b. Cambuslang 1894

Club	Season	Apps	Gls	Lge
Cambuslang R				
Kilmarnock	14/15	4		
Linfield Swifts	14/15			
Army	15/16			
Linfield	16/17			IL
	17/18			IL
	18/19			IL
	19/20			IL
Rangers	20/21	1		
	21/22			
Airdrieonians	22/23	6		

MORTON James D

Club	Season	Apps	Gls	Lge
Queen's Park	23/24	5		
	24/25	1		

MORTON John

Club	Season	Apps	Gls	Lge
Abercorn	95/96	4	?	D2
	96/97	6	1	
Cambuslang	96/97			

MORTON John
b. Glasgow

Club	Season	Apps	Gls	Lge
Airdrieonians	19/20	5	1	
Albion R	20/21	4	2	

MORTON John
b. Kilmarnock 7.12.1899

Club	Season	Apps	Gls	Lge
Mossblown Jnrs				
Prestwick Glenburn R				
Clydebank	19/20	29		
	20/21	20		
	21/22	41		
Kilmarnock	22/23	23		
	23/24	38		
	24/25	1		

MORTON Robert M
b. Glasgow

Club	Season	Apps	Gls	Lge
Queen's Park	12/13	1		
	13/14	31	22	
	14/15			
	15/16	31	15	
	16/17	12	5	
	17/18	19	15	
	18/19	26	21	
	19/20	14	4	

MORTON W H

Club	Season	Apps	Gls	Lge
Morton	27/28	15		

MOTHERWELL James Oliver
b. Kelvin 1887

Club	Season	Apps	Gls	Lge
Yoker A				
Third Lanark	07/08	14	2	

MOULDS Francis J
b. Kilmarnock 13.10.1910 d. Kilmarnock 31.12.1958

Club	Season	Apps	Gls	Lge
Kilmarnock Academicals				
Cambuslang R	32/33			
St Johnstone	33/34	31	1	
	34/35	15		
	35/36	18		
	36/37	36		
	37/38	30		
	38/39	37	2	

MOUNTFORD Harry Washington
b. Hanley 1884
Hanley Swifts
Burslem Port Vale 03/04 7 2 FL
04/05 26 3 FL
05/06 33 16 FL
06/07 32 8 FL
Everton 07/08 10 3 FL
08/09 2 FL
09/10 12 2 FL
10/11 1 FL
Burnley 10/11 2 2 FL
11/12 10 6 FL
12/13 14 1 FL
13/14 2 1 FL
Third Lanark 13/14 21 3
14/15 24 1

MOWATT Magnus James
b. Fraserburgh 13.3.1917
St Francis
Morton Jnrs
Clyde 35/36 8 2
Dumbarton 36/37 D2
Brentford 37/38 FL
Lincoln C 38/39 6 1 FL
Morton
Clyde

MOYES David
b. Cowdenbeath 14.11.1895 d. 1984
Cardwell
Kingseat Jnrs
Leicester C T 19/20 FL
Raith R 19/20 8
20/21 34 2
21/22 33 1
22/23 36 1
23/24 33 1
24/25 37
25/26 36 3
Leicester C 26/27 3 FL
Cowdenbeath 27/28 34
28/29 35
29/30 34
East Fife 30/31 20
31/32 D2
Cowdenbeath 32/33 18
Rosyth Dockyard Rec

MOYES John
b. Fife
Hearts o'Beath
Dundee 16/17 5
Scots Guards
West Ham U 19/20 2 1 FL
Clackmannan 20/21

MOYES William
b. Glasgow
Bridgeton Waverley
Rangers 26/27 1
27/28 2
Albion R L 27/28 D2
28/29 D2
Third Lanark 29/30 D2
Partick T 30/31

MUIR
Motherwell 03/04 3

MUIR Archibald
b. Strathaven c1902
Larkhall Thistle
Ayr U 21/22 14 3
22/23 5
Queen of the South
Bathgate

MUIR Archibald
b. Strathaven
Third Lanark 28/29 37 4
Airdrieonians 29/30 13

MUIR D
Cambuslang 90/91 2 1
91/92 6

MUIR David
Preston NE
Third Lanark 98/99 9 4

MUIR David
b. Paisley c1914
Mossvale YMCA
St Mirren 31/32 5
32/33 2
33/34 9 1
34/35 3
35/36 D2
36/37 9
Dumbarton T 37/38 D2

MUIR E
Queen's Park 17/18 7 3

MUIR Forbes A
Queen's Park 24/25 3

MUIR Harry
Alloa A
Rangers 12/13 2
13/14 17
14/15 15
Renton 14/15
Rangers 15/16 30
Clackmannan
Raith R 16/17 25
17/18 15

MUIR J
Rangers 85/86
86/87
87/88
88/89
89/90
90/91 8
91/92 5 2
92/93 1
93/94 4
94/95
95/96 1

MUIR James
b. c1884
Muirkirk A
Hamilton A 06/07 11 1

MUIR James
Maryhill
Aberdeen 07/08 18 2
08/09 11 5
Retired for 4 years 09/10
10/11
11/12
12/13
Aberdeen 13/14 1

MUIR James
b. Longcroft 1904
Kilsyth R
Third Lanark 22/23 16
Solway Star
Third Lanark 23/24 5
24/25
25/26 D2
Bo'ness * 26/27 D2
Luton T * 27/28 10 FL
Bo'ness *

MUIR James
Dumbarton A
Raith R 27/28 17

MUIR James Shanks
b. Garngad
Montrose 29/30 D2
30/31 D2
Kilmarnock 30/31 13 1
31/32 10 1
32/33 9 2
Excelsior Roubaix
Margate 34/35
Dumbarton 34/35 D2

MUIR John
Heart of Midlothian 04/05 2
Middlesbrough

MUIR John
Falkirk 18/19 11 ?

MUIR John
Kilwinning R
Queen of the South 38/39 3

MUIR John Baker
b. Hamilton 18.11.1903
Ayr U
Queen of the South
Broxburn U 24/25 D2
Stockport Co 25/26 FL
26/27 FL
Dumbarton 27/28 D2
Armadale 27/28 D2
Falkirk 28/29 24 1
29/30 20
Luton T 30/31 4 FL
Bristol R 30/31 8 1 FL
31/32 13 2 FL
Bo'ness 32/33 D2
Arbroath 32/33 18 2 D2
33/34 34 1 D2
34/35 23 D2
East Stirlingshire 35/36 D2

MUIR Malcolm McKenzie
b. Campbelltown 20.1.1903
Kirkintilloch Rob Roy
Aberdeen 25/26 1
26/27 5
27/28 5
28/29 3
Peterhead 29/30
Northampton T 30/31 2 FL
Peterhead 31/32

MUIR Robert
Churches league football
St Mirren 30/31 1

MUIR Robert
b. St Ninians
Rutherglen Glencairn
Celtic T
Hamilton A T
Portsmouth 34/35 1 FL
Third Lanark 35/36 38
36/37 30
37/38 32
38/39 4
Rochdale

MUIR Robert Bruce
b. Kilmarnock 23.9.1876 d. Toronto 1953
Kilmarnock Deanpark
Clyde 96/97 7 2
Kilmarnock 97/98 9 5 D2
98/99 16 6 D2
99/00 16 2
00/01 20 3
Bristol R 01/02 25 3 SL
02/03 21 3 SL
Celtic 03/04 20 4
Notts Co 04/05 19 FL
Norwich C 05/06 32 5 SL
06/07 11 SL
07/08 21 SL
Toronto Eatonia

MUIR Ross
Hibernian 98/99 2

MUIR Thomas
b. Pencaitland
Tranent Jnrs
Airdrieonians 27/28 24 15
28/29 21 6
29/30 9 2
30/31 22 15
31/32 2
Bo'ness 32/33 D2
Chirnside U

MUIR William 1 cap
b. Ayr 22.9.1877 d. ?.10.1941
Glenbuck A
Third Lanark 95/96 3
Kilmarnock 96/97 12 D2
Everton 97/98 21 FL
98/99 33 FL
99/00 32 FL
00/01 34 FL
01/02 7 FL
Dundee 02/03 22
03/04 23
04/05 24
05/06 30
06/07 32
Bradford C 07/08 33 FL
Heart of Midlothian 08/09 33
09/10 26
Dundee Hibs 10/11
Dumbarton 11/12 D2

MUIRHEAD John

Duntocher Hibs
Partick T 00/01 9 3
01/02 22 12 D2
02/03 19 2
03/04 9 4
Clyde

MUIRHEAD John

Partick T 06/07 1
Dumbarton

MUIRHEAD Robert

Kilwinning R
Port Glasgow A 06/07 1
07/08

MUIRHEAD Thomas Allan 8 caps
b. Cowdenbeath 31.1.1897 d. ?.6.1979
Hearts of Beath
Hibernian 15/16 5 1
16/17 23 2
Rangers 17/18 7 5
18/19
19/20 34 10
20/21 19 4
21/22 36
22/23 31 4
23/24 27 2
24/25 12
Boston Wonder Workers 24/25 14 ASL
Rangers 25/26 27 2
26/27 24 3
27/28 26 1
28/29 28 6
29/30 20 1

MUIRHEAD William

St Bernards 95/96 3

MULHALL John
b. Dykehead 3.10.1902
Cleland
Burnley 23/24 FL
Dykehead 24/25 D3
Brighton 24/25 2 FL
Falkirk 25/26 21 5
Bethlehem Steel
Dykehead 26/27

MULHOLLAND David

Denny Hibs
St Mirren 17/18 2

MULLEN

Hibernian 08/09 1

MULLEN Matthew

St Mirren 93/94 18 10
94/95
95/96 11 2
96/97 16 7
97/98 15 2
98/99 8 5
Dunblane

MULLIGAN George

Clyde 14/15 14 5

MULROONEY John
b. Hamilton 1.8.1886 d. 26.7.1914
Cadzow Hibernian
Quarter Huttonbank
Burnbank A
Earnock R
Celtic 11/12 16
12/13 26
St Johnstone 13/14 19 D2

MULVEY Michael
b. Shettleston 3.7.1869
Drumpellier
Hibernian
Newcastle EE
Airdrieonians
Newcastle EE
Airdrieonians
Carfin Shamrock
Celtic 92/93 3 3
Dundee Harp

MUNN

Third Lanark 90/91 1

MUNN Stuart
b. Greenock 22.12.1872 d. Shotts 21.8.1959
Maryhill
Third Lanark 93/94 4
Burnley 94/95 2 FL
Grimsby T 95/96 28 FL
96/97 28 FL
97/98 7 FL
Manchester C 97/98 8 FL
98/99 7 FL
99/00 6 FL
00/01 FL
Watford 01/02 20 SL
02/03 16 SL
03/04 1 SL
Hitchin T

MUNNOCK John
b. Bannockburn 1901
Falkirk 23/24 2

MUNRO

Abercorn 91/92 9 1
92/93 10 2
93/94 9 ? D2

MUNRO Alexander Dewar 3 caps
b. Carridon 6.4.1912 d. Blackpool 29.8.1986
Bo'ness U
Champfleurie
Newtongrange Star
Linlithgow Rose
Heart of Midlothian 32/33 1
33/34 15 2
34/35 34 6
35/36 32 8
36/37 24 6
Blackpool 36/37 7 2 FL
37/38 42 4 FL
38/39 33 5 FL
46/47 24 3 FL
47/48 23 1 FL
48/49 8 2 FL

MUNRO Daniel
b. Peterhead 2.3.1887
Forres Mechanics
Celtic 07/08
08/09 18 6
09/10 7
10/11 5
Bradford PA 10/11 27 1 FL
11/12 21 1 FL
12/13 31 2 FL
13/14 6 FL
Port Vale 14/15 11 2 CL
Clydebank 18/19 1

MUNRO David
b. 1880
Petershill
Third Lanark 04/05 16 7
05/06 24 9
06/07 17 5
Notts Co 07/08 12 1 FL
Glentoran 08/09

MUNRO Donald

Forres Mechanics
Heart of Midlothian 08/09
09/10 1

MUNRO James

Port Glasgow A 08/09 22 1
09/10 18

MUNRO James

Dundee 09/10 2

MUNRO James Auchterlonie
b. Glasgow 20.5.1905 d. Liverpool 18.5.1978
Ardrossan Winton R
St Johnstone 25/26 14 1
26/27 35 29
27/28 22 18
Raith R L 27/28 17 1
St Johnstone 28/29 13 7
Cardiff C 28/29 11 2 FL
29/30 4 1 FL
Millwall 29/30 5 2 FL
St Johnstone 30/31 5 5 D2
Cork 30/31 LI
Reds U

MUNRO James B

Queen's Park 15/16 5 1

MUNRO John
b. Invergordon c1898 K.I.A. ?.5.1917
Aberdeen East End
Aberdeen 14/15 13
15/16 1

MUNRO John Scott
b. Burnside 13.8.1914
Burnside R
Dundee NE
Dundee Violet
Dundee 31/32 4
32/33 30 3
Birmingham T 33/34 FL
Heart of Midlothian 34/35
35/36 9 1
Hibernian L 35/36 10
Nottingham F 36/37 18 FL
37/38 34 FL
38/39 41 FL
39/40 3 FL

MUNRO Mungo W

Clyde 31/32 10 2
32/33 14 1

MURDOCH

Abercorn 90/91 2 1

MURDOCH Andrew C

Falkirk 05/06 14
06/07 3

MURDOCH George
b. Ayrshire
Lugar Boswell
St Bernards
Third Lanark 91/92 22 2
92/93
St Bernards 93/94 16
94/95 18 4
95/96 17
96/97 1

MURDOCH James

Albion R 94/95
95/96
Hibernian 95/96 1

MURDOCH John

Banknock Jnrs
Falkirk 19/20 6
20/21 4

MURDOCH John B

Douglasdale
Clyde 31/32 4 1
Larne 32/33 IL
Bo'ness 32/33 D2

MURDOCH John Livingstone 1 cap
b. New Stevenston 6.2.1901 d. ?.9.1962
Kirkintilloch Rob Roy
Airdrieonians 21/22 18 1
22/23 13 1
23/24 11 2
24/25 6 1
25/26 31 13
26/27 29 6
27/28 34 5
28/29 10
Motherwell 28/29 25 7
29/30 38 9
30/31 35 18
31/32 26 10
32/33 18 6
Dundee 33/34 37 10
Dunfermline A 34/35 16 1

MURDOCH Mungo

Kilmarnock A
Rangers 95/96 1

MURPHY

Vale of Leven 91/92 1

MURPHY

Third Lanark 92/93 1

MURPHY Arthur

Baillieston
Airdrieonians
Dundee
Bathgate L 10/11
Airdrieonians 10/11 19
11/12 31
12/13 31 1
13/14 22 1
14/15 30 1
Dumbarton 15/16 17

MURPHY Francis 1 cap
b. Gartcosh 6.12.1915 d. Airdrie 12.2.1984
Glenboig BG
Coatbridge BG
Croy Celtic
Celtic 32/33
St Roch L 32/33
Celtic 33/34 2 2
34/35 6 2
35/36 29 14
36/37 30 6
37/38 37 10
38/39 35 12
Limerick

MURPHY Hugh

Clydebank
Falkirk 15/16 16 3
16/17 16 1
17/18 7 ?
Dumbarton 17/18 1
Falkirk 18/19 3 ?
Dumbarton 18/19 8 ?
Clydebank 18/19

MURPHY James

Hibernian 97/98 1
98/99 2
Cowdenbeath

MURPHY James B
b. Possil 20.9.1897
Glasgow Perthshire
Abercorn L 15/16
Parkhead Jnrs
Celtic 20/21 18
21/22 10
22/23
Clydebank L 22/23
23/24 33
24/25
25/26 35
Glasgow Perthshire

MURPHY James J
b. Kilbirnie 25.1.1902
Glasgow Perthshire
East Kilbride Thistle
Parkhead
Celtic 21/22 4 2
22/23
Ayr U L 22/23
Celtic 23/24
Clydebank L 23/24 9
Ayr U 23/24 19
24/25 15
Mid Rhondda L 25/26
Charlton A 26/27 17 FL
Merthyr T T 27/28
Morton 27/28 D2
28/29 D2

MURPHY John
b. Airdrie ?.4.1896 d. Rotherham 28.11.1921
Airdrie Shamrock
Glasgow Ashfield
Croy Celtic
Hamilton A 16/17 33 3
17/18 25 7
18/19 11 1
Airdrieonians 18/19 1
Hamilton A 19/20 20 12
Bury 20/21 21 5 FL
Rotherham U 21/22 2 FL

MURPHY John
b. Govan 1898
St Anthonys
Heart of Midlothian 19/20 19 12
20/21 38 13
21/22 8 1
St Mirren L 21/22
Heart of Midlothian 22/23 16
23/24 33 6
24/25 21 7
25/26 7 2
Motherwell 25/26 13 3
26/27 5
Kilmarnock 26/27 16 4
27/28 29 6
Coleraine 28/29 IL
Ballymena 29/30 IL
30/31 IL
Shelbourne 31/32 LI
Ballymena 31/32 IL

MURPHY John S

Queen's Park 04/05 2
05/06 3

MURPHY Joseph
b. Stockton 1873
Hibernian 93/94 17 D2
94/95 16 D2
95/96 18 1
96/97 14 1
Stoke 97/98 30 FL
98/99 19 1 FL
Woolwich Arsenal 99/00 27 FL
Raith R

MURPHY Patrick

Hibernian 97/98 18

MURRAY

Vale of Leven 90/91 2

MURRAY

Abercorn 92/93 3
93/94 5 ? D2

MURRAY

Leith A 92/93 1

MURRAY

Third Lanark 17/18 1 ?

MURRAY

Clyde 18/19 1 ?

MURRAY

Raith R 19/20 1

MURRAY

Third Lanark 19/20 1

MURRAY Andrew
b. Newarthill
Falkirk 34/35 3
Glenavon 34/35 IL
35/36 IL
36/37 IL
Partick T T 37/38
Motherwell 37/38 9
38/39 28

MURRAY Arthur Farquhar
b. Aberdeen 1880 d. Inverness 27.7.1930
forfar A
Queen's Park 05/06 2
06/07 28 3
07/08 27 1
08/09 27 1
09/10 17 1
10/11 26
11/12 4

MURRAY Charles

Ferguslie
St Mirren 04/05 1

MURRAY Charles G

Kilmarnock 22/23 1

MURRAY David
b. c1892 d. Motherwell 24.7.1918
Slamannan
Vale of Clyde
Motherwell 13/14 12
14/15
15/16 20 1
16/17 24
17/18 31

MURRAY Donald
b. Walkerburn
Vale of Leithen
Peebles R
Ayr U 29/30 13 8
30/31 14 2
Peebles R L
St Bernards 31/32 D2
32/33 D2
33/34 D2
34/35 D2
35/36 D2
Peebles R 36/37

MURRAY Frank
b. Dundee
Dunfermline A
Dundee 16/17 21 2
17/18
18/19
West Ham U 19/20 2 FL
Dundee Hibs

MURRAY Fred

Perth Roselea
Cowdenbeath 32/33 20 6
Dundee U 33/34 5 D2

MURRAY George

Dundee 16/17 5

MURRAY George
b. Glasgow
Cambuslang R
Hibernian 22/23 17
23/24 25 3
24/25 12
Peebles R L 24/25 D3
Hibernian 25/26 29 5
26/27 22 1
27/28 37 5
28/29 13

MURRAY George
b. Stirlingshire c1907
Camelon
Falkirk 29/30 1
Armadale

MURRAY Herbert
b. Aberdeen 11.12.1886 K.I.A. ?.7.1918
Aberdeen University
Arbroath
East Stirlingshire 05/06
Clyde 06/07 24 3
07/08 22 2
Aberdeen 08/09 9 2
09/10 31 1
Queen's Park 10/11 11
St Johnstone 11/12 12 1 D2
Aberdeen 12/13 5 2
13/14 2
14/15
15/16
16/17 1

MURRAY Hugh

Kelty R
St Mirren 23/24 1

MURRAY Hugh

Cambuslang R
Motherwell 33/34 1
34/35
Airdrieonians 35/36 32 1
36/37 33 6 D2
37/38 31 8 D2
38/39 32 1 D2
Falkirk

MURRAY J

Motherwell 11/12 1

MURRAY James

Royal Albert
Rangers 97/98 3

MURRAY James Marshall
b. Kilmacrenan 14.3.1884
Shettleston
Distillery 04/05 IL
05/06 IL
06/07 IL
07/08 IL
08/09 IL
Motherwell 09/10 22 19
Sheffield W 09/10 8 2 FL
10/11 5 2 FL
Derry Celtic 11/12 IL
Motherwell 11/12

MURRAY John 1 cap
b. c1874 d. Hillhead 17.10.1933
Renton 91/92 20 2
92/93 14 4
93/94 17 1
94/95 12 ? D2
95/96 10 ? D2
96/97 ? ? D2
Dundee

MURRAY John
Newmilns
Riccarton Jnrs
Kilbirnie Ladeside
Kilmarnock 12/13 9
13/14 28
Galston L 13/14
Kilmarnock 14/15
15/16 12 1
Stevenston U
Galston 19/20
Queen of the South 19/20
20/21
21/22
Kilmarnock

MURRAY John
Renton
Dumbarton 13/14 9 6
14/15 6 1

MURRAY John
b. Edinburgh
St Rochs
Falkirk 24/25 5
25/26 15 2

MURRAY John Black Ritchie
b. Auchterderran 9.11.1915
Bowhill Jnrs
Hamilton A 34/35 1 1
35/36 1
East Stirlingshire 36/37 D2
Plymouth A 36/37 FL
37/38 FL
38/39 4 FL

MURRAY John James
b. Saltcoats 10.8.1908
Saltcoats V
Rangers 30/31 4
31/32 6 2
Newcastle U 32/33 26 1 FL
33/34 24 2 FL
34/35 34 7 FL
35/36 8 FL
Albion R 36/37 16 3

MURRAY Joseph
b. Uddingston c1914 d. ?.10.1990
Overton A
Hamilton A 32/33
33/34 23
34/35 12
35/36 11 1
Brentford 36/37 1 FL
37/38 FL
Partick T 38/39 1

MURRAY Michael
b. Stirling 3.11.1872 d. 31.1.1925
Campsie
Celtic 90/91
Glasgow Hibernian 91/92
Celtic 92/93 2
Abercorn 93/94
Johnstone
Campsie
Hibernian 94/95 3 ? D2
St Mirren 94/95 1
95/96 5 1
Johnstone 95/96
Hibernian 95/96 8 2

MURRAY P
Partick T 31/32
32/33 3

MURRAY Patrick 2 caps
b. Edinburgh c1868 d. ?.12.1925
St Patricks CYMS
Campsie
Hibernian 93/94 17 ? D2
94/95 16 ? D2
95/96 18 10
96/97 18 6
97/98 17 6
98/99 10 3
99/00 9 1
00/01 11 2

MURRAY Patrick
b. Currie 13.3.1874 d. Edinburgh 25.12.1925
Quarter Huttonbank
Royal Albert 95/96
Hibernian 95/96 8 2
Darwen 96/97 5 1 FL
East Stirlingshire 97/98
Preston NE 98/99 31 9 FL
99/00 20 3 FL
East Stirlingshire 99/00
Wishaw Thistle 99/00
Royal Albert 00/01
Nottingham F 00/01 12 2 FL
01/02 14 FL
Celtic 02/03 11 2
Portsmouth 03/04 19 3 SL
East Stirlingshire 04/05 D2
Royal Albert

MURRAY Peter
b. Aberdeen 1897
Aberdeen
Kilmarnock 19/20 6
20/21 11 3
21/22 14
Hurlford

MURRAY Robert
Dykehead
Airdrieonians 03/04 1

MURRAY Robert
b. Kilmarnock
Riccarton Jnrs
Kilbirnie Ladeside
Arthurlie
Aberdeen 04/05 20 D2
05/06 7
Forfar A 05/06
06/07
Kilmarnock 07/08 1

MURRAY Robert
Ayr U 13/14 2

MURRAY Robert A C
b. Livingstone
Niddrie Thistle
Bo'ness Cadora
Heart of Midlothian 34/35 2
Clyde 35/36 7
Dundee U L 35/36 21 1 D2
Winchburgh Jnrs 36/37

MURRAY Robert D
b. Newhaven 27.3.1915
Niddrie Strollers
Bo'ness Cadora
Newtongrange Star
Heart of Midlothian 33/34
Dunfermline A L 34/35
Heart of Midlothian 35/36 22 4
36/37 9
Manchester U 37/38 4 FL
Bath C 38/39 SL
Colchester U 38/39 21 4 SL

MURRAY Stephen
b. Dumbarton 1913
Kirkintilloch Rob Roy
Falkirk 32/33 17 2
33/34 23 1
34/35 22
Stenhousemuir 35/36 D2
Dumbarton 36/37 D2
37/38 D2
38/39 D2
Dunfermline A

MURRAY Thomas
Southend U
Portsmouth 03/04 18 4 SL
Parkhead
Maryhill
Partick T 08/09 20
? 09/10
10/11
11/12
Portsmouth 12/13 5 SL
Airdrieonians 12/13 5
13/14 15
Motherwell 14/15 9

MURRAY Thomas
b. Middlesbrough 7.4.1889 d. 1976
Middlesbrough 05/06 3 1 FL
06/07 10 1 FL
Aberdeen 07/08 32 14
Rangers 08/09 14 11
Aberdeen 09/10 15 6
10/11 29 9
Heart of Midlothian 11/12 28 12
12/13
Bradford C 13/14 6 1 FL
Hull C 13/14 2 FL

MURRAY Thomas
b. Auchtermuchty
Newburgh WE
Dundee 28/29
29/30 5
30/31 2
Newburgh WE
Raith R 33/34 D2

MURRAY William
b. Cheshire
Everton
Partick T L 12/13 5 1

MURRAY William
Loanhead Mayflower
Falkirk 18/19 3 ?
19/20 2

MURRAY William
St Mirren 21/22 1
Paterson Silk Sox 22/23 13 4 ASL

MURRAY William
b. South Church 1898
Bishop Auckland
Derby Co 20/21 31 3 FL
Middlesbrough 21/22 3 FL
22/23 12 1 FL
Heart of Midlothian 23/24 34 1
24/25 18
25/26 31 10
26/27 33 11
27/28 36 9
28/29 33 11
29/30 33 6
30/31 33 11
31/32 38 8
32/33 30 6
33/34 17 5
Dunfermline A 34/35 20 5
35/36 31 5

MURRAY William
b. Aberdeen 10.3.1901 d. Aberdeen 14.12.1961
Hall Russells
Aberdeen
Cowdenbeath 21/22
22/23
23/24
24/25 38 1
25/26 36
26/27 37 2
Sunderland 27/28 41 FL
28/29 32 FL
29/30 38 FL
30/31 32 FL
31/32 40 FL
32/33 31 FL
33/34 37 FL
34/35 32 FL
35/36 21 FL
St Mirren 36/37 11
37/38 38
38/39 26

MURRAY William Thomas

b. Alexandria 9.11.1904 d. 1940

Bonhill Celtic					
Vale of Clyde					
Clydebank		25/26	1		
Preston NE	T	25/26			FL
Clydebank		26/27			D2
New Brighton		26/27	2		FL
Liverpool		27/28	2		FL
		29/30	2	1	FL
Barrow		29/30	18	1	FL
		30/31	37		FL
		31/32	38	1	FL
		32/33	26	1	FL
		33/34	18	6	FL
Bristol R		33/34	21		FL
		34/35	19		FL
Folkestone					
Racing Club de Roubaix		37/38			

MUTCH Adam

b. Aberdeen 7.3.1901 d. Aberdeen 12.1.1930

Aberdeen BL					
Aberdeen		23/24	6	1	
Accrington S		24/25	40	7	FL
Lincoln C		25/26	8	2	FL
Forfar A		25/26			D2
Arbroath		25/26			D2
Walsall		25/26	4		FL
Montrose		26/27			D2
Marsh Lane Electric					
Banks o'Dee					

MUTCH Alexander

b. Aberdeen 9.12.1884 d. Newcastle 16.9.1967

Inverurie Loco					
Aberdeen		06/07	3		
		07/08	5		
		08/09	33		
		09/10	34		
Huddersfield T		10/11	28		FL
		11/12	13		FL
		12/13	37		FL
		13/14	32		FL
		14/15	28		FL
		19/20	35		FL
		20/21	41		FL
		21/22	15		FL
Newcastle U		22/23	15		FL
		23/24	19		FL
		24/25	2		FL

MYLES Matthew

Leith A					
Heart of Midlothian		97/98	1		

McADAM

Vale of Leven		90/91	3		
		91/92	6		

McADAM Peter

b. Glasgow 1897 d. Hillhead 1926

St Anthonys					
Rutherglen Glencairn					
Clydebank		19/20	16	1	
Lochgelly U					

McAFFREY Edward

Clydebank Jnrs					
Third Lanark		37/38	6		
		38/39	34		

McALLAN James

Rangers		95/96	1		
		96/97			
Kilmarnock		97/98			
Airdrieonians		98/99			
		99/00			
		00/01			
		01/02			
		02/03			
Leith A		03/04			

McALLISTER

Third Lanark		91/92	2		

McALLISTER Alexander

Bearsden RUFC					
Partick T		02/03	3	2	
Bearsden RUFC					
Queen's Park		03/04	17	5	
		04/05	3		
Partick T		05/06	1		

McALLISTER James

b. Newmilns

Newmilns					
St Johnstone		29/30	8	1	
Partick T		30/31	12		
		31/32	4		
		32/33	28		
		33/34	24	3	
		34/35	3		
Airdrieonians		34/35	12	5	
		35/36	36	1	
Dunfermline A		36/37	32	1	
Dumbarton		37/38			D2
		38/39			D2
Carlisle U					

McALLISTER John

b. Kilmarnock 8.1.1889 d. 9.11.1944

Riccarton Kirkstyle					
Riccarton Celtic					
Ardeer Thistle					
Kilmarnock		07/08	7		
		08/09	5		
		09/10	9	3	
Bathgate		10/11			
		11/12			
		12/13			
St Bernards		12/13			D2
		13/14			D2
Kilmarnock		13/14			
Galston		13/14			
Bathgate		14/15			
		15/16			
Armadale		15/16			
		16/17			
		17/18			
Arthurlie		17/18			
Kilmarnock		18/19	2		
		19/20			
		20/21			
Stevenston U					

McALLISTER Robert

Clyde		28/29	2		

McALLISTER William

b. Glasgow 1900

Milngarvie Allander					
Maryhill					
Hamilton A		16/17	15		
		17/18	22		
		18/19	15		
Renton		19/20			
St Mirren		20/21	4		
Johnstone	L	20/21			
Ebbw Vale		21/22			
Brighton		21/22	21	3	FL
		22/23	8	1	FL
		23/24	41	2	FL
		24/25	19		FL
Middlesbrough		24/25	15		FL
		25/26	18		FL
QPR		26/27	26	1	FL
Raith R		27/28	26		
		28/29	35		
Heart of Midlothian		29/30	1		
Dolphin		30/31			LI
		31/32			LI
Glentoran *		32/33			IL

McALPINE Andrew

b. Paisley 5.6.1888

Ayrshire jnr football					
St Mirren		07/08	4	2	
		08/09			
		09/10			
		10/11			
Alloa A		11/12			

McALPINE James B

b. London

Queen's Park		19/20	15	2	
		20/21	42	10	
		21/22	41	5	
		22/23	38	13	D2
		23/24	36	11	
		24/25	35	4	
		25/26	35	14	
		26/27	36	8	
		27/28	35	15	
		28/29	38	26	
		29/30	30	19	
		30/31	38	19	
		31/32	32	13	
		32/33	20	4	
		33/34	2		

McALPINE James Walker

b. Ravenscraig 5.2.1887 d. Wishaw 8.10.1946 (?)

Craigneuk Heatherbell					
Dalziel R					
Vale of Clyde					
Strathclyde Jnrs		09/10			
		10/11			
Southampton		11/12	33		SL
		12/13	36		SL
		13/14	31	1	SL
		14/15	32	1	SL
Kilmarnock		15/16	3		
Wishaw Thistle					
Millwall		19/20	31	1	SL
		20/21	17		FL
Gillingham		21/22	40		FL
		22/23	7		FL

McALPINE Thomas

Hibernian		24/25	7		
Tottenham H					

McALPINE William

Yoker A					
Motherwell		06/07	13	1	

McALPINE William F

Benburb					
Dumbarton		13/14	24		
		14/15	4		

McANDREW William

b. Kirkintilloch

Kirkintilloch Rob Roy					
Queen's Park		06/07	2		
		07/08	31		
		08/09	28		
		09/10	27		
		10/11	17		
Clyde		10/11	16		
		11/12	30		
		12/13	32	1	
		13/14	32		
		14/15	17		
		15/16	1		
		16/17	4		
		17/18	5	?	
		18/19			
		19/20	22		
Third Lanark		19/20	10		
		20/21	40	1	
		21/22	7	1	

McARDLE John

b. Gorbals 1905

St Francis Jnrs					
St Anthonys		23/24			
		24/25			
		25/26			
Celtic		26/27	1		
St Rochs					
Blantyre Celtic					
St Francis Jnrs					
Rothesay Royal V					

McARDLE Patrick

Cambuslang Hibs					
Falkirk		05/06	5	2	
Broxburn Shamrock		06/07			
		07/08			
Bathgate		07/08			
Dumbarton Harp		07/08			
Bathgate		08/09			
Dumbarton Harp		09/10			
Watford		09/10	1		SL
		10/11	10		SL
Dumbarton Harp		11/12			
Broxburn Shamrock		12/13			
Pontypridd					

McARTHUR Daniel 3 caps

b. Old Monkland 9.8.1867 d. Shettleston 11.11.1943

Parkhead Star					
Parkhead Jnrs					
Cowlairs	T	91/92			
Celtic		92/93	1		
		93/94			
		94/95	14		
		95/96	17		
		96/97	11		
		97/98	17		
		98/99	15		
		99/00	11		
		00/01	17		
		01/02	1		
		02/03			
Clyde		03/04			D2
Queen's Park		04/05			

McARTHUR Edward Stanley Smith

b. Cowdenbeath 30.4.1908

Edinburgh Emmet					
Crossgates Primrose					
Raith R		29/30			D2
Alloa A					
Crossgates Primrose					
Raith R		33/34			D2
Middlesbrough		33/34			FL
Exeter C		34/35	15	5	FL
		35/36	8	2	FL
Dawlish					
Torquay U		36/37	14		FL
Bath C		37/38			SL
Raith R		38/39	16	3	

McARTHUR John

Strathclyde					
Clyde		27/28	2		

McARTHUR John C

Queen's Park		04/05	1		
Falkirk		05/06	17		
		06/07	2		
Partick T		06/07	8		
Rangers		07/08	6		
		08/09	3		
Bathgate		09/10			

McARTHUR John C

Third Lanark		10/11	1		

McARTHUR Peter

b. Campbelltown

Port Glasgow Jnrs					
Morton		29/30	3		
		30/31			
		31/32	1		
		32/33	17		
		33/34			D2
Motherwell		34/35	3		
		35/36			
		36/37	30		
		37/38	29		
Clyde		38/39			

McARTHUR Robert

Shotts U					
Motherwell		08/09	17	1	

McARTHUR William

b. Lintmill 17.8.1870

Renton Union					
Sunderland A					
Middlesbrough I					
Bolton W		93/94	19	6	FL
Leicester F		94/95	28	16	FL
		95/96	27	11	FL
Dundee		96/97	11	4	
		97/98	14	1	
Brighton U		98/99	20	11	SL
		99/00	12		SL
Worthing					

McATEE Andrew 1 cap

b. Cumbernauld 2.7.1888 d. Condorrat 15.7.1956

Croy Celtic					
Mossend Hibernian		10/11			
Celtic		10/11	17	6	
		11/12	32	6	
		12/13	32	4	
		13/14	36	7	
		14/15	38	9	
		15/16	34	11	
		16/17	32	4	
		17/18	28	5	
Ayr U	L	17/18	1	?	
Celtic		18/19	13	4	
		19/20	22	4	
		20/21	29	4	
		21/22	37	5	
		22/23	28	1	
		23/24	28	2	
New Bedford Whalers		25/26	3	1	ASL
Newark Skeeters		25/26	4		ASL

McATEE R

Falkirk		38/39	1		

McATEER Thomas

b. Smithson 18.11.1881

Kilsyth W					
Smithson Hibernian		97/98			
Bolton W		98/99	8	3	FL
		99/00	17	5	FL
		00/01	29	2	FL
		01/02	5		FL
West Ham U		02/03	13		SL
Brighton		03/04	33	6	SL
Dundee		04/05	22	3	
		05/06	4		
Carlisle U		06/07			
Clyde	L	06/07	24	4	
		07/08	8	2	
Carlisle U		07/08			
Clyde		08/09	30	4	
		09/10	26	2	
Celtic		10/11	13	3	
		11/12	11	1	
Wishaw Thistle		11/12			
Albion R		12/13			D2
Abercorn		13/14			D2
Broxburn U		14/15			
Cameron Highlanders					

McAULAY

Renton		92/93	1		

McAULAY Andrew

Camelon					
East Stirlingshire		32/33	19	3	

McAULAY Archibald

Maryhill					
Raith R		09/10			D2
		10/11	29	9	
		11/12			
Abercorn		12/13			D2
Dumbarton Harp					
Vale of Leven		21/22			D2
Johnstone		21/22			D2

MacAULAY Archibald Renwick 7 caps

b. Falkirk 30.7.1915 d. Knowle 10.6.1993

Comely Park					
Laurieston Villa					
Camelon Jnrs					
Rangers		34/35	16	4	
		35/36	6	1	
		36/37	9	1	
West Ham U		37/38	39	10	FL
		38/39	36	16	FL
		39/40	3		FL
		46/47	8	3	FL
Brentford		46/47	26	2	FL
Arsenal		47/48	40		FL
		48/49	39	1	FL
		49/50	24		FL
Fulham		50/51	29	2	FL
		51/52	19	2	FL
		52/53	1		FL
Guildford C		53/54	32	4	SL
		54/55	24	4	SL
		55/56	5	2	SL

McAULAY Frank

Dunoon A					
St Mirren		33/34	5		
		34/35	1		

McAULAY James

Morton		18/19	18	6	
		19/20	12	1	

MACAULAY James Lowry

b. Portarlington 24.11.1889 d. Preston 8.10.1945

Cloughfern					
Cliftonville Olympic					
Cliftonville		07/08			IL
		08/09			IL
		09/10			IL
Rangers		10/11	1		
Huddersfield T		10/11	24	6	FL
		11/12	35	11	FL
		12/13	26	13	FL
		13/14	10	2	FL
Preston NE		13/14	22	8	FL
		14/15	37	16	FL
Belfast Celtic	L	17/18			IL
Leicester C		19/20	19	2	FL
Grimsby T		20/21	16	4	FL
Lancaster T		21/22			
		22/23			
Morecambe		23/24			

McAULAY John

Glasgow Perthshire					
Airdrieonians		09/10	8		

McAULAY William

b. Glasgow 1.11.1879 d. Scotland

Cambuslang Hibernian					
Celtic		98/99	1	1	
Sheffield W		98/99			FL
Dundee		98/99			
Walsall		99/00	24	7	FL
Aston Villa		00/01	5		FL
Portsmouth		01/02	11	5	SL
Middlesbrough		02/03	20	2	FL
Aberdeen		03/04	20	13	D2
		04/05	19	3	D2
		05/06	24	4	
Falkirk		06/07	23	4	
Hibernian		06/07	2		
		07/08	4	1	
		08/09			
Alloa A		09/10			

McAULEY

St Mirren		90/91	17	2	
		91/92	4		

McAULEY James

St Mirren		20/21	3		

McAULEY John

Glenbuck Cherrypickers					
Heart of Midlothian		08/09	3		

MACAULEY Robert 2 caps

b. Wishaw 28.8.1904 d. Edinburgh 1993

Bellshill					
Carsteel (Montreal)		20/21			
		21/22			
Grenadier Guards		22/23			
Providence Clamdiggers		25/26	35	1	ASL
		26/27	34		ASL
		27/28	23		ASL
Fall River Marksmen		27/28	32		ASL
		28/29	45	6	ASL
		29/30	26		ASL
Clyde	T	30/31			
Rangers		30/31	3		
		31/32	36		
Chelsea		32/33	10		FL
		33/34	13		FL
		34/35	38	1	FL
		35/36	5		FL
Cardiff C		36/37	4		FL
Sligo R		37/38			LI
Workington		38/39			
Raith R					

McAULEY William

Leith A					
Dundee		03/04	2		
Leith A	L	04/05			D2

McAVOY Douglas Haig

b. Kilmarnock 29.11.1918 d. Kilmarnock 15.4.1988

Kilmarnock Academicals					
Cumnock Jnrs					
Kilmarnock		36/37	1		
		37/38	26	5	
		38/39	32	7	
		45/46	8	2	
		46/47	17	5	
		47/48	10	3	
Liverpool		47/48	1		FL
		48/49	1		FL
Queen of the South		48/49			
		49/50	15	2	
		50/51			D2

McAVOY Michael

St Mirren		96/97	18	1	
		97/98	14		
		98/99	18	2	
		99/00	6		
		00/01	20		
		01/02	18		
		02/03	22	1	
		03/04	26		
		04/05	20		
		05/06	27	2	
		06/07	31	2	
		07/08	26	2	
		08/09	17		
Abercorn		09/10			D2

McAVOY Richard
b. Paisley
Kilbarchan A
St Mirren 19/20 10
20/21 7
St Bernards 21/22 D2

McAVOY Robert
b. Stevenston
Irvine Meadow
St Mirren 25/26 1
26/27 3
Raith R 26/27 D2
? 27/28
28/29
29/30
Saltcoats V 30/31

McBAIN A
St Mirren 90/91 14
91/92 1

McBAIN Edward 1 cap
b. Paisley
St Mirren 87/88
88/89
89/90
90/91 17 1
91/92 22 2
92/93 14
93/94 18
94/95 18
95/96 16
96/97 14
97/98 17 2
98/99 1

McBAIN John
b. Leith
Bo'ness
Ayr U 29/30 8
30/31 9

MacBAIN Laurence Durkie
b. Dundee 1907 d. Dundee 20.9.1937
Queen's Park 24/25 2
25/26 17 4
26/27 24 17
St Johnstone 27/28 16 6
28/29 8 3
Raith R L 28/29 6 1
St Johnstone 29/30 19 4
30/31 36 1 D2
31/32 16 2 D2
32/33 10
Dundee U 33/34 15 3 D2

McBAIN Neil 3 caps
b. Campbelltown 15.11.1895 d. Ayr 13.5.1974
Campbelltown A
Hamilton A T
Ayr U 14/15 1
15/16 7 2
16/17
17/18
18/19 29 8
19/20 35 1
20/21 27
21/22 18
Kilmarnock T 21/22
Third Lanark T 21/22
Manchester U 21/22 21 FL
22/23 21 2 FL
Everton 22/23 15 FL
23/24 37 FL
24/25 35 FL
25/26 10 1 FL
St Johnstone 26/27 27 4
27/28 11
Liverpool 27/28 10 FL
28/29 2 FL
Watford 28/29 27 2 FL
29/30 33 2 FL
30/31 25 1 FL
New Brighton 46/47 1 FL

McBAIN W
St Mirren 90/91 5 1

McBAIN W
Rangers 91/92 3 2

McBEAN James L
Ayr 05/06 D2
06/07 D2
07/08 D2
Queen's Park 08/09 4
09/10 17
10/11 25
11/12
Kilmarnock L 11/12
Queen's Park 12/13 24
Stevenston U
Queen's Park
St Mirren 18/19 6 ?

McBEAN Robert C
Queen's Park 14/15 6 1
St Mirren 15/16 1 1
16/17
Linfield 17/18
18/19
Partick T 18/19 1
Linfield 20/21 IL
Hamilton A 20/21 5

McBEATH Alexander
b. West Calder
Broomhill
Raith R 21/22 2
22/23 6
23/24 12
St Bernards 24/25 D2

McBETH John
b. Glasgow
Pollok Jnrs
Albion R 21/22 2
22/23 18

McBIRNIE William Samuel
Derry Celtic 07/08
Linfield 08/09 IL
St Mirren 08/09 1
09/10 12
Derry Celtic 09/10 IL
10/11 IL
11/12 IL
12/13 IL
Johnstone 13/14 D2

McBLANE James
Cowlairs 94/95 6 ? D2
St Mirren 94/95 5
95/96 12 1
96/97 15 1
97/98 16
98/99 17

McBOYLE James
b. Aberdeen
Aberdeen 21/22 1
22/23 3
23/24 8
St Johnstone 24/25 23
25/26 2

McBRIDE Alex
Port Glasgow A
Morton 15/16 2
Partick T 15/16
Dumbarton Harp L 15/16
16/17

McBRIDE Edward
Hamilton A 11/12 4
12/13 17 5
13/14 5 1
14/15
St Mirren 15/16 1 1

McBRIDE Hugh
Ayr U Jnrs
Ayr U 13/14 1
Girvan A 14/15
Prestwick Glenburn R

McBRIDE Hugh
East Fife
Dumbarton 21/22 11
Plymouth A FL
East Fife 22/23 D2
23/24 D2
Raith R 24/25 1
Hamilton A 24/25 9
Dundee U 25/26 20
East Fife 26/27 D2

McBRIDE James
b. Renton 30.12.1873
Renton W
Renton 91/92 22 1
Liverpool 92/93 20 4 LL
93/94 25 3 FL
94/95 5 FL
Manchester C 94/95 17 1 FL
95/96 25 FL
96/97 28 FL
Ashton NE

McBRIDE James
Kilbarchan
Morton 02/03 1 1
03/04 5 1
Kilbarchan

McBRIDE Patrick
Dundee 12/13 1

McBRIDE William
Ayr Parkhouse 07/08 D2
Clyde 08/09 2

McBRYDE Thomas Hardy W
Solway Star
Clyde 29/30 1

McBRYER James
Queen's Park 14/15 1
15/16
16/17 3

McCABE James
b. Paisley 1907
Kilbirnie Ladeside
Hamilton A 26/27 13 2
27/28 1
28/29 8
Barrow 29/30 12 FL
East Stirlingshire 30/31 D2
31/32 D2
32/33 36 1
St Mirren 33/34 17
34/35 14 1
Babcock & Wilcox 35/36

McCABE Patrick
Laurieston Villa
East Stirlingshire 11/12 D2
12/13 D2
13/14 D2
14/15 D2
Celtic 15/16 2
East Stirlingshire L 15/16
Vale of Leven L 15/16
East Stirlingshire 19/20
Banknock Jnrs 20/21

McCAFFER James
Kirkintilloch Rob Roy
Dundee U 31/32
Kirkintilloch Rob Roy
Airdrieonians 35/36 37 1
36/37 D2
37/38 34 1 D2
38/39 15 D2

McCAFFERTY James
b. Beith 1900
Wishaw Jnrs
Larkhall Thistle
Duntocher Hibs
Shieldmuir Celtic
Motherwell 24/25 8
25/26 11
Halifax T 25/26 1 FL
26/27 19 6 FL
Brentford 27/28 1 FL
28/29 FL
Gillingham 29/30 14 FL
Vale of Leithen

McCAFFERTY William
b. Rutherglen 9.12.1882
Rutherglen Glencairn
Celtic 01/02
02/03 1
Bolton W 02/03 8 FL
Stenhousemuir 03/04
Dunfermline A 04/05
Bathgate 05/06
Reading 05/06 19 13 SL
06/07 12 5 SL
Birmingham 06/07 4 FL
Bathgate 07/08
Portsmouth 07/08 14 6 SL
08/09 28 7 SL
09/10 5 SL
Brentford 09/10 16 3 SL
Bathgate 10/11

McCAIG Alexander Reid
b. Larbert 18.10.1895
Larbert Central
Law Volunteers
Newarthill Thistle
Falkirk 18/19 4
Alloa A 19/20
Stenhousemuir 20/21
Coventry C 21/22 10 2 FL
Reading 22/23 17 2 FL
Cowdenbeath 23/24 D2
Stenhousemuir 23/24 D2
24/25 D2
25/26 D2
26/27 D2
27/28 D2
St Bernards 28/29 D2
Stenhousemuir 28/29 D2

McCAIG David
b. Carluke 26.11.1906
Law Scotia
Raith R 26/27 D2
27/28 11
Bristol R 28/29 8 FL
29/30 7 FL
30/31 FL
East Fife 31/32 6 D2

McCAIG James

Bellshill A
Partick T 13/14 19
Wishaw Thistle 14/15
15/16

McCALL

Morton 21/22 1

McCALL Adam

Partick T 05/06 4 2
Ayr Parkhouse 05/06
Nithsdale W

McCALL Andrew Johnstone
b. Cumnock 12.10.1908
Cumnock Juveniles
Cumnock Townend Thistle
Ayr U 27/28 4 D2
28/29 19 3
29/30 20 2
30/31 37 2
31/32 37 4
32/33 36 3
33/34 30 2
34/35 34 11
35/36 11 3
St Johnstone 35/36 18 11
36/37 36 28
37/38 38 20
38/39 25 21
Huddersfield T 38/39 5 FL
Nottingham F 39/40 3 1 FL
Huntly

McCALL Archibald 1 cap
b. Renton 8.5.1867 d. Dumbarton 17.4.1936
Renton 84/85
85/86
86/87
87/88
88/89
89/90
90/91
91/92 21
92/93 14
93/94 17
94/95 14 ? D2

McCALL D

Third Lanark 95/96 1 1

McCALL James 5 caps
b. Renton 2.3.1865 d. Millburn 16.2.1925
Renton 82/83
83/84
84/85
85/86
86/87
87/88
88/89
89/90
90/91
91/92 22 5
92/93 16 7
93/94 16 5
94/95 1 ? D2

McCALL James F
b. Cumnock
Cumnock Jnrs
Kilmarnock 25/26 13 4
26/27 10 2
Alloa A 27/28 D2
28/29 D2
Cumnock Jnrs 29/30
30/31
31/32
Lugar Boswell

McCALL John
b. Muirkirk 1877
Murikirk A
Strathclyde
Kilmarnock Dean Park
Hibernian 01/02 12 1
Bristol R 02/03 7 SL
Notts Co 03/04 3 FL

McCALL Patrick

Motherwell
Hibernian 95/96 8
96/97 16
97/98 16
98/99 15
99/00 1

McCALL Thomas

Queen of the South 32/33 ? 32 D2
33/34 11 4
Ayr U 34/35 6 1

McCALLUM

Vale of Leven 90/91 1

McCALLUM Alexander

Glasgow Ashfield
Motherwell 05/06 23
06/07 29 1
07/08 15 1

McCALLUM Cornelius Joseph 1 cap
b. Bonhill 3.7.1868 d. Glasgow 5.11.1920
Renton A
Renton
Rangers L 87/88
Celtic 88/89
89/90
Blackburn R 89/90 2 FL
Celtic 90/91
91/92 20 10
Nottingham F 92/93 19 5 FL
93/94 18 5 FL
Loughborough 94/95 FL
Newark T
Notts Co 95/96 13 3 FL
Heanor T 96/97
Middleton 97/98
Folkestone 98/99
99/00
00/01
01/02
02/03
Gravesend U 03/04
04/05
Celtic

McCALLUM Denis
b. Alexandria 4.5.1908
Dumbarton St Patricks
Bonhill Celtic
St Anthonys 25/26
Dumbarton
Celtic 26/27 3
27/28 1
Clydebank L 27/28 D2
Nithsdale W L 27/28
Celtic 28/29 22 2
29/30 11
30/31 2 2
Dundee U L 30/31 24 9 D2
St Bernards L 30/31 D2
Celtic 31/32 1
Glentoran 32/33 IL
Bangor 32/33 IL
Coleraine 32/33 IL
33/34 IL
Sligo R 34/35 LI

McCALLUM Donald
b. Scotland c1880
Strathclyde Jnrs
Queen's Park 00/01
01/02
Liverpool 02/03 1 FL
Morton 03/04 21
04/05 5
Sunderland 04/05 3 FL
Middlesbrough 04/05 19 FL
05/06 6 FL
Port Glasgow A 05/06 1
Kilmarnock 05/06 2
06/07 20
07/08 3
Renton 08/09
Lochgelly U 09/10
East Fife
Mid Rhondda 13/14
East Fife 14/15

McCALLUM Hugh

Queen's Park 10/11 1

McCALLUM William

Carnoustie Panmure
YM Anchorage
Dundee U
Arbroath 30/31 2 D2
Dundee U 30/31 17 D2
31/32 3
Brechin C

McCALLUM William Donald
b. Kilbirnie 24.10.1870
Wishaw Thistle
Elm Park
Dumbarton A
Hibernian
Celtic 90/91 1
WBA 91/92 FL
Dumbarton
Wishaw Thistle
Dundee Harp 93/94
Coatdyke Gaelic

McCAMON Patrick Logan
b. Kilmarnock 23.5.1912
Irvine V
Largs Thistle 34/35
St Mirren 35/36 D2
36/37 14 3
Barrow 37/38 7 1 FL
Dundee U 38/39 3 D2

McCANDLESS John
b. Coleraine 29.2.1892 d. Coleraine 12.10.1940
Coleraine Alexandra
Belfast Celtic 11/12 IL
Linfield 11/12 IL
Bradford PA 11/12 4 1 FL
12/13 16 3 FL
13/14 28 5 FL
14/15 38 5 FL
Hibernian L 17/18 20 ?
Linfield L 18/19 IL
Bradford PA 19/20 36 5 FL
20/21 34 2 FL
21/22 29 2 FL
22/23 4 FL
Accrington S 23/24 2 FL
Barn 23/24 IL
Mid Rhondda
Lovells A
Coleraine 27/28 IL
28/29 IL

McCANDLESS William
b. Portglenone 20.12.1892 d. Corkett 18.7.1955
Ligoniel
Barn A
Linfield 15/16 IL
16/17 IL
17/18 IL
18/19 IL
19/20 IL
Rangers 20/21 26
21/22 41 1
22/23 22
23/24 33
24/25 32 5
25/26 7 1
26/27 22 1
27/28 17
28/29
29/30 2
Ballymena 30/31 IL
31/32 IL
32/33 IL

McCANN
Clyde 92/93 2 1

McCANN Daniel
b. Hurlford 18.3.1888
Hurlford Thistle
Galston 06/07
Nithsdale W 07/08
Hurlford Thistle 07/08
Dundee 08/09 7 1
09/10 10 4
Celtic 10/11 7 1
Ayr U L 10/11 D2
Dundee Hibs 10/11 D2
Nottingham F 11/12 1 FL
Hurlford A 11/12
12/13
13/14
Galston 13/14
Dundee 14/15 4 2
15/16
16/17
17/18 12 1

McCANN Edward
Broxburn Shamrock 89/90
Bathgate R 90/91
Newcastle EE 90/91
Broxburn Shamrock 91/92
Celtic 92/93 1
Broxburn Shamrock

McCANN Henry
b. Falkirk 1889
Glasgow Ashfield
Hibernian 05/06 4 2
06/07 15

McCANN James
Kilsyth W
Hibernian 95/96 1
Kilsyth W

McCANN John
b. Uphall 6.9.1867
Broxburn Shamrock
Bathgate R 90/91
Newcastle WE 90/91
Broxburn Shamrock 91/92
Celtic 92/93 3
Hibernian
Preston NE 93/94 6 1
Broxburn Shamrock

McCANN William
d. Alexandria ?.10.1904
Abercorn 92/93 9
93/94 12 D2
Liverpool 94/95 15 FL

McCANN William
Strathclyde
Celtic 94/95 3
Clydebank U 95/96
Abercorn 96/97 1
Partick T 96/97 1 D2
97/98
Kilsyth W

McCARTHY Joseph
Irvine V 31/32
32/33
33/34
Kilmarnock 33/34
34/35 1
Irvine V 34/35
Lancaster T 35/36
Galston 36/37
Glentoran 36/37 IL

McCARTHY Thomas
b. Dundee
Dundee Logie
Lochee U
Dundee 28/29 1
Montrose L 28/29 D2
Dundee 29/30 38 1
30/31 33 1
31/32 22
32/33 38 1
33/34 31 1
34/35 11
Brighton 35/36 1 FL
Dundee U 36/37 4 D2
Fraserburgh 36/37

McCARTNEY
Leith A 91/92 22
92/93 18 1
93/94 17
94/95 16

McCARTNEY
Third Lanark 94/95 4

McCARTNEY Andrew
b. Glasgow
Queen's Park 28/29
29/30
30/31 7
31/32 13
32/33 23
Edinburgh C 33/34 D2
34/35 D2
35/36 D2

McCARTNEY Andrew J
Queen's Park
Partick T 33/34 1
Cowdenbeath

McCARTNEY Charles
b. Glasgow
Old Kilpatrick Jnrs
Morton 25/26 27 7
26/27 36 11
27/28 D2
28/29 D2
29/30 38 19
30/31 38 12
31/32 27 6
Cowdenbeath 32/33 6

McCARTNEY David
Rutherglen Glencairn
St Mirren 00/01 7 2

McCARTNEY James
Clyde 96/97 2

McCARTNEY John
b. Mauchline 1866 d. Edinburgh 18.1.1933
Cartvale
Glasgow Thistle 85/86
Rangers 86/87
87/88
Cowlairs 88/89
89/90
90/91 16
91/92
92/93
93/94 D2
Newton Heath 94/95 20 2 FL
Luton T 94/95 2 SL
95/96 14 SL
97/98 27 FL
Barnsley 98/99 32 1 FL
99/00 26 1 FL
00/01 5 FL
01/02 4 FL
02/03 3 FL
03/04 1 FL
04/05 1 FL

McCARTNEY John
b. Newmilns
Newmilns
St Mirren 90/91 16 2
91/92 19 1
Liverpool 92/93 18 LL
93/94 19 1 FL
94/95 28 FL
95/96 21 FL
96/97 30 1 FL
97/98 27 2 FL
New Brighton Tower 98/99 17 FL
99/00 1 FL

McCARTNEY Robert
b. c1871 d. Edinburgh ?.3.1937
Heart of Midlothian 95/96 5
96/97 17
97/98 15
98/99 16
99/00 1
Leith A

McCARTNEY William 1 cap
b. Newmilns d. ?.11.1945
Rutherglen Glencairn
Ayr 98/99 D2
99/00 D2
Hibernian 99/00 15 4
00/01 16
01/02 17 7
02/03 17 5
Manchester U 03/04 14 1 FL
West Ham U 04/05 18 3 SL
Broxburn 05/06
Lochgelly U 05/06
06/07
Clyde 06/07 27 4
07/08 24 6
08/09 26 7
09/10 22 2
10/11 18 3
11/12 10
Broxburn
Clyde 13/14

McCHESNIE Hugh
Clyde 99/00 2
Hurlford

McCLAIR
Third Lanark 92/93 5

McCLORY Allan 3 caps
b. Armadale 11.11.1899 d. 9.7.1983
Shotts U
Motherwell 24/25 35
25/26 38
26/27 36
27/28 35
28/29 37
29/30 38
30/31 38
31/32 38
32/33 38
33/34 13
34/35 35
35/36 38
36/37 8
Brideville 37/38
Albion R L 38/39 23
Montrose

McCLOUNIE James
Clydebank Jnrs
Kilmarnock 05/06 3
06/07
Dumfries
Broxburn

McCLOY Henry
Shawfield Jnrs
Ayr U 37/38 1

McCLOY James
b. Uddingston 1911
Petershill
Clyde 32/33 2
St Mirren 33/34 23
34/35 12
35/36 D2
36/37 33
37/38 29
Bradford C 38/39 37 FL
Swansea T

McCLOY Philip 2 caps
b. Uddingston ?.4.1896 d. 1972

Baillieston Jnrs					
Mossend Hibs					
Kilsyth Emmet					
Parkhead					
Ayr U		18/19	25		
Clyde	L	18/19	1		
Ayr U		19/20	41		
		20/21	39	4	
		21/22	41	1	
		22/23	37	2	
		23/24	37	1	
		24/25	26		
		25/26	2		D2
Manchester C		25/26	37		FL
		26/27	30		FL
		27/28	38		FL
		28/29	31		FL
		29/30	11		FL
Cork C		30/31			
Chester		30/31	34		CCL
Stade Rennais Universite					
Workington					
Kidderminster H					

McCLUNE D

St Johnstone		26/27	1		

McCLURE David
b. Perth

Dunipace Jnrs					
St Johnstone		24/25	19		
		25/26	13		
		26/27	4		
Nelson		27/28	28	1	FL
Dundee U		28/29	35		
		29/30	9		
Portadown		30/31			IL
		31/32			IL
		32/33			IL
Glentoran		32/33			IL
		33/34			IL
Montrose					

McCLURE Duncan
b. Troon 10.6.1913 d. Grangemouth ?.5.1991

Parkhead					
Heart of Midlothian		33/34	26		
		34/35	29		
		35/36	14		
		36/37	29		
		37/38	27	1	
		38/39	37		
		46/47	16		
		47/48	1		
		48/49			
		49/50			
		50/51			

McCLURE James
b. Glasgow

Parkhead Jnrs					
Kilmarnock		35/36	11		
		36/37	25		
		37/38	25		
Albion R	L	38/39	22		
Kilmarnock		46/47	5		
Albion R		46/47			D2
		47/48			D2

McCLURE James A

Clyde		21/22	20	1	
		22/23	23	4	
		23/24	4		

McCLYMONT Hugh
b. c1897

Douglas Water Thistle					
Hibernian		19/20	3	1	

McCLYMONT James

St Mirren		03/04	1		

McCOLGAN Daniel
b. Baillieston 22.2.1903

Baillieston Jnrs					
Celtic		25/26	2		
		26/27			
Third Lanark	L	26/27			D2
Celtic		27/28			
Third Lanark	L	27/28			D2
Raith R	L	27/28			
Ayr U	L	27/28	29	1	D2
Celtic		28/29			
Third Lanark		28/29	14	7	
Belfast Celtic	L	29/30			IL
Third Lanark		29/30			D2
		30/31			D2
Albion R		31/32			D2

McCOLGAN John
b. Tollcross 2.1.1898

Vale of Clyde					
Albion R		20/21	21		
		21/22	42		
		22/23	32		
Portsmouth		23/24	17		FL
		24/25	40		FL
		25/26	38		FL
		26/27	29		FL
		27/28	42		FL
		28/29	17		FL
		29/30	7		FL
Waterford		30/31			
		31/32			

McCOLL

Third Lanark		90/91	1		

McCOLL Connell

Hibernian		13/14	11	1	
		14/15	24		
Broxburn U		14/15			

McCOLL James
b. Glasgow 14.12.1892 d. Edinburgh 7.3.1978

Anderston Thornbank					
St Anthonys		11/12			
		12/13			
Celtic		13/14	18	7	
Peebles R	L	13/14			
Celtic		14/15	33	25	
		15/16	32	34	
		16/17	31	24	
		17/18	14	10	
		18/19	29	17	
		19/20	8		
Stoke		20/21	26	5	FL
Partick T		21/22	32	10	
		22/23	3		
Hibernian		22/23	25	12	
		23/24	33	21	
		24/25	38	23	
		25/26	31	11	
		26/27	31	17	
		27/28	38	26	
		28/29	33	11	
		29/30	31	8	
		30/31	29	4	
Leith A		31/32	14	3	

McCOLL Robert Smith 13 caps
b. Glasgow 13.4.1876 d. Glasgow 25.11.1959

Benmore					
Queen's Park		00/01	15	7	
		01/02	4	3	
Newcastle U		01/02	10	7	FL
		02/03	29	9	FL
		03/04	25	5	FL
Rangers		04/05	12	7	
		05/06	13	6	
		06/07	1		
Queen's Park		07/08	17	9	
		08/09	15	4	
		09/10	25	17	

McCOLL William

Dundee		98/99	5		

McCOMBE James
b. Bothwell 4.6.1915

Bothwellhaugh A					
Wishaw Thistle					
Wishaw Jnrs					
Heart of Midlothian		34/35			
Clyde		35/36	6		
Kings Park		35/36			D2
Clapton Orient		36/37	27	8	FL
		37/38	18		FL
Chelmsford C		38/39			SL
Dartford					

McCOMBIE

Clyde		92/93	1	1	

McCOMBIE Alec

Aberdeen		20/21	2		

McCONNACHEY Jacob

Larkhall Thistle					
Third Lanark		18/19	16	?	
		19/20	5		

MacCONACHIE John

Hibernian		13/14	1		

McCONACHY Frederick J

Queen's Park		14/15	12	1	
		15/16	3	1	
		16/17	3	2	
		17/18	1		

McCONNACHIE Alexander

Glasgow Ashfield					
Derby Co		97/98	23	7	FL
Notts Co		98/99	33	14	FL
		99/00	33	12	FL
		00/01	10		FL
Third Lanark		01/02	18	6	
Ripley A		02/03			
Newton R		03/04			
		04/05			
Ilkeston U					
Alfreton T					
Tibshelf					

McCONNACHIE Alexander
b. Gourock

Gourock FP					
Hibernian		27/28	4		
		28/29	2		
Morton		29/30	13		

McCONNACHIE James
b. Mossend

Irvine Meadow					
Kings Park					
Clyde		23/24	4		
Stenhousemuir		24/25			D2

MacCONNACHIE John

Newtongrange Star					
Raith R		21/22	1		

MacCONNACHIE John Smith Jackson
b. Aberdeen 8.5.1885 d. Swindon 24.11.1956

Glasgow Perthshire					
Hibernian		03/04	14	1	
		04/05	15		
		05/06	24	4	
		06/07	24	3	
Everton		07/08	21		FL
		09/09	38		FL
		09/10	31		FL
		10/11	22		FL
		11/12	31		FL
		12/13	23	4	FL
		13/14	35		FL
		14/15	28		FL
Shelbourne		18/19			IL
Everton		19/20	16	2	FL
Swindon T		20/21	29		FL
		21/22	26	3	FL
Djurgaardens					
Swindon T		22/23	1		FL
Foleshill Great Heath					
Barrow		27/28	2		FL
Lowestoft T					

McCONNELL Hugh
b. c1919

Kilwinning R					
Watford	T	37/38			FL
Kilwinning R		37/38			
Ayr U		38/39	19	9	

McCONNELL James

Hibernian		99/00	1		
Leith A					

McCONNELL James
b. Ayr 23.2.1899 d. Carlisle 15.5.1949

Auchinleck Talbot					
Kilmarnock		20/21	1	1	
Stevenston U		20/21			
Nithsdale W		20/21			
		21/22			
		22/23			
		23/24		14	D3
		24/25		45	D3
		25/26		37	D2
Celtic	L	25/26			
Nithsdale W		26/27		10	D2
Springfield Babes		26/27	3		ASL
Providence Clamdiggers		26/27	21	17	ASL
J & P Coats		27/28	22	12	ASL
Bethlehem Steel		27/28	10	7	ASL
Carlisle U		28/29	42	43	FL
		29/30	33	27	FL
		30/31	41	37	FL
		31/32	34	19	FL
Crewe A		32/33	35	20	FL
Rotherham U		33/34	21	4	FL
Nithsdale W					

McCONNELL John
b. Mossend 1881
Glenbuck A
Kilmarnock 02/03 12
Grimsby T 03/04 7 FL
04/05 14 FL
05/06 27 FL
Brentford 06/07 2 SL
Grimsby T 07/08 6 FL
Nithsdale W
St Cuthbert W
Hurlford

McCONNELL John
Cronberry
Third Lanark 10/11 3

McCONNELL John Morrison
b. Cambusnethan
Motherwell Hearts
Glasgow Ashfield
Motherwell 06/07 6
07/08 28 2
Airdrieonians 08/09 22
Liverpool 09/10 13 FL
10/11 29 FL
11/12 8 1 FL
Aberdeen 12/13 19

McCONNELL Thomas
b. Motherwell
Glasgow Ashfield
Motherwell 10/11 23 2

McCONNELL Thomas
Dumbarton 13/14 23 4
Galston 14/15
Airdrieonians 14/15 5 3

McCORKINDALE John 1 cap
Partick T 87/88
88/89
89/90
90/91
91/92 12 SA
Clyde 91/92 11
92/93 17
93/94 15 D2

McCORMACK Arthur Terence
b. Perth 25.2.1887
Perth St Leonards
St Johnstone 09/10
10/11
Celtic 11/12 1
St Johnstone L 11/12 7 D2
Merthyr T 12/13 SL
13/14 SL
14/15 SL

McCORMACK Charles
b. Coatbridge
Third Lanark 15/16 6
16/17 32
17/18 31 ?
18/19 18 ?
19/20 34 1
20/21 35
21/22 17
22/23 28
23/24 25 2
24/25 8
Hamilton A 24/25 16
25/26 32 1
26/27 28 3
27/28 25 3
Ayr U 28/29 2

McCORMACK Henry
b. c1897
Denny Hibernian
Celtic 17/18 2 1
18/19
Albion R 19/20 4
Bathgate

McCORMACK Hugh
b. Yoker
Yoker A
St Mirren 23/24 8 1

McCORMACK John
b. Glasgow
Anniesland Social Welfare
Alloa A 32/33 D2
Third Lanark 33/34 11

McCORMACK Johnston
Rutherglen Glencairn
Third Lanark 20/21 16 2
21/22 7

McCORMICK
Abercorn 92/93 1

McCOSH John McLauchlan
b. Colyton 29.3.1904
Auchinleck Talbot
Ayr U 25/26 20 6 D2
26/27 11 6 D2
Nithsdale W 26/27 D2
Ayr U 27/28 3 D2
Cowdenbeath 28/29 6 3
Clydebank T 28/29 D2
Third Lanark T 28/29
East Stirlingshire T 28/29 D2
Morton T 28/29 D2
Queen of the South 29/30 D2
Exeter C 30/31 1 FL
New Brighton 31/32 24 2 FL
Drumcondra

McCOSH Thomas C
St Mirren 13/14 1
Johnstone 14/15 D2

McCOURT James
b. Bellshill 23.10.1901
St Pauls Jnrs
Bedlay Jnrs
Mossend Hibs
Third Lanark 19/20 1
20/21 14
Sheffield U 20/21 7 FL
21/22 39 3 FL
22/23 14 1 FL
23/24 2 FL
Manchester C 24/25 4 FL
Dykehead 25/26 D3
26/27

McCOURT William
Blantyre Celtic
Hibernian 18/19 18 ?
Blantyre Celtic 19/20
Partick T 19/20 4

McCRACKEN
St Mirren 92/93 1

McCRACKEN
Morton 04/05 5

McCRACKEN James
Queen's Park 36/37 8

McCRACKEN Thomas
St Bernards *
Heart of Midlothian 00/01 3

McCRAE Andrew B
Queen's Park 13/14 14

McCRAE Andrew Bowie
Falkirk 12/13 5 1

McCRAE D
St Mirren 16/17 1

McCRAE David 2 caps
b. Bridge of Weir 23.2.1901 d. Kilmalcolm 1976
Kilmalcolm Jnrs
Beith 17/18
18/19
19/20
20/21
21/22
Manchester C T 21/22 FL
Bury T 21/22 FL
Gainsborough T 21/22
Denaby Main 22/23
Beith 22/23
St Mirren 23/24 5 3
24/25 35 29
25/26 33 24
26/27 37 30
27/28 37 32
28/29 36 25
29/30 34 18
30/31 34 16
31/32 19 9
32/33 32 29
33/34 17 7
Stade Rennes Universite 33/34
Morton T 34/35 D2
New Brighton 34/35 11 1 FL
Queen of the South 34/35 6 2
Stranraer
Darlington 34/35 4 3 FL
Beith
Glentoran 35/36 IL

McCRAE James Clark Fulton
b. Bridge of Weir 2.9.1894 d. Paisley 3.9.1974
Port Glasgow Jnrs
Clyde 12/13 3
13/14 2
14/15 5 1
Rangers 15/16 3
Clyde 15/16 16 2
18/19 1
West Ham U 19/20 35 FL
20/21 15 FL
Bury 20/21 26 1 FL
21/22 34 4 FL
22/23 24 5 FL
Wigan B 23/24 32 FL
New Brighton 24/25 6 FL
Manchester U 25/26 9 FL
Third Lanark L 26/27
Watford 26/27 2 FL
Clyde 27/28 3

McCREADIE Andrew 2 caps
b. Girvan 19.11.1870
Cowlairs
Rangers 89/90
90/91 15 2
91/92 19 5
92/93 14 1
93/94 18 1
Sunderland 94/95 FL
95/96 FL
Rangers 96/97 18 1
97/98 4
Bristol St Georges 98/99
Wishaw Thistle

McCREADIE Hugh
Rangers 89/90
90/91 14 5
91/92 16 2
92/93 15 10
93/94 9 2
94/95 13 2
95/96 10 6

McCREADIE Hugh
Third Lanark 96/97 11

McCREADIE Richard
b. c1915
Forth R
East Stirlingshire 37/38 D2
Raith R 38/39 13

McCREADY John
Port Glasgow Clydeville
Port Glasgow A 07/08 2
08/09 14 1
09/10 6 1
10/11 20 ? D2

McCRINDLE Hugh
Rutherglen Glencairn
St Mirren 25/26 7 2

McCRINDLE William Davidson
b. Hurlford 1915 d. Partick ?.3.1941
Clydebank Jnrs
Partick T 36/37 2
37/38 2
38/39 19 10

McCRINSON
Clyde 91/92 1

McCRONE Thomas
Kilmarnock Thistle
Kilmarnock 96/97
97/98
98/99
Galston 98/99
Kilmarnock 99/00 3
Galston

McCRONE William
St Mirren 97/98 7
98/99
Galston 98/99

McCRORIE Thomas Shanks
b. Cumlachie 1.3.1902
Renfrew St James
Kirkintilloch Rob Roy
Dundee
Hamilton A 24/25 20 6
Charlton A 25/26 5 FL
Aberdare A 26/27 2 FL
Dunfermline A 26/27 1
Gurney (Canada)
Dunfermline A
Birmingham T 27/28 FL
Alloa A 28/29 D2
Merthyr T 28/29 1 FL
Dumbarton 28/29 D2
Olympique Marseilles 28/29
New Bedford Whalers 29A 5 1 ASL
Barrow 29/30 5 FL
Arbroath 29/30 1 D2
Linfield 30/31 IL
Shelbourne 31/32 LI
Pawtucket Rangers 31A 2 1 ASL
QPR 32/33 FL
Beith T 33/34
Ards 33/34 IL

McCUBBIN Alexander
b. East Greenock 1887
Volunteer Amateurs
Morton 05/06 21 1
06/07 34 4
07/08 33 7
Bristol R 08/09 SL
Morton 09/10 32 8
Huddersfield T 10/11 11 5 FL
Lincoln C 11/12 31 16 ML
12/13 34 9 FL
13/14 26 6 FL
Newland A
Lincoln Corinthians

McCUISH Angus
Queen's Park 12/13 13

McCULLEY David R
b. Glasgow
Cumnock Jnrs
Ayr U 19/20 8
20/21 4

McCULLOCH
St Mirren 17/18 1 1

McCULLOCH Alexander
b. Edinburgh 1886
Bonnyrigg Rose A
Leith A 06/07
Middlesbrough 07/08 4 1 FL
Newcastle U 07/08 1 FL
Brentford 08/09 12 3 SL
Bradford PA 08/09 7 1 FL
Swindon T 09/10 21 3 SL
Reading L 10/11 SL
Swindon T 11/12 15 3 SL
Coventry C 12/13 23 4 SL
Raith R 13/14 5
Alloa 14/15
St Bernards 15/16
Broxburn U 15/16
Dunfermline A 18/19
Heart of Midlothian 18/19 8 2
Lincoln C 19/20 13 3 FL
Merthyr T 20/21 3 FL
Llanelly 21/22
Dundee Hibs 21/22 9 1 D2
Gala Fairydean

McCULLOCH Alexander
Arbroath 38/39 8 2

McCULLOCH Archie
St Mirren 05/06 2
06/07 10
Bo'ness 07/08
08/09
Dumbarton Harp 09/10

McCULLOCH David 7 caps
b. Hamilton 5.10.1911 d. Hamilton ?.5.1979
Hamilton Amateurs
Hamilton A T
Partick T T
Shotts U
Third Lanark 32/33 11 7
33/34 23 15
Heart of Midlothian 34/35 35 38
35/36 18 17
Brentford 35/36 26 26 FL
36/37 41 31 FL
37/38 41 26 FL
38/39 9 2 FL
Derby Co 38/39 31 16 FL
39/40 3 FL
Leicester C 46/47 4 2 FL
Bath C 46/47 SL
47/48 SL
48/49 SL
49/50 SL
Waterford 49/50
50/51
Alloa A

McCULLOCH James
b. Bellshill
Bellshill A
Airdrieonians 10/11
11/12
12/13 3
Dunfermline A L 12/13 D2

McCULLOCH James
b. Cumnock c1897
Parkhead Jnrs
Carluke
Clyde 19/20 3

McCULLOCH John
Morton 16/17 3 1
17/18 1

McCULLOCH John
b. Dumbarton
Strathclyde
Clyde 32/33 26 7
33/34 32 9
34/35 18 7
35/36 24 11
36/37 17 5

McCULLOCH John
Motherwell 36/37 10 1
37/38 28 6
38/39 32 11
Dumbarton 46/47 D2

McCULLOCH John Gray
b. Rutherglen 15.7.1896
Vale of Clyde
Dumbarton 17/18 17 13
Rangers 17/18 2 1
Glentoran * 18/19 IL
Vale of Clyde
Dykehead
Exeter C 21/22 1 FL
Airdrieonians 21/22 1
J & P Coats ASL

McCULLOCH John Kelly
Ayr U 37/38 2
38/39 1

McCULLOCH Joseph
b. Ardrossan 30.12.1918 K.I.A. 24.2.1945
South Beach
Ardrossan Winton R
Third Lanark 37/38 1
38/39 13 1

McCULLOCH Michael
b. Denny 26.4.1891
Denny Hibs
Falkirk 13/14 13 3
14/15 10 3
15/16 18 2
16/17 20 5
17/18 23 ?
18/19 28 ?
19/20 28 2
20/21 21
Heart of Midlothian 21/22
Nelson 22/23 28 6 FL
23/24 21 2 FL
Chesterfield 24/25 3 FL
Bournemouth 24/25 10 FL
St Bernards 25/26

McCULLOCH Peter
Hibernian 01/02 6 2

McCULLOCH Robert
Dundee 97/98 1

McCULLOCH Robert
Clyde Jnrs
Hibernian 01/02
Broxburn 01/02
Hibernian 01/02
Airdrieonians 02/03 17 9 D2
03/04 2
Stenhousemuir 04/05
Vale of Leven 05/06

McCULLOCH Robert Gray
b. Cathcart 20.4.1900 d. Glasgow 24.4.1964
Auchinleck Talbot
Kilmarnock 22/23 14 3
23/24
Arbroath L 23/24 5 D2
Bournemouth 24/25 38 4 FL
Watford 25/26 14 2 FL

McCULLOCH Thomas
Dundee 13/14 11 2
14/15 30 1
15/16 33 6
16/17 31 6

McCULLOCH William
Parkhead
Ayr U 22/23 1
Glasgow Churches League
Dennistoun Jnrs 25/26

McCURDIE Alexander
b. Mauchline c1895 K.I.A., France 24.4.1917
Kilmarnock 13/14 5 2
Stevenston U L 13/14
Kilmarnock 14/15 6

McCURDIE Robert
Morton 16/17 8

McCURLEY John
b. Kelty 17.3.1906 d. Morpeth 1969
Kelty R
Third Lanark 26/27 D2
27/28 D2
Newcastle U 27/28 4 3 FL
28/29 25 4 FL
29/30 14 1 FL
East Fife 30/31 34 7
31/32 35 4 D2
32/33 29 5 D2
Cowdenbeath 33/34 33 2
34/35 D2
35/36 D2
36/37 D2
37/38 D2

McDADE James
Port Glasgow Jnrs
Dumbarton 13/14 8 1
Dumbarton Harp

McDANIEL
Dumbarton 95/96 1

McDERMID Robert
b. Scotland 1870
Renton Thistle
Renton
Newcastle WE
Sunderland 88/89
Sunderland A
Accrington 90/91 22 FL
Burton Swifts
Stockton
Lincoln C 92/93 2 FL
Renton 93/94 18
Dundee W 94/95 5 ? D2
Newcastle U 94/95 20 1 FL
95/96 30 1 FL
96/97 6 FL
Hebburn A 97/98
Warmley 98/99
South Shields

McDERMID Robert Forsyth
b. Alexandria 1895 d. Largs 19.8.1952
Rangers 17/18 28 4
18/19 7 1
19/20
20/21 2
21/22 15 7
22/23
Queen of the South L 22/23
23/24 D3
24/25 D3
Aberdeen 25/26 34 8
26/27 38 8
27/28 34 4
28/29 35 3
29/30 35 4
30/31 36 13
31/32 28 4
32/33 7 1

McDERMOTT Thomas
b. Bridgeton 12.1.1878 d. Rutherglen 1961
Rutherglen Rosebank
Cambuslang Hibs
Dundee 99/00 18 7
00/01 18 4
Celtic 01/02 2
02/03 10 2
Everton 03/04 29 7 FL
04/05 28 7 FL
05/06 6 1 FL
Chelsea 05/06 23 7 FL
06/07 9 3 FL
Dundee 06/07 20 7
07/08 17 9
Bradford C 07/08 4 2 FL
08/09 4 FL
Gainsborough T 08/09 FL
Kilmarnock 08/09 3 2
Bradford C 08/09
Dundee Hibernian 09/10
Anfield Royal 10/11
St Helens Rec 11/12
Wirral Railway 11/12
Vale of Leven
Broxburn Shamrock
Clyde 13/14 2

McDEVITT James
Third Lanark 19/20 16 3

McDIARMID Fred
b. Dundee 1880
Partick T 97/98 15 4
98/99
Dundee 99/00 12 7
00/01 19 3
01/02 16 1
02/03 22 3
03/04 26 1
04/05 19
05/06 29 1
Tottenham H 06/07 7 SL
Northampton T 07/08 33 7 SL
08/09 39 9 SL
09/10 41 SL
10/11 18 2 SL
Distillery 10/11
11/12

McDIARMID George
b. Garterage 1880 d. 1946
Cambuslang
Nottingham F 00/01 4 FL
Northampton T 01/02
Airdrieonians 01/02 7 D2
02/03 21 D2
Grimsby T 03/04 27 FL
04/05 34 1 FL
05/06 4 FL
Glossop 05/06 28 2 FL
06/07 21 FL
Clyde 07/08 2
Grimsby T 07/08 7 FL

McDIARMID Robert F
b. Alexandria
Vale Glenoak
Queen's Park 16/17 29 11
17/18
Dumbarton 18/19 16 ?
19/20 41 17
20/21 38 5
Rangers 20/21
21/22
Queen of the South 22/23
23/24 D3
24/25 D3
25/26 D2

McDONALD
Dumbarton 90/91 2
91/92 9 1
92/93 5

McDONALD
Third Lanark 98/99 1

McDONALD
Morton 07/08 5

McDONALD
Raith R 12/13 1

McDONALD A (either Alex or Archie?)
Clyde 96/97 8
97/98 11

McDONALD Alexander
b. 1876
Clyde 97/98
98/99 8
Bristol C 99/00 19 SL
Clyde 99/00 4
00/01 16 ? D2
01/02 D2
02/03 D2

McDONALD Alexander
Denbeath
Raith R 19/20 17

McDONALD Angus
Glasgow Perthshire
Rangers 02/03 13 5
03/04 1
Johnstone 03/04

McDONALD Archibald
Clyde 92/93 3
93/94 1 D2
94/95 1

McDONALD Archibald
Clyde 97/98
98/99 16 1

McDONALD Archibald G
Queen's Park 19/20 1
20/21 25 10
21/22 27 1
22/23 2 D2
Partick T 22/23 5 1
23/24 5

McDONALD Daniel McIlroy
b. East Wemyss 12.7.1894
Wemyss A
Kirkcaldy U
Dundee 13/14 23
14/15 30
15/16 37 4
16/17 14 1
19/20 8
Tottenham H 20/21 FL
Bradford PA 21/22 22 FL
22/23 5 FL

McDONALD David
Dundee W 94/95 1 ? D2
Dundee 95/96 12 6
Everton 95/96 FL
Leicester F 96/97 16 7 FL
Dundee 97/98
Millwall 97/98 2 1 SL
Dundee W 98/99
99/00
00/01

McDONALD David
b. Wemyss
Dundee 19/20 23 4
20/21 13 1
21/22 4 1
22/23
23/24 6 2

McDONALD David T
Dundee 98/99 9 1
99/00 2 1
00/01 5 1

McDONALD Donald
Renfrew Jnrs
Cowdenbeath 32/33 23
33/34 12
Morton 34/35 D2

McDONALD Hector
Leith A
Heart of Midlothian 03/04 3

McDONALD Hugh
St Mirren 02/03 1
03/04 7 3
04/05 9 3
05/06 2 1
Abercorn 05/06 D2
Port Glasgow A 06/07 5 1
07/08 1
08/09 1
09/10 3 3
10/11 9 ? D2

McDONALD Hugh Lachlan
b. Kilwinning 20.12.1881 d. Plumstead 27.8.1920
Ayr Academicals
Ayr Westerlea
St Bernards 98/99 1
Hearts of Beath 98/99
Ayr 99/00 D2
Hearts of Beath 00/01
01/02
Ayr 02/03 D2
Beith 03/04
04/05
05/06
Woolwich Arsenal 05/06 2 FL
Brighton 06/07 38 SL
07/08 33 SL
Woolwich Arsenal 08/09 38 FL
09/10 36 FL
Oldham A 10/11 38 FL
11/12 3 FL
Bradford PA 11/12 21 FL
12/13 5 FL
Woolwich Arsenal 12/13 18 FL
Fulham 13/14 8 FL
Bristol R 13/14 2 SL

McDONALD J
Heart of Midlothian 94/95 2

McDONALD James

Baillieston Thistle					
Aberdeen		06/07	20	4	
		07/08	24	5	
QPR					

McDONALD James

Dumbarton A *					
Renfrew *					
Dumbarton		19/20	5		
Bo'ness	L	19/20			
Dumbarton		20/21	17	1	

MacDONALD James

Heart of Midlothian		16/17	3	1	

McDONALD James
b. Kilmarnock

Johnstone					
St Mirren		22/23	2		
		23/24	37	1	
		24/25	33	1	
		25/26	8	4	
		26/27	5	2	
		27/28	7	5	
		28/29	11	2	
		29/30	3	1	
Queen of the South		30/31			D2
		31/32			D2
		32/33			D2
		33/34	22	1	
		34/35	3		
		35/36			
Raith R		36/37			D2

MacDONALD James A

Port Glasgow A		09/10	7		

McDONALD James Alexander

Morton		07/08	1		

McDONALD James Alexander
b. Old Machar 8.12.1883 d. Keighley ?.8.1924

Inverness Citadel					
Inverness Thistle					
Aberdeen Favourites					
St Bernards		04/05			D2
		05/06			D2
		06/07			D2
Bradford C		06/07	3	3	FL
		07/08	36	10	FL
		08/09	17	2	FL
		09/10	7		FL
		10/11	18		FL
		11/12	32	1	FL
		12/13	34		FL
		13/14	20	1	FL
		14/15	32	4	FL
		19/20	3		FL
Raith R		20/21	15	2	
Wakefield C		20/21			
Keighley Parkwood					

McDONALD John

Nithsdale W		03/04			
Kilmarnock		03/04	3		
		04/05	3		
Lanemark		04/05			
Maxwelltown Volunteers		05/06			
Lanemark		05/06			
		06/07			
		07/08			
		08/09			
		09/10			
		10/11			
		11/12			
		12/13			
		13/14			
		14/15			

McDONALD John
b. Kirkcaldy 1886

Wemyss Harp					
Vale of Wemyss					
Raith R					
Rangers		06/07	5		
		07/08	19	4	
		08/09	22	6	
Liverpool		09/10	34	2	FL
		10/11	25	1	FL
		11/12	18	1	FL
Newcastle U		12/13	19	2	FL
		13/14	12	2	FL
		14/15			FL
Raith R		19/20	5		

McDONALD John

Vale of Leven					
Third Lanark		09/10	6	2	
		10/11	1		
Vale of Leven		11/12			D2
Arthurlie		12/13			D2

McDONALD John

Dundee		14/15	13	1	

McDONALD John
b. Glasgow d. 18.8.1943

Army					
Linfield		17/18			IL
Partick T		17/18	1		
Linfield		18/19			IL
		19/20			IL
Blackburn R		19/20	1		FL
		20/21	16	4	FL
		21/22	16	3	FL
Dundee		22/23	25	3	
		23/24	36	4	
		24/25	29	3	
Dundee U		25/26	36	4	
		26/27	36	3	
		27/28	31	5	

McDONALD John
b. Dykehead 4.1.1896

Dykehead					
Shotts U					
Barnsley		13/14			FL
Motherwell		14/15	2		
		15/16			
Airdrieonians		16/17	35		
		17/18	27		
		18/19	15	1	
		19/20	37	1	
Everton		20/21	39		FL
		21/22	26		FL
		22/23	29		FL
		23/24	24		FL
		24/25	29		FL
		25/26	37		FL
		26/27	24		FL
New Brighton		27/28	39		FL
		28/29	42	2	FL
		29/30	41	1	FL
		30/31	38		FL
Connahs Quay		31/32			
Colwyn Bay U		31/32			

McDONALD John B
b. Edinburgh

Queen's Park		21/22	13	1	
		22/23	7	1	D2
		23/24	33	1	
		24/25	31	3	
		25/26	22	13	
		26/27	32	8	
		27/28	33		
		28/29	38	3	
		29/30	13	1	
		30/31	1		
Heart of Midlothian		30/31			
Edinburgh C		31/32			D2

McDONALD John W

Inverness Thistle					
Penicuik A					
St Mirren		36/37	2		

McDONALD Joseph
b. Irvine

Irvine Meadow					
Motherwell	T	23/24	14		
Ayr U		24/25			
Dumbarton		25/26			D2
Cowdenbeath		25/26	5		
		26/27	24	1	
		27/28	37		
		28/29	30		
Bethlehem Steel		29/30	3		ASL
Dolphin		30/31			LI
New York Giants		31A	1		ASL
Brigg T		31/32			
Montrose		31/32			D2

McDONALD Kenneth
b. Llanrwst 24.4.1898

Inverness Citadel					
Invernes Clachnacuddin					
Aberdeen		19/20	16	3	
		20/21	7	2	
Caerau					
Cardiff C		21/22	4	2	FL
		22/23	7	5	FL
Manchester U		22/23	2	1	FL
		23/24	7	1	FL
Bradford PA		23/24	28	17	FL
		24/25	12		FL
		25/26	39	43	FL
		26/27	33	28	FL
		27/28	33	31	FL
Hull C		28/29	32	23	FL
		29/30	9	6	FL
Halifax T		29/30	8		FL
Inverness Caledonian		30/31			
Coleraine		30/31			IL
Walker Celtic		30/31			
Spennymoor U		30/31			
		31/32			
Walker Celtic		31/32			
Blyth Spartans					

McDONALD M

Partick T					
St Mirren		11/12	21		

MacDONALD Malcolm
b. Glasgow 26.10.1913 d. 26.9.1999

Linwood St Convals					
St Anthonys		31/32			
Celtic		31/32	1	2	
		32/33	7		
		33/34	15	1	
		34/35	30	1	
		35/36	10		
		36/37	12	1	
		37/38	27	12	
		38/39	30	14	
Kilmarnock		46/47	8		
Brentford					

McDONALD Murdoch
b. Redding 1.7.1901 d. Falkirk 22.12.1934

Grange R					
St Ninians Thistle					
Cowdenbeath		21/22			D2
Bo'ness		22/23	8	3	D2
Rangers		23/24	1		
Bo'ness		24/25			D2
		25/26			D2
Reading		26/27	24	5	FL
		27/28	21	5	FL
		28/29	15	1	FL
		29/30	4	1	FL
Brighton		29/30	6		FL
		30/31	4	1	FL
Bo'ness		31/32			D2
Bray Unknowns		31/32			LI
Bo'ness		32/33			D2

MacDONALD Robert

Beith					
St Mirren		99/00	3	1	

McDONALD Robert Logan
b. Omagh 11.8.1902 d. Millport 7.6.1956

Hamilton Thistle					
Toronto Ulster					
Bethlehem Steel		24/25	36		ASL
		25/26	35	3	ASL
		26/27	22	2	ASL
		27/28	26		ASL
Rangers		28/29	3		
		29/30	13		
		30/31	13		
		31/32	7		
		32/33	29		
		33/34	38		
		34/35	35		
		35/36	22		
		36/37	22		
		37/38	3		

McDONALD Ronald
b. Bridgeton 1912

Kilsyth R					
Lanark U					
Pollok Jnrs		32/33			
Kilmarnock		32/33	1		
		33/34	3		
Swindon T					

McDONALD Stephen
b. Dundee
Dundee
Brechin C
Aston Villa 08/09
Falkirk 09/10 32
10/11 34
11/12 31
12/13 27 1
13/14 35 2
14/15 28
15/16 28 3
16/17 6

McDONALD Stephen
Dunoon A
Cowdenbeath 33/34 21 1
34/35 D2
East Stirlingshire 35/36 D2
East Fife 35/36 D2

McDONALD Stuart
Dundee 06/07 13

McDONALD Thomas
b. Longtown 28.11.1887 d. 1947
High Blantyre A
Bellshill A
Blantyre V
Motherwell 06/07 23
07/08 34
Portsmouth 08/09 27 SL
Motherwell 09/10 30
Carlisle U 10/11
Bury 11/12 29 FL
12/13 38 FL
13/14 38 FL
14/15 37 FL

MacDONALD Thomas
b. Portobello c1897
Musselburgh Comrades
Musselburgh Bruntonians
Portobello Thistle
Doncaster R 20/21
Rossington Main Colliery
Wigan B 21/22 1 FL
Hibernian 21/22 1

McDONALD Thomas Henry
b. Inverness 25.9.1895 d. Newcastle 1969
Inverness Thistle
Rangers 20/21 2
Newcastle U 20/21 13 2 FL
21/22 39 16 FL
22/23 36 15 FL
23/24 36 9 FL
24/25 33 11 FL
25/26 40 11 FL
26/27 41 17 FL
27/28 41 13 FL
28/29 30 1 FL
29/30 29 5 FL
30/31 3 FL
York C 31/32 34 6 FL
32/33 40 5 FL
Goole T 33/34
York C 34/35 1 FL
Usworth Colliery

MacDONALD Walter
St Mirren 98/99 1 1
Abercorn 99/00 D2
Longriggend 00/01
Abercorn 01/02 D2
Longriggend

McDONALD William
Dumbarton Fern
Celtic 93/94 1
94/95 2
Everton

McDONALD William
b. c1872 d. ?.8.1936
Partick T 94/95 6 2 D2
95/96 7 1 D2
96/97 14 1 D2
97/98 5
Bedminster 98/99 SL
Partick T 99/00 9 1 D2

McDONALD William
Vale of Gurnock Strollers
Third Lanark 02/03 5 1
Ayr 02/03

McDONALD William
b. c1883
Nithsdale W
Kilmarnock 03/04 2
04/05 23 1
05/06 20 1
Lanemark L 05/06
Brighton 06/07 33 SL
07/08 37 SL
Leeds C 08/09 14 FL
Nithsdale W 08/09
Lanemark

MacDONALD William
Inverness Citadel
Port Glasgow A 07/08 27 1

McDONALD William
b. c1891
Maryhill
Vale of Leven
Partick T 09/10 17
10/11 19
11/12 2
St Mirren 12/13
Aberdeen 13/14

MacDONALD William
b. Coatbridge 9.7.1905
Law Scotia
Dundee U 25/26 3
Broxburn U 26/27 D2
Armadale 26/27 D2
27/28 D2
Airdrieonians 28/29 31 6
29/30 28 2
30/31 36 8
31/32 31 10
Manchester U 31/32 2 FL
32/33 21 4 FL
33/34 4 FL
Tranmere R 34/35 41 10 FL
35/36 39 9 FL
Coventry C 36/37 36 8 FL
37/38 36 12 FL
38/39 19 3 FL
Plymouth A 39/40 2 FL

McDONALD William
b. Kilmarnock
St Mirren 25/26 36
26/27 34 2
27/28 34
28/29 29 1

McDONALD William James
b. Inverness 1877
Dundee 98/99 14 3
Derby Co 98/99 16 4 FL
99/00 7 1 FL
Dundee 00/01 6 2
Stoke 01/02 7 1 FL
Dundee 01/02
Montrose 02/03

McDONALD William S
b. Wick
Queen's Park 36/37 10
37/38 10
38/39 29 5

McDONNELL Alistair
St Johnstone YMCA
St Johnstone 31/32 D2
32/33 1
33/34
34/35
35/36
Kings Park 36/37 D2

McDONNELL John
Bonnyrigg Rose A
Hibernian 33/34 1
34/35 5
35/36 2

McDOUGALL Angus McKinnon
b. Old Kilpatrick 1911
Burnbank A
St Mirren 29/30
30/31 1
Kilmarnock 31/32 5
32/33 1
Alloa A 33/34 D2
Dunfermline A 34/35 D2
Kings Park

McDOUGALL David
b. Irvine
Irvine Meadow
Partick T
Rangers
Bristol C 00/01 11 2 SL
Rangers 01/02 4 3
Distillery 01/02 IL
Vale of Atholl 01/02
Distillery 02/03 IL
03/04 IL
04/05 IL
Glentoran 05/06 IL
06/07 IL
07/08 IL
08/09 IL
09/10 IL

McDOUGALL David B
Bonnyrigg Rose A
St Bernards
Hibernian 16/17 1
17/18 7 ?

McDOUGALL Hugh Ross
b. Fort William
Stenhousemuir
Falkirk 06/07 3
Dunfermline A 07/08
08/09
09/10
10/11
11/12
12/13
East Stirlingshire 12/13 D2

McDOUGALL James
Shettleston
Ayr U 13/14 22
14/15 6

McDOUGALL James 2 caps
b. Port Glasgow 23.1.1904 d. Liverpool ?.7.1984
Port Glasgow A
Partick T 25/26 11 1
26/27 16 3
27/28 32 17
Liverpool 28/29 36 8 FL
29/30 34 1 FL
30/31 40 1 FL
31/32 39 FL
32/33 26 FL
33/34 32 FL
34/35 38 1 FL
35/36 38 1 FL
36/37 39 FL
37/38 17 FL
South Liverpool

McDOUGALL John
b. Hamilton 8.12.1900
Hamilton Intermediates
Larkhall Thistle
Motherwell 21/22 4
Port Vale
Accrington S 26/27 1 FL
Vale of Leven 26/27
27/28
28/29
New Bedford Whalers 29/30 1 ASL

McDOUGALL John 1 cap
b. Port Glasgow 21.9.1901 d. Port Glasgow 26.9.1973
Kilmalcolm Amateurs
Port Glasgow A
Airdrieonians 21/22 21 1
22/23 38 2
23/24 34 5
24/25 30 4
25/26 34 2
26/27 37 2
27/28 34
28/29 33
Sunderland 29/30 37 1 FL
30/31 40 1 FL
31/32 34 FL
32/33 33 1 FL
33/34 23 1 FL
Leeds U 34/35 11 FL
35/36 29 FL
36/37 12 FL

McDOUGALL John Lindsay
b. Buckhaven 24.2.1902 d. Slough ?.1.1976

Club		Season	Apps	Goals	Lge
Wellesley Jnrs					
Raith R		22/23	4		
Forfar A	L				
Raith R		23/24			
		24/25			
		25/26			
		26/27			D2
		27/28			
		28/29	7		
Aldershot		28/29	12	1	SL
		29/30	27		SL
		30/31	16		SL
		31/32	18	1	SL
		32/33	39	1	FL
		33/34	41	2	FL
		34/35	22	1	FL
		35/36	5		FL

McDOUGALL Malcolm

Club	Season	Apps	Goals	Lge
Petershill				
St Mirren	10/11	21	6	
	11/12	6	2	
Coventry C	12/13			SL
Arthurlie	13/14			D2

McDOUGALL Neil
b. Kirn

Club	Season	Apps	Goals
Rothesay Jnrs			
Overtown A			
Airdrieonians	28/29	17	2
	29/30	23	2
	30/31		
	31/32		
Morton	32/33		

McDOUGALL Robert
b. Kirkcudbright

Club	Season	Apps	Goals	Lge
St Cuthberts W				
Liverpool	13/14	6	1	FL
	14/15	1		FL
Falkirk	15/16	18	2	
	16/17			
	17/18			
	18/19			
	19/20	38	6	
	20/21	36	5	
Ayr U	21/22	35	3	

McDOUGALL W

Club	Season	Apps
Airdrieonians	20/21	1

McDOUGALL William

Club	Season	Apps
Hibernian	13/14	4

McDOUGALL William
b. Gourock d. Glasgow 28.3.1923

Club	Season	Apps	Goals
Motherwell	18/19	1	?
	19/20	4	
	20/21	36	
	21/22	30	
	22/23	2	

McDOWALL

Club	Season	Apps	Goals
Dumbarton	18/19	1	?

McDOWALL Isaac McCandlish
b. Glasgow

Club	Season	Apps	Goals	Lge
Dunoon A				
Glasgow Perthshire	34/35			
Airdrieonians	34/35	5	2	
	35/36	1		
Dumbarton	36/37			D2
Kings Park	37/38			D2
Cowdenbeath	38/39			D2
	46/47			D2
Coleraine	47/48			IL
Linfield	48/49			IL
	49/50			IL
	50/51			IL
Ards	51/52			IL
	52/53			IL
Linfield	53/54			IL

McDOWALL John

Club	Season	Apps
Falkirk	19/20	4

McEACHRAN David
b. Clydebank 5.12.1903

Club		Season	Apps	Goals	Lge
Browns Welfare					
Yoker Rob Roy					
Clydebank Jnrs					
Vale of Leven					
Clydebank		24/25			D2
		25/26	24	3	
Preston NE	T	25/26	1		FL
Clydebank		26/27			D2
Fall River Marksmen		26/27	34	10	ASL
		27/28	40	16	ASL
Boston Wonder Workers		27/28	7	6	ASL
		28/29	24	9	ASL
		29A	19	10	ASL
New Bedford Whalers		29/30	8	4	ASL
Providence Clamdiggers		29/30	13	5	ASL
Montreal Carsteel					
Beith					
St Johnstone	T	32/33	4	1	
Linfield		32/33			IL
		33/34			IL

McECHERN Victor A C

Club	Season	Apps	Goals
Aberdeen University			
Aberdeen	07/08	6	
	08/09	14	2
	09/10	5	1

McELENY Charles
b. Glasgow 6.2.1872 d. Greenock 1.8.1908

Club	Season	Apps	Goals	Lge
Greenock Volunteers				
Abercorn				
Celtic	93/94	1		
	94/95	15		
	95/96	3		
Burnley	95/96	15	1	FL
Celtic	96/97	10	1	
New Brighton Tower	96/97			
	97/98			
	98/99	31		FL
Aston Villa	99/00	1		FL
Swindon T	00/01	28	1	SL
Brentford	01/02	27	2	SL
Morton	02/03	3		

McELHANEY Ralph
b. c1877

Club	Season	Apps	Goals	Lge
Dreghorn Jnrs				
Third Lanark	94/95			
Celtic	94/95	2		
Clyde	95/96			
Partick T	95/96			
Tottenham H	96/97	19	6	SL
Swindon T	97/98	3		SL
Beith	98/99			
East Stirlingshire	99/00			
Dunipace	99/00			
	00/01			
Brentford	01/02	18		SL
	02/03			
Grays U	02/03			
Southall				

McEVOY

Club	Season	Apps
Clydebank	23/24	1

McEVOY Patrick George
b. Glasgow 2.5.1899

Club		Season	Apps
St Anthonys			
Celtic		17/18	
		18/19	10
Dumbarton Harp	L	19/20	
Celtic		19/20	
		20/21	

McEWAN

Club	Season	Apps	Goals
Cowlairs	90/91	6	1

McEWAN

Club	Season	Apps
Third Lanark	99/00	1

McEWAN A

Club	Season	Apps	Goals
Glasgow Ashfield			
Raith R	13/14	8	1

McEWAN Alexander

Club	Season	Apps
Albion R	20/21	1

McEWAN Francis Fowler
b. Airdrie c1915 K.I.A., 21.9.1944

Club	Season	Apps	Goals	Lge
Whitburn				
Airdrieonians	35/36	3		
	36/37	20	11	D2
	37/38	28	11	D2
	37/38			D2
	38/39	8	2	D2
Tottenham H	38/39			FL

McEWAN John

Club	Season	Apps	Goals
Heart of Midlothian	15/16	21	6
	16/17	28	3
Partick T	17/18	11	1

McEWAN John
b. Crookedholm 16.9.1903 d. Kilmarnock 10.10.1957

Club	Season	Apps	Goals
Darvel Jnrs			
Irvine Meadow			
Kilmarnock	23/24	19	
	24/25	34	3
	25/26	31	
	26/27	28	1
	27/28	27	1
	28/29	33	1
	29/30	37	4
	30/31	32	2
	31/32	36	8
	32/33	38	10
	33/34	36	2
	34/35	2	

McEWAN John McK

Club	Season	Apps	Goals
Dumbarton	18/19	10	?

McEWAN Neil

Club	Season	Apps
Clydebank Jnrs		
Hamilton A	13/14	17
	14/15	9

McEWAN Robert
b. Edinburgh 1881

Club	Season	Apps	Goals	Lge
St Bernards	02/03			D2
Bury	03/04	29		FL
	04/05	6		FL
Rangers	04/05	9		
Heart of Midlothian	04/05			
Chelsea	05/06	21		FL
Glossop	06/07	35		FL
	07/08	19	1	FL
QPR	08/09	1		SL
Dundee	09/10	10		
	10/11	2		

McEWAN Robert

Club	Season	Apps	Goals	Lge
Kilsyth Emmet				
Dumbarton	21/22	29	1	
	22/23			D2
Dundee Hibs	23/24	10		D2

McFADYEN William 2 caps
b. Overtown 23.6.1898 d. 1971

Club		Season	Apps	Goals	Lge
Wishaw YMCA					
Motherwell		21/22			
Bo'ness	L	22/23			D2
Motherwell		23/24	15	3	
		24/25	3		
Clyde	L	24/25			
Motherwell		25/26	36	16	
		26/27	21	12	
		27/28	31	2	
		28/29	35		
		29/30	28	3	
		30/31	20	24	
		31/32	34	53	
		32/33	38	45	
		33/34	37	38	
		34/35	38	33	
		35/36	22	7	
		36/37	20	13	
Huddersfield T		36/37	16	8	FL
		37/38	32	10	FL
		38/39			FL
Clapton Orient		39/40	3		FL

McFARLAND A D

Club	Season	Apps
Dunoon		
Clydebank	21/22	7

McFARLANE (poss G or S)

Club	Season	Apps
Cambuslang	90/91	1

McFARLANE (poss J or R)

Club	Season	Apps
St Mirren	90/91	8

McFARLANE

Club	Season	Apps	Goals
Vale of Leven	91/92	16	2

McFARLANE

Club	Season	Apps	Goals
Leith A	93/94	4	3
	94/95	4	

McFARLANE

Club	Season	Apps
Rangers	06/07	1

McFARLANE A (John?)

Partick T 19/20 1
Fall River

MacFARLANE Alexander 5 caps
b. Dundee ?.7.1878 d. 1945
Bailleston
Woolwich Arsenal 96/97 5 FL
Airdrieonians 97/98 13 8 D2
98/99 7 6 D2
Newcastle U 98/99 21 5 FL
99/00 31 4 FL
00/01 30 8 FL
01/02 2 FL
Dundee 01/02 6
02/03 22 5
03/04 26 8
04/05 24 6
05/06 24 8
06/07 34 6
07/08 33 9
08/09 33 9
09/10 20 3
10/11 30 5
11/12 21 5
12/13 20 4
Chelsea 13/14 3 FL
14/15 1 FL

McFARLANE G

Cambuslang 91/92 13 1

MacFARLANE George

Aberdeen 08/09 2
09/10 6
10/11 2

MacFARLANE Hugh
b. Wellesley
Cardenden
Hibernian 26/27 9
27/28 2
28/29 8
29/30 31 1
30/31 38 2
31/32 D2
32/33 D2
33/34 34 3
34/35
Albion R 35/36 29 1
36/37 26
Dunfermline A 37/38 D2

McFARLANE Hugh Morton
b. Rutherglen 1917
Rutherglen Academy
Rutherglen Amateurs
Rutherglen Glencairn
Clyde 35/36 5
Dumbarton 36/37 D2
Clyde 37/38 4
Alloa A 38/39 D2

McFARLANE J

St Mirren 91/92 11

McFARLANE J

Third Lanark 96/97 14

McFARLANE James

Wishaw Amateurs
Hamilton A 06/07 32
07/08 14
Distillery IL

MacFARLANE James
b. Rutherglen
Cambuslang R
Clyde 27/28 12

McFARLANE James

Third Lanark 31/32 13 1
32/33 6 1
33/34 13

McFARLANE James L

Leith A 31/32 4

McFARLANE John
b. Bathgate 21.11.1899 d. Ardrossan 25.2.1956
Denbeath Star Jnrs
Wellesley Jnrs
Cowdenbeath T 19/20
Raith R T 19/20
Celtic 19/20 3
20/21 13
21/22 16 4
22/23 36 3
23/24 36 2
24/25 37 1
25/26 34 2
26/27 34
27/28 35
28/29 23
Middlesbrough 29/30 30 FL
30/31 41 FL
31/32 20 FL
32/33 4 FL
Shelbourne 33/34 LI
Dunfermline A 34/35 26

McFARLANE John
b. Shettleston 24.12.1911
Cambuslang R
Shawfield Jnrs
Aberdeen 26/27 1
27/28 5
28/29 1
Liverpool 28/29 1 FL
29/30 1 FL
Halifax T 30/31 42 9 FL
31/32 21 5 FL
Northampton T 32/33 3 1 FL
Kidderminster H 33/34
34/35
Darlington 35/36 11 FL
36/37 7 2 FL
Kidderminster H
Worcester C 37/38 SL
Bath C 38/39 SL

McFARLANE John McD
b. Glasgow d. ?.10.1929
St Johnstone 26/27 6
27/28 2
28/29 1

McFARLANE Peter

Heart of Midlothian 97/98 1

McFARLANE Robert
b. c1866 d. Pawtucket ?.1.1941
Thornliebank *
Third Lanark 90/91 4 1
91/92 10 1
Port Glasgow A
Thornliebank

MACFARLANE Robert

St Mirren 91/92 14
92/93
Blackburn R 93/94 2 FL
Nelson 93/94
Blackburn R 94/95 FL
Everton 94/95 FL
Liverpool 94/95 FL

MacFARLANE Robert 1 cap
b. Greenock 16.1.1874 d. 27.7.1943
Greenock Rosebery
Morton 94/95 12 D2
95/96 2 D2
Third Lanark 96/97
Everton 97/98 9 FL
East Stirlingshire 97/98
Bristol St Georges
New Brompton 00/01
Grimsby T 00/01 18 FL
Celtic 01/02 17
Middlesbrough 02/03 18 FL
Aberdeen 03/04
04/05 21 D2
05/06 30
06/07 31
07/08 29
Motherwell 08/09 4

McFARLANE Robert A
b. Glasgow
Parkhead
Queen's Park 18/19 6
19/20 21 2
Partick T 19/20 8 1
20/21 10 2
21/22 13 2
22/23 19 9
23/24 4
Arbroath 23/24 21 9 D2
24/25 34 15 D2
25/26 7 2 D2
Dundee U L 25/26 2
Arbroath 26/27 12 1 D2
Abbey FC

MacFARLANE Robert D

Queen's Park 36/37 1
37/38 3
Falkirk 37/38 1

McFARLANE S

Cambuslang 91/92 5

McFARLANE Thomas
b. Davidsons Mains
Muirhouse R
Hibernian 93/94 10 ? D2
94/95 15 ? D2
95/96 18
96/97 18
97/98 18
98/99 6

McFARLANE William
b. c1886
St Johnstone
Rangers 06/07
Third Lanark 07/08 8
East Fife

McFIE John

Maryhill Jnrs
Queen's Park
Rangers 05/06 4 1
06/07 12 2
Third Lanark 07/08 24 4
08/09 20 5
09/10 9 2
10/11
11/12
12/13
13/14 5 3

McFIE Peter

Glasgow Perthshire
Pollok Jnrs
Airdrieonians 11/12 7 1
12/13 23
Dumbarton 13/14 30
14/15 22 2
15/16 8

McGACHIE Arthur
b. Lochore 1904 d. Dunfermline 20.12.2002
Crossgates Primrose
East Fife T
Alloa A T
Sunderland T
Preston NE T
Heart of Midlothian T
East Fife 27/28 11 D2
28/29 34 28 D2
29/30 36 37 D2
30/31 34 14
31/32 30 26 D2
32/33 31 9 D2
Dunfermline A 33/34 D2
Cowdenbeath 33/34 9 1
Kings Park 34/35 D2
Leith A 34/35 D2

McGARRITY Francis
b. West Calder (?) c1887 d. Kelty 28.1.1941
Queensferry
St Andrews U
Kelty R
St Bernards
Airdrieonians 15/16 15

McGARRY Daniel
b. Lochwinnoch 9.2.1911
Port Glasgow Jnrs

Club		Season	Apps	Gls	Lge
Dunfermline A		30/31			D2
		31/32			D2
		32/33			D2
Arthurlie		33/34			
Morton		34/35			D2
		35/36			D2
		36/37			D2
		37/38	35	15	
Barnsley		38/39	41	12	FL
		39/40	3	1	FL
Morton		46/47	7		
Stirling A		47/48			D2

McGARRY Edward

Club		Season	Apps	Gls	Lge
Dundee		27/28	1		

McGATHAN George

Club		Season	Apps	Gls	Lge
St Mirren		94/95	2		
		95/96	16		
Johnstone		95/96			

McGEACHAN Andrew
b. Glasgow 1882 d. Milton of Campsie ?.11.1943
Cambuslang Hibernian

Club		Season	Apps	Gls	Lge
Hibernian		98/99			
		99/00			
		00/01			
		01/02	7	4	
		02/03	10		
		03/04	17	1	
Bradford C		04/05	21	8	FL
		05/06	13	1	FL
Clyde		06/07	6	2	

McGEACHAN Andrew

Club		Season	Apps	Gls	Lge
Clyde		09/10	6	3	

McGEACHAN Andrew

Club		Season	Apps	Gls	Lge
Morton		09/10	3		

McGEACHAN James
b. Govan 1873 d. 4.4.1903

Club		Season	Apps	Gls	Lge
Hibernian		93/94	17	?	D2
		94/95	8	?	D2
Bolton W		94/95	16	2	FL
		95/96	27	2	FL
		96/97	24	1	FL
		97/98	2		FL
Stoke		97/98	4		FL
Hibernian		98/99	1		
Bolton W		99/00			FL
Belfast Celtic		00/01			IL

McGEACHIE George
b. c1919
Gairdoch Juveniles

Club		Season	Apps	Gls	Lge
St Johnstone		37/38	16	1	
		38/39	9		

McGEACHY Edward

Club		Season	Apps	Gls	Lge
Campbelltown					
Port Glasgow A		09/10	1		

McGEE Robert
b. Mearns 2.9.1903
Corkerhill Jns
Eaglesham
East Kilbride Thistle

Club		Season	Apps	Gls	Lge
Celtic		22/23			
		23/24	1		
St Mirren	L	23/24			
Stenhousemuir	L	23/24			D2
Dumbarton	L	23/24			D2
Celtic		24/25			
Ards		24/25			IL
		25/26			IL
		26/27			IL
		27/28			IL
Bangor	L	27/28			IL
Ards		28/29			IL
		29/30			IL
		30/31			IL
		31/32			IL
Bangor		32/33			IL

McGEE Thomas
b. c1916
Blantyre V
Sheffield W
Blantyre V

Club		Season	Apps	Gls	Lge
Hamilton A		37/38	1		

McGEOCH Archibald Craig
b. Scotland
Dunblane

Club		Season	Apps	Gls	Lge
Woolwich Arsenal		97/98	10	8	FL
		98/99	26	6	FL
		99/00			
Dundee		00/01	14	3	
		01/02	1		
Dunblane		01/02			
Portsmouth		01/02			SL

McGETTIGAN Neil

Club		Season	Apps	Gls	Lge
Levern V					
St Bernards		03/04			
Royal Albert					
Hamilton A		06/07	11	3	

McGHEE

Club		Season	Apps	Gls	Lge
Cowlairs		90/91	4		

McGHEE

Club		Season	Apps	Gls	Lge
Abercorn		92/93	5	1	

McGHEE James 1 cap
b. Lugar d. USA c1945

Club		Season	Apps	Gls	Lge
Cronberry		78/79			
		79/80			
Lugar Boswell		80/81			
		81/82			
		82/83			
Hibernian		83/84			
		84/85			
		85/86			
		86/87			
		87/88			
		88/89			
St Bernards	L	88/89			
Celtic		89/90			
		90/91	9	4	
		91/92	1	1	
Dykebar	L	91/92			
Abercorn	L	91/92			

McGHEE James H

Club		Season	Apps	Gls	Lge
Queen's Park		00/01	7	4	
		01/02	6	2	

McGHEE Joseph
b. Galston 12.7.1911
Galston R
Hurlford Juveniles

Club		Season	Apps	Gls	Lge
Celtic		29/30			
Maryhill Hibernian		29/30			
Celtic		30/31			
		31/32	5	2	
Sheffield W	L	32/33			FL
Airdrieonians		32/33	5		

McGHIE Constantine

Club		Season	Apps	Gls	Lge
Dumbarton Harp					
Rangers		05/06	1		
Third Lanark		06/07	19		
Ayr Parkhouse		06/07			D2
Reading		07/08			SL
		08/09			SL
		09/10			SL
Renton		09/10			

McGHIE Joseph

Club		Season	Apps	Gls	Lge
Clyde		16/17	17		

McGIBBON Terence
b. Irvine
Irvine Meadow

Club		Season	Apps	Gls	Lge
Galston	L				
Kilmarnock					
St Mirren					
Partick T					
Ayr U		33/34	38	35	
		34/35	36	13	
		35/36	29	11	
		36/37	34	39	D2
		37/38	34	21	
Preston NE		38/39	22	2	FL
Ayr U					

McGILL Charles
b. Kilmarnock 3.2.1903 d. ?.2.1988
Queen of the South

Club		Season	Apps	Gls	Lge
Heart of Midlothian		23/24	6		
Third Lanark		24/25	25		
Fall River Marksmen		25/26	31		ASL
		26/27	32		ASL
		27/28	51		ASL
		28/29	53		ASL
Boston Bears		29A	20		ASL
Boston		29/30	3		ASL
Fall River Marksmen		29/30	20		ASL
		30A	21		ASL
New York Yankees		31S	15		ASL
Aberdeen		31/32	23		
		32/33	38	1	
		33/34	38		
		34/35	38		
		35/36	35		
		36/37	25		
		37/38	21		
Glentoran		38/39			

McGILL J P

Club		Season	Apps	Gls	Lge
Dundee Violet					
Queen's Park		08/09	1		

McGILL Patrick
b. Baillieston 1911
Baillieston

Club		Season	Apps	Gls	Lge
Clyde		30/31	11	2	
		31/32	11	2	
Maryhill Hibs		32/33			
		33/34			
		34/35			
Heart of Midlothian		35/36	3		
Raith R	L	35/36			D2
Exeter C		36/37	25	1	FL
		37/38	9		FL
Distillery		38/39			

McGILLIVRAY Charles
b. Kinlochleven 5.7.1912 d. Bangor 7.11.1986
Dreghorn Jnrs

Club		Season	Apps	Gls	Lge
Ayr U		30/31	19	11	
		31/32	25	8	
Celtic		32/33	4	2	
Manchester U		33/34	8		FL
Motherwell		33/34	2	1	
		34/35	7		
		35/36	10	5	
		36/37	14	10	
		37/38	7	5	
		38/39	1		
Dundee		38/39	26	29	D2
Dundee U					
Stirling A					
Arbroath		46/47			D2

McGIMPSEY James
b. Partick
Renfrew V

Club		Season	Apps	Gls	Lge
Kilmarnock		03/04	8		
Distillery		04/05			
Vale of Leven		05/06			D2
		06/07			D2
		07/08			D2
		08/09			D2
		09/10			D2
Johnstone		09/10			D2

McGINLAY George

Club		Season	Apps	Gls	Lge
Queen of the South		34/35	19	5	
		35/36	9	1	
St Mirren		35/36			D2

McGINN David

Club		Season	Apps	Gls	Lge
Ardrossan Winton R					
Ayr U		18/19	1	?	

McGINN Hugh
b. Hewood 17.8.1896 d. ?.1.1937
Glengarnock Vale

Club		Season	Apps	Gls	Lge
Arsenal		23/24			FL
Charlton A		24/25	2		FL
		25/26	9		FL
Dundee		26/27	30	2	
Portadown *		30/31			
Glentoran		31/32			

McGINN James
b. Rehfrew Abbey 27.6.1868 d. Johnstone ?.8.1932
Paisley Celtic
Abercorn

Club		Season	Apps	Gls	Lge
Hibernian		94/95	3	?	D2
		95/96	10		
		96/97	2		
Clyde		97/98	1		
Johnstone					

McGINN James

Baillieston					
Mossend Celtic					
Celtic		93/94	2		
Airdrieonians		94/95			D2
Bolton W		94/95	15	3	FL
Airdrieonians		94/95	4	2	D2
		95/96			D2
		96/97	2		D2

McGINNIGLE Hugh

b. Coatbridge 1.7.1906

Minerva Hibs					
Falkirk		27/28	1		
		28/29	16	1	
		29/30	24	10	
Luton T		30/31	25		FL
		31/32	36		FL
		32/33	40		FL
		33/34	40	2	FL
		34/35	14		FL
		35/36	3		FL
		36/37	1		FL
Aldershot		37/38	2		FL

McGINNIGLE William George

b. Paisley 5.6.1892 d. Paisley 11.10.1947

Cambuslang R					
Hibernian		18/19	30	?	
Celtic	L	18/19	1		
Hibernian		19/20	27	2	
		20/21	29		
		21/22	29		
		22/23	38		
		23/24	31		
		24/25	34		
		25/26	8		
		26/27	23		
		27/28	30		
		28/29	19		
Coleraine		29/30			
		30/31			
Larne		30/31			

McGIRR William

Lochgelly Celtic					
Cowdenbeath		29/30	2		
		30/31			
Dartford		30/31			
Leith A		31/32	35	2	
		32/33			D2
		33/34			D2
		34/35			D2
St Bernards					
Rhyl					

McGLADE James

Blantyre V					
Motherwell		13/14	1		
		14/15	20		

McGLASHAN

Third Lanark		91/92	1		
		92/93	1		

McGLYNN George A

Dundee U		31/32	12		
St Bernards		32/33			D2

McGOLDRICK Edward

Bowhill R					
Pollok Jnrs					
Dundee		33/34	3		
		34/35	1		
Raith R		35/36			D2

McGOLDRICK William

St Rochs					
Third Lanark		23/24	21		

McGONAGLE Bernard

St Mirren		18/19	2	?	

McGONAGLE Peter William 6 caps

b. Hamilton 30.4.1904 d. Cheltenham 20.12.1956

St Josephs BG					
Greenhead Thistle					
Duntochter Hibernian					
Celtic		26/27			
Nithsdale W	L	26/27			D2
Celtic		27/28	29		
		28/29	38	1	
		29/30	35		
		30/31	37		
		31/32	35		
		32/33	31	1	
		33/34	35	5	
		34/35	31		
		35/36	13		
Dunfermline A		35/36	6		
Hamilton A		36/37	20	1	
Cheltenham T		37/38			
		38/39			
Sunningend					

McGORAM James

b. Old Kipatrick 5.11.1908

St Leonards					
Cowdenbeath					
Singer					
Raith R		28/29	10	1	
Partick T		29/30	1		

McGOURTY John

b. Addiewell 10.7.1912 d. Birkenhead ?.11.1999

Fauldhouse St Johns					
Partick T		31/32	26	4	
Edinburgh C	L				
Everton		32/33	14	2	FL
		33/34	1		FL
Hamilton A		34/35	4		
		35/36			
Waterford		36/37			
		37/38			
Ipswich T		38/39	1		FL

McGOVERN Bernard

Vale of Bannock					
Falkirk		21/22	1		
Clydebank		22/23			D2

McGOVERN Thomas

b. Old Kilpatrick 6.2.1901

Clydebank					
Millwall		21/22			
Clydebank		22/23			D2
		23/24	30	1	
Bristol C		24/25	3	1	FL
Merthyr T		25/26	28	8	FL
Sheppey U		26/27			
Queen of the South					
Torquay U		27/28	18	1	FL
Sheppey U		28/29			
Northfleet U		29/30			
Sittingbourne					
Devon General Bus Co					
Paignton T					

McGOWAN

Rangers		91/92	1	1	

McGOWAN Harry

Ayr U		12/13			D2
		13/14	9	3	
		14/15			
Johnstone		14/15			
Clyde		15/16	14	2	
		16/17	31	14	
		17/18	22	?	
		18/19			
		19/20	14	4	
Bo'ness		20/21			

McGOWAN James

Cambuslang R *					
Third Lanark		17/18	21	?	
		18/19	32	?	
		19/20	13		
		20/21			
Royal Albert		21/22			

McGOWAN Robert Nivison

b. Sanquhar 2.6.1908 d. Dunfermline 1984

Nithsdale W		26/27	?	2	D2
Kello R		27/28			
Carlisle U		27/28			
Crewe A		28/29			
Rangers		28/29			
Kilmarnock	L	29/30	15	18	
Rangers		30/31	12	10	
		31/32			
Bournemouth		32/33	6	2	FL
Queen of the South		33/34	27	20	
Ballymena U		33/34			IL
Dunfermline A		34/35	19	16	
		35/36	32	23	
		36/37	23	17	
Kilmarnock		37/38	12	8	

McGOWN John

b. Renton

Vale of Leven Academy					
Vale of Emmet					
Rutherglen Glencairn					
Ayr U		35/36	2	1	

McGOWN Peter

Petershill					
Clyde		34/35			
		35/36	9	2	
Larne		36/37			IL
Luton T		37/38			FL

McGRAIN Charles S

Shawfield					
Partick T		20/21	2		

McGRAIN Thomas

Parkhead					
Third Lanark		05/06	11	3	
		06/07	10	2	

McGRAN William

b. Lochwinnoch 1879 d. Lochwinnoch 12.12.1922

Lochwinnock North British					
Barnsley		02/03	9	1	FL
Beith		03/04			
Rangers		03/04			
Airdrieonians		04/05	24	1	
		05/06	30	1	
		06/07	32	1	
		07/08	30	1	
		08/09	30		
		09/10	25		
		10/11	3		
Hibernian					
Glasgow Ashfield					

McGRATH John

b. Clydebank

Duntocher Hibs					
Motherwell		24/25	19	3	
		25/26	15	2	
Dumbarton		25/26			D2

McGRATH William

Kilbirnie Ladeside					
Ayr U		32/33	24	3	
		33/34	3		
Morton		34/35			D2
Galston		35/36			
Alloa A		35/36			D2

McGRAW Thomas

Common Thistle					
Hamilton A		06/07	5	4	
		07/08	18	2	
Workington		08/09			

McGREGOR

Vale of Leven		90/91	2		
		91/92	2		

McGREGOR

Renton		92/93	15	3	

McGREGOR

Dumbarton		93/94	3		

McGREGOR

St Mirren		93/94	1		
		94/95	1		

McGREGOR

Hibernian		07/08	2		

McGREGOR

Club		Season	Apps	Goals	
Morton		18/19	1		

McGREGOR A
b. Paisley

Club		Season	Apps	Goals	
St Mirren		28/29	2		

McGREGOR Alexander

Club		Season	Apps	Goals	
Queen's Park		00/01	1		
		01/02			
		02/03	1		
Dunblane					

McGREGOR Alexander

Club		Season	Apps	Goals	
Ashfield					
Partick T		04/05	1	1	
		05/06	3		
		06/07	33	12	
		07/08	31	7	
		08/09	28	2	
		09/10	28	2	
		10/11	23	3	
		11/12	12		
St Mirren		12/13	16	2	

McGREGOR Alexander
b. Renfrew 9.5.1896

Club		Season	Apps	Goals	
Renfrew Jnrs					
Clydebank Jnrs					
Celtic		13/14	1		
St Mirren	L	13/14	13		
Dumbarton	L	14/15	32	5	
St Mirren	L	14/15	1		
Dumbarton	L	15/16	35	10	
Clydebank		17/18	1		
Vale of Leven		18/19			
Stevenston U					

McGREGOR Alexander W

Club		Season	Apps	Goals	
Petershill					
Queen's Park		14/15	8		

McGREGOR Charles S

Club		Season	Apps	Goals	
Dunbar U					
Partick T		38/39	26		

McGREGOR Donald M

Club		Season	Apps	Goals	
Queen's Park		10/11	1		

McGREGOR George W
b. Saltcoats

Club		Season	Apps	Goals	
Saltcoats V					
St Mirren		27/28	5		
		28/29			
Sunderland		29/30	1		FL
Benburb		30/31			
Norwich C	T	30/31			FL
India of Inchinnan					

McGREGOR Henry
b. Inverkeithing

Club		Season	Apps	Goals	
2nd Black Watch					
Dundee		23/24	3		
Arbroath		24/25	12		D2
Forfar A		25/26			D2
East Stirlingshire		26/27			D2
		27/28			D2
Dundee U		28/29	31		D2
		29/30	12		
Alloa A		30/31			D2
		31/32			D2
Forfar A		32/33			D2

McGREGOR James
b. Scotland

Club		Season	Apps	Goals	
Queen's Park		01/02	5		
		02/03	20	1	
		03/04	10		
Vale of Leven		03/04			D2
Grimsby T		04/05	22		FL
		05/06	38	1	FL
		06/07	33	1	FL
Glossop		07/08	37	1	FL
		08/09	34		FL
		09/10	6		FL

McGREGOR James

Club		Season	Apps	Goals	
Cambuslang R					
Dumbarton		17/18	17		
		18/19	12	?	
Kilmarnock	L	18/19	2		

McGREGOR James B

Club		Season	Apps	Goals	
Benburb					
St Mirren		32/33	3		
		33/34	32	14	
		34/35	28	9	
		35/36			D2
		36/37	12	4	
		37/38	5	1	

McGREGOR John

Club		Season	Apps	Goals	
Musselburgh Bruntonians					
Armadale		23/24			D2
Rangers		23/24	2		
		24/25	1		
		25/26	6		

McGREGOR Michael
b. Dundee

Club		Season	Apps	Goals	
Stobswell Jnrs					
Dundee U		25/26	1		
		26/27	29	3	
		27/28	25	2	
Montrose		28/29			D2
Arbroath		28/29	8	3	D2
		29/30	4	1	D2
Falkirk		29/30	34	6	
		30/31	28	3	
		31/32	12	1	
Dartford		32/33			

McGREGOR Robert
b. Govan c1897

Club		Season	Apps	Goals	
Pollok					
Morton		19/20	22		
		20/21	42	2	
		21/22	42	2	
		22/23	27		
Bethlehem Steel		23/24	22	1	ASL
		24/25	29	4	ASL
		25/26	31	3	ASL
		26/27	34	3	ASL
		27/28	44	2	ASL
		28/29	7		ESL
		29/30	23	1	ASL
Newark Americans		30A	28	2	ASL
		31S	13	1	ASL
Fraserburgh		31/32			
		32/33			

McGREGOR T

Club		Season	Apps	Goals	
St Johnstone		28/29	1		

McGREGOR Thomas
b. Laurieston 23.11.1893

Club		Season	Apps	Goals	
Laurieston Villa					
Kilsyth Emmet					
Celtic		10/11	2		
		11/12	8		
		12/13	6		
		13/14	13		
Motherwell	L	13/14			
Celtic		14/15	15		
		15/16	15		
		16/17	1		
		17/18	10		
Dumbarton Harp	L	17/18			
Celtic		18/19	5		
Clydebank	L	18/19	2	?	
Dumbarton	L	18/19	6	?	
Motherwell		19/20	36		
		20/21	22		
Alloa A		21/22			D2
		22/23	31		

McGRILLEN John Joseph
b. Belfast 4.7.1902

Club		Season	Apps	Goals	
Rosario					
Linfield		21/22			IL
		22/23			IL
Clyde		23/24	26	1	
Cliftonville		24/25			IL
Belfast Celtic		25/26			IL
		26/27			IL
		27/28			IL
		28/29			
Bethlehem Steel		28/29	3		ESL
Shamrock R		29/30			LI
		30/31			LI
		31/32			LI
Belfast Celtic		31/32			IL
Newry T		31/32			IL
?		32/33			
Dundela		33/34			

McGROGAN Felix
b. Dumbarton 27.7.1914

Club		Season	Apps	Goals	
Duntocher His					
Maryhill Hibs					
Renfrew Jnrs					
Blackburn R		35/36	4	1	FL
Dunfermline A		36/37	36	11	
Cumbernauld U					
Falkirk		37/38	7	1	
Kilmarnock		37/38	12	6	
		38/39	31	9	
Dumbarton					
Third Lanark					

McGROGAN Vincent
b. Paisley 12.11.1901

Club		Season	Apps	Goals	
Glenburn R					
Largs Thistle					
Celtic		24/25	5		
		25/26			
Ayr U	L	25/26			D2
Armadale Thistle	L	25/26			
Celtic		26/27			

McGRORY Hugh

Club		Season	Apps	Goals	
Blackburn R					
St Mirren		14/15	24	1	
		15/16	25		

McGRORY James Edward 7 caps
b. Garngad 26.4.1904 d. Glasgow 20.10.1982

Club		Season	Apps	Goals	
St Roch BG					
St Roch Jnrs					
Bury	T	21/22			FL
Celtic		22/23	3	1	
Clydebank	L	23/24			
Celtic		24/25	25	17	
		25/26	37	32	
		26/27	33	48	
		27/28	36	47	
		28/29	21	21	
		29/30	26	32	
		30/31	29	36	
		31/32	22	28	
		32/33	25	22	
		33/34	27	17	
		34/35	27	18	
		35/36	32	50	
		36/37	25	21	
		37/38	10	5	

McGRORY Robert Gerard
b. Erskine 17.10.1891 d. Kelvingrove 23.5.1954

Club		Season	Apps	Goals	
Bishopton Boys Brigade					
Houston St Fillans					
Cumbernauld U					
Kilbarchan A					
Dumbarton		14/15	33		
		15/16	37		
		16/17	37		
		17/18	34		
Partick T	L	17/18	1		
Dumbarton		18/19	33		
		19/20	38		
Burnley		20/21	3		FL
Stoke		20/21	2		FL
		21/22	41		FL
		22/23	32		FL
		23/24	29		FL
		24/25	40		FL
		25/26	36		FL
		26/27	42		FL
		27/28	42		FL
		28/29	38		FL
		29/30	21		FL
		30/31	30		FL
		31/32	41		FL
		32/33	7		FL
		33/34	26		FL
		34/35	42		FL

McGRORY Thomas

Club		Season	Apps	Goals	
Kirkintilloch Rob Roy					
Dundee		23/24	12	2	

McGRORY W

Club		Season	Apps	Goals	
Clydebank		23/24	30	11	

McGUIGAN Andrew
b. Newton Stewart 24.2.1878

Club		Season	Apps	Goals	
Newton Stewart					
Hibernian		98/99	17	4	
		99/00	18	12	
Liverpool		00/01	14	5	FL
		01/02	18	9	FL
Middlesbrough		02/03	1		FL
		03/04	2		FL
Southport Central					
Barrow					
Exeter C		08/09	28	16	SL
		09/10	16	4	SL

McGUIRE Charles

Falkirk 25/26 7
26/27 8 3

McGUIRE Edward

Heart of Midlothian 15/16 2 1

McGUIRE Edward

Newry T
Cowdenbeath 24/25 1

McGUIRE George
b. Blantyre
St Rochs
Strathclyde
Clyde 26/27 38
27/28 37
28/29 36
29/30 8
Portadown 29/30 IL
Morton 30/31 35
31/32 37 1
Kirkcaldy U

McGUIRE James

Abercorn 96/97 8

McGUNNIGLE Thomas
b. Glasgow 31.3.1905
Maryhill Hibernian
Celtic 31/32 1
Glentoran 32/33
Bangor 32/33
Dumbarton 32/33 D2
33/34 D2
Cork 33/34 LI
Brideville 34/35 LI
35/36 LI
Dumbarton 36/37 D2
Brechin C 36/37 D2
37/38 D2
38/39 D2
St Roch

McGURDY Robert Nelson
b. c1917 d. 27.8.1998
Heart of Midlothian 38/39 2 3
Falkirk

McGURK Francis Reynolds 1 cap
b. Eddlewood 15.1.1909 d. Birmingham 2.3.1978
Blantyre Celtic
Clyde 31/32 37 7
32/33 37 12
Birmingham 33/34 18 3 FL
34/35 1 FL
Bristol C 35/36 3 FL
Whittaker Ellis 36/37
37/38
38/39

McGURK James

Stonehouse Violet
Hamilton A 37/38 13
38/39 11
46/47 26
47/48 D2
48/49 D2

McHALE John
b. Maryhill
Maryhill Hibs
Aberdeen 25/26 3
26/27 13
27/28 22 2
28/29 20 1
29/30 6
St Johnstone L 29/30 7
Falkirk 30/31 4
Shelbourne 31/32 LI
Keith 31/32
Doncaster R 32/33 31 FL
33/34 22 FL
Crewe A 34/35 7 FL

McHALLUM Joseph
b. Galston
Hurlford Thistle
Kilmarnock 18/19 12 2
19/20 9 2
20/21 1
Galston 21/22
New Cumnock U 21/22
Ayr U 22/23 1
Nithsdale W 23/24 D3

McHARDY John

Montrose
Dundee 04/05 3
Montrose
Aberdeen University 06/07

McHUGH James

Maryhill
Glasgow St Anthonys
Maryhill
Morton 29/30 3

McHUGH John
b. Hamilton 13.8.1909 d. Bushey 9.10.1966
Strathclyde
Burnbank A
Dundee U 27/28 6 D2
28/29 5 D2
29/30 26
30/31 15 D2
31/32
Portsmouth 32/33 3 FL
Watford 33/34 2 FL
34/35 1 FL
35/36 4 FL
36/37 6 FL
37/38 3 FL
38/39 22 FL
39/40 3 FL

McILHENNY

Clyde 95/96 5

McILHENNY Hugh

Dumbarton 95/96 6 1
96/97 4 ? D2

McILVENNY Henry Joseph
b. Gorbals 1876 d. Cathcart ?.1.1934
Parkhead Jnrs
Celtic 95/96 1
Dumbarton L 95/96
Burnley 96/97
Celtic 96/97 1
New Brighton Tower 96/97
Victoria U 97/98
Belfast Celtic 98/99 IL
99/00 IL
00/01 IL
St Bernards 00/01 D2
01/02 D2
Hamilton A 02/03 D2
03/04 D2
Partick T 04/05 6 1
Celtic 04/05 7 1
Hamilton A 05/06 D2
Ayr 06/07 D2

McILWAINE John
b. Bellodyke 12.6.1904 d. Grimsby 24.4.1980
Irvine V
Falkirk 25/26 7
26/27 34 5
27/28 21 3
Portsmouth 27/28 15 FL
28/29 32 FL
29/30 10 1 FL
Southampton 30/31 26 7 FL
31/32 20 2 FL
Llanelly 32/33
Southampton 33/34 11 1 FL
34/35 24 7 FL
35/36 33 1 FL
36/37 3 FL

McILWRAITH J C

Queen's Park 08/09 3

McILWRAITH Stewart
b. Airdrie
Bellshill A
Third Lanark 22/23 13
Sunderland T 23/24 FL
Hamilton A 23/24 18 5
24/25
Broxburn U 25/26 D2

McINALLY Arthur
b. Barrhead 15.9.1900
St Mungos Academy
Barrhead Belmont
Kirkintilloch Rob Roy 13/14
14/15
15/16
St Mirren 16/17
Croy Celtic
Celtic 17/18 1
Ayr U L 17/18 1 ?
Dumbarton Harp L 17/18
St Mirren 18/19 18 ?
Abercorn 19/20
Dunfermline A 19/20
20/21
Armadale 21/22 D2
Alloa A 22/23 32
23/24 D2
Clyde L 23/24 9
St Bernards 24/25 D2

McINALLY James

Heart of Midlothian 18/19 4 ?

McINALLY John Joseph
b. Blantyre 17.5.1915
Wishaw Jnrs
Celtic 34/35 7 3
35/36 1 1
36/37 1 1
Arbroath 37/38 33 15
38/39 37 13
46/47 D2
Queen of the South 46/47 D2
Cowdenbeath 46/47 D2
Ballymena U 47/48
Albion R 48/49 D2
Los Angeles
Wigtown & Bladnoch 51/52

McINALLY Thomas Bernard 2 caps
b. Partick ?.12.1899 d. Paisley 29.12.1955
St Mungos Academy
Croy Celtic
St Anthonys
Barrhead
Rangers T 18/19
Celtic 19/20 32 30
20/21 37 28
21/22 24 16
Third Lanark 22/23 30 12
23/24 30 13
24/25 27 15
Celtic 25/26 37 17
26/27 31 8
27/28 27 15
Sunderland 28/29 31 3 FL
29/30 4 FL
Bournemouth 29/30 10 1 FL
Morton 30/31 7
Derry C 30/31 IL
Coleraine 30/31 IL
31/32 IL
Armadale 32/33 D2
Nithsdale W 32/33
33/34
34/35
35/36
36/37

McINDEWAR

Dumbarton 91/92 1

McINDEWAR

Dumbarton 94/95 2

McINDOE John

Queen's Park 28/29 1

McINDOE Robert Whyte

Troon A
St Mirren 31/32 31 1
32/33 22 2
Ayr U 33/34
Morton T 34/35 D2
Ayr U 34/35
35/36
Glentoran 35/36 IL
36/37 IL
Airdrieonians 37/38 D2

McINNES

Abercorn 90/91 1

McINNES

Third Lanark 90/91 14 4

McINNES

Abercorn 92/93 1

McINNES

Rangers 92/93 4 2

McINNES Angus

St Bernards 97/98 13 6
Burnley 97/98 3 1 FL
98/99 3 1 FL
99/00 FL
00/01 FL
01/02 FL
02/03 32 2 FL
Padiham
Kings Park

McINNES David

Jeanfield
St Johnstone 19/20
Raith R 20/21 9
Dundee Hibs 21/22 8 D2

McINNES James Sloan
b. Ayr 17.2.1912 d. Liverpool 5.5.1965
Glasgow University
Ardeer Rec
Third Lanark 35/36 34 1
36/37 38 1
37/38 31 5
Liverpool 37/38 11 1 FL
38/39 34 FL
39/40 3 1 FL
Distillery 43/44 IL

McINNES John
d. ?.6.1914
Thornliebank
St Mirren 99/00
Thornliebank 99/00
00/01
Beith 01/02
Morton 02/03 14 1

McINNES John

Falkirk 05/06 10 6
Vale of Leven 06/07 D2

McINNES John

Johnstone
Motherwell 11/12 1
Johnstone 11/12
12/13 D2

McINNES Peter

Clyde 08/09 1

McINNES Thomas
b. Glasgow 22.3.1870 d. Luton ?.1.1939
Cowlairs
Notts Co 89/90 7 1 FL
90/91 22 9 FL
91/92 25 8 FL
Rangers 91/92
Notts Co 92/93 19 5 FL
Third Lanark 93/94 18 8
Everton 94/95 23 10 FL
95/96 19 6 FL
Luton T 96/97 FL
97/98 29 10 FL
98/99 31 7 FL
99/00 33 2 FL
Bedford Queen Works

McINNES Thomas 1 cap
b. Glasgow 29.8.1870
Dalmuir Thistle
Cowlairs
Newcastle EE
Clyde 91/92 22 6
Nottingham F 92/93 30 10 FL
93/94 2 12 FL
94/95 17 5 FL
95/96 30 9 FL
96/97 28 4 FL
97/98 23 4 FL
98/99 11 1 FL
Third Lanark 99/00
Lincoln C 00/01 27 7 FL
01/02 32 10 FL
02/03 19 2 FL
03/04
Port Glasgow A 04/05 1

McINROY David
b. Dundee 16.12.1874 d. Lochee 11.7.1940
Dundee Our Boys
Dundee 93/94 9 4
94/95 5 1
Millwall A 95/96 5 1 SL
Tottenham H 95/96
Dundee 95/96
96/97
97/98
98/99 1
Dundee W 98/99
99/00
00/01
01/02
Lochee U

McINTOSH

Clyde 91/92 21 6
92/93 8 1

McINTOSH

Falkirk 07/08 1

McINTOSH

Falkirk 16/17 1

McINTOSH Alexander

Clydebank 21/22 16 2

McINTOSH Alexander
b. Port Glasgow c1903
Aberdeen East End
St Johnstone 25/26 4

McINTOSH Angus Munro
b. Birkenhead 1884
Inverness Thistle
Sunderland 05/06 4 1 FL
06/07 19 4 FL
07/08 16 5 FL
08/09 1 FL
Bury 08/09 22 7 FL
09/10 14 5 FL
Aberdeen 10/11 34 16
11/12 22 5
12/13
13/14 9 1
Buckie Thistle 14/15

McINTOSH Charles K
b. c1911
Logie Jnrs
Dundee U 31/32 35
32/33 33 D2
33/34 23
Preston NE 34/35 FL
Luton T 35/36 FL
Cowdenbeath 36/37 D2

McINTOSH David

Queen's Park 14/15 3 1
15/16 1
16/17
17/18
18/19 2

McINTOSH George
b. Govan 1899
Govan YMCA
Renfrew Jnrs
Hibernian 18/19 10
19/20
20/21
Solway Star 21/22
Workington 22/23
Exeter C 23/24 16 FL
Accrington S 24/25 17 1 FL
Boston T

McINTOSH Hugh D
b. Aberdeen
St Mirren 19/20 5 2
20/21 9
Lochgelly U 21/22 D2

McINTOSH James

Abercorn
Morton 03/04 1
04/05 25 3
05/06 28
06/07 31 1
07/08 31
08/09 29 1
09/10 25 1
10/11 8

McINTOSH James Boyd
b. Glasgow 25.5.1886 d. 1959
Wellwood Juveniles
Petershill
Scots Guards
Reading T 02/03 SL
Glasgow Perthshire
Third Lanark 06/07 20 1
Aberdeen 07/08 32
08/09 31 1
Celtic 09/10 6
Hull C 10/11 30 FL
11/12 11 FL
12/13 18 2 FL
13/14 32 FL
Scots Guards
Heart of Midlothian 16/17 9
17/18 12
Hibernian 17/18
Dumbarton T 18/19 5 ?

McINTOSH Ralph

Partick T 20/21 3
Clydebank 20/21 15 1

McINTOSH Robert Anderson
b. Dundee 1.8.1892 d. Dundee 9.1.1952
Thistle
Dundee Fairfield
Dundee 12/13
13/14 37 1
14/15 38 3
15/16 27 2
16/17 27
Motherwell L 17/18 32 1
18/19 31 1
Dundee 19/20 39
Newcastle U 20/21 33 FL
21/22 24 1 FL
22/23 27 1 FL
23/24 17 FL
Stockport Co 24/25 8 FL

McINTOSH Robert G

Queen's Park 20/21 1

McINTOSH William 1 cap

Third Lanark 01/02 9
02/03 18 1
03/04 23
04/05 21
05/06 18
06/07 12
07/08 23
Partick T

McINTOSH William

Third Lanark 08/09 28 1
09/10 7
Vale of Leven 10/11 6 D2

McINTOSH William

Glasgow Meat Market
Clydebank 20/21 3
21/22
Strathclyde
St Mirren 22/23 13 3
23/24 19 2
Clyde 24/25
Blackpool 24/25 1 FL

McINTOSH William Dowlin

Petershill
St Johnstone 38/39 14 9
Preston NE
Blackpool

McINTYRE

Abercorn 90/91 1

McINTYRE

Vale of Leven 90/91 1

McINTYRE

Dumbarton 95/96 1

McINTYRE Donald S

Queen's Park 00/01 1

McINTYRE James 1 cap
b. Glasgow c1863 d. Townhead ?.3.1943
Glasgow St Andrews
Alexandra A
Rangers 79/80
80/81
81/82
82/83
83/84
84/85
85/86
86/87
87/88
88/89
89/90
90/91 9
91/92 2

McINTYRE John

Galston
Kilmarnock L 37/38 2
East Stirlingshire 38/39 D2

McINTYRE John McGregor
b. Glasgow 4.1.1895 d. Blackpool ?.2.1974
Denny A
Partick T 12/13 10 1
13/14 15 1
14/15 10 2
Vale of Leven 15/16
St Mirren L 15/16 2
Partick T 16/17 4
17/18
18/19 2
Fulham 19/20 26 9 FL
Sheffield W 19/20 9 1 FL
20/21 41 27 FL
21/22 17 8 FL
Blackburn R 21/22 16 2 FL
22/23 31 10 FL
23/24 40 10 FL
24/25 30 12 FL
25/26 35 3 FL
26/27 21 1 FL
27/28 2 FL
Blackpool 27/28 6 2 FL
Chorley

McINTYRE Murdoch

Glasgow Ashfield
Partick T 25/26 2
26/27
Alloa A 26/27 D2

McINTYRE Peter

Rangers 95/96 3
96/97
Abercorn 96/97

McINTYRE Peter
b. Glenbuck ?.11.1875
Preston NE 98/99 22 2 FL
99/00 33 2 FL
00/01 32 2 FL
Sheffield U 01/02 3 FL
Portsmouth 02/03 2 SL
Hamilton A 03/04 D2
04/05 D2
05/06 D2
06/07 20 1
07/08 22 4
Abercorn 08/09

McINTYRE Robert
b. Greenock
Morton 15/16 34 1
16/17 34 4
17/18 27 3
18/19 34 5
19/20 36 1
20/21 34
21/22 34
22/23 28
23/24 35
Boston Wonder Workers 24/25 39 1 ASL
25/26 18 1 ASL
26/27 29 ASL
27/28 39 ASL
28/29 42 1 ASL
Coleraine 29/30 IL
Boston Bears 31A 4 2 ASL

McINTYRE Thomas
b. Livingston 1919
Portobello Renton
Hibernian 36/37
37/38 38 11
38/39 33 15
Kilmarnock

McINTYRE William

Maryhill
Partick T 07/08 3
08/09
09/10
Workington 10/11

McIVER John

Dykehead
Hamilton A 21/22 1

McIVOR Neil

Tranent Jnrs
Airdrieonians 31/32
32/33 12 2
33/34
34/35
Newry T 34/35 IL
35/36 IL
36/37 IL
37/38 IL
38/39 IL
Derry C 39/40 IL
40/41 IL

McKAY

Vale of Leven 91/92 1

McKAY

Abercorn 92/93 1

McKAY

Third Lanark 92/93 10 3

MacKAY

Morton 01/02 1

McKAY

Hibernian 05/06 2

MacKAY

Heart of Midlothian 30/31 1

McKAY Colin Campbell
b. Portobello 24.8.1895 d. Edinburgh 1978
Denbeath Star
Cowdenbeath
Raith R 16/17
Heart of Midlothian 16/17 4
17/18
18/19 6 3
19/20 2
Sheffield W 19/20 12 3 FL
Huddersfield T 20/21 4 FL
21/22 14 2 FL
Bradford C 22/23 20 4 FL
23/24 6 FL
Aberavon 24/25

MacKAY David

Dundee 00/01 9 6
01/02 13 3

MacKAY Donald Morgan
b. Edinburgh 23.6.1909
Clerwood Amateurs
Queen's Park 29/30 3 3
Plymouth A
Northampton T 32/33 FL
Dundee 33/34 31 17
34/35 7 3
Barnsley 35/36 1 FL
Queen of the South 36/37 D2
37/38 D2
Leith A T 37/38 D2

McKAY Duncan
b. Troon 1894
Troon Ailsa
Rutherglen Glencairn 10/11
Dreghorn 10/11
Irvine Meadow 11/12
Kilmarnock 12/13 2

MacKAY Eric

St Andrews
Cowdenbeath 33/34 2 1

MacKAY George

Bannockburn
Stenhousemuir
St Johnstone 10/11
Kilmarnock 11/12 2
Bo'ness 11/12
St Johnstone 11/12 10 4 D2

McKAY George

Aberdeen 15/16 2
16/17 10

MacKAY George K

Forres Mechanics
Partick T 12/13 1
Forres Mechanics 13/14

McKAY Hector

Gordons Regt
Aberdeen 09/10 2 2

McKAY Hugh

Vale of Midlothian
Heart of Midlothian 87/88
88/89
89/90
90/91 2

McKAY John Reid 1 cap
b. Maryhill 1.11.1898 d. Glasgow 6.2.1970
Townhead Benburb
St Anthonys
Celtic 19/20 6 5
20/21 4 1
Blackburn R 21/22 12 5 FL
22/23 38 12 FL
23/24 33 12 FL
24/25 39 12 FL
25/26 11 1 FL
26/27 17 4 FL
Middlesbrough 26/27 7 1 FL
27/28 9 3 FL
28/29 8 FL
29/30 28 6 FL
30/31 25 7 FL
31/32 16 2 FL
32/33 1 FL
33/34 10 FL
34/35 FL
35/36 FL
Hibernian 36/37 11 2

McKAY Neil

Renfrew V
Kilmarnock 02/03 7 1
03/04 11
Vale of Leven 04/05
05/06 D2

MacKAY Norman

Leith Amateurs
Gala Fairydean
Hibernian 20/21 4
St Bernards 21/22 D2
Lochgelly U 22/23 D2
Broxburn U 23/24 D2
Aston Villa 23/24 FL
24/25 FL
Clydebank 25/26 4 2

McKAY Robert 1 cap
b. Govan 2.9.1900
Parkhead White Rose
Vale of Clyde
Parkhead
Neilston V
Morton 21/22 36 4
22/23 38 9
23/24 32 8
24/25 36 7
Rangers 25/26 22 6
26/27 3 1
Newcastle U 26/27 25 10 FL
27/28 32 12 FL
28/29 5 FL
Sunderland 28/29 34 15 FL
29/30 14 2 FL
30/31 1 FL
Charlton A 30/31 21 4 FL
31/32 28 4 FL
Bristol R 32/33 27 2 FL
33/34 39 14 FL
34/35 25 1 FL
Newport Co 35/36 16 3 FL

McKAY Robert

Raith R 37/38 6 3 D2
38/39 7

McKAY Stewart

Clyde 30/31 6 1
31/32 16

McKAY Thomas Galloway
b. Glasgow 16.7.1909 d. Southport 16.10.1988
Dreghorn
Glasgow Ashfield
Lyon St Church
Nottingham F 30/31 2 FL
31/32 2 FL
Queen of the South 32/33 D2
33/34 18 2
34/35 27 2
35/36 24 2
36/37 3 1
Southport 36/37 40 5 FL
37/38 25 FL
38/39 3 FL
Wigan A

McKAY William
b. West Benhar 24.8.1906
Shotts Battlefield
East Stirlingshire 25/26 D2
26/27 D2
Hamilton A 27/28 28 8
28/29 31 8
29/30 17 6
Bolton W 29/30 22 5 FL
30/31 28 2 FL
31/32 13 FL
32/33 22 4 FL
33/34 19 4 FL
Manchester U 33/34 10 FL
34/35 38 3 FL
35/36 35 FL
36/37 29 4 FL
37/38 37 7 FL
38/39 20 1 FL
39/40 2 FL
Stalybridge C

McKEARY Francis
b. Milngarvie
St Rochs
Hamilton A 26/27 17

McKECHNIE D

Renton 92/93 8

McKECHNIE James
b. Bonhill 15.4.1899
Duntocher Hibs
Helensburgh
Luton T 20/21 1 FL
Mid Rhondda 21/22
Manchester C T 21/22 FL
Partick T T 21/22 1
22/23 6 1
Raith R 22/23 4
Helensburgh
Reading 23/24 1 FL
Helensburgh 23/24 D3
Falkirk 23/24
East Stirlingshire 24/25 D2
Helensburgh

McKEE Robert

Camelon
Hibernian T 30/31
East Fife 30/31 1
31/32 13 D2

McKELLAN William B (or McLELLAN)

Clyde 17/18 14 ?
18/19 2 ?

McKELLAR Daniel
K.I.A., Flanders 13.4.1918
Ashfield
Bellshill A
Airdrieonians 13/14 3
Kilmarnock 14/15 24 1
15/16 13

McKELLAR H David

Queen's Park 09/10 5
St Mirren 09/10 3 1
Vale of Leven 10/11 19 D2
11/12 D2

McKELVIE James

Beith
Hamilton A 31/32 6
Queen's Park 32/33 1
33/34 1

McKENDRICK Charles
b. Greenock
St Anthonys
Clydebank 22/23 D2
23/24 37
24/25 D2
25/26 38
Partick T 26/27 14
27/28
Morton 28/29 D2
Partick T 29/30 5
Dunfermline A 29/30 D2
Morton 30/31 38
31/32 18

McKENNA Harold
b. Yoker
Glasgow Ashfield
Rangers 16/17 24
17/18 12
Glasgow Ashfield
St Mirren 18/19 26
19/20 24
Rangers 20/21 4
Third Lanark 21/22 28 1
22/23 34
23/24 31 1
Brighton 24/25 7 FL
Alloa A 25/26 D2

McKENNA Thomas

St Cuthberts W
Fauldhouse U
Airdrieonians 31/32 4

McKENNA W

Partick T 11/12 1

McKENNA William

Bellshill A
Bo'ness 23/24 D2
Albion R 24/25 D2
25/26 D2
26/27 D2
27/28 D2
Airdrieonians 27/28 12 4
28/29
Queen of the South 28/29 D2

McKENNA William C

Falkirk
Queen's Park 07/08 17
Falkirk 08/09
Port Glasgow A 09/10 7
Morton 09/10 1
Queen's Park 10/11 17
11/12 1
Falkirk
Clydebank 14/15 D2

McKENNAN Hugh
b. Airdrie 8.2.1905 d. Airdrie 1962
Airdrie Merchants
Nottingham F 27/28 1 FL
28/29 FL
St Johnstone 29/30 5 1
Morton 30/31 13 4
Cowdenbeath 31/32 16 3

McKENNAN Peter Stewart
b. Airdrie 16.7.1918 d. Dundonald 28.9.1991
Whitburn Jnrs
Partick T 35/36 19 6
36/37 33 20
37/38 35 20
38/39 34 24
Linfield 39/40 IL
Glentoran 40/41 IL
41/42 IL
Partick T 46/47 4 1
47/48 6 5
WBA 47/48 11 4 FL
Leicester C 47/48 11 4 FL
48/49 7 3
Brentford 48/49 24 6 FL
Middlesbrough 49/50 33 15 FL
50/51 7 3 FL
Oldham A 51/52 38 16 FL
52/53 32 10 FL
53/54 8 2 FL
Coleraine

McKENNY David

Benburb
St Mirren 32/33 2
Larne 33/34 IL
Glentoran 33/34 IL

McKENZIE

Cowlairs 90/91 1

McKENZIE

Vale of Leven 90/91 3

McKENZIE Alick B

Rangers 89/90
90/91 3 3
91/92 2 2
93/94
93/94 1

McKENZIE Archibald

Bo'ness
Partick T 04/05 1
05/06 6
06/07 7
07/08 29 1
08/09 29
09/10 33
10/11 32
11/12 31
12/13 13
13/14 16
14/15 10

McKENZIE Archibald Denny F
b. Greenock 1.5.1863
Clyde 92/93 9 1
93/94 15 ? D2
Millwall 94/95 16 18 SL
Sunderland 95/96 2 1 FL
Millwall 96/97 19 8 SL
WBA 97/98 30 2 FL
98/99 21 6 FL
Portsmouth

MacKENZIE Daniel
b. Aberdeen
Aberdeen Parkvale
Aberdeen 27/28
28/29 1
29/30 1
30/31 1

McKENZIE Donald H

Leith A 31/32 2
Edinburgh C 32/33 D2

MacKENZIE George

Buckie Thistle
Aberdeen 09/10 1

McKENZIE George Duncan
b. Buckie 27.1.1908 d. Bolton 11.12.1974
Buckie Thistle
Aberdeen University
Queen's Park 29/30 28 3
30/31 20 2
31/32 31 5
32/33 25 5
Hull C 33/34 9 4 FL
Stockport Co 34/35 7 3 FL
Macclesfield T 34/35

McKENZIE Gilbert
d. c1982
Pollok
Rangers 35/36
Queen of the South L 36/37 20 2
Rangers 37/38
Queen of the South 37/38 15
Hamilton A 38/39 26
Dundee 46/47 24 2 D2
47/48 1
Airdrieonians 47/48 9
Dundee U 47/48 10 D2
48/49 3 D2
Berwick R 49/50
50/51
Bangor 51/52 IL
52/53 IL
Linfield 52/53 IL
53/54 IL

McKENZIE Hugh

Rothesay
Morton 00/01 1
01/02
02/03 8

McKENZIE J

Queen's Park 14/15 9

McKENZIE J Hector

Queen's Park 10/11 2
11/12 31
12/13 33 4
13/14 23 2

McKENZIE James

Clyde 97/98 14 2

McKENZIE John

St Bernards 98/99 6 1
99/00 10

McKENZIE John

Elgin C
Forres Mechanics
Rangers 08/09 2
09/10 24
Cowdenbeath 10/11 D2
11/12 D2
12/13 D2
13/14 D2
14/15 D2
15/16

MacKENZIE John
b. Douglas 28.7.1885
Glenbuck Cherrypickers
Carlisle U
Norwich C 10/11 38 2 SL
11/12 36 SL
12/13 38 SL
13/14 36 SL
14/15 38 SL
Heart of Midlothian 15/16 25
Millwall T
Walsall 20/21 32 BDL
21/22 4 FL

McKENZIE John

Dunniker Jnrs
Raith R 24/25 1

McKENZIE John
b. Glasgow
Montrose
Maryhill Hibs
Third Lanark 31/32 32 3
32/33 32 10
33/34 34 13
Heart of Midlothian 34/35 30 13
Aberdeen 35/36 35 8
36/37 36 4
37/38 26 3
38/39 10 4
Ayr U 38/39 25 9

MacKENZIE John Alick
b. Altbea
Ross Co
Nairn Co
St Mirren 34/35 18 12
35/36 D2
36/37 11 4
37/38 19 13
Manchester U 38/39 FL
Swindon T 39/40 1 FL

McKENZIE John Wilson
b. Montrose ?.9.1885 d. Scotland 1943
Montrose 02/03
03/04
Dundee 04/05 9
05/06 24
06/07 34
07/08 31
Aston Villa 08/09 5 FL
Bristol R 09/10 19 SL

McKENZIE Kenneth Wilson
b. Montrose 1.5.1898 d. Glasgow 1960
Whitehill School
Queen's Park 17/18 21
18/19 31
19/20 41 2
Chelsea 20/21 3 FL
21/22 18 FL
22/23 FL
Cardiff C 23/24 FL
Dalkeith

McKENZIE Lewis

Inverness Thistle
Clyde 13/14
14/15
15/16 1

McKENZIE Murdoch
b. Ayr 17.11.1899
Yoker A
Ayr U 16/17 4
17/18
18/19
Stevenston U L 18/19
Ayr U 19/20
20/21 14 8
21/22 19 5
22/23 32 14
23/24 33 12
24/25 34 17
Darlington 25/26 37 17 FL
Portsmouth 26/27 4 1 FL
Hamilton A 27/28 10 1
Ashfield

McKENZIE Robert Copeland

Cumbernauld U
Morton 10/11 17
Queen's Park 10/11 9 2
11/12 31
Linfield 12/13 IL
Rangers 13/14

McKENZIE Thomas
b. Shieldmuir
Cambuslang R *
Kilwinning R
Motherwell 31/32 1
32/33 12
33/34 6
34/35 23
35/36 14
36/37 22
37/38 31 1
38/39 35 1

McKENZIE Thomas A
b. Petershill
Petershill
Third Lanark 03/04 21 11
04/05 23 14
05/06 6 4
Sunderland 05/06 8 1 FL
Plymouth A 06/07 20 10 SL
Portsmouth 06/07 4 1 SL
Glossop 07/08 6 2 FL
QPR 08/09 9 SL
Dunfermline A

McKENZIE William

Queen's Park 24/25 5
25/26 2
26/27
27/28
Clydebank 28/29 D2
29/30 D2
Clyde 30/31 2 1
Clydebank 30/31 D2

McKEOWN Patrick

Cronberry
Kilmarnock 05/06 1
06/07 4
07/08
Lanemark 08/08
Leeds C 08/09 FL
09/10 FL
Dumbarton Harp 10/11
Royal Albert

McKEOWN Thomas Michael 2 caps
b. Dalmellington ?.3.1870 d. Glasgow 25.10.1903
Lugar Boswell
Hibernian 87/88
Celtic 88/89
89/90
90/91 15
Blackburn R 91/92 19 FL
Cowlairs 92/93
Fair City A 92/93
Motherwell 92/93
Morton 93/94 4 ? D2
Ayr Parkhouse 94/95
95/96
Hamilton Harp 95/96
Lugar Boswell 96/97
Hibernian 97/98
Carfin Shamrock 97/98
Camelon 97/98
Fair City A
Lugar Boswell

McKERLEY James McIlvenny
b. c1893 d. Old Monkland 4.10.1917
Bellshill A
Armadale
Raith R 15/16 26
Airdrieonians 16/17 13 1

McKERRELL Daniel
b. Blantyre
Bedlay Jnrs
Shawfield
Hamilton A 36/37 2 2
Falkirk 37/38 10 3
East Fife L 37/38 D2
Falkirk 38/39 3
East Fife 38/39 17 10 D2
46/47 1 D2

MacKIE

Heart of Midlothian 92/93 1

MacKIE

St Mirren 94/95 2 1

MacKIE

Clyde 95/96 3

MacKIE

Clyde 18/19 9 ?

MacKIE Alexander

Raith R
Rangers 02/03 8 4
03/04 23 12
04/05 20 8

MacKIE Archibald S

Rutherglen Glencairn
Parkhead Jnrs
Kilmarnock 13/14 23
14/15 37
15/16 37
Clydebank 15/16
Kilmarnock 16/17 28
17/18 26
18/19 30 2
19/20 20 1
Dumbarton 20/21 11
Clydebank 20/21
East Stirlingshire 21/22 D2
22/23 D2
Peebles R 23/24 D2

MacKIE Charles
b. Peterhead 1882
Peterhead
Aberdeen 02/03
03/04 21 9 D2
Manchester U 04/05 5 3 FL
West Ham U 05/06 10 3 SL
Aberdeen 05/06 6 1
Lochgelly U 06/07

McKIE David

Queen's Park 11/12 6

MacKIE G

Queen's Park 16/17 1

McKIE Gilbert

Alva Albion R
St Ninians Thistle
Falkirk 37/38 38
38/39 25

McKIE James 1 cap
b. Arbroath
Dykehead
Heart of Midlothian 95/96 2 1
Darwen 96/97
East Stirlingshire 96/97
97/98
98/99
99/00
Bolton W 00/01 32 8 FL
01/02 33 7 FL
02/03 16 3 FL
Luton T 03/04 32 8 SL
New Brompton 04/05 27 6 SL
05/06 19 1 SL

MacKIE James

Raith R 12/13 2
13/14
14/15
15/16 4

MacKIE James
b. Ayr
Cumnock Jnrs
Aberdeen 20/21 3 2
21/22 1
Ton Pentre T 22/23
Bo'ness 22/23 D2
Dundee Hibs 23/24 D2
Kings Park 23/24 D2
24/25 D2
Clydebank 25/26
26/27 D2
Cumnock Jnrs 27/28

MacKIE Lewis

Clyde 99/00 7

MACKIE Robert
b. Dalry ?.8.1882 d. Airdrie 1943
Bannockburn
Stenhousemuir 02/03
03/04
Heart of Midlothian 04/05 17
Chelsea 05/06 35 1 FL
06/07 3 FL
07/08 6 FL
Leicester F 07/08 18 FL
08/09 15 FL
Darlington 09/10
Airdrieonians 10/11 22
11/12 32 2
12/13 34
13/14 32
14/15 35
15/16 38
Third Lanark 16/17 32
17/18 15 ?
Albion R 17/18

McKIE Robert

Parkhead Jnrs
Airdrieonians 17/18 2
18/19 10

MACKIE Thomas

Benburb
Partick T 22/23 1

McKIE William

Montrose
Dundee 93/94 10
Montrose 94/95

McKILLOP Thomas Boyd 1 cap
b. Dreghorn 27.10.1917 d. Bromley 14.2.1984
Dreghorn
Rangers 35/36 2
36/37 17 1
37/38 29
38/39 25
Asturias (Mex)
Rhyl A 47/48
48/49
49/50
50/51
51/52
52/53

McKIM James

St Mirren 94/95 4
95/96 15

McKIM John

Abercorn 92/93 1
93/94 4 ? D2
94/95 1 ? D2
95/96 D2
96/97 11 3
97/98 4 ? D2

McKIM John

Petershill
Dumbarton 16/17 33 2
17/18 20 4
18/19 7 ?
Hamilton A 19/20
Vale of Leven 20/21

McKINLAY J

Falkirk 22/23 2

McKINLAY Robert
b. Glencraig c1905
Thornton R
Dunfermline A 27/28 13
Cowdenbeath 27/28 1
Hearts of Beath
Lochgelly Amateurs

MacKINLAY William H

Albion R 38/39 16 1

McKINLEY

Clyde 94/95 10

McKINLEY David
b. Dumbarton
Dumbarton Harp
Aberdeen 06/07 14 5
07/08 4
Watford 08/09 23 5 SL
Pontypridd 09/10
Aberdare A 10/11
11/12
Rochdale

McKINLEY John F

Port Glasgow A
Rangers 99/00 2
Port Glasgow A

McKINLEY Roger

Dunfermline A 35/36 1

McKINNELL James Templeton Broadfoot
b. Dalbeattie 27.3.1895 d. Brixworth 1972
Dalbeattie Star
Ayr U 13/14 6
Nithsdale W 14/15
Queen of the South
Blackburn R 20/21 10 FL
21/22 7 FL
22/23 41 FL
23/24 27 FL
24/25 20 FL
25/26 6 FL
Darlington 26/27 32 1 FL
27/28 36 FL
28/29 33 FL
Nelson 29/30 10 FL

McKINNON Hugh

St Bernards 95/96 6

McKINNON Hugh H

Falkirk 10/11 4 1
11/12 2

McKINNON Robert S

Airdrieonians 10/11 1

McKINNON Robert S

Clyde 11/12 3

McKINVEN Andrew
b. Harthill
Shotts U
Hibernian 33/34 5
34/35 6 1
Arbroath 35/36 6
Ross Co 35/36

McKIRN John

Hamilton A 18/19 1

McKNIGHT John

St Bernards 95/96 5 1
Lanemark

McKNIGHT Robert J A

Hurlford
Dundee 11/12 1
12/13 3
Barrow 13/14
Bury 14/15 22 5 FL
Kilmarnock 15/16 4 2

McKNIGHT Thomas

Douglas Water Thistle
Broxburn
Peebles R
Morton 09/10 7
Wishaw Thistle 10/11

McLACHLAN Albert James
b. Kirkcudbright ?.2.1892 d. Edinburgh 1956
St Cuthberts W
Aston Villa 13/14 3 FL
Aberdeen 14/15 36
15/16 25 1
16/17 1
17/18
Abercorn L 18/19
Aberdeen 19/20 30 2
20/21 25 1
21/22 39
22/23 32 1
23/24 38 1
24/25 35
25/26 3 1
26/27 24 5
Heart of Midlothian 27/28
28/29
Elgin C 29/30
30/31
31/32

McLACHLAN Archibald

Glasgow Perthshire
Partick T 17/18 7
Dumbarton 18/19 12 ?

McLACHLAN David

Heart of Midlothian
Chatham 99/00
Heart of Midlothian 00/01 15 4
01/02 2 2

McLACHLAN Edward Rolland
b. Glasgow 24.9.1903 d. Leicester 16.3.1970
Glasgow Boys Brigade
Hibernian
Queen's Park 21/22 2
Clyde 22/23
23/24
Third Lanark 24/25 3 2
Vale of Leven 25/26 D3
26/27
Leicester C 26/27 FL
Nottingham F 27/28 8 2 FL
Mansfield T 28/29 41 16 ML
29/30 32 23 ML
Northampton T 30/31 11 1 FL
Mansfield T 31/32 FL

MacLACHLAN Frederick
b. Kirkcudbright 21.8.1896 d. Dumfries 1982
St Cuthberts W
KOSB
Austin Motor Works
Manchester U T
Harold Johnson Motor Works
Partick T 19/20 4
20/21 9
Aberdeen 21/22 6
Maidstone U 22/23
Coventry C 23/24 42 FL
24/25 24 FL
25/26 1 FL
Grimsby T 25/26 22 FL
26/27 30 FL
Bury 27/28 2 FL
Halifax T 28/29 42 FL
29/30 28 FL
30/31 15 FL
31/32 9 1 FL

McLACHLAN George Herbert
b. Glasgow 21.9.1902
Crosshill Amateurs
Parkhead Jnrs
Rutherglen Glencairn
Quens Park Strollers
Clyde 22/23 6
Kings Park L 22/23 D2
23/24 D2
Clyde 23/24 8 1
Peebles R L 24/25 D3
Cardiff C 25/26 19 2 FL
26/27 38 5 FL
27/28 42 11 FL
28/29 32 2 FL
29/30 8 2 FL
Manchester U 29/30 23 2 FL
30/31 42 2 FL
31/32 28 FL
32/33 17 FL
Chester 33/34 29 7 FL
Le Havre

McLACHLAN Herbert

Aberdeen
Heart of Midlothian 27/28
Airdrieonians 28/29 2
Elgin C 29/30

McLACHLAN Ian

Queen's Park 21/22 5

McLACHLAN Ian

Falkirk 38/39 4 1

McLACHLAN John Andrew
b. Dumfries ?.7.1888 d. Glasgow ?.1.1944
St Cuthberts W
Dundee 10/11 16 3
11/12 27 3
Aston Villa 12/13 8 2 FL
13/14 8 1 FL
14/15 1 FL
Dundee
Partick T 19/20 7

McLAFFERTY

Vale of Leven 91/92 3

McLAINE Edward
b. Coatbridge
Albion R 22/23 6
Dykehead
Grenadier Guards
Montreal Maroons
Carsteel
Providence Clamdiggers 26/27 32 21 ASL
27/28 3 ASL

McLAINE James
b. Govan 11.7.1881 d. Glasgow 22.7.1930
Ashfield
Clyde 05/06 D2
06/07 11 12
07/08 17 6
Watford 08/09 37 10 SL
09/10 42 11 SL
10/11 20 6 SL

McLARDIE A

Renfrew Jnrs
St Mirren 20/21 3
Vale of Leven 21/22 D2
22/23 D2
23/24 D2

McLARDIE Alexander
b. Paisley 1868
St Mirren
Burnley 89/90 2 FL
90/91 17 14 FL
91/92 24 11 FL
Abercorn 92/93 14 8
93/94 5 ? D2

McLARDIE Archibald

John Neilsons FP
St Mirren 10/11 3
11/12 2

McLAREN

Abercorn 90/91 11 1
91/92 8 1

McLAREN Alexander 5 caps
b. Tibbermore 25.2.1910 d. Perth 5.2.1960
Muirton
St Johnstone 26/27 1
27/28 21
28/29 38
29/30 35
30/31 38 D2
31/32 38 D2
32/33 28
Leicester C 32/33 13 FL
33/34 42 FL
34/35 42 FL
35/36 40 FL
36/37 37 FL
37/38 34 FL
38/39 31 FL
39/40 3 FL
Morton
St Johnstone

McLAREN Andrew D

Queen's Park 14/15 24 2
15/16 12 1
16/17 2

McLAREN Benjamin G
b. Bishopbrigg
Cadder Jnrs
East Fife 20/21
Hamilton A 21/22 30 11

McLAREN David

Cambuslang Hibs
Hibernian 06/07 3

McLAREN Duncan

Queen's Park 14/15 14
15/16 13

McLAREN Frank

Heart of Midlothian 04/05 2 1
05/06 21 2
06/07 24 2
07/08 21 1
08/09 3 2
09/10 30 1
10/11 28 8
11/12 10
12/13 2
Hamilton A 12/13 20
13/14 18

McLAREN George
d. 1964
Plymouth A 12/13 2 SL
Royal Albert
Hamilton A 19/20 12 3
Royal Albert 20/21
Armadale 20/21

McLAREN Hugh McDonald
b. Kilbirnie 13.1.1901 d. Littleborough 8.3.1971
Dalry Thistle
Nithsdale W 24/25 ? 1 D3
25/26 ? 3 D2
26/27 ? 4 D2
27/28
Aberdeen 28/29 17
Kilmarnock L 28/29
Aberdeen 29/30 33 2
30/31 36 2
31/32 19
Workington 32/33
Bradford C 33/34 19 1 FL
34/35 5 FL
Tranmere R 35/36 39 3 FL
36/37 4 1 FL
Rochdale 36/37 30 FL
37/38 34 1 FL
Astley Bridge

McLAREN James 3 caps
b. Lugar 1860 d. Vancouver 3.1.1927
Cronbery Eglington
Lugar Boswell Thistle
Hibernian 83/84
84/85
85/86
St Bernards 86/87
87/88
Celtic 88/89
89/90
90/91 4
Morton 91/92
Clyde 91/92 15 1
92/93 4
93/94 D2
94/95
Celtic 95/96

McLAREN John A

Queen's Park 14/15 15 2

McLAREN Robert

Bainfield
Heart of Midlothian 92/93 4 3
93/94 3
94/95 18 7
95/96 13 4
96/97 16 1
97/98 11 6

McLAREN Robert

Heart of Midlothian 99/00 14 1
00/01 3

McLAREN Robert

Airdrieonians 00/01 16 D2
01/02 22 D2
02/03 22 1 D2
03/04 22

McLAREN William
b. Glasgow
Shettleston
Hamilton A 31/32 26 15
32/33 31 7
33/34 19 3
34/35 31 1
35/36 27 3
36/37 5 2
St Johnstone 36/37 20 8
37/38 23 7
Morton T 38/39 D2

McLAUCHLAN

Falkirk 16/17 1 1

McLAUCHLAN Edward R

Partick T 22/23 1

McLAUGHLAN

Benburb
Celtic 91/92 1
92/93
Albion R

McLAUGHLAN

Clyde 92/93 6
93/94 4 ? D2

McLAUGHLAN

Hibernian 07/08 1

McLAUGHLAN George

Glengowan R
Port Glasgow A 02/03 3
Johnstone

McLAUGHLAN James

Kilwinning R
Ayr U 10/11 22 7 D2
11/12 ? ? D2
12/13 ? ? D2
13/14 31 4
14/15 38 5
Partick T L 14/15
Ayr U 15/16 36 5
16/17 37 1
17/18 32 ?
18/19 33 4
Stevenston U 19/20
20/21
Kilwinning R 21/22
Kilwinning Eglington 22/23

McLAUGHLAN James

Rothesay junior football
Vale of Clyde
Bradford PA 13/14 1 FL
14/15 FL
Airdrieonians 15/16 2
Vale of Clyde
Dundee 19/20 18 5
Aberdeen 19/20 8 2
20/21 5
Clydebank 20/21

McLAUGHLIN George
b. Calton 24.3.1902
Greenhead Thistle Juveniles
Celtic 23/24 1
Clydebank L 23/24 5 1
Stenhousemuir L 23/24 D2
Clydebank 24/25 D2
Mid Rhondda 24/25
Clyde 25/26 D2
Darlington 25/26 1 FL
Hull C 26/27 8 2 FL
Accrington S 27/28 41 10 FL
28/29 35 11 FL
Nelson 29/30 29 3 FL
Morecambe

McLAUGHLIN James

Benburb
Morton 01/02 5
02/03 6
Cartvale 02/03
Renton 03/04
04/05
05/06
Cowdenbeath 06/07 D2

McLAUGHLIN James

Ayr U 19/20 30 3

McLAUGHLIN John

Strathclyde
Third Lanark 16/17 23
17/18 20 ?
18/19 18 ?
Armadale *

McLAUGHLIN John H

Hamilton Academy
Blantyre V
Strathclyde
Hamilton A 10/11 21 3
11/12 30 4
12/13 27 2
Morton 13/14 6 1
14/15 16 8
15/16 3 1
Dumbarton Harp 16/17
Hamilton A 19/20 15 3

McLAUGHLIN Patrick

Kirkintilloch Rob Roy
Heart of Midlothian 02/03 1
Falkirk 02/03
Renton

McLAUGHLIN William
b. Dumbarton
Dumbarton Welfare
Renfrew
Dumbarton Harp
Benburb
Morton 32/33 22 1

McLAUGHLIN William Joseph
b. Cambuslang 22.6.1882 d. Cambuslang 20.7.1946
Hamilton A 03/04 D2
Everton 04/05 7 3 FL
05/06 8 2 FL
Plymouth A 06/07 31 1 SL
Preston NE 07/08 1 FL
Hamilton A 08/09 11 4
09/10 27 3
10/11 19 2
11/12 19 1
Shelbourne 12/13 IL
13/14 IL

McLAURIN J
b. Calmyle
Albion R 21/22 6
22/23 9

McLAVIN Michael
b. Glasgow
Croy Celtic
Clydebank 19/20 15 4
20/21 25 8
21/22 29 7
Dunfermline A 22/23 D2
East Stirlingshire 22/23 D2
Kings Park 23/24 D2
Royal Albert 24/25 D3

McLAY David S
b. c1898
Queen's Park 15/16 1
16/17
17/18
18/19
19/20
20/21 3
21/22 7
22/23 1 D2

McLAY George
b. Glencraig c1889 K.I.A., Passchendale 22.10.1917
Glencraig Celtic
Raith R 10/11 9 2
11/12 19
12/13 30 2
13/14 21 1
14/15 10

McLAY James

Clackmannan
Dundee 98/99 9 2
Abercorn 98/99 D2

McLAY Raeburn

Rutherglen Glencairn
Airdrieonians 05/06 5
06/07 9
07/08 11
08/09 28 1
09/10 12
Albion R 10/11 D2
11/12 D2
12/13 D2
Dumbarton 13/14 1
Johnstone 14/15 D2

McLEAN

Clyde 92/93 1

McLEAN

Clyde 94/95 1

McLEAN

Clyde 06/07 3

McLEAN

Hibernian 06/07 1

McLEAN Adam 4 caps
b. Coatbridge 27.4.1898 d. Glasgow 29.6.1973
Whiteinch Oaklea Juveniles
Broomhill YMCA
Anderston Benburb Juveniles
Anderston Thornbank Juveniles
Celtic 16/17 6 1
17/18 24 13
18/19 33 14
19/20 40 12
20/21 38 10
21/22 34 9
22/23 31 4
23/24 33 10
24/25 27 12
25/26 32 16
26/27 32 18
27/28 36 8
Sunderland 28/29 39 8 FL
29/30 25 7 FL
30/31 2 FL
Aberdeen 30/31 24 11
31/32 25 8
32/33 25 5
Partick T 33/34 7 3

McLEAN Andrew

Abercorn 00/01 D2
Heart of Midlothian 01/02 6
Renton 02/03
Preston NE 03/04 FL

McLEAN Andrew

Third Lanark 10/11 2

McLEAN Andrew L

Third Lanark 06/07 2
07/08 2 1

McLEAN Angus

Wishaw Thistle
Heart of Midlothian 99/00 2
Airdrieonians

McLEAN Daniel R

Rothesay Royal V
St Mirren 09/10 6 1
Partick T 10/11
Wishaw Thistle 10/11

McLEAN David

Broxburn A
Heart of Midlothian 16/17 16
17/18 8

McLEAN David Forrester

Third Lanark 38/39 16

McLEAN David Prophet 1 cap
b. Forfar 13.12.1890 d. Forfar 21.12.1967
Forfar Half-Holiday 03/04
Forfar WE 03/04
Forfar Celtic
Forfar A 06/07
Celtic 07/08 10 11
08/09 14 6
Ayr U L
Preston NE 09/10 27 18 FL
10/11 22 7 FL
Sheffield W 10/11 11 2 FL
11/12 37 25 FL
12/13 36 30 FL
Forfar A 13/14
Sheffield W 13/14 15 9 FL
14/15 33 22 FL
Dykehead L 15/16
Third Lanark L 15/16 21 17
16/17 37 28
17/18 27 ?
Rangers 18/19 24 29
Linfield L 18/19
Sheffield W 19/20 3 FL
Bradford PA 19/20 23 18 FL
20/21 40 22 FL
21/22 23 9 FL
Dundee 22/23 25 22
23/24 33 12
24/25 33 5
25/26 23 4
Forfar A 26/27 D2
27/28 D2
28/39 D2
29/30 D2
30/31 D2
31/32 D2
Dykehead

McLEAN Duncan 2 caps

b. Dumbarton 12.9.1869					
Renton Union					
Renton		88/89			
		89/90			
Everton		90/91	5		FL
		91/92	20		FL
Liverpool		92/93	22	1	LL
		93/94	27	4	FL
		94/95	24		FL
St Bernards		95/96	10		
		96/97	17		
		97/98	14		

McLEAN Duncan

Hibernian		04/05	16	1	
Albion R		05/06			

McLEAN Finlay

b. 1879					
Maryhill					
Glasgow Perthshire					
Hamilton A		02/03			D2
		03/04			D2
Celtic		04/05	15	3	
Hamilton A		05/06			D2
		06/07	24	3	
		07/08	31	10	
		08/09	31	5	
Workington		09/10			
Hamilton A		10/11			
Abercorn		11/12			D2
Renton					

McLEAN George

b. Ayr					
Dalmellington U					
Ayr U		30/31	9	3	
		31/32	10	1	
Dunfermline A	T	32/33			D2

McLEAN James

St Mirren		91/92	1		
		92/93	14	10	
		93/94	14	14	
		94/95	6	4	
Liverpool					

McLEAN James

Ayr Parkhouse					
Rangers		08/09	1		
		09/10	1	1	
Morton		10/11	21	3	
		11/12	26	4	
		12/13	18		
		13/14	24	2	
		14/15	26	1	
		15/16	35	2	
		16/17	35	1	
		17/18	24		
		18/19	31		
		19/20	6	2	

McLEAN James

b. Forfar 1896					
Dykehead					
Motherwell		14/15	6	2	
		15/16			
		16/17			
		17/18			
Dumbarton Harp		18/19			
Vale of Leven					
Kilmarnock		19/20	13	5	
Beith					
Troon A					
Ayr U		21/22			
		22/23			
Forfar A		23/24			D2
Queen of the South					

McLEAN James

Cowdenbeath					
Hibernian		17/18	1	?	

McLEAN James

b. Ayr					
Troon					
Ayr U		22/23	33	1	
		23/24	13	2	
		24/25	4		

McLEAN James

b. Fife					
Cowdenbeath		27/28	4		
		28/29	8		

McLEAN James

Hibernian		36/37	29		
		37/38	16	2	
		38/39	12	2	
Dundee U					

McLEAN John

Motherwell		04/05	14		
		05/06	20		
		06/07	30		
		07/08	27		
		08/09	31		
		09/10	10		
Vale of Leven		10/11	18		D2

McLEAN John

Kilwinning R					
Ayr U		21/22	17	2	
		22/23	19	8	
		23/24	21	6	
		24/25			
		25/26			D2
Nithsdale W		26/27			D2
Cumnock		27/28			

McLEAN John

Lochgelly U		24/25			D3
		25/26			D3
Dunfermline A		26/27	1		
Lochgelly U					

McLEAN John A

Queen's Park		00/01	6	3	
		01/02	7	2	
Ayr Parkhouse		02/03			
Queen's Park		03/04	4	2	
		04/05	20	1	
		05/06	10	4	
		06/07	15	5	
		07/08	19	3	
		08/09	19	6	

McLEAN Lauchlan

b. Inverness					
Inverness Clachnacuddin		07/08			
		08/09			
Celtic		09/10	7	2	
Preston NE		10/11	1		FL
St Mirren		11/12	2		
		12/13			
Inverness Caledonian					

McLEAN Robert

Glasgow Perthshire					
St Mirren		06/07	6		
Hamilton A					
Royal Albert					

McLEAN Robert

b. Glasgow 9.6.					
Army Service Corps					
St Bernards					
Airdrieonians		20/21	14	3	
Alloa A		21/22			D2
Doncaster R		22/23			FL
		23/24	41	1	FL
		24/25	36	2	FL
		25/26	33	1	FL
		26/27	15		FL
		27/28	6		FL
		28/29	4		FL
		29/30	1		FL
Waterford Celtic		30/31			
Hatfield Main Colliery		30/31			
Doncaster R		30/31			

McLEAN Thomas

Abercorn		95/96	7	?	D2
		96/97	4		
Airdrieonians		96/97			D2

McLEAN Thomas

b. Lochgelly 26.12.1903 d. Canada ?.7.1983					
Crosshill U					
Bowhill Jnrs					
Arbroath		23/24	13	1	D2
Lochgelly U		23/24			D2
		24/25			D3
St Johnstone		25/26	17	1	
		26/27	15	2	
Blackburn R		26/27	10	1	FL
		27/28	33	4	FL
		28/29	28	5	FL
		29/30	26	10	FL
		30/31	33	7	FL
		31/32	35	10	FL
		32/33	37	5	FL
		33/34	28	2	FL
		34/35	17		FL
Exeter C		35/36	21	1	FL
Barrow		36/37	11	2	FL

McLEAN William M

b. Hamilton					
Kilmarnock		18/19	1		
Raith R		19/20	22	3	
St Mirren		20/21	4	1	
Dundee		20/21	30	6	
		21/22	31	7	
		22/23	10	2	
Heart of Midlothian		23/24	26	7	
		24/25			
Ayr U		25/26			

McLEAVY Michael

b. Rutherglen 1898					
Rutherglen Glencairn					
Falkirk		21/22	15	4	
Kilmarnock		22/23	2		
Bo'ness		22/23	1	1	D2
Vale of Leven		23/24			D2
J & P Coats		23/24	15	4	ASL
		24/25	12	8	ASL
Providence Clamdiggers		24/25	7		ASL
Dykehead		25/26			D3
New Bedford Whalers		25/26	35	21	ASL
		26/27	30	20	ASL
		27/28	36	17	ASL
		28/29	31	11	ASL
		29A	14	6	ASL
		29/30	29	9	ASL
		30A	21	4	ASL
		31S	11	3	ASL
Fall River		31S	6	4	ASL
New Bedford Whalers		31A	2	1	ASL

McLELLAN

Clydebank		19/20	1		

McLELLAN James

b. c1903					
Rosslyn					
Raith R		22/23	1		

McLELLAN James

Saltcoats V					
St Mirren		26/27	10	3	
		27/28	12	4	

McLELLAN James

Third Lanark		31/32	29	1	
		32/33	33	1	
		33/34	30	1	
		34/35			D2
Dunfermline A	T	35/36	2		

McLELLAN John R

Partick T		10/11	1		
		11/12	1		
		12/13			
Abercorn		13/14			D2

McLELLAN Robert

b. c1917					
Rutherglen Glencairn					
Third Lanark		37/38	2		
		38/39	16		
Cowdenbeath					

McLELLAN William B

Johnstone					
Morton		19/20	13		
		20/21	8		
Helensburgh					
Peterborough U		24/25			
		25/26			
		26/27			
		27/28			

McLELLAND Douglas
b. Glasgow
Queen's Park 27/28 23 19
28/29 29 27
29/30 30 19
30/31 24 10
31/32 16 7
32/33 1
33/34 10 5

McLENNAN Alexander G
b. Elgin
Buckie Thistle
Partick T 33/34 12 11
34/35 23 15
Buckie Thistle L 34/35
Partick T 35/36 12 6
Excelsior de Roubaix T 36/37
Albion R 36/37 4 2

McLENNAN James

Mossend Hibs
Hamilton A 16/17 26 1
17/18 6

McLEOD

Vale of Leven 90/91 8 1

McLEOD

Leith A 91/92 11 3
92/93 14 6

McLEOD

Renton 92/93 2

McLEOD Angus

Inverness Caledonian
Aberdeen 13/14 12 5
14/15 6 1
15/16 4

McLEOD Archibald G
b. Townhead
Parkhead Jnrs
Glasgow Ashfield
Partick T 33/34 3 2
Derry C 34/35 IL
35/36 IL
36/37 IL
37/38 IL
38/39 IL

McLEOD D

Dumbarton 93/94 5 1

McLEOD Donald 4 caps
b. Laurieston 28.5.1882 d. Flanders 6.10.1917
Stenhouse Thistle
Stenhousemuir 01/02
Ayr 01/02 D2
Celtic 02/03 20
03/04 10
04/05 25
05/06 20
06/07 25
07/08 27
08/09 4
Middlesbrough 08/09 32 FL
09/10 35 FL
10/11 34 FL
11/12 24 FL
12/13 13 FL
Inverness Caledonian L 13/14

McLEOD Donald A
b. Edinburgh 1.11.1917 d. Penicuik 20.6.1999
Arniston Star
Whithorn Jnrs
Motherwell 38/39 2
46/47 30
47/48 29
48/49 17
49/50 21 1
50/51 29
51/52 17 1

McLEOD Edward
b. Prestonpans
St Bernards
Falkirk 17/18 23 ?
18/19 9 ?

McLEOD Edward McCormick
b. Springburn 28.7.1907
Ashfield
Port Glasgow Jnrs
Partick T 26/27 37 1
27/28 22
28/29 32 1
29/30 29
30/31 37
31/32 36 1
32/33 35 1
33/34 36
34/35 30 1
35/36 30 1
36/37 32
37/38 17
38/39 21

McLEOD Hugh P
b. Tain
Queen's Park 27/28 12
28/29 1

McLEOD James

Kilmaurs
Kilmarnock 03/04 4 1
Maybole 03/04

McLEOD James
b. New Cumnock 1898
Cumnock Jnrs
Rotherham U T
Merthyr T T
Ayr U 21/22 20
22/23 31
23/24 31
24/25 33 2
25/26 30 2 D2
Kilmarnock 26/27 33
27/28 27
Ayr U 28/29 24
29/30 30 2
30/31 22 2
31/32 35
32/33 18
Galston L 32/33
Distillery 33/34 IL
Dalbeattie Star 33/34

McLEOD James
b. Glasgow 26.11.1905
Petershill
Partick T 27/28
28/29 6 2
Carlisle U 29/30 9 1 FL
Raith R 30/31 D2
Havana 30/31

McLEOD James Rae
b. Clydebank 1906
Dreghorn Jnrs
Kilmarnock 29/30 2
30/31
31/32 19
Dumbarton

McLEOD John 5 caps
b. Dumbarton 12.3.1866 d. 4.2.1953
Dumbarton A
Dumbarton 87/88
88/89
89/90
90/91 18 1
91/92 13 1
92/93 16
93/94 15
94/95 18
Rangers 95/96 5

McLEOD John Simpson
b. Gorbals 20.4.1912
Neilston V
Rangers
Heart of Midlothian 34/35 1
Queen of the South L 34/35 4 2
Larne 35/36 IL
Manchester C 35/36 9 7 FL
36/37 3 2 FL
Millwall 37/38 10 7 FL
38/39 17 5 FL
Hibernian

McLEOD Murdo

Queen's Park 25/26 1

McLEOD Murdo

Johnstone A
Hibernian 38/39 2

McLEOD Robert

7th Scottish Rifles
Raith R 11/12 33
12/13 32
Newport Co 13/14 26 SL
Q P R 14/15 38 SL
Armadale
Vale of Leven 16/17
Clyde 17/18 3

McLEOD Thomas
b. Airdrie c1904
Kirkintilloch Rob Roy
Aberdeen 25/26 8 2
26/27 1
27/28 6 1
28/29 23 1
29/30 2
30/31 4
Charlton A 30/31 3 FL
31/32 1 FL

McLEOD William
b. Springburn c1860 d. Townhead ?.11.1943
Queen's Park
Cowlairs 90/91 16 1

McLEOD William
b. Aberdeen
Parkvale
Aberdeen 22/23 1

MacLEOD William S

Beith Amateurs
Port Glasgow A 06/07 1

McLEOD William S

Clyde 09/10 2 1
Beith 10/11

McLETCHIE Alex M

Kirkmuirhill
Airdrie Jnrs
Albion R 38/39 35 5

McLINTOCK Alexander 3 caps
b. c1854 d. Alexandria ?.5.1931
Vale of Leven 91/92 2

McLINTOCK William
b. c1919
Dunipace Jnrs
St Mirren 37/38 5 2
38/39 35 21
Kings Park

McLOUGHLIN James

Clydebank 20/21 8 1

McLOY James

Clyde 31/32 4

McLUCKIE Alexander
b. Burnbank
Clydebank Jnrs
Third Lanark 16/17 1
Renton

McLUCKIE James
b. Glasgow 1877 d. New York ?.8.1924
Jordanhill
Bury 98/99 28 3 FL
99/00 30 13 FL
00/01 32 13 FL
01/02 5 1 FL
Aston Villa 01/02 21 14 FL
02/03 21 18 FL
03/04 15 8 FL
Plymouth A 04/05 20 6 SL
Dundee 05/06 28 10
Third Lanark 06/07 30 3
07/08
Hamilton A 08/09 6 2

McLUCKIE James Sime 1 cap

b. Stonehouse 2.4.1908 d. Ipswich ?.11.1986

Tranent Jnrs					
Hamilton A		28/29	25	10	
		29/30	14	1	
		30/31	21	2	
		31/32	28	3	
		32/33	18		
Manchester C		33/34	27		FL
		34/35	5	1	FL
Aston Villa		34/35	1		FL
		35/36	14	1	FL
Ipswich T		36/37			SL
		37/38			SL
		38/39	41	1	FL
		39/40	3		FL
		46/47			FL
Clacton T		47/48			
		48/49			

McLUNG Robert

Abercorn		91/92	20	6	
		92/93			
		93/94	9		D2
		94/95	13		D2
		95/96	13		D2

McLURG Charles

Barrhead South YMCA					
East Stirlingshire		32/33	19		

McMAHON Alexander 6 caps

b. Selkirk 1871 d. Glasgow 25.1.1916

Harp Juveniles					
Hibernian					
Queen's Park Jnrs					
Woodburn					
Leith Harp		87/88			
Darlington St Augustines		88/89			
Hibernian		88/89			
		89/90			
Celtic		90/91	11	5	
		91/92	20	17	
		92/93	13	11	
		93/94	15	10	
		94/95	11	8	
		95/96	15	10	
		96/97	12	8	
		97/98	14	5	
		98/99	17	11	
		99/00	10	5	
		00/01	20	12	
		01/02	13	6	
		02/03	6	2	
Partick T		03/04	3	1	

McMAHON Hugh

b. Saltcoats 7.7.1906 d. Saltcoats 22.12.1997

Saltcoats V					
Cowdenbeath		27/28	1		
		28/29	28		
		29/30	24		
Blackpool		30/31	26	1	FL
Stoke C		31/32	8	1	FL
Wrexham		32/33	32	2	FL
		33/34	40	2	FL
		34/35	38	2	FL
		35/36	34	1	FL
Workington		35/36			
Doncaster R		36/37	5		FL
Albion R		36/37	7	1	

McMAHON John

b. c1877 d. Possilpark ?.9.1933

Clyde		99/00	10		
		00/01	9	?	D2
Preston NE		00/01	21		FL
		01/02	32		FL
		02/03	12		FL
Manchester C		02/03	17		FL
		03/04	27		FL
		04/05	31		FL
		05/06	26	1	FL
Bury		06/07	14		FL
		07/08	24		FL
		08/09	10		FL
		09/10	13		FL

McMAHON John

Glencraig Celtic					
Celtic					
Dumbarton Harp		13/14			
East Fife		14/15			
		19/20			
Hamilton A		19/20	8	2	
Dundee Hibs		20/21			
Lochgelly U					

McMAHON Patrick

b. Glasgow 26.10.1908 d. Wrexham 28.1.1992

Pollokshaws Hibs					
St Anthonys					
West Ham U		32/33	13		FL
		33/34	3		FL
St Mirren		34/35	25		
Wrexham		34/35	2		FL
		35/36	30		FL
		36/37	36		FL
		37/38	42		FL
		38/39	3		FL
Stoke C		39/40	3		FL

McMANUS Edward

Queen's Park		20/21	12		
		21/22	2		

McMANUS Harry

Parkhead Jnrs					
Hibernian		15/16	15		
		16/17	34		
		17/18	25	?	

McMANUS Peter Thomas

b. Winchburgh ?.4.1873 d. 1936

Hibernian		91/92			
		92/93			
Mossend Swifts		93/94			
St Bernards		94/95	15		
Celtic		95/96	1		
St Bernards		95/96			
WBA		96/97	17		FL
		97/98	11	1	FL
Warmley		98/99	11		SL
Thames Ironworks		98/99	5		SL
		99/00	5		SL

McMASTER John

b. Port Glasgow 4.1.1893 d. Greenock 27.12.1954

Menstrie Thistle Juveniles					
Port Dundas Acrehill Juveniles					
Carron Juveniles					
Clydebank Jnrs					
Vale of Leven		10/11	1	?	D2
Dumbarton Harp		11/12			
Clydebank Jnrs		12/13			
Celtic		13/14	33	1	
		14/15	33		
		15/16	37	3	
		16/17	4		
		17/18	8		
		18/19			
		19/20	27		
		20/21	33	1	
		21/22	27		
Birmingham	L	21/22			FL
Celtic		22/23	4		
Ayr U	L	22/23			
Queen of the South		23/24			D3
		24/25			D3

McMASTER Thomas

Port Glasgow A		97/98	16		D2
		98/99	14		D2
		99/00	13		D2
		00/01	12		D2
		01/02			D2
		02/03	5		

McMATH Henry E

Kilsyth R *					
Portadown *		34/35			IL
		35/36			IL
		36/37			IL
		37/38			IL
Queen of the South		38/39	1		

McMEEKIN John

Maryhill Hibernians					
Airdrieonians		28/29	8		

McMEEKIN John G

Mossfield Amateurs					
Glasgow Perthshire		10/11			
		11/12			
		12/13			
		13/14			
		14/15			
		15/16			
		16/17			
Dumbarton		17/18	1		

McMEEKIN Joseph N

Parkhead Jnrs					
Aberdeen		31/32	5		
Montrose		31/32			D2
Dumbarton	T	32/33			D2
Airdrieonians		32/33			
Edinburgh C		33/34			D2

McMEEKIN W

Petershill					
Airdrieonians		09/10	1		
Bathgate					

McMENEMY Francis

b. Hamilton 5.12.1906

Burnbank A					
Hamilton A		29/30	3		
		30/31	4		
St Cuthberts W	L	30/31			
Hamilton A		31/32	8		
Nithsdale W	L				
Airdrieonians					
Tunbridge Wells R		32/33			
Northampton T		33/34	10		FL
		34/35	28	2	FL
		35/36	19	1	FL
Crystal Palace		36/37	25	3	FL
Guildford C *					

McMENEMY Henry

b. Glasgow 26.3.1910

Strathclyde					
Newcastle U		31/32	29	4	FL
		32/33	39	9	FL
		33/34	17	3	FL
		34/35	23	7	FL
		35/36	20	5	FL
		36/37	10	4	FL
Dundee		37/38	36	9	

McMENEMY James 12 caps

b. Rutherglen 23.8.1880 d. Robroyston 23.6.1965

Rutherglen Young Celtic		98/99			
Cambuslang Bluebell		99/00			
Dundee	T	99/00			
Cambuslang Hibernian		00/01			
Rutherglen Glencairn		01/02			
Everton	T	01/02			
Celtic		02/03	6	2	
East Stirlingshire	L	02/03			D2
Stenhousemuir	L	02/03			
Celtic		03/04	22	9	
		04/05	15	6	
		05/06	28	10	
		06/07	31	7	
		07/08	30	7	
		08/09	31	14	
		09/10	29	9	
		10/11	30	10	
		11/12	21	7	
		12/13	21	7	
		13/14	20	9	
		14/15	36	14	
		15/16	32	9	
		16/17	34	5	
		17/18	24	5	
		18/19	19	4	
Linfield	L	18/19			IL
Celtic		19/20	28	2	
Partick T		20/21	29	1	
		21/22	27	2	
Stenhousemuir	L	21/22			D2

McMENEMY John 1 cap

b. Glasgow 9.2.1908 d. 5.2.1983

St Mungos Academy					
St Anthonys					
St Rochs					
Celtic		25/26			
		26/27	4	1	
Motherwell	L	26/27			
Celtic		27/28	9	1	
		28/29	2		
Motherwell		28/29	25	5	
		29/30	36	13	
		30/31	36	11	
		31/32	31	6	
		32/33	29	10	
		33/34	37	6	
		34/35	31	8	
		35/36	15	3	
		36/37	1		
Partick T		36/37	28	3	
		37/38	4	1	
St Mirren		37/38	5	1	
		38/39	5	1	

McMILLAN

Vale of Leven		90/91	3		

McMILLAN

St Mirren 92/93 1

McMILLAN Archibald

Dumbarton Harp
Celtic
Dumbarton Harp 13/14
Ayr U 14/15 4

McMILLAN Archibald
b. Glasgow
Clyde 28/29 1

McMILLAN Charles
b. Lugar
Lugar Boswell
St Johnstone 29/30 14
Heart of Midlothian 30/31 1

McMILLAN David

Rangers 05/06 9 1
Motherwell 06/07 3

McMILLAN George
b. Edinburgh
Leith A 91/92 2
St Bernards 91/92
Millwall A 92/93
Lincoln C 93/94 3 FL

McMILLAN George
b. Armadale 28.3.1904
Fauldhouse U
Armadale
Rangers 26/27 13 6
27/28 8 4
28/29 6 2
29/30 5
30/31 1
Bradford PA 30/31 23 6 FL
31/32 28 4 FL
32/33 3 FL
Bath C 33/34 SL
34/35 SL
Lovells A 35/36 SL
Albion R 36/37 7 1
East Stirlingshire 36/37 D2

McMILLAN Hubert A

Glasgow Ashfield
Queen's Park 15/16 7
16/17 27 7
17/18 7 1

McMILLAN James 1 cap

St Bernards 96/97 18 4
97/98 7

McMILLAN James
b. Rothesay c1884 d. Falkirk ?.9.1935
Bute A
Rothesay Royal V
Falkirk 07/08 2
08/09
09/10 23 1
10/11 32 1
11/12 30 2
12/13 27 1
13/14 10
14/15 35 1
15/16 33
16/17 20
17/18 16 ?
Stenhousemuir

McMILLAN James

Clyde 33/34 1
Derry C 34/35 IL

McMILLAN James Hunter

Ross Co
Third Lanark 36/37 3
Cardiff C

McMILLAN John
b. Whiteinch
Kirkintilloch Rob Roy
Bellshill A
Dumbarton
Distillery 17/18 IL
Clydebank 17/18 3
Distillery 18/19 IL
Clydebank 19/20 22 1
20/21 15 1
21/22 42 3
Ayr U T 22/23

McMILLAN John

Armadale
Duntocher Hibs
Dumbarton 20/21 1
Renton 20/21
Vale of Leven 21/22 D2

McMILLAN John K
b. Motherwell
Royal Albert
Hamilton A 26/27 2 1
Alloa A 26/27 D2

McMILLAN Lachlan
b. Hamilton
Rutherglen Glencairn
Hamilton A 20/21 16 3
21/22 38 9
22/23 27 8
23/24 30 13
Heart of Midlothian 24/25 35 11
25/26 12 4
26/27 27 3
27/28 38 19
28/29 16 3
29/30 18 7
30/31 9 1
Aberdeen 30/31 1 1
Heart of Midlothian 31/32 8
Partick T 32/33 22 5
Heart of Midlothian 33/34 1
Third Lanark 33/34 9
Elgin C 34/35

McMILLAN Peter

Dundee U 25/26 3 1

McMILLAN Thomas 1 cap
b. Mauchline 11.10.1866 d. 2.1.1928
Dumbarton A
Dumbarton 86/87
87/88
88/89
89/90
90/91 13 2
91/92 16 2
92/93 16
93/94 16
94/95 10

McMILLAN William
b. Dykehead 6.9.1876 d. Paisley * 3.4.1906 *
Dykehead 94/95
Heart of Midlothian 94/95
Dykehead 94/95
Heart of Midlothian 95/96 11
Southampton 95/96 4 SL
96/97 20 1 SL
97/98 7 2 SL
Burnley 98/99 2 FL
99/00 1 FL
St Mirren 00/01 2
Kilbarchan
Arthurlie
Morton 03/04
Arthurlie

McMILLAN William W

Linlithgow * 30/31
Whifflet Emerald * 31/32
Heart of Midlothian * 31/32
Strathclyde 32/33
Millwall T 32/33 FL
East Stirlingshire 32/33 1 3
33/34 D2

McMINN James A
b. Glasgow
Morton 21/22 31 4
22/23 7
23/24 3
Ayr U 23/24 13

McMULLAN James 16 caps
b. Denny 26.3.1895 d. Sheffield 28.11.1964
Denny Hibs
Third Lanark 11/12
12/13
Partick T 13/14 19
14/15 18
15/16 31
16/17 35 1
17/18 32 2
18/19 27 1
19/20 27 2
20/21 29 2
Maidstone U 21/22
22/23
Partick T 23/24 25 1
24/25 30 2
25/26 23
Manchester C 25/26 10 FL
26/27 35 3 FL
27/28 38 4 FL
28/29 38 FL
29/30 25 2 FL
30/31 27 FL
31/32 26 FL

McMURDO Alexander Brown
b. Cleland 9.4.1914
West Calder
Bury 35/36 1 FL
Queen of the South 36/37 26 2
Rochdale 37/38 2 FL

McMURDO Thomas

Dumbarton Corinthians
Third Lanark 03/04 1 1
04/05 4

McMURRAY Alexander

Dumbarton Corinthians
Rangers 02/03
Motherwell 03/04 13 1
04/05 8 1

McMURRAY Patrick

Hibernian 95/96 1

McMURTRIE Andrew
b. Dreghorn 30.10.1906
Dreghorn
Motherwell 26/27 27 9
27/28 30 2
28/29 7 2
Bristol C 29/30 10 1 FL
Cork 30/31 LI
Kings Park T 30/31 D2
Rotherham U 31/32 FL
32/33 FL
Dreghorn 33/34

McMURTRIE Peter S

Dreghorn
Ayr U 28/29 1

McNAB

St Bernards 93/94 13 4

McNAB

Leith A 94/95 6 1

McNAB

Hibernian 06/07 1

McNAB Alexander 2 caps
b. Gourock 27.12.1895 d. St Louis 3.4.1960
Morton 15/16 4
16/17 33 6
17/18 26 5
18/19 32 7
19/20 42 8
20/21 32 7
21/22 42 7
22/23 38 8
23/24 35 5
Boston Wonder Workers 24/25 20 1 ASL
25/26 40 12 ASL
26/27 39 8 ASL
27/28 50 14 ASL
Fall River Marksmen 28/29 44 9 ASL
29A 18 3 ASL
29/30 26 7 ASL
30A 18 3 ASL
New York Yankees 31S 7 1 ASL
New Bedford Whalers 31A 21 3 ASL
St Louis Stix,Baer & Fuller 32/33
St Louis Central Breweries
St Louis Shamrocks

McNAB Andrew

Club		Season	Apps	Goals	League
Dalziel R					
Motherwell		02/03			D2
		03/04	20	1	
		04/05	16		
Glossop		05/06	18		FL

McNAB Colin Duncan 6 caps

b. Portobello 6.4.1902 d. 25.11.1970

Club		Season	Apps	Goals	League
Musselburgh Bruntonians					
Heart of Midlothian	T				
Dundee		24/25	21		
		25/26	33		
		26/27	24	3	
		27/28	34	3	
		28/29	34	3	
		29/30	37	3	
		30/31	31	1	
		31/32	32	2	
		32/33	17	2	
		33/34			
Arbroath		34/35	29	6	D2
		35/36	28	4	

McNAB D

Club		Season	Apps	Goals	League
Albion R					
Airdrieonians		07/08	10	1	

McNAB Duncan

Club		Season	Apps	Goals	League
Queen's Park		02/03	8	1	
Hamilton A					

McNAIR Alexander 15 caps

b. Bo'ness 26.12.1883 d. Larbert 18.11.1951

Club		Season	Apps	Goals	League
Stenhouse Thistle					
Stenhousemuir Hearts		02/03			
Celtic	T	02/03			
Stenhousemuir		03/04			
Celtic		04/05	3		
		05/06	22	4	
		06/07	29	2	
		07/08	19	2	
		08/09	26		
		09/10	29		
		10/11	34		
		11/12	29		
		12/13	30		
		13/14	32		
		14/15	35		
		15/16	31		
		16/17	37		
		17/18	31		
		18/19	31		
		19/20	35		
		20/21	29		
		21/22	39		
		22/23	25		
		23/24	29		
		24/25	12		

McNAIR Andrew

Club		Season	Apps	Goals	League
Queen's Park		01/02	17		
		02/03	19		
		03/04	3		
South Africa					
Queen's Park		06/07	4		

McNAIR Hugh

b. Glasgow

Club		Season	Apps	Goals	League
Benburb					
Vale of Clyde					
Falkirk		20/21	8		
		21/22	39	2	
		22/23	38		
		23/24	25	2	
		24/25	37	1	
		25/26	11		
Springfield Babes		26/27	24	1	ASL
Providence Clamdiggers		26/27	7		ASL

McNAIR James

Club		Season	Apps	Goals	League
Falkirk		33/34	16	5	
		34/35			
		35/36			D2
Stenhousemuir		36/37			D2
		37/38			D2

McNAIR John

Club		Season	Apps	Goals	League
Aberdeen		15/16	2		

McNAIR William

b. Renfrew 28.4.1885

Club		Season	Apps	Goals	League
Forth Rangers					
Celtic		05/06	1		
Hamilton A	L	05/06			D2
East Stirlingshire		06/07			D2
Tottenham H		07/08	15	5	SL
Aberdeen		08/09	15	3	
Reading		09/10	7		SL
Alloa A		09/10			

McNAIRN William J

Club		Season	Apps	Goals	League
Castle Douglas					
Hamilton A		07/08	1		
St Bernards		07/08			

McNAIRN William John

Club		Season	Apps	Goals	League
Morton		08/09	2		

McNALLY J

Club		Season	Apps	Goals	League
Motherwell Jnrs					
Dundee U		29/30	19		

McNALLY Owen

b. Denny 20.6.1906 d. Denny 1973

Club		Season	Apps	Goals	League
Denny Hibs					
Celtic		26/27	2		
Arthurlie	L	27/28			D2
Hamilton A	L	28/29	10	7	
Celtic		28/29	5	1	
		29/30	5	2	
Bray Unknowns		30/31			
Norwich C	T	30/31			FL
Cardiff C		31/32	6		FL
Bray Unknowns		32/33			LI
Lausanne		33/34			
Sligo R		34/35			LI
Distillery		35/36			IL
Leicester C		35/36	10	5	FL
		36/37	6	2	FL
Racing Club de Calais		37/38			
Shamrock R		38/39			LI

McNAMEE

Club		Season	Apps	Goals	League
Heart of Midlothian		93/94	1		

McNAMEE

Club		Season	Apps	Goals	League
Clyde		18/19	1	?	

McNAMEE William

b. c1892 d. Hamilton ?.6.1935

Club		Season	Apps	Goals	League
Strathclyde					
Hamilton A		12/13	20		
		13/14	36	5	
		14/15	37	4	
		15/16	34	2	
		16/17	27	2	
		17/18	13	2	
		18/19	22	1	
		19/20	26		
Barrow		20/21			
Alloa A	L	20/21			
Airdrieonians		20/21	17	1	

McNAUGHT Hugh

Club		Season	Apps	Goals	League
Glasgow University					
Queen's Park		03/04	3		
Dundee		04/05	7		
Heart of Midlothian		05/06	26		
Sheffield U		06/07	1		FL
Heart of Midlothian					
Nottingham F		09/10			FL

McNAUGHT James Rankin

b. Dumbarton 8.6.1870 d. West Ham ?.3.1919

Club		Season	Apps	Goals	League
Dumbarton		90/91	16	2	
		91/92	21	8	
		92/93	11	2	
Linfield					
Newton Heath		93/94	26	1	FL
		94/95	26	2	FL
		95/96	29	3	FL
		96/97	30	4	FL
		97/98	30	2	FL
Tottenham H		98/99	19		SL
		99/00	24		SL
		00/01	18		SL
		01/02	17		SL
		02/03			SL
		03/04	13		SL
		04/05	8		SL
		05/06			SL
Maidstone U		06/07			
		07/08			
		08/09			

McNAUGHT John A

b. Glasgow 1892 d. Ayr 1972

Churches league football

Club		Season	Apps	Goals	League
Cambuslang R					
Falkirk		11/12	27	5	
		12/13	28	3	
		13/14	35	6	
		14/15	31	2	
		15/16	5		
		16/17	4		
		17/18			
		18/19			
Vale of Leven	L	18/19			
St Mirren		18/19	3	?	
Kilmarnock		19/20	32	2	
		20/21	33	3	
		21/22	22	1	
Johnstone		22/23			D2
		23/24			D2
Clyde		24/25			
Johnstone		25/26			D3
East Stirlingshire		25/26			D2

McNAUGHTON Alan

Club		Season	Apps	Goals	League
Dundee		93/94	2		

McNAUGHTON Douglas

Club		Season	Apps	Goals	League
Arthurlie					
Ayr U		17/18	15	?	
		18/19	4	1	

McNAUGHTON Gibson Norrie

b. Broughty Ferry 30.7.1911 d. West Bridgford 16.9.1991

Club		Season	Apps	Goals	League
Dundee Violet					
Clyde		33/34	21	2	
Dundee		34/35	30	8	
		35/36	17	5	
East Fife		36/37			D2
Nottingham F		36/37	21	3	FL
		37/38	27	7	FL
		38/39	18	2	FL
Notts Co					
Ilkeston T					

McNAUGHTON Harry

b. Canongate 6.4.1894

Club		Season	Apps	Goals	League
Tolbooth Juveniles					
Edinburgh Renton					
Army					
Heart of Midlothian		18/19	1		
St Bernards					
Liverpool		20/21	1		FL
Broxburn U					
Leith A					

McNEE

Club		Season	Apps	Goals	League
Renton		93/94	12	4	

McNEE Christopher

Club		Season	Apps	Goals	League
Shawfield					
Blantyre V					
Hamilton A		35/36			
		36/37	29	10	
		37/38	37	8	
		38/39	34	5	
Rangers		46/47	10	3	
		47/48			
Dumbarton		48/49			D2

McNEIL

Club		Season	Apps	Goals	League
Hibernian		06/07	1		

McNEIL Donald

Club		Season	Apps	Goals	League
St Bernards		96/97	17	3	
Partick T *		97/98			
Dunblane *					

McNEIL Hugh

Club		Season	Apps	Goals	League
Dalziel R					
Motherwell		99/00			
Celtic		00/01	2		
Hamilton A		01/02			
Morton		02/03			
		03/04			
Motherwell		04/05	19		
		05/06	30	1	
		06/07	31	1	
		07/08	29	1	
		08/09	16		
		09/10	30		
		10/11	33		
		11/12	27	1	
		12/13	22		
		13/14	12		
Wishaw Thistle		14/15			
Royal Albert		15/16			

McNEIL Hugh
b. Motherwell
Parkhead Jnrs
Larkhall Thistle
Hamilton A 23/24 29
24/25 22
25/26 19
Motherwell 26/27 30 1
27/28 12
28/29 32
29/30 11

McNEIL James
Falkirk 26/27 7
Third Lanark
Glasgow Perthshire *

McNEIL John Law
b. Inverkeithing c1906
Bo'ness
Musselburgh Bruntonians
Heart of Midlothian 25/26 15 12
26/27 14 6
Raith R L 26/27 D2
Heart of Midlothian 27/28 1
28/29 1
Portsmouth 28/29 9 4 FL
29/30 3 1 FL
Reading 29/30 8 2 FL
Airdrieonians T 30/31
Reading 30/31 26 3 FL
Shelbourne T 30/31 LI
Reading 31/32 5 FL
Guildford C 32/33
Heart of Midlothian 33/34
Inverness Caledonian 33/34
Plymouth A 34/35 31 FL
35/36 34 3 FL
36/37 37 3 FL
37/38 31 5 FL
38/39 5 1 FL
Clapton Orient 39/40 3 FL

McNEIL Malcolm
Limited Liability FC
Partick T 25/26 4 1
Albion R 26/27 D2

McNEIL Neil
Hurlford
Kilmarnock 09/10 1
Hurlford 10/11
11/12
12/13
13/14
14/15

McNEIL Robert
Motherwell 18/19 1

McNEIL Robert William
b. Partick 10.3.1889 d. Hamilton c1970
Wishaw Caledonians
Shettleston Jnrs
Hamilton A 10/11 13 2
11/12 24 1
12/13 34 5
13/14 29 5
Chelsea 14/15 37 3 FL
Bathgate
Motherwell 15/16 12 3
Wishaw Thistle 16/17
Hamilton A 16/17 25 4
17/18 31 4
18/19 31 8
Chelsea 19/20 26 3 FL
20/21 39 6 FL
21/22 42 2 FL
22/23 41 4 FL
23/24 29 FL
24/25 35 3 FL
25/26 24 5 FL
26/27 6 1 FL

McNEIL William
Cumnock Jnrs
Kilmarnock 18/19 1

McNEIL William
b. c1914 d. Isle of Arran ?.02.2001
Cambuslang R
Hamilton A 36/37 9 4
37/38 7 3
38/39 25 3

McNEILL
Abercorn 91/92 4

McNEILL
Renton 91/92 1

McNEILL
Lochgelly U
Heart of Midlothian 04/05 7

McNEILL Alexander
Port Glasgow A 00/01 D2
01/02 D2
02/03 11
03/04 21
04/05 19 1
05/06 2

McNEILL Duncan
b. Glasgow 1886 d. Glasgow 25.6.1931
Kirkintilloch Rob Roy
Raith R 10/11 27 6
11/12 26 8
Linfield 11/12 IL
12/13 IL
13/14 IL
Distillery 14/15 IL
Hamilton A 15/16
Motherwell 15/16 2
Morton 16/17 9 3

McNEILL John
b. Lochgelly
Leith A 30/31 31
31/32 25

McNEILL Robert
b. Glasgow
Port Victoria
Port Glasgow A
Vale of Leven
Clyde 92/93 3
93/94 16
Sunderland 94/95 22 FL
95/96 18 FL
96/97 26 FL
97/98 14 FL
98/99 32 FL
99/00 28 FL
00/01 1 FL
Morton 01/02 4
02/03 19 3
03/04 26

McNEILL Thomas
b. Lochgelly
Dunfermline A 27/28 4

McNEILL William
Hibernian 05/06 17 6
06/07 9 1
07/08 6
Heart of Midlothian 07/08 2

McNEILL William
b. Clydebank
Yoker A
Dundee 27/28 1

McNEILLAGE
Hibernian 17/18 1 ?

McNEILLY James
St Mirren 98/99 9 8
99/00 3 2
00/01 5 2
Johnstone 00/01
Abercorn 01/02 D2
Johnstone

McNEISH
Clyde 96/97 1

McNICHOL Duncan
b. Alexandria
St Bernards 97/98 8
98/99 10
Woolwich Arsenal 99/00 30 FL
00/01 30 FL
01/02 20 FL
02/03 21 FL
Aberdeen 03/04
04/05 18 D2

McNICOL
Clyde 94/95 5

McNICOL John
b. c1864 d. Alexandria ?.7.1933
Vale of Leven *
Dumbarton 94/95 3 1
95/96 4
96/97 1 D2

McNICOLL
Vale of Leven 90/91 10
91/92 19

McNICOLL George
Falkirk
Partick T 98/99 1
99/00 13 2 D2
00/01 8 2
Port Glasgow A 01/02 D2
02/03 20 2
03/04 22 10
Aberdeen 04/05 14 5 D2
05/06 12 9

McNIVEN Archibald
Dundee 31/32 1

McNIVEN Daniel
Alva Albion R
Partick T 21/22 5 1
Bethlehem Steel 22/23 22 28 ASL
New York Field Club 23/24 19 11 ASL
New York Giants 23/24 4 2 ASL
Indiana Flooring 24/25 7 1 ASL

McNULTY
Third Lanark 96/97 1 1

McNULTY Bernard
b. Craigneuk
Sheildmuir Celtic
Dundee 25/26 8 1
Bathgate 26/27 D2
Brighton T 26/27 FL

McOUSTRA William
Heather R
Glasgow Ashfield
Celtic 99/00
Stenhousemuir L 99/00
Celtic 00/01 14 3
01/02 9 4
Manchester C 01/02 13 2 FL
02/03 32 4 FL
03/04 2 FL
04/05 2 FL
05/06 7 FL
06/07 10 FL
Blackpool 07/08 FL
08/09 FL
Stenhousemuir 09/10
Abercorn 09/10 D2
Alloa 10/11

McPAKE James
Third Lanark 15/16 24

McPARTLIN James
b. Edinburgh c1908
Edinburgh Emmet
Hibernian 27/28 6
Ayr U 28/29

McPHAIL Angus
b. Blantyre
Blantyre Celtic
Clyde 31/32 11 1
32/33 37 1
33/34 37
34/35 22 2
35/36 19 2
36/37 7
37/38 1

McPHAIL Daniel
Broxburn U
Hibernian 13/14 1

McPHAIL Malcolm Wright
b. Cathcart 2.2.1896
Barrhead Churches League
Arthurlie 14/15 D2
Kilmarnock 15/16 21 2
16/17 38 13
17/18 32 11
18/19 34 9
19/20 40 11
20/21 31 3
21/22 28 2
22/23 18 3
23/24 3 1
Morton 24/25 31 3
25/26 5

McPHAIL Robert Low 17 caps
b. Barrhead 25.10.1905 d. Glasgow 24.8.2000
Barrhead Ashvale
Pollok Jnrs
Arthurlie 23/24 D3
Airdrieonians 23/24 9 1
24/25 33 14
25/26 36 23
26/27 31 34
Rangers 27/28 36 17
28/29 33 18
29/30 23 17
30/31 34 20
31/32 35 22
32/33 31 29
33/34 25 22
34/35 30 14
35/36 26 23
36/37 33 25
37/38 25 10
38/39 23 13

McPHEE
St Mirren 90/91 1 1
91/92 3 1
92/93 1

McPHEE
Clyde 91/92 1

McPHEE John
Queen's Park 01/02 1
02/03 10 3
03/04
04/05 3
05/06 7
06/07 1
07/08
08/09 1
09/10
10/11 9 4
11/12 2

McPHEE John
b. Stirling 17.6.1909 (?)
Cowie Thistle Juveniles
Sunderland 29/30 4 FL
Brentford 30/31 FL
Albion R 31/32 D2
32/33 D2
33/34 D2
34/35 34 3
35/36 25 6

MacPHEE Magnus George
b. Edinburgh 30.4.1914 d. Basingstoke 1960
Wellington R
Heart of Midlothian 32/33
Edina L 32/33
Heart of Midlothian 33/34
Leith A L 33/34 D2
Dunfermline A 34/35 12 5
Bangor 35/36
Belfast Celtic 35/36 IL
Workington 36/37
Bradford PA 36/37 FL
Coventry C 37/38 12 6 FL
Reading 38/39 42 25 FL
39/40 3 3 Ex
46/47 41 3 FL
47/48 25 16 FL
48/49 24 16 FL
Banbury Spencer

McPHERSON
Third Lanark 92/93 3 3

McPHERSON Andrew Forbes
b. Greenock 22.9.1879
Morton Jnrs
Morton 98/99 18 ? D2
99/00 18 ? D2
00/01 19
01/02 18
Celtic 02/03 22
03/04 5
Hibernian 03/04 1
04/05
Stenhousemuir 05/06
Port Glasgow A

McPHERSON Archibald
b. Alva 10.2.1910 d. 1969
Alva Albion R
Rangers 27/28
28/29
29/30 6 2
Bathgate L
Liverpool 29/30 25 5 FL
30/31 42 10 FL
31/32 28 2 FL
32/33 24 1 FL
33/34 9 FL
34/35 2 FL
Sheffield U 34/35 22 1 FL
35/36 25 FL
36/37 10 FL
Falkirk 37/38 30 1
38/39 12 1
East Fife 38/39 9 D2
Dundee U

McPHERSON David Murray 1 cap
b. Kilmarnock 22.8.1872
Kilmarnock 91/92
Rangers 91/92 2
92/93 8 1
Kilmarnock 93/94
94/95
95/96 19 2 D2
96/97 17 1 D2
97/98 17 6 D2
98/99 15 4 D2
99/00 16 1
00/01 18 2
01/02 18 2
02/03 18 1
03/04 18 3
Beith

McPHERSON Duncan
b. c 1881
Beith
Belfast Celtic 03/04
Beith
Woolwich Arsenal T
St Mirren 05/06 1

McPHERSON Francis Comber
b. Barrow 14.5.1901 d. Daveyhulme 5.3.1953
Barrow Shipbuilders
Partick T 18/19 1
Barrow Shipbuilders
Chesterfield Municipal 19/20
Barrow Shipbuilders
Barrow 21/22 21 1 FL
22/23 32 2 FL
Manchester U 23/24 34 1 FL
24/25 38 7 FL
25/26 29 16 FL
26/27 32 15 FL
27/28 26 6 FL
Manchester Central 28/29
Watford 28/29 33 33 FL
29/30 28 22 FL
Reading 29/30 11 8 FL
30/31 31 7 FL
31/32 23 7 FL
32/33 14 7 FL
Watford 33/34 11 4 FL
34/35 6 1 FL
35/36 16 7 FL
Barrow 36/37 3 2 FL

McPHERSON Herbert
Inverness Thistle
Partick T 08/09 15 1
09/10
Dumbarton 10/11 11 D2
11/12 D2
12/13 D2

McPHERSON Hugh
Kenmuir Church
Third Lanark 29/30 D2
30/31 D2
31/32 3 1

McPHERSON James
Falkirk 05/06 5 1

McPHERSON James Adam
b. c1865 d. Hillhead 10.3.1926
Cowlairs 90/91 18

McPHERSON James Milne
b. Bathgate ?.2.1909
Bathgate
Rangers 28/29
St Johnstone 29/30 5
Albion R 30/31 D2
31/32 D2
Ballymena 32/33 IL
Sheppey U 33/34
Waterford 34/35 LI
Queen of the South 35/36

McPHERSON John 9 caps
b. Kilmarnock 19.6.1868 d. Glasgow 31.7.1926
Kilmarnock
Cowlairs
Rangers 89/90
90/91 18 15
91/92 18 10
92/93 18 7
93/94 15 3
94/95 17 9
95/96 16 7
96/97 10 11
97/98 12 10
98/99 15 7
99/00 13 9
00/01 18 7
01/02 5 3

McPHERSON John 1 cap
b. Motherwell 28.2.1867 d. Saskatchewan c1935
Cambuslang
Heart of Midlothian 88/89
89/90
90/91 8 3
91/92 1
Nottingham F 91/92 19 4 FA
Heart of Midlothian 92/93 4 1
Nottingham F 92/93 21 3 FL
93/94 29 7 FL
94/95 28 3 FL
95/96 24 1 FL
96/97 27 2 FL
97/98 27 4 FL
98/99 30 2 FL
99/00 28 2 FL
00/01 11 1 FL
Motherwell 01/02 D2
Cambuslang

McPHERSON Joseph
b. Livingston
Armadale Thistle
Queen of the South 35/36 3
36/37 8
37/38 38 2
38/39 33

McPHERSON Noble
St Johnstone 00/01
Rangers 01/02 2
St Johnstone 02/03
03/04
04/05
05/06
06/07
07/08

McPHERSON Robert
Falkirk 11/12 1

McPHERSON Roderick
Kings Park
St Mirren 11/12 5 1

McPHERSON William
b. Beith
Beith
St Mirren 04/05 12 3
05/06 28 2
Liverpool 06/07 28 9 FL
07/08 20 6 FL
Rangers 08/09 26 12
09/10 25 12
10/11
Heart of Midlothian 11/12 18 3
12/13 16 4

McPHERSON William
b. Greenock 22.9.1897
Morton 19/20 3 1
20/21 3
Beith 21/22
Fall River Marksmen 22/23 4 1 ASL
23/24 26 10 ASL
24/25 38 13 ASL
25/26 39 7 ASL
26/27 40 3 ASL
27/28 57 5 ASL
28/29 51 7 ASL
29A 22 5 ASL
29/30 27 1 ASL
30A 27 1 ASL
New York Yankees 31S 17 ASL
New Bedford Whalers 31A 18 1 ASL
St Louis Stix,Baer & Fuller
Pawtucket Rangers

McPHIE James
b. Bonnybridge 25.8.1920 d. Falkirk 24.2.2002
Falkirk 37/38 1
38/39 9 2
46/47 24
47/48 28
48/49 30
49/50 21
50/51 19 1
51/52 28 D2
52/53 6

McPHILLIPS Charles
Broxburn U
Heart of Midlothian 10/11 20
Broxburn U 11/12
12/13
Dundee Hibs 13/14 11 D2

McPHILLIPS Laurence
b. Bathgate 6.5.1914 d. Wallington ?.1.1994
Avonbridge Juveniles
Musselburgh A
Heart of Midlothian 36/37
37/38
Albion R 38/39 6
Belfast Celtic 38/39 IL
Cardiff C 39/40 3 FL

McQUADE John D
Neilston V
St Mirren 17/18 3
18/19
Renton L 18/19
Neilston V 19/20

McQUADE Thomas
Renfrew
Partick T 20/21 2

McQUADE Thomas
b. Glasgow
St Anthonys
Albion R 22/23 7 1

McQUAKER Robert
Newton Stewart
Third Lanark 07/08 15
08/09
Dumbarton 09/10 D2
10/11 D2
11/12 D2
12/13 D2
Abercorn 13/14 D2
Thornhill

McQUE Joseph
b. Scotland
Celtic
Liverpool 92/93 18 2 LL
93/94 25 2 FL
94/95 29 1 FL
95/96 26 FL
96/97 8 FL
97/98 14 2 FL
Third Lanark 97/98 15 1
98/99 16
99/00 16
00/01 12 2
01/02 12

McQUEEN
St Mirren 17/18 1

McQUEEN
Third Lanark 18/19 1 ?

McQUEEN George
b. Dalserf 1896
Rangers 17/18 12
18/19 7
Partick T 18/19 2
Kilmarnock L 18/19 1
Rangers 19/20
20/21 4
Airdrieonians 21/22 41
22/23 38 10
23/24 31 1
24/25 20
25/26 35 2
26/27 18
27/28 34 1
28/29 33
29/30 36 6
30/31 38 4
31/32 31 1
32/33 33 3

McQUEEN Hugh
b. Harthill 1.10.1867 d. Norwich 8.4.1944
Leith A 91/92 21 4
92/93 7
Liverpool 92/93 16 3 LL
93/94 26 11 FL
94/95 12 3 FL
Derby Co 95/96 29 6 FL
96/97 30 6 FL
97/98 30 3 FL
98/99 18 1 FL
99/00 20 FL
00/01 23 3 FL
QPR 01/02 26 9 SL
Gainsborough T 02/03 30 2 FL
Fulham 03/04 10 SL
Kilmarnock T 04/05 7
Hibernian 04/05 2
Norwich C

McQUEEN Matthew 2 caps
b. Harthill 18.5.1863 d. Liverpool 29.9.1944
Leith A
Heart of Midlothian 87/88
88/89
Leith A 89/90
90/91
91/92 21 3
92/93 8
Liverpool 92/93 16 5 LL
93/94 25 1 FL
94/95 23 FL
95/96 22 2 FL
96/97 1 FL
97/98 2 FL
98/99 2 FL

McQUEEN William
Hurlford
Kilmarnock 05/06 2
Abercorn 06/07 D2
Hurlford

McQUILKIE Archibald (?)
Renton 91/92 3
92/93 3
93/94 3

McREYNOLDS J B
Abercorn 96/97 2
Morton

McRITCHIE William
St Marys UF *
St Johnstone *
Benburb *
Clyde 33/34 6
Dundee U 34/35 D2
35/36 D2
Brechin C 36/37 D2

McROBBIE Alan
b. Elgin 13.11.1886
Elgin C
Dundee 10/11
Middlesbrough 11/12 1 FL
12/13 6 FL
Swindon T 13/14 12 SL
14/15 SL
Aberdeen 15/16 2
16/17
17/18
18/19
19/20 6

McROBERTS John
b. Glasgow
Kirkintilloch Rob Roy
Heart of Midlothian 19/20 12
20/21 5
21/22 13
St Johnstone 22/23 37 4 D2
23/24 35 2 D2
Dundee U 24/25 37 1
25/26 3
East Stirlingshire 25/26 D2
26/27 D2
27/28 D2
Forfar A T 27/28 D2

McRORIE Daniel 1 cap
b. Hutchesontown 25.6.1906
d. Newton Mearns 26.7.1963
Queen's Park Strollers
Queen of the South 24/25 D3
Airdrieonians 25/26 4 4
26/27 3 1
Stenhousemuir 27/28 D2
28/29 D2
Morton 29/30 27 6
30/31 13 18
Liverpool 30/31 3 1 FL
31/32 25 5 FL
32/33 5 FL
Millwall T 33/34 FL
Rochdale 33/34 5 FL
Morton 33/34 D2
Runcorn
Workington

McSEVICH Peter
b. Stevenston 14.5.1902 d. Walsall 1979
Newmains Jnrs
Shieldmuir Celtic
Celtic 24/25
Aberdeen 25/26 2
26/27 20
27/28 12
Bournemouth 28/29 33 FL
29/30 40 FL
30/31 42 FL
31/32 27 1 FL
Coventry C 32/33 34 FL
Walsall 33/34 35 FL
34/35 39 FL
35/36 28 FL
Wellington T

McSHEA Ernest
b. Glasgow
Strathclyde
Port Glasgow A 06/07 30 7
Barnsley 07/08 20 8 FL
Clyde 08/09 1
Rochdale 09/10 3 LC

McSKIMMING Robert
b. Glenboig 1888 d. Dunedin ?.12.1952
Douglas Park
Albion R
Sheffield W 09/10 9 FL
10/11 28 FL
11/12 25 FL
12/13 36 FL
13/14 32 FL
14/15 34 FL
Motherwell 15/16 11
16/17 28
17/18 28 3
18/19 23
Sheffield W 19/20 16 FL
Albion R 20/21 26
21/22 36
22/23 9
Ayr U 23/24
Helensburgh 23/24 D3
New Zealand

McSORLAND John
Coats Jnrs
Partick T T 32/33
St Mirren 32/33 4 2
Played at Partick under the name Smith.

McSPADYEN Alexander McLuckie 2 caps
b. Holytown 19.12.1914 d. Holytown 31.10.1978
Holytown Thistle
Partick T 34/35 6
35/36 16
36/37 32 6
37/38 31 1
38/39 38 5
46/47
47/48 1
Portadown 48/49 IL
49/50 IL

McSPADYEN James

Chapelhall U					
Airdrieonians		28/29	1		

McSTAY Francis

b. Carluke 1892 d. Townhead 18.11.1935

Larkhall U					
Motherwell		11/12	30	1	
		12/13	31		
		13/14	35	3	
		14/15	37	2	
		15/16	29		
		16/17	36		
		17/18	6		
		18/19	8		

McSTAY James

b. Netherburn 1.4.1895 d. 3.1.1974

Larkhall Thistle					
Celtic		20/21			
		21/22			
		22/23	24		
		23/24	36		
		24/25	36	2	
		25/26	36	1	
		26/27	26		
		27/28	38		
		28/29	38		
		29/30	32	1	
		30/31	37	2	
		31/32	37		
		32/33	33		
		33/34	33	1	
Hamilton A		34/35	25		
		35/36	23		
Celtic	L	35/36			
Hamilton A		36/37	15		
Brideville					

McSTAY William 13 caps

b. Netherburn 21.4.1894 d. 3.9.1960

Larkhall Thistle					
Ashgill R					
Larkhall Thistle					
Tottenham H	T	11/12			FL
Celtic		11/12			
Vale of Leven	L	11/12			D2
Celtic		12/13			
Ayr U	L	13/14	38		
	L	14/15	37		
	L	15/16	34		
Celtic		16/17	37		
		17/18			
Belfast Celtic	L	17/18			IL
Celtic		18/19	20	1	
		19/20	40	7	
		20/21	37	5	
		21/22	30	4	
		22/23	33	6	
New York Giants		22/23			
Celtic		23/24	32	4	
		24/25	33	5	
		25/26	36	2	
		26/27	33	2	
		27/28	34	1	
		28/29	36		
Heart of Midlothian		29/30	14		
Kirkmuirhill Jnrs					

McTAGGART William

Queen's Park		05/06	4		
East Stirlingshire		06/07			D2
		07/08			D2
Port Glasgow A		08/09	5		

McTAVISH John

Heart of Midlothian		17/18	5		

McTAVISH John Kay 1 cap

b. Govan 7.6.1885 d. Glasgow 1926

Petershill					
Falkirk		05/06	29	5	
		06/07	31	9	
		07/08	34	12	
		08/09	25	6	
		09/10	32	3	
Oldham A		10/11	10		FL
Tottenham H		10/11	7		FL
		11/12	30	3	FL
Newcastle U		11/12	1		FL
		12/13	33	6	FL
Partick T		13/14	33	5	
		14/15	34	8	
		15/16	30	5	
		16/17	26		
Falkirk	L	17/18	11	?	
East Fife		19/20			
Dumbarton		20/21	22	3	
East Stirlingshire		21/22			D2
Dumbarton					

McTAVISH Robert

b. 26.10.1888 d. 8.5.1972

Ibrox Roselie					
Petershill					
Falkirk		07/08	7	4	
		08/09	8	3	
		09/10	2		
Tottenham H		10/11	2		FL
Brentford		11/12	12	5	SL
		12/13	25	1	SL
Third Lanark		13/14	22	4	
York C		14/15			

McTAVISH Robert

Raith R		15/16	14	2	

McTURK George

Renton					
Clyde		07/08	8		
		08/09	32		
		09/10	33		
		10/11	20		
Partick T	L	11/12			
Clyde		11/12	13		
Partick T		12/13	29		
St Mirren	L	12/13	1		
Clyde		13/14	29		
		14/15	30		
Clydebank		15/16			
		16/17			
		17/18	34		
		18/19	32		
		19/20	13		
		20/21	13		

McVAY T

St Mirren		24/25	3		

McVEAN M

Vale of Leven		90/91	4		

McVEAN Malcolm

b. Jamestown 7.3.1871 d. Bonhill 6.6.1907

Vale of Leven W					
Clydebank					
Rangers		90/91			
Clydebank		90/91			
Third Lanark		91/92	20	6	
Liverpool		92/93	21	9	LL
		93/94	21	9	FL
		94/95	20	4	FL
		95/96	24	9	FL
		96/97	23	5	FL
Burnley		96/97	4		FL
Dundee		97/98	16	7	
Bedminster		98/99	24	4	SL

McVEIGH Samuel

b. Glasgow

Kirkintilloch Rob Roy					
St Mirren		23/24	6		
		24/25	3		
Arthurlie		24/25			D3

McVEIGH William

b. Ardrossan

St Mirren		20/21	13	7	
Stevenston U		21/22			

McVEY Alexander

St Mirren		30/31	1	1	
		31/32			
Beith		31/32			

McWALKER

St Mirren		96/97	2		

McWATT William

b. Denny

Dunipace Thistle					
Heart of Midlothian		27/28			
		28/29			
		29/30			
Airdrieonians		30/31	4		

McWATTIE George Chappell 2 caps

b. Arbroath 22.4.1875

Arbroath					
Hibernian		98/99	3		
		99/00	17		
Queen's Park		00/01	18		
Heart of Midlothian		01/02	17		
		02/03	18		
		03/04	19		
		04/05	6		

McWHINNIE William G

b. Wiltshire ?.7.1872 d. USA 1936

Reading		97/98	7	4	SL
		98/99	6	2	SL
Third Lanark		99/00	16	7	
Sheffield W		00/01	9		FL
		01/02			FL
		02/03			FL
		03/04			FL
		04/05			FL
Hibernian		05/06	3		
Third Lanark		05/06			
Aberdeen		06/07	1		

McWILLIAMS Robert McMillan

b. Camelon 24.5.1909

Auchinsharry Juveniles					
Denny Hibs		28/29			
Celtic		28/29	5		
Watford		29/30	12	1	FL
		30/31	10		FL
Leith A		31/32	15		
Celtic		31/32	1		
		32/33			
Yeovil T		32/33			
Newry T	T	32/33			IL
Celtic		32/33			
Larne		33/34			IL
Coleraine		33/34			IL

NAIRN William James

b. Cowdenbeath 23.8.1898 d. Scotland ?.9.1970

Cowdenbeath					
Dundee		19/20	3		
Ebbw Vale		20/21			
		21/22			
Newport Co		22/23	29		FL
		23/24	29		FL
		24/25	34	5	FL
		25/26	34	1	FL
		26/27	36	7	FL
		27/28	3		FL
		28/29	20		FL
		29/30	33		FL
		30/31	8		FL

NAISMITH James

Clyde		98/99	1		

NAISMITH Matthew

b. c1920

Morrison Church					
Falkirk		36/37	1		
		37/38			
Kings Park		38/39			D2

NAPIER Charles Edward 5 caps

b. Bainsford 8.10.1910 d. Falkirk 5.9.1973

Grangemouth Sacred Heart					
Cowie Thistle Juveniles					
Alva Albion R		28/29			
Celtic		28/29			
Maryhill Hibernian	L	28/29			
Celtic		29/30	29	15	
		30/31	37	19	
		31/32	33	21	
		32/33	35	20	
		33/34	16	5	
		34/35	27	2	
Derby Co		35/36	26	6	FL
		36/37	32	13	FL
		37/38	22	5	FL
Sheffield W		37/38	7		FL
		38/39	41	9	FL
		39/40	3	2	FL
Falkirk					
Stenhousemuir		46/47			
		47/48			

NAPIER George G

b. Falkirk

Camelon Jnrs					
Maryhill Hibernian					
Alva Albion R		30/31			
Kilmarnock		30/31	18	1	
		31/32	11	2	
		32/33	6	1	
Cowdenbeath		33/34	30	1	
East Stirlingshire		34/35			D2
Airdrieonians		35/36			
Beith					

NASH W

Dumbarton		92/93	5		
		93/94	12		
		94/95	16	3	
		95/96	15	1	

NASH William

Clyde 97/98 14
98/99 18
99/00 13 3
00/01 11 ? D2

NEAL Herbert
b. Daventry 1882
Northampton T 01/02 11 SL
02/03 15 SL
03/04 32 2 SL
04/05 32 2 SL
05/06 29 3 SL
06/07 34 1 SL
Dundee 07/08 17 2
08/09 30
09/10 10
10/11 30 1
11/12 33
12/13 18 2
St Johnstone 13/14 18 7 D2
14/15 21 6 D2

NEAL John T

Motherwell *
Airdrieonians * 98/99 D2
St Mirren 99/00 2
Hamilton A 99/00 D2

NEAVE

Hibernian 18/19 2 ?

NEAVE David
b. Arbroath 1883 d. Arbroath 14.11.1990
Forfar A 01/02
Montrose
Arbroath
Woolwich Arsenal 04/05 3 FL
Leyton 05/06 SL
Woolwich Arsenal 05/06 18 6 FL
06/07 33 4 FL
07/08 35 6 FL
08/09 25 5 FL
09/10 21 5 FL
10/11 15 3 FL
11/12 4 FL
Merthyr T 12/13 8 SL
13/14 SL
14/15 SL
Dunfermline A L 17/18
Heart of Midlothian L 18/19 23 2
Clyde L 18/19 3

NEAVE Robert
b. Lochee 23.5.1894 d. Glasgow 3.7.1951
Glasgow Perthshire
Sheffield U 12/13 11 FL
Chesterfield T 13/14 32 3 ML
Rochdale 14/15 37 7 CL
Clyde 15/16 30
16/17 34
Abercorn 16/17
Clyde 17/18 6 ?
Kilmarnock 17/18 9
18/19 24
19/20 16
20/21 34
21/22 4
Johnstone 22/23 D2
23/24 D2
24/25 D2
Helensburgh 25/26 D3

NEAVES

Clyde 91/92 1
92/93 6 1

NEEDHAM Anthony

Glasgow Perthshire
Third Lanark 05/06 2
06/07 1

NEEDHAM Anthony

Port Glasgow A 08/09 1

NEEDHAM Thomas

Moss Rose 02/03
03/04
Christ Church 04/05
05/06
06/07
West Hartlepool 07/08
08/09
Hartlepool U T 08/09
Port Glasgow A 09/10 1
Dumbarton 10/11 D2
Hartlepool U 11/12

NEIL

Clyde 92/93 1 1

NEIL Andrew
b. Crosshouse 18.11.1892 d. Kilmarnock 14.8.1941
Ardeer Thistle
Kilmarnock 12/13 2
Galston L 12/13
Kilmarnock 13/14 32 12
14/15 33 20
Clydebank L 14/15 D2
Third Lanark 15/16
Kilmarnock 15/16 5
16/17
17/18
18/19 3
Galston 19/20
Stevenston U
Brighton 20/21 18 2 FL
21/22 40 3 FL
22/23 42 10 FL
23/24 29 7 FL
Arsenal 23/24 11 2 FL
24/25 16 2 FL
25/26 27 6 FL
Brighton 25/26 12 2 FL
26/27 26 4 FL
QPR 27/28 41 1 FL
28/29 29 FL
29/30 36 FL

NEIL David

Queen's Park 18/19 8

NEIL James

Glasgow Perthshire
Portsmouth SL
Partick T 15/16 19
16/17 10
17/18
18/19
19/20 3

NEIL James

Old Kilpatrick
Dumbarton 18/19 3 ?

NEIL James

Morton 20/21 3

NEIL James
b. Kilmarnock
Glasgow Perthshire
Kilmarnock 21/22 29

NEIL Peter W H
b. Methil 1898
Cambuslang R
East Fife
Birmingham 21/22 5 FL
Heart of Midlothian 22/23 8
Alloa A

NEIL Robert

Benburb
Vale of Clyde
St Rochs
Partick T 26/27 12

NEIL Robert Scott Gibson 2 caps
b. Govan 24.9.1875 d. 2.3.1913
Ashfield
Hibernian 94/95 14 ? D2
95/96 17 6
Liverpool 96/97 22 2 FL
Rangers 97/98 12 3
98/99 18 6
99/00 15 3
00/01 9 1
01/02 16 3
02/03 17 8
03/04 5
Airdrieonians 04/05

NEIL Samuel

Motherwell
Clyde 97/98 6
98/99 1

NEIL Thomas W R

Pollok
Morton 12/13 3

NEIL William

Parkhead Jnrs
Airdrieonians 19/20 20 3
20/21 31 8
21/22 25 3
22/23 36
23/24 12
24/25 12
Third Lanark L 24/25 4
Airdrieonians 25/26 24 1
26/27 34 8
27/28 33 8
Ayr U 28/29 30 4
Derry C 29/30 IL
Cowdenbeath 30/31 2
Airdrieonians 31/32 6 1

NEILL James

Hurlford
Kilmarnock 06/07 2
07/08
Johnstone 08/09
Morton 08/09 1
09/10
Galston 10/11
Hurlford 11/12
Johnstone 12/13 D2
13/14 D2
14/15 D2

NEILL John

Shotts U *
Motherwell 15/16 21 12

NEILSON

Motherwell 03/04 2

NEILSON Adam

Abbotshill U
Raith R 19/20 2

NEILSON Adam

Lochgelly U 23/24 D2
Falkirk 24/25 26 1

NEILSON Andrew

Kilmarnock 09/10 1

NEILSON Charles
b. Ellon c1890 K.I.A. 1.6.1916
Aberdeen 10/11 5
11/12 3

NEILSON J H

Aberdeen 11/12 1 1

NEILSON James

St Bernards 96/97 8 3

NEILSON James

Parkhead Jnrs
Queen's Park 15/16 27
16/17 20
17/18 7

NEILSON John
b. Renfrew 26.12.1874
Renfrew V
Abercorn 96/97 1
Celtic 96/97 1
Abercorn 97/98 14 ? D2
98/99 D2
Third Lanark 99/00 15
Bristol R 00/01 27 3 SL
01/02 22 3 SL
Third Lanark 02/03 15 1
03/04 25 3
04/05 24 7
05/06 23 3
06/07 14
Wishaw Thistle 07/08
Albion R 08/09 D2

NEILSON John
b. Fauldhouse
St Ninians
Kilmarnock 07/08 1
Hurlford 08/09

NEILSON John
Hibernian 08/09 1

NEILSON Peter M
b. Glasgow 1890
Kilbirnie Ladeside
Airdrieonians 08/09 9 7
09/10 5 2
10/11 23 11
11/12 10
12/13 3
Birmingham 13/14 3 1 FL
Wallyford

NEISH Emerson
Vale of Grange
Bo'ness
St Mirren 13/14 5
Clydebank 14/15 D2
15/16
16/17
17/18 31 2
18/19 26 ?
19/20 40 3
20/21 15
21/22 2

NEISH James B
Dunniker Jnrs
Raith R 24/25 10 2
25/26 5 3
East Fife 25/26 D2

NEISH John
Denbeath Star
Raith R 13/14 17
14/15 23
15/16
16/17 12
17/18
18/19
19/20
East Fife 20/21
21/22 31 D2
22/23 18 D2
23/24 34 D2
24/25 35 D2
25/26 4 D2
Broxburn U 25/26 D2
East Fife 26/27 D2

NEISH John
b. Elgin 1911
Elgin C
Coleshill Hall 31/32
32/33
Buckie Thistle 32/33
Morton T 33/34 D2
Buckie Thistle 33/34
Partick T 34/35 9 2
Hull C 35/36 1 FL
Buckie Thistle 36/37
Coleshill Hall 36/37
Elgin Corinthians 37/38
Inverness Thistle 37/38

NEISH Thomas
Kirkcaldy U 12/13
Cowdenbeath
Dundee 13/14 2 1
14/15
19/20
20/21
East Fife 21/22 28 8 D2
Lochgelly U 22/23 D2
Burntisland Shipyard

NELLIES Peter 2 caps
b. Kingseat 24.4.1886 d. 15.7.1930
Douglas Water Thistle
Heart of Midlothian 07/08 1
08/09 28
09/10 18 2
10/11 20
11/12 30 1
12/13 26 2
13/14 35 2
14/15 35 1
15/16 32 1
16/17 27 1
17/18 13
18/19 19
19/20 34
20/21 21
Kings Park 21/22 D2
Berwick R 22/23
Carlisle U

NELLIS Walter (or NEILLIES)
Douglas Water Thistle
Motherwell 03/04 8 1

NELSON
Dumbarton 92/93 1

NELSON Andrew Burt
b. 1876
Cambusnethen
Wishaw Thistle
Hibernian 98/99 13 1
Reading 99/00 10 SL

NELSON John
Airdrieonians 09/10 1
10/11
Galston 10/11

NELSON John
b. Dundee
Dundee Violet
Dundee 29/30 9 1
Dundee U 30/31 1 D2

NESBITT Thomas
Blyth Spartans
Queen of the South 33/34 5 5
34/35 12 4

NESS David
b. Irvine 15.8.1902
Irvine V
Nithsdale W 22/23
Partick T 23/24 31 3
24/25 33 4
25/26 29 10
26/27 32 6
27/28 26 4
28/29 38 15
29/30 24 4
30/31 32 3
31/32 28 8
32/33 31 12
33/34 24 6
34/35 12 1

NEVIN John
b. Lintz 20.2.1886
Lintz Institute
Gateshead T
Sunderland
Hobson W
WBA 10/11 2 FL
11/12 FL
Bristol R 12/13 18 SL
13/14 5 SL
Lintz Institute
Ayr U 14/15 33 1
15/16 17
16/17
17/18
18/19
19/20 8
West Stanley 20/21
Workington 21/22
Barrow 22/23 29 3 FL
23/24 27 FL
West Stanley
Crewe A 24/25 23 1 FL
Hobson W 25/26
Lintz Colliery
York C T
Inverness Thistle
Fraserburgh

NEWALL John White
b. Ayr 21.7.1917 d. 21.1.2004
Irvine V
Burnfoothill Primrose
Ayr U 36/37 1 D2
37/38 3 D2
38/39 6 2
Retired
Wellington (NZ) 51
52
53
54

NEWALL Thomas
Annbank
Ayr U 12/13 D2
13/14 1

NEWBIGGING Alexander
b. Leadhills 12.9.1876
Lanark A
Abercorn 97/98 4 ? D2
98/99 18 ? D2
Lanark U 00/01
QPR 00/01 5 SL
Nottingham F 01/02 4 FL
02/03 1 FL
03/04 22 FL
04/05 2 FL
Reading 05/06 34 SL
Rangers 06/07 34
07/08 26
Reading 08/09 38 SL
Coventry C 09/10 7 SL
Inverness Thistle

NEWBIGGING Archibald
Denbeath Star
Heart of Midlothian 17/18 5

NEWBIGGING Henry
Douglas Water Thistle
Blantyre V
Cambuslang R
Raith R 14/15
Cambuslang R 15/16
Hamilton A 15/16 7 3
Raith R 15/16 4 2

NEWBIGGING William
Larkhall Thistle
Motherwell 21/22 17
22/23 22
23/24 25

NEWBIGGING William
b. Larkhall
St Mirren 24/25 20
25/26 38
26/27 9
27/28 17

NEWLANDS
Aberdeen 06/07 1

NEWLANDS David George
b. Kinning Park 1879
Parkhead Oaklea
Parkhead A
Vale of Clyde
Parkhead Jnrs
St Mirren 98/99
99/00
Fulham 99/00 2 SL
QPR 00/01 22 SL
01/02 25 1 SL
02/03 26 SL
03/04 32 SL
04/05 27 SL
05/06 27 SL
06/07 15 SL
Norwich C 07/08 34 SL
08/09 35 1 SL
09/10 27 SL
Dunfermline A 10/11
Airdrieonians 11/12 3
12/13 8

NEWLANDS Malcolm
Campbelltown
Port Glasgow A 09/10 1

NEWMAN
Dundee 16/17 1

NEWMAN

Clyde 16/17 1

NEWMAN

Clydebank 18/19 1 ?

NEWMAN Stanley B

Queen's Park 06/07 1

NEWTON Francis
b. Menston 28.10.1902
Menston
Kilsyth R
Clydebank
Hibernian 15/16 26 3
16/17 11
Abercorn 16/17
Clyde 17/18 2
18/19 1
19/20 2

NEWTON James Israel
b. Horsforth 1898
Anderston V
Glasgow Perthshire
Rutherglen Glencairn
Queen's Park 21/22 29
22/23 37 D2
Bradford C 23/24 FL
24/25 5 FL
Halifax T 25/26 40 FL
Coventry C 26/27 42 FL
27/28 28 FL
28/29 FL
Brighton 29/30 1 FL
Otley
Burley Grove U 35/36
Otley

NEWTON John

Kirkintilloch Rob Roy
Aberdeen 35/36
36/37
37/38 8

NEWTON William R
b. c1914
Kirriemuir Thistle
Dundee 31/32
32/33 2

NIBLO Thomas Bruce D 1 cap
b. Dunfermline 24.9.1877 d. Tynemouth ?.7.1933
Cadzow Oak
Hamilton A
Linthouse 96/97 12 ? D2
97/98 16 ? D2
Newcastle U 97/98 1 FL
98/99 10 FL
99/00 11 2 FL
Middlesbrough 99/00 3 2 FL
Newcastle U 00/01 26 2 FL
01/02 12 FL
Aston Villa 01/02 12 2 FL
02/03 17 FL
03/04 16 6 FL
Nottingham F 04/05 29 6 FL
05/06 18 3 FL
Watford 06/07 30 7 SL
Newcastle U 07/08 FL
Hebburn A 08/09
Aberdeen 08/09 9 2
Raith R 09/10 D2
10/11
Cardiff C 10/11 SL
Blyth Spartans

NIBLOE Joseph 11 caps
b. Corkerhill 23.11.1903 d. Doncaster 25.10.1976
Shawfield Jnrs
Rutherglen Glencairn
Kilmarnock 24/25 6
25/26 31
26/27 38
27/28 38
28/29 35
29/30 36
30/31 33
31/32 31 1
Aston Villa 32/33 12 FL
33/34 36 FL
Sheffield W 34/35 34 FL
35/36 42 FL
36/37 23 FL
37/38 17 FL

NICHOL

Heart of Midlothian 91/92 2

NICHOL George M
b. Stenhousemuir
St Ninians Thistle
St Mirren 28/29 1

NICHOL John

Queen's Park 05/06 3
06/07 2
Clyde

NICHOL William
b. Coldstream
Sunderland
St Mirren 34/35 12
East Stirlingshire 34/35 D2
Babcock & Wilcox

NICHOL William Douglas
b. Easington ?.1.1887
Royal Warwickshire Regt
Northumberland Fusiliers
Nottingham F
Notts Co
Seaforth Highlanders 09/10
Fort George 09/10
Aberdeen 09/10 2
10/11 7 2
Celtic 10/11
11/12 16 8
Stenhousemuir L 11/12
Ayr U L 11/12 D2
Bristol C 12/13 3 FL
Queen's Park Wednesday 13/14
Seaforth Highlanders

NICHOLL Henry
b. Enniskillen 30.11.1875 d. Belfast 21.8.1911
Belfast Celtic 99/00 IL
00/01 IL
01/02 IL
02/03 IL
Third Lanark 02/03 1
Belfast Celtic 03/04 IL
04/05 IL
05/06 IL
06/07 IL
07/08 IL
08/09 IL
09/10 IL

NICHOLL James
b. Port Glasgow
Morningside R
Cambuslang R
Airdrieonians 08/09 24 7
09/10 17 5
Middlesbrough 10/11 24 8 FL
11/12 4 FL
12/13 11 2 FL
13/14 13 3 FL
Liverpool 13/14 14 3 FL
14/15 38 10 FL
Wishaw Thistle
Hamilton A 16/17 9 1

NICHOLSON Donald

Bedlay Jnrs
Kilmarnock 31/32 1

NICHOLSON Harry
b. Perth c1910
Strathallan Hawthorn
Bridge of Allan
St Johnstone 26/27 2
27/28 30 8
28/29 7
29/30 24 4
30/31 37 9 D2
31/32 34 15 D2
32/33 18 5
Hibernian 33/34 6 2
Dundee U 33/34 4 1 D2
Alloa A 34/35 D2

NICHOLSON Henry
b. West Ham
Crystal Palace
Dundee 24/25 10 2
25/26 12 2

NICHOLSON Henry

Dundee 28/29 9

NICHOLSON John Andrew
b. Ayr 8.3.1888 d. Weston Super Mare 13.6.1970
Glasgow Ashfield
Bristol C 11/12 37 FL
12/13 33 FL
13/14 31 FL
14/15 33 1 FL
19/20 29 2 FL
20/21 34 1 FL
Rangers 21/22 17 1
22/23 10
23/24 3
St Johnstone 24/25 12

NICHOLSON Sidney
b. Shildon 1912
Cardiff C
Merthyr T
Bournemouth 31/32 4 FL
32/33 4 FL
Scunthorpe U 33/34
34/35
Chesterfield 34/35 FL
Barnsley 35/36 4 FL
36/37 2 FL
37/38 1 FL
Aberdeen 37/38 15
38/39 35 4

NICHOLSON William G
b. Glasgow
Bellahouston Academy
Queen's Park 24/25 32 2
25/26 37 10
26/27 29 5
27/28 34 7
28/29 25 5
Rangers 29/30 12 2
30/31 6
31/32 11 3
32/33 2 1
33/34 26 8
34/35 13 1
St Johnstone 35/36 30 8
36/37 12 3

NICOL

Abercorn 90/91 16 6
91/92 18 5

NICOL

Heart of Midlothian 93/94 1
94/95 1

NICOL

Motherwell 06/07 9

NICOL

Falkirk 23/24 1

NICOL David
b. 20.9.1907
Cadder U
Maryhill Hibernian
Celtic 27/28
Ayr U L 27/28 D2
Celtic 28/29 1
Third Lanark L 28/29
Montrose L 28/29 D2
Hamilton A 29/30 20
30/31 6
Stranraer 31/32
Maryhill Jnrs

NICOL George
d. Moderfontain, SA ?.8.1929
Ardeer Thistle
Motherwell 04/05 15 2
05/06 27 5
06/07 25 7
07/08 32 7
08/09 20
09/10 28 2
10/11 33 2
11/12 23 3
12/13 26 8
13/14 20 4
14/15 26 7

NICOL Hugh

Falkirk 19/20 3

NICOL James Couttie
b. Edinburgh 26.1.1908
Murrayfield Amateurs
Leith A 30/31 20 6
31/32 29 19
Portsmouth 32/33 3 1 FL
Aldershot 33/34 20 10 FL
St Mirren 34/35
Burton T 35/36
Hull C 35/36 6 1 FL
Burton T
York C 36/37 11 3 FL
Scarborough 37/38

NICOL Robert
b. Darconner 1908
Kello R
Kilmarnock 30/31 3 1
31/32 1
Queen of the South 32/33 D2

NICOLL Dyken
b. Forfar
Forfar A
Dundee 19/20 33 2
20/21 30 1
21/22 39 1
22/23 16
Forfar A 23/24 D2
24/25 D2
Dundee U 25/26 2
Forfar A 26/27 D2

NICOLL George M
St Mirren 27/28 1

NIMMO
Heart of Midlothian 18/19 1 ?

NIMMO Allan
Dundee 05/06 3 1
06/07 2
Cowdenbeath 07/08
08/09
East Fife 09/10

NIMMO Michael
b. Bothwell 27.10.1892
Glasgow Ashfield
Hamilton A 19/20 15
Barrow 20/21
21/22 34 FL
22/23 21 1 FL
Chatham 23/24

NISBET
Vale of Leven 90/91 1

NISBET Alexander H
Queen's Park 03/04 1
04/05 17
05/06 10 3

NISBET David B
Darvel Jnrs
Galston 06/07
Kilmarnock 07/08 2
08/09
Galston

NISBET George
b. Glasgow
Petershill
Ayr U 16/17 12
17/18 3
18/19 2
19/20 15
20/21 42 3
21/22 42
22/23 38
23/24 19
24/25 15
25/26 28 D2
26/27 14 4 D2
Raith R 26/27 D2
Ayr U 27/28 37 13 D2
28/29
Petershill 29/30
30/31
31/32
Montreal Verdun 32/33
Toronto Scottish 32/33

NISBET J
Queen's Park 17/18 1

NISBET James 3 caps
b. Glenbuck 27.8.1904
Cumnock Jnrs
Ayr U 26/27 D2
27/28 D2
28/29 36 6
29/30 36 7
30/31 6
31/32
Falkirk T 32/33

NISBET Robert
b. Falkirk c1910
Camelon Jnrs
Motherwell 29/30 6
30/31 2
Dolphin 31/32 LI
Preston NE 32/33 39 1 FL
East Stirlingshire T 32/33 4
Falkirk 32/33 5 1
33/34 28
34/35 27
35/36 D2
36/37 36 1
37/38 30 1
38/39 28
Dumbarton

NISBET Robert G
Queen's Park 03/04 3
04/05 4 1

NISBET T
Auchinleck Talbot
Ayr U 20/21 5

NIVEN Alexander F
b. c1893
Kilwinning R
Queen's Park 14/15 7 3
15/16 2
16/17
17/18
18/19
19/20 16 2
20/21 1

NIVEN James
Kilwinning R
Partick T 19/20 4 2
20/21 4 3
Kilwinning R

NIXON Andrew M
b. Paisley
Paisley Vulcan
Ayr U 20/21 4
21/22 6
Forth River
Shawsheen Indians 25/26 6 1 ASL

NIXON John
b. Bathgate 1885
Hibernian 05/06 9
06/07
Bristol C 07/08 7 FL
Croydon Common 08/09 11 6 SL
Stockport Co 09/10 30 5 FL
10/11 8 1 FL
Halifax T 11/12 ML
12/13 ML
Belfast Celtic 13/14 IL
Halifax T 14/15 ML
19/20 ML

NOBLE
Clyde 16/17 1

NOBLE David
b. Queensferry
St Bernards 34/35 D2
35/36 D2
36/37 D2
Clyde 36/37 28 6
37/38 37 9
38/39 38 14

NOBLE George
Broxburn A
Heart of Midlothian 16/17 13 3

NOBLE Rankin
Heart of Midlothian 16/17 2

NOBLE Rankin
Albion R 18/19
19/20 17
20/21 9
21/22 1
22/23 1
Mid Annandale 23/24 D3

NOBLE Robert
b. Broxburn
Broxburn A
Rangers 07/08 8 1
08/09 2
Carlisle U
Portsmouth 10/11 31 3 SL
Accrington S

NOBLE Thomas M
Queen's Park 24/25 5 1

NOON Robert
Hibernian 04/05 2
Leith A 04/05

NORTON Alfred
b. England
Clydebank Jnrs
Yoker A
Third Lanark 13/14 12 1
Clydebank 14/15 D2

NORWOOD Arthur
Stevenston Thistle
Kilmarnock 01/02 3 1
Stevenston Thistle 01/02
Maybole

NUGENT John
Vale of Clyde
Morton 07/08 6
08/09 29
09/10 25 1
Derby Co T 10/11 FL
Third Lanark 10/11 1
Port Glasgow A 10/11 D2
11/12 D2
Abercorn 12/13 D2

NUTLEY Robert
b. Paisley 10.9.1916 d. Paisley 1996
Blantyre V
Hibernian 37/38 26 8
38/39 37 12
Portsmouth 46/47 9 1 FL
Queen of the South

NUTTALL Thomas Albert B
b. Bolton ?.2.1889 d. Wandsworth 1963
Heywood U
Manchester U 11/12 6 2 FL
12/13 10 2 FL
Everton 13/14 14 7 FL
14/15 5 FL
St Mirren 19/20 11
Northwich V 19/20
Southend U 20/21 35 9 FL
21/22 22 1 FL
Leyland 21/22
Northwich V 22/23
Eccles U
Chorley

OAKES John
b. c1919
St Marys School, Hamilton
Wolverhampton W
Queen of the South 36/37 1
37/38 33 5
38/39 23 4

O'BRIEN
Hibernian 18/19 1 ?

O'BRIEN Edward
Clyde 97/98 5

O'BRIEN James
Oldham A
Falkirk L 17/18 4 ?

O'BRIEN John
b. Blantyre 3.8.1877
Mossend Brigade Jnrs
Celtic L 94/95 1
Benburb 95/96

O'BRIEN Michael

Vale of Leven
Renton 02/03
Port Glasgow A 03/04 15 1
04/05 26 4
05/06 22 5
Vale of Leven

O'BRIEN P J
b. 8.2.1894
St Aloysius
Queen's Park 12/13 2

O'BYRNE Fergus
b. West Calder 19.8.1871
Broxburn Shamrock
Newcastle WE 90/91
Broxburn Shamrock 91/92
Celtic L 92/93 1
Broxburn Shamrock 92/93
Celtic 93/94 5
Broxburn Shamrock 93/94
94/95
95/96

O'CONNELL Patrick
b. Dublin 8.3.1887 d. St Pancras 27.2.1959
Frankfort
Stanville R
Belfast Celtic 08/09 IL
Sheffield W 08/09 1 FL
09/10 3 FL
10/11 10 FL
11/12 4 FL
Hull C 12/13 30 FL
13/14 28 1 FL
Manchester U 14/15 34 2 FL
Rochdale 18/19
Dumbarton 19/20 32
Ashington 20/21
21/22 19 1 FL

O'CONNOR John
b. Greenock 7.1.1867
Vale of Leven Hibernian
Celtic 88/89
Glasgow Hibernian 89/90
Renton 89/90
Warwick Co 89/90
Hibernian 89/90
Aston Villa 89/90 FL
Burslem Port Vale 90/91
Celtic 91/92 1
Nottingham F

O'DONNELL

Abercorn 92/93 1 1

O'DONNELL

Abercorn 96/97 1

O'DONNELL Daniel
b. Renfrew
St Pauls U
Hibernian 18/19 17 ?
19/20 5

O'DONNELL Francis 6 caps
b. Buckhaven 31.8.1911 d. Macclesfield 4.9.1952
Denbeath Violet Juveniles
Wellesley Jnrs 30/31
Celtic 31/32 9 9
32/33 13 5
33/34 32 22
34/35 23 15
Preston NE 35/36 39 13 FL
36/37 39 16 FL
37/38 14 7 FL
Blackpool 37/38 17 10 FL
38/39 13 7 FL
Aston Villa 38/39 29 14 FL
39/40 3 FL
Nottingham F 46/47 11 5 FL
Buxton

O'DONNELL Hugh

Hibernian 99/00 1

O'DONNELL Hugh
b. Buckhaven 15.2.1913 d. Preston 10.5.1965
Denbeath Violet Jnrs
Wellesley Jnrs
Blantyre V
Celtic 32/33 27 4
33/34 19 5
34/35 28 11
Preston NE 35/36 39 15 FL
36/37 38 7 FL
37/38 35 5 FL
38/39 20 2 FL
Blackpool 38/39 10 1 FL
39/40 3 FL
46/47 1 1 FL
Rochdale 46/47 14 5 FL
47/48 26 9 FL
Halifax T 47/48 8 FL
48/49 5 1 FL

O'GARA James
b. Maryhill 1888
Airdrieonians 07/08 3
Middlesbrough 07/08 FL
Clapton Orient 08/09 1 FL
Preston NE T 09/10 FL
Dundee Hibernian 10/11 20 5 D2
11/12 3 D2
Portsmouth 11/12 1 SL

OGDEN Rowland

Dumbarton 18/19 3 ?

OGILVIE Charles Scott

Queen's Park 07/08 1 1

OGILVIE Duncan Henderson 1 cap
b. Shettleston 8.10.1912 d. Stirling 1977
St Ninians Thistle
Alva Albion R 30/31
31/32
Motherwell 32/33 19 8
33/34
34/35
Huddersfield T 35/36 10 FL
36/37 18 4 FL
Motherwell 37/38 36 18
38/39 36 9
Hamilton A 46/47 12 4
47/48 3 D2
Dundee U 48/49 19 D2

OGILVIE John
b. 5.10.1912
Motherwell Boys Brigade
Motherwell 33/34 30 13
34/35 27 6
35/36 28 7
36/37 17 11
37/38
38/39 3

O'HAGAN Charles
b. Buncrara 28.7.1881 d. New York 1.7.1931
St Columbs Court
Derry Celtic 00/01 IL
01/02 IL
Old Xavierans
Everton 02/03 FL
03/04 FL
Tottenham H 04/05 14 5 SL
05/06 7 SL
Middlesbrough 06/07 5 1 FL
Aberdeen 06/07 13 4
07/08 29 5
08/09 28 8
09/10 29 5
Morton 10/11 28 7
11/12 27 15
Third Lanark 12/13 3

O'HAGAN William
b. Buncrara 8.8.1890 d. Prescot 29.6.1972
St Columbs College
Londonderry Guild
Derry Celtic
St Mirren 11/12 1
12/13 33
13/14 38
14/15 36
Third Lanark
Linfield 181/9 IL
St Mirren 18/19 12
19/20 31
20/21 29
Airdrieonians 21/22 7
Norwich C 21/22 14 FL
22/23 39 FL
Fordsons 23/24
Aberdare A 24/25 3 FL
Fordsons

O'HARA John

Law Volunteers
Hibernian 08/09 25 1
09/10
10/11
11/12
Peebles R 12/13
Pontypridd 13/14
Peebles R 14/15
Wishaw Thistle 15/16
Bathgate 16/17

O'HARE Denis
b. Renton 21.1.1900
Renfrew
Partick T 22/23 21
23/24 22
24/25 3
Celtic 24/25
Partick T 25/26 17
26/27 28
27/28 34
28/29 33
29/30 30
30/31
Cork C 31/32
Circle Athletic de Paris 32/33
Southport T 33/34

O'HARE D

Third Lanark 24/25 4

O'HARE William
b. Hamilton 27.6.1904
Dalkeith Thistle
Dundee 27/28 29 14
28/29 21 7
29/30 34 8
30/31 4 1
St Mirren L
Portsmouth 31/32 1 FL
Brechin C

O'HENLY Donald

St Mirren 26/27 8 1

O'KANE Joseph
b. Milngavie 12.1.1896
Maryhill Jnrs
Celtic 14/15
Clydebank L 14/15 D2
Celtic 15/16 5 8
Clydebank L 15/16
Celtic 16/17 15 5
17/18
Clydebank L 17/18 8 4
Clyde L 17/18 7 ?
Celtic 18/19
Airdrieonians L 18/19 8 5
Celtic 19/20
20/21
Stevenston U L 20/21
Stockport Co L 21/22 16 12 FL
Celtic 21/22
Stalybridge C L 22/23 23 5 FL
Celtic 22/23
23/24
Dundee Hibernian L 23/24 29 10 D2
24/25 13 5 D2
Arthurlie L 24/25 D2
Celtic 25/26
Helensburgh

O'KEEFE Timothy James
b. Cork 1910 d. Cork ?.4.1943
Blackrock R
Cork 30/31 LI
31/32 LI
32/33 LI
33/34 LI
34/35 LI
Waterford 35/36 LI
36/37 LI
37/38 LI
Hibernian 38/39 4
Raith R L 38/39 18 8
Waterford 39/40 LI
40/41 LI
Cork 41/42 LI
42/43 LI

OLDMAN P

Motherwell 13/14 1

OLIPHANT Thomas

Shettleston
Queen's Park 10/11 3
11/12 2

OLIVER Alexander

Clyde 96/97 2
Hamilton A 97/98 D2

OLIVER James
b. Dumfries 1.8.1889
Creetown Volunteers
Morton L 06/07 2
07/08 6
08/09 1
Celtic L 08/09 2
Girvan A 09/10
Creetown Volunteers 09/10
Port Glasgow A 10/11 22 ? D2
Morton 10/11
Maybole 11/12

O'NEILL Felix
b. Motherwell 21.12.1889
Shotts U
Celtic 10/11 1
Alloa A L 10/11
Celtic 11/12
Bathgate 12/13
Dykehead

O'NEILL Hugh
b. Motherwell 15.2.1913 d. 24.9.1964
Holytown U Juveniles
St Anthonys 36/37
Celtic T 36/37
St Andrews U 37/38
Celtic 37/38
Wishaw Jnrs L 37/38
Celtic 38/39 4
Arthurlie
Dunfermline A
Comrie Colliery
Lochgelly Albert 46/47

O'NEILL James

Blackburn R
Raith R 16/17 6

O'NEILL James
b. c1904
Rosyth Rec
Dundee 23/24 3

O'NEILL James

Ferniegair Violet
Dundalk
Hamilton A 33/34 2
Cork 34/35 LI

O'NEILL John
b. c1913
Motherwell Higher Grade Schoo
Heart of Midlothian 31/32 3

O'NEILL Patrick

Mossend Hibs
Burnbank A
Dumbarton 15/16 26 14
Dumbarton Harp 16/17

O'NEILL Thomas
b. Coatbridge c1907
Bellshill A
Heart of Midlothian 26/27
27/28
28/29 1
29/30 8
30/31 35
31/32 20 1
32/33 35
33/34 3
34/35
35/36
Newry T 36/37 IL

O'REILLY Joseph
b. c1914
Brideville 31/32 LI
Aberdeen 32/33 23
33/34 15
34/35
Brideville 35/36 LI
St James Gate 35/36 LI
36/37 LI
37/38 LI
38/39 LI

ORMISTON James

Queen's Park 00/01 7
01/02 4
02/03 1
03/04 2

ORMOND George

Rangers 11/12 12
12/13 24
13/14 17
Morton 14/15 32
15/16 37
16/17 37
17/18 31
18/19 29
19/20 11

O'ROURKE Frank 1 cap
b. Bargeddie 5.12.1878 d. Bargeddie 24.12.1954
Kirkwood Jnrs
Airdrieonians 98/99 5 2 D2
Albion R 99/00
Airdrieonians 00/01 18 7 D2
01/02 13 6 D2
02/03 19 3 D2
03/04 24 5
04/05 25 7
05/06 28 13
06/07 28 7
Bradford C 06/07 5 4 FL
07/08 36 23 FL
08/09 38 19 FL
09/10 35 20 FL
10/11 32 13 FL
11/12 21 4 FL
12/13 18 5 FL
13/14 7 2 FL

O'ROURKE Henry

Airdrieonians 00/01 1 D2
01/02 17 3 D2
02/03 15 2 D2
03/04 9

O'ROURKE Henry

Port Glasgow A 05/06 19 5

O'ROURKE Peter
b. Newmilns 22.9.1876 d. Bradford 10.1.1956
Mossend Celtic
Hibernian T 94/95
Celtic 94/95 3
95/96 6
96/97
Burnley 97/98 16 FL
98/99 2 FL
Lincoln C 99/00 32 FL
Third Lanark 00/01
01/02
Chesterfield T 01/02 19 1 FL
02/03 20 1 FL
Bradford C 03/04 25 1 FL
04/05 6 FL
05/06 12 FL

ORR

Third Lanark 94/95 5

ORR Andrew

Morton 96/97 1 D2
97/98 16 D2
98/99 18
99/00 16
00/01 18
01/02 16
02/03 18
Heart of Midlothian 03/04 25
04/05 17

ORR Andrew

Morton 04/05 5

ORR Andrew

Airdrieonians 09/10 1

ORR Andrew

Airdrieonians 20/21 3

ORR J

Dumbarton 92/93 1

ORR James 1 cap
b. Dalry 24.7.1871 d. Knockintiber 2.10.1942
Kilmarnock Winton
Kilmarnock Roslyn
Kilmarnock Shawbank
Kilmarnock A 89/90
Kilmarnock 90/91
91/92
Darwen 92/93 22 1 FL
93/94 29 1 FL
94/95 26 1 FL
Celtic 95/96
96/97 1
97/98 4
Kilmarnock A 98/99
Galston 99/00

ORR James

Cambuslang Hibernian
Hibernian 00/01 3
01/02
Airdrieonians 01/02 D2
02/03 D2
Hibernian 03/04 1

ORR James

Yoker A
Kilmarnock 11/12 11

ORR James

Northampton T
Dundee 19/20 3

ORR Robert

Barnsley
Falkirk 12/13 4

ORR Robert John
b. Hardgate 1888
Clydebank Jnrs
Third Lanark 09/10 18
10/11 26
11/12 23
12/13 32
13/14 33 3
14/15 12 4
15/16 35 4
16/17 6
17/18
18/19 11 ?
19/20 40 5
20/21 40 5
21/22 40 2
22/23 38 3
23/24 29 3
Morton 24/25 37 5
25/26 31 1
Crystal Palace 26/27 38 2 FL
27/28 32 FL
Dumbarton 28/29 D2
Clydebank 29/30 D2

ORR Ronald 2 caps
b. Bartonholm 6.8.1880 d. Kilwinning ?.3.1924
Kilwinning Eglington
St Mirren 98/99 17 9
99/00 18 6
00/01 20 12
Newcastle U 01/02 32 9 FL
02/03 23 5 FL
03/04 12 10 FL
04/05 20 9 FL
05/06 36 17 FL
06/07 19 4 FL
07/08 19 6 FL
Liverpool 07/08 7 5 FL
08/09 33 20 FL
09/10 31 5 FL
10/11 30 5 FL
11/12 7 1 FL
Raith R 11/12 5 1
South Shields

ORR William 3 caps

b. Shotts 20.6.1873 d. 26.2.1946

Airdrie Fruitfield					
Airdrieonians					
Preston NE		94/95	10	1	FL
		95/96	27	1	FL
		96/97	25		FL
Celtic		97/98	11		
		98/99	11	1	
		99/00	8		
		00/01	18	1	
		01/02	14		
		02/03	19	1	
		03/04	18	5	
		04/05	20		
		05/06	24	5	
		06/07	17	4	
		07/08	1		

ORR William

Bellshill A					
Airdrieonians		17/18	8	1	

ORROCK Robert Abbie 1 cap

b. Kinghorn 25.5.1885

Forth Rangers					
Bainsford					
East Stirlingshire					
Falkirk		09/10	1		
		10/11	23	1	
		11/12	22		
		12/13	29		
		13/14	28		
		14/15	15		
		15/16	30		
		16/17	27		
St Mirren		17/18	20		
		18/19	18	?	
Alloa A		19/20			
		20/21			
		21/22			D2
		22/23	29		
East Stirlingshire		23/24			

OSBORNE A

Clyde		94/95	8		

OSBORNE James

b. Greenock

Rangers		25/26	9	1	
		26/27			
		27/28	1		
Morton	L	27/28			D2
Rangers		28/29	1		
		29/30	1		
Northampton T					
Dumbarton		33/34			D2

OSBORNE John Edward

b. Dundee 24.4.1902 d. Dundee 2.4.1968

Lochee Central					
Dundee U		24/25	28		
		25/26	1		
Forfar A		26/27			D2
		27/28			D2
Brighton		28/29	3		FL
Brechin C		29/30			D2
Morton		30/31	19		
		31/32	6		
Norwich C	T				

O'SHEA John James

b. c1904

Blantyre Celtic					
Cowdenbeath		25/26	?		
Alloa A		26/27			D2
		27/28			D2
Kings Park		28/29			D2

OSWALD

Third Lanark		92/93	1		

OSWALD Albert

Tayport *					
Dundee		06/07	13		
		07/08			
		08/09	4		
East Fife		09/10			

OSWALD James 3 caps

b. Greenock 3.1.1868 d. 26.2.1948

Clydebank					
Govan Hill					
Kilbirnie					
Third Lanark		88/89			
Notts Co		89/90	19	11	FL
		90/91	22	12	FL
		91/92	24	15	FL
		92/93	30	11	FL
St Bernards		93/94	16	8	
		94/95	16	10	
Rangers		95/96	17	11	
		96/97	5	2	
		97/98	4		
Leith A		97/98			D2
		98/99			D2
Morton		99/00	14	?	D2
		00/01	17	9	
Leith A		00/01			D2
Raith R		01/02			
Morton		01/02	10	3	
Raith R		01/02			
Leith A					

OSWALD John McGill

Queen's Park		23/24	1		

OSWALD Joseph

Morton		99/00	17	?	D2
		00/01	13		

OSWALD Robert Ray Broome

b. Linlithgow 20.12.1910 d. Rochford 1961

Linlithgow Rose					
Heart of Midlothian		24/25			
East Stirlingshire					
Bo'ness		25/26			D2
		26/27	?	17	D2
		27/28	32	12	
Reading		28/29	42	10	FL
		29/30	41	5	FL
Sheffield U		30/31	9		FL
		31/32	26	7	FL
		32/33	41	13	FL
		33/34	30	3	FL
Southend U		34/35	27	2	FL
		35/36	33	5	FL
		36/37	27	5	FL
		37/38	23	8	FL
		38/39	13	1	FL

OSWALD William

Abercorn *					
Third Lanark		99/00	1		

OSWALD William

b. Dundee 3.8.1900

Dundee Celtic					
Dundee U	T	21/22	1		
Gillingham		22/23	13	3	FL
St Johnstone		23/24	1		
Dundee U		24/25	30	11	
		25/26	19	5	
Brighton		26/27	11	1	FL
		27/28	3	1	FL
Providence Clamdiggers		28/29	41	9	ASL
		29A	1		ASL
		29/30	11	5	ASL
		30A	25	8	ASL
Fall River		31S	11	1	ASL
New York Yankees		31S	1		ASL

OTHER A N

Ayr U		17/18	14	?	
		18/19	3	?	

OTHER A N

Clyde		17/18	1	?	
		18/19	4	?	

OTHER A N

Falkirk		17/18	2	?	
		18/19	3	?	

OTHER A N

Third Lanark		17/18	4	?	
		18/19	2	?	

OTHER A N

Dumbarton		18/19	4	?	

OTHER A N

Heart of Midlothian		18/19	10	?	

OTHER A N

Hibernian		18/19	2	?	

OWEN John Russell

b. Busby 1883 d. 25.12.1924

Rutherglen V					
Leven V					
Hibernian					
Aberdeen	L	03/04			
Barnsley		03/04	1		FL
Morton		04/05	8		
Barnsley		05/06	22	5	FL
		06/07	15		FL
Sheffield W		06/07	19	5	FL
		07/08	22	5	FL
		08/09	26	8	FL
		09/10	19	1	FL
		10/11	4		FL
Chorley					

OWEN William

St Mirren		98/99	3		
Ayr					

OWERS Ebenezer Harold

b. West Ham 21.10.1888 d. ?.6.1951

Bashford					
Leytonstone					
Leyton		06/07			SL
Blackpool		07/08	9	3	FL
WBA		07/08	4		FL
Chesterfield T		08/09	15	3	FL
Darlington		09/10			
Bristol C		10/11	31	16	FL
		11/12	8	3	FL
		12/13	23	13	FL
Clyde		12/13	8	5	
Celtic	L	13/14	13	8	
Clyde		13/14	10	3	
		14/15	8	1	

PAGE Samuel

b. Blackheath 10.6.1901 d. Warley 1973

Blackheath V					
Halesowen T					
Burnley		23/24	6		FL
		24/25	6		FL
St Johnstone		25/26	27		
		26/27	35		
		27/28	17		
Raith R	L	27/28	7		
St Mirren		28/29	25		
Halesowen T		29/30			
Willenhall					
Brierley Hill A		31/32			

PAGE Thomas

b. Kirkdale 15.11.1888 d. Gloucester 26.10.1973

Pembroke					
Selwyn					
Carada					
Liverpool	T				
Rochdale		11/12	17	15	LC
		12/13	25	15	CL
Everton		13/14	7	2	FL
St Mirren		14/15	32	12	
		15/16	8	4	
		16/17			
		17/18	2		
		18/19	4		
		19/20	27	9	
Port Vale		20/21	39	10	FL
		21/22	37	9	FL
		22/23	25	1	FL
		23/24	37	9	FL
		24/25	28	5	FL
		25/26	36	9	FL
		26/27	33	9	FL
		27/28	33	8	FL
		28/29	17		FL
New Brighton		29/30	8	1	FL
Chorley		30/31			

PALMER John

Hibernian		97/98	2		
		98/99			
		99/00			
		00/01	1		

PARK

Cambuslang		90/91	1		

PARK James

Clyde		98/99	1		
Lanemark		98/99			

PARK James R
b. Strathaven
Hamilton A 37/38 4 1
38/39 14 1

PARK John
b. Douglas Water 7.10.1913
Douglas Water Thistle
Partick T T 31/32
Douglas Water Thistle 32/33
Hamilton A 33/34 26 4
Nithsdale W L 33/34
Hamilton A 34/35 4 1
35/36 13 13
Newcastle U 36/37 9 2 FL
37/38 37 9 FL
38/39 14 FL

PARKER Robert Norris
b. Maryhill 27.3.1891 d. Provan ?.12.1950
Glasgow Ashfield
Third Lanark 08/09
Glasgow Ashfield
Rangers 10/11 2 1
11/12 3 2
12/13 9 12
13/14 3 2
Everton 13/14 24 17 FL
14/15 35 35 FL
Rangers 15/16 1
Morton L 16/17 18 9
Everton 19/20 8 4 FL
20/21 17 11 FL
Nottingham F 21/22 32 7 FL
22/23 14 3 FL
Fraserburgh

PARKINSON Walter
Heart of Midlothian 00/01 3

PARLANE James
Queen's Park 38/39 2

PARLANE John McK
Queen's Park 33/34 2

PARLANE William
St Mirren 33/34 4

PARLANE William
Queen's Park 33/34 2
34/35 1
Dumbarton 35/36

PARRY Maurice Pryce
b. Oswestry 1877 d. Bootle 24.3.1935
Oswestry U 95/96
96/97
97/98
Nottingham F T 97/98 FL
Long Eaton R 98/99
Leicester F 98/99 1 FL
Loughborough 98/99 12 FL
Brighton U 99/00 22 SL
Liverpool 00/01 8 FL
01/02 13 FL
02/03 31 FL
03/04 29 FL
04/05 30 2 FL
05/06 36 1 FL
06/07 19 FL
07/08 21 FL
08/09 20 FL
Partick T 09/10 23 1
Wrexham 10/11
South Africa
Oswestry U

PARRY Robert
b. Glasgow
Queen's Park 27/28 3 1
28/29 6 1
29/30 8
Kilmarnock 30/31 1
? 31/32
32/33
Edinburgh C 33/34 D2

PATERSON
Vale of Leven 90/91 6
91/92 5

PATERSON
Cambuslang 91/92 15 2

PATERSON
Clyde 91/92 6
92/93 1

PATERSON Andrew
Dalziel R
Motherwell 01/02 D2
02/03 D2
03/04 5

PATERSON Andrew
Kirkcaldy U
Raith R 15/16 11

PATERSON Archibald B
Dunfermline A 27/28 9

PATERSON Daniel
b. Cambuslang
Cambuslang R
Kings Park 21/22 D2
Hamilton A 22/23 24 3
23/24 5
Alloa A 23/24 D2
24/25 D2
Falkirk 24/25 9 1
25/26 36 16
26/27 38 25
27/28 22 6
28/29 1
Kilmarnock 28/29 24 6
29/30 26 6
Dolphin 30/31 LI
31/32 LI
Ballymena 32/33 IL
Dundee 33/34 11 2
Brechin C 33/34 D2
Dolphin 34/35 LI
Distillery 35/36 IL

PATERSON George Denholm 1 cap
b. Denny 26.9.1914 d. New Zealand ?.12.1985
Denny YMCA
Carrowbank Juveniles
Dunipace Thistle
Celtic 32/33
33/34
34/35 30 7
35/36 36
36/37 36 3
37/38 37
38/39 37
Brentford 46/47 FL
47/48 FL
48/49 FL
Yeovil T 49/50
50/51
Stirling A 51/52

PATERSON Henry (?)
Heart of Midlothian 96/97 1

PATERSON James
St Mirren 99/00 6

PATERSON James
Queen's Park 16/17 11
17/18
18/19 8 1
19/20 1

PATERSON James 3 caps
b. St Ninians 1908
Causewayhead
Camelon Jnrs
Everton 26/27 FL
St Johnstone 27/28 2 4
28/29 22 8
29/30 21 6
Cowdenbeath 30/31 38 26
31/32 36 27
Leicester C 32/33 19 11 FL
33/34 24 6 FL
34/35 5 FL
Reading 35/36 25 12 FL
36/37 40 11 FL
37/38 8 FL
Clapton Orient 38/39 5 FL

PATERSON James Alexander
b. Chelsea 9.5.1891
Bellahouston Academy
Queen's Park
Rangers 10/11 2
11/12 4
12/13 21 7
13/14 32 6
14/15 30 7
15/16 31 7
16/17
17/18
18/19
19/20 36 11
Arsenal 20/21 20 FL
21/22 2 FL
22/23 26 FL
23/24 21 FL
24/25 FL
25/26 1 1 FL

PATERSON John
Leith A 94/95 14 7
Burton Swifts 94/95 10 2 FL

PATERSON John
b. Linwood
St Mirren 26/27 6

PATERSON John
b. Cowie
St Ninians
Airdrieonians 28/29 12 1
29/30 14 4
30/31 14 2
31/32 28 10
32/33
33/34 5

PATERSON John M
Renfrew
Hamilton A 23/24 3 1
24/25 2
St Bernards 25/26 D2

PATERSON Matthew
b. Douglas Water c1888
Bellshill A
Hibernian 08/09 31 2
09/10 30 2
10/11 33 17
11/12 28 2
12/13 31 1
13/14 31 2
14/15 38 1
15/16 38
16/17 32 2
17/18 23 ?
18/19 13 ?
19/20 26 1
20/21 32 1
21/22 23 3
22/23 5 1
St Bernards

PATERSON Matthew
Burnbank A
Morton 13/14 17 4
14/15 1
15/16 17 6
16/17 13 6
Aberdeen L 16/17 1

PATERSON Matthew
Renfrew
Arthurlie 21/22 D2
Morton 21/22 2
Third Lanark 21/22 3

PATERSON R
Leith A 94/95 9

PATERSON Robert
b. Glasgow
Clyde 95/96 12 2
96/97
Derby Co 97/98 5 FL
98/99 8 FL
99/00 4 FL
Coventry C

PATERSON T
Abercorn 96/97 3

PATERSON Walter

Larkhall Thistle
Airdrieonians 13/14 34 8
14/15 32 3
15/16 28 8
16/17 35 7
17/18 14 5
Third Lanark 18/19 26 ?
Larkhall Thistle

PATERSON William

Hibernian 95/96 1
Manchester C 96/97 1 FL
Stockport Co

PATERSON William
b. Hill o'Beath 5.3.1897 d. Cowdenbeath ?.8.1970
White Rose
Cowdenbeath W 14/15
Cowdenbeath 14/15 D2
15/16
Rangers 16/17 5 3
17/18
18/19
Cowdenbeath 19/20
Derby Co 20/21 17 8 FL
21/22 15 2 FL
22/23 20 5 FL
23/24 2 FL
Armadale L 23/24 D2
Cowdenbeath 24/25 9 2
Coventry C 25/26 40 25 FL
Springfield Babes 26/27 13 7 ASL
Fall River Marksmen 26/27 20 15 ASL
New Bedford Whalers 26/27 7 8 ASL
27/28 34 20 ASL
28/29 7 ASL
Providence Clamdiggers 28/29 35 32 ASL
29A 8 6 ASL
29/30 22 27 ASL
New Bedford Whalers 29/30 20 21 ASL
Brooklyn Wanderers 30A 13 5 ASL
Fall River Marksmen 31S 17 11 ASL
Gold Bugs
New York Nationals

PATERSON William
b. Dunfermline 1902 d. Edinburgh 30.7.1967
Bungalow C 19/20
Broomhall Swifts
Dunfermline A
Clydebank L
Boston Wonder Workers 24/25 21 ASL
Dunfermline A 24/25 D2
Dundee U 25/26 38
26/27 25
27/28 14
Arsenal 27/28 5 FL
28/29 10 FL
Airdrieonians 29/30 38
30/31 37
31/32 36
Dundee U

PATERSON William

Springburn UF Church
Aberdeen 30/31 1
31/32 1

PATERSON William
b. Hamilton 4.3.1914
Quarter U
Denny Hibs
Morton 31/32 2
32/33
Belfast Celtic 33/34 IL
Distillery 33/34 IL
East Fife T 33/34 D2
Broadway U 33/34
Dundee 34/35
Arbroath 34/35 D2
Raith R 35/36 D2
Stenhousemuir 35/36 D2
Lincoln C 36/37 2 FL
Mansfield T 37/38 40 FL
38/39 21 FL
39/40 2 FL

PATERSON William Francis
b. Hamilton
Earnock R
Petershill
Hamilton A 13/14 20
14/15 33 1
15/16 36 1
16/17 34 1
17/18 9
18/19
Motherwell 19/20 35
20/21 34
21/22 40 1
Bo'ness L 22/23 D2
Motherwell 22/23 3
23/24
24/25 13
Charlton A 25/26 32 FL
26/27 37 FL
27/28 24 FL
Bostall Heath

PATON

Clyde 95/96 1
96/97 12 1

PATON

Clyde 19/20 1

PATON Andrew

Motherwell 04/05 7 1
Royal Albert 05/06

PATON Daniel John Ferguson 1 cap
b. Auchencorrach Moor 1871
Vale of Leven 89/90
Aston Villa
Vale of Leven 90/91
91/92 17 2
92/93
St Bernards 93/94
94/95 11 4
95/96 18 5
96/97 9 1
97/98 17 9
Aston Villa
Clyde 98/99 13 3

PATON Harold D
b. Larkhall 23.5.1897
Larkhall Thistle
Queen's Park 17/18 15 3
Motherwell 18/19 7
Clydebank 19/20 37
20/21 39 11
Newcastle U 21/22 13 2 FL
St Mirren 22/23 5

PATON James Arklay Jackson
b. Mains 14.2.1903 d. Dundee 3.1.1994
Kilmarnock 26/27 5
27/28 1
Dundee 28/29 32
Watford 29/30 5 FL
Training Battn RE

PATON John

Larkhall U
St Mirren 06/07 1 1
07/08 7 4
08/09 8

PATON John
b. Leith
Hibernian 10/11 3
11/12 4
12/13 7
13/14 4

PATON John

Aberdeen 15/16 3
16/17 28 2
17/18
18/19
Hall Russells 19/20

PATON John
b. Glasgow
Celtic 21/22
Third Lanark 22/23 14 1
New York Giants 23/24 6 ASL
Aberdeen 23/24 16 1
24/25 17 4
25/26
26/27
Clydebank 27/28 D2
28/29 D2
Alloa A 29/30 D2
Waterford T 30/31 LI
Shelbourne 30/31 LI
Cork 31/32 LI
Stranraer 32/33
33/34

PATON Robert

Larkhall Thistle
Airdrieonians 14/15 17 4
15/16 10 2

PATON Robert P S
b. Glasgow 9.7.1902
Moorpark Amateurs
Partick T 24/25 28
25/26 13
26/27 6
27/28 28
28/29 19
St Johnstone 29/30 13
Shelbourne 30/31 LI
Queen of the South 31/32 D2
Third Lanark 32/33 8
Worcester C 33/34

PATON Samuel

Hibernian 07/08 2

PATON Thomas H
b. Larkhall
Hamilton A 01/02 D2
Royal Albert 02/03
Rangers 03/04 2
Derby Co 04/05 14 1 FL
05/06 21 3 FL
Sheffield U 05/06 4 FL
06/07 17 4 FL
St Mirren 07/08 28 4
08/09 25 6
09/10 16 4
10/11 33
11/12 18 1
Airdrieonians 12/13 26
13/14 30
St Johnstone 14/15 D2
Stevenston U 18/19

PATRICK

Dumbarton 18/19 1 ?

PATRICK Alexander

Petershill
Kilmarnock 16/17 25 1
17/18 2
Renton 18/19
Solway Star
Royal Albert

PATRICK John 2 caps
b. Kilsyth 10.1.1870
Grangemouth
Falkirk
St Mirren 92/93 17
93/94 17
94/95 18
95/96 18
96/97 16
Everton 96/97 1 FL
St Mirren 97/98 18
98/99 16
99/00 12
00/01 17

PATTERSON George W
b. Glasgow
Queen's Park 30/31 9 2
31/32 6

PATTILLO John Timothy
b. Aberdeen 1914 d. Perth ?.8.2002
Mugiemoss
Hall Russells
Aberdeen 38/39 9 11
Dundee 46/47 23 14 D2
47/48 26 13
48/49 25 9
49/50 21
50/51 13 4
51/52 15 3
Aberdeen 52/53
St Johnstone 52/53 8 2 D2

PATTISON John Morris
b. Glasgow 19.12.1918
St Anthonys
Motherwell 36/37 1
QPR 37/38 3 1 FL
38/39 14 FL
46/47 37 12 FL
47/48 20 8 FL
48/49 11 3 FL
49/50 7 2 FL
Leyton Orient 49/50 15 4 FL
50/51 28 6 FL
Dover A

PATTON Alexander
b. Belfast
Rockville
Mount Cuba
Ormiston
Glentoran 19/20 IL
20/21 IL
Belfast Ormiston 21/22
22/23
Falkirk 23/24 11 3
Ards 24/25 IL
25/26 IL
26/27 IL
27/28 IL
Barrow 28/29 27 4 FL
29/30 30 6 FL
Ards 30/31 IL
31/32 IL
Scunthorpe U T 32/33
Macclesfield T

PATTON John H
Belfast Ormiston
Falkirk 22/23 3 1

PAUL
St Mirren 91/92 1
92/93 1

PAUL Harold McDonald 3 caps
b. Gourock 31.8.1886 d. 19.4.1948
Crieff Morrisonians
Queen's Park 05/06 23 5
06/07 16 4
07/08 23 4
08/09 29 8
09/10 12 4
10/11 10
11/12 13
12/13 15 2
13/14 22 4

PAUL James
Glasgow Transport
Queen's Park 32/33 14 6
33/34 5 5

PAUL William 3 caps
b. Partick c1869 d. 23.10.1911
Elm
Partick
Partick T 86/87
87/88
Clyde G 88/89
Partick T 88/89
89/90
Queen's Park G 89/90
Partick T 90/91
91/92 17 5 SA
92/93 10 6 SA
93/94 16 7 D2
94/95 13 10 D2
95/96 10 11 D2
96/97 15 8 D2
97/98 16 5
98/99 16 3
99/00 14 11 D2
00/01 3

PEACOCK
Cowlairs 90/91 4

PEAKE Ernest
b. Aberystwyth 1888 d. Bridgend 19.11.1931
Aberystwyth
Liverpool 08/09 1 FL
09/10 3 FL
10/11 8 3 FL
11/12 8 FL
12/13 26 2 FL
13/14 5 FL
Third Lanark 14/15 11 1
Blyth Spartans 19/20

PEARSON David
Partick T 97/98 1
Linthouse

PEARSON David
Morton 00/01 18 9
01/02 9 3

PEARSON David
Newtongrange Star
Dundee 16/17 4

PEARSON Isaac
b. Castle Ward 28.2.1908 d. Newcastle 1972
Hebburn Colliery
Hamilton A 28/29 1
Barrow 29/30 4 FL

PEARSON John
b. Arbroarh 22.1.1892 d. Arbroath 13.4.1937
Arbroath Fairfield
Arbroath 09/10
10/11
11/12
12/13
Tottenham H 12/13 FL
13/14 FL
14/15 17 FL
Partick T L 18/19 6
Tottenham H 19/20 21 FL
20/21 5 FL
21/22 3 FL
22/23 1 FL
Luton T 23/24 1 FL

PEARSON Thomas
b. Penrith
Gala
Leith A T
Heart of Midlothian 06/07 13 2

PEARSON Thomas
Wemyss A
St Mirren 12/13 30 1
13/14 28 1
Armadale

PEAT Alexander
Falkirk 36/37 14
37/38 34
38/39 37

PEAT William
Bo'ness Cadora
Falkirk 33/34 10 2
34/35 8 3
Bo'ness L 34/35 D2
East Stirlingshire 34/35 D2
Leith A 35/36 D2
Bo'ness 36/37

PEATTIE William
b. St Monance c1908 d. 1990
St Monance Swifts
Raith R 36/37 D2
37/38 7 D2
38/39 11

PEDDIE John Hope
b. Glasgow 21.3.1877 d. Detroit ?.10.1928
Glasgow Benburb
Third Lanark 95/96 17 7
96/97 17 4
97/98 5
Newcastle U 97/98 20 17 FL
98/99 29 17 FL
99/00 27 15 FL
00/01 33 13 FL
01/02 16 FL
Manchester U 02/03 30 11 FL
Plymouth A 03/04 28 8 SL
Manchester U 04/05 32 17 FL
05/06 34 17 FL
06/07 15 6 FL
Heart of Midlothian 06/07 6 4
07/08 6 1
USA

PEDEN Robert
St Bernards 95/96
96/97 3

PEDEN Robert G C
b. Dundee
East Fife 26/27 10 D2
27/28 D2
Queen's Park 28/29 35
29/30 35
30/31 32
31/32 7
32/33
Dundee 33/34 1

PEEBLES Andrew
Clyde 06/07 4
Ayr Parkhouse

PEGGIE James Nesbit
b. Fife
Saline
Lochgelly U
East Fife
Hibernian 05/06 4 1
Dunfermline A 06/07
Hibernian 07/08 12 6
08/09 22 10
09/10 28 7
10/11 7 1
Middlesbrough 10/11 6 FL
East Fife 11/12

PENDER Robert
b. Coatbridge 5.11.1891
Kirkintilloch Harp
Dumbarton 12/13 D2
13/14 6 2
St Mirren T 13/14 1
Johnstone 14/15 D2
Dumbarton Harp 14/15
15/16
Raith R 16/17 12
Johnstone 16/17
Dumbarton Harp L 16/17
Renton 18/19
Middlesbrough 19/20 23 5 FL
20/21 18 3 FL
21/22 21 1 FL
22/23 33 1 FL
23/24 9 FL
St Johnstone 24/25 25

PENMAN James
Dunfermline A 27/28 5

PENMAN Robert
b. Holytown
Motherwell 14/15 35
15/16 36
16/17 12
17/18
18/19
Albion R 19/20 23
20/21 37
21/22 42
22/23 32
23/24 D2
St Johnstone 24/25 38
25/26 38
26/27 30
27/28 10
28/29 10

PENNIE Robert
Bedlay Jnrs
Airdrieonians 18/19 2

PENSON Frank S
b. Dundee c1910
Dundee Fairfield
Dundee U 30/31 37 D2
31/32 35
32/33 25 D2

PERRY John
Kilsyth R
Third Lanark 27/28 D2
28/29 5
29/30 D2
30/31 D2
Arbroath 30/31 2 D2
Kings Park 31/32 D2

PERRY Private
Aberdeen 15/16 6
16/17 16

PETERS Martin R
b. Kirkintilloch
Maryhill
Hamilton A 23/24 9 1
St Bernards
Helensburgh
Dumbarton 25/26 D2

PETRIE Robert
b. Dundee 25.10.1874 d. Arbroath 15.3.1947
Arbroath
Dundee East End
Dundee 93/94 13 1
Sheffield W 94/95 18 1 FL
95/96 19 1 FL
96/97 15 FL
Southampton 97/98 20 4 SL
98/99 8 SL
99/00 21 1 SL
New Brighton Tower 00/01 28 FL
? 01/02
02/03
03/04
Arbroath 04/05
05/06
06/07
07/08
08/09
Dundee W 08/09

PETTIGREW Alexander
Queen's Park 08/09 2
09/10 8 3
10/11
Arthurlie 11/12 D2

PETTIGREW John
Cambuslang Hibs
Falkirk 04/05 D2
05/06 13
Dunfermline A L 06/07

PHILIP David C
b. c1881
Edinburgh Myrtle
Heart of Midlothian 03/04
04/05 14
05/06 14
06/07 16 1
07/08 19
08/09 9
Leith A 09/10 D2
Raith R 10/11 25
11/12 28
12/13 28
13/14 2

PHILIP George
Dundee 94/95 2
95/96 1

PHILIP George
Dundee 98/99 3
99/00 1

PHILIP George C
b. Newport, Fife
Heart of Midlothian
Dundee 08/09 1
09/10 3
10/11 1
11/12 5
12/13 28 2
13/14 37 14
Sunderland 14/15 37 22 FL
St Mirren 15/16 13
16/17
Dundee 17/18 1 1
18/19
Sunderland 19/20 FL
Dundee 20/21 25

PHILIP George G
Rangers 16/17 1

PHILLIP George
b. 1880
Heart of Midlothian 00/01 14
Cowdenbeath 01/02
Heart of Midlothian 02/03 4
03/04 18
04/05 20
05/06 29
Portsmouth 06/07 30 SL
07/08 9 SL

PHILLIP William
St Johnstone 09/10
Dundee 10/11 2

PHILLIPS
Cambuslang 90/91 1

PHILLIPS
Heart of Midlothian 94/95 1 1

PHILLIPS Charles
Ayr Parkhouse *
West Ham U
Ayr U 10/11 17 22 D2
11/12 ? ? D2
12/13 ? ? D2
13/14 17 5
14/15 2
Clydebank 15/16
Dumbarton 15/16
Ayr U 16/17 7 2

PHILLIPS John
b. c1915
Camelon
Partick T T 31/32
St Mirren 31/32
32/33 10
33/34 23
Bo'ness 34/35 D2
East Fife 34/35 13 3 D2

PHILLIPS Robert
St Bernards 99/00 1
Lochgelly U 99/00

PHILLIPS William
Aberdare A
Dundee 35/36 26 7
36/37 34 5
37/38
Heart of Midlothian 38/39 8 2
St Johnstone 46/47 1 D2

PICKEN Samuel
b. Twechar d. 1993
Bridgetown Waverley
Partick T 37/38 15
38/39 10 1
Airdrieonians 46/47
47/48 18 2
48/49 D2
49/50 14 3 D2
50/51 11 3

PICKERING William
b. Glasgow d. 1917
Burnley 13/14 3 1 FL
14/15 10 5 FL
Morton 15/16 5 4

PIGG Albert
b. Medomsley 6.4.1903 d. Consett 22.9.1944
Allendale Park
Newcastle U T 24/25
Crewe A
Carlisle U
Raith R 27/28 28 22
28/29 27 13
Barnsley 29/30 5 1 FL
Consett 30/31
Annfield Plain 31/32

PILLAR Robert
St Bernards 95/96 6
96/97 3

PINKERTON Henry
b. Dunipace 7.5.1916 d. Toronto 1986
Kilsyth A
Banknock
Dunipace Jnrs
Hull C 34/35 2 1 FL
Port Vale 35/36 3 FL
Burnley 36/37 1 FL
37/38 2 FL
Falkirk 38/39 6
Bo'ness U

PINKERTON James Ross
b. Rothesay 21.9.1911
Rothesay Royal V
Bute A
Partick T 33/34 5
Montrose 34/35 D2
Blackburn R 35/36 1 FL
St Bernards 36/37 D2
Dundee U

PIPER John
b. Carluke
Carluke R
Hamilton A
Airdrieonians 30/31 26 7
St Mirren 31/32 4
Brechin C 32/33 D2
Coleraine 32/33 IL
33/34 IL
Dumbarton 34/35 D2

PIRIE James
b. Kinghorn
Kinghorn St Leonards
Dunniker
Dundee 27/28 2 1
Charlton A 28/29 FL
Montrose 29/30 D2
Portadown 30/31 IL

PIRIE Robert (or PIRRY)
St Mirren 18/19 5 ?

PIRIE Thomas Stuart
b. Gorbals 9.12.1896
Battlefield Jnrs
Bathgate
Queen's Park 20/21 27 2
21/22 38 1
22/23 26
23/24 2
Manchester U 23/24 FL
Aberdeen 24/25 12 5
25/26 25 1
Cardiff C 26/27 5 FL
27/28 FL
Bristol R 28/29 12 FL
Brighton 28/29 FL
Ross Co

PIRRIE Robert
b. Kilwinning
Kilwinning Eglington
Beith 25/26 D3
26/27
Kilmarnock 27/28 8
Third Lanark 27/28 D2
Arthurlie 28/29
Beith 28/29
29/30
30/31
Irvine V

PITCAIRN John Watt
b. Kelvinside 29.1.1904 d. Gravesend ?.7.1987
Maryhill Jnrs
Raith R 25/26 3
26/27 D2
27/28 32 1
28/29 30
Connahs Quay 29/30
Charlton A 30/31 30 FL
31/32 25 FL
Chester 32/33 22 FL
33/34 37 FL
34/35 42 FL
35/36 20 FL
36/37 14 FL
Wigan A 37/38 25 CCL

PLANK John
Yoker A *
Clydebank *
Derby Co *
Third Lanark * 12/13
Dumbarton 13/14 3

PLAYFAIR Andrew S
Kilmarnock 19/20 4
20/21 4
Stevenston U L 20/21
East Stirlingshire

PLAYFAIR Peter
b. c1918
Crosshill Hearts
Lochore Welfare
Heart of Midlothian 37/38
38/39 1
Cowdenbeath

PLENDERLEITH
Cambuslang 90/91 3 3
91/92 7 1

POCOCK William Thomas
b. Bristol 24.2.1884 d. 4.2.1959
Reading
Army
Bristol C 19/20 39 10 FL
20/21 40 14 FL
21/22 40 3 FL
22/23 40 7 FL
23/24 40 5 FL
24/25 18 2 FL
25/26 21 5 FL
St Johnstone 26/27 24 1
Bath C 27/28
28/29
Bedminster Down Sports

POLE Robert
St Mirren 31/32 3

POLLAND John
Cowiebank
Partick T 02/03 4
Nithsdale W 03/04
Dunfermline A *
Ayr Parkhouse *
Lanemark *

POLLAND John
Longriggend Rob Roy
Aberdeen 28/29 1

POLLOCK Adam
Renfrew Jnrs
St Mirren 17/18 5
18/19 5 ?

POLLOCK Alexander
b. Blantyre d. High Blantyre 1945
Blantyre V
Hamilton A 20/21 17 1

POLLOCK Jacob
Dundee 97/98 6 1

POLLOCK James
b. Govan
Cambuslang R
Kilmarnock 20/21 2
21/22 2 1
Pollok Jnrs

POLLOCK James
b. Cambuslang
Hamilton A 32/33 1
33/34 1
34/35 2
Motherwell 35/36 2

POLLOCK John
Glenboig Cameronians
Airdrieonians 28/29 1
Kings Park 28/29 D2
29/30 D2
30/31 D2
31/32 D2
32/33 D2
33/34 D2
Coleraine * 34/35 IL

POLLOCK John
Sheppey U
Queen of the South 33/34 2

POLLOCK Robert
b. Wishaw
Wishaw Thistle
Third Lanark 97/98 1
98/99
99/00
Bristol C 99/00 7 SL
Kettering T 00/01 18 SL
Notts Co 01/02 FL
Leicester F 02/03 28 1 FL
03/04 33 4 FL
04/05 32 FL
05/06 33 2 FL
06/07 34 1 FL
07/08 35 5 FL
08/09 16 1 FL
Leyton 09/10 4 SL
Leicester Imperial

POLLOCK William
b. Netherton, Wishaw 1911
Royal Albert
Cambuslang R 32/33
Chelsea 32/33 FL
33/34 FL
Dunfermline A 34/35 11
Dundee 34/35 3
Stockport Co 35/36 7 FL
Hamilton A 36/37 2

POOLE George
Bonnyrigg Rose
Heart of Midlothian 13/14
Armadale
Linlithgow
Hamilton A 19/20 1

POPE Alfred Leslie
b. Lofthouse 8.1.1913 d. Blackpool ?.8.1987
Harrogate T
Leeds U 31/32 FL
32/33 FL
33/34 FL
Rotherham U T 34/35 FL
Leeds U 34/35 FL
Halifax T 35/36 28 FL
36/37 26 FL
Heart of Midlothian 36/37 5 1
37/38 5
38/39 2
Darwen

POPE Fred
b. Moorpark
Partick T 30/31 6 1
31/32 4 1
Brentford 32/33 FL
Beith
Ayr U 35/36 11 2
Beith

PORTEOUS George
b. Glasgow
Govan St Anthonys
Blackburn R 12/13 5 FL
13/14 1 FL
Clyde 14/15
15/16 3

PORTEOUS William 1 cap
Vale of Grange
Bo'ness
Heart of Midlothian 99/00 3
00/01 13 1
01/02 16 6
02/03 21 9
03/04 16 13
Bathgate 04/05
Portsmouth 04/05 13 6 SL
Falkirk 05/06 12 4
06/07 1
Bathgate

PORTER
Hibernian 98/99 10 2

PORTER
Morton 17/18 1

PORTER
St Mirren 18/19 1 ?

PORTER A
Heart of Midlothian 11/12 1

PORTER Frederick James
Queen's Park 09/10 8
10/11 1
11/12 32
12/13 29
13/14 1

PORTER James
b. Dysart c1900
Rosslyn Jnrs
Heart of Midlothian 22/23 8
Dundee Hibs 23/24 36 2 D2
24/25 3 D2
Bathgate 24/25 D2

PORTER William
Third Lanark 99/00 11 3

PORTER William
b. Kirkintilloch
Kirkintilloch Rob Roy
Raith R 13/14 30 4
14/15 33 1
15/16 19 1
Armadale 15/16
Ayr U 18/19 7
Raith R 19/20 30 4
20/21 10 1
Heart of Midlothian 20/21 18
Philadelphia Field Club 21/22 11 ASL
Guildford U 22/23
Weymouth 23/24

PORTERFIELD
Clyde 91/92 2

POTTER Andrew
Dumbarton 13/14 3

POTTS Thomas
Maryhill Jnrs
Kilmarnock 18/19 8
19/20
20/21
Todd Shipyards 21/22 3 ASL
Fall River U 21/22 10 ASL

POWER Patrick
b. Glasgow 11.7.1876
Blantyre V
Celtic 94/95 1
Airdrieonians 94/95 1 D2
Blantyre

PRATT
Morton 19/20 1

PRATT Archibald G
b. Edinburgh
Tranent Jnrs
Heart of Midlothian 27/28 7
28/29 1
29/30 3
30/31 2
Bo'ness L 31/32 D2
Heart of Midlothian 31/32 2
32/33 2
East Fife 33/34 D2
34/35 D2
35/36 D2
Montrose 36/37 D2
Penicuik A 37/38

PRATT David
b. Lochore 5.3.1896
Lochore Welfare
Lochgelly U
Hearts o'Beath 18/19
Celtic 19/20 1
Bo'ness L 19/20
Celtic 20/21 19
Bradford C 21/22 27 1 FL
22/23 23 4 FL
Liverpool 22/23 7 FL
23/24 15 FL
24/25 26 FL
25/26 15 1 FL
26/27 14 FL
Bury 27/28 26 FL
28/29 25 FL
Yeovil T 29/30 SL
30/31 SL
31/32 SL
32/33 SL

PRATT William James

Third Lanark 33/34 1
Ballymena U 34/35 IL

PRAY Jack
b. Falkirk d. 1948
Rangers 94/95 3
Bury 95/96 30 FL
96/97 30 1 FL
97/98 28 2 FL
98/99 30 FL
99/00 32 1 FL
00/01 31 4 FL
01/02 5 FL

PRENTICE

St Mirren 90/91 1

PRENTICE Charles

Strathclyde
Third Lanark 09/10 20 1
10/11 30 9
11/12 25 2
Motherwell 12/13 7
Albion R 13/14 D2

PRENTICE David
b. Alloa 29.7.1908 d. Trowbridge 10.11.1984
Alva Albion R 27/28
Celtic 28/29 4 3
Stranraer L 28/29
Celtic 29/30 2
Ayr U L 29/30
Nithsdale W L 29/30
Plymouth A 30/31 FL
Walsall 31/32 23 4 FL
Bournemouth
Raith R 32/33 D2
Mansfield T 33/34 21 1 FL
Bath C 34/35 SL
35/36 SL

PRENTICE James

St Mirren 06/07 2

PRENTICE James N

Port Glasgow A 07/08 2

PRESDEE Albert John
b. Gloucester 15.9.1906 d. Cardiff ?.12.1999
Linfield Swifts
Bangor 29/30 IL
30/31 IL
31/32 IL
32/33 IL
33/34 IL
Hereford U 34/35
Bath C 35/36 SL
Dundee 35/36 2

PRESTON James
b. Glasgow
Benburb
Hibernian 27/28 8 1
28/29 6 3
29/30 15 2

PRESTON James S

St Mirren 30/31 6 1

PRESTON Robert
b. Loanhead 1895 d. Co Antrim ?.5.1945
Loanhead Mayflower
Heart of Midlothian 18/19 8
19/20 39 1
20/21 38 4
21/22 42 4
Torquay U 22/23 SL
Plymouth A 23/24 38 2 FL
24/25 41 1 FL
25/26 20 FL
26/27 25 FL
27/28 19 FL
Torquay U 28/29 15 FL
Llanelly 29/30
30/31
Bray Unknowns 31/32 LI
Shelbourne
Sligo R

PRESTON Thomas
b. Bathgate d. 1971
Loanhead Mayflower
Airdrieonians 21/22 26
22/23 1
23/24 26
24/25 37 1
25/26 26 2
26/27 28
27/28 36 1
28/29 37 1
29/30 33
30/31 37 1
31/32 37 1

PRICE James
b. Annbank 24.4.1896
Cumnock Jnrs
Celtic 18/19 5
Dumbarton L 18/19
Celtic 19/20
20/21 2
Airdrieonians 21/22 2
Nelson 21/22 20 FL
22/23 4 FL
Ashington 22/23 9 3 FL
23/24 37 1 FL
24/25 39 2 FL
25/26 41 FL
26/27 40 3 FL
27/28 28 2 FL
28/29 41 FL
29/30
North Shields 30/31
Ashington

PRICE Norman Malcolm
b. Dumfries 2.3.1904
Dumfries
Ashfield
Ayr U 27/28 2 D2
28/29 38
29/30 13
Bristol R 30/31 FL
Nithsdale W L 30/31
Accrington S 31/32 30 3 FL
32/33 18 2 FL
33/34 31 3 FL
Coleraine 34/35 IL
Stalybridge C 35/36
Oldham A 36/37 40 FL
37/38 33 FL
Gainsborough T 38/39

PRIESTLEY John
b. Johnstone 19.8.1900 d. Johnstone 9.1.1980
Johnstone
Chelsea 20/21 1 FL
21/22 FL
22/23 20 1 FL
23/24 40 2 FL
24/25 35 1 FL
25/26 39 4 FL
26/27 39 6 FL
27/28 17 4 FL
Grimsby T 28/29 36 1 FL
29/30 41 1 FL
30/31 36 2 FL
31/32 26 3 FL
St Johnstone 32/33 24 2
Cowdenbeath 33/34 18 1
Keith

PRINGLE

Bathgate
Heart of Midlothian 05/06 1

PRINGLE Charles

Heart of Midlothian 00/01 2
Cowdenbeath 01/02

PRINGLE Charles Ross 1 cap
b. Nitshill 18.10.1894
Inkerman R
Maryhill
St Mirren 16/17 35 5
17/18 32 1
18/19 2 ?
19/20 33
20/21 32
21/22 1
Manchester C 22/23 42 FL
23/24 28 FL
24/25 35 FL
25/26 36 FL
26/27 34 1 FL
27/28 22 FL
Manchester Central 28/29
Inkerman R 28/29
Bradford PA 29/30 31 1 FL
30/31 13 FL
Lincoln C 31/32 35 3 FL
32/33 23 FL
Stockport Co 32/33 FL
FC Zurich 33/34
Hurst 33/34
Waterford 34/35 LI

PRINGLE David
b. Wallsend ?.9.1908
Tranent Jnrs
Stoke C
Hamilton A 29/30
30/31 6 1
Coleraine 31/32 IL
32/33 IL
33/34 IL
Derry C 33/34 IL
Coleraine 34/35 IL
35/36 IL

PRIOR Alexander L
b. Aboyne
Dunfermline A
Stenhousemuir
Partick T 33/34 17 1
34/35 4
35/36 4
Hibernian 36/37 33
37/38 25
38/39 37 4

PRIOR George
b. Edinburgh
St Bernards 00/01 14 ? D2
Sunderland 01/02 5 FL
Third Lanark 02/03 10 2

PRITCHARD Andrew Smart
b. Airdrie 23.6.1912
Ashfield
Partick T 33/34 14 3
34/35 1
Ards 35/36 IL
36/37 IL
Halifax T 37/38 15 1 FL
Clapton Orient 38/39 1 FL

PRITCHARD George
b. Shettleston 1875 d. Blantyre ?.3.1936
Burnbank A
Clyde 99/00 1

PRITCHARD Robert
d. Barachnie (?) ?.7.1914
Burnbank A
Motherwell 02/03 D2
03/04 25
Luton T 04/05 SL
Stenhousemuir
Motherwell 05/06 4
Hamilton A 06/07 24 1
07/08 7 1
Port Glasgow A 08/09
09/10 1

PROCTOR William
b. Dundee
Dundee Violet
Dundee 29/30 2

PROSSER Matthew

Campbelltown
Port Glasgow A 09/10 1

PROUDFOOT

Club		Season	Apps	Gls	Lge
Clyde		91/92	6		
		92/93	13		
		93/94	1		D2

PROUDFOOT David

b. c1873

Club		Season	Apps	Gls	Lge
Whiteinch Jnrs					
Partick T		93/94			
		94/95			
		95/96	14		D2
		96/97	7		D2
Leicester F		96/97	6		FL
		97/98			FL
Bedminster		98/99	17		SL
Partick T		99/00	16	3	D2
		00/01	15		

PROUDFOOT John

b. Airdrie 27.10.1874 d. Glasgow 22.4.1934

Club		Season	Apps	Gls	Lge
Partick T		93/94			D2
		94/95	17	13	D2
		95/96	18	9	D2
		96/97	9	3	D2
Blackburn R		96/97	7	5	FL
		97/98	28	9	FL
Everton		98/99	28	13	FL
		99/00	20	8	FL
		00/01	29	9	FL
		01/02	7		FL
Watford		02/03	12	5	SL
Partick T		03/04	17	5	
Hamilton A		04/05			

PROUDFOOT Peter

b. Wishaw 25.11.1880 d. Wishaw 4.3.1941

Club		Season	Apps	Gls	Lge
Wishaw V					
Airdrieonians		98/99			
Wishaw Thistle		98/99			
Wishaw U		99/00			
Sheffield W		99/00			FL
Lincoln C		00/01	18	6	FL
		01/02	34	6	FL
		02/03	27	8	FL
St Mirren		03/04	2		
Albion R		04/05			
Millwall		04/05	16		SL
Clapton Orient		05/06	26		FL
Chelsea		05/06	4		FL
		06/07	7		FL
		07/08	1		FL
Stockport Co		08/09	34	1	FL
Morton	T	09/10	1		
Stockport Co		10/11	10		FL
		11/12			FL
		12/13	1		FL

PROVAN John

Club		Season	Apps	Gls	Lge
St Bernards		96/97	9	9	
		97/98	3	1	

PROVAN Thomas B

Club		Season	Apps	Gls	Lge
Queen's Park		10/11	4	1	

PRYCE John

b. Renton 25.1.1874 d. ?.12.1905

Club		Season	Apps	Gls	Lge
Renton		93/94	6		
		94/95	15	?	D2
		95/96	15	?	D2
Hibernian		96/97	18	11	
		97/98	16	5	
Glossop NE		98/99	20	6	FL
Sheffield W		98/99	7		FL
		99/00	31	4	FL
		00/01	16	1	FL
QPR		01/02	14	2	SL
		02/03	5		SL
Brighton		03/04	21	5	SL
		04/05	2		SL

PRYDE George

Club		Season	Apps	Gls	Lge
St Andrews Jnrs					
Brechin C		30/31			D2
Leith A		30/31	5		

PRYDE James

b. Dundee

Club		Season	Apps	Gls	Lge
Dundee		29/30	4	1	

PRYDE Robert Ireland

b. Methil 25.4.1913 d. Blackpool 30.6.1998

Club		Season	Apps	Gls	Lge
Windygates Thistle					
Thornton R					
East Fife	T	29/30			D2
St Johnstone		29/30	1		
		30/31	24		D2
		31/32	3		D2
Brechin C	L	32/33			D2
Blackburn R		33/34	10		FL
		34/35	40	2	FL
		35/36	36	4	FL
		36/37	41		FL
		37/38	35	2	FL
		38/39	41	1	FL
		39/40	3		FL
		46/47	40	1	FL
		47/48	40	1	FL
		48/49	37		FL
Wigan A		49/50	22	2	LC

PUDDEFOOT Leonard F

Club		Season	Apps	Gls	Lge
West Ham U					
FC Cete					
Falkirk		22/23	1		

PUDDEFOOT Sydney Charles

b. Limehouse 17.10.1894 d. Rochford 2.10.1972

Club		Season	Apps	Gls	Lge
Condor A					
Limehouse T					
West Ham U		12/13	4	1	SL
		13/14	16	10	SL
		14/15	35	18	SL
Falkirk	L	18/19	5	7	
West Ham U		19/20	39	21	FL
		20/21	38	29	FL
		21/22	26	14	FL
Falkirk		21/22	12	4	
		22/23	32	12	
		23/24	37	16	
		24/25	26	13	
Blackburn R		24/25	14	5	FL
		25/26	37	10	FL
		26/27	39	14	FL
		27/28	35	13	FL
		28/29	40	9	FL
		29/30	37	12	FL
		30/31	41	15	FL
		31/32	7	1	FL
West Ham U		31/32	7		FL
		32/33	15	3	FL
Fenerbahce					

PULLAR William

b. Edinburgh

Club		Season	Apps	Gls	Lge
Cowdenbeath		21/22			D2
		22/23			D2
		23/24			D2
		24/25	33	8	
		25/26	37	7	
		26/27	35	6	
		27/28	36	5	
		28/29	26	3	
		29/30	34	5	
Leith A		30/31	20	2	
		31/32	13		
Raith R					

PULLEN

Club		Season	Apps	Gls	Lge
Motherwell		15/16	1		

PURDIE Alexander

Club		Season	Apps	Gls	Lge
Larkhall Thistle					
Hamilton A		10/11	6		
		11/12	18		
Wishaw Thistle		12/13			
Pontypridd		13/14			
Hamilton A		14/15	16		
		15/16	34		
		16/17	23		
		17/18	25	1	
		18/19	28	1	
		19/20	21		
		20/21	27		
		21/22	2		
Dykehead					
USA					

PURDIE Hugh

Club		Season	Apps	Gls	Lge
Lanemark					
Airdrieonians		11/12	1		

PURDIE William B

Club		Season	Apps	Gls	Lge
Queen's Park		07/08	2		
Third Lanark *		08/09			
Kings Park *		08/09			

PURDON James Small

b. Springburn 14.3.1906 d. Govan 20.12.1985

Club		Season	Apps	Gls	Lge
Baillieston Jnrs					
Tweedhill					
Rangers		24/25			
		25/26			
		26/27	2		
Clyde	L	26/27	5		
Ayr U	L	27/28	34		D2
Celtic	L				
Rangers		27/28			
		28/29			
		29/30	4		
		30/31			
Bradford PA		31/32	9		FL
		32/33	14		FL
		33/34	21		FL
Crystal Palace		34/35	11	2	FL
		35/36	3		FL
Southport		36/37	28		FL
Montrose		37/38			D2

PURSELL Peter 1 cap

b. Campbelltown 1.7.1894 d. Old Kilpatrick 14.8.1968

Club		Season	Apps	Gls	Lge
Campbelltown Academicals					
Queen's Park		13/14	26		
Rangers		14/15	31		
		15/16	20		
		16/17	30	1	
		17/18	24		
		18/19	23		
Port Vale		19/20	8		CL
		19/20	33		FL
		20/21	34		FL
		21/22	30		FL
		22/23	40		FL
		23/24	24		FL
Wigan B		24/25	32		FL
		25/26	3		FL
Congleton T					
Dordrecht					

PURSELL Robert Russell

b. Campbelltown 18.3.1889 d. Hanley 24.5.1974

Club		Season	Apps	Gls	Lge
Aberdeen University					
Queen's Park		09/10	27	2	
		10/11	23		
Liverpool		11/12	24		FL
		12/13	24		FL
		13/14	26		FL
		14/15	27		FL
		19/20	2		FL
Port Vale		20/21	38		FL
		21/22	28		FL

PURVES Alex

Club		Season	Apps	Gls	Lge
Clyde		10/11	6		

QUIGHLEY John

Club		Season	Apps	Gls	Lge
Dykehead					
Hamilton A		19/20	1	1	

QUIGLEY

Club		Season	Apps	Gls	Lge
Abercorn		92/93	1		

QUIGLEY Dennis

b. St Andrews 7.12.1913 d. Newmarket 1.1.1984

Club		Season	Apps	Gls	Lge
St Andrews U					
Dundee		34/35	2		
Brechin C		35/36			D2
Grimsby T		36/37	9		FL
		37/38	12	2	FL
		38/39	2		FL
Hull C		39/40	2		FL

QUIGLEY Hugh

b. Ireland

Club		Season	Apps	Gls	Lge
Clydebank					
Third Lanark *	T	12/13			
Partick T		12/13	2		

QUIN William John Joseph
b. Barrhead 1890 d. Leicester 1957
Manchester Xaverian College
Higher Broughton
Cheetham Hill
Manchester C 07/08
Manchester U 08/09 1 FL
09/10 1 FL
Nelson 10/11
Chorley 10/11
Ecclesborough 11/12
Grimsby T 12/13 21 2 FL
13/14 30 1 FL
14/15 11 2 FL
Arthurlie 15/16
Clyde 15/16 4 2
16/17
17/18
18/19
19/20 17 10
20/21 8 5
Ayr U 20/21 7 10
21/22 13 9
22/23 7 2

QUINN James 11 caps
b. Croy 8.7.1878 d. Croy 20.11.1945
Smithson A
Celtic 00/01 1 1
01/02 12 2
02/03 18 3
03/04 18 10
04/05 21 19
05/06 27 20
06/07 26 29
07/08 24 20
08/09 28 22
09/10 28 24
10/11 27 14
11/12 10 8
12/13 23 11
13/14 1 2
14/15 6 4

QUINN James

Kilwinning R
Alloa A 21/22 D2
22/23 26 1
23/24 D2
Queen of the South 24/25 D3
25/26 D2
26/27 D2
Kilwinning R 27/28
Largs Thistle 27/28

QUINN John G

Auchinleck Talbot
Ayr U 13/14 9
Arthurlie 14/15 D2
Clyde 15/16 4 2

QUINN John P
b. Motherwell
New Stevenston Jnrs
Broxburn U 22/23 D2
Motherwell 22/23 8 1
23/24 4
Hamilton A L 23/24 3 4
Third Lanark 24/25 1

RADCLIFFE George
b. Armadale
Selkirk
Albion R
Dundee U 31/32 15 1
Falkirk 31/32 12 2
32/33 4
Armadale 32/33 D2
Alloa A 33/34 D2

RAE

Heart of Midlothian 93/94 1 1

RAE Alexander

Queen's Park 37/38 12
38/39 1

RAE George

Falkirk Ath
Hibernian 10/11 22 3
11/12 27 7
12/13 16 2
Partick T 13/14 12
Kirkcaldy U 13/14
Dunfermline A
Falkirk 19/20 2
Dumbarton 20/21 12

RAE Henry S
b. Glasgow c1896
Benburb
Clyde 17/18 32 ?
Morton 18/19 7 5
Clyde 19/20 22
20/21 42 2
21/22 37
22/23 32 3
23/24 32 3
24/25 D2
Brentford 25/26 37 4 FL
26/27 30 2 FL
Hamilton A 27/28 7

RAE J

Third Lanark 92/93 5
93/94 6

RAE James Clarkson
b. Bothkennar 22.11.1907 d. Shirley 4.7.1958
Gairdoch U
Kings Park 24/25 D2
25/26 D2
26/27 D2
27/28 D2
28/29 D2
Partick T 29/30 27 1
30/31 32 1
31/32 29
Plymouth A 32/33 37 FL
33/34 35 FL
34/35 37 FL
35/36 39 FL
36/37 30 FL
37/38 29 FL
38/39 3 FL

RAE John

Vale of Clyde
Motherwell 11/12 6

RAE John
b. Blackmill 1912
Camelon
Clyde 35/36 6 2
East Stirlingshire L 35/36 D2
Dumbarton 36/37 D2
East Stirlingshire 36/37 D2
Partick T
Bristol C 37/38 2 FL
BAC

RAE Livingstone

Dunipace Jnrs
St Mirren 02/03 16
03/04 15
04/05 22
05/06 30
06/07 24
East Stirlingshire *
Clackmannan 11/12
12/13

RAE Robert
b. c1916
Uphall
Motherwell 35/36 1
36/37
Clyde 37/38

RAE Thomas
b. Kilwinning 1883
Morton 04/05 16
05/06 15 1
06/07 23 2
Bury 06/07 9 FL
07/08 33 FL
08/09 14 FL
09/10 14 1 FL
10/11 2 FL
St Mirren 11/12 3

RAEBURN James
b. Edinburgh
Leith Benburb
Tranent Jnrs
Raith R 20/21 13
21/22 31
22/23 36 2
23/24 37 1
24/25 30 1
25/26
St Bernards 26/27 D2

RAESIDE H

Abercorn 90/91 8 4
91/92 5 2

RAESIDE H

Vale of Leven 90/91 1

RAESIDE James Smith 1 cap
b. Glasgow 1879 d. Glasgow 17.1.1946
Parkhead
Third Lanark 99/00 16
00/01 20
01/02 7
02/03 20
03/04 26
04/05 26
05/06 28
Bury 06/07 30 FL
07/08 36 FL
08/09 34 FL
09/10 38 3 FL
10/11 17 FL
11/12 1 FL

RAESIDE Thomas
b. Old Kilpatrick
Old Kilpatrick
Ashfield
Dumbarton 16/17 34 1
17/18 29 2
18/19
19/20 11
20/21 33 1
Kings Park 21/22 D2
Bethlehem Steel 22/23 17 ASL
Fall River Marksmen 23/24 19 ASL
24/25 43 2 ASL
Brooklyn Wanderers 26/27 5 1 ASL
J & P Coats 27/28 9 ASL
Fall River Marksmen 27/28 4 2 ASL

RAFFERTY Daniel

Blantyre V
Everton 07/08 3 FL
08/09 1 FL
09/10 3 FL
Royal Albert 10/11
Airdrieonians 11/12 30
12/13 27
13/14 38 2
14/15 34
15/16 18

RAISBECK

Cambuslang 91/92 1

RAISBECK Alexander Galloway 8 caps
b. Wallacetown 26.12.1878 d. 12.3.1949
Larkhall Thistle
Royal Albert
Hibernian 96/97 8
97/98 16 2
Stoke 97/98 4 FL
Liverpool 98/99 32 1 FL
99/00 32 3 FL
00/01 31 1 FL
01/02 28 FL
02/03 26 1 FL
03/04 30 1 FL
04/05 33 2 FL
05/06 36 1 FL
06/07 27 4 FL
07/08 23 2 FL
08/09 15 2 FL
Partick T 09/10 22 2
10/11 29 2
11/12 27 3
12/13 23
13/14 12
Hamilton A

RAISBECK Andrew

Hibernian 00/01 11 4

RAISBECK William
b. Wallacetown 22.12.1875 d. Taber, Alberta 2.11.1946
Larkhall Thistle
Hibernian 96/97
Clyde 96/97 7 1
Sunderland 96/97 FL
Royal Albert 97/98
Clyde 97/98 11 1
Sunderland 98/99 26 4 FL
99/00 30 3 FL
00/01 14 2 FL
01/02 1 FL
Derby Co 01/02 3 FL
New Brompton 02/03 26 2 SL
03/04 30 SL
Reading 04/05 14 3 SL
Falkirk 05/06 20
06/07 13 1
Canada

RAITT David
b. Buckhaven 7.12.1894 d. Dundee 8.5.1969
Buckhaven V
Buckhaven Thistle
Elgin C
Dundee 19/20 41
20/21 38
21/22 37
Everton 22/23 36 FL
23/24 19 FL
24/25 20 FL
25/26 30 FL
26/27 11 FL
27/28 6 FL
Blackburn R 28/29 4 FL
Forfar A 29/30 D2

RAITT William D

Cambuslang R
Third Lanark 11/12 7
12/13 8 1
13/14 4 1
14/15
15/16
16/17
17/18
18/19
19/20
Johnstone 19/20
20/21
21/22 D2
Kings Park 22/23 D2
23/24 D2
24/25 D2
USA

RALSTON Joseph

St Mirren Jnrs *
Paisley V *
Bridgeton Waverley
Clyde 26/27 1
Nithsdale W 27/28
Bathgate 28/29 D2

RAMAGE

Rangers 09/10 6 2
Cowdenbeath 10/11 19 D2
Royal Albert

RAMAGE Andrew
b. Canongate 27.2.1904
Orwell U
Musselburgh Bruntonians 23/24
Dunfermline A T 24/25 D2
Musselburgh Bruntonians 24/25
25/26
Dundee 26/27 7 4
South Shields 27/28 3 FL
Penicuik A

RAMAGE John
b. Lasswade 4.10.1899
Bonnyrigg Rose
Heart of Midlothian 19/20 2
20/21 15 1
21/22 11 1
22/23 30
23/24 28
24/25 22
25/26 35 4
26/27 2
Coventry C 26/27 8 1 FL
27/28 3 1 FL
Luton T 27/28 9 FL
Heart of Midlothian 28/29
29/30
30/31
Ross Co 31/32
32/33
33/34
Chirnside U 34/35

RAMSAY

Cambuslang 90/91 7
91/92 12 1

RAMSAY Aaron

Glasgow Ashfield
Kilmarnock 08/09 26 6
09/10 15 5
Raith R 10/11 27 3

RAMSAY Andrew
b. East Benhar 1877
Newcastle EE
Newcastle U 92/93
Stockton
Newcastle U 93/94 1 FL
Dundee 93/94 2
East Benhar
Middlesbrough 99/00 28 FL
00/01 29 FL
01/02 33 1 FL
02/03 30 FL
03/04 5 FL
04/05 FL
Leyton 05/06 SL

RAMSAY David
b. Glasgow
Shettleston
Bo'ness 26/27 D2
27/28 34
28/29 D2
Airdrieonians 29/30 1
30/31
Queen of the South 31/32 D2

RAMSAY George

Larkhall Thistle
Motherwell 16/17 14 1

RAMSAY George Strachan
b. Kilpatrick 1892
Clydebank Jnrs
Queen's Park 10/11 10 3
11/12 31 4
Carlisle U 12/13
Queen's Park 12/13 1
Rangers 12/13 3
13/14
Ayr U 13/14 15 11
Partick T 14/15 27 3
15/16 13 7
16/17 2

RAMSAY James Howie
b. Old Kilpatrick 7.8.1898 d. Maidstone 26.1.1969
Moor Park
Arthurlie
Renfrew V
Kilmarnock 20/21 26 6
21/22 26
22/23 29 4
23/24 28 6
Arsenal 23/24 11 3 FL
24/25 30 6 FL
25/26 16 FL
26/27 12 2 FL
Kilmarnock 26/27 17 5
27/28 38 10
28/29 28 8
29/30 20 2
30/31 13 3
Galston

RAMSAY John Bishop
b. Dalkeith 1892 K.I.A. 18.7.1916
Falkirk 14/15 25 10

RAMSAY Joseph
b. Springburn
Petershill
Partick T 23/24 10
24/25 36
25/26 33
Crystal Palace 26/27 FL
Arbroath 26/27 24 D2
Petershill 27/28
28/29
Parkhead 29/30
30/31

RANKIN

Renton 92/93 6

RANKIN A
b. Glasgow
Anderston Thornbank
Clydebank 18/19 13 ?

RANKIN Arthur
b. Milton 30.4.1898 d. Bishops Lydeard 1.11.1962
Rutherglen Glencairn
Clyde 20/21 8 1
21/22 3 1
Dykehead 22/23
23/24 D3
24/25 D3
25/26 D3
Bristol C 26/27 41 9 FL
27/28 28 3 FL
28/29 1 FL
Charlton A 29/30 FL
Yeovil T 30/31 SL
31/32 SL
32/33 SL

RANKIN Gilbert 2 caps
b. Bonhill 20.3.1870 d. Hornsey 28.11.1927
Vale of Leven 90/91 7
91/92 3

RANKIN John
b. Govan
Strathclyde
Third Lanark 09/10 31 14
10/11 32 9
11/12 28 5
12/13 20 2
13/14 20 2
14/15
15/16 15 1
Airdrieonians 16/17 38 7
17/18 29 5
18/19 29 7
19/20 11 1

RANKIN John Patterson
b. Coatbridge 10.5.1901 d. Glasgow 1989
Bellshill A
Hamilton A 22/23 21 3
23/24 17
24/25 2
Doncaster R 24/25 6 FL
Dundee 24/25 11 1
25/26 2
Charlton A 25/26 32 5 FL
26/27 41 8 FL
27/28 32 7 FL
28/29 41 9 FL
29/30 41 5 FL
Chelsea 30/31 6 1 FL
31/32 24 4 FL
32/33 29 4 FL
33/34 3 FL
Notts Co 34/35 23 2 FL
35/36 2 FL
Burton T 36/37
37/38
38/39

RANKIN Robert 3 caps
b. Paisley 7.4.1905 d. 25.8.1954
Albert Star
Kilwinning R
Strathclyde
St Mirren 26/27 14 4
27/28 17 7
28/29 36 10
29/30 36 13
30/31 28 7
31/32 26 8
32/33 30 9
Beith 33/34
Dundee 33/34 11 4
34/35 16 3
Clyde 35/36 29 10
36/37 29 7
St Mirren 37/38 32 10
38/39 30 10

RANKIN William

Burnbank
Parkhead Jnrs
Motherwell 17/18 29 11
18/19 30 5
19/20 39 12
20/21 36 6
21/22 36 8
22/23 27 6
23/24 32 6
Cowdenbeath 24/25 35 4
25/26 29
26/27
27/28 2
28/29
Clyde 29/30 35 4
30/31 29 5
31/32 15
Montrose T 32/33 D2
Balmoran (SA)

RANKIN William

b. Dumbarton 20.3.1901 d. Burton on Trent 1968

Club	Season	Apps	Goals	League
Parkhead Jnrs				
Vale of Clyde				
Dundee	22/23	27		
	23/24	33		
	24/25	32	1	
	25/26	33		
	26/27	30	1	
Blackburn R	26/27	2	1	FL
	27/28	31		FL
	28/29	33	1	FL
	29/30	38	1	FL
	30/31	30	1	FL
	31/32	10		FL
Charlton A	31/32	8		FL
	32/33	18		FL
Burton T				

RANKINE Andrew

Club	Season	Apps	Goals	League
Banks o'Dee				
Aberdeen	20/21	30	6	
	21/22	33	7	
	22/23	38	13	
	23/24	24	6	
	24/25	11	1	
Cowdenbeath	24/25	24	7	
	25/26	22		
	26/27	35	8	
	27/28	30	5	
	28/29	38	6	

RANKINE John

Club	Season	Apps	Goals	League
Cowdenbeath				
Rangers	05/06	8	1	
	06/07	7	2	

RARITY James

Club	Season	Apps	Goals	League
Portobello Thistle				
East Fife	28/29			D2
	29/30			D2
Dunfermline A	30/31			D2
	31/32			D2
	32/33			D2
	33/34			D2
	34/35	6		
	35/36	1		
East Stirlingshire	36/37			D2

RATTRAY Hardie Wilson

b. Glasgow 11.7.1901

Club	Season	Apps	Goals	League
Benburb				
Kilmarnock	22/23	13	3	
	23/24	7		
Bournemouth	24/25	11	1	FL
	25/26			FL
Arthurlie	25/26			

RATTRAY John

Club	Season	Apps	Goals	League
Montrose				
Motherwell	06/07	27		
	07/08	28		
	08/09	29		
	09/10	11		

RATTRAY John

b. Cowdenbeath

Club	Season	Apps	Goals	League
Lumphinnans Swifts				
Falkirk	10/11	3	2	
	11/12	12	7	
	12/13	21	6	
Raith R	13/14	31	7	
	14/15	34	9	
Ayr U	15/16	8	1	
Raith R	16/17	29	1	
	17/18			
	18/19			
Dumbarton	18/19	1	?	
Raith R	19/20	33	2	
	20/21	32	3	
	21/22	8	1	
	22/23			
Bethlehem Steel	23/24			ASL

RAWLINGS Archibald James

b. Leicester 2.10.1891 d. Preston 11.6.1952

Club	Season	Apps	Goals	League
Wombwell				
Shirebrook				
Barnsley	11/12			FL
Northampton T	12/13	4		SL
	13/14	13	1	SL
Rochdale	14/15	35	4	CL
Shirebrook				
Dundee	19/20	27	3	
Preston NE	20/21	42	6	FL
	21/22	40	2	FL
	22/23	38	6	FL
	23/24	27	3	FL
Liverpool	23/24	11		FL
	24/25	40	7	FL
	25/26	12	1	FL
Walsall	26/27	23		FL
Bradford PA	26/27	15	4	FL
	27/28	5	1	FL
Southport	28/29	9	3	FL
Dick Kerrs	28/29			
	29/30			
Fleetwood	29/30			
	30/31			
Burton T	31/32			

RAY William R

Club	Season	Apps	Goals	League
Morton	32/33	11		

RAYNE James

Club		Season	Apps	Goals	League
Anstruther R					
East Fife	T	27/28			D2
Bo'ness	T	28/29			D2
Raith R		28/29	4	1	

READ William Henry

b. Blackpool 1885 d. Blackpool c1955

Club	Season	Apps	Goals	League
Lytham				
Blackpool	07/08	15	1	FL
	08/09	15	3	FL
Colne	09/10			
Sunderland	09/10	1		FL
	10/11	3	2	FL
Chelsea	11/12	2		FL
Dundee	12/13	5		
	13/14	7	1	
Swansea T	14/15			SL

REAY George Turnbull

b. East Howden ?.2.1903 d. York 15.8.1962

Club	Season	Apps	Goals	League
Percy Main Amateurs				
South Shields	22/23	2		FL
Blyth Spartans	23/24			
Reading	23/24	4		FL
Kettering T	24/25			
Raith R	25/26	16	1	
	26/27			D2
	27/28	6		
Bristol R	28/29	29	4	FL
	29/30	38	5	FL
Coventry C	30/31	11	3	FL
Burton T	31/32			
	32/33			
	33/34			
Rushden T	34/35			
Kettering T	34/35			
Gresley R	34/35			

REAY Wilfred

b. Dunoon (?) 1913 K.I.A., Burma ?.5.1944

Club	Season	Apps	Goals	League
Dunoon A				
Partick T	34/35			
Arthurlie				
Bridgeton Waverley	36/37			
Dunoon A				
Morton	37/38	7	1	
Kings Park				

REDDISH John

b. Nottingham 22.12.1904 d. Manchester 18.10.1989

Club	Season	Apps	Goals	League
Boots A				
Tottenham H	29/30	3		FL
	30/31			FL
	31/32	3		FL
	32/33			FL
Lincoln C	33/34	39		FL
	34/35	15		FL
Notts Co	35/36			FL
Dundee	36/37	14		

REEKIE James G

Club	Season	Apps	Goals	League
Newburgh WE				
Partick T	24/25	1		
East Stirlingshire				

REFORD Frank Duncan

b. Partick 1907

Club	Season	Apps	Goals	League
Alva Albion R				
St Ninians Thistle				
Third Lanark	30/31			
	31/32	5		
	32/33	6		

REGAN Robert Hunter

b. Falkirk 21.8.1915

Club	Season	Apps	Goals	League
Grangetown Thistle				
Queen of the South				
Linlithgow Rose				
Partick T	32/33			
	33/34	5	1	
	34/35	20	5	
	35/36	25	8	
	36/37	3		
Manchester C	36/37	4		FL
Dundee	37/38	6	5	
Rhyl A	38/39			

REID

Club	Season	Apps	Goals	League
Abercorn	90/91	18		
	91/92	20	1	
	92/93	16		
	93/94	5	?	D2
	94/95	1	?	D2

REID

Club	Season	Apps	Goals	League
Vale of Leven	90/91	2		

REID

Club	Season	Apps	Goals	League
Heart of Midlothian	92/93	1	1	

REID

Club	Season	Apps	Goals	League
Dumbarton	95/96	2		
	96/97	6	?	D2

REID

Club	Season	Apps	Goals	League
Clyde	97/98	2		

REID

Club	Season	Apps	Goals	League
Alloa A	22/23	1		

REID

Club	Season	Apps	Goals	League
Raith R	22/23	1		

REID

Club	Season	Apps	Goals	League
Clyde	26/27	1		

REID Alexander

b. West Calder 9.2.1897

Club	Season	Apps	Goals	League
Ashfield				
Airdrieonians	17/18			
	18/19	15	11	
	19/20	35	10	
	20/21	17	1	
Third Lanark	20/21	18	11	
	21/22	40	8	
	22/23	32	4	
	23/24	37	13	
	24/25	35	8	
Aberdeen	25/26	30	10	
	26/27	38	11	
Preston NE	27/28	33	13	FL
	28/29	41	13	FL
	29/30	39	7	FL
	30/31	41	13	FL
	31/32	32	4	FL
	32/33	7		FL
Blackpool	32/33	13	1	FL
Chorley	33/34			
Darwen				
Aberdeen NE				
Tunbridge Wells R				
Babcock & Wilcox				

REID Alexander S

b. Carlisle

Club	Season	Apps	Goals	League
Carluke Milton R				
Airdrieonians	22/23	16	3	
St Johnstone	22/23	4	1	D2
Dykehead	23/24			D3

REID Allan

b. Irvine

Club	Season	Apps	Goals	League
Irvine Meadow				
St Mirren	20/21	32		
	21/22	1		

REID Andrew
b. Mauchline
Kilmarnock Shawbank
Kilmarnock 00/01 20 7
01/02 4
Galston
Annbank

REID Andrew
St Bernards
St Mirren 08/09 20
09/10 26
10/11 28
11/12 32
12/13 30
13/14 34 1
14/15 21
15/16 31
16/17 20 1
Airdrieonians 17/18 5
Wishaw Thistle

REID B
Rangers 92/93 2

REID Charles
Abercorn 96/97 8 1

REID Charles
Dundee Albert
Partick T 04/05 1

REID David
Hibernian 00/01 1
Motherwell 01/02 D2
02/03 D2
Hibernian 02/03 16 13
03/04 5 4
04/05
05/06 2

REID David G
Rangers
Kilmarnock 88/89
Rangers 89/90
90/91 16

REID David M
Rankinston Seaview *
Galston *
Craigview A
Ayr U 32/33 6 1
33/34 5
34/35 2

REID Edward J
Heart of Midlothian 11/12 3

REID George
Dundee 93/94 6 3
94/95
95/96 1

REID George McC
b. Aberfoyle
Tranent Jnrs
Celtic 35/36
Dunfermline A L 36/37 24 7
Kilmarnock 37/38 14 3
38/39 38 17
45/46
46/47 17 1

REID George McN
b. Tranent
Leith A 30/31 37 2
31/32 25
Dunfermline A 32/33 D2
33/34 D2
34/35 22

REID George T
b. Blackland Mill 1884
St Mirren 02/03 1
03/04 15 4
04/05 8 3
Middlesbrough 05/06 24 6 FL
Johnstone 06/07
Bradford PA 07/08 33 12 SL
08/09 5 FL
Brentford 08/09 24 17 SL
09/10 39 17 SL
10/11 35 21 SL
11/12 4 3 SL
Clyde 11/12 4 1
12/13 15 6
Johnstone 13/14 D2
Clydebank 14/15 D2

REID Hugh
Glasgow Ashfield
Partick T 25/26 1

REID Isaac
b. Mauchline
Auchinleck Talbot
Dundee 20/21 6
Kello R *
Solway Star * 26/27

REID James
b. Bellshill 18.11.1879
Petershill
Hibernian 98/99 7 3
Burslem Port Vale 99/00 17 2 FL
West Ham U 00/01 13 5 SL
Fulham
Gainsborough T 01/02 31 6 FL
Worksop T 02/03
Notts Co 03/04 5 FL
04/05 11 2 FL
Watford 05/06 19 7 SL
Tottenham H 06/07 26 16 SL
07/08 11 2 SL
New Brompton 08/09 20 6 SL
Worksop T

REID James
Third Lanark 99/00 2 1

REID James
East Stirlingshire
Falkirk 05/06 20 1
06/07 32 6
06/07 27
07/08 27 2
08/09 21 1
09/10 4

REID James
Dundee 06/07 1

REID James
d. Blantyre 16.3.1933
Blantyre V
Motherwell 16/17 1
17/18 4
Blantyre Celtic

REID James
Queen's Park 17/18 13

REID James
b. Letham
Forfar Celtic
Heart of Midlothian 33/34 5 3

REID James Greig 3 caps
b. Peebles 1.5.1890 d. 22.4.1938
Peebles R
Partick T T 09/10 3
Chelsea T 09/10 FL
Lincoln C 09/10 5 1 FL
10/11 31 3 FL
11/12
Airdrieonians 12/13 32 31
13/14 37 27
14/15 37 15
15/16 23 4
16/17 3
17/18 5 4
18/19 5 4
19/20 39 17
20/21 24 5
21/22 25 5
22/23 32 1
23/24 30 4
24/25 32 1
25/26 12 2
26/27 15 1
Clydebank

REID James McD
Queen's Park 18/19 2
Dumbarton 18/19 1 ?

REID John
b. Motherwell
Burnbank
Motherwell 20/21 19 2
21/22 25 5
22/23 33 3
23/24 27
24/25 9 1
25/26
Third Lanark 25/26 D2
Motherwell 25/26
26/27
27/28 1

REID John B F
b. South Queensferry
Broxburn A
Heart of Midlothian 21/22
22/23 1
Alloa A 23/24 D2
St Bernards * 24/25 D2

REID John C
b. Mauchline
Glenafton A
Rangers 35/36
* 36/37 1
37/38 8 3
38/39 2
Airdrieonians

REID Peter
b. Holytown c1905
Parkhead Jnrs
Rhyl
Swansea T 26/27 FL
Caernarvon T 27/28
28/29
Partick T 29/30 2 1
Sittingbourne 30/31
Caernarvon T 30/31

REID Robert
Parkhead
Hibernian 13/14 11 4
14/15 2 2
15/16
16/17 1
Hamilton A 17/18 1 1
Royal Albert

REID Robert
Portsmouth SL
St Mirren 14/15 38 5
15/16 26 4
16/17 9 7
Dumbarton 16/17 21 2
Vale of Leven

REID Robert 2 caps
b. Hamilton 19.2.1911 d. East Kilbride 16.11.1987

Fernigar Violet					
Hamilton A		32/33	3		
		33/34	9	2	
		34/35	36	12	
		35/36	14	5	
Stranraer	L	35/36			
Brentford		35/36	18		FL
		36/37	28	10	FL
		37/38	40	17	FL
		38/39	17	3	FL
Sheffield U		38/39	13	4	FL
		46/47	1		FL
Bury		46/47	17	1	FL

REID Thomas
b. Calderbank 1901

Bedlay Jnrs					
New Stevenston U					
Clyde	T				
Albion R	T				
Dundee	T				
Ayr U		20/21	16	2	
		21/22	1		
Port Vale		22/23	6	1	FL
		23/24	17	2	FL
		24/25	1		FL
		25/26	5		FL
Clapton Orient		26/27	7	2	FL
Northwich V		27/28			
New Brighton		28/29	5	1	FL
		29/30	2		FL

REID Thomas Joseph
b. Motherwell 15.8.1905 d. Prescot 1972

Blantyre V					
Clydebank		25/26	30	17	
Liverpool		25/26	1	2	FL
		26/27	20	12	FL
		27/28	25	15	FL
		28/29	5	2	FL
Manchester U		28/29	17	14	FL
		29/30	13	5	FL
		30/31	30	17	FL
		31/32	25	17	FL
		32/33	11	10	FL
Oldham A		32/33	13	9	FL
		33/34	31	16	FL
		34/35	23	9	FL
Barrow		35/36	31	17	FL
Prescot Cables					
Rhyl A					

REID Thomas S
b. Kingseat

Kingseat					
Rangers		20/21	3		
		21/22			
		22/23	13		
		23/24	10		
		24/25	3		
Heart of Midlothian		24/25	9		
		25/26	26		
		26/27	19		
		27/28			
		28/29	7		

REID William
b. Mauchline 1876 d. Scotland 12.4.1923

Stevenston Thistle					
Kilmarnock A					
Kilmarnock		96/97	3	2	
		97/98	14	5	
		98/99	16	12	
Newcastle U	L	98/99	4	1	FL
Kilmarnock		99/00	11	3	
		00/01	14	1	
Partick T		00/01	3		
		01/02	17	5	D2
Galston					
Thornhill					
Kilmarnock		06/07			
Galston					

REID William 9 caps
b. Baillieston c1884 d. ?.05.1964

Baillieston Thistle					
Morton		03/04	1		
		04/05	25	11	
		05/06	18	9	
Motherwell		06/07	27	16	
		07/08	32	19	
Portsmouth		08/09	32	27	SL
Rangers		08/09	2		
		09/10	20	12	
		10/11	33	38	
		11/12	32	33	
		12/13	25	22	
		13/14	33	24	
		14/15	37	28	
		15/16	25	21	
		16/17			
		17/18	1	2	
		18/19			
		19/20	9	8	
Albion R		20/21	29	16	
		21/22	33	20	

REID William

Heart of Midlothian		05/06	1		
		06/07	23		
		07/08	28		

REID William

Blantyre					
Partick T		16/17	7	4	
		17/18	4	1	
Motherwell		17/18			

REID William

Ashfield Jnrs					
Airdrieonians		17/18	3		

REID William
b. Belfast

Bloomfield Olympia					
Queens Island					
Glentoran		22/23			IL
		23/24			IL
		24/25			IL
		25/26			IL
Willowfield		26/27			
Bethlehem Steel		26/27	10	1	ASL
		27/28	44	3	ASL
		28/29			
		29/30	27	2	ASL
Glentoran		30/31			IL
Heart of Midlothian		30/31	21	2	
		31/32	5		
		32/33	3		
		33/34	22		
		34/35	34		
		35/36	36		
		36/37	12		
		37/38			
Dundalk		38/39			LI
Distillery		38/39			IL

REID William
b. c1916

Hall Russells					
Aberdeen					
Dundee U		36/37	6		D2
Forfar A		36/37			D2
Hibernian		37/38	8		

REILLY Francis
b. Perth 26.5.1894 d. Burnley ?.10.1956

Perth Roselea					
Falkirk		12/13	1		
		13/14	34	2	
		14/15	37	3	
		15/16	35	2	
		16/17	1		
		17/18	1		
		18/19			
		19/20	8		
Blackburn R		19/20	26	1	FL
		20/21	38	2	FL
		21/22	34	4	FL
		22/23	29	1	FL
Llanelly					
Swansea T					
Llanelly		23/24			
Weymouth		24/25			
Lancaster C					

REILLY John

Dennistoun					
Clydebank		25/26	3		

REILLY Joseph

Maryhill Hibs					
Celtic					
St Mirren		30/31	27	9	
Alloa A		31/32			D2

REILLY Matthew Michael
b. Donnybrook 22.3.1874 d. Dublin 9.12.1954

Benburb					
RA (Portsmouth)					
Southampton	L	95/96	2		SL
Freemantle	L				
RA (Portsmouth)		97/98	20		SL
		98/99	22		SL
Portsmouth		99/00	27		SL
		00/01	28		SL
		01/02	18		SL
		02/03	27		SL
		03/04	28		SL
Dundee		04/05	3		
Notts Co		05/06	16		FL
Tottenham H		06/07	19		SL
Shelbourne		07/08			IL
		08/09			IL

REILLY Robert

Saltcoats V					
St Johnstone		38/39	2		

REILLY William
b. Lanark 24.12.1902

Lanark U					
Shieldmuir Celtic		23/24			
St Rochs		24/25			
Kilmarnock		25/26	9		
		26/27	19	1	
		27/28	11		
South Shields		28/29	37	3	FL
		29/30	37	1	FL
Gateshead		30/31	26	1	FL
Chester		31/32	33	1	FL
Southend U		32/33	2		FL
Hartlepools U		33/34	7		FL
Ashington		34/35			
Jarrow		34/35			

RENFREW J Stewart M

Dunblane R					
Rangers		30/31			
Sheffield W					
Dunblane R					
Cowdenbeath		32/33	15	12	
		33/34	30	15	
Queen of the South		34/35	11	5	
Derry C		35/36			IL

RENNIE Alexander

Broxburn Shamrock					
Linlithgow Rose					
Heart of Midlothian		38/39	10	9	

RENNIE Gordon

St Mirren		37/38	9		
		38/39	33		

RENNIE Henry George 13 caps
b. Greenock 1.6.1873 d. 1954

Greenock Volunteers					
Belgrove Ramblers					
Greenock WE					
Morton		94/95	1		D2
		95/96	10		D2
		96/97	5		D2
		97/98	17		D2
Heart of Midlothian		98/99	18		
		99/00	18		
Hibernian		00/01	19		
		01/02	17		
		02/03	22		
		03/04	25		
		04/05	25		
		05/06	28		
		06/07	33		
		07/08	26		
Rangers		08/09	31		
		09/10	2		
Inverness Thistle		09/10			
Morton		09/10	1		
Kilmarnock		10/11	32		
Morton		11/12	1		

RENNIE James

Alva Albion R					
Falkirk		19/20	6	1	

RENNIE Robert

Inverkeithing Jnrs
Dundee 33/34 8 6
34/35 3
35/36 30
36/37 36 2
37/38 19
38/39 31 D2

RENNIE Thomas S

Arthurlie
Albion R
Ayr U 13/14 5
Clydebank 14/15 D2
Abercorn 16/17

RENWICK Arthur Douglas

Petershill
Queen's Park 19/20 3
20/21 9

RENWICK John Loudon
b. Larkhill 1906
Royal Albert
Dumbarton T
Falkirk T
East Stirlingshire 29/30 D2
30/31 D2
Gillingham T 31/32 5 3 FL
Albion R 31/32 D2
32/33 D2
33/34 D2
34/35 23 17
Distillery 35/36 IL
Excelsior de Roubaix 35/36
Queen of the South 36/37 29 9
Barrow 37/38 25 4 FL

RESIDE John
b. Old Monkland 1877
Clyde 97/98 17 3
Kilsyth W 98/99
Clyde 99/00 3

REYNOLDS Arthur
b. Dartford 30.6.1889 d. South Kensington 14.3.1970
Dartford A
Dartford 05/06
06/07
07/08
08/09
Fulham 09/10 2 FL
10/11 38 FL
11/12 38 FL
12/13 36 FL
13/14 30 FL
14/15 20 FL
Heart of Midlothian T 16/17
Hibernian L 16/17 1
Fulham 19/20 38 FL
20/21 40 FL
21/22 42 FL
22/23 42 FL
23/24 41 FL
24/25 33 FL
Clapton Orient

REYNOLDS Jeremiah
b. Maryhill 15.4.1867 d. Springburn 26.12.1944
Drumpelier
Cowlairs 84/85
85/86
Hibernian 86/87
Cowlairs 86/87
87/88
Carfin Shamrock 88/89
Celtic L 88/89
Glasgow Hibernian L 88/89
Celtic 89/90
90/91 17
91/92 22
92/93 11
93/94 18
94/95 7
Burnley 95/96 27 FL
96/97 22 FL
97/98 29 1 FL
98/99 27 FL
99/00 2 FL
Mossend Swifts

REYNOLDS John
b. Blackburn 21.2.1869 d. Sheffield 12.3.1917
Park Road
Witton
Blackburn R 84/85
85/86
Park Road 86/87
East Lancs Regt 86/87
87/88
Distillery 88/89
89/90
Ulster 90/91 IL
WBA 91/92 17 2 FL
Droitwich T 91/92
WBA 92/93 19 1 FL
Aston Villa 93/94 26 7 FL
94/95 24 6 FL
95/96 22 2 FL
96/97 24 2 FL
Celtic 97/98 4 1
Southampton 97/98 2 SL
Bristol St George 89/99
New Zealand
Stockport Co 03/04 1 FL
Willesden T

REYNOLDS William

Heart of Midlothian 07/08 20 3
Albion R *
Reading *
Bathgate * 10/11

RHIND Robert

Queen's Park 13/14 12 2
14/15 4 2
15/16
16/17
Linfield 17/18 IL

RHODIE J Andrew
b. c1913
Parkhead
Third Lanark 35/36 1
36/37
37/38 3
Cowdenbeath 38/39 D2
Partick T

RIBCHESTER William
b. Govan 28.7.1898
Partick St Peters
St Mungos Academy
Townhead Benburb
Parkhead Jnrs 16/17
Celtic 16/17 2
17/18
18/19
Albion R 19/20 33 6
20/21 11 2
21/22 12 2
St Johnstone 22/23 35 7 D2
23/24 37 14 D2
24/25 3
Dunfermline A 24/25 D2
Armadale 25/26 D2
26/27 D2
St Mirren

RICE

Vale of Leven 90/91 3

RICE James

Holytown U
Manchester U T
Wrexham 34/35 5 5 FL
Albion R 35/36 32 21
36/37 15 8
Falkirk 37/38 2 2
Alloa A 38/39 D2

RICE William

Western U
Partick T T
Dumbarton Harp 35/36
Glasgow Perthshire 36/37
Hibernian 37/38 29
38/39 35 2

RICHARDS Leonard George
b. Barry 13.4.1911 d. Newport 27.12.1985
Canton Institute
Cardiff C 32/33 1 FL
Dundalk 33/34 LI
Belfast Celtic 33/34 IL
Dundalk 34/35 LI
Dundee 35/36 29
36/37 22
Barry T 36/37
Dundee 37/38 23
Newport Co 38/39 30 FL

RICHARDSON

St Mirren 90/91 1

RICHARDSON

Heart of Midlothian 94/95 1

RICHARDSON

St Mirren 94/95 2

RICHARDSON

Dumbarton 95/96 1

RICHARDSON Jack

Dundee 94/95 11 3
95/96 3 1

RICHARDSON James
b. Bridgeton 1885 d. Glasgow 31.8.1951
Glenitter
Blantyre V
Kirkintilloch Rob Roy
Third Lanark 07/08 13 1
08/09 24 23
09/10 31 20
10/11 11 10
Huddersfield T 10/11 22 14 FL
11/12 20 10 FL
Sunderland 12/13 18 11 FL
13/14 17 9 FL
Ayr U 13/14 9 9
14/15 37 28
Partick T L 14/15
Ayr U 15/16 34 27
16/17
17/18 1
18/19 20 16
19/20 34 22
20/21 24 8
Millwall 21/22 19 4 FL

RICHARDSON John
b. Walker c1894 d. Crosshill 22.2.1919
Walker Cl
Newcastle C
Lincoln C 13/14 FL
St Mirren 14/15 3 1
Queen's Park 15/16 26
16/17 14
Abercorn L 16/17
Ayr U L 17/18 1
St Mirren 17/18 10
18/19 16

RICHARDSON John

Burnbank A
Hamilton A 23/24 1
Tottenham H FL

RICHARDSON John
b. Johannesburg 1909
Wallacetown Wesleyans
Wallacetown Welfare
Bristol R 30/31 8 FL
Falkirk 31/32 16
32/33 33
33/34 11
Alloa A 34/35 D2
Leith A 35/36 D2
36/37 D2
37/38 D2
38/39 D2
East Stirlingshire 38/39 D2

RICHARDSON Joseph

Vale of Clyde
Albion R 38/39 3

RICHMOND

Dumbarton 91/92 7

RICHMOND

Club		Season	Apps	Goals	
St Mirren		96/97	1		
		97/98	1		

RICHMOND Andrew 1 cap

Club		Season	Apps	Goals	
Parkhead Jnrs					
Queen's Park		03/04	22		
		04/05	18	2	
		05/06	24	2	
		06/07	28	2	
		07/08	27	1	
		08/09	20		
		09/10	25		
Rangers		10/11	20		
		11/12	12		

RICHMOND David

Club		Season	Apps	Goals	
Arderr Thistle					
Motherwell		05/06	28	4	
		06/07	6	1	
		07/08	7	2	
Hurlford		08/09			

RICHMOND James

Club		Season	Apps	Goals	
Dumbarton					
Partick T		98/99	9	1	

RICHMOND James Hart
b. Auchinleck 12.12.1903 d. ?.11.1967

Club		Season	Apps	Goals	
Kello R					
Partick T		25/26	16		
		26/27	26	1	
		27/28	4		
		28/29	17	2	
Morton		29/30	18		
Luton T		30/31	2		FL
Cork		31/32			LI
Linfield		31/32			IL
		32/33			IL
		33/34			IL
Larne		34/35			IL
		35/36			IL

RIDDELL Edward Hunter
b. Glasgow 1885

Club		Season	Apps	Goals	
Queen's Park					
Rangers					
St Mirren		04/05	3	1	
		05/06	7	1	
		06/07	3	1	
		07/08	1		
Partick T		07/08	18	4	
		08/09	12	1	
St Mirren		09/10	4		
		10/11	26	1	
		11/12	4		
Clyde		12/13	1		
St Mirren		13/14	2		

RIDDELL James Hamilton
b. Hutchesontown 6.2.1891 d. Glasgow 7.7.1952

Club		Season	Apps	Goals	
Fern Thistle					
Bellevue Hearts					
Glasgow Ashfield					
Rangers		12/13	1		
Dumbarton		13/14	28		
		14/15	36	3	
		15/16	31	3	
Renton		16/17			
Rangers		16/17	23	3	
Clyde		17/18	3		
Rangers		18/19	4		
Partick T	L	18/19	1		
Kilmarnock		18/19	3		
Dumbarton	L	18/19	11	?	
St Mirren		18/19	2	?	
		19/20	28	2	
Millwall		20/21	31	3	FL
		21/22	35	1	FL
		22/23	39	1	FL
Fulham		23/24	15		FL
		24/25	20		FL
		25/26	2		FL
Wigan B		25/26	26	1	FL
		26/27	33	1	FL
		27/28	30	1	FL
Caernarvon T					

RILEY John

Club		Season	Apps	Goals	
Queen's Park		06/07	25	1	
		07/08	21	1	
		08/09	11		
		09/10			
		10/11	11		
Morton		10/11	2		
Rangers					
St Mirren					
Hamilton A		11/12	2		

RILEY Joseph J
b. Bonnybridge

Club		Season	Apps	Goals	
St Mungos Academy					
Cardown St Josephs					
Cambuslang Bluebell					
Rutherglen Glencairn					
Maryhill Hibernian		27/28			
Hibernian	T	27/28			
Celtic		28/29	10	2	
Ayr U	L	28/29	7	3	
Celtic		29/30			
Nithsdale W	L	29/30			
St Mirren		30/31			
Alloa A		31/32			D2

RILEY Richard

Club		Season	Apps	Goals	
Colne					
Burnley		12/13	3	1	FL
Third Lanark		13/14	15	2	
		14/15	9	3	
		15/16			
		16/17			
		17/18			
		18/19	1	?	

RINTOUL David

Club		Season	Apps	Goals	
Crieff Earngrove					
St Johnstone	T	33/34			
Crieff Earngrove		34/35			
Kings Park	T	35/36			D2
Dundee		36/37	2	1	

RIPLEY Wiliam S

Club		Season	Apps	Goals	
Raith R		16/17	7		

RIPPON Willis
b. Beighton 15.5.1886 d. Rotherham 1956

Club		Season	Apps	Goals	
Kilnhurst T					
Bristol C		07/08	7	2	FL
		08/09	23	8	FL
		09/10	6	4	FL
Woolwich Arsenal		10/11	9	2	FL
Brentford		11/12	24	17	SL
Hamilton A		12/13	29	20	
		13/14	10	2	
Grimsby T		13/14	23	11	FL
Rotherham T		14/15			

RISK Charles D

Club		Season	Apps	Goals	
Queen's Park		08/09	8	1	

RISK Ralph

Club		Season	Apps	Goals	
Glasgow Ashfield					
Queen's Park		12/13	3		
		13/14	2		
		14/15	12		

RITCHIE

Club		Season	Apps	Goals	
Hibernian		98/99	3		

RITCHIE Alexander Watson
b. Airdrie 2.4.1904 d. Mossend 13.7.1954

Club		Season	Apps	Goals	
Glasgow Ashfield					
Fauldhouse U					
Airdrieonians		22/23			
Armadale		22/23			D2
Raith R		22/23			
St Bernards		23/24			D2
Peebles R	L	23/24			D3
Raith R		23/24	9		
		24/25	30	?	
		25/26	23	5	
Dunfermline A	L	25/26			D2
Raith R		26/27			D2
		27/28	16	2	
Blackpool		28/29	12		FL
		29/30	17	5	FL
		30/31	2		FL
Reading		30/31	4	1	FL
		31/32	40	19	FL
		32/33	28	16	FL
Watford		33/34	17	3	FL
Bournemouth		34/35	33	11	FL
Third Lanark		35/36	14	4	
Hibernian		36/37	26	4	
Albion R					

RITCHIE Andrew

Club		Season	Apps	Goals	
Greenock Volunteers					
Morton		01/02	1		
		02/03	16		
		03/04	7		
Port Glasgow A		04/05	11		
		05/06	19	4	
		06/07	29	1	
		07/08	20	1	
		08/09	28		
St Mirren		09/10	20		

RITCHIE Archibald
b. Stenhousemuir 11.5.1894 d. Guildford 24.11.1973

Club		Season	Apps	Goals	
Denny Hibs					
Stenhousemuir					
Dumbarton		14/15	29		
		15/16	1		
		16/17			
		17/18	3		
		18/19	2		
Rangers		19/20	21		
Derby Co		20/21	39	1	FL
		21/22	30		FL
		22/23	1		FL
		23/24	2		FL
		24/25			FL
		25/26	14		FL
		26/27	1		FL
Guildford C		27/28			
		28/29			

RITCHIE Charles
b. Glasgow

Club		Season	Apps	Goals	
Falkirk		24/25	1		
		25/26	13		
		26/27	29	1	

RITCHIE Duncan

Club		Season	Apps	Goals	
Strathleven					
Renton		05/06			
		06/07			
Hibernian		07/08	32	2	
		08/09	8		
Dumbarton		09/10			D2
		10/11	16	?	D2
Raith R		11/12	32	3	
Sheffield U		12/13	13	1	FL
Derby Co		13/14	2		FL

RITCHIE George

Club		Season	Apps	Goals	
Airdrieonians		09/10	10	2	

RITCHIE George
b. Aberdeen

Club		Season	Apps	Goals	
Montrose		21/22			D2
Arbroath		22/23	30	13	D2
Aberdeen		23/24	1		
		24/25			
		25/26	6		
		26/27	8		
		27/28	3		

RITCHIE George Thompson
b. Maryhill 16.1.1904 d. Leicester 10.9.1978

Club		Season	Apps	Goals	
Maryhill					
Blackburn R		22/23	2		FL
Royal Albert		23/24			D3
		24/25			D3
		25/26			D3
Falkirk		27/28	31	1	
		28/29	7	1	
Leicester C		28/29	28		FL
		29/30	21		FL
		30/31	36	2	FL
		31/32	33	3	FL
		32/33	40	3	FL
		33/34	26		FL
		34/35	35	1	FL
		35/36	15	2	FL
		36/37	10	1	FL
Colchester U		37/38	21	1	SL

RITCHIE Henry McGill 2 caps
b. Scone 27.10.1898 d. ?.7.1941
Perth Violet
Hibernian 18/19 3 ?
19/20 29 3
20/21 15 3
21/22 35 7
22/23 34 11
23/24 38 11
24/25 32 10
25/26 37 15
26/27 36 9
27/28 25 4
Everton 28/29 19 4 FL
29/30 9 1 FL
Dundee 29/30 10 2
30/31 31 11
St Johnstone 31/32 22 5 D2
32/33 35 7
33/34 6
Brechin C 33/34 D2
Arbroath 34/35 2 D2

RITCHIE James M

Cowdenbeath
Aberdeen 20/21 7
Dundee Hibs 21/22 23 2 D2

RITCHIE John

Dundee 93/94 2 4

RITCHIE John

Dundee 98/99 2

RITCHIE John L

St Mirren 99/00 1

RITCHIE Peter

Wemyss A
Airdrieonians 15/16 5

RITCHIE Richard T

Gourock FP
Morton 31/32 35 1
32/33 23 1
Dumbarton 33/34 D2
Aberdeen 34/35 2
35/36 3
36/37 2
37/38 2

RITCHIE Robert

Clydebank Jnrs
Heart of Midlothian 07/08 12 3

RITCHIE Robert J
b. Kilmarnock
Darvel Jnrs
Kilmarnock 25/26 1
26/27
Queen of the South 27/28 D2
28/29 D2
29/30 D2
30/31 D2
31/32 D2

RITCHIE Robert Young

St Bernards 97/98 1
98/99 16 4
99/00 5
00/01 14 ? D2

RITCHIE William

Dundee 98/99 3
Arbroath
Orion

RITCHIE William
b. Renton 1895
Renton
Dumbarton 15/16 35 10
16/17 36 6
17/18 28 4
18/19 23 ?
Bury 19/20 37 11 FL
20/21 12 4 FL
21/22 12 1 FL
Grimsby T 22/23 25 4 FL

ROBB A O

Third Lanark 96/97 1

ROBB Andrew

Rutherglen Glencairn
Morton 33/34 D2
34/35 D2
35/36 D2
36/37 D2
37/38 28 1

ROBB David
b. Leith 18.2.1903 d. Burnley ?.7.1992
Leith Unitas
Musselburgh Bruntonians
Dundee 24/25 3
Arbroath L 24/25 7 D2
Dundee 25/26 4
Charlton A T 26/27 FL
Wigan B 26/27 17 FL
27/28 27 FL
28/29 28 2 FL
29/30 35 1 FL
Chesterfield 30/31 23 1 FL
31/32 FL
New Brighton 32/33 34 FL

ROBB John

Bridgeton Waverley *
Third Lanark 33/34 4
Beith
Clyde 36/37 21
37/38 28
Kings Park *

ROBB Thomas
b. Bellshill 25.1.1895
Kirkintilloch Harp 19/20
Bradford C 19/20 FL
Bathgate 20/21
Bradford C 21/22 11 1 FL
Bathgate 21/22 D2
Hamilton A 22/23 22 2
New York Giants 23/24 6 ASL

ROBB William 2 caps
b. Rutherglen 20.3.1895 d. Aldershot 18.2.1976
Rutherglen Welfare
Eastern Burnside
Kirkintilloch Rob Roy
Birmingham 13/14 2 FL
14/15 38 FL
Vale of Leven 15/16
Royal Albert
Third Lanark 17/18 31
18/19 13
Armadale 19/20
Rangers 19/20 7
20/21 42
21/22 42
22/23 38
23/24 38
24/25 38
25/26 22
Hibernian 26/27 37
27/28 36
28/29 32
29/30 23
Aldershot 30/31 15 SL
31/32 18 SL
32/33 42 FL
33/34 42 FL
34/35 40 FL
35/36 32 FL
36/37 20 FL
Guildford C 37/38 22 SL
38/39 SL
Regent Star

ROBBIE Charles

St Johnstone 38/39 3

ROBERTS

St Mirren 91/92 1

ROBERTS

Hibernian 98/99 2 1

ROBERTS John T
b. Glasgow
Cadzow St Annes *
Queen's Park 13/14 18
14/15 20 1
15/16
16/17 3
17/18
18/19
19/20 15
20/21 17

ROBERTS Lawrence
b. Kirkintilloch
Dykehead
Rangers
St Mirren L 18/19 1
Renton 19/20
Burnley T 19/20 1 FL
Hamilton A 19/20 7 2
Dumbarton Harp 20/21
Dykehead
Airdrieonians 21/22 4 2
Vale of Leven 22/23 D2
Old Kilpatrick
Helensburgh
Dumbarton Harp
Helensburgh

ROBERTS Robert

Johnstone
Morton 02/03 20 6
03/04 25 3
04/05 23 5
Port Glasgow A 05/06 15 2
Johnstone 06/07

ROBERTS Robert

Dundee 16/17 3

ROBERTS Samuel
b. Connahs Quay
Holywell
Connahs Quay 29/30
Flint T U
Rhyl A
Halifax T 32/33 10 1 FL
Rhyl A
Newry T 34/35 IL
Rangers 34/35 5 1
35/36 3
Kilmarnock 35/36 25 7
36/37 34 8
37/38 12 1
Dundee 38/39 21 2
Benburb

ROBERTS Thomas

Heart of Midlothian 06/07 1

ROBERTSON

Cambuslang 90/91 1
91/92 3

ROBERTSON

Dumbarton 92/93 2

ROBERTSON

Leith A 94/95 1

ROBERTSON

St Mirren 94/95 1

ROBERTSON

Hibernian 98/99 1

ROBERTSON

Heart of Midlothian 05/06 1

ROBERTSON

Morton 06/07 1

ROBERTSON

Clyde 16/17 1

ROBERTSON

Clyde 32/33 10 2

ROBERTSON A

Queen's Park 02/03 3

ROBERTSON A

Queen's Park 15/16 2

ROBERTSON A
b. c1912
Kilsyth R
Airdrieonians 31/32 3 1
St Bernards 32/33 D2

ROBERTSON Abraham
b. Greenock
Port Glasgow Juveniles
Pollok Jnrs
Cowdenbeath 32/33 16 1
33/34 34 8
Heart of Midlothian 34/35 10 1
Morton 35/36 D2
Dumbarton 36/37 D2

ROBERTSON Alexander
Dundee 96/97 4 1

ROBERTSON Alexander
b. Perth c1880
Fair City A
Hibernian 96/97 18
Fair City A 96/97
Hibernian 97/98 17 2
98/99 17 3
99/00 12
00/01 18
01/02 14
02/03 20
Manchester U 03/04 23 FL
04/05 8 1 FL
05/06 1 FL
Fair City A L

ROBERTSON Alexander
b. Dundee 1878
Dundee Violet
Dundee 99/00 15 9
00/01 11 7
Middlesbrough 00/01 29 9 FL
01/02 8 9 FL
02/03 13 6 FL
Manchester U 03/04 27 10 FL
04/05 1 FL
05/06 FL
06/07 FL
Bradford PA 06/07

ROBERTSON Alexander
Shotts U
Partick T T
Cowdenbeath 26/27 4 4
The match for Partick was played under the name of Gray

ROBERTSON Alexander
b. Kilbirnie 1911
Beith A
Aberdeen 32/33 2
33/34 3 1
Kilmarnock 34/35 1
Hartlepools U 35/36 30 4 FL
36/37 36 11 FL
37/38 13 1 FL
Horden CW 37/38

ROBERTSON Arthur
b. Dundee
Aberdeen East End
Aberdeen 13/14 4
14/15
15/16 5 2
16/17 26
17/18
18/19
19/20 19 2
20/21 16
21/22 8 2
22/23 18 1
Bethlehem Steel 23/24 13 1 ASL
24/25 27 6 ASL
25/26 15 4 ASL
26/27 11 ASL
27/28 14 3 ASL
29/30 7 ASL

ROBERTSON David S
b. Kilmarnock
Dreghorn Jnrs
Kilmarnock 20/21 6
21/22 19
Queen of the South 21/22
Brooklyn Wanderers 22/23 25 3 ASL
23/24 26 3 ASL
24/25 8 ASL
25/26 36 ASL
26/27 15 ASL
27/28 44 4 ASL
28/29 38 15 ASL
29A 3 ASL
29/30 28 8 ASL
Aberdeen 30/31

ROBERTSON David Vallance
b. Kirkcaldy 16.8.1906
Tranent Jnrs
Rosslyn Jnrs
St Mirren 26/27 2
27/28 6
York C
Rosslyn Jnrs
Celtic 30/31 2
Clydebank L 30/31 D2
Cowdenbeath
Rosslyn Jnrs

ROBERTSON Ernest
Cambuslang R
Clyde 38/39 3

ROBERTSON Fred
Partick T 07/08 24 4
08/09 28 8
Johnstone

ROBERTSON Frederick
Morton 11/12 14 2
12/13 20 3

ROBERTSON George
b. Glasgow 1883
Rutherglen Glencairn
Clyde 01/02 D2
02/03 D2
Blackburn R 02/03 9 FL
Clyde 03/04 D2
04/05 D2
05/06 D2
06/07 32
07/08 29 2
08/09 25
09/10 28
10/11 12
Birmingham 10/11 19 FL
11/12 29 3 FL
Bloxwich Strollers
Brierley Hill A

ROBERTSON George
Port Glasgow A
South Africa
Port Glasgow A 04/05 20 3
05/06 30 2
06/07 25
Motherwell 07/08 15

ROBERTSON George
Pollok Jnrs
Partick T 16/17 7
Dumbarton Harp 17/18

ROBERTSON George
b. Dundee
Dundee Violet
Cowdenbeath 29/30 6

ROBERTSON George 1 cap
b. Kilmarnock 7.9.1915 d. Irvine 2006
Bartenholme Juveniles
Dalry Thistle
Irvine Meadow
Kilmarnock 36/37 32
37/38 36 1
38/39 4

ROBERTSON George C 4 caps
b. Stonefield 1884 d. 1962
Yoker A
Port Glasgow A
Motherwell 06/07 31 4
07/08 32 4
08/09 33 7
Sheffield W 09/10 8 3 FL
10/11 35 7 FL
11/12 36 4 FL
12/13 33 10 FL
13/14 21 4 FL
14/15 24 2 FL
19/20 5 FL
East Fife 20/21

ROBERTSON
Aberdeen 03/04 4 D2
04/05 1 D2
05/06 4
06/07 2

ROBERTSON Graham Baird
b. Buckhaven 22.9.1907
Kirkland W
Milton Violet
Denbeath Star
Thornton R
Wellesley Jnrs
Partick T T 28/29
St Mirren T 28/29
East Fife T 28/29
Celtic 29/30 28 1
30/31 6
Cowdenbeath 31/32 20 1
St Mirren 31/32
Cowdenbeath 32/33 7
33/34
Cardiff C T 33/34 FL
Alloa A T 34/35 D2

ROBERTSON Hugh
b. Perth
St Johnstone YMCA
Wrexham 36/37 1 FL
37/38 5 FL
St Johnstone 38/39 1

ROBERTSON J
Motherwell 15/16 1

ROBERTSON J M
Queen's Park 06/07 3

ROBERTSON James
Dunblane
Dundee 00/01 1 1
Dunblane

ROBERTSON James
Abercorn
Third Lanark 00/01 8 2
01/02 11 1
Middlesbrough 01/02 2 FL
02/03 30 3 FL

ROBERTSON James
b. Glasgow 1880
Glasgow U
Crewe A 01/02
02/03
Small Heath 03/04 6 2 FL
04/05 FL
Chelsea 05/06 17 13 FL
06/07 13 8 FL
Glossop 07/08 33 4 FL
08/09 33 11 FL
Partick T 09/10 17 10
10/11 17 1
Ayr U 11/12 D2
Barrow 12/13
Leeds C 12/13 FL
Gateshead 13/14
14/15

ROBERTSON James
New Brompton 03/04 18 4 SL
Aberdeen 04/05 19 1 D2
05/06 29 2
06/07 6

ROBERTSON James
Arthurlie
Port Glasgow A 05/06 12 3
06/07 16 2

ROBERTSON James
b. Scotland
Vale of Leven
Blackburn R 05/06 26 9 FL
06/07 36 9 FL
07/08 16 5 FL
Brighton 08/09 23 5 SL
Vale of Leven 09/10 D2
Falkirk 10/11 11 9
11/12 29 12
12/13 31 15
13/14 37 27
14/15 35 11
Dunfermline A 15/16
Armadale 15/16
Falkirk 15/16 9 3
16/17
17/18 1 ?
18/19 7 ?
Vale of Leven L 18/19
19/20
Dumbarton Harp 20/21
Dumbarton 21/22 30 2

ROBERTSON James				
Aberdeen	10/11	1		
Wallsend				
Aberdeen	16/17	1		

ROBERTSON James				
b. c1909				
Pollok Jnrs				
Chelsea				
Cowdenbeath	32/33	27	3	
Larne	33/34			IL
Brechin C	34/35			D2

ROBERTSON James E			2 caps	
b. Dundee 1910				
Logie U				
Logie Thistle				
Dundee	28/29	10	1	
	29/30	34	2	
	30/31	32	14	
	31/32	30	4	
	32/33	31	22	
	33/34	20	4	
Birmingham	33/34	6	1	FL
Kilmarnock	34/35	34	23	
	35/36	36	18	
	36/37	26	12	
	37/38	11	1	
Elgin C				

ROBERTSON James G				
Motherwell				
Heart of Midlothian				
Glasgow Ashfield				
Woolwich Arsenal	12/13			FL
Ayr U	13/14	24	3	

ROBERTSON James S				
Petershill				
Ashfield				
Ayr U	18/19	4	3	
Vale of Clyde	19/20			
Bo'ness	20/21			

ROBERTSON John				
Third Lanark	06/07	5		
	07/08	3		

ROBERTSON John				
b. c1887				
Dalbeattie Star				
Blackpool				FL
Dumfries				
Hamilton A	08/09	27	8	
Workington				
Motherwell	09/10	27	10	
	10/11	31	7	
	11/12	20	8	
	12/13	11	4	
	13/14	1	1	
Stevenston U				

ROBERTSON John				
Queen's Park	10/11	1		
	11/12	1		
	12/13			
	13/14	1		

ROBERTSON John				
Motherwell	17/18	1	?	
	18/19	2	3	
	19/20	17	8	
	20/21	10	3	

ROBERTSON John				
Motherwell				
Falkirk	35/36			
	36/37	14		
Albion R	37/38			D2
	38/39	5		

ROBERTSON John B				
Hibernian	14/15	18	1	
St Mirren	15/16	3		

ROBERTSON John Nicol				
b. Coylton 1884 d. Maybole 23.1.1937				
Drogan				
Rangers				
Bolton W	03/04	1		FL
	04/05			FL
	05/06	14		FL
Southampton	06/07	23		SL
	07/08	25	1	SL
	08/09	20		SL
	09/10	36		SL
	10/11	21		SL
	11/12	28		SL
Rangers	11/12	2		
	12/13	12		

ROBERTSON John Tait			16 caps	
b. Dumbarton 25.2.1877 d. Milton 24.1.1935				
Poinfield				
Sinclair Swifts				
Morton	94/95	15	?	D2
	95/96	9	?	D2
	96/97			
Everton	97/98	26	1	FL
Southampton	98/99	19		SL
Rangers	99/00	15	4	
	00/01	20	3	
	01/02	8	3	
	02/03	20	2	
	03/04	18	2	
	04/05	20	4	
Chelsea	05/06	32	4	FL
	06/07	3		FL
Glossop	06/07	14	6	FL
	07/08	31	4	FL
	08/09	3		FL

ROBERTSON John Thomas				
b. Newton Mearns 1877				
Newton Thistle				
St Bernards				
Stoke	94/95	13	1	FL
Hibernian	94/95	3		D2
	95/96	16		
	96/97	18		
Stoke	97/98	23		FL
	98/99	31		FL
	99/00	34	2	FL
Liverpool	00/01	25		FL
	01/02	5		FL
Southampton	02/03	26	1	SL
	03/04	19		SL
Brighton	04/05	26	1	SL

ROBERTSON Peter				
b. Kilmarnock d. By 1926				
Kilmarnock Rugby XI				
Kilmarnock	00/01	1		
Kilmarnock A	01/02			
	02/03			
Ayr Parkhouse	03/04			D2
Kilmarnock	03/04			
	04/05			
	05/06			
Hurlford	06/07			

ROBERTSON Peter			1 cap	
b. Dundee 1881				
Providence				
Dundee	01/02	18	1	
	02/03	20		
	03/04	13	1	
Nottingham F	04/05	7		FL
	05/06			FL
Dundee				

ROBERTSON Peter				
b. Port Glasgow 1891				
Port Glasgow A				
Morton	13/14	3		
	14/15	4	2	
	15/16	1		
	16/17	2		
	17/18	4	1	
	18/19	2	?	
Hartlepools U	21/22	26	12	FL
	22/23	10	6	FL
Doncaster R	23/24	16	4	FL

ROBERTSON Peter				
b. Dundee ?.2.1908 d. Dundee 6.6.1964				
Lochee U				
Dundee	27/28	3		
	28/29	5		
Charlton A	29/30	41		FL
	30/31	42		FL
	31/32	25		FL
	32/33	9		FL
Crystal Palace	33/34	4		FL
Dundee U	34/35	33		D2
Brechin C	35/36			D2
Arbroath	36/37	18		
	37/38	38		
	38/39	26		
Rochdale				

ROBERTSON Peter				
Blantyre V				
Clyde	32/33			
	33/34	21	4	
	34/35	12	5	
Hamilton A	35/36	2	1	

ROBERTSON R George				
Third Lanark	13/14	1		

ROBERTSON Robert				
d. ?.4.1940				
Renfrew V				
St Mirren	01/02	18	2	
	02/03	16	5	
	03/04	25	3	
	04/05	24		
	05/06	21		
	06/07	33	2	
	07/08	30		
	08/09	31	3	
	09/10	16		
	10/11	32		
	11/12	5		

ROBERTSON Robert				
b. Nottingham				
Ayr Academicals				
Morton	04/05	17		
	05/06	30		
	06/07	32		
	07/08	28		
	08/09	33		
	09/10	25		

ROBERTSON Robert				
Motherwell	15/16	11	1	

ROBERTSON Robert C				
Cambuslang R				
Hamilton A	12/13	10		
	13/14	27		
	14/15	28		
	15/16	34		
	16/17	28		
	17/18	14		
	18/19	16		
Bo'ness	19/20			
	20/21			
Dumbarton	21/22	14		

ROBERTSON Samuel				
b. Bridge of Allan				
Alva Albion R				
Alloa A	08/09			
Heart of Midlothian	09/10	8		
	10/11	12		
Cowdenbeath	11/12			D2

ROBERTSON T				
Heart of Midlothian	98/99	1		

ROBERTSON Theodor				
Edinburgh C				
Falkirk	32/33	3		

ROBERTSON Thomas				
St Bernards	95/96	5		
	96/97	18		
	97/98	6		

ROBERTSON Thomas 1 cap

East Benhar Heatherbell
Motherwell
Fauldhouse
Heart of Midlothian 96/97 8 7
97/98 17 9
Liverpool 97/98 3 2 FL
98/99 33 9 FL
99/00 34 8 FL
00/01 34 6 FL
01/02 31 5 FL
Heart of Midlothian 02/03 3
Dundee 02/03 13 1
Manchester U 03/04 4 FL
04/05 FL
Bathgate 05/06

ROBERTSON Thomas
b. Paisley
Maryhill
Partick T 08/09 14 3
Abercorn 09/10 D2
Vale of Leven

ROBERTSON Thomas
b. Leith
Edinburgh Emmet
Morton
St Bernards 21/22 D2
Middlesbrough 22/23 FL
23/24 FL
24/25 FL
25/26 FL
St Bernards 26/27 D2
Heart of Midlothian 27/28
28/29
29/30 4 1
St Bernards 29/30 D2
30/31 D2

ROBERTSON Thomas
b. c1905
Edinburgh Emmet
Morton 25/26 5
St Bernards 26/27

ROBERTSON Thomas
b. Patna
Tongue Row Juveniles
Ayr U 30/31 13 2
31/32 35
32/33 12 8
Galston L 32/33
Ayr U 33/34 26 7
Dundee 34/35 36 11
35/36 37 13
Clyde 36/37 25 5
37/38 21 5
38/39 27 4

ROBERTSON Thomas G
b. Stevenston
Ardeer Thistle
Kilmarnock 27/28 18
28/29 35
29/30 28
30/31 26
31/32 2
32/33
Queen of the South 32/33 D2
Galston

ROBERTSON W

Queen's Park 20/21 1

ROBERTSON W

St Mirren 22/23 1

ROBERTSON W T

St Bernards 93/94 1
94/95 4

ROBERTSON William

Hibernian 18/19 11 ?

ROBERTSON William J

Oatlands
Morton 16/17 1

ROBERTSON William P
b. Glasgow
Oatlands
Morton 18/19 10 3
Bury 19/20 6 FL
Beith
Vale of Clyde 24/25

ROBERTSON William S
b. Falkirk 20.4.1907
Camelon Jnrs
Kings Park
Third Lanark
Ayr U 27/28 38 1 D2
28/29 36 3
29/30 32 3
Stoke C 29/30 9 1 FL
30/31 20 1 FL
31/32 38 1 FL
32/33 39 FL
33/34 11 FL
Manchester U 33/34 10 FL
34/35 36 1 FL
Reading 35/36 7 FL
36/37 16 FL
East Stirlingshire 37/38 D2

ROBERTSON William Smith
b. Stirling 7.6.1887 d. Preston 24.8.1960
Denny Hibernian
Celtic 09/10 3
Preston NE 10/11 2 FL
St Mirren 11/12 12 1
12/13
York C 13/14

ROBERTSON William W

Kirkintilloch Rob Roy
Hamilton A T
Rangers
Partick T T
Aberdeen T
Clydebank 21/22 18 2

ROBEY James Henry
b. Radcliffe ?.1.1911
Heywood St James
Stalybridge C
Aston Villa 36/37 3 FL
Aberdeen 37/38 2
Wigan A

ROBINSON Charles A

Dalkeith Thistle
Leith A 28/29 D2
29/30 D2
30/31 14 2
31/32 9

ROBSON

Morton 17/18 1

ROBSON George A

Raith R 15/16 18
16/17 16

ROBSON George Arnold
b. Blyth 22.4.1897 d. Blyth 12.3.1984
Cambois U
Blyth Spartans
Raith R 19/20 16
St Mirren
South Shields 19/20 10 FL
20/21 14 FL
21/22 2 FL
22/23 4 FL
23/24 15 FL
24/25 29 FL
25/26 8 FL
Southampton 26/27 FL
Ashington 27/28 7 FL
28/29 14 FL
Blyth Spartans

ROBSON George Chippendale
b. Newcastle 17.6.1908
St Peters A
Newcastle U 25/26 FL
26/27 FL
West Ham U 27/28 1 FL
28/29 5 1 FL
29/30 10 1 FL
30/31 1 FL
Brentford 30/31 13 5 FL
31/32 38 9 FL
32/33 24 6 FL
33/34 4 FL
34/35 27 10 FL
35/36 18 3 FL
Heart of Midlothian 35/36 13 1
36/37 38 3
37/38 31 1
38/39 33

ROCK Robert Munro
b. Camlachie 1905
Kilsyth R
Kilsyth Emmet
Glasgow Ashfield
Kilmarnock 24/25 10 4
25/26 8 3
Airdrieonians 25/26 6 5
Alloa A 26/27 D2
Fall River Marksmen 26/27 9 8 ASL
J & P Coats 26/27 11 3 ASL
Philadelphia Field Club 26/27 10 10 ASL
Airdrieonians 27/28 6 3
28/29
Barrow 29/30 25 FL
Stenhousemuir 30/31 D2
Armadale 30/31 D2

RODGER Charles Gordon
b. Ayr 3.3.1909 d. Ayr 26.5.1982
Craigview A
Ayr U 31/32 3 1
32/33 10 4
33/34 35 10
34/35 15 2
35/36 18 6
Manchester C 35/36 4 FL
36/37 9 7 FL
37/38 6 FL
Northampton T 37/38 11 FL
38/39 24 4 FL
Ipswich T

RODGER Donald S
b. Paisley
Paisley YMCA
St Mirren 29/30
Morton 30/31 3
31/32
32/33
33/34 D2
Dunfermline A 34/35 7 1
Kings Park 35/36 D2
East Fife 35/36 D2

RODGER William
b. c1914
Pumpherston U
Motherwell 34/35 1
35/36
Babcock & Wilcox 35/36
St Bernards 36/37 D2

RODGERSON Ralph
b. Sunderland 1892
Pallion Institute
Burnley 12/13 FL
Huddersfield T 13/14 FL
14/15 1 FL
Dundee L 16/17 2
Huddersfield T 19/20 11 FL
20/21 14 FL
Leeds U 20/21 3 FL
21/22 24 FL
Sunderland WE
Dundee 22/23 5
Spennymoor U
Carlisle U

ROGERS Thomas R
b. Pumpherston
Pumpherston R
Heart of Midlothian 26/27 14 2
27/28 25 8

ROGERSON Robert

Law Volunteers
Carluke Milton R
Wishaw Thistle
Kings Park
Hibernian 11/12 4 1
Cowdenbeath 11/12 D2
Abercorn 12/13 D2

ROLLO James

Glasgow Perthshire
Renton
Hamilton A 08/09 9
Third Lanark 08/09 4
Carlisle U 09/10
Abercorn 10/11 D2
11/12 D2

ROLLO Robert
d. 30.4.1917
Petershill
Clydebank Jnrs
Hibernian 07/08 10 1

ROMBACH David Sutherland
b. Glasgow 1874 d. Pollok 3.4.1943
Petershill
Clyde 98/99 3
Albion R 98/99
99/00
Airdrieonians 00/01 18 D2
01/02 21 D2
02/03 21 1 D2
03/04 25 6
04/05 23 3
05/06 30 2
06/07 31 7
07/08 30 1
08/09 28
09/10 7

RONEY Peter
b. Rutherglen 15.1.1887 d. Clydebank 25.8.1930
Petershill
Stratchclyde
Cambuslang Hibs
Ayr 06/07
Norwich C 07/08 22 SL
08/09 31 SL
Bristol R 09/10 42 1 SL
10/11 29 SL
11/12 38 SL
12/13 37 SL
13/14 22 SL
14/15 9 SL
Army
Albion R 19/20 10
Ayr U 20/21

RORRISON James Armstrong
b. Kirkconnel 21.6.1908 d. Scotland 1981
Kello R
St Mirren 28/29 2 1
29/30 7 2
Carlisle U 30/31 2 FL
Doncaster R 31/32 1 FL
Cork 32/33 LI
Workington 33/34
Distillery 33/34 IL
Dolphin 33/34 LI
Bray Unknowns 34/35 LI

ROSS

Heart of Midlothian 90/91 12 3
91/92 7 2
92/93 7 3

ROSS

Leith A 93/94 12 4
94/95 4

ROSS Alexander
b. Aberdeen
Aberdeen Richmond
Dundee 23/24 1
Arbroath L 24/25 6 2 D2
Dundee 25/26 18 9
Rochdale 26/27 1 1 FL

ROSS Alexander

Cameron Highlanders
Inverness Caledonian
Hibernian 30/31 6 3

ROSS Andrew
b. Hurlford 17.2.1878
Hurlford T
Kilmarnock T 97/98
Celtic 98/99 1
99/00
Galston 00/01
Barrow

ROSS Daniel
b. Lundin Links d. ?.1.1965
St Andrews U
Partick T 28/29
29/30 2
30/31 1

ROSS David
b. Over Darwen 8.1.1883 d. Luton 2.1.1947
Heywood U
Bury 03/04 4 1 FL
Luton T 04/05 32 12 SL
Norwich C 05/06 33 18 SL
06/07 24 19 SL
Manchester C 06/07 6 1 FL
07/08 10 3 FL
08/09 22 5 FL
09/10 12 6 FL
10/11 10 4 FL
11/12 2 FL
Dundee 12/13 17
13/14
14/15
Rochdale 19/20 2 CL

ROSS Dennison
b. Glasgow 21.10.1910 d. Clydebank 1.7.1966
Eastern A
Clyde 29/30
Portadown 29/30 IL
Linfield 30/31 IL
Clyde 30/31 12
Portadown 30/31 IL
Linfield 31/32 IL

ROSS Duncan

Clyde 94/95 6
95/96 17
96/97 8

ROSS George

Port Glasgow A 00/01 D2
01/02 D2
02/03 13 1
03/04 23
04/05 26
05/06 17
06/07 24 6
07/08 32 2
Falkirk 08/09
Morton 09/10 8
Port Glasgow A 10/11 18 D2

ROSS George Adams
b. Bonnyrigg 21.2.1908 d. Edinburgh 1980
Dalkeith Thistle
Arbroath T 27/28 D2
Dundee U 28/29 5 2 D2
29/30 16 6
Portsmouth 29/30 3 FL
30/31 2 2 FL
Bray Unknowns 31/32 LI
32/33 LI
Dundee U 33/34 34 17 D2
34/35 34 18 D2
35/36 26 10 D2
36/37 30 7 D2
Leith A 37/38 D2

ROSS Henry
b. Brechin 4.4.1881 d. Brechin 28.11.1953
Lochee Harp
Brechin
Burnley 99/00 1 FL
00/01 4 FL
01/02 34 FL
02/03 34 2 FL
03/04 32 1 FL
Fulham 04/05 29 2 SL
05/06 33 1 SL
06/07 36 6 SL
07/08 28 2 FL
08/09 1 1 FL
St Mirren 08/09 9
Southport Central 09/10
Darwen 09/10
Brechin C

ROSS James
b. c1914
Arthurlie
Airdrieonians 33/34 24 5
34/35 36 6
35/36 29 2
Stenhousemuir 36/37 D2
East Stirlingshire 37/38 D2

ROSS John B
b. Paisley
Pollok Jnrs
Dundee 21/22 23 2
22/23 27
23/24 29
24/25 32
25/26 16
26/27 15
27/28 20
28/29 17
Dundee U 29/30 35
Connahs Quay

ROSS Kenneth

Aberdeen University
Aberdeen 07/08 1

ROSS Robert
b. Glasgow
Rutherglen Glencairn
Clyde 15/16 12

ROSS Robert
b. Govan 2.2.1917
Benburb
Rangers 37/38 7
38/39 1
Ayr U 38/39 20
Rangers
Watford 46/47 FL
Dumbarton 47/48 D2

ROSS S H

Third Lanark 94/95 13
95/96 2

ROSS Samuel Young
b. Darvel 13.11.1914 d. Newmilns 1973
Darvel Jnrs
Kilmarnock 33/34 3
34/35 29
35/36 36 2
36/37 35 3
37/38 38 5
38/39 25 10
Dundee U 46/47 25 2 D2
47/48 4 D2
Morton 47/48
Newton Stewart 48/49
Tarff R 49/50
Newton Stewart

ROSS Sidney

Cambuslang 90/91 17
91/92 21

ROSS Thomas
b. Musselburgh
Heart of Midlothian 16/17 36
17/18 26 1
18/19 25
19/20 4 1

ROSS William

Parkhead
Clydebank Jnrs
Cambuslang R
Hamilton A 15/16 17

ROSS William
b. Aberdeen c1902 d. ?.4.1992
Mugiemoss
Aberdeen 25/26
26/27 10
27/28 8
Mugiemoss

ROSS William
Shotts Battlefield
Airdrieonians 30/31 2
31/32 7
32/33
33/34 1
Derry C 34/35 IL
35/36 IL
36/37 IL
37/38 IL
Cork C 38/39 LI
39/40 LI
40/41 LI
Derry C 41/42 IL
42/43 IL
43/44 IL
44/45 IL
45/46 IL
46/47 IL
47/48 IL
48/49 IL
49/50 IL
50/51 IL
51/52 IL

ROUGHEAD Malcolm
Hibernian 08/09 2

ROUGVIE David
Denbeath Star
Raith R 16/17 9 2

ROUTLEDGE William
Duntocher Hibs
St Mirren 36/37 4 1
East Stirlingshire *

ROWAN John G
b. Coatbridge
Glasgow Perthshire
Dumbarton 10/11 1 ? D2
11/12 D2
12/13 D2
13/14 37 11
14/15 17 7
15/16 2 1
16/17
17/18
18/19 5 ?
19/20 5 1
Hamilton A 19/20 8 2
Bathgate 20/21
Played some matches under the assumed name of J G Robertson

ROXBURGH George
b. Charleston
Renfrew V
Hamilton A 07/08 20
08/09 22
09/10 3
Abercorn 10/11 16 ? D2
Motherwell 11/12 1
12/13
Stevenston U 13/14

ROY
Third Lanark 91/92 2 1

ROYAN William Osgood Hamlett
b. Findhorn 9.12.1914
Greenhead Thistle
Glasgow Perthshire 35/36
Heart of Midlothian 35/36
Chirnside U L 35/36
QPR 36/37 FL
Queen of the South 37/38 3 1
Rochdale 38/39 5 1 FL
Glasgow Perthshire

RUDDIMAN Thomas
Rangers 05/06 4 3
06/07 3
Aberdeen 06/07
Airdrieonians 06/07 3
Port Glasgow A 07/08 27 11
08/09 8 1
Vale of Leven 09/10 D2
Third Lanark 10/11 1 1

RUNDELL George
Kilmarnock 18/19 5
Nithsdale W
Arthurlie

RUNDELL John
b. Larkhall
Motherwell 15/16 4
16/17 38
17/18 34
18/19 4
19/20 42
20/21 33
21/22 42
22/23 38
23/24 28
24/25 3
Arthurlie 24/25 D2
25/26 D2

RUSSELL
Third Lanark 91/92 3

RUSSELL
Leith A 92/93 6 1

RUSSELL
Third Lanark 17/18 1 ?

RUSSELL
Hamilton A 18/19 1

RUSSELL Alexander
St Mirren 04/05 8
Beith

RUSSELL Andrew
b. Airdrie 3.9.1904
Harthill A
Airdrieonians 24/25 1
25/26 2 1
26/27 1
Ayr U L 26/27 8 D2
Airdrieonians 27/28 2
Leicester C 27/28 FL
Falkirk 28/29
28/30
Morton 30/31 28 2
Queen of the South 31/32 D2
32/33 D2
33/34 18 1
Coleraine 34/35 IL
35/36 IL

RUSSELL B
Queen's Park 32/33 3
33/34 1

RUSSELL Balsillie
b. Glasgow
Queen's Park 26/27 2 1
27/28 10 3
28/29 2
29/30 5

RUSSELL David Kennedy 6 caps
b. Airdrie 6.4.1868
East Benhar Heatherbell
Shotts Minors
Stewarton
Broxburn
Heart of Midlothian 90/91 13 6
91/92 19 14
92/93 5 4
Preston NE 92/93 18 11 FL
Heart of Midlothian 92/93
93/94 15 6
94/95 14 3
95/96 15 3
Celtic 96/97 16 1
97/98 18 8
Preston NE 98/99 27 3 FL
Celtic 99/00 16
00/01 17 1
01/02 3
02/03
Broxburn

RUSSELL David Wallace
b. Dundee 7.4.1914 d. Birkenhead 12.6.2000
Dundee Violet
Forthill A
Dundee 34/35 1
East Fife 35/36 29 3 D2
36/37 33 2 D2
37/38 30 D2
Sheffield W 38/39 42 FL
39/40 1 FL

RUSSELL George
b. Ayrshire
Ayr
Aston Villa
Rangers 95/96 2
Ayr 95/96

RUSSELL Henry R
Queen's Park 00/01 10
01/02
Port Glasgow A 02/03 16
Albion R

RUSSELL J 1 cap
Cambuslang 90/91 16 1

RUSSELL J
Leith A 92/93 1
93/94 10
94/95 4

RUSSELL J R
b. Airdrie
Falkirk 28/29 24 1
29/30 18 2

RUSSELL James
St Bernards 95/96 4
96/97 1

RUSSELL James L
Stenhousemuir
Morton 01/02 12 3
02/03 15 4

RUSSELL John
Clyde 94/95 1 1

RUSSELL John
b. Carstairs 29.12.1872 d. Glasgow ?.8.1905
Glasgow Thistle
Leith A
St Mirren 95/96 7 2
Woolwich Arsenal 96/97 23 4 FL
Bristol C 97/98 22 6 SL
98/99 22 6 SL
99/00 9 2 SL
00/01 FL
Blackburn R 01/02 1 FL
Brighton 01/02 13 2 SL
Port Glasgow A 02/03
Motherwell 03/04 12 3
Doncaster R 04/05 3 FL

RUSSELL John
St Bernards 95/96 7
96/97 17
97/98 10

RUSSELL John
Strathclyde
Rangers
Dundee 34/35 13
35/36 13
Arbroath 36/37 3

RUSSELL John L
Port Glasgow Jnrs
Airdrieonians 23/24 3

RUSSELL John M
b. Glasgow
Queen's Park 23/24 4 2
24/25 29 10
25/26 31 5
26/27 23 1
27/28 16

RUSSELL John M
Queen's Park 31/32 9 1
32/33 1

RUSSELL John M
Kenmure Church
Queen's Park 35/36
36/37 7 2

RUSSELL John W
Invergowrie
Dundee 06/07 9 3
07/08
Queen's Park 08/09 2

RUSSELL Joseph
b. c1905
Forth R
Alva Albion R
Airdrieonians 27/28 8

RUSSELL Joseph V

Queen's Park 19/20 12 1

RUSSELL Robert
b. Paisley
Bo'ness
Glasgow Perthshire
Heart of Midlothian 09/10 8
10/11 3
Stockport Co 11/12 27 FL

RUSSELL Robert
b. Glasgow
Rothesay Royal V
Airdrieonians 29/30 2 1
30/31 2 1

RUSSELL Robert M

Galston
Maryhill
Clyde 31/32 11
32/33 19
33/34 18
34/35 5
Ayr U 34/35 1

RUSSELL Thomas
b. Cowdenbeath 23.11.1909
Cowdenbeath Wednesday
Cowdenbeath 28/29 1
29/30 4
30/31 32
31/32 33
32/33 11
Rangers 32/33 5
33/34 3
Newcastle U 34/35 7 FL
35/36 FL
36/37 FL
Horden CW 37/38
38/39

RUSSELL William
b. Hamilton 1903
Larkhall Jnrs
Blantyre Celtic 25/26
26/27
Chelsea 27/28 3 FL
28/29 13 FL
29/30 20 FL
30/31 17 1 FL
31/32 24 5 FL
32/33 31 1 FL
33/34 29 FL
34/35 14 1 FL
Heart of Midlothian 35/36 16
36/37
37/38 1
Rhyl A 38/39

RUSSELL William Fraser 2 caps
b. Falkirk 6.12.1901
Petershill
Glasgow Benburb
Airdrieonians 20/21 7 1
21/22 19 1
22/23 29 7
23/24 35 14
24/25 35 16
25/26 2
Preston NE 25/26 40 12 FL
26/27 40 5 FL
27/28 25 10 FL
28/29 8 6 FL
29/30 14 2 FL
30/31 7 1 FL
Shelbourne 31/32

RUTHERFORD Alexander

Leith A 94/95 2

RUTHERFORD James

St Cuthberts W 29/30
Dalbeattie Star 30/31
Queen of the South 30/31 D2
31/32 D2
32/33 D2
33/34 9 3
34/35 3 1
Stranraer 34/35
Alloa A 34/35 D2

RUTHERFORD John Burnet
b. Newbottle 9.11.1899
Winchburgh Violet
Hibernian 18/19 1 ?
Falkirk 18/19 3
19/20 4
20/21
21/22
22/23
Workington 22/23
Aberaman 23/24
Bridgend T 23/24
Swindon T 24/25 5 FL

RUTHERFORD Walter
d. ?.11.1944
Maryhill Jnrs
Singers Works
Yoker A
Kilmarnock 16/17 36 8
17/18 16 4
18/19
Alloa A 19/20
Ayr U 20/21 10 3
21/22 2
Johnstone

RUTHERFORD Walter

Rangers 16/17 1 1

SAEGER Harry B

Queen's Park 10/11 2

SALISBURY William
b. Govan 23.2.1899 d. Glasgow ?.1.1965
St Anthonys
Partick T 18/19 32 7
19/20 9 1
20/21 31 6
21/22 29 6
22/23 37 1
23/24 30
24/25 33 8
25/26 34 6
26/27 10 1
27/28 35 15
28/29 3
Liverpool 28/29 16 2 FL
Bangor 29/30 IL
Distillery 29/30 IL
Shelbourne 30/31 LI
Bangor 31/32 IL
32/33 IL
Partick T 33/34

SANDERS Robert
b. Maybole
Lugar Boswell
Clyde 29/30 8 2
East Stirlingshire 29/30 D2
30/31 D2
31/32 D2
St Cuthberts W 32/33

SANDERSON James N
b. Edinburgh
St Johnstone 24/25 17 2
25/26 3 1
St Bernards 26/27 D2

SANDERSON Robert Turnbull
b. Peebles 15.3.1887
Vale of Leithen
Peebles R
Celtic 07/08 1
08/09 1
Kilmarnock L 08/09
Spennymoor U
Barnsley 09/10 FL
Heart of Midlothian 10/11 10

SANKEY Stanley

Queen's Park 14/15 6
15/16
16/17 1

SANKEY Stanley

Albion R 19/20 1

SATTERTHWAITE James

Gateshead
Dundee 12/13 3

SAUNDERSON A

Dumbarton 92/93 8
93/94 13 2
94/95
95/96 16 5
96/97 13 ? D2

SAUNDERSON Albert

St Mirren 94/95 1

SAVAGE

Clyde 95/96 1

SAVAGE William
d. c1961
Motherwell Jnrs
Queen of the South 32/33 D2
33/34 36
34/35 36
35/36 32
36/37 36
37/38 36 3
38/39 35 1
46/47 28
47/48 8

SAWERS Alexander

Kilmarnock 85/86
86/87
87/88
88/89
89/90
Third Lanark 90/91 4
Clyde 91/92 22
92/93 4
Burnley 92/93 3 FL

SAWERS William 1 cap
b. Calton 13.6.1871 d. Glasgow 24.10.1927
Clyde 88/89
89/90
90/91
91/92 22 8
92/93 2
Blackburn R 92/93 24 11 FL
Stoke 93/94 17 5 FL
Dundee 94/95 14 6
Stoke 95/96 1 FL
Dundee 95/96 9 3
Kilmarnock 95/96 4 D2
Abercorn
Clyde 96/97 1

SCANLON Edward A
b. Hebburn 14.5.1890
Wallsend
North Shields A
Jarrow
Lincoln C 09/10 19 3 FL
10/11 10 FL
South Shields
Jarrow
Swindon T 14/15 9 2 SL
Hamilton A 19/20 16

SCARFF Peter 1 cap
b. Linwood 29.3.1908 d. Kilbarchan (?) 9.12.1933
Linwood St Convals
Celtic 28/29 16 6
Maryhill Hibernian L 28/29
Celtic 29/30 25 18
30/31 37 18
31/32 19 6
32/33

SCHOFIELD Charles

Barrhead Auburn V *
Bute A *
St Mirren 17/18 12 2

SCHOLES Alexander

Burnbank A
Hamilton A 06/07 6
08/09
09/10

SCLATER Robert

b. Polton 1908					
Polton Welfare					
Hibernian		29/30	8	2	
Dunfermline A		30/31			D2
Albion R		31/32			D2
		32/33			D2
Alloa A		33/34			D2
		34/35			D2
		35/36			D2
Waterford		36/37			LI
Shelbourne		36/37			LI
Ballymena U		37/38			IL
		38/39			IL
		39/40			IL
Derry C		40/41			IL

SCOBIE George H

b. Falkirk					
Falkirk		24/25	3		
		25/26	9		
		26/27	7		
		27/28	8		
		28/29	7		
		29/30	6		
		30/31	18		
		31/32	32		
		32/33			
East Stirlingshire		33/34			D2
Ayr U		34/35	11		

SCORGIE John

b. Aberdeen 9.1.1892					
Aberdeen Parkvale					
Aberdeen		12/13	7	2	
		13/14	16	1	
		14/15	1		
Birmingham		19/20			FL
Nuneaton T		20/21			
Hartlepools U		21/22	4	2	FL
Redditch T					
Tranmere R		22/23			FL
Aberdeen					
Worcester C	T	23/24			
Aberdeen Parkvale					

SCOTT

Third Lanark		90/91	17		

SCOTT

St Bernards		93/94	6	2	

SCOTT

St Mirren		93/94	1		

SCOTT

Clydebank		18/19	2	?	

SCOTT Alexander

Milton Parish Church League *					
Albion R *		30/31			D2
		31/32			D2
		32/33			D2
Cowdenbeath		33/34	25		

SCOTT Allan

Orion		97/98			
Forfar A		97/98			
Orion		98/99			
Dundee		98/99	6		
Forfar A		98/99			
Dundee					

SCOTT Archibald

Glasgow Ashfield					
Third Lanark		96/97	5	1	
Beith					
St Bernards		02/03			

SCOTT Archibald Teasdale

b. Airdrie 27.7.1905 d. Gosport 2.5.1990					
Bellshill A					
Gartsherrie A					
Airdrieonians		25/26			
		26/27	9		
Derby Co		27/28	9		FL
		28/29	3		FL
		29/30	6		FL
		30/31	4		FL
		31/32	1		FL
		32/33			FL
		33/34	4		FL
Brentford		34/35	2		FL
		35/36	1		FL
		36/37	2		FL
		37/38	1		FL

SCOTT Charles

K.I.A. 12.4.1917					
Lochee Central					
Forfar A					
Rangers		13/14	3		
St Johnstone		14/15	25	1	D2

SCOTT Edward R

b. Glasgow					
Battlefield					
Queen's Park		20/21	40	5	
		21/22	20	2	
		22/23	37	10	D2
		23/24	23	5	
		24/25			
		25/26	5	1	
		26/27	11	1	
		27/28	9	1	
		28/29	6	2	

SCOTT George

K.I.A.					
Lochgelly Celtic					
East Fife		33/34	31	7	D2
		34/35	33	13	D2
		35/36	33	14	D2
		36/37	27	6	D2
Aberdeen		36/37	5	1	
		37/38	10	1	
		38/39	8		

SCOTT George Archibald

b. Scoonie (?) 1865 d. Bishopbriggs 14.1.1937					
Abercorn					
Cowlairs					
Heart of Midlothian		90/91	18	6	
		91/92	20	4	
		92/93	16	6	
Cowlairs		93/94			D2
Leith A		93/94			
St Bernards		93/94			
Heart of Midlothian		94/95	16	6	
		95/96	3	1	
		96/97	1		
Kilmarnock	L	96/97			
Clyde		97/98	13	4	

SCOTT James

b. 1881					
St Mirren		03/04	8		
		04/05			
		05/06	2		FL

SCOTT James

b. Airdrie 1895 K.I.A., Somme 1.7.1916					
Craigton Thistle					
Petershill		12/13			
Raith R		13/14	28	14	
		14/15	31	11	

SCOTT James

Hamilton A		17/18	4		
		18/19	2		

SCOTT James

b. Stevenston c1882					
Ardeer Thistle					
Liverpool		10/11			FL
		11/12			FL
		12/13			FL
		13/14			FL
		14/15			FL
Dumbarton		19/20	29	1	
		20/21	34	1	
Third Lanark		21/22	2		
New York Giants		23/24	19		ASL
		24/25	22		ASL

SCOTT James

b. Edinburgh					
Wemyss A					
Raith R		25/26	9	3	
Arbroath		25/26	12	3	D2
Raith R		26/27			D2
Kettering T		26/27			
St Bernards		27/28			D2
Bathgate	T	27/28			D2
?		28/29			
		29/30			
		30/31			
Peebles R	T	31/32			

SCOTT James

Hamilton A		32/33	6		

SCOTT James A B

Queen's Park		31/32	1		
		32/33	4		
		33/34	2		
		34/35	3		

SCOTT James Mc

b. c1897					
Newtongrange U					
Scone Thistle					
Dalkeith Hibs					
Hibernian		19/20	16		

SCOTT John

Queen's Park		04/05	2		

SCOTT John

b. Shieldmuir					
Wishaw R					
Cambuslang R					
Hamilton A		08/09	17		
		09/10	27	2	
Bradford PA		09/10	7		FL
		10/11	24		FL
		11/12	32		FL
		12/13	38	1	FL
		13/14	38		FL
		14/15	38	1	FL
Clydebank	L	18/19			
Bradford PA		19/20	41		FL
		20/21	27	1	FL
Manchester U		21/22	23		FL
St Mirren		22/23	23		
New York Giants		23/24	19		ASL
		24/25	22		ASL

SCOTT John

b. Auchinleck					
Auchinleck Bluebell					
Ayr A					
Ayr U		19/20	7		
		20/21	13		

SCOTT John

b. Crieff c1898					
Muirkirk A					
Argyll & Sutherland Highlanders					
Norwich C					
East Stirlingshire		19/20			
Ayr U		20/21	6		
Reading		21/22	27	6	FL
		22/23	27	1	FL

SCOTT John

Kilmarnock		21/22	12		

SCOTT John

Douglasdale					
Hamilton A		36/37	16		
		37/38	28		
		38/39	34	3	

SCOTT John C

Cameron Highlanders					
Leith A		91/92	9	4	
		92/93	1		
		93/94	10	4	
Sheffield U		94/95			
		95/96			
Gainsborough T		96/97	29	10	FL
		97/98	27	6	FL
		98/99	32	4	FL
		99/00	4		FL

SCOTT Matthew McLintock 1 cap

b. Airdrie 11.7.1872					
Airdrieonians		91/92			
		92/93			
		93/94			
		94/95	17	1	D2
		95/96	9	1	D2
		96/97	14		D2
		97/98	9		D2
		98/99	13	1	D2
		99/00	13		D2
Newcastle U		00/01	5		FL
Albion R		01/02			
		02/03			
		03/04			D2
Airdrieonians		04/05	10		
		05/06	4		

SCOTT R

Rangers		91/92	12	1	
		92/93	10	1	

SCOTT Robert 1 cap

b. Airdrie 2.10.1870

Airdrieonians		88/89			
		89/90			
		90/91			
		91/92			
Celtic	L	92/93	1		
Airdrieonians		93/94			
		94/95	18	18	D2
		95/96	17	10	D2
		96/97	8	5	D2
		97/98	14	9	D2
		98/99	11	3	D2
		99/00	1		D2

SCOTT Robert W

Cumnock					
Kilmarnock		26/27	1		
Preston NE	T	27/28			FL

SCOTT Samuel

Port Glasgow A		95/96			D2
Bolton W		96/97	10		FL
		97/98	9		FL
Rangers		98/99			
Port Glasgow A		98/99			D2
		99/00			D2
		00/01			D2
Barrow		01/02			
Port Glasgow A		02/03	13		
		03/04	1		

SCOTT Thomas

b. Denny

Denny Hibs

Falkirk		17/18	34	?	
		18/19	30	?	
		19/20	37	3	
		20/21	34	3	
		21/22	41	2	
		22/23	37	4	
		23/24	26		
		24/25	35		
		25/26	28	1	
		26/27	34	2	
		27/28	29		
		28/29	24		
		29/30			
Morton		29/30	23		
Cork		30/31			LI

SCOTT Thomas M

Musselburgh A					
Hibernian		38/39	3		

SCOTT Thomas Mc

Mercantile Academy					
Cliftonville Olympic		92/93			
Cliftonville		93/94			IL
		94/95			IL
		95/96			IL
		96/97			IL
		97/98			IL
Partick T		98/99	4		
Cliftonville		99/00			IL
		00/01			IL
		01/02			IL
		02/03			IL

SCOTT Walter J

b. Willington Quay 1893 d. 1975

Bedlington U					
Heart of Midlothian		12/13	2		
		13/14	4		
		14/15	32		
Raith R		15/16	16		
St Bernards		15/16			
Dunfermline A		16/17			
Broxburn U		17/18			
Falkirk		18/19	7	?	
Hartlepools U		19/20			
Blyth Spartans		20/21			
South Shields		21/22	3		FL
Close Works					
Ashington		21/22	1		FL
New Delaval Villa					

SCOTT Walter P

Queen's Park		10/11	1		

SCOTT William

Lochgelly U *					
Falkirk		05/06	2		

SCOTT William

Lochgelly U		06/07			
Falkirk		07/08	7	3	
Lochgelly U	L	07/08			
Heart of Midlothian		08/09	16	7	
Lochgelly U		09/10			

SCOTT William

b. Bucksburn 10.10.1916 d. Bridge of Don 7.8.1994

Woodside					
Aberdeen		35/36	5	3	
		36/37	6	3	
		37/38	12	2	
Newcastle U		38/39	6	2	FL
		39/40	3	1	FL
Linfield *		41/42			IL
Consett					

SCOTT William John

Aberdeen		09/10	1		

SCOULAR

Cambuslang		90/91	1		
		91/92	1		

SCOULAR James Donald (or SCOULLIER)

b. c1888 d. Stornoway ?.4.1944

Queen's Park		07/08	7		
		08/09	5		
Morton		09/10	8		
Kilmarnock		10/11			
Lanemark *		10/11			

SCOULLAR

Abercorn		91/92	2	2	

SCOULLER Samuel S

Corkerhill					
Glasgow Perthshire					
Third Lanark		11/12	10	2	
		12/13	12	1	
Abercorn	T	13/14			D2
		14/15			D2
Clyde		15/16	20	7	
		16/17			
		17/18			
		18/19	2		
Armadale		19/20			
		20/21			
Beith		21/22			

SCRAGGS Matthew John Hoffman

b. Clogher 26.3.1889 d. Belfast 21.9.1960

Glentoran		09/10			IL
		10/11			IL
		11/12			IL
		12/13			IL
		13/14			IL
		14/15			IL
		15/16			IL
		16/17			IL
		17/18			IL
		18/19			IL
		19/20			IL
		20/21			IL
		21/22			IL
Clydebank		21/22	22		
		22/23			D2
		23/24	27	4	
		24/25			D2
		25/26	23		
Arbroath		26/27	14		D2
Dundee	L	26/27			
Glentoran		27/28			IL
Bangor		28/29			IL

SCULLION James

Kirkintilloch Rob Roy					
Hamilton A		21/22	29		
Carluke R *		22/23			
Bury *		22/23			FL
Kings Park *		23/24			D2

SEATON John

b. c1862 d. Pollokshields ?.9.1910 *

Dumbarton		94/95	4		
		95/96	8		
		96/97	2		D2
Clyde *					

SELFRIDGE James

Cadzow Oak					
Airdrieonians		06/07	4		
		07/08	8		

SELLARS William

Morton		02/03	2		
		03/04	7		
Renton					

SEMPLE John

b. Kirkintilloch 28.5.1889

Kirkintilloch Rob Roy					
Ayr U		14/15	10		
		15/16	14	2	
Dumbarton	L	16/17	34	1	
		17/18	1		
Renton	L	17/18			
Ayr U		17/18	19	?	
		18/19	30		
		19/20	37		
Luton T		20/21	7		FL
		21/22			FL
		22/23			FL

SEMPLE William

b. West Maryston 18.4.1886 d. Southport 4.6.1965

Baillieston Thistle					
Rutherglen Glencairn					
Celtic		07/08	7	2	
		08/09	1		
Millwall		09/10	39	3	SL
Carlisle U		10/11			
Haslingden		11/12			
Southport		12/13			
		13/14			
		14/15			
		19/20			
		20/21			
		21/22	32	2	FL
		22/23	7	1	FL

SERVICE D

Third Lanark		93/94	1		

SEYMOUR George Stanley

b. Kelloe 16.5.1892 d. Newcastle 24.12.1978

Newcastle U					
Shildon T					
Coxhoe					
Bradford C		11/12	1		FL
		12/13			FL
Morton		12/13	8	1	
		13/14	32	12	
		14/15	36	11	
		15/16	36	11	
		16/17	33	16	
		17/18	24	8	
		18/19	29	10	
		19/20	35	16	
Newcastle U		20/21	30	9	FL
		21/22	18	1	FL
		22/23	28	4	FL
		23/24	33	16	FL
		24/25	35	7	FL
		25/26	24	6	FL
		26/27	42	18	FL
		27/28	29	12	FL
		28/29	3		FL

SHANDLEY Joe

Queen of the South		24/25			
Dundee U		25/26	2	1	
Dundee	T	25/26			

SHANKLAND John

b. Kirkconnel 13.2.1893

Kilmarnock Juveniles					
Ardeer Thistle		14/15			
Kilmarnock		18/19	6	1	
		19/20	2		
Hurlford	L	19/20			
Nithsdale W		20/21			
Luton T		20/21	3		FL
Galston		21/22			
		22/23			
		23/24			D3

SHANKLY Alexander

b. Glenbuck 29.1.1897

Glenbuck Cherrypickers					
Ayr U		16/17	18	2	
		17/18	11	?	
Nithsdale W					

SHANKLY John D
b. Glenbuck 4.11.1903 d. Glasgow 18.5.1960
Glenbuck Cherrypickers
Nithsdale W
Portsmouth 22/23 2 1 FL
23/24 1 FL
Luton T 24/25 28 11 FL
25/26 18 9 FL
Carlisle U
Alloa A
Blackpool 30/31 5 FL
Morton 30/31 9 2
31/32 22 4
32/33 15 3
Kings Park 33/34 D2
Alloa A
Dalbeattie Star

SHANKLY Robert
b. Glenbuck
Douglasdale *
Douglas Water Thistle * 30/31
Falkirk T
Alloa A
Tunbridge Wells R
Falkirk 33/34 34 5
34/35 36 2
35/36 D2
36/37 36
37/38 37
38/39 38

SHANKS (John?)
Cowlairs 90/91 12 2

SHANNON William John
Partick T 97/98 4
Clydebank

SHARKEY John H
b. c1906
Shettleston
Heart of Midlothian 26/27 1

SHARP
Clyde 17/18 1 ?

SHARP Alexander
St Bernards 94/95 8 1
Bathgate 95/96

SHARP Alexander
b. Prestonpans 12.11.1910
Tranent Jnrs
Heart of Midlothian 27/28
Ayr U 28/29 7
29/30 7
Southampton 29/30 1 FL
East Fife T 30/31 2
Tranmere R 30/31 3 FL
Leith A 31/32 D2
Duns 31/32

SHARP Alexander
b. Dundee 12.10.1910
Dundee Violet
East Fife 32/33 29 4 D2
33/34 32 D2
34/35 12 6 D2
Blackburn R 34/35 7 1 FL
35/36 2 FL
Hull C 35/36 18 4 FL
Falkirk 36/37 28 4
37/38 33 1
Raith R 38/39 9 1

SHARP Alexander
b. c1917
Musselburgh A
Heart of Midlothian 36/37
Leith A L 36/37 D2
Glenavon 36/37 IL
37/38 IL
Albion R 38/39 33 2

SHARP Andrew
Motherwell
Rangers 98/99 4 3
99/00 3 1
00/01 2 2
Morton 00/01 14 7
01/02 9 1
Hamilton A

SHARP Andrew
Motherwell 03/04 17 5

SHARP Andrew
Motherwell 08/09 8
09/10 2

SHARP B
Vale of Leven 91/92 1 1

SHARP Claude Young
b. Springburn 3.11.1909
Kirkintilloch Rob Roy
Aberdeen 31/32 3
32/33
33/34
34/35
Doncaster R 35/36 FL
36/37 1 FL
37/38 1 FL
Clyde 38/39

SHARP David
b. Wishaw c1900
Cleland Jnrs
Heart of Midlothian 20/21 2 3
Stenhousemuir L

SHARP G
Vale of Leven 90/91 14

SHARP J
Vale of Leven 90/91 11

SHARP James
Broxburn A
Heart of Midlothian 96/97 10 4
97/98 11 8
98/99
99/00 1

SHARP James 5 caps
b. Jordanstone 11.10.1880 d. Fulham 18.11.1949
East Craigie
Dundee 99/00 17
00/01 20 1
01/02 18
02/03 22 1
03/04 16 3
Fulham 04/05 16 SL
Woolwich Arsenal 05/06 34 2 FL
06/07 36 1 FL
07/08 32 1 FL
Rangers 07/08 1
08/09 18
Fulham 08/09 15 FL
09/10 28 FL
10/11 18 FL
11/12 25 FL
12/13 11 FL
Chelsea 12/13 23 FL
13/14 21 FL
14/15 17 FL
Fulham 19/20 1 1 FL

SHARP James
K.I.A.
Grange R
Falkirk 13/14 5

SHARP James
Dalkeith Thistle
Hibernian 25/26 20

SHARP James
b. Motherwell
Craigneuk Jnrs
Hamilton A 28/29 4
Rotherham U 28/29 4 1 FL
29/30 2 FL

SHARP James
Dunfermline A 34/35 4

SHARP James N
Dunfermline A 26/27 10

SHARP James N
Third Lanark 33/34 11
Rhyl A

SHARP John
b. Edinburgh (?)
Leith Amateurs
Hibernian 09/10 13 5

SHARP John
b. Bathgate
Bathgate
Heart of Midlothian 15/16 13
16/17 17 3
17/18 32 10
18/19 31 5
19/20 24 1
20/21 20
21/22 16 3
Albion R 22/23 37 9
23/24 D2
Bathgate 24/25 D2

SHARP John P C
Rangers 98/99 1

SHARP Wilfred
b. Bathgate 8.4.1907 d. Sefton South ?.6.1981
Pumpherston R
Kirkintilloch Rob Roy
Clydebank 25/26 10
26/27 D2
27/28 D2
28/29 D2
Airdrieonians 29/30 38
30/31 38 2
31/32 37 2
Tunbridge Wells R 32/33
Airdrieonians 33/34 35 2
Sheffield W 34/35 24 1 FL
35/36 24 1 FL
Bradford PA 36/37 17 1 FL
Burton T

SHARP William M
Johnstone
Kilbirnie Ladeside
Clyde 09/10 4
10/11 1
11/12
St Mirren 12/13
Kilbirnie Ladeside 12/13
Johnstone 13/14 D2

SHARPE Drummond
Third Lanark 98/99 1

SHARPE Hugh
b. c1915
Northern Glenburn
Third Lanark 36/37 2

SHAW
Third Lanark 90/91 2

SHAW
Abercorn 91/92 1

SHAW
St Mirren 92/93 18 6
93/94 8 1
94/95 4

SHAW
Abercorn 96/97 3

SHAW Charles
b. Twechar 21.9.1885 d. New York 27.3.1938
Baillieston Thistle
Kirkintilloch Harp
Port Glasgow A 05/06 3
06/07 33
QPR 07/08 38 SL
08/09 40 SL
09/10 42 SL
10/11 38 SL
11/12 37 SL
12/13 37 SL
Celtic 13/14 38
14/15 38
15/16 38
16/17 38
17/18 34
18/19 32
19/20 39
20/21 42
21/22 40
22/23 33
23/24 38
24/25 11
Clyde L 24/25
New Bedford Whalers 25/26 27 ASL

SHAW David
b. Annathill 5.5.1917 d. 1977
Banknock Juveniles
Grange R
Hibernian 38/39 1
46/47 28
47/48 28
48/49 14
49/50 15
Aberdeen 50/51 23
51/52 14 1
52/53 13

SHAW Hugh
b. Clydebank d. ?.2.1976
Clydebank Corinthians
Clydebank Jnrs
Hibernian 18/19 20 ?
19/20 25 1
20/21 24 3
21/22 37 3
22/23 31 1
23/24 29 1
24/25 35 2
25/26 33 2
Rangers 26/27 36 2
Heart of Midlothian 27/28 33 2
28/29 18
29/30 6 2
East Fife 30/31 27
31/32 D2
Leith A 32/33 D2
Elgin C 33/34
Buckie Thistle T 33/34

SHAW Hugh Crawford
b. Uddingston 31.7.1879
Queen's Park 03/04
Hamilton A 04/05 3 1 D2
Albion R 05/06 D2
Rangers 05/06 6 3
Celtic 05/06 1
Kilmarnock L 06/07
Albion R

SHAW John
Scotstoun Jnrs
Queen's Park 15/16 2

SHAW John 4 caps
b. Annathill 29.11.1912 d. Glasgow 13.6.2000
Benburb
Airdrieonians 33/34 37
34/35 37
35/36 35 1
36/37 31 2 D2
37/38 34 2 D2
Rangers 38/39 36
46/47 28
47/48 28 1
48/49 27
49/50 29
50/51 18
51/52 2
52/53 1

SHAW Robert
Pollok
Queen's Park 11/12 8 3
QPR 12/13 SL
Partick T 12/13

SHAW Robert
Battlefield
Queen's Park
Clydebank 20/21 7 1

SHAW Robert
b. Kilsyth
Kilsyth R
Clyde 22/23 4
23/24 1 1

SHAW Thomas
Airdrieonians 12/13 1

SHAW William
b. Kilmarnock
Kilmarnock Oakvale
Kilmarnock 05/06 23 2
06/07 21 1
07/08 26
08/09 9
Bristol R 09/10 38 3 SL
10/11 34 3 SL
11/12 31 SL
Dumbarton Harp 12/13
Cowdenbeath

SHEA Daniel
b. Wapping 6.11.1887 d. Wapping 25.12.1960
Builders Arms, Stepney
Manor Park A
West Ham U 07/08 13 3 SL
08/09 36 16 SL
09/10 38 29 SL
10/11 35 25 SL
11/12 36 24 SL
12/13 22 16 SL
Blackburn R 12/13 15 12 FL
13/14 36 27 FL
14/15 21 14 FL
Celtic L 18/19 1
Blackburn R 19/20 25 9 FL
West Ham U 20/21 16 1 FL
Fulham 20/21 23 4 FL
21/22 38 11 FL
22/23 39 8 FL
Coventry C 23/24 39 6 FL
24/25 21 5 FL
Clapton Orient 24/25 10 3 FL
25/26 23 5 FL
Sheppey U

SHEARER
St Mirren 92/93 3 1

SHEARER Robert
Cambuslang R
Third Lanark 15/16 16
Abercorn 15/16

SHEARER Robert C
Falkirk 14/15 6
15/16 25 10
16/17 21 5
17/18 10 ?

SHEDDEN Alexander
Bridge of Weir
Dumbarton 21/22 1

SHEPHERD Bert
Dundee 94/95 1

SHEPHERD James
Third Lanark 10/11 2 1
Renton 11/12

SHERIDAN James
b. Downpatrick 15.5.1882 d. Glasgow ?
Cambuslang Hibernian
Everton 02/03 18 2 FL
03/04 2 2 FL
Stoke 04/05 12 1 FL
New Brompton 05/06 8 1 SL
06/07 SL
07/08 SL
Shelbourne 08/09 IL
09/10 IL
Hamilton A T 10/11 5

SHERIDAN James
Clyde 09/10 2 4

SHEPHERD John
Third Lanark 97/98 7

SHERLAW David Drummond
b. Penicuik 17.9.1901
Dalkeith Thistle
Bathgate 24/25 D2
St Bernards 24/25 D2
Bristol C 25/26 20 6 FL
Charlton A 26/27 41 19 FL
27/28 35 13 FL
28/29 2 FL
Brentford 28/29 27 7 FL
29/30 1 1 FL
30/31 6 2 FL
31/32 FL
St Johnstone 32/33 8 4
Montrose L 32/33 D2

SHERRINGTON Edward R
Queen's Park 38/39 6

SHEVLIN Peter
b. Wishaw 18.11.1905 d. Manchester 10.10.1948
Uddingston St Johns
Pollok Jnrs
St Rochs 24/25
Celtic 24/25 27
25/26 38
26/27 23
South Shields 27/28 27 FL
28/29 39 FL
Nelson 29/30 37 FL
30/31 16 FL
Shelbourne 31/32 LI
Hamilton A 32/33 5
33/34 29
Celtic L 33/34
Hamilton A 34/35 37
Albion R 35/36 16

SHIELS Denis
b. Ireland
Clyde 15/16 1
16/17
Shelbourne 17/18
18/19
19/20 IL
20/21
21/22 LI
22/23 LI

SHIELS Thomas
Clyde 96/97 12
Stevenston Thistle
Wishaw U 01/02

SHIMMONS William G
b. Belfast
Cambuslang R
Clyde 16/17 35 9
17/18 17 ?
18/19 4 ?

SHINGLETON Thomas
b. Glasgow
Shettleston
Clyde 15/16 37
16/17 38
17/18 30
Rangers L 17/18 2
Clyde 18/19 28
19/20 39
20/21 42
21/22 33
22/23 18
Clydebank 22/23 D2
Clyde 23/24 38
24/25 D2
25/26 D2
Dunfermline A 26/27 21

SHORTT Joseph
b. Johnston
Shettleston Jnrs
Albion R 19/20 32
Armadale 20/21
Airdrieonians 21/22 35
22/23 9
Armadale 23/24 D2
24/25 D2
Stenhousemuir 25/26 D2

SHORTT Matthew
b. Dumfries 5.2.1889
Nithbank
Balmoral
Skares Burnock
Dumfries
Dalbeattie Star 09/10
Millwall T 09/10 SL
Woolwich Arsenal T 10/11 4 FL
Kilmarnock 10/11 6 1
11/12 20 2
12/13 30
13/14 27
14/15 36
15/16 27 1
Clydebank 16/17
17/18 23 5
Kilmarnock 18/19 29 1
19/20 37
20/21 25
21/22 25 1
Llanelly 22/23
Fall River Marksmen 23/24 2 ASL
Brooklyn Wanderers 23/24 2 ASL
24/25 36 2 ASL
25/26 10 ASL
Philadelphia Field Club 25/26 8 ASL
Boston Wonder Workers 26/27 10 ASL
Brooklyn Wanderers 26/27 10 ASL
27/28 20 ASL

SIBBALD

St Bernards 93/94 14
Leith A 94/95 3

SIBBALD Robert S

Queen's Park 14/15 6
15/16 38 12
16/17 11 2
Partick T 17/18 6
USA

SIM James B

Queen's Park 05/06 6 1
06/07 5 4
07/08 16 9
Sheffield U

SIM John

St Mirren 33/34 9 1

SIM Robert

Petershill
St Mirren 16/17 3

SIM W R

Queen's Park 16/17 1

SIME Thomas

Falkirk 17/18 12 ?

SIMMS Ernest
b. c1896
Vale of Clyde
Clyde 18/19 9
Vale of Leven 19/20
Abercorn
Vale of Clyde
Reading 20/21 1 FL

SIMPSON

Clyde 99/00 1

SIMPSON George

Duntochter Hibs
Ayr U 21/22 2

SIMPSON Henry C
b. Aberdeenshire
Peterhead
St Bernards 07/08 D2
08/09 D2
09/10 D2
Leicester Fosse 09/10 7 FL
Raith R 10/11 4
Ayr U 10/11 16 11 D2
11/12 D2
12/13 D2
East Stirlingshire 13/14 D2

SIMPSON Hugh

Shettleston
Bo'ness
Glossop 04/05 12 2 FL
Raith R 05/06 D2
06/07 D2
07/08 D2
08/09 D2
09/10 D2
10/11 20 2
11/12 12
Leith A 12/13 D2
Abercorn 13/14 D2
Cowdenbeath 14/15 D2

SIMPSON J

Queen's Park 09/10 1

SIMPSON James 3 caps
b. Ardrossan 2.4.1873
Saltcoats V
Third Lanark 94/95 16
95/96 18
96/97 17 2
97/98 16
98/99 5 1
99/00 17 1
00/01 16

SIMPSON James

Cowdenbeath 32/33 2

SIMPSON James McMillan 14 caps
b. Ladybank 29.10.1908 d. 1972
Auchtermuchty Bellevue
Newburgh WE
Dundee U 25/26 21 2
26/27 30 4
Rangers 27/28 7 1
28/29 5
29/30 8
30/31 12
31/32 33
32/33 32
33/34 29 1
34/35 37 1
35/36 35
36/37 31 2
37/38 34
38/39 25
Buckie Thistle

SIMPSON James W
b. Leven c1909
Wellesley Jnrs
Third Lanark T 28/29 4
Wellesley Jnrs 29/30
30/31
Third Lanark 31/32 38
32/33 33
33/34 7
34/35 D2
35/36 2
Morton 36/37 D2
37/38 28

SIMPSON John
b. Pendleton 25.12.1886 d. Falkirk 4.1.1959
Grange R
Laurieston Jnrs
Rangers T
Falkirk 05/06 30 9
06/07 33 21
07/08 33 33
08/09 32 24
09/10 32 24
10/11 18 4
Blackburn R 10/11 11 FL
11/12 35 2 FL
12/13 34 9 FL
13/14 34 2 FL
14/15 37 3 FL
Falkirk 15/16 5
16/17 32 8
17/18 34 ?
18/19 21 ?

SIMPSON John

Dundee 16/17 1

SIMPSON John
b. Glasgow 2.2.1908 d. 13.5.1999
Queen's Park district league
Maryhill Jnrs
Partick T 27/28
28/29 7 5
29/30 23 22
30/31 29 25
31/32 18 7
Plymouth A 32/33 5 2 FL
33/34 4 FL
34/35 2 1 FL
Ayr U 35/36 2
Stranraer 35/36
Sligo R 35/36 LI
Stranraer 36/37

SIMPSON John A G

Beardmore's (Mossend)
Mossend A
Ayr U 27/28 D2
28/29 14 3
East Stirlingshire 29/30 D2

SIMPSON John J

Aberdeen 06/07
07/08 1

SIMPSON Peter Robb

Crieff Earngrove
St Johnstone 36/37 3 1
37/38 24 17
38/39 35 12

SIMPSON Robert Albert
b. Chorlton cum Hardy 1888
Westburn
Aberdeen 06/07 10 3
07/08 22 6
08/09 24 10
09/10 30 10
Bradford PA 10/11 25 2 FL
11/12 24 6 FL
12/13 4 FL
Brighton 12/13 22 8 SL
13/14 8 3 SL

SIMPSON Thomas M
b. Dundee 1904
Dundee Osborne
Dundee U 23/24 20 D2
24/25 37 4 D2
25/26 28 6
26/27 16 4
Brighton 27/28 30 6 FL
Montrose

SIMPSON William A

Ruchil UF Church
Glasgow Perthshire
Third Lanark 36/37
37/38 8
38/39 19 1

SIMPSON William C

Grange R
Bo'ness 27/28 14
28/29 D2
Norwich C

SIMPSON William Stewart
b. Annan 1897
Solway Star
Blackburn R 21/22 4 FL
Aberaman A 22/23
Aberavon 23/24
Morton 24/25 2

SIMPSON William Swan
b. Cowdenbeath 30.10.1907 d. Erdington 27.02.1986
Donisbristle Colliery
Cowdenbeath YMCA
Fulford White Rose
Dunbar
Musselburgh Bruntonians
Clyde 27/28 2 1
28/29 27 9
29/30 31 6
30/31 36
31/32 16 1
Aston Villa 31/32 2 FL
32/33 13 1 FL
33/34 11 FL
34/35 3 FL
Cowdenbeath 35/36 D2
Northampton T 36/37 42 FL
Walsall 37/38 36 1 FL
38/39 31 3 FL
Bromsgrove R

SIMS Alexander

St Johnstone 24/25 2

SINCLAIR

Cowlairs 90/91 3

SINCLAIR

Dumbarton 95/96 8

SINCLAIR

Clydebank 20/21 3

SINCLAIR Andrew
b. c1910
Clydebank
Motherwell 33/34 3
34/35 4
35/36
Bury 35/36 FL
Cowdenbeath 36/37 D2

SINCLAIR George William Lloyd 3 caps
b. Leith 25.9.1889
Kings Park (Edinburgh)
Leith A
Heart of Midlothian 08/09 33 7
09/10 31 7
10/11 30 2
11/12 22 3
12/13 30 3
13/14 25 3
14/15
15/16 27 2
16/17 14 1
17/18 32 2
18/19 27 6
19/20 37 8
20/21 18 1
Dunfermline A 21/22 D2
Cowdenbeath 22/23 D2
23/24 D2
New Bedford Whalers 24/25 22 3 ASL
J & P Coats 25/26 13 ASL
Philadelphia Field Club 25/26 10 ASL
Montreal Scottish

SINCLAIR Henry

St Johnstone 36/37 2
37/38 3

SINCLAIR Malcolm J M

Dundas Congregational Churches
Renfrew Jnrs
Third Lanark 38/39 3
46/47 2
Falkirk 46/47 10 1
Dundee U 47/48 16 2 D2

SINCLAIR Robert Dunlop
b. Winchburgh 29.6.1915 d. 1993
Musselburgh A
Heart of Midlothian
Musselburgh A 35/36
36/37
Falkirk 37/38 10 1
38/39 7
Chesterfield 39/40 2 FL
Darlington 46/47 40 4 FL
47/48 29 7 FL

SINCLAIR Thomas Mackie
b. Alva 13.3.1907
Alva Albion R 27/28
Celtic 27/28 2
South Shields 28/29 42 FL
29/30 42 FL
Gateshead 30/31 41 1 FL
31/32 40 FL
32/33 12 FL
Alloa A T 34/35 D2

SINCLAIR Thomas S
b. Glasgow
Rutherglen Glencairn 00/01
01/02
02/03
Morton 03/04 26
Rangers 04/05 16
05/06 30
Celtic L 06/07 6
Newcastle U 06/07 3 FL
07/08 FL
08/09 FL
09/10 1 FL
10/11 2 FL
11/12 2 FL
Dumbarton Harp 12/13
Dunfermline A 12/13 D2
Stevenston U 16/17
Kilmarnock 16/17 3
Stevenston U 17/18
18/19

SINCLAIR William

Broxburn U
Airdrieonians 13/14 5
14/15 10 2
15/16 6

SKENE Clydesdale Duncan
b. Larbert 1884 d. ?.1.1946
Falkirk Amateurs
Queen's Park 03/04 1
04/05
05/06 4 1
St Johnstone 06/07
Falkirk 06/07 3 4
07/08 28 23
08/09
Queen's Park 09/10 16 6
10/11 4 1
Stenhousemuir 11/12
Glentoran 12/13 IL
Dundee 13/14 12 7
Match played for Stenhousemuir under the name Jackson

SKENE James

Lochee U
Dundee 98/99 6

SKENE Leslie Henderson 1 cap
b. Larbert 22.8.1882
George Watson's College
Bromage A
Edinburgh University
Queen's Park 01/02 1
Hibernian 01/02 1
Stenhousemuir 02/03
Queen's Park 02/03 1
03/04 23
04/05 16
05/06 11
Stenhousemuir 06/07
Fulham 07/08 36 FL
08/09 27 FL
09/10 25 FL
Glentoran 10/11 IL
11/12 IL

SKILLEN James
b. Ballochmyle 27.5.1893
Auchinleck Talbot
Kilmarnock 22/23 1
23/24 19 4
Accrington S 24/25 25 8 FL
Barrow 25/26 28 14 FL
Morton 26/27 1
Royal Albert 26/27

SKILLEN John
b. 1879 d. 1942
Kilbirnie Ladeside
Kilmarnock 06/07 11 5
07/08 6 2
Ayr Parkhouse 07/08 D2
Swindon T 08/09 2 SL
Ayr Parkhouse 09/10 D2
Lanemark 09/10

SKINNER J

Morton 24/25 1

SKINNER Robert
b. Glasgow
Clydebank Jnrs
Kilmarnock 21/22 7 2
22/23
St Mirren 23/24 4 1
Morton 23/24 16
Dunfermline A 23/24 D2
Ayr U 24/25 14 7
Dunfermline A 24/25 D2
25/26 38 53 D2
26/27 33 24
27/28 16 10
Cowdenbeath L 27/28
Airdrieonians 27/28 1
28/29 22 9
29/30 33 24
30/31 23 9
Shelbourne 31/32 LI

SLACK James

Glasgow Perthshire
Raith R 11/12 21 4
Cowdenbeath 12/13 D2

SLADE Donald
b. Southampton 26.11.1888 d. Southampton 24.3.1980
Shirley Warren
Southampton Ramblers 07/08
Blackpool T 08/09 FL
09/10 FL
Southampton 10/11 2 SL
11/12 1 SL
Lincoln C 12/13 14 7 FL
13/14 9 2 FL
Arsenal 13/14 12 4 FL
Fulham 14/15 17 4 FL
Dundee 19/20 29 13
20/21 6
Ayr U 20/21 30 11
21/22 37 18
22/23 19 5
23/24 3

SLATER John B C

Hibernian 05/06 1

SLAVEN Patrick
b. Rutherglen 22.4.1878
Fauldhouse Hibernian
Celtic 96/97 1
Motherwell 97/98 D2
Dykehead 98/99
99/00
Carfin Shamrock 99/00
Dykehead 99/00
Albion R 00/01
East Benhar A

SLAVIN John
b. Carnoustie
Forthill
Raith R 21/22 2
22/23 1
23/24 14
24/25 11 1
Arbroath 25/26 6 10 D2
Heart of Midlothian 25/26 14 7
26/27 15
New York Nationals 27/28 39 1 ASL
28/29 29 2 ASL
29A 20 ASL
29/30 26 2 ASL
New York Giants 30A 20 ASL
31S 17 1 ASL
31A 20 2 ASL

SLAVIN Maurice
b. Lanarkshire
Strathclyde
Hamilton A 07/08 33
Broxburn 08/09
Hamilton A 09/10 16
Dykehead

SLAVIN Thomas
b. Maryhill 1894 d. Maryhill 30.1.1944
Petershill
Raith R * L 14/15
Benburb
Third Lanark 21/22 27
Aberdeen 22/23
Arbroath 23/24 2 D2

SLEIGH Arthur Robert

Edinburgh C
Queen's Park 38/39 6 2

SLIGO James

St Bernards 97/98 2

SLIMMON David Glencross
b. Muirkirk 1892 (or 1896) K.I.A.,France 23.7.1917
Kilmarnock Hazelburn
Kilmarnock V
St Andrews U
Auchinleck Talbot 11/12
12/13
13/14
Kilmarnock 14/15 16
15/16 1

SLOAN

St Mirren 90/91 1
91/92 1

SLOAN

Third Lanark 93/94 1

SLOAN

Port Glasgow A 06/07 1

SLOAN

Dumbarton 14/15 1

SLOAN Eric

India of Inchinnan
St Mirren 30/31 3
31/32 2
Queen's Park 32/33 1
India of Inchinnan

SLOAN P Robertson

Bolton W
Aberdeen 15/16 2
Raith R 16/17 1

SLOAN Thomas Parker 1 cap
b. Eastwood 4.10.1880
Thornliebank
Glasgow Perthshire
Third Lanark 00/01 14 2
01/02 15
02/03 9 1
03/04 23 1
04/05 24
05/06 15
06/07 28 2
07/08 25 5
08/09 29
09/10 29
10/11 23

SMART David
b. Sorn 1887
Cronberry Eglington
Kilmarnock 11/12 23
Lanemark 12/13
Nithsdale W 13/14

SMEATON John Raymond
b. Perth 29.7.1914 d. Cleveland ?.2.1984
Scone Thistle
St Johnstone 34/35 2
35/36 6 1
Blackburn R 36/37 18 4 FL
37/38 20 5 FL
Sunderland 38/39 28 4 FL
39/40 3 FL
Jeanfield Swifts
Albion R 46/47 D2
East Fife 46/47 6 1 D2
St Johnstone 47/48 22 9 D2
48/49 12 2 D2
49/50 24 4 D2

SMELLIE Robert

Clyde 96/97 1 1
97/98 1
Beith

SMELLIE Robert M

Bo'ness Cadora
St Johnstone 36/37 10
37/38 22 1
38/39 4 1
46/47 7 D2

SMILLIE Henry J
b. Yoker
Yoker A
Heart of Midlothian 20/21 6 1
21/22 9 3
St Johnstone 22/23 16 5 D2
Dundee Hibs 22/23 D2
St Mirren 23/24 7 2
Armadale 24/25 D2
Helensburgh 24/25 D3
25/26 D3
Clydebank

SMITH

Abercorn 90/91 1

SMITH

Cowlairs 90/91 1

SMITH

St Mirren 90/91 2
91/92 4 1

SMITH

Vale of Leven 90/91 7

SMITH

Dumbarton 91/92 8
92/93 17
93/94 15

SMITH

Abercorn 92/93 6 2

SMITH

Clyde 92/93 5

SMITH

St Bernards 96/97 1

SMITH

Clyde 06/07 1

SMITH

Third Lanark 14/15 2

SMITH

Ayr U 15/16 3 3
16/17 2

SMITH

Morton 15/16 1

SMITH

Raith R 16/17 3

SMITH

Ayr U 17/18 3 ?

SMITH

Dumbarton 17/18 1

SMITH

Partick T 18/19 1

SMITH

Dumbarton 20/21 1

SMITH A

Dumbarton 92/93 3

SMITH Adam C

Canada
Cowdenbeath
Clyde 12/13 1
Kilmarnock 13/14 1

SMITH Albert Charles
b. Dromoyne 1905
Barclay Curle
Third Lanark T
Petershill
Manchester U 26/27 4 1 FL
Preston N E 27/28 8 FL
28/29 15 3 FL
29/30 10 3 FL
30/31 7 4 FL
Morton T 30/31
Dolphin 31/32 LI
Carlisle U 32/33 39 1 FL
Glenavon 33/34 IL
Belfast Celtic 33/34 IL
Derry C 34/35 IL
35/36 IL
Ayr U 36/37 23 11 D2
37/38 20 7

SMITH Alexander
b. Old Kilpatrick 7.11.1873 d. Old Kilpatrick ?.1.1908
St Mirren 93/94 4
94/95 3 1
Lincoln C 95/96 28 8 FL
96/97 15 1 FL
Third Lanark 97/98
Swindon T 98/99 21 1 SL
99/00 25 SL

SMITH Alexander 20 caps
b. Darvel 7.11.1876 d. 12.11.1954
Darvel
Rangers 94/95 6 3
95/96 17 13
96/97 17 5
97/98 17 12
98/99 18 12
99/00 16 13
00/01 17 7
01/02 18 5
02/03 22 6
03/04 16 4
04/05 26 7
05/06 24 3
06/07 25 8
07/08 22 3
08/09 28 9
09/10 21 2
10/11 29 4
11/12 27 2
12/13 22 5
13/14 11 5
14/15 7

SMITH Alexander

Port Glasgow A
Third Lanark 00/01 17
01/02 13
02/03 1

SMITH Alfred
b. Bury 1890
Bury Tradesmen
Bury 08/09 1 2 FL
09/10 1 1 FL
Stalybridge C
Hamilton A 13/14 11 3
Stalybridge C

SMITH Alfred
b. Dundee c1917
Partick T 35/36 1
36/37 16 7
37/38 11 4
Dundee Logie
Cowdenbeath 38/39 D2

SMITH Augustus
b. Woolwich
Ebbw Vale
Dundee 27/28 29 24
28/29 19 12

SMITH Charles James
b. Cardiff 26.8.1915 d. Torquay 31.3.1984
Exeter Toc-H
Exeter C 36/37 5 FL
Yeovil T 37/38 SL
Aberdeen 37/38 8 2
38/39 13 3
Torquay U 46/47 23 FL

SMITH David
d. ?.3.1915
Jordanhill
Maryhill
Glasgow Perthshire
Clydebank
Heart of Midlothian 02/03 3
Abercorn 02/03

SMITH David

Glasgow Ashfield
Hamilton A 19/20 17 5
Armadale 19/20

SMITH David B
b. c1917
Wemyss U
Third Lanark 37/38
38/39 1

SMITH David Lamont McQueen
b. Coatbridge 6.7.1903
Pollok
Albion R 22/23
Mid Annandale 23/24 D3
Albion R 24/25 D2
Queen of the South 24/25 D2
25/26 D2
26/27 D2
27/28 D2
Hamilton A 28/29 34
Gillingham 29/30 20 FL
30/31 6 FL
Brentford 31/32 7 FL

SMITH E

Ayr U 34/35 5

SMITH Edward Clark
b. c1907
Carluke R
Dundee U 29/30 8 2

SMITH Effingham G
Partick T 05/06 1
Vale of Leven
Beith
St Bernards

SMITH Frank
St Bernards 98/99 1
99/00 1

SMITH Frederick
Liverpool
Heart of Midlothian 10/11 13 1
11/12 7 4

SMITH G
Cambuslang 91/92 14 1

SMITH George
Dundee 13/14 7
14/15 5

SMITH George C
Morton 37/38 11

SMITH George L
Inverness Caledonian
St Johnstone 33/34 3
34/35
35/36 6
Falkirk 36/37 24

SMITH George M C
Buckie Thistle
Clyde 34/35 10
Galston L 34/35
Montrose 35/36 D2
36/37 D2
37/38 D2

SMITH H
Third Lanark 90/91 15
91/92 20
92/93 13
93/94 12
94/95 17
95/96 1

SMITH Harry
Queen's Park 10/11 2 1
Thornhill 11/12

SMITH Harry McPherson
b. Dundee 5.5.1911
Logie Jnrs
Dundee U
Dunfermline A
Dundee 30/31 7
31/32 12 2
32/33 15 3
33/34 2
Raith R 33/34 D2
Clapton Orient 34/35 11 1 FL
35/36 28 5 FL
36/37 38 10 FL
37/38 40 11 FL
38/39 31 7 FL
39/40 1 FL

SMITH Henry J
Queen's Park 19/20 3

SMITH Hugh
b. Port Glasgow c1913
Clyde U
Port Glasgow Jnrs
Celtic 30/31 3 1
31/32 9
32/33 9 1
33/34 4
Ayr U 34/35
Tunbridge Wells R 35/36
Morton 35/36 D2
36/37 D2
37/38 27 4
Alloa A 38/39 D2

SMITH J D
Clydebank 20/21 1

SMITH James
Dundee 96/97 17 7

SMITH James
Third Lanark 97/98 17 5
98/99 1
99/00
00/01 2

SMITH James
St Mirren 03/04 16 3
04/05 5
Bo'ness 05/06

SMITH James
Rangers
Morton 09/10 23 5
10/11 2
Arthurlie 11/12 D2

SMITH James
Falkirk 19/20 3
Dunfermline A 19/20

SMITH James
b. Darvel 1896
Glasgow Highlanders
Larkhall Thistle
Rangers 19/20 6
20/21 9
21/22 2 1
Aberdeen 22/23 35 4
23/24 35 7
24/25 37 3
25/26 37 9
26/27 27 5
27/28 35 11
28/29 33 8
29/30 36 5
30/31 22 2
Shamrock R 31/32 LI
32/33 LI
33/34 LI
Glentoran 34/35 IL
Brora R 35/36

SMITH James 2 caps
b. Slamannan 24.9.1911 d. 4.12.2003
Argyll Rob Roy
Denny Hibs
Longriggend Rob Roy
Middlesbrough T
East Stirlingshire 28/29 15 17 D2
Rangers 28/29 2
29/30 1 1
30/31 21 21
31/32 8 5
32/33 34 33
33/34 32 41
34/35 32 36
35/36 28 31
36/37 37 31
37/38 32 22
38/39 7 4

SMITH James B
b. Clydebank
St Anthonys
Dunfermline A 21/22 D2
Clydebank 22/23 D2
23/24 37 3
Heart of Midlothian 24/25 34 2
25/26 37 11
26/27 23 4
27/28 10 8
Raith R 27/28 8 2
Heart of Midlothian 28/29 36 15
29/30 15 7
30/31 8 1
31/32 22 7
32/33 26 7
33/34 14 1

SMITH James B
Cork C 31/32
Dalry Thistle 31/32
Benburb
Heart of Midlothian
East Stirlingshire 32/33 29 11
33/34 D2
Dundee U 34/35 31 15 D2
35/36 20 4 D2

SMITH James D
b. Glasgow 26.7.1882 (?)
Rutherglen Hawthorn
Rutherglen Glencairn
Third Lanark 11/12 23 11
12/13 8 1
Abercorn 12/13 D2
Glentoran 13/14 IL
13/14 IL
Third Lanark 14/15 27 19
15/16 4
16/17
17/18
Clydebank L 18/19 2 ?
Clyde 18/19 3 ?
19/20 14 5
20/21 10 2
Dunfermline A L
Plymouth A 21/22 1 FL
Port Vale 22/23 7 2 FL
Fulham 22/23 5 1 FL
Dartford
Dundee Hibs 24/25 3 3 D2
Dumbarton Harp 24/25 D3
Clydebank 25/26

SMITH James D
b. Inverness
Rutherglen Glencairn *
Clyde 30/31 27 10
31/32 30 3
32/33 7
Dundee T 33/34
Inverness Thistle 33/34
St Mirren 33/34 4

SMITH James McQueen Anderson
b. Leith 28.11.1901 d. Scotland 9.4.1964
Rosyth Rec
East Fife
Tottenham H 25/26 7 FL
26/27 23 FL
27/28 FL
28/29 FL
St Johnstone 29/30 3
Norwich C 30/31 31 FL
Ayr U 31/32 17
32/33 17 3

SMITH James Terence
b. Old Kilpatrick 12.3.1902 d. Bridgeport,USA 1975
Dumbarton Harp
Clydebank 25/26
Rangers 26/27 2
Ayr U 27/28 38 66 D2
28/29 33 26
29/30 5 5
Liverpool 29/30 37 23 FL
30/31 21 14 FL
31/32 3 1 FL
Tunbridge Wells R 32/33
Bristol R 33/34 11 6 FL
34/35 14 7 FL
Newport Co 35/36 26 10 FL
Notts Co 36/37 4 1 FL
Dumbarton

SMITH John
b. Stewarton
Ardrossan Winton R
Beith T
Newcastle U T
Rangers 08/09 7 5
Ayr Parkhouse 09/10 D2
10/11 D2
Arthurlie 11/12 D2

SMITH John
b. Tollcross
Vale of Clyde
Millwall 09/10 SL
10/11 2 SL
Hamilton A 11/12 23 7
Linfield 12/13 IL
Glentoran * 13/14 IL

SMITH John 1 cap
b. Beith 7.12.1898
Beith
Neilston Victoria 14/15
Ayr U 19/20 33 11
20/21 35
21/22 39
22/23 36
23/24 27
24/25 36
25/26 36 6 D2
Middlesbrough 26/27 33 FL
27/28 41 FL
28/29 33 FL
29/30 6 FL
Cardiff C 30/31 35 FL
31/32 29 FL
Distillery 32/33 IL
33/34 IL
34/35 IL

SMITH John
b. Hurlford
Dalbeattie Star
Queen of the South 31/32 D2
32/33 D2
33/34 7
Middlesbrough 33/34 1 FL
Nithsdale W L 35/36
Queen of the South 35/36 23
36/37 11 1
37/38
Dumbarton 38/39 D2

SMITH John
Queen of the South 35/36 4
36/37 22 11

SMITH John
Raith R 37/38 30 1 D2
38/39 19 1

SMITH John F
Queen's Park 05/06 9
06/07 4

SMITH John Joseph
b. Clydebank 1910
Clydebank Jnrs
Heart of Midlothian 31/32
32/33
Hibernian 33/34 10 3
34/35 33 8
35/36 29 4
Wrexham 36/37 12 1 FL
Bray Unknowns
Babcock & Wilcox

SMITH John M
Queen's Park 08/09 2

SMITH John Reid
b. Pollokshaws 2.4.1896 d. Whitchurch 3.9.1946
Battlefield Swifts
Kilmarnock 19/20 15 8
20/21 38 24
Cowdenbeath 21/22 D2
Rangers 21/22
22/23 3 2
Bolton W 22/23 22 7 FL
23/24 32 17 FL
24/25 21 13 FL
25/26 22 12 FL
26/27 32 13 FL
27/28 18 10 FL
Bury 27/28 9 10 FL
28/29 33 20 FL
29/30 34 29 FL
30/31 37 27 FL
31/32 35 13 FL
32/33 8 7 FL
Rochdale 33/34 25 8 FL
Whistons Temperence

SMITH Jonathan William
b. Bolton 1891
Wirksworth
Burton T
Manchester C 10/11 14 5 FL
11/12 4 1 FL
Mansfield Mechanics
Chesterfield 12/13
Rotherham Co
Hartlepools U 13/14
Third Lanark 13/14 10 3
14/15 36 12
15/16 10 1
Q P R 19/20 42 15 SL
20/21 42 18 FL
21/22 33 10 FL
Swansea T 22/23 38 23 FL
23/24 29 13 FL
Brighton 24/25 14 4 FL
Burton T
Burton Wednesday

SMITH Matthew
b. Stevenston 31.12.1897 d. Glasgow 15.5.1953
Ardeer Thistle
Kilmarnock 16/17 35 11
17/18 29 13
18/19
19/20 30 6
20/21 38 10
21/22 34 7
22/23 36 5
23/24 32 6
24/25 36 14
25/26 35 8
26/27 1
27/28 26 3
28/29 31 13
29/30 37 10
30/31 15 3
Ayr U 31/32
32/33
Galston

SMITH Matthew
b. Johnstone
Rutherglen Glencairn
Clyde 27/28 17
28/29 8 1
29/30 32
30/31 34
Morton 31/32 21
Clyde 32/33 34 1
33/34 32
34/35 35 10
35/36 16 2
36/37 7 1
Ayr U 36/37 D2
37/38

SMITH Nicol 12 caps
b. Darvel 25.12.1873 d. Kilmarnock 5.1.1905
Vale of Irvine
Royal Albert
Darvel
Rangers 92/93 2
93/94 17
94/95 13
95/96 17
96/97 9
97/98 13
98/99 13
99/00 10 1
00/01 18
01/02 15 1
02/03 7
03/04 22 1
04/05 12

SMITH P
Ayr U 38/39 9

SMITH R
Rutherglen Glencairn
Clyde 99/00 11
00/01 17 ? D2

SMITH Richard
b. Nigg 1911
Aberdeen Mugiemoss
Aberdeen East End
Aberdeen 32/33
33/34
34/35 29 9
35/36 4 1
36/37 3 1
37/38 14 5
Cardiff C 38/39 11 2 FL
Clyde 38/39 4
Arbroath

SMITH Robert
Rutherglen Glencairn
Hibernian 15/16 28
16/17
17/18 21 ?

SMITH Robert
Heart of Midlothian 16/17 2

SMITH Robert
Hibernian 20/21 1

SMITH Robert
Raith R 28/29 22 1

SMITH Robert
Beith Caledonians
Ayr U 36/37 33 D2
37/38 19
Dundee U 38/39 30 D2

SMITH Stephen
b. Aberdeen
Hall Russells
Chicago Thistle
Chicago All Scots
Brooklyn Wanderers 23/24 9 ASL
24/25 44 ASL
25/26 36 ASL
26/27 25 ASL
27/28 46 ASL
28/29 49 ASL
29A 16 ASL
29/30 21 ASL
Aberdeen 30/31 31
31/32 37
32/33 38
33/34 33
34/35 36
35/36 30
36/37 28

SMITH Sydney E
Glossop 08/09 1 FL
Partick T 09/10 17 6

SMITH Thomas
Gourock Thistle
Clyde 14/15 8 1

SMITH Thomas Craig
b. Glasgow
Shawlands YMCA
Queen's Park 29/30 3
30/31 5
31/32 31
32/33 34
33/34 37
34/35 30
35/36 4
Ayr U 35/36 18
St Bernards 36/37 D2
37/38 D2
38/39 D2

SMITH Thomas F
b. Luncarty 1911
Luncarty
Dundee 31/32 2
32/33 21 1
33/34 19
34/35 22
35/36 35 1
36/37 38
37/38 27 2
38/39 17 1 D2
Hull C 39/40 2 FL

SMITH Thomas McCall 2 caps
b. Fenwick 4.10.1908 d. Preston 21.6.1998
Cumnock Juveniles
Sinclair Celtic
Cumnock Townhead Thistle
Kilmarnock 27/28 26 3
Galston L 28/29
Kilmarnock 28/29 3
29/30 12
30/31 29 1
31/32 32
32/33 30
33/34 34
34/35 34
35/36 31
36/37 13
Preston N E 36/37 9 FL
37/38 34 FL
38/39 1 FL

SMITH W

Cambuslang		90/91	12		
		91/92	22		

SMITH W

Vale of Leven		91/92	1		

SMITH Walter
b. Airdrie 1914

Fruitfield					
Kirkintilloch Rob Roy					
St Mirren		33/34	16	5	
		34/35	4		
Kirkintilloch Rob Roy		35/36			
East Stirlingshire		35/36			D2
Stranraer		36/37			
Portadown	T	37/38			IL
New Brighton		37/38	8		FL
		38/39	8	3	FL
		39/40	2		FL

SMITH William
b. Scotland 1873 d. 1914

Hibernian		93/94	15	?	D2
		94/95	2	?	D2
		95/96	18	13	
		96/97	18	7	
		97/98	6	1	
Newcastle U		97/98	10	4	FL
		98/99	5		FL

SMITH William

Clyde		98/99	4		
		99/00	4		

SMITH William
b. Wishaw

Shettleston					
Hibernian		08/09	33	4	
		09/10	26	3	
		10/11	30	4	
		11/12	29	6	
		12/13	27	10	
		13/14	33		
		14/15	37	10	
		15/16	32	4	
Wishaw Thistle		16/17			
Hibernian		16/17	20	5	
		17/18	9	?	
		18/19	12	?	
		19/20	30	1	

SMITH William

Larkhall Thistle					
Third Lanark		09/10	4		
Royal Albert					
Albion R		13/14			D2

SMITH William

Heart of Midlothian					
Hamilton A		11/12	4		

SMITH William
b. Kirkcaldy 1914

Newburgh WE					
Hartlepools U		37/38	28	1	FL
Queen of the South		38/39	19	7	

SMITH William A
b. Auchinleck

Auchinleck Talbot					
Cowdenbeath		24/25	4	1	
		25/26	3	1	
Queen of the South		26/27			D2

SMITH William G

Hibernian		38/39	3		

SMITH William John

Port Glasgow A		04/05	13		

SNAPE Alfred
b. Armagh 14.1.1896 d. Belfast 13.11.1931

Glentoran		15/16			IL
		16/17			IL
		17/18			IL
Airdrieonians		18/19	5		
Glentoran		18/19			IL
Airdrieonians		19/20	8	2	
Belfast U		19/20			
Wallsend		20/21			
Glentoran		20/21			IL
Belfast U		21/22			
Manchester U		22/23			FL
Willowfield		22/23			
		23/24			
Glentoran		24/25			IL
Glenavon		25/26			IL
Ards		25/26			IL
Barn		26/27			IL
Willowfield		26/27			
Grove Mens Club					

SNEDDON

Leith A		93/94	8		

SNEDDON Alexander

Raith R		19/20	5		

SNEDDON George

West Benhar					
Hibernian		04/05	3		
		05/06			
		06/07	3	1	

SNEDDON George

Armadale					
Rangers		15/16	5	1	
Airdrieonians		16/17	10		
Armadale					

SNEDDON Harry

Blairhall					
Dundee		37/38	11		
		38/39	29	4	D2

SNEDDON James
b. Newington 1871 d. Edinburgh ?.7.1931

Broxburn A					
Leith A					
St Bernards		94/95	17		
		95/96	8		

SNEDDON James

Dalziel R					
Motherwell		05/06	27		
		06/07	26	1	
		07/08	12		
		08/09	28		
		09/10	3		
Wishaw Thistle		10/11			

SNEDDON James

Motherwell		13/14	1		
		14/15			
		15/16	2		

SNEDDON John

Vale of Clyde					
Port Glasgow A		02/03	3	1	

SNEDDON John

Larkhall Thistle					
Airdrieonians		09/10	3		
Royal Albert		10/11			

SNEDDON Robert
b. Kilwinning 1908

Kilwinning Eglington					
Kilmarnock		31/32	5		
		32/33	30	7	
Carlisle U		33/34	17	3	FL
Beith		34/35			
Galston					

SNEDDON Thomas

Wishaw Thistle					
Motherwell		15/16	21		

SNEDDON Thomas
b. Livingstone 22.8.1912 d. Chadwell Heath 11.12.1972

Whithorn Jnrs					
Queen of the South		36/37	1		
Rochdale		37/38	34		FL
		38/39	31		FL
		39/40	3		FL
		46/47	2		FL

SNEDDON Thomas D
b. Glasgow

Queen's Park		21/22	39		
		22/23	37		D2
		23/24	37		
		24/25	33		
		25/26	8		
		26/27	3		

SNEDDON Walter

St Ninians Thistle					
Kilsyth R					
St Mirren Jnrs					
St Mirren		18/19	6	?	
		19/20	5		

SNEDDON William Cleland
b. Wishaw 1.4.1914 d. Bangor 1.4.1995

Rutherglen Glencairn					
Falkirk		36/37	36	8	
Brentford		37/38	31	5	FL
		38/39	27	2	FL
Swansea T		39/40	3		FL
		46/47	2		FL
Newport Co		46/47	18		FL
Milford U					

SNODDY Thomas

Vale of Clyde					
Raith R		10/11	12		
		11/12	28	4	
St Mirren		12/13	30		
		13/14	1		
East Stirlingshire		14/15			D2
Johnstone		15/16			

SNOWDEN Emerson

Burnbank A					
Hamilton A		17/18	4		

SODDON William

Dunaskin					
Ayr U		23/24	1		

SOLIS Jerome Andrew
b. Glasgow 6.10.1909

St Aloysius College					
Woodside R					
Dennistoun Amateurs					
Maryhill Hibernian					
Celtic		31/32	9	3	
Coleraine		32/33			IL
Linfield		32/33			IL
Newry T		32/33			IL

SOMERS John
b. Hamilton

Coalburn					
Heart of Midlothian		28/29	5	1	
		29/30			
Dolphin		30/31			LI
		31/32			LI

SOMERS Peter 4 caps
b. Avondale 3.6.1878 d. Glasgow 27.11.1914

Mossend Celtic					
Cadzow Oak					
Hamilton A		97/98	3	?	D2
Celtic		97/98	3	3	
		98/99	8	8	
		99/00	3	1	
Clyde	L	99/00	6	3	
Blackburn R		99/00	14	2	FL
		00/01	31	3	FL
		01/02	31	9	FL
Celtic		02/03	14	4	
		03/04	20	2	
		04/05	25	8	
		05/06	22	4	
		06/07	27	9	
		07/08	30	12	
		08/09	25	4	
		09/10	6	1	
Hamilton A		09/10	8	1	
		10/11	15	1	

SOMERVILLE Archibald
b. Cleland

Club	Season	Apps	Goals	Notes
Pollok Jnrs	12/13			
	13/14			
	14/15			
	15/16			
	16/17			
Ayr U	16/17	1		
	17/18	18	?	
	18/19	4		

SOMERVILLE Ernest
b. Dalmuir

Club	Season	Apps	Goals	Notes
Clydebank	19/20	4		
	20/21	1		
	21/22	4		
	22/23			D2
	23/24	1		

SOMERVILLE Ernest

Club	Season	Apps	Goals	Notes
Dumbarton	20/21	14	2	

SOMERVILLE James
b. Stenhousemuir

Club	Season	Apps	Goals	Notes
Falkirk	17/18	4	?	
	18/19	15	?	
	19/20	5		
Stenhousemuir	20/21			
	21/22			D2
Airdrieonians	22/23	30	8	
	23/24	34	5	
	24/25	29	4	
	25/26	38	14	
	26/27	36	9	
	27/28	31	11	
	28/29	33	10	
	29/30	28	3	

SOMERVILLE James

Club	Season	Apps	Goals	Notes
Peebles R				
Morton	21/22	2		

SOMERVILLE R

Club	Season	Apps	Goals	Notes
Tranent Jnrs				
Hibernian	33/34	11	3	

SOMMEN James (Daniel?)

Club	Season	Apps	Goals	Notes
Stevenston Thistle				
Motherwell	01/02			D2
	02/03			D2
	03/04	19	3	
Partick T	04/05	20	1	
	05/06	19	3	
	06/07	18	1	
Dumbarton	07/08			

SOMMERVILLE George Douglas Liddell
b. Dalziel 21.12.1900 d. Bristol ?.12.1984

Club	Season	Apps	Goals	Notes
Holytown Violet				
Strathclyde				
Hamilton A	21/22	4		
	22/23	21		
	23/24	38		
	24/25	38		
	25/26	37		
Burnley	26/27	41		FL
	27/28	13		FL
	28/29	4		FL
	29/30	28		FL
	30/31	13		FL
	31/32	19		FL
Bristol C	32/33	31		FL
	33/34	3		FL
Burton T	34/35			
Yeovil T	35/36			

SOUTER John
b. c1910

Club	Season	Apps	Goals	Notes
Hamilton A	T			
Kings Park	30/31			D2
	31/32			D2
	32/33			D2
	33/34			D2
	34/35			D2
Hibernian	35/36	22		
Alloa A	36/37			D2
	37/38			D2
Montrose	38/39			D2

SOUTER Thomas Hoggan
b. Blair Atholl 26.3.1912 d. 1990s

Club	Season	Apps	Goals	Notes
Glasgow University				
Queen's Park	34/35	10	1	
	35/36	26	3	
Rangers	36/37	10		

SOWERBY Frederick

Club	Season	Apps	Goals	Notes
Bishop Auckland				
Heart of Midlothian	11/12	8		
St Mirren	12/13	30	6	
	13/14	18	6	
	14/15	37	1	
	15/16	32	3	
	16/17	18	5	
Clydebank	16/17			
Stevenston U	17/18			
Abercorn	17/18			
Morton *	17/18	1		
Third Lanark *	18/19	14	?	

SOWERBY John
b. NE of England

Club	Season	Apps	Goals	Notes
Army				
Ipswich T	32/33			
	33/34			
	34/35			
	35/36			
	36/37	12	2	SL
Rangers	37/38	3	1	
Third Lanark	38/39	7	1	
Carlisle U				

SOYE James
b. Govan 14.4.1885 d. Lurgan ?.10.1975

Club	Season	Apps	Goals	Notes
Rutherglen Glencairn				
Celtic				
Hibernian	T			
Distillery	03/04			IL
	04/05			IL
Southampton	05/06	17	4	SL
Newcastle U	06/07	1		FL
	07/08	6	2	FL
	08/09			FL
Aberdeen	09/10	23	5	
	10/11	33	5	
	11/12	32	5	
	12/13	32	2	
	13/14	35	2	
	14/15	32	1	
Distillery	15/16			IL
	16/17			IL
Glenavon	17/18			

SPALDING Thomas

Club	Season	Apps	Goals	Notes
Bonnyrigg Rose A				
Aberdeen	23/24	1		
Forfar A	24/25			D2

SPEEDIE Finlay Ballantyne 3 caps
b. Dumbarton 18.8.1880 d. Dumbarton 5.2.1953

Club	Season	Apps	Goals	Notes
Artizan Thistle				
Dumbarton	95/96			
Duntochter Hibs				
Strathclyde				
Rangers	00/01	11	5	
	01/02	16	6	
	02/03	18	4	
	03/04	23	10	
	04/05	26	13	
	05/06	2		
	06/07	1		
Newcastle U	06/07	27	10	FL
	07/08	25	3	FL
Oldham A	08/09	15	6	FL
Bradford PA	08/09	5	1	FL
Dumbarton	09/10			D2
	10/11	18	?	D2
	11/12			D2
	12/13			D2
	13/14	32	5	
	14/15			
	15/16			
	16/17			
	17/18	2		
	18/19			
	19/20	1		

SPEEDIE James Hodge
b. Edinburgh 17.11.1893 K.I.A., Loos 25.9.1915

Club	Season	Apps	Goals	Notes
Tranent Jnrs				
Heart of Midlothian	13/14	1	2	
St Mirren L	13/14	7		
Heart of Midlothian	14/15	8	3	

SPEEDIE William

Club	Season	Apps	Goals	Notes
Third Lanark	99/00	10		
Dumbarton *	00/01			
East Stirlingshire *	01/02			D2
Renton				

SPEIRS James H

Club	Season	Apps	Goals	Notes
Morton	07/08	27	8	
	08/09	28	4	
Johnstone	09/10			
Morton	10/11	8	2	

SPEIRS James Hamilton 1 cap
b. Glasgow 22.3.1886 K.I.A. 20.8.1917

Club	Season	Apps	Goals	Notes
Glasgow Annandale				
Maryhill				
Rangers	05/06	18	6	
	06/07	22	13	
	07/08	13	5	
Clyde	08/09	15	6	
Bradford C	09/10	38	6	FL
	10/11	25	7	FL
	11/12	10	7	FL
	12/13	13	9	FL
Leeds C	12/13	19	10	FL
	13/14	29	12	FL
	14/15	25	10	FL

SPEIRS John C
d. 1918

Club	Season	Apps	Goals	Notes
Ardeer Thistle				
Port Glasgow A	08/09	10		
	09/10	21	4	
Hamilton A	09/10	8	1	
	10/11	12	2	
Abercorn	11/12			D2
	12/13			D2
	13/14			D2
	14/15			D2
	15/16			
	16/17			
Stevenston U	17/18			

SPEIRS Robert

Club	Season	Apps	Goals	Notes
Abercorn				
Third Lanark	12/13	22	11	
Motherwell	13/14			
Vale of Leven	14/15			
Abercorn	15/16			

SPENCE Alexander Ronald

Club	Season	Apps	Goals	Notes
Glasgow Perthshire				
Heart of Midlothian	06/07	12	4	
Bradford PA	07/08			SL
Girvan A				

SPENCE George
b. Rothesay 27.9.1877

Club	Season	Apps	Goals	Notes
St Mirren	97/98	1	1	
Derby Co	98/99			FL
	99/00			FL
Reading	00/01	20	6	SL
Preston NE	01/02	19	7	FL
Reading	02/03	19	4	SL
Southampton	03/04	14	3	SL
	04/05			SL
Hull C	05/06	19	2	FL
Clyde	06/07	8		
Cowdenbeath				

SPENCE John Couper
b. c1874 d. Paisley ?.10.1932

Club	Season	Apps	Goals	Notes
Partick A				
Partick T	95/96	3		D2
	96/97	14		D2
	97/98	18		
	98/99	12		
	99/00			D2
	00/01	1		

SPENCER Samuel
b. Stoke 18.1.1902 d. Wallasey 3.1.1987

Club	Season	Apps	Goals	Notes
Trent Vale				
Oakhill				
Stoke	21/22	1		FL
New Brighton	23/24	3		FL
	24/25	5		FL
Mid Rhondda	25/26			
Aberdeen	25/26	1		
	26/27	7		
	27/28	1		
Bristol R	28/29	2		FL
Port Vale	29/30			FL
Newry T	30/31			IL
New Brighton	31/32	8		FL
Winsford U				

SPINK Thomas William
b. Dipton 13.11.1887 d. Grimsby 6.8.1966

Club	Season	Apps	Goals	Notes
Dipton U				
Craghead U	08/09			
	09/10			
Fulham	10/11	2	1	FL
	11/12	7		FL
Rochdale	12/13	37	3	CL
	13/14	34	1	CL
Grimsby T	14/15	34		FL
Hibernian	18/19	7		
Grimsby T	19/20	35	2	FL
	20/21	22		FL
	21/22	25	1	FL
Worksop T				

SPITTAL John

Rosslyn Jnrs				
Aberdeen	33/34			
	34/35	8	1	

STAFFORD James

b. Glasgow

St Anthonys				
Clydebank	22/23			D2
	23/24	3		
Dumbarton Harp	24/25			D3
Vale of Leven	24/25			D3

STAGE William

b. Whitby 22.3.1893 d. Blackley 12.5.1957

Willington				
Middlesbrough	13/14	3		FL
	14/15			FL
Hibernian	19/20	42	5	
St Bernards	20/21			
Bury	21/22	22	2	FL
	22/23	40	7	FL
	23/24	31	4	FL
	24/25	32	7	FL
	25/26	27	7	FL
	26/27	29	5	FL
	27/28	22	2	FL
Burnley	28/29	19		FL
	29/30	6	1	FL
Southampton	30/31	4	1	FL
Darwen	31/32			
Rossendale U	32/33			
Fleetwood	32/33			

STALKER Robert

Edinburgh University				
Queen's Park	03/04	6	2	
Hibernian	03/04	1	1	
	04/05	1		
Heart of Midlothian	04/05	1		
Motherwell	04/05	2		

STALKER William

Dunipace Jnrs				
Everton				
Falkirk	16/17	8		
Dundee Hibs				
Dunblane R	22/23			

STANDRING Wilfred

St Mirren	13/14	3		
	14/15			
	15/16			
	16/17			
	17/18			
Ayr U	18/19	7	1	

STANEX Wilfred Page

b. Belfast 6.2.1917 d. Belfast 15.3.1977

Glentoran				
Dundela				
Clyde	38/39	8		
Coleraine	39/40			IL
Dundela	40/41			
Linfield	40/41			IL
Larne	41/42			IL
Dundela	42/43			
Alexandra Works	42/43			
	43/44			
Dundela	44/45			
	45/46			
	46/47			
	47/48			
	48/49			
Brantwood	49/50			
	50/51			
Queens Island	51/52			

STANLEY

Raith R	16/17	1		

STANNAGE William

b. Motherwell

Newarthill				
Motherwell	26/27	2		

STARK James 2 caps

b. Glasgow 1880 d. Leith 1949

Mansewood				
Pollokshaws Eastwooc				
Glasgow Perthshire				
Rangers	00/01	12		
	01/02	16		
	02/03	12	2	
	03/04	22	2	
	04/05	13	1	
	05/06	28	3	
	06/07	22	3	
Chelsea	07/08	30	2	FL
Rangers	08/09	17	1	
	09/10	24		
Morton	10/11	30		
	11/12	31	2	
	12/13	32		
	13/14	28	1	
	14/15	28	2	

STARK James

Bellshill A				
St Mirren	01/02	12		
	02/03	5		
	03/04	3		

STARK James H

b. Edinburgh

Murrayfield Amateurs				
Hibernian	25/26	19		
	26/27	39		
	27/28	35	1	
	28/29	30		
	29/30	9		

STARK Peter McKinnon

b. Cambuslang

Rothesay Royal V				
Albion R	36/37	24	2	
Airdrieonians	37/38			D2
	38/39			D2
Heart of Midlothian	38/39			

STARK Thomas

b. ?.3.1919

Kirkintilloch Rob Roy				
Motherwell	35/36	1		
	36/37			
	37/38	1	1	
Stenhousemuir	38/39			D2

STARK Walter

Clyde	26/27	7		

STEAD Angus W

b. c1920 d. Glasgow 1999

Mossvale Jnrs				
St Mirren	37/38	6		
	38/39	6		
Dumbarton				
Rangers	46/47	3		
Morton	47/48	4		

STEEL

St Bernards	93/94	4	2	

STEEL

Dumbarton	16/17	3		

STEEL Alexander

b. Newmilns 25.7.1886

Newmilns				
Ayr U				
Manchester C	05/06	4		FL
	06/07	23	1	FL
	07/08	3		FL
	08/09			FL
Tottenham H	09/10	1		FL
	10/11			FL
Kilmarnock	11/12	3		
	12/13			
Southend U	13/14	32		SL
	14/15	32		SL
Gillingham	19/20	23		SL

STEEL Daniel

b. Newmilns 2.5.1884 d. Marylebone 29.4.1931

Newmilns				
Airdrieonians	03/04	1		
	04/05			
Rangers	05/06	2		
Tottenham H	06/07	6		SL
	07/08	25	1	SL
	08/09	38	1	FL
	09/10	36	2	FL
	10/11	26		FL
	11/12	29		FL
Third Lanark	12/13	34		
	13/14	13	1	
Clapton Orient	14/15	23		FL

STEEL David

Dumbarton	13/14	5		
	14/15	16	2	

STEEL George G

Queen's Park	21/22	1		

STEEL J

Rangers	91/92	3		
	92/93	2	1	
	93/94	14	7	

STEEL James

Third Lanark	95/96	14	7	
	96/97	9	1	
Linthouse	96/97	1	?	D2
	97/98	8	?	D2

STEEL James

Lanemark				
Partick T	10/11	5	3	
	11/12	19	1	
	12/13	6	2	
	13/14			
	14/15			
Johnstone	15/16			

STEEL James S

b. Dumfries

Roslyn				
Maxwelltown Volunteers				
Lanemark	09/10			
5th KOSB (Dumfries)				
Kilmarnock	12/13	12		
	13/14	4		
5th KOSB (Dumfries) L	13/14			
Kilmarnock	14/15			
Johnstone				
Queen of the South	19/20			
	20/21			

STEEL John

b. Denny 24.10.1902

Banknock Jnrs				
Hamilton A	20/21	6		
	21/22	35	5	
	22/23	34	2	
	23/24	21	2	
	24/25	21	1	
	25/26	10		
Burnley	25/26	25		FL
	26/27	38	5	FL
	27/28	25		FL
	28/29	33		FL
	29/30	22		FL
	30/31	2		FL
Hamilton A	31/32			

STEEL John Hay

b. Glasgow

Queen's Park	19/20	38	1	
Third Lanark	20/21	12		
Nelson	21/22	25		FL
	22/23	24		FL
	23/24	1		FL
Arsenal T	23/24			FL
Brentford	24/25	16		FL

STEEL Peter

b. Leith

Tranent				
Raith R	21/22	1		

STEEL Robert Loudoun
b. Newmilns 25.6.1888 d. 28.3.1972
Newmilns
Kilwinning
Port Glasgow A 06/07 16 3
07/08 34 6
Tottenham H 08/09 37 12 FL
09/10 38 9 FL
10/11 29 9 FL
11/12 30 7 FL
12/13 19 1 FL
13/14 37 FL
14/15 36 2 FL
Gillingham 19/20 19 3 SL

STEEL William
b. Glasgow 20.5.1875 d. Johnstone 20.10.1962
Royal Albert 95/96
96/97
St Mirren 97/98 13 5
98/99 16 3
99/00 14 5
00/01 2
Royal Albert 00/01
Abercorn * 01/02 D2
Johnstone * 01/02
Chesterfield T 02/03 32 7 FL

STEEL William Gilbert
b. Blantyre 6.2.1908
Bellhaven Oak
Bridgeton Waverley
St Johnstone 26/27 10
27/28 38
28/29 38
29/30 38
30/31 38 D2
Liverpool 31/32 22 FL
32/33 42 FL
33/34 40 FL
34/35 16 FL
Birmingham 34/35 11 FL
35/36 36 FL
36/37 17 FL
37/38 16 FL
38/39 12 FL
Derby Co 38/39 11 FL

STEELE

St Mirren 15/16 1

STEELE David Morton 3 caps
b. Carluke 29.7.1894 d. 23.5.1964
Armadale
St Mirren 13/14 1
14/15 11
15/16 18 4
Douglas Water Thistle
Bristol R 19/20 22 1 SL
20/21 29 FL
21/22 38 2 FL
Huddersfield T 22/23 33 1 FL
23/24 31 FL
24/25 39 FL
25/26 18 FL
26/27 20 FL
27/28 24 FL
28/29 21 FL
Preston NE 29/30 28 2 FL
Bury
Ashton National

STEELE Gilbert
b. Prestwick 12.2.
Glenburn R
Ayr U 17/18 10 ?
18/19 6 1
Glenburn R 19/20
20/21
Stockport Co 21/22 15 4 FL
Crewe A 22/23 4 2 FL
23/24 12 FL
24/25 5 FL

STEELE James

Co-operative U
Morton 04/05 11

STEELE James
b. c1911
Buckhaven V
St Andrews U
East Fife 30/31 11
31/32 4 D2
Rosslyn Jnrs

STEELE John
b. Camlachie 24.11.1916 d. 23.12.1989
Barony Parish Church
Lesmagahow Jnrs 34/35
East Fife 34/35 16 2 D2
35/36 11 1 D2
Raith R L 35/36 D2
Ayr U 35/36 21 2
36/37 5 D2
Raith R L 36/37
Ayr U 37/38 19 5
Barnsley 38/39 39 17 FL
39/40 3 2 FL
46/47 5 1 FL
47/48 3 3 FL
48/49 1 FL

STEELE Peter
b. Leith
Leith A 29/30 D2
30/31 32
31/32 D2
Dunfermline A 32/33 D2
33/34 D2
34/35 34
35/36 18

STEIN James
b. Coatbridge 7.11.1904
Blackburn R (W Lothian)
Dunfermline A 25/26 D2
26/27 27 6
27/28 34 4
Everton 28/29 4 FL
29/30 29 10 FL
30/31 28 10 FL
31/32 37 9 FL
32/33 40 16 FL
33/34 42 8 FL
34/35 19 4 FL
Burnley 36/37 27 3 FL
37/38 15 5 FL
New Brighton 38/39 39 5 FL
39/40 3 FL

STEVEN

Heart of Midlothian 07/08 1

STEVEN David
b. Dundee 16.3.1878 d. Dundee 28.4.1903
Dundee Violet
Dundee
Bury 96/97 3 FL
Dundee 96/97
Southampton 97/98 8 3 SL
98/99 8 1 SL
Dundee 99/00 18 3
00/01 17 8
01/02 7 1
Montrose

STEVEN George
b. Dundee 24.2.1891
Dundee Violet
Dundee
St Johnstone L 11/12 20 4 D2
Dundee 12/13 17 6
13/14 28 4
14/15 32 8
15/16 38 3
16/17 26 6
Third Lanark 17/18 3 ?
Dundee
Darlington 21/22 19 5 FL
22/23 30 14 FL
23/24 41 13 FL
24/25 32 5 FL
25/26 8 1 FL
Crewe A 26/27 7 FL

STEVENS Robert C
b. Maryhill 1886
John St FP
Maryhill
Rangers 07/08 9 1
08/09
Woolwich Arsenal 09/10 7 1 FL

STEVENS Thomas

Aylesbury U
Chesterfield T 09/10
Clyde 10/11 7 1
11/12 27 4
12/13 16 1
Everton 12/13 5 FL
Chesterfield T 13/14
Doncaster R 14/15

STEVENSON

Clyde 92/93 16 1

STEVENSON

Third Lanark 96/97 1

STEVENSON

Dumbarton 14/15 1

STEVENSON A

Clyde 94/95 1

STEVENSON Alexander
b. Airdrie 24.10.1906
Airdrieonians
Detroit R
Airdrieonians 26/27 14 2
Armadale 26/27 D2
Brentford 27/28 2 FL
28/29 21 FL
29/30 32 FL
30/31 26 FL
31/32 14 FL
32/33 27 FL
33/34 3 FL
Southend U 34/35 11 FL
Ards 35/36 IL
Ross Co 35/36

STEVENSON Alexander

Petershill
Partick T 35/36 20
36/37 3
37/38 3

STEVENSON Alexander Ernest
b. Dublin 9.8.1912 d. Liverpool ?.9.1985
St Barnabas
Dolphin 31/32 LI
Rangers 32/33 1
33/34 11 7
Everton 33/34 12 1 FL
34/35 36 15 FL
35/36 29 10 FL
36/37 41 19 FL
37/38 35 13 FL
38/39 36 11 FL
39/40 3 FL
46/47 30 8 FL
47/48 17 3 FL
48/49 19 2 FL

STEVENSON Archibald
b. Glasgow
Kirkintiloch Rob Roy
Queen's Park 17/18 25
18/19 30
Clydebank 19/20 41
20/21 38
21/22 35
J & P Coats 22/23 24 ASL
23/24 23 ASL
24/25 36 ASL
25/26 20 ASL
26/27 25 ASL
27/28 38 3 ASL
28/29 18 ASL
Pawtucket Rangers 29A 19 ASL
29/30 3 ASL

STEVENSON David
b. Newhaven
Leith A
Hibernian 13/14 2
14/15 4
Lochgelly U 15/16
Hibernian 18/19 7
19/20 21
St Bernards 20/21
21/22 D2
Bo'ness 22/23 D2
Cowdenbeath 23/24 D2
24/25 24
25/26 1

STEVENSON David
b. Leith
Dunfermline A 26/27 7
27/28 9

STEVENSON George 12 caps
b. Kilbirnie 4.4.1905 d. ?.5.1990

Club	Season	Apps	Goals	
Lochwinnoch Viewfield				
Kilbirnie Ladeside				
Motherwell	23/24	10	1	
	24/25	35	5	
	25/26	37	5	
	26/27	36	10	
	27/28	35	21	
	28/29	33	8	
	29/30	35	13	
	30/31	35	16	
	31/32	35	12	
	32/33	29	8	
	33/34	37	14	
	34/35	27	12	
	35/36	33	11	
	36/37	31	11	
	37/38	31	12	
	38/39	31	10	

STEVENSON Harry

Club	Season	Apps	Goals	
Kilbarchan A				
Morton	08/09	3	1	
	09/10	7		

STEVENSON Hugh
b. Paisley

Club	Season	Apps	Goals	
Woolwich				
Maryhill				
Blackburn R	06/07	2		FL
	07/08	23		FL
	08/09	8	1	FL
	09/10	6	2	FL
	10/11	19		
Great Harwood T	11/12			
St Mirren	12/13			
	13/14	30	4	

STEVENSON Hugh

Club	Season	Apps	Goals	
Strathclyde				
Clyde	33/34	8	2	
Arbroath	33/34	4		D2
Alloa A	34/35			D2

STEVENSON J

Club	Season	Apps	Goals	
Queen's Park	07/08	10	2	
	08/09	1		

STEVENSON James
b. Bonhill 1875 d. 3.3.1925

Club	Season	Apps	Goals	
Dumbarton	94/95	11	1	
	95/96	12	2	
Preston NE	95/96	12	4	FL
	96/97	14	7	FL
	97/98	25	11	FL
Bristol St George	98/99			
Preston NE	99/00	28	5	FL
	00/01	2		FL
WBA	00/01	24	3	FL
	01/02	34	2	FL
	02/03	34	3	FL
	03/04	28	1	FL
Dumbarton				

STEVENSON James
b. Govan 2.2.1881 d. Greenock 9.7.1946

Club		Season	Apps	Goals	
Abington					
Leith A					
Morton		00/01	14	5	
		01/02	9	2	
Nottingham F		02/03	6	1	FL
New Brompton		03/04	28	6	SL
Morton		04/05	9		
Belfast Celtic					
Port Glasgow A		06/07	1		
Morton					
Arthurlie					
Morton		12/13	11	4	
		13/14	30	6	
		14/15	7		
		15/16	4		
		16/17	8		
		17/18	11		
Kilmarnock	L	18/19	2		
Clyde	L	18/19	1	?	
Morton		19/20	7	1	
		20/21			
Arthurlie		21/22			D2

STEVENSON James Trevit
b. Newmains 10.11.1903 d. Stockport 5.11.1973

Club	Season	Apps	Goals	
Newmains				
Overtown R				
Third Lanark	24/25	8		
	25/26			D2
South Shields	26/27	8	3	FL
	27/28	21	6	FL
	28/29	35	15	FL
Bradford C	29/30	8	1	FL
	30/31	2		FL
Aldershot	31/32	12	5	SL
Stockport Co	32/33	35	13	FL
	33/34	37	15	FL
	34/35	24	10	FL
Walsall	35/36	3		FL
Stockport Co	35/36	1		FL
Macclesfield				

STEVENSON James W
b. Paisley 1876

Club	Season	Apps	Goals	
Clyde	94/95	15	4	
Derby Co	94/95	1		FL
	95/96	25	15	FL
	96/97	19	16	FL
	97/98	23	5	FL
	98/99	4		FL
Newcastle U	98/99	24	7	FL
	99/00	10	6	FL
Bristol C	00/01	23	5	SL
Grimsby T	01/02	8	1	FL
Leicester F	01/02	7	1	FL
Clyde	02/03			D2
St Mirren				

STEVENSON John

Club	Season	Apps	Goals	
Rangers				
Kilbirnie				
St Mirren	95/96	5	2	
	96/97	16	10	

STEVENSON John

Club	Season	Apps	Goals	
Beith				
St Mirren	04/05	3		
	05/06	13		
Beith				

STEVENSON John

Club		Season	Apps	Goals	
Broxburn					
Rangers	L				
Partick T		12/13	25	1	
		13/14	17		
Reading		14/15			SL
Partick T		15/16	7		
Bathgate		16/17			

STEVENSON John Alexander
b. Wigan 27.2.1898 d. Carlisle 12.3.1979

Club		Season	Apps	Goals	
Kilbirnie Ladeside					
Sunderland	T				
Ayr U		20/21	14	4	
Aberdeen		21/22	2		
Middlesbrough	T				
Beith		22/23			
Bury		22/23	3		FL
		23/24	2		FL
		24/25	3	1	FL
Nelson		24/25	13	2	FL
		25/26	25	5	FL
		26/27	34	17	FL
St Johnstone		27/28	30	9	
		28/29	35	6	
		29/30	26	9	
Falkirk		30/31	28	9	
		31/32	31	8	
Chester		32/33	11	2	FL
Bristol R		32/33	7	1	FL
Carlisle U		33/34	34	6	FL
		34/35	31	5	FL

STEVENSON Malcolm

Club	Season	Apps	Goals	
Queen of the South	38/39	1		

STEVENSON Neil

Club	Season	Apps	Goals	
Irvine Meadow				
Kilmarnock	08/09	1		
	09/10	6		

STEVENSON P

Club	Season	Apps	Goals	
Leith A	91/92	21		
	92/93	11		
	93/94	7		

STEVENSON Robert
b. Barrhead 10.5.1869

Club	Season	Apps	Goals	
Third Lanark	92/93	10		
	93/94	15	2	
Royal Arsenal	94/95	8		FL
Old Castle Swifts	94/95			
Thames Ironworks	95/96			
	96/97			
Arthurlie	96/97			
	97/98			
	98/99			
	99/00			
	00/01			

STEVENSON Robert

Club	Season	Apps	Goals	
Maryhill				
Petershill				
Morton	13/14	2		
	14/15	37	7	
	15/16	37	16	
	16/17	35	10	
	17/18	21	4	
	18/19	27	8	
	19/20	35	6	
	20/21	28	6	
St Mirren	21/22	39	8	
	22/23	22	4	
	23/24	8	1	
Arthurlie	24/25			

STEVENSON Robert

Club	Season	Apps	Goals	
Clydebank	23/24	6	1	

STEVENSON Samuel

Club	Season	Apps	Goals	
Glentoran	06/07			IL
	07/08			IL
Motherwell	08/09	1		

STEVENSON Thomas (or STEVENSTON)
b. Glasgow c1873 d. Glasgow c1951

Club	Season	Apps	Goals	
Clyde	96/97	7		
	97/98	12	1	
Sheffield W	97/98	2		FL
Clyde				

STEVENSON William

Club	Season	Apps	Goals	
Bathgate				
Clyde	07/08	1		
Albion R				

STEVENSON William

Club	Season	Apps	Goals	
Vale of Clyde				
Third Lanark	22/23	2		

STEVENSON William
b. Glasgow

Club	Season	Apps	Goals	
Strathclyde				
Arthurlie	26/27			
Providence Clamdiggers	27/28	14		ASL
	28/29			
Clyde	29/30	37		
	30/31	26		
	31/32	34		
	32/33	36		
	33/34	38		
	34/35	38		
	35/36	16		
	36/37	7		
	37/38			
Dunfermline A	38/39			D2

STEVENSON William
b. Glasgow

Club	Season	Apps	Goals	
Lochgelly U	26/27			D2
	27/28			D2
Third Lanark	28/29	35		

STEWART

Club	Season	Apps	Goals	
Clyde	91/92	1	1	

STEWART

Club	Season	Apps	Goals	
Abercorn	92/93	1		

STEWART

Club	Season	Apps	Goals	
Hamilton A	17/18	1	1	

STEWART A William

Club	Season	Apps	Goals	
Queen's Park	19/20	1		
	20/21	3		

STEWART Alexander
b. East Benhar

Club	Season	Apps	Goals	
Partick T	06/07	1		
Ayr	06/07			

STEWART Alexander

Club	Season	Apps	Goals	
Perth Roselea				
Falkirk	09/10	34		
	10/11	34		
	11/12	33		
	12/13	34		
	13/14	36		
	14/15	28		
	15/16	36		
	16/17	34		
	17/18			
Partick T	18/19	29		
	19/20	3		
St Johnstone	20/21			
	21/22	11		D2
	22/23	30		D2
	23/24	22		D2
Arbroath	24/25	24		D2
	25/26	35		D2
	26/27	6		D2

STEWART Alexander

Club	Season	Apps	Goals	
Heart of Midlothian	15/16	1		

STEWART Alexander

Club	Season	Apps	Goals	
Raith R	16/17	1		
East Fife				

STEWART Alexander
b. Perth

Club	Season	Apps	Goals	
Queen's Park	28/29	6	1	
St Mirren	29/30	24	17	
	30/31	33	6	
Rhyl	31/32			
Sheffield U	31/32			FL
St Johnstone	32/33	8		
	33/34	33	3	
	34/35	28	16	
	35/36			
Motherwell	36/37	24	28	
	37/38	33	17	
	38/39	8	6	
Falkirk	38/39	19	13	

STEWART Alistair J

Club	Season	Apps	Goals	
Heart of Midlothian	08/09	4	1	
	09/10	4		

STEWART Allan

Club	Season	Apps	Goals	
Johnstone				
Third Lanark	13/14	2		
Johnstone				

STEWART Andrew

Club	Season	Apps	Goals	
Third Lanark	91/92	1		
	92/93	1		
	93/94	15	8	
	94/95	1		
	95/96			
Queen's Park				
St Bernards	96/97	2		

STEWART C

Club	Season	Apps	Goals	
Falkirk	16/17	1		

STEWART Charles

Club	Season	Apps	Goals	
Linfield	03/04			IL
	04/05			IL
	05/06			IL
	06/07			IL
	07/08			IL
	08/09			IL
Airdrieonians	09/10	28	1	
Linfield	10/11			IL
	11/12			IL
	12/13			IL

STEWART David

Club	Season	Apps	Goals	
Yoker A				
Morton	32/33	15	2	

STEWART F Harry

Club	Season	Apps	Goals	
Dundee	98/99	4	1	
	99/00	5	1	
Derby Co	99/00	2	1	FL
Blackburn R				

STEWART George 4 caps
b. Wishaw 1883

Club	Season	Apps	Goals	
Strathclyde				
Hibernian	02/03	19	9	
	03/04	23	8	
	04/05	24	2	
	05/06	24	3	
Manchester C	06/07	36	8	FL
	07/08	10	1	FL
	08/09	9	1	FL
	09/10	22	1	FL
	10/11	17		FL
Partick T	11/12	15	2	

STEWART George

Club	Season	Apps	Goals	
Circle Amateurs				
Petershill				
Buckie Thistle				
Aberdeen University				
Third Lanark	34/35			
	35/36	7	1	
Clyde	35/36	15	4	
	36/37	24	1	
	37/38	24	5	
Dundee	38/39			D2

STEWART J

Club	Season	Apps	Goals	
Queen's Park	20/21	1		

STEWART J W
b. Renton

Club	Season	Apps	Goals	
Dumbarton Academy				
Hamilton A	25/26	14		
	26/27	7		

STEWART James
b. Gateshead 7.6.1883 d. Gateshead 23.5.1957

Club	Season	Apps	Goals	
Todds Nook				
Gateshead NER				
Sheffield W	02/03	1		FL
	03/04	10	1	FL
	04/05	20	13	FL
	05/06	37	20	FL
	06/07	23	6	FL
	07/08	32	14	FL
Newcastle U	08/09	25	8	FL
	09/10	17	8	FL
	10/11	30	19	FL
	11/12	33	14	FL
	12/13	16	9	FL
Rangers	13/14	19	10	
North Shields A				

STEWART James

Club	Season	Apps	Goals	
Quarter Huttonbank				
Strathclyde				
Hamilton A	09/10	16		
	10/11	5		

STEWART James

Club	Season	Apps	Goals	
Luncarty				
St Johnstone	29/30	10	9	
Aberdeen	30/31			

STEWART James

Club	Season	Apps	Goals	
Cowdenbeath	32/33	1		

STEWART James Luke

Club	Season	Apps	Goals	
Fauldhouse U				
Partick T	36/37	16		
	37/38	31		
	38/39	22		
Falkirk	46/47	9	1	

STEWART James Maxwell
b. Hurlford

Club		Season	Apps	Goals
Hurlford Juveniles				
Irvine Meadow				
Kilmarnock		28/29	6	
Galston	L	28/29		
Kilmarnock		29/30	8	
		30/31	6	
Irvine Meadow				

STEWART James Munro
b. Dumbarton

Club	Season	Apps	Goals	
Motherwell	06/07	8		
	07/08	31	9	
	08/09	33	17	
Liverpool	09/10	37	18	FL
	10/11	11	4	FL
	11/12	9	4	FL
	12/13	4	1	FL
	13/14	3		FL
Hamilton A	13/14	8	3	
	14/15	34	20	
	15/16	25	11	
	16/17	13	3	
Dumbarton	16/17	6	1	
	17/18	14	9	
Hamilton A	18/19	25	11	

STEWART John

Club	Season	Apps	Goals	
Third Lanark	99/00	10	2	

STEWART John

Club	Season	Apps	Goals	
Buckie Thistle				
Raith R	12/13	8	2	
Dunfermline A				

STEWART John A

Club	Season	Apps	Goals	
Morton	24/25	14		
Bathgate	25/26			D2

STEWART John E

Club	Season	Apps	Goals	
Queen's Park Strollers				
Queen's Park	33/34	15		
	34/35	14		
	35/36	1		

STEWART John George
b. Glasgow

Club	Season	Apps	Goals	
Queen's Park				
Rangers	33/34			
	34/35			
	35/36			
	36/37			
Kilmarnock	37/38	11		
	38/39	28		

STEWART Peter M

Club	Season	Apps	Goals	
Queen's Park				
Bathgate	04/05			
Queen's Park	05/06	1		
	06/07	3		
	07/08			
Morton	08/09	34	1	
	09/10	7		
Port Glasgow A	09/10	1		
Third Lanark	09/10	2		

STEWART Robert

Club	Season	Apps	Goals	
Kilbarchan A				
Morton	02/03	21	4	
	03/04	25		
	04/05	25		
	05/06	28	1	
	06/07	33	1	
	07/08	32	1	
	08/09	34	1	
	09/10	29		
	10/11	16		
	11/12	7	1	

STEWART Robert
b. Motherwell

Club	Season	Apps	Goals	
Larkhall Thistle				
Motherwell	16/17	34	4	
	17/18	31	1	
	18/19	30		
	19/20	36		
	20/21	39	2	
	21/22	40		
	22/23	34	1	
	23/24	28		
Ayr U	23/24	8		
	24/25			
	25/26	30	5	D2
	26/27	1		D2
Royal Albert	27/28			

STEWART Robert

Club	Season	Apps	Goals	
Blantyre V				
Hamilton A	17/18	3		

STEWART Robert Whyte
b. Paisley 19.12.1899

Club	Season	Apps	Goals	
Stevenston U				
St Mirren	20/21	22	3	
	21/22			
Norwich C	22/23	15		FL

STEWART Thomas Earley
b. Renfrew 28.6.1888
Cambuslang R
Rutherglen Glencairn 11/12
Fulham 12/13 6 FL
13/14 6 FL
14/15 FL
Dumbarton Harp 15/16
Celtic L 17/18 1
St Mirren L 18/19 5 ?
Dumbarton Harp

STEWART Thomas M D
Dundee 96/97
Lochee U L 96/97
Dundee 97/98
98/99 14
99/00 16
00/01 20
01/02 1

STEWART W
Clyde 96/97 2

STEWART William
Rangers 95/96 7 2
Mothewell

STEWART William
Bridgeton Waverley
St Mirren 34/35 1
St Anthonys
Bridgeton Waverley
Morton 36/37 D2
37/38 26

STEWART William Graham 2 caps
b. Glasgow 29.2.1876
Third Lanark
Queen's Park 97/98
98/99
99/00
00/01 7 1
Newcastle U 01/02 25 4 FL
02/03 12 2 FL

STEWART William R
Bent Royal Oak
Hamilton A 13/14 5
14/15 3
Motherwell L 14/15
Royal Albert 14/15

STEWART William Todd
b. Glasgow 29.4.1910
Shettleston Jnrs
Cowdenbeath 31/32 35 6
32/33 16 4
Manchester U 32/33 21 3 FL
33/34 25 4 FL
Motherwell 33/34 3 4
34/35 4
35/36 11 3
36/37 12 2
Albion R 36/37 11 1
Alloa A 37/38 D2

STEWART William W
Queen's Park 00/01 12
01/02 14 1
02/03 10

STIRLING
Heart of Midlothian 90/91 11 1
91/92 1

STIRLING James
b. Larkhall
Clyde 27/28 9
Third Lanark 28/29

STIRLING John
b. Clydebank 1894 d. Hillhead 13.3.1924
Clydebank Jnrs
Rangers T
Clyde 08/09 21 4
09/10
10/11
Middlesbrough 11/12 36 3 FL
12/13 33 2 FL
13/14 33 4 FL
Bradford PA 14/15 31 1 FL
Coventry C 19/20 5 FL
Stoke 19/20 20 1 FL
Alloa A 20/21 D2
21/22 12 2

STIRLING John
Dundee 14/15 12 1
15/16 20 2
16/17 31 2
17/18
18/19
Dundee Hibernian 19/20
20/21
Arbroath 21/22 34 3 D2
22/23 D2
Dundee Hibernian 23/24 D2

STIRLING John
Third Lanark 17/18 3 ?

STIRLING Robert Laidlaw
b. Kelvin 26.2.1883
Heart of Midlothian 06/07 13
Plymouth A 07/08 SL
Blackpool 08/09 2 FL
Morton 09/10 2
Millwall 09/10 SL

STIRLING William
Falkirk 24/25 4

STIVEN
Third Lanark 95/96 1

STOCKMAN
Third Lanark 95/96 1

STODDART George Graham
b. Kirkcaldy 9.3.1897 d. Kirkcaldy 14.10.1961
Inverkeithing U
Leslie Hearts
Raith R 14/15
15/16
16/17
17/18
18/19
19/20
20/21 4
Hull C 20/21 7 FL
Dundee Hibs

STODDART John
Stenhousemuir
Clyde 99/00 1
Stenhousemuir
Morton 02/03 9
Stenhousemuir

STODDART Robert
b. Falkirk c1900
East Stirlingshire
Falkirk 25/26 2
East Stirlingshire 26/27 D2
Stranraer
Ballymena 31/32 IL
Montrose 32/33 D2
Morton 33/34 D2
East Stirlingshire 34/35 D2
35/36 D2
36/37 D2
Bo'ness 37/38

STODDART William H
Wishaw Jnrs
St Mirren 34/35 14

STORMONT Robert
b. Dundee 12.4.1872
Dundee 96/97 6
Tottenham H 97/98 22 2 SL
98/99 23 SL
99/00 25 1 SL
00/01 23 5 SL
Brentford 01/02 22 1 SL
Maidstone

STORRIER David 3 caps
b. Arbroath 25.10.1872 d. Arbroath 27.1.1910
Arbroath Dauntless
Arbroath
Everton 93/94 1 FL
94/95 1 FL
95/96 3 FL
96/97 25 FL
97/98 25 FL
Celtic 98/99 14 1
99/00 7
00/01 12
Dundee 01/02 7
Millwall 02/03 18 SL
03/04 9 1 SL

STORROCK Alex (or STERRICKS)
Falkirk 15/16 1

STOTHERS James
Shelbourne 10/11 IL
Airdrieonians 10/11 6 2
11/12 1
Alloa A 12/13
Distillery 12/13 IL
Shelbourne 12/13 IL

STRACHAN
St Mirren 92/93 2 1

STRACHAN
Heart of Midlothian 97/98 1

STRACHAN Hugh
Bungalow C
Dunfermline A 20/21
21/22 D2
22/23 D2
23/24 D2
24/25 D2
USA 25/26
Alloa A 25/26 D2
Dunfermline A 26/27 24
27/28 2
Cowdenbeath 28/29
Edinburgh C 28/29 D2

STRACHAN James
Dundee Violet
Dundee Hibs
Brechin C
Dundee 11/12
12/13 1

STRACHAN Stuart
Nithsdale W 03/04
Dumfries 04/05
Partick T L 04/05 1
Maxwelltown Volunteers 05/06
Lanemark 06/07
Ayr Parkhouse 07/08 D2
Kilmarnock 07/08 13
Maxwelltown Volunteers 08/09
Lanemark

STRAIN David
b. Kilmarnock 1909
Galston
Irvine Meadow
St Mirren 30/31 4
31/32 2
32/33 7
York C 33/34 13 FL
Galston 34/35
Ayr U 34/35 8
35/36 22
36/37 34 D2
37/38 38
38/39 37

STRAIN Joseph
b. Baillieston 25.7.1894 d. Glasgow 23.1.1973
Baillieston Jnrs
Shettleston Jnrs
Bo'ness T 21/22 1 D2
Watford 21/22 26 1 FL
22/23 26 2 FL
23/24 19 2 FL
24/25 41 FL
25/26 39 FL
26/27 27 1 FL
Hamilton A T 27/28 3
Baillieston Jnrs

STRANG Alexander
b. Leith
Arniston R
Hibernian 19/20 3
20/21 6
21/22 15

STRANG Thomas
b. West Calder
Plains
Celtic
Bolton W 02/03 3 FL
Aberdeen 03/04 20 1 D2
04/05 20 D2
05/06 30 1
06/07 21
Bristol R 07/08 24 SL
08/09 37 2 SL
New Brompton 09/10 SL
10/11 32 1 SL
11/12 7 SL

STRANG William
b. Dunfermline 16.9.1878
Dunfermline A
Orion
Dunfermline A 01/02
02/03
Celtic 03/04 2
Renton L 03/04
Calgary Caledonian

STRATFORD Nelson R
Inverkeithing U
Queen's Park 13/14 11

STRATHEARN Colin M K C
b. Aberdeen 1887
Aberdeen East End
Aberdeen 16/17 1

STRATHIE James William
b. Beancross 12.2.1913 d. Hatfield 23.6.1976
Camelon Jnrs
Falkirk 33/34 3
34/35 16
Kings Park 35/36 D2
St Bernards 36/37 D2
Luton T 37/38 1 FL
38/39 1 FL
Northampton T 39/40 3 FL
Kettering T
Corby T
Rothwell T

STRAUSS William Henry
b. Benoni 6.1.1916 d. 1987
South African football
Aberdeen 35/36
36/37 30 24
37/38 19 6
38/39 31 12
Plymouth A 46/47 23 11 FL
47/48 41 5 FL
48/49 31 10 FL
49/50 37 10 FL
50/51 15 3 FL
51/52 9 1 FL
52/53 0 0 FL
53/54 2 0 FL

STRINGFELLOW John Francis
b. Sutton in Ashfield ?.3.1888 d. Lincoln 1966
Ilkeston U
Sheffield W 08/09 7 FL
09/10 6 2 FL
10/11 7 3 FL
Portsmouth 11/12 27 1 SL
Mansfield T 11/12
12/13
Portsmouth 12/13 31 7 SL
13/14 21 9 SL
14/15 35 18 SL
19/20 42 20 SL
20/21 37 13 FL
21/22 23 13 FL
Heart of Midlothian 21/22 12 3
22/23 30 5
Weymouth 23/24
Pontypridd
Bournemouth 25/26 33 8 FL
26/27 41 13 FL
27/28 37 8 FL
28/29 6 FL
Scunthorpe U

STRUTHERS
Clyde 95/96 2

STRUTHERS John D
b. Falkirk
Army
Queen's Park 19/20 2
20/21 41
Partick T 21/22 35

STUART Charles M
b. Lauriston
Falkirk 23/24 22
24/25 3

STURROCK Robert H
Heart of Midlothian
Dunfermline A 27/28 7 1

SUGGETT Ernest James
b. Pelaw 3.12.1905 d. Slough 29.3.1971
Crawcrook A
Ayr U 30/31 13 2
Gateshead T 30/31
Barrow 31/32 35 21 FL
Bradford PA 32/33 42 22 FL
33/34 35 10 FL
34/35 25 8 FL
35/36 6 1 FL

SUMMERS
Heart of Midlothian 95/96 2

SUMMERS David
Strathclyde
Hamilton A 36/37 2
37/38 3
Morton 38/39 D2
Ballymena U 39/40 IL
Strathclyde

SUMMERS Edward
b. Burnbank
Burnbank A
Clyde 27/28 20 1
28/29 38 1
29/30 23
30/31 23 1
31/32 35
32/33 33 1
33/34 31 1
34/35 36
35/36 27
36/37 12
Ayr U 36/37 21 D2
37/38 12

SUMMERS William 1 cap
b. Burnbank 14.7.1893 d. Burnbank 23.2.1972
Burnbank A
Bellshill A
Airdrieonians 18/19 29
19/20 25
St Bernards L 20/21
St Mirren 21/22 39
22/23 34 1
23/24 36 1
24/25 26
25/26 28 2
26/27 18
27/28 4
Bradford C 27/28 23 1 FL
28/29 38 FL
29/30 20 FL
30/31 31 FL
31/32 9 FL
Newport Co 32/33 36 FL

SURGENOR Jack
Queen's Park 21/22 4
Brooklyn Wanderers 22/23 13 ASL
23/24 18 ASL
Providence Clamdiggers 24/25 36 ASL
25/26 30 ASL
26/27 13 ASL

SURGEONOR Robert
Port Glasgow A
Morton 30/31 1
31/32 3

SUTHERLAND Charles Christison
b. Brechin 4.2.1898
Petershill
Third Lanark 16/17 28 3
Abercorn L 16/17
Clydebank 17/18 20 10
St Mirren 18/19 30 ?
19/20 28 6
Millwall 20/21 39 4 FL
21/22 18 4 FL
Bristol C 22/23 36 9 FL
23/24 22 1 FL
24/25 34 11 FL
25/26 11 2 FL
Merthyr T 26/27 34 6 FL
St Mirren 27/28 10 5

SUTHERLAND David
Newtongrange
Airdrieonians 03/04 9

SUTHERLAND George
Aberdeen 20/21 4

SUTHERLAND George
b. Musselburgh
Linlihgow Rose
East Stirlingshire 33/34 D2
East Fife 33/34 D2
34/35 D2
35/36 D2
Partick T 35/36 32
36/37 32
37/38 35
38/39 18
Leyton Orient FL

SUTHERLAND George
Benburb
Falkirk 36/37 3
Alloa A 36/37 D2
37/38 D2
Dundee U 38/39 D2

SUTHERLAND Hugh
b. Ayr c1900
Ayr Ballantyne
Ayr U 19/20 1
Queen of the South 20/21
English football
Ayr Fort 25/26

SUTHERLAND Kenneth
Queen's Park 21/22 3

SUTHERLAND Kenneth
Aberdeen 23/24 2
24/25 1

SUTHERLAND M
Leith A 94/95 2

SUTHERLAND Stanley
b. Earleston 21.1.1906
Grange R
Partick T 29/30 2
30/31 2
Bournemouth

SUTTON Joseph
b. Glasgow
Dunfermline A 23/24 D2
24/25 D2
25/26 D2
26/27 19 4
Luton T

SWALLOW Andrew
b. Bellshill 23.11.1906 d. Perth 15.6.1969
Shettleston Celtic
Shettleston Jnrs
St Johnstone 24/25 19
25/26 36 3
26/27 35 1
27/28 35 1
28/29 25 1
29/30 29
Millwall 30/31 21 3 FL
31/32 1 FL
32/33 3 FL
33/34 5 FL
34/35 10 FL
Morton 35/36 D2
Of Polish extraction: real first name was Andras

SWAN Andrew
b. Dalbeattie
Dalbeattie Star
6th GRV
St Mirren 02/03 12 1
03/04 21 7
04/05
Partick T 05/06 16 3
Blackpool
Workington

SWAN Edward
b. Glasgow 28.7.1897
St Rochs
Aberdeen 22/23 7
New York Giants 23/24 1 ASL
Barnsley 24/25 2 FL
Dumbarton 25/26 D2
Nairn Co 26/27
Forres Mechanics

SWANN Andrew McE

Glasgow University					
Queen's Park		00/01	20		
		01/02	13		
		02/03	3		
		03/04	10		
Partick T		03/04			

SWANN John Whyte

b. c1914

Larne		34/35			IL
		35/36			IL
Partick T		35/36			IL
		36/37	9		
		37/38	5		
		38/39	1		
Ballymena U		39/40			IL
Larne		40/41			

SWANSON Adam

Old Kilpatrick					
Clydebank		24/25			D2
		25/26	3		
Dumbarton		25/26			D2
Dumbarton A		26/27			
Rutherglen Glencairn		27/28			
		28/29			
Dunoon A					

SWIFT Henry

b. Accrington

Accrington S					
Burnley		09/10	1		FL
		10/11	33	1	FL
		11/12	17		FL
		12/13	13	1	FL
Third Lanark		13/14	29		
		14/15	28		
		15/16			
		16/17			
		17/18			
		18/19			
		19/20			
Pontypridd		19/20			

SYME David

b. Govan 11.12.1891 d. Irvine 20.4.1962

Irvine Meadow		13/14			
		14/15			
		15/16			
St Anthonys		16/17			
		17/18			
Celtic		18/19	2		
Stevenston U	T	18/19			
Irvine Meadow		19/20			

SYME Robert Graham

b. South Queensferry 13.12.1907 d. Cupar 1972

Hearts of Beath					
Blairhall					
Dunfermline A		28/29			D2
		29/30			D2
		30/31			D2
Manchester C		31/32	1		FL
		32/33	3		FL
		33/34	7	2	FL
Burnley		34/35	9		FL
Dunfermline A		34/35	3	1	
		35/36	34	3	
		36/37	36	2	
Dundee U					

SYMERS Stuart

Dundee		98/99	3	1	

SYMON James Scotland 1 cap

b. Errol 9.5.1911 d. Glasgow 30.4.1985

Errol Amateurs					
Perth NE					
Dundee Violet					
Dundee		30/31	21		
		31/32	32	2	
		32/33	26		
		33/34	35		
		34/35	36		
Portsmouth		35/36	34	3	FL
		36/37	23	2	FL
		37/38	9	1	FL
Rangers		38/39	22	3	
		46/47	10		

TAGGART T

Clyde		26/27	19	2	

TAGGART Thomas

Inkerman R					
Clyde		13/14	5	1	
East Stirlingshire		14/15			D2

TAIT

Third Lanark		92/93	2		
		93/94	1		

TAIT Alexander Gilchrist

b. Glenbuck 1873 d. Croydon 6.4.1949

Glenbuck A					
Ayr					
Royal Albert	L				
Rangers		91/92	6		
Motherwell		92/93			
		93/94	17		D2
Preston NE		94/95	3		FL
		95/96	25		FL
		96/97	15		FL
		97/98	7		FL
		98/99	26		FL
Tottenham H		99/00	28		SL
		00/01	22		SL
		01/02	26		SL
		02/03	25	1	SL
		03/04	25		SL
		04/05	24	1	SL
		05/06	27	1	SL
		06/07	24		SL
		07/08	1		SL
Leyton		08/09	6		SL

TAIT David

Renton		92/93	1		
		93/94	18		
		94/95	15	?	D2
		95/96	12	?	D2
Manchester C		96/97	4	2	FL
		97/98			FL
Darwen		98/99	4		FL

TAIT James

b. Edinburgh

Petershill					
Bo'ness					
Heart of Midlothian		20/21			
		21/22	2		
		22/23	1		
Broxburn U	L	22/23			D2
Bournemouth		23/24	12	4	FL

TAIT John B

Heart of Midlothian		03/04	2		

TAIT Joseph

Pollok Jnrs					
Dumbarton		16/17	3		

TAIT Robert

Carlisle U					
Motherwell		08/09	30	5	
Nithsdale W		09/10			
		10/11			
Cowdenbeath		11/12			

TAIT Thomas Somerville 1 cap

b. Carluke 13.9.1879

Cambuslang R					
Airdrieonians		99/00	7		D2
		00/01	17	2	D2
		01/02	22	1	D2
		02/03	21	2	D2
Bristol R		03/04	34	1	SL
		04/05	32	1	SL
		05/06	30		SL
Sunderland		06/07	35	1	FL
		07/08	30		FL
		08/09	26		FL
		09/10	35		FL
		10/11	35	1	FL
		11/12	19		FL
Dundee		12/13	22		
Wishaw Thistle		13/14			
Jarrow					
Armadale		14/15			

TALLAS Charles

Dunfermline A		27/28	5	1	
Alloa A		28/29			D2
Kings Park		28/29			D2
?					
East Stirlingshire		31/32			D2
Bo'ness					

TANNER Andrew

Morton		20/21	2		

TARBAT Edward McKenzie

b. Forfar 1881 d. Old Ardrossan ?.7.1933

Forfar A		00/01			
Dundee		00/01	1		
Forfar A		01/02			
Bathgate		02/03			
Airdrieonians		03/04	20	6	
		04/05	24	12	
		05/06	23	8	
		06/07	10	3	
Third Lanark		07/08	24	5	
		08/09	6	1	

TAYLOR

Renton		92/93	1		

TAYLOR Andrew

b. c1910

Shawfield Jnrs					
Third Lanark		32/33	32		
		33/34	16		

TAYLOR Archibald

b. Dundee 1882

Dundee		00/01	1		
East Craigie					
Bolton W		04/05	3		FL
Bristol R		05/06	9		SL
West Ham U		06/07	4		SL
		07/08	25		SL
		08/09	34		SL
Dundee					Sc
Falkirk		09/10			Sc
Huddersfield T		10/11	29		FL
Barnsley		11/12	34		FL
		12/13	23		FL
York C					

TAYLOR Archibald

b. Dumbarton *

Vale St Andrews *					
Heart of Midlothian *		35/36			
		36/37			
		37/38			
Clyde		38/39	4	5	

TAYLOR David

b. Bannockburn 29.7.1883 d. Logie 6.8.1949

Bannockburn Jnrs					
Falkirk	T				
Glasgow Ashfield		06/07			
Rangers		06/07	9		
		07/08	12		
		08/09	6		
Motherwell	L	09/10	34	4	
Rangers		10/11	1		
Bradford C		10/11	33	1	FL
		11/12	12		FL
Burnley		11/12	21		FL
		12/13	30	1	FL
		13/14	30		FL
		14/15	34	1	FL
Ayr U	L	15/16	1		
Rangers	L	15/16	1		
Falkirk	L	17/18	2		
Celtic	L	18/19	5		
Burnley		19/20	3		FL
		20/21	11		FL
		21/22	15		FL
		22/23	40	1	FL
		23/24	37	1	FL

TAYLOR David

b. c1904

Anstruther R					
Raith R		24/25	1		

TAYLOR David W

b. c1890

Hull C					
Darlington					
Heart of Midlothian		11/12	24		
		12/13	33		
		13/14	32		
Bristol R		14/15			SL

TAYLOR Francis P

b. Glasgow

Queen's Park		29/30	8	3	
		30/31	15	6	
		31/32	3		
		32/33	1		
		33/34	8		
		34/35	13	5	

TAYLOR George
b. Aberdeen 9.6.1913
Hall Russells
Aberdeen 36/37
37/38 1
38/39 5
46/47 28 3
47/48 29 3
Plymouth A

TAYLOR Henry
K.I.A.
Kings Park
Falkirk 11/12 2
Stenhousemuir 12/13

TAYLOR James
b. Kirkoswald
Kilwinning R
Kilmarnock 32/33 2
Dalbeattie Star

TAYLOR James K
b. Dumbarton
Dumbarton 21/22 8 1

TAYLOR John
Falkirk 08/09
09/10 30

TAYLOR John
b. Glasgow
Strathclyde
Dundee
Hibernian 28/29 2 1
29/30 31 3
30/31 17 3
Ayr U 31/32 36 4
32/33 37 2
33/34 25 4
34/35 36
35/36 20 3
36/37 26 3 D2
37/38 38 2
38/39 8 1

TAYLOR John B
Queen's Park 03/04 17 2
04/05 11 2

TAYLOR John Davidson 4 caps
b. Dumbarton 27.1.1872 d. West Kirby 1949
Dumbarton A
Dumbarton 90/91 15 10
91/92 18 13
92/93 12 3
93/94 13 6
St Mirren 93/94 1
94/95 15 9
95/96 11 3
Everton 96/97 30 12 FL
97/98 30 2 FL
98/99 34 3 FL
99/00 32 7 FL
00/01 25 10 FL
01/02 26 8 FL
02/03 33 3 FL
03/04 22 6 FL
04/05 34 4 FL
05/06 36 5 FL
06/07 34 1 FL
07/08 23 2 FL
08/09 27 FL
09/10 14 FL
South Liverpool

TAYLOR John M
Port Glasgow Jnrs
Port Glasgow A 07/08 2 1
08/09

TAYLOR Robert
Parkhead Jnrs
Hibernian 15/16 30 3

TAYLOR Robert S
Glasgow Perthshire
Clyde 32/33 2
Dumbarton 32/33 D2
33/34 D2

TAYLOR Thomas
Third Lanark 05/06 1

TAYLOR Thomas
Dundee 16/17 1

TAYLOR William 1 cap
b. Edinburgh 1870 d. 23.7.1949
Dalry Primrose
Heart of Midlothian 90/91 18 5
91/92 21 10
92/93 10 5
Blackburn R 92/93 10 1 FL
Heart of Midlothian 93/94 16 8
94/95 1
95/96 4 6
96/97 16 12
97/98 8 4
98/99 15 10
99/00 8 3
Leith A 00/01 9 ? D2

TAYLOR William
b. Edinburgh c1885
Gainsborough T 05/06 4 FL
West Ham U 06/07 4 SL
Croydon Common 07/08 18 SL
08/09 12 SL
09/10 22 SL
Airdrieonians 10/11 11
Dunfermline A 11/12
Newport Co 12/13 21 SL
Glentoran 13/14 IL
Hartlepool U 14/15

TAYLOR William
b. Longriggend
Longriggend Thistle
Slamannan Hearts
Dundee U 27/28 18 D2
28/29 31 D2
29/30 32
30/31 38 1 D2
31/32 37 1
32/33 30 D2
St Johnstone 32/33 1
33/34 23
34/35 25
35/36 28
36/37 26
37/38 30
Arbroath 38/39 3

TELFER Robert
Clyde 20/21 1

TELFER William 2 caps
b. Shotts 23.3.1909 d. 15.5.1986
Blantyre Celtic
Motherwell 29/30 27
30/31 37
31/32 37
32/33 27
33/34 37
34/35 23 1
35/36 16
36/37 25
37/38 20
38/39 35
Airdrieonians

TELFER William
Grange R
Dundee T
Falkirk 37/38
38/39 1

TELFORD John
Maryhill Hibs
Maryhill Jnrs 36/37
Arthurlie 37/38
Clyde 38/39 6

TEMPLE
Ayr U 17/18 1 ?

TEMPLE Robert
Grangemouth Boys Brigade
Cowie Juveniles
Kings Park
Aberdeen 35/36
36/37 10
37/38 10
Dundee U 38/39 34 9 D2

TEMPLEMAN David
Arthurlie 13/14 D2
Airdrieonians 14/15 1
15/16 3

TEMPLEMAN William
Kames A
Glasgow Perthshire 10/11
Airdrieonians 11/12 26 4
12/13 32 8
13/14 31 4
14/15 14

TEMPLETON
Clyde 92/93 11 3
93/94 10 ? D2

TEMPLETON A
Ayr U 13/14 1

TEMPLETON Andrew
Queen's Park 06/07 20 7
07/08 5
08/09 4

TEMPLETON Daniel
Queen's Park 16/17 19 2

TEMPLETON Daniel
b. Glasgow
Queen's Park 20/21 13
21/22 35 5
Partick T 22/23 13 1
Ayr U 23/24 10 1
24/25 13

TEMPLETON James F
Queen's Park 00/01 19
01/02 14 1
02/03 15 1
03/04 7

TEMPLETON Robert
b. Paisley
Neilston V
Hibernian 11/12 12
12/13 33
13/14 34
14/15 19
15/16 7
16/17 4
17/18 15 ?
18/19 14 ?
19/20 25 1
20/21 24 3
21/22 13
22/23 4
23/24 13
24/25 11
25/26 5
26/27 1

TEMPLETON Robert Bryson 11 caps
b. Coylton 22.6.1879 d. Kilmarnock 2.11.1919
Irvine Heatherbell
Westmount
Kilmarnock Roslin
Neilston V
Kilmarnock RUFC 97/98
Hibernian 97/98
98/99
Aston Villa 98/99 1 FL
99/00 11 5 FL
00/01 17 2 FL
01/02 24 FL
02/03 11 1 FL
Newcastle U 02/03 10 1 FL
03/04 31 3 FL
04/05 10 FL
Woolwich Arsenal 04/05 16 1 FL
05/06 17 FL
Celtic 06/07 25 6
07/08 4
Kilmarnock 08/08 19 7
08/09 29 3
09/10 24
10/11 33
11/12 30 1
12/13 29 1
Fulham 13/14 10 FL
14/15 23 FL
Kilmarnock 14/15

TENNANT A K
Partick T 04/05
05/06
06/07 1 1
Queen's Park 06/07 1

TENNANT David
b. c1882 d. Glasgow ?.1.1945
Cambuslang R
Airdrieonians 02/03 1 D2
03/04 18 4
04/05 19 1
05/06 12
06/07
07/08
Albion R 08/09 D2

TENNANT James
b. Parkhead 1878
Linton Villa
Parkhead
St Bernards 97/98 8 3
98/99 17 8
Woolwich Arsenal 99/00 26 5 FL
00/01 25 2 FL
Middlesbrough 01/02 16 8 FL
Watford 02/03 31 6 SL
03/04 20 7 SL
04/05 32 2 SL
Royal Albert 05/06
Stenhousemuir 06/07
St Bernards 07/08 D2
09/09 D2

TENNANT James

Kilwinning R
Canada
St Johnstone 33/34 34 6
34/35 31 4
35/36 22
36/37 35 3
37/38 31 3
38/39 19 8

TENNANT John

Ashgill
Motherwell 08/09 1
09/10 7 4
10/11 16 3
Royal Albert 11/12

TENNANT Thomas

St Bernards 95/96 12
Motherwell 95/96 D2

TENNANT Thomas

Clydebank Jnrs
Motherwell 27/28 2
28/29 14 8

TENNANT William
b. Coatbridge 1874
Arthurlie 95/96
96/97
97/98
98/99
QPR 99/00 12 5 SL
Arthurlie 99/00
Third Lanark 00/01 1

TENNANT William Shields
b. Carluke 26.10.1902
Motherwell Welfare
Motherwell 21/22 16 3
22/23 8 2
23/24
24/25 28 7
25/26 31 11
26/27 18 18
27/28 8 9
28/29 3
Norwich C 30/31 10 1 FL

TENNANT William W

Partick T 04/05 9
Queen's Park 05/06 16 5

TERRAS Samuel

Kilmarnock Winton
Galston
Kilmarnock 99/00 1
00/01
Galston 00/01
Hurlford 01/02
02/03
03/04
04/05
Galston 05/06
06/07
Nithsdale W 07/08

TERRIS James Lonie
b. Cowdenbeath 21.12.1894
Victoria Hawthorn
Inverkeithing Jnrs
Cowdenbeath
Heart of Midlothian 18/19 8
Cowdenbeath 19/20
20/21
Millwall 21/22 3 FL
Falkirk
Liverpool
New York Field Club 23/24 25 2 ASL
Indiana Flooring 24/25 41 2 ASL
25/26 39 ASL
26/27 32 ASL
New York Giants 27/28 10 1 ASL
28/29 3 ESL

TERRIS Robert

Bowhill Thistle
Falkirk 10/11 3 3
11/12 10 1
12/13 24 8
13/14 13 1
Liverpool 13/14 FL
14/15 FL
East Fife 15/16
Falkirk 16/17 5

THACKERAY David
b. Hamilton 16.11.1902 d. Portsmouth 21.7.1954
Banknock Jnrs
Law Winnings
Alloa A 21/22 D2
22/23 D2
23/24 D2
24/25 D2
Motherwell 25/26 37 1
26/27 35 2
27/28 38 1
Portsmouth 28/29 40 1 FL
29/30 41 4 FL
30/31 40 2 FL
31/32 39 1 FL
32/33 41 1 FL
33/34 35 FL
34/35 40 FL
35/36 3 FL

THOM Alexander
b. Ardrossan 11.10.1890 d. Glasgow 1.10.1973
Leven Academy
Leven Amateurs
Yoker A
Dumbarton 13/14 23 2
14/15 34 6
15/16 38 8
16/17 36 11
17/18 33 8
Kilmarnock L 17/18 1
Dumbarton 18/19
Ayr U L 18/19 2 1
Motherwell L 18/19 1
Dumbarton 19/20 27 4
Morton 20/21 14 7
Airdrieonians 21/22 40 7
Hull C 22/23 35 5 FL
23/24 32 4 FL
24/25 30 3 FL
25/26 34 6 FL
Swindon T 26/27 27 8 FL
27/28 29 9 FL
28/29 37 6 FL
29/30 7 1 FL

THOM Hugh

Queen's Park 19/20 16
20/21 12

THOM James

Parkhead Jnrs
Celtic T 94/95 1
Parkhead Jnrs

THOM Matthew

Ardeer Thistle
Kilmarnock 17/18 5
Stevenston U 18/19
Dalbeattie Star

THOMAS Daniel
b. Glasgow 30.3.1872
Mossend Celtic
Celtic T 94/95 1
Hibernian 95/96
Motherwell 95/96 D2
96/97 D2
Carfin R 97/98
Albion R 98/99
Carfin R 98/99

THOMAS Daniel
b. Falkirk
Forfar A
St Johnstone 24/25 24 8
25/26 12 1

THOMAS William A

Queen's Park 02/03 4
03/04 1
04/05
05/06 2 1

THOMPSON Francis William
b. Ballynahinch 2.10.1885 d. Ayr 4.10.1950
Cliftonville 05/06 IL
06/07 IL
07/08 IL
08/09 IL
09/10 IL
10/11 IL
Black Diamonds 10/11
Linfield 10/11 IL
Bradford C 10/11 10 2 FL
11/12 23 6 FL
12/13 17 2 FL
Clyde 13/14 27 2
14/15 34 9
15/16
16/17
17/18
18/19
19/20 31 11
20/21 33 5
21/22 13
22/23 20 3
23/24 16 2

THOMPSON George Wilfred
b. Witton le Wear 15.4.1896 d. Sunderland 1976
Castletown
Southwick
Norwich C 14/15 2 SL
Croydon Common
Durham C
Norwich C 19/20 3 SL
Aberdare A 20/21
Dundee 21/22 12
Torquay U 22/23
Reading 23/24 23 2 FL
Coventry C 24/25 2 FL
Nuneaton T 24/25
25/26
Walsall 25/26 1 FL
Caernarvon T 26/27
27/28
Scarborough 28/29
Rhyl A 28/29
Larne 29/30 IL

THOMPSON J

Falkirk 12/13 1

THOMPSON James Edward H
b. Thornaby 1908
Marsden
Weymouth 26/27
27/28
28/29
Whitby U 29/30
Hartlepools U 29/30 18 10 FL
30/31 37 9 FL
31/32 12 3 FL
Falkirk T 32/33 6 1

THOMPSON James H

Raith R 16/17 7 1

THOMPSON Peter
b. Rothesay 23.4.1877
Bute R
St Mirren
Partick T 98/99 1
99/00
00/01
Chesterfield T 01/02 4 FL

THOMSON

Cambuslang 90/91 1
91/92 4

THOMSON

Heart of Midlothian 90/91 2

THOMSON

St Mirren 91/92 4

THOMSON

Abercorn 92/93 2
93/94 7 ? D2
94/95 3 ? D2

THOMSON

Third Lanark 93/94 3

THOMSON

St Mirren 95/96 1

THOMSON

Third Lanark 95/96 7 1

THOMSON

Queen's Park 09/10 1

THOMSON

Rangers 14/15 3

THOMSON

Falkirk 15/16 1

THOMSON

Heart of Midlothian 15/16 1
16/17 2 1

THOMSON

St Mirren 16/17 1

THOMSON (see BENNETT, Alexander)

Ayr U 17/18 3 ?
18/19 2 2

THOMSON

Heart of Midlothian 18/19 2

THOMSON

Hibernian 19/20 1

THOMSON

Raith R 22/23 5 1
Lochgelly U 23/24 D2

THOMSON A

Queen's Park 15/16 2

THOMSON (Alex?)

Falkirk 18/19 4 ?

THOMSON Alexander

St Bernards 97/98 3
Kings Park 97/98
St Ninians Thistle
Falkirk
Dunblane 02/03

THOMSON Alexander 1 cap
b. Coatbridge?
Coatbridge Caledonians
Airdrieonians 99/00 18 4 D2
00/01 14 11 D2
01/02 19 9 D2
02/03 21 11 D2
03/04 4
04/05 25 8
05/06 29 8
06/07 29 8
07/08 33 16
08/09 33 14
09/10 33 12
10/11 33 7
11/12 32 7
12/13 33 6
13/14 36 12
14/15 36 6
15/16 28 3
16/17 8 1

THOMSON Alexander

Baillieston Thistle
Falkirk 07/08 2

THOMSON Alexander
b. Glasgow
Rutherglen Glencairn
Airdrieonians 22/23 1
Armadale 23/24 D2

THOMSON Alexander 3 caps
b. Buckhaven 14.6.1901 d. 1975
Glencraig Celtic
Wellesley Jnrs
Celtic 22/23 9 1
23/24 33 3
Ayr U L 23/24
Celtic 24/25 38 12
25/26 37 16
26/27 37 12
27/28 36 12
28/29 37 5
29/30 35 4
30/31 36 6
31/32 35 9
32/33 36 6
33/34 22 2
Dunfermline A 34/35 38 4
35/36 34 9
36/37 7

THOMSON Alick

Falkirk 13/14 3 1
14/15 9 1

THOMSON Andrew 1 cap
b. Barrhead d. Prestwick 2.6.1936
Arthurlie
Third Lanark 90/91 13 1
91/92 17 1
92/93 12

THOMSON Archibald
b. Glasgow
Linlithgow Port
Bo'ness 26/27 D2
27/28 29
Cowdenbeath 28/29 25

THOMSON Benjamin
b. Saltcoats 8.6.1913 d. 1944
Kilwinning R 30/31
31/32
32/33
33/34
Kilmarnock 34/35 10
35/36 36 8
36/37 38 11
37/38 36 12
38/39 27 8

THOMSON C

Queen's Park 06/07 1

THOMSON Charles Bellamy 21 caps
b. Prestonpans 12.6.1878 d. Edinburgh 6.2.1936
Prestonpans
Heart of Midlothian 98/99 1
99/00 3 1
00/01 17
01/02 13 6
02/03 10 1
03/04 25 1
04/05 24 3
05/06 35 7
06/07 22 5
07/08 25 7
Sunderland 08/09 36 2 FL
09/10 35 FL
10/11 35 FL
11/12 30 FL
12/13 35 1 FL
13/14 29 FL
14/15 36 FL

THOMSON Charles Marshall
b. Perth 25.10.1905
Perth YMCA
Arbroath T 25/26 1 D2
Raith R 27/28 4
Alloa A 28/29 D2
29/30 D2
Falkirk 30/31 12
31/32 34
32/33 38
33/34 38
Brighton 34/35 42 FL
35/36 35 FL
36/37 39 FL
37/38 27 FL
38/39 26 FL
Exeter C 39/40 3 FL
Dundee U 46/47 D2

THOMSON Daniel

Dumbarton 92/93 10
93/94
94/95 13 2
95/96 16 2
96/97 13 ? D2

THOMSON Daniel
b. Stirling
California Celtic
Falkirk 20/21 6 1
21/22 14 5
22/23 27 4
Aberdeen 23/24 11 1
Forfar A

THOMSON David

Glasgow Ashfield
Queen's Park 05/06 4

THOMSON David

Port Glasgow A 07/08 18
08/09 24
Everton 09/10 FL
10/11 FL
Kilmarnock 11/12 4
Ayr U 11/12 D2
12/13 D2
Airdrieonians 13/14
Stevenston U 13/14

THOMSON David 1 cap
b. Dundee 1892 d. c1950
Fairfield Jnrs
Dundee 13/14 19
14/15 33
15/16 14
16/17 29 3
17/18
18/19
19/20 40 1
20/21 35 4
21/22 29
22/23 30 2
23/24 28
24/25 36 2
25/26 32 2
26/27 25 1

THOMSON Douglas
b. Dundee 10.8.1891
Dundee Violet
Minnedosa (Canada)
Winnipeg Scottish
Dundee Hibs
Millwall 19/20 16 4 SL
Aberdeen 20/21 36 6
21/22 30 10
22/23 29 11
Grimsby T 23/24 25 3 FL
Aberdeen 23/24
Dartford

THOMSON E

Morton Amateurs
Port Glasgow Jnrs
Morton 12/13 3

THOMSON F

St Bernards 99/00 1 1

THOMSON G S

Falkirk 14/15 5 2

THOMSON George
b. Glasgow
Alloa A
East Stirlingshire 26/27 D2
27/28 D2
28/29 D2
29/30 D2
30/31 D2
31/32 D2
32/33 22

THOMSON George
b. Campsie
Yoker A
Clydebank

Club		Season	Apps	Goals	League
Newcastle U	T	29/30			FL
Dundee U		29/30	15	2	
		30/31			D2
		31/32			D2
Bo'ness		31/32			D2
Aberdeen		32/33	3		
		33/34	33	2	
		34/35	36	2	
		35/36	34	6	
		36/37	36		
		37/38	33	2	
		38/39	38	4	

THOMSON George
b. Kilmarnock
Clydebank

Club		Season	Apps	Goals	League
St Mirren		30/31	2		

THOMSON Hugh

Club		Season	Apps	Goals	League
Clyde		09/10	1		

THOMSON Hugh

Club		Season	Apps	Goals	League
Hibernian		10/11	2		

THOMSON Hugh M

Club		Season	Apps	Goals	League
Partick T		11/12	1		
St Bernards		12/13			D2
Ayr U		12/13			D2

THOMSON J

Club		Season	Apps	Goals	League
Port Glasgow A		06/07	26	2	
		07/08	25		
		08/09	12	1	
		09/10	25	1	

THOMSON J

Club		Season	Apps	Goals	League
Queen's Park		14/15	4		

THOMSON James
b. Dumbarton
Clydebank
Renton

Club		Season	Apps	Goals	League
Manchester U		13/14	6	1	FL
Dumbarton Harp		14/15			
Clyde		15/16	10	4	
		16/17	16	2	
Dumbarton Harp		16/17			
St Mirren		17/18			
		18/19			
		19/20	42	12	
		20/21	38	7	
		21/22	42	11	
		22/23	32	7	
		23/24	38	13	
		24/25	35	9	
		25/26	32	4	
		26/27	32	7	
		27/28	5	3	
		28/29	2	1	

THOMSON James

Club		Season	Apps	Goals	League
Falkirk		14/15	2		

THOMSON James

Club		Season	Apps	Goals	League
Aberdeen		16/17	11		

THOMSON James Hunter
b. Shetland 9.5.1884 d. ?.11.1959
Edinburgh Myrtle
Leith A

Club		Season	Apps	Goals	League
Heart of Midlothian		02/03	16	8	
Abercorn					
Leith A		03/04			
		04/05			
		05/06			
Portsmouth		06/07	36	1	SL
		07/08	35	1	SL
		08/09	14	1	SL
		09/10	24		SL
		10/11	29		SL
Coventry C		11/12	31		SL
		12/13	38		SL
Bury		13/14	25		FL
		14/15	33		FL
Nelson					

THOMSON James Pender
b. Larkhall 10.11.1908 d. Larkhall 1984
Larkhall Academy
Larkhall Thistle

Club		Season	Apps	Goals	League
Strathclyde Jnrs		26/27			
Kilmarnock		26/27	17	2	
		27/28	23	3	
Third Lanark		28/29	21	1	
Carlisle U		29/30	15	3	FL
Dunfermline A		30/31			D2
		31/32			D2
		32/33			D2
Newry T		33/34			IL
Larne		34/35			IL
		35/36			IL
Blairhall Colliery		36/37			

THOMSON James S

Club		Season	Apps	Goals	League
Queen's Park		05/06	26		
		06/07	22		
		07/08	8		
		08/09	23	1	
		09/10	16		
		10/11	12		
Third Lanark		11/12	26		
		12/13	24		
Dumbarton		13/14	23		
		14/15	22		

THOMSON James William

Club		Season	Apps	Goals	League
Queen's Park		36/37	5		
		37/38	1		

THOMSON John

Club		Season	Apps	Goals	League
Carlisle U					
Dalbeattie Star					
Hamilton A		08/09	1		

THOMSON John

Club		Season	Apps	Goals	League
Loanhead Mayflower					
Raith R		14/15	7	1	

THOMSON John

Club		Season	Apps	Goals	League
Third Lanark		16/17	21	1	
		17/18	8	?	

THOMSON John

Club		Season	Apps	Goals	League
Hamilton A		18/19	16	2	

THOMSON John 4 caps
b. Buckhaven 28.1.1909 d. Glasgow 5.9.1931

Club		Season	Apps	Goals	League
Bowhill WE		24/25			
Bowhill R		24/25			
Wellesley Jnrs		25/26			
Celtic		26/27	15		
Ayr U	L	26/27			
Celtic		27/28	38		
		28/29	37		
		29/30	29		
		30/31	36		
		31/32	8		

THOMSON John
K.I.A. 1944

Club		Season	Apps	Goals	League
Hamilton A		32/33	4		
		33/34	12		
		34/35	27	1	
		35/36	37		
		36/37	35		
		37/38	36	1	
		38/39	16	3	

THOMSON John
b. c1915
Blairhall Jnrs

Club		Season	Apps	Goals	League
Dunfermline A		35/36	5		

THOMSON John B

Club		Season	Apps	Goals	League
Arbroath		37/38	1		

THOMSON John Ross 1 cap
b. Thornton 6.7.1906 d. Montrose 21.10.1979
Thornton R

Club		Season	Apps	Goals	League
Dundee		24/25	1		
		25/26	2	1	
		26/27	23		
		27/28	38	1	
		28/29	35	3	
		29/30	26	2	
Everton		29/30	9		FL
		30/31	41		FL
		31/32	39		FL
		32/33	41	3	FL
		33/34	38		FL
		34/35	42	1	FL
		35/36	25		FL
		36/37	2		FL
		37/38	9	1	FL
		38/39	26		FL
Carnoustie Panmuir					

THOMSON John S

Club		Season	Apps	Goals	League
Leith A		31/32	10		

THOMSON John Youngman
b. West Greenock 27.6.1896
Caledonian Jnrs
Benburb

Club		Season	Apps	Goals	League
Bristol R		21/22	5		FL
Alloa A		22/23	35		
Partick T		23/24	28		
Aberaman		24/25			
Aberdare A		24/25	20		FL
Brentford		25/26	40		FL
Plymouth A		26/27	7		FL
Chesterfield		27/28	22		FL
Coventry C		27/28	3		FL
New York Nationals		28/29			
Nuneaton T		29/30			

THOMSON Norman Shaw
b. Glasgow 20.2.1901 d. Ferring 6.6.1984
St Anthonys

Club		Season	Apps	Goals	League
Dumbarton		21/22	7	2	
		22/23			D2
		23/24			D2
Hibernian	L	24/25	5		
Luton T		25/26	27	5	FL
		26/27	17	4	FL
Clapton Orient		26/27	10	2	FL
Brighton		27/28	11	5	FL
Walsall		28/29	38	13	FL
Norwich C		29/30	16		FL
Brentford		30/31	1		FL
Swindon T		32/33	3		FL
Folkestone T		33/34			

THOMSON Robert

Club		Season	Apps	Goals	League
Dumbarton Corinthians					
Heart of Midlothian		05/06	11		
		06/07	8		

THOMSON Robert 1 cap
b. Falkirk 24.10.1903 d. Ipswich
Laurieston Villa
Falkirk Amateurs

Club		Season	Apps	Goals	League
Falkirk		25/26	13		
		26/27	25		
Sunderland		27/28	19		FL
Newcastle U		28/29	29		FL
		29/30	23		FL
		30/31	16		FL
		31/32	3		FL
		33/34	2		FL
Hull C		34/35	4		FL
Marseilles		34/35			
Racing Club de Paris		35/36			
Marseilles		35/36			
Ipswich T		36/37	27		SL
		37/38	1		SL

THOMSON Robert Austin 1 cap
b. Johnstone 12.7.1907 d. Blythswood 17.9.1937
Broomfield Juveniles
Possil Hawthorn

Club		Season	Apps	Goals	League
Glasgow Perthshire		26/27			
		27/28			
		28/29			
Celtic		29/30	20	3	
		30/31	34	10	
		31/32	28	5	
		32/33	29	6	
Blackpool		33/34	24	1	FL
Motherwell		34/35	8	1	
		35/36			
Brideville		35/36			LI

THOMSON Robert Rayburn
b. Kilmarnock 1875 d. Dalziel 1934

Hamilton A		95/96			
Celtic					
Third Lanark		98/99	12		
		99/00	17		
		00/01	17		
		01/02	17	1	
		02/03	17		
		03/04	1		
Hamilton A		03/04			
Albion R					

THOMSON Samuel J

Camphill School					
Queen's Park		35/36	2		
		36/37	12		
		37/38			
		38/39	10		

THOMSON Thomas J
d. ?.8.1910

Parkhead					
Morton		03/04	1		
		04/05	17		
		05/06	30		
		06/07	2		
		07/08	32		
		08/09	25		
Johnstone		09/10			

THOMSON W

Third Lanark		90/91	10	4	
		91/92	6	5	
		92/93	1		

THOMSON W

St Mirren		17/18	13		
		18/19	33	?	

THOMSON W

Clyde		32/33	3		

THOMSON Walter
b. Glasgow

Benburb					
Hamilton A		20/21	15		
		21/22	38	1	
		22/23	32		
		23/24	37	1	
		24/25	35		
		25/26	35	5	
		26/27	30	1	
		27/28	20		
		28/29	6		
Alloa A		28/29			D2

THOMSON William 4 caps

Dumbarton		90/91	2	1	
		91/92	20	3	
		92/93	8	1	
		93/94	17		
		94/95	10		

THOMSON William 1 cap
b. Dundee?

Clydemore					
Dundee Our Boys					
Dundee		93/94	17	2	
		94/95	16	3	
		95/96	18	2	
Bolton W		96/97	22	4	FL
		97/98	15	1	FL
		98/99	8		FL

THOMSON William

Wishaw Hibernian					
Celtic	T	94/95	1		
Wishaw Hibernian					

THOMSON William

Clyde		98/99	17		
		99/00	7	1	
		00/01	1	?	D2

THOMSON William

Queen's Park		02/03	1		

THOMSON William

Queen's Park		05/06	2		
		06/07			
		07/08	1		

THOMSON William
b. Glasgow c1895

Blantyre V					
Parkhead					
Clyde		12/13	10		
		13/14	4		
Leicester F		14/15	35	1	FL
Arthurlie					
Leicester C		19/20	34	1	FL
		20/21	27		FL
		21/22	39	1	FL
		22/23	38		FL
		23/24	24		FL
Bristol R		24/25	21		FL
Inverness Citadel					

THOMSON William
b. Kilsyth

Kilsyth St Patricks					
Hibernian		19/20	9		
		20/21	4		

THOMSON William

Victoria					
Third Lanark		19/20	3		
		20/21	1		

THOMSON William

Clyde		20/21	1	1	

THOMSON William
b. c1913

Barrhead YMCA					
Hibernian		30/31			
		31/32			D2
Airdrieonians		32/33	21	2	
		33/34	21		
		34/35	35	1	
Queen of the South		35/36	25		
		36/37	30	5	
		37/38	21		
Kilmarnock		38/39			

THOMSON William
b. North Berwick c1916

Berwick R					
Sunderland					
Norwich C					
Ashington					
Leeds U		35/36			FL
		36/37			FL
		37/38			FL
Ayr U		38/39	1		

THOMSON William I

Dundee					
Arthurlie		09/10			D2
		10/11	19	?	D2
Raith R		11/12	4		

THOMSON William S
b. Baillieston

Wellshot Albion					
Parkhead					
Morton					
Dundee		04/05	5		
		05/06			
Hamilton A		06/07	5	1	

THORBURN Alexander
b. Glasgow

East Fife					
Hibernian		12/13	9		
East Fife		13/14			
Dumbarton		13/14			
Abercorn		14/15			D2

THORBURN Harry

Buckhaven					
Raith R		10/11	8	1	
East Fife		11/12			

THORBURN Harry H

Co-operative U					
Queen's Park		03/04	1		
Everton		04/05			
Motherwell		05/06	3		
Port Glasgow A		06/07	4	1	

THORNLEY Irvine
b. Glossop 1883 d. South Shields 24.4.1955

Glossop Villa					
Glossop St James					
Glossop		01/02	13	5	FL
		02/03	34	14	FL
		03/04	32	21	FL
Manchester C		03/04	4		FL
		04/05	4	2	FL
		05/06	36	21	FL
		06/07	30	13	FL
		07/08	31	14	FL
		08/09	31	18	FL
		09/10	22	12	FL
		10/11	18	6	FL
		11/12	19	6	FL
South Shields Adelaide		12/13			
		13/14			
		14/15			
Clydebank		17/18	3	1	
Hamilton A		18/19			
		19/20	27	16	
Houghton					

THORNTON W

Third Lanark		11/12	1		

THORNTON William 7 caps
b. Winchburgh 3.3.1920

Winchburgh A					
Rangers		36/37	5	1	
		37/38	14	5	
		38/39	36	23	
		46/47	25	18	
		47/48	30	17	
		48/49	29	22	
		49/50	19	11	
		50/51	21	12	
		51/52	28	18	
		52/53	4	4	
		53/54	8	7	

THORPE Peter
b. Glasgow

Queen's Park		14/15	22	1	
		15/16	34	4	
		16/17	35	3	
Clyde		17/18	28	?	
		18/19	24	?	
		19/20	4		
		20/21	6		
Morton		20/21	9		
		21/22	23		

THOW Lewis K
b. c1921

Ardeer Recreation					
Ayr U		37/38	6	3	
		38/39	23	10	

TIERNEY Cornelius
b. Kilbirnie 22.4.1909

Rosewell Rosedale					
Bo'ness		29/30			D2
Celtic		29/30			
		30/31	7		
St Johnstone	L	30/31	11	1	D2
Celtic		31/32			
Forfar A	L	31/32			D2
Belfast Celtic	L	31/32			IL
Guildford C		32/33			
		33/34			
Exeter C		34/35	18	1	FL
?		35/36			
		36/37			
Glenavon		37/38			

TILL Ernest

Crossgates Primrose					
Hamilton A	T				
Raith R		38/39	26	1	

TILL Joseph
b. Stoke c1895

Wellington T					
Dumbarton		19/20	39		
		20/21	35		
St Mirren		20/21	3		
		21/22	35		
		22/23			
Luton T		23/24	34		FL
		24/25	22		FL
		25/26	37	1	FL
		26/27	37		FL
		27/28	8		FL
Crewe A	T				

TIMMINS John

Fauldhouse U					
Airdrieonians		26/27	2		

TODD

Third Lanark	95/96	2		

TODD Alan

b. Leslie c1912

Wellesley				
Leith A	31/32	22		
Cowdenbeath	32/33	4		
Port Vale	32/33	9		FL
	33/34	28		FL
	34/35			FL
	35/36	2		FL
	36/37	39		FL
Nottingham F	37/38	5		FL
	38/39	12		FL
Darlington	39/40	3		FL

TODD Alexander

Clydebank Jnrs				
Queen's Park	12/13	32		
	13/14	37		
St Mirren	14/15	17		

TODD Archibald

Larkhall Thistle				
Airdrieonians	15/16	22	4	

TODD Harold

b. Kirkcaldy c1914

Newtongrange Star				
Airdrieonians	33/34	32	2	
	34/35	19		
Margate	35/36			

TODD Hugh

Falkirk	24/25	13	1	
	25/26	23		
Raith R	26/27			D2

TODD James Colin

b. Canongate 1895 K.I.A. Flanders 12.3.1916

Raith R	14/15	22	1	

TODD John A

Nithsdale W					
Clyde		10/11	2		
		11/12	10	4	
Hamilton A		12/13	1	2	
Motherwell	L				
Armadale		13/14			
Airdrieonians		13/14	3		
Nithsdale W					
Airdrieonians *		16/17	3	1	

TOLAND Daniel (or TOLLAND)

b. Coatbridge 31.12.1902 d. Hillhead 26.6.1945

Well Park					
Shettleston					
Ayr U		24/25	13	2	
		25/26	29	9	D2
		26/27	31	12	D2
		27/28	32	9	D2
		28/29	25	4	
		29/30	37	5	
		30/31	33	6	
		31/32	23	3	
Galston	L	32/33			
Ayr U		32/33	5		
Northampton T		33/34	27	6	FL
		34/35	35	5	FL
		35/36	31	5	FL
		36/37	35	9	FL
		37/38	11	1	FL
Bristol R		37/38	19	2	FL
		38/39	15	1	FL
USA					

TOLLAN Francis

b. Baillieston

Baillieston				
Hamilton A	26/27	12	3	
	27/28	20	5	
	28/29	8		
Cowdenbeath	28/29	21	6	
New Bedford Whalers	29/30	14	1	ASL
New York Nationals	29/30	1		ASL
Bethlehem Steel	29/30	22	3	ASL
New York Giants	30A	22	3	ASL
	31S	9	1	ASL
	31A	17	2	ASL

TOMAN Wilfred

b. Bishop Auckland 1874 K.I.A. ?

Aberdeen				
Victoria A				
Dundee	95/96	1		
Victoria U	96/97			
Burnley	96/97	8	6	FL
	97/98	29	14	FL
	98/99	26	9	FL
Everton	98/99	2	1	FL
	99/00	25	8	FL
Southampton	00/01	19	7	SL
Everton	01/02	2	1	FL
	02/03			FL
Stockport Co	03/04	5	1	FL
Newcastle U				

TOMLINSON

St Mirren	90/91	2		
	91/92	4		

TOMLINSON Isaac

b. Clay Cross 16.4.1880 d. Bournemouth 24.8.1970

North Wingate Red Rose				
Chesterfield T	00/01	1		FL
	01/02	25	3	FL
	02/03	33	8	FL
Woolwich Arsenal	03/04			FL
Chesterfield T	04/05	33	9	FL
Southampton	05/06	29	6	SL
Portsmouth	06/07	5		SL
Heart of Midlothian	07/08	22	4	
Clay Cross Works				

TONER Joseph

b. Castlewellan 30.3.1894 d. Castlewellan 18.11.1954

Castlewellan				
Whitehaven A				
Whitehaven Rec				
Annsboro				
St Peters Swifts				
Belfast Celtic				
Belfast U	18/19			
Arsenal	19/20	15	1	FL
	20/21	12	3	FL
	21/22	24	1	FL
Belfast U	22/23			
Arsenal	22/23	7		FL
	23/24	3		FL
	24/25	26	1	FL
	25/26	2		FL
St Johnstone	25/26	7		
	26/27	22	2	
	27/28			
Coleraine	28/29			IL
?	29/30			
Castlewellan Star	30/31			
Annsboro	31/32			
Castlewellan Star	32/33			

TONNER Arthur Edward McSorley

b. Govanhill 10.3.1909

Stafford				
St Anthonys				
West Ham U	35/36	1		FL
St Mirren	36/37	12		
Swindon T	37/38	26		FL
	38/39	15		FL
Swansea T				

TONNER James

b. Bridgeton 31.3.1896

Bungalow C				
Inverkeithing U				
Dunfermline Jnrs				
Dunfermline A				
East Fife				
Linlithgow Rose				
Clapton Orient	19/20	12		FL
Lochgelly U	20/21			
	21/22			D2
Bo'ness	22/23			D2
	23/24			D2
Burnley	24/25	27	2	FL
	25/26	10		FL
Hamilton A	26/27	24	4	
	27/28	20	3	

TOOLE John M

Bellshill A				
St Mirren	11/12	8		

TOOLE Richard

St Mirren	20/21	3		

TORBET John McDowell

b. Port Glasgow 26.9.1903 d. 1957

New Cumnock U				
Partick T	24/25	5	1	
	25/26	9	3	
	26/27	28	11	
	27/28	3		
	28/29	30	18	
	29/30	36	18	
	30/31	33	11	
	31/32	38	13	
	32/33	30	17	
Preston NE	33/34	11	4	FL
Burton T	34/35			
Stockport Co	35/36	6	1	FL
Ayr U	35/36	11	4	
	36/37	22	23	D2
	37/38	2		
Alloa A	37/38			D2
Leith A	37/38			D2

TORRANCE David A

Beith				
Morton	10/11	26	2	
	11/12	26	7	
	12/13	27	5	
	13/14	32	5	
	14/15	28	1	
	15/16	19	1	

TOSH Joseph

b. Edinburgh 1917

Hibernian	37/38	2		
Linfield	37/38			IL

TOSH Robert

Morton	00/01	8		

TOTTEN Isaac

St Bernards	98/99	16		
	99/00	8		

TOUGH Alexander S

b. c1917

Beardmores Welfare				
Yoker A	35/36			
Ayr U	35/36	7	1	
Yoker A	36/37			

TOWIE Thomas

Dumbarton Union				
Preston NE	91/92	22	8	FL
Renton	91/92	1		
	92/93	7	2	
Celtic	92/93	7	2	
Derby Co	93/94	8	1	FL
Rossendale	94/95			
Renton	95/96			D2

TOWNROW Frank Albert

b. West Ham ?.11.1902 d. West Ham 10.8.1958

Barking T				
Chelsea				
Northfleet				
Arsenal	22/23	1		FL
	23/24	7	2	FL
	24/25			FL
	25/26			FL
Dundee	26/27	23	5	
	27/28	26	3	
	28/29	31	9	
	29/30	10	2	
Bristol C	30/31	22	5	FL
Bristol R	31/32	38	5	FL
	32/33	10		FL
Taunton T	33/34			

TOWNSLEY Thomas 1 cap

b. Polmont 28.4.1898 d. Peterhead 10.4.1976

Laurieston Villa				
Cowie W				
California Celtic				
Falkirk	19/20	36		
	20/21	41	3	
	21/22	41	1	
	22/23	37	4	
	23/24	35	2	
	24/25	37	3	
	25/26	17	1	
Leeds U	25/26	21	1	FL
	26/27	42		FL
	27/28	42	1	FL
	28/29	38		FL
	29/30	9		FL
	30/31	7		FL
Falkirk	31/32	17		
	32/33	7		
Bo'ness	33/34			
Peterhead	34/35			

TRAILL William

Club		Season	Apps	Gls	
Raith R		19/20	9	1	

TRAIN Wiliam

Club		Season	Apps	Gls	
Carluke Milton R					
Cambuslang R					
Kilmarnock		10/11	8		
		11/12	3		
Hurlford		12/13			
Bathgate		13/14			

TRAVERS Martin

Club		Season	Apps	Gls	
Bedlay Jnrs					
Dumbarton		20/21	16		
		21/22	1		

TRAVERS Patrick

b. Beith 28.5.1883 d. Dublin 5.2.1962

Club		Season	Apps	Gls	
Renfrew V					
Thornliebank		00/01			
Barnsley		01/02	13	4	FL
Thornliebank		02/03			
Barnsley		03/04	8		FL
New Brompton		04/05	11	2	SL
		05/06	27	1	SL
Renton		06/07			
		07/08			
Clyde		08/09	18	6	
		09/10	18	2	
Aberdeen		10/11	34	10	
Celtic		11/12	18	5	
Aberdeen		12/13	32	7	
		13/14	31	4	
Dumbarton		14/15	37	8	
		15/16	21	1	
		16/17	35		
Clydebank		17/18	31	4	
		18/19	28	?	
Vale of Leven		19/20			
Dumbarton Harp					
Dumbarton		20/21			

TRAYNOR Arthur James

b. New Monkton 5.4.1874

Club		Season	Apps	Gls	
Longriggend W					
Hibernian		96/97	1		
Millwall		97/98			SL
		98/99			SL
Grasshoppers					

TRAYNOR Bernard Charles

b. New Kilpatrick 11.2.1872

Club		Season	Apps	Gls	
Longriggend W					
Airdrieonians					
Abercorn		95/96	14	?	D2
		96/97	15		
Millwall		97/98			SL
Abercorn		97/98			D2

TRODDEN Patrick

Club		Season	Apps	Gls	
Shawbank					
Kilsyth Hibernian					
Kilmarnock	T	93/94			
Queen's Park	T	94/95			
Celtic		94/95	1		
Kilmarnock A		95/96			

TROTTER Alexander Elliott

b. Jarrow 1893 d. St Pancras 1948

Club		Season	Apps	Gls	
Jarrow		13/14			
		14/15			
Raith R		16/17	2	1	
Dumbarton		17/18	16		
Renton		18/19			
Ashington					
Leicester C		20/21	22	2	FL
		21/22	38	7	FL
		22/23	15	1	FL
		23/24	21		FL
South Shields		24/25	41	4	FL
		25/26	42	7	FL
		26/27	37	4	FL
Port Vale		27/28	16	3	FL
Manchester Central		29/29			
Bedlington U					
West Stanley					

TROTTER Alexander John

b. Renfrew 9.7.1910

Club		Season	Apps	Gls	
Ashfield					
Wolverhampton W		30/31			FL
Arsenal		31/32			FL
Preston NE		32/33			FL
Carlisle U		33/34	2		FL
Shelbourne		33/34			LI
Portadown		33/34			IL
Shelbourne		34/35			LI
Morecambe	T	35/36			
Albion R		36/37	22	4	

TROTTER Thomas

b. c1915

Club		Season	Apps	Gls	
Bo'ness					
Hibernian	T	32/33			D2
Bo'ness		33/34			
Bo'ness Cadora		34/35			
		35/36			
		36/37			
Falkirk		37/38	1		
		38/39	1		

TROUP Alexander 5 caps

b. Forfar 4.5.1895 d. Forfar 1951

Club		Season	Apps	Gls	
Forfar N E					
Forfar A					
Dundee		15/16	30	6	
		16/17	11	2	
Ayr U	L	16/17	4		
Dundee		19/20	40	4	
		20/21	39	6	
		21/22	38	3	
		22/23	16	2	
Everton		22/23	17	2	FL
		23/24	41	1	FL
		24/25	32	2	FL
		25/26	38	6	FL
		26/27	37	5	FL
		27/28	42	10	FL
		28/29	38	5	FL
		29/30	4	1	FL
Dundee		29/30	9	5	
		30/31	35	8	
		31/32	36	3	
		32/33	28	3	
Forfar A					

TRUEMAN Albert Harry Cowell

b. Leicester 1882 d. Leicester 24.2.1961

Club		Season	Apps	Gls	
Grasmere Swifts					
Leicester F		99/00			FL
Grasmere Swifts		00/01			
		01/02			
Hinckley T		02/03			
Coalville T		03/04			
		04/05			
Leicester F		05/06	17	2	FL
		06/07	18		FL
		07/08	8		FL
Southampton		08/09	30		SL
		09/10	30	2	SL
		10/11	29	2	SL
Sheffield U		10/11	5		FL
		11/12	26		FL
		12/13	24		FL
Darlington		13/14			
Leicester Imperial					
Clydebank		17/18	7		
		18/19	1		
		19/20	12		

TULIP Joseph J

Club		Season	Apps	Gls	
Crawcrook A					
Queen of the South		33/34	22	5	
		34/35	32	11	
		35/36	30	15	
		36/37	12	4	
		37/38	21	7	
		38/39	2		

TULIPS James

Club		Season	Apps	Gls	
Vale of Clyde					
Partick T		33/34			
St Mirren		34/35	4	1	
		35/36			
Ards		36/37			IL
Falkirk		37/38	7	1	
		38/39			
Alloa A					

TULLIS

Club		Season	Apps	Gls	
Leith A		92/93	4		

TULLIS David

Club		Season	Apps	Gls	
Leith A		94/95	2		

TULLOCH

Club		Season	Apps	Gls	
St Bernards		97/98	1		

TURNBULL

Club		Season	Apps	Gls	
Clyde		18/19	1	?	

TURNBULL Adam S

Club		Season	Apps	Gls	
Morton		04/05	26	4	
		05/06	27	5	
		06/07			
Arthurlie		07/08			
Reading		07/08			
Ayr Parkhouse		07/08			D2
Distillery		07/08			IL
Morton		08/09	9	5	

TURNBULL Alexander Stewart

b. Partick 1917

Club		Season	Apps	Gls	
Yoker A					
Albion R		34/35	14		
		35/36	1		
East Stirlingshire		36/37			D2
Manchester C		37/38			FL
Droylsden	L	37/38			
Exeter C		38/39	13		FL

TURNBULL David

b. Hurlford 4.4.1904

Club		Season	Apps	Gls	
Kilbirnie Ladeside					
Celtic		26/27	2		
		27/28			
Ayr U		28/29	27		
		29/30	28		
		30/31	30		
		31/32	11		
Glentoran		31/32			IL
		32/33			IL
Distillery		33/34			IL

TURNBULL James

b. Hurlford

Club		Season	Apps	Gls	
Kilmarnock Parkvale					
Queen of the South W		21/22			
Kilmarnock		22/23	23		
Nithsdale W		23/24			D3
		24/25			D3
Queen of the South					

TURNBULL James

b. Kelty c1913

Club		Season	Apps	Gls	
Blairhall Jnrs					
East Stirlingshire		32/33	17	9	
		33/34			D2
		34/35			D2
Cowdenbeath		35/36			D2
Rangers		35/36	16	5	
		36/37			
		37/38	3	1	
		38/39	6	1	
Cowdenbeath					

TURNBULL James McLachlan

b. Bannockburn 23.5.1884 d. Manchester 1945

Club		Season	Apps	Gls	
Falkirk					
East Stirlingshire		00/01	12	?	D2
Dundee		01/02	13	4	
		02/03	12	2	
Falkirk		03/04			
Rangers		04/05	1	1	
Preston NE		04/05	8		FL
		05/06	5		FL
Leyton		06/07	36	13	SL
Manchester U		07/08	26	10	FL
		08/09	22	17	FL
		09/10	19	9	FL
Bradford PA		10/11	21	10	FL
		11/12	28	9	FL
Chelsea		12/13	19	7	FL
		13/14	1		FL
Manchester U	T	14/15			FL
Hurst		14/15			

TURNBULL John

b. Carronshore 1905

Club		Season	Apps	Gls	
Dunblane R					
Bonnyrigg Rose					
Leith A					
Stenhousemuir	L	30/31			D2
Leith A		30/31	6	2	
		31/32	9	3	
Stenhousemuir					
York C		32/33	1		FL

TURNBULL John Mackay

b. Kilmarnock 1916

Club		Season	Apps	Gls	
Glenafton A		36/37			
Kilmarnock		37/38	2		
		38/39	26	3	
		46/47	27	7	
		47/48	26	11	
Queen of the South		48/49	6	1	
Ayr U	T	49/50			D2
Dumbarton		49/50			D2
Stirling A	T	50/51			D2

TURNBULL Maxwell
b. Barrhead
Clydebank Jnrs
Motherwell 38/39 8
46/47
Ayr U 46/47 D2

TURNBULL Peter
b. Sanquhar 30.12.1873
Rangers 91/92 1
92/93 2 1
Glasgow Thistle
Burnley 92/93 6 3 FL
93/94 27 18 FL
94/95 14 3 FL
Bolton W 94/95 4 5 FL
Blackburn R 95/96 25 7 FL
Rangers 96/97 11 10
97/98 4 3
Blackburn R 97/98 1 FL
Millwall 98/99 19 17 SL
QPR 99/00 19 6 SL
00/01 3 SL
Brentford 00/01 13 15 SL
01/02 9 SL
Barrow 01/02
Tranmere R 01/02

TURNBULL Thomas
Falkirk 93/94
94/95
95/96
96/97
97/98
98/99
East Stirlingshire 98/99
Celtic 99/00 11
Partick T 00/01
Sheffield U 00/01 2 FL
01/02 FL
02/03 FL
Stenhousemuir 03/04
Partick T 03/04 1

TURNBULL Thomas
b. Kirkconmel
Lugar Boswell
Third Lanark 18/19 31
19/20 17
20/21
21/22 6
Nithsdale W 22/23

TURNBULL Wilfred
b. Jarrow
Blantyre V
Ayr U 23/24 3
24/25 7

TURNBULL William W
Denny Hibs
Parkhead Jnrs
Petershill 10/11
Morton 11/12 8 1
Rochdale 12/13 5 CL
York C 13/14
Plymouth A 14/15 SL

TURNER
Clyde 93/94 11 ? D2
94/95 1

TURNER
Rangers 97/98 1

TURNER Archibald Donald
b. Hillhead 1910
Partick T 29/30 9 2
30/31 4 2
31/32 7 1
Dumbarton 31/32 D2
Kilmarnock 32/33 4

TURNER George
b. c1897
Peebles R
Airdrieonians T 14/15 1
Inverleithen
Airdrieonians 19/20 15 5
20/21 8 3
Peebles R 20/21
Preston NE 21/22 FL
Peebles R 22/23
23/24 D3
24/25 D3
25/26 D3

TURNER James
Black Watch
Dundee 98/99 6 2
Third Lanark *

TURNER Matthew
b. Newcastle *
Dundee T
Hibernian 07/08 4
Everton 07/08

TURNER Neil McD
b. Hutchesontown 7.10.1892
Petershill
Leeds C 13/14 4 2 FL
Raith R 14/15 19 3
15/16 31 7
16/17 8 1
St Mirren 16/17 11 4
Vale of Leven 17/18
Kilmarnock 18/19 9 5
Sunderland 19/20 1 FL
Aberdare A 20/21 SL
21/22 20 1 FL
Dundee 22/23 8
Bethlehem Steel 23/24 20 5 ASL
24/25 23 12 ASL
New Bedford Whalers 25/26 32 14 ASL
Springfield Babes 26/27 21 6 ASL

TURNER Peter
b. Glasgow 18.12.1876 d. East Kilbride 8.2.1870
Parkhead
St Bernards 98/99 17 5
99/00 17 6
Woolwich Arsenal 00/01 32 5 FL
Middlesbrough 01/02 23 6 FL
02/03 FL
Royal Albert 03/04
Luton T 03/04 25 3 SL
Watford 04/05 34 5 SL
05/06 31 8 SL
06/07 34 7 SL
Clyde 06/07
Leyton 07/08 28 5 SL
08/09
Doncaster R 08/09

TURNER Thomas Stuart
b. Glasgow
Commercial A
St Rochs 23/24
Raith R 23/24 1
24/25 10 1
25/26 9
26/27 D2
27/28 33 6
28/29 35 4
Blackburn R 29/30 23 2 FL
30/31 10 2 FL
31/32 6 1 FL
32/33 6 2 FL
33/34 26 6 FL
34/35 15 3 FL
35/36 27 8 FL
Arbroath 36/37 20 2
Albion R * 37/38 D2

TUTTY James
Johnstone
Rangers 00/01 1
Port Glasgow A 00/01 D2
Clyde 00/01
Kilbarchan A 01/02
Clyde
Rangers T 03/04

UNDERWOOD Albert
b. Glencartra
Rutherglen Glencairn
Barnsley 02/03 15 3 FL
Airdrieonians 03/04 7 1

UPWARD George
b. Old Kilpatrick 1911
Kilwinning R
Glenafton A
St Mirren 36/37 3

URE William
b. Linlithgowshire
Baillieston
Kirkintilloch Rob Roy
Ayr U 32/33 24 1
33/34 38 4
34/35 29 3
35/36
Bo'ness 36/37
37/38
Penicuik A 38/39

URQUHART
St Bernards 95/96 1

URQUHART Arthur
Ashfield
Linthouse
Morton 06/07 19 2
07/08 16 3
Middlesbrough 07/08 4 FL
Johnstone 08/09
Dumbarton 09/10 D2

URQUHART Duncan 1 cap
b. Gorgie 18.8.1908
Clinton Vale
Newtongrange Star
Hibernian 28/29 11
29/30 32
30/31 29
31/32 D2
32/33 D2
33/34 38
34/35 33
35/36 6
Aberdeen 35/36 3
36/37 2
Barnsley T 37/38 FL
Barrow 37/38 19 FL
Cork C
Clapton Orient T 38/39

URQUHART George
b. Paisley
St Johnstone YM
St Mirren 33/34 1
34/35 5
Hamilton A T 34/35
Arbroath 34/35 6 D2
35/36 38 1
36/37 33 1
37/38 36
38/39 38

URQUHART John
Aberdeen 06/07 3

URQUHART William
Inverness Thistle 32/33
Millwall T 32/33 FL
Inverness Thistle 33/34
34/35
St Mirren T 35/36
Morton T 36/37 D2
Clyde 36/37 9
37/38 9 2
38/39 16

VAIL Thomas
Lochgelly U 94/95
95/96
Dundee 95/96 9 4
Bolton W 95/96 3 1 FL
Lochgelly U 96/97
Chatham 96/97 19 13 SL
97/98 21 5 SL
Walsall 98/99 30 16 FL
Gainsborough T 99/00 22 12 FL
Doncaster R 00/01
Lochgelly U 01/02
02/03
Dunfermline A

VALLANCE James
Postal A
Glasgow Civil Service
Queen's Park 06/07 8
07/08 5 1
Bradford C 07/08 3 FL
08/09 FL
09/10 FL
St Johnstone 10/11
11/12 D2
Beith 12/13

VALLIS Henry John
b. Bristol 1901
Horfield U
Dundee 19/20 5
Barry T 20/21
Bristol C 21/22 10 FL
Yeovil T 22/23 SL
23/24 SL
24/25 SL
25/26 SL
26/27 SL

VANDELEUR Patrick

b. Hamilton 1909

Stonehouse Violet					
Morton		33/34			D2
Dunfermline A		34/35	1		
Drumcondra		34/35			LI

VANNETT Joseph T B

Dundee Violet					
Arbroath		38/39	17		

VENTERS Alexander 3 caps

b. Cowdenbeath 9.6.1913 d. 30.4.1959

Southend R					
St Andrews U		29/30			
Cowdenbeath		30/31	13	3	
		31/32	33	11	
		32/33	37	12	
		33/34	13	10	
Rangers		33/34	15	5	
		34/35	28	10	
		35/36	32	17	
		36/37	33	10	
		37/38	34	12	
		38/39	33	35	
Third Lanark		46/47	8	2	
Blackburn R		46/47			FL
		47/48			FL
Raith R		47/48			D2

VENTERS John Cook

b. Cowdenbeath 22.8.1910

Lochore Thistle					
Dunniker Jnrs					
Preston NE		27/28			FL
Nottingham F		28/29			FL
		29/30	1		FL
Thames		30/31	1		FL
Morton		30/31	6		
Young Boys Berne					

VERRILL George

b. Staithes

Middlesbrough					
Hibernian		19/20	1	1	

VICKERS Charles

b. Hutchesontown 1891 K.I.A. 21.6.1917 (?)

Kilsyth Emmet					
Kilmarnock		13/14	7		
		14/15	9	1	
Renton		15/16			

WADDELL Andrew

Armadale					
Shotts Battlefield		28/29			
Tranent Jnrs					
Albion R		32/33			D2
		33/34			D2
		34/35	34		
		35/36	29		
		36/37	25		
		37/38			D2
		38/39	36		

WADDELL Frank

St Bernards		99/00	7	2	

WADDELL George Boyd

b. Lesmagahow 29.11.1888 d. Sible Hedingham 17.9.1966

Dalziel R					
Burnbank A					
Larkhall U					
Rangers		08/09	1		
		09/10	11		
		10/11			
		11/12	5		
		12/13	4		
Kilmarnock	L	13/14	30	1	
Bradford C		14/15	6		FL
Royal Albert	L	15/16			
Stevenston U	L	15/16			
Ayr U		16/17	36	4	
		17/18	2	?	
Abercorn	L	17/18			
Bradford C		19/20	15		FL
		20/21	2		FL
Preston NE		20/21	32	2	FL
		21/22	18		FL
Oldham A		22/23	1		FL
Birmingham		22/23	2		FL
Hamilton A		23/24	5		
New Brighton		23/24	3		FL
Wolverhampton W		23/24			FL
Aberaman A		24/25			
Chorley					
Fraserburgh					
Dick Kerrs		30/31			
Ribble Motors					

WADDELL James

b. Cornsilloch 19.2.1908 d. Belfast 3.8.1995

Larkhall Thistle					
Third Lanark		32/33	14		
		33/34	4		
		34/35			D2
		35/36			
Albion R		36/37	19		
		37/38			D2
Kings Park		38/39			D2
Linfield		38/39			IL
		39/40			IL
		40/41			IL
Limerick		41/42			LI
Alexandra Works		42/43			

WADDELL John McAllister

St Bernards		99/00	6	1	
Glentoran		00/01			
		01/02			
		02/03			
Morton		03/04	4		

WADDELL Peter

Clyde		99/00	9		
		00/01	14	?	D2

WADDELL William

b. Glasgow 7.12.1918

Strathclyde					
Renfrew Jnrs					
Aberdeen		38/39	3		
		46/47	12		
		47/48	23		
		48/49	25		
		49/50	11		
Kettering T					

WADDELL William 17 caps

b. Forth 7.3.1921 d. Glasgow 13.10.1992

Forth W					
Eastfield Heatherbell					
Strathclyde					
Rangers		37/38			
		38/39	27	7	
		46/47	22	5	
		47/48	12	2	
		48/49	20	3	
		49/50	7	4	
		50/51	28	6	
		51/52	24	5	
		52/53	16	2	
		53/54	29	3	
		54/55	11		

WAITE George

b. Bradford 1.3.1894 d. Bradford 1972

Royal Artillery					
Bradford PA		19/20	6		FL
Heart of Midlothian	L	20/21			
Raith R		20/21	24	12	
Clydebank		20/21	3	2	
Pontypridd		21/22			
Leicester C		21/22	1		FL
		22/23	27	12	FL
Clapton Orient		22/23	10	2	FL
		23/24	30	3	FL
		24/25	16	3	FL
		25/26	6		FL
Hartlepools U		26/27	26	7	FL
York C		27/28			

WAKEMAN Christopher

Clydebank					
Motherwell		08/09	2		
Wishaw Thistle		09/10			

WALES Abraham

b. Bridgeton 14.6.1874

Motherwell					
Third Lanark		99/00			
Motherwell		99/00			
Third Lanark		00/01	18	1	
		01/02			
		02/03			
Morton		03/04	18	2	
Fulham		03/04			SL
		04/05			SL
Morton		04/05	1		
Luton T		05/06			SL

WALES Abraham

b. Kilwinning 1909

Bartonholm U					
Kilwinning R					
Kilmarnock		29/30	8	3	
Galston	L	29/30			
Kilmarnock		30/31	6	6	
Montrose		30/31			D2
Luton T		31/32	3		FL
Kilwinning Eglington		31/32			
Leicester C	T	32/33			FL
Kilwinning Eglington		32/33			
Queen of the South		33/34	4	1	
Scottish Aviation					

WALES Hugh Morrison 1 cap

b. Kilwinning 4.10.1907 d. Kilwinning 24.7.1976

Kilwinning Eglington					
Motherwell		29/30	10		
		30/31	38	2	
		31/32	30	1	
		32/33	37	2	
		33/34	37	1	
		34/35	36		
		35/36	35	3	
		36/37	28	2	
		37/38	30	1	
		38/39	30	3	

WALKER

Albion R		19/20	1		

WALKER Alexander

Heart of Midlothian		99/00	4	1	
		00/01	4		
		01/02	5	1	
		02/03			
Motherwell		03/04	17	1	

WALKER Andrew

b. Paisley 27.9.1900 d. Paisley 17.9.1963

Renfrew Jnrs					
Bo'ness		26/27			D2
		27/28			D2
St Mirren	T	27/28			
Bo'ness		27/28	24	2	
Reading		28/29			FL
Bo'ness		29/30			
Watford		30/31	2		FL
Dunfermline A		31/32			D2
		32/33			D2

WALKER Andrew McQueen

b. Dalkeith ?.6.1892 d. USA 1961

Lumphinnans Swifts					
Dundee		10/11	3	1	
		11/12	1		
		12/13	19	7	
Chelsea		13/14	3	2	FL
		14/15	12		FL
Raith R		15/16	2		
Chelsea		19/20	3		FL
Newport Co		20/21	40	6	FL
		21/22	35	8	FL
Accrington S		22/23	13		FL
USA					

WALKER Archibald

Beith					
Morton		09/10	10	1	
Galston					
Beith					
Pontypridd		12/13			
		13/14			
		14/15			

WALKER David

Lanemark					
Partick T		02/03	11	1	
		03/04	18		
		04/05	16	2	
		05/06	22	2	
		06/07	23	1	
Kilmarnock		07/08	25	2	
Lanemark		08/09			
		09/10			
		10/11			
Nithsdale W		11/12			

WALKER David C
b. Paisley 1898
Benburb
Kilmarnock 20/21 5
Queen of the South L 21/22
St Johnstone 22/23 37 3 D2
23/24 34 9 D2
24/25 23 4
Dundee U 25/26 37 3
St Johnstone L 25/26
Dundee U 26/27 28 1
27/28 37 12 D2
28/29 10 2 D2

WALKER Dawson
b. Bo'ness
Kilmarnock 26/27 3 1
27/28 1
Raith R 28/29
Partick T 28/29
Clydebank 29/30 D2
30/31 D2
Stenhousemuir 30/31 D2

WALKER Duncan Campbell
b. Alloa 12.9.1902
Army
Kilsyth R
Dumbarton 18/19 3 ?
19/20 26 18
Bo'ness L 19/20
Dumbarton 20/21 33 15
St Mirren 20/21 3
21/22 38 45
22/23 34 20
Nottingham F 23/24 39 17 FL
24/25 35 7 FL
25/26 6 3 FL
26/27 2 2 FL
Bo'ness L 27/28 4

WALKER Frank 1 cap
b. Paisley
Paisley GSFP
Abercorn 14/15
15/16
Queen's Park 16/17 11 5
17/18 1 1
18/19
19/20
Third Lanark 19/20 28 12
20/21 35 18
21/22 39 14
22/23 30 3
23/24 30 12
24/25 25 9

WALKER George
b. Peterhill
West Calder School
Hibernian 05/06 2

WALKER George
Hibernian 17/18 2 ?

WALKER George 4 caps
b. Musselburgh 24.5.1904
Rosslyn Jnrs
St Mirren 26/27 7
27/28 29
28/29 36 1
29/30 35 1
30/31 29 1
31/32 37
32/33 37 3
Notts Co 33/34 41 FL
34/35 34 FL
35/36 25 1 FL
Crystal Palace 36/37 41 FL
37/38 40 1 FL
38/39 21 FL
Watford

WALKER Harry
Kings Park *
St Mirren 22/23 1
East Stirlingshire 23/24 D3
Bo'ness 24/25 D2

WALKER Isaac
b. Glasgow
Third Lanark 14/15 33 1
15/16
16/17 26
17/18 24 ?
18/19 22 ?
19/20 35 2
20/21 29
21/22 3

WALKER James
Cambuslang R
Clyde 06/07 2
07/08 6

WALKER James
b. Paisley
Paisley Grammar School
Queen's Park 13/14 2
14/15 13 4
15/16
16/17
Linfield 17/18 IL
18/19 IL
Queen's Park 18/19 4
Third Lanark 19/20 40
20/21 33 1
21/22 39 1
22/23 30 2
23/24 19 1
24/25 28 1
Dundee U 25/26 33 3

WALKER James
b. Glasgow c1902
Bathgate Northern
Livingstone Jnrs
Arniston R
Dundee 23/24 1
Dundee U 23/24 22 2 D2
Broxburn U 24/25 D2
Coventry C 25/26 16 1 FL
Bathgate 26/27 D2
Bo'ness 26/27 D2
Armadale

WALKER James T
b. Paisley
Third Lanark 24/25 6

WALKER John
Burnley 90/91 21 FL
91/92 19 FL
Clyde 92/93 18
Sunderland 93/94 5 FL
Stoke

WALKER John 5 caps
b. Coatbridge 31.5.1874
Armadale
Heart of Midlothian 92/93 7
93/94 12 7
94/95 15 8
95/96 17 8
96/97 18 5
97/98 12 4
Liverpool 97/98 3 2 FL
98/99 32 12 FL
99/00 27 10 FL
00/01 29 9 FL
01/02 17 1 FL
Rangers 02/03 17 7
03/04 21 11
04/05 12 5
Morton 05/06 8 6

WALKER John
b. c1878 d. South Leith 1.8.1900
Leith Primrose
Leith A 97/98 5 ? D2
98/99 6 ? D2
Heart of Midlothian 98/99 7 1
Lincoln C 99/00 6 FL

WALKER John 9 caps
b. Beith 8.10.1882 d. Swindon 16.12.1968
Eastern Burnside
Cambuslang R
Burnbank A
Raith R
Beith
Rangers 05/06 14
06/07
Swindon T 07/08 38 SL
08/09 39 SL
09/10 38 SL
10/11 35 SL
11/12 31 SL
12/13 30 SL
Middlesbrough 13/14 37 FL
14/15 33 FL
19/20 34 FL
20/21 2 FL
Reading 21/22 33 FL
22/23 29 FL

WALKER John
Morton 05/06 28 6

WALKER John
Buckhaven
Motherwell 07/08 6

WALKER John
b. Clydebank
Kirkintilloch Rob Roy
Rangers
Hibernian 20/21 22 6
21/22 41 6
22/23 35 4
23/24 34 7
24/25 36 9
25/26 22 8
26/27 6 1
Swindon T 27/28 12 2 FL
28/29 8 2 FL
Ebbw Vale

WALKER Joseph
Aberdeen 11/12 20 3
12/13 17 1
13/14 26 5
14/15 34 8
15/16 19 5
16/17 16 2

WALKER Joseph
English football
Falkirk 19/20 15

WALKER Robert
Abercorn 95/96 13 ? D2
96/97 13 5

WALKER Robert 29 caps
b. Dalry 10.1.1879 d. 28.8.1930
Dalry Primrose
Heart of Midlothian 96/97 3 3
97/98 10 8
98/99 18 13
99/00 16 8
00/01 15 3
01/02 18 5
02/03 21 7
03/04 26 12
04/05 20 13
05/06 27 16
06/07 26 5
07/08 22 7
08/09 28 4
09/10 21 3
10/11 24 8
11/12 22 4
12/13 11 7

WALKER Robert
b. Coatbridge
Bedlay Jnrs
Airdrieonians 21/22 2
Albion R 22/23 11 1

WALKER Robert
b. Paisley 1906
St Rochs
Kilmarnock 24/25 36 4
25/26 22 4
26/27 7 2
East Stirlingshire 26/27 D2
New York Nationals 27/28 47 14 ASL
28/29 13 2 ASL
J & P Coats 28/29 26 7 ASL
Pawtucket Rangers 29A 5 1 ASL

WALKER Robert R
Falkirk *
Motherwell 33/34 3

WALKER Roderick
b. Buckhaven
Buckhaven
Heart of Midlothian 00/01 2
Hill of Beath 01/02
Aberdeen 02/03
Heart of Midlothian 03/04
Motherwell 03/04 19
Portsmouth 04/05 25 2 SL
05/06 32 7 SL
06/07 32 SL
07/08 20 SL
Heart of Midlothian 08/09 27 2
09/10 28
10/11 22
11/12 17
York C 12/13

WALKER Thomas 20 caps

b. Livingston Station 26.5.1915 d. Edinburgh 11.1.1993

Berryburn R				
Livingstone Violet				
Broxburn R				
Heart of Midlothian	32/33	17	8	
	33/34	27	15	
	34/35	36	19	
	35/36	35	18	
	36/37	37	11	
	37/38	37	10	
	38/39	37	23	
	46/47	9	3	
Chelsea	46/47			FL
	47/48			FL
Heart of Midlothian	48/49	1		

WALKER William

b. Broxburn d. Leith ?.1.1907

Cardross Swifts				
Broxburn A				
Leith A	92/93	1		
	93/94	11	3	
	94/95	13	4	
	95/96	13	?	D2
	96/97	12	?	D2
	97/98	5	?	D2
Liverpool	97/98	12	4	FL
Leith A	98/99	17	?	D2
	99/00	16	?	D2
	00/01	18	?	D2
	01/02			D2
	02/03			D2
	03/04			D2
	04/05			D2
	05/06			D2
	06/07			D2

WALKER William 2 caps

b. Glasgow c1884 d. Whiteinch 2.5.1945

Rangers	02/03	2		
Clyde	03/04			D2
	04/05			D2
	05/06			D2
	06/07	33	4	
Reading	07/08	37	2	SL
Clyde	08/09	33	1	
	09/10	29	2	
	10/11	32	1	
	11/12	31	2	
	12/13	30	1	
	13/14	36	1	
	14/15	26		
	15/16	35	4	
	16/17	31	1	
Clydebank	17/18	25		
	18/19	26	?	
	19/20	30	1	
	20/21	27	1	
Fraserburgh				

WALKER William

b. Leith

Leith A	30/31	10	1	
Bo'ness	30/31			D2

WALKER William

Rosewell Rosedale				
St Bernards				
East Fife	32/33	33	8	D2
	33/34	33	12	D2
Falkirk	33/34	22	1	
	34/35	29	4	
Arbroath	35/36	23	3	
Leith A	36/37			D2

WALKER William F

Paisley GSOB				
Queen's Park	11/12	4	1	
	12/13	13	7	
	13/14	3		
	14/15	3	1	

WALKER William O

b. Glasgow

Queen's Park	27/28	6		
	28/29	24		
	29/30	19		
	30/31	37		
	31/32	32		
	32/33	16		
	33/34	6		
	34/35	14		

WALL George

b. Boldon Colliery 20.2.1885 d. Manchester 1962

Boldon Royal R				
Whitburn	01/02			
	02/03			
Jarrow	03/04			
Barnsley	03/04	18	4	FL
	04/05	30	6	FL
	05/06	29	15	FL
Manchester U	05/06	6	3	FL
	06/07	38	11	FL
	07/08	36	19	FL
	08/09	35	11	FL
	09/10	32	14	FL
	10/11	27	5	FL
	11/12	33	3	FL
	12/13	36	10	FL
	13/14	29	11	FL
	14/15	17	2	FL
Cowdenbeath L	16/17			
Oldham A	19/20	40	4	FL
	20/21	34	7	FL
Hamilton A	21/22	34	6	
Rochdale	22/23	29	2	FL
Ashton National				
Manchester Ship Canal				

WALL Leonard John

b. Ditherington 1889 d. Shrewsbury 1951

Ditherington A				
Shrewsbury All Saints				
Welshpool				
Shrewsbury T				
Glossop	09/10	5		FL
	10/11	5	2	FL
Manchester C	10/11	10	1	FL
	11/12	20	1	FL
	12/13	7		FL
	13/14	4		FL
Dundee	13/14	17	1	
Crystal Palace	14/15			SL
Wellington T				
Shrewsbury T				
Walsall	21/22	3		FL
Bargoed				
Bloxwich Strollers				
West Cannock Colliery				

WALLACE Alexander

Abercorn	90/91	12	4	
	91/92	13	4	
Sheffield U	92/93	16	3	FL
Middlesbrough I	93/94	12	2	FL

WALLACE David

b. c1917

Irvine Royal Academy				
Dreghorn Jnrs				
Rangers	33/34			
	34/35			
	35/36	1		

WALLACE David

b. c1917

Ardeer Rec				
St Mirren	38/39	6	1	
Hamilton A				

WALLACE Douglas H

b. S Africa

Clyde	37/38	2		
	38/39	36	16	
	46/47	2		
Dunfermline A	47/48			D2
Albion R	47/48			D2
	48/49	14	6	

WALLACE James

b. Milton of Campsie

Milton Battle				
Pollok				
Clyde	23/24	21	4	
	24/25			D2
	25/26			D2
	26/27	38	12	
	27/28	28	9	
	28/29	24	2	
Burnley	28/29	6	1	FL
	29/30	33	7	FL
Chester	30/31	1		CCL
Bo'ness	30/31			D2
Hibernian	30/31	12		
Rutherglen Glencairn	31/32			
	32/33			
Clyde	33/34	5	1	

WALLACE John

Morton	03/04	3		

WALLACE John

b. Falkirk 20.6.1912 d. Fallin 17.11.1992

Blantyre V				
Stonehouse Violet				
Celtic	32/33	10		
	33/34	5		
East Stirlingshire L	33/34			D2
Coleraine	34/35			IL
Derry C	35/36			IL
	36/37			IL
	37/38			IL
Hartlepols U	38/39	31		FL
	39/40	1		FL
Belfast Celtic	41/42			IL

WALLACE John

b. Glenbuck c1917

Cumnock Jnrs				
Partick T	35/36	1		
	36/37	36	26	
	37/38	31	23	
	38/39	37	28	
Ayr U	46/47			D2

WALLACE Joseph

Glasgow Perthshire				
Raith R	03/04			D2
	04/05			D2
Third Lanark	05/06	1		
Alloa A	06/07			
	07/08			
Hamilton A	08/09	2		
Albion R				

WALLACE Joseph

Albion R	15/16			
	16/17			
	17/18			
	18/19			
	19/20	23	1	
	20/21			
Renton	20/21			

WALLACE Robert

b. Kilmarnock 27.10.1904

Muirkirk Ex-Servicemen				
Hamilton A	23/24	2		
Bathgate	23/24			D2
Plymouth A	24/25	1		FL
	25/26			FL
Torquay U	26/27			
Taunton T				
Falkirk				

WALLACE Robert

Hibernian	33/34	21	1	

WALLACE Robert

b. Paisley c1905

Cambuslang R				
Cowdenbeath	27/28	6	1	
Sunderland	28/29	5		FL
Third Lanark	29/30			D2
	30/31			D2
Bo'ness	31/32			D2
Raleigh A				
Blantyre V				
Hamilton A	33/34	13		
	34/35	35		
	35/36	25		
	36/37	33		
	37/38	35		
	38/39	31		
Bathgate L				
Plymouth A				

WALLACE William

b. Dunoon 1875 d. Dunoon 19.5.1934

Third Lanark	98/99	1		
Partick T	99/00	2		D2
Port Glasgow A				
Heart of Midlothian	01/02	1		
Abercorn				
Rangers	02/03	1		

WALLACE William

Vale of Grange				
Raith R	13/14	21		
	14/15	15		
Airdrieonians	15/16	17		
Vale of Leven	15/16			

WALLACE William
b. Glasgow
Motherwell 20/21 9
21/22
Clydebank 22/23 D2
23/24 29

WALLS Alexander

St Bernards 98/99 1
99/00 1

WALLS George
b. Edinburgh 20.1.1874
Heart of Midlothian 95/96 4 6
Sheffield U 96/97 16 5 FL

WALLS James
b. Beith 7.6.1883
Dalmuir Thistle
Duntochter Harp
Beith
Hamilton A
Celtic 01/02
Beith L 01/02
Celtic 02/03 4
Ayr 03/04 D2
Johnstone
Beith 04/05
Morton 04/05 2

WALLS James
b. Baillieston 1892
Shettleston
Portsmouth 12/13 8 SL
13/14 30 1 SL
14/15 31 SL
Rangers 18/19 34
19/20 39 2
20/21 23 2
21/22
22/23 1
23/24 1
Cowdenbeath 23/24 D2

WALLS James

Bathgate
St Mirren 16/17 26
17/18 33

WALLS Murdoch
b. Baillieston
Parkhead White Rose
Vale of Clyde 20/21
Albion R 20/21 3
21/22 27 2
22/23 37 5

WALLS Murdoch

Albion R 34/35 2

WALLS Robert Mackenzie
b. Leith 13.7.1908 d. 1992
Leith Emmet
Rosslyn Jnrs
Wemyss A
Heart of Midlothian 28/29 6 3
29/30 1
St Bernards 30/31 D2
31/32 D2
Hibernian 32/33 D2
33/34 38 11
34/35 31 11
35/36 24 6
Aldershot 36/37 20 8 FL
Waterford 37/38 LI
Cowdenbeath 37/38 ? 34 D2
38/39 54 D2

WALSH William
b. Blackpool 1909 d. Blackpool 3.11.1965
South Shore Wednesday
Fleetwood
Bolton W 31/32 FL
Fleetwood 32/33
Oldham A 33/34 6 6 FL
34/35 31 11 FL
35/36 41 32 FL
Heart of Midlothian 36/37 28 22
37/38 8 4
Millwall 37/38 21 11 FL
38/39 21 8 FL

WALTERS

Falkirk 17/18 9 ?

WALTERS Charles

Petershill
Third Lanark 15/16 15 1
16/17
17/18
18/19
Raith R 19/20 1
20/21 10
Petershill
Birmingham T 23/24 FL

WANN Robert

Edinburgh University
Cowdenbeath 29/30 1
30/31 7

WANN Robert

Arbroath 36/37 1

WARD Alfred
b. Eastwood 1883 d. Burton on Trent ?.8.1926
Clowne White Star
Notts Co 03/04 7 FL
Brighton 04/05 3 SL
Aberdeen 05/06 8 4
06/07 18 6
Bradford PA 07/08 2 SL
Southampton 08/09 4 2 SL

WARD John

Cronberry Eglington
Airdrieonians 06/07 1
07/08 21 3
Kirkcaldy U

WARD Richard

Kirkintilloch Rob Roy
Queen's Park 15/16 4
16/17 20
17/18 11
18/19 4
19/20
Kilsyth Emmet
USA

WARD Robert
b. Glasgow c1881
Abercorn 00/01 D2
01/02 D2
Port Glasgow A 02/03 8
03/04 26
04/05 26
05/06 27
Sunderland 06/07 35 FL
07/08 13 FL
Bradford PA 08/09 8 FL
Marsden Rescue

WARD Samuel
b. Dennistoun 1.6.1906
Shawfield Jnrs
Morton 26/27 18
Brentford 27/28 7 FL

WARDEN James

Renfrew
Dumbarton
New York Nationals 27/28 43 3 ASL
28/29 41 ASL
29A 16 ASL
29/30 29 4 ASL
Third Lanark 30/31 D2
31/32 30 5
32/33 24 3
33/34 30 2
Bath C T 34/35
Dunfermline A 34/35 20 2
35/36 38 3
36/37 25 2
Bray Unknowns 37/38 LI
Alloa A 37/38 D2

WARDLAW Peter
b. Linlithgow
Vale of Grange
Airdrieonians 10/11 11
Falkirk 11/12 4 1

WARDROP James
b. Motherwell
Wishaw YMCA
Armadale
Bo'ness
Motherwell 22/23 26 1
23/24 3 1
Broxburn U 23/24 D2
Brooklyn Wanderers 25/26 18 6 ASL
Philadelphia Field Club 26/27 33 4 ASL
Newark Skeeters 27/28 32 2 ASL
28/29 7 2 ESL
Philadelphia 28/29 30 6 ASL
Bridgeport Bears 29A 5 1 ASL
Philadelphia 29A 1 ASL
Brooklyn Wanderers 29A 6 ASL
30A 12 3 ASL
31S 14 ASL

WARDROPE Alexander
b. Stewarton 1886
Broxburn
Kilbirnie Ladeside
Airdrieonians 07/08 14
08/09 10
09/10 14 1
Middlesbrough 10/11 10 FL
Portsmouth 11/12 26 SL
12/13 3 SL
Nithsdale W 13/14

WARDROPE Alexander F
b. 30.8.
Camelon Jnrs
Broxburn U
Kings Park
Bolton W
Armadale 27/28 D2
Bo'ness 27/28 8 5
Ayr U 28/29 3 1

WARDROPE William
b. Wishaw 14.2.1876
Dalziel R
Motherwell
Linthouse
Newcastle U 95/96 30 15 FL
96/97 29 11 FL
97/98 26 13 FL
98/99 23 1 FL
99/00 18 5 FL
Middlesbrough 99/00 2 FL
00/01 33 9 FL
01/02 27 11 FL
Third Lanark 02/03 17 6
03/04 25 9
Fulham 04/05 27 16 SL
05/06 31 12 SL
Swindon T 06/07 38 8 SL
Hamilton A 07/08 31 6
Third Lanark 07/08 2
Raith R 08/09 D2
09/10 D2

WARK Isaac

St Bernards 95/96 6
96/97 11 1
97/98 5

WARNOCK David
b. c1911
Banks o'Dee
Aberdeen 30/31
31/32 14 2
32/33 12 2
33/34 30 6
34/35 20 3
35/36 18 9
36/37 8 3
37/38 13 8
38/39 18 6
Dundee
Huntly

WARREN Emrys John
b. Troedyrhiw 9.4.1909 d. Hereford ?.1.1988
Troedyrhiw Welfare
Bristol C T
Troedyrhiw
Tranmere R 33/34 1 FL
34/35 6 FL
Aberaman 35/36
Dundee 35/36 7
Hereford U 36/37

WARREN Frederick Windsor
b. Cardiff 23.12.1907 d. Milton Keynes ?.7.1986
Whitchurch
Cardiff C 27/28 4 2 FL
28/29 22 1 FL
29/30 13 5 FL
Middlesbrough 29/30 16 4 FL
30/31 35 18 FL
31/32 10 5 FL
32/33 25 4 FL
33/34 31 9 FL
34/35 39 9 FL
35/36 4 FL
Heart of Midlothian 36/37 38 17
37/38 35 9
38/39 37 4

WASSON Frank
Port Glasgow A
Morton 24/25 5

WATERS Samuel
b. Croy c1918
Camelon Jnrs
Third Lanark 38/39 22 10

WATERSON John
Queen's Park 06/07 1

WATERSTON
Heart of Midlothian 90/91 10
91/92 13 1
92/93 14 4
93/94 12

WATERSTON
Leith A 94/95 1

WATERSTON Archibald Rutherford
b. Musselburgh 13.10.1902 d. Haddington 13.5.1982
Musselburgh Bruntonians
Leicester C 23/24 FL
24/25 FL
25/26 FL
Cowdenbeath 26/27 18 11
Newport Co 27/28 30 27 FL
28/29 13 9 FL
Southampton 28/29 6 1 FL
Tranmere R 29/30 30 18 FL
Southport 30/31 29 31 FL
31/32 30 13 FL
Doncaster R 32/33 36 24 FL
33/34 7 3 FL
Aldershot 34/35 19 4 FL
Edinburgh C

WATERSTON Thomas
Heart of Midlothian 09/10 1
Dundee Hibs 10/11 9 3 D2

WATSON
Abercorn 91/92 5 3

WATSON
St Mirren 21/22 1

WATSON Alexander
b. Stirling 2.8.1889
St Ninians Thistle
Clyde 07/08 1
08/09
09/10 29
10/11 26
11/12 6
Bradford PA 11/12 28 FL
12/13 38 FL
13/14 35 FL
14/15 34 FL
19/20 16 FL
Pontypridd 20/21
Halifax T 21/22 8 FL

WATSON Andrew
Clyde 06/07 30
07/08 29
08/09 27

WATSON Andrew
Morton 08/09 3

WATSON Charles
b. Coatbridge 21.5.1895
Ashfield
Airdrieonians 13/14 8
Albion R 14/15 D2
15/16
Clyde 15/16 11 8
16/17 9 1
Albion R 16/17
Stevenston U 17/18
Johnstone 17/18
Dumbarton Harp 18/19
Celtic 19/20 15 4
20/21 3
Bathgate 21/22 D2
Dykehead 22/23
Albion R 23/24 D2

WATSON Charles G
Army football
Aberdeen 19/20 1

WATSON D
Dumbarton 90/91 18
91/92 8

WATSON David
Glasgow Ashfield
Clyde 13/14
14/15 4
Clydebank T 14/15
Clyde 15/16 33
16/17 4
Stevenston U 17/18
Albion R

WATSON David
Cowie W
Falkirk 16/17 35 10
17/18 15 ?

WATSON David
b. c1915
Dalmarnock Parish Church
Raith R 31/32 D2
32/33 D2
33/34 D2
34/35 D2
35/36 D2
36/37 D2
37/38 14 D2
38/39 10
East Stirlingshire 38/39 D2

WATSON Edwin
b. Pittenweem 28.5.1914
Crossgate Primrose
Partick T 36/37 1
37/38 10 5
Huddersfield T 37/38 3 FL
38/39 FL
Bradford PA 39/40 1 1 FL

WATSON Fred
d. ?.7.1917
Aberdeen Shamrock
Aberdeen 12/13 1
13/14 1

WATSON Gavin
b. Coatbridge
Leith A 10/11 19 ? D2
11/12 D2
Kilmarnock 11/12 1
12/13 9 2
Albion R 13/14 D2
14/15 D2
Airdrieonians 14/15 1
15/16 1
Wishaw Thistle 15/16
Clyde 15/16 13 2
16/17 33 6
17/18 32 ?
18/19 23 ?
19/20 1
Dumbarton Harp 19/20
Albion R 19/20 16 2

WATSON George
b. Errol c1912 d. Canada 1998
Dundee Violet
Dundee U 29/30 8
30/31 17 D2
31/32 23
32/33 13 D2
Bradford C T

WATSON George B
St Johnstone 32/33 1

WATSON George Whyte
b. Newcastle
Army
Motherwell 28/29 13 12
29/30 2
30/31 1
31/32
Partick T 32/33 10 3
Halifax T 33/34 2 FL
Coleraine 33/34 IL
Dunfermline A 34/35 8 4
Cowdenbeath

WATSON Hugh
b. Maybole 20.8.1882
Trabboch Thistle
Celtic 01/02 12
02/03 19
03/04 17
04/05 1
05/06 1
Kilmarnock 05/06 13
Belfast Celtic 06/07 IL
07/08 IL

WATSON James
Glasgow Perthshire
Partick T 98/99 12
Morton

WATSON James Marshall
b. Maryhill 1886
Cambuslang R
Earnock R
Hamilton A 10/11 16
11/12 34
12/13 29
13/14 36
14/15 38
15/16 10
Ayr U L 15/16
Hamilton A 16/17
17/18 1
18/19 4
Glasgow Highlanders
Dundee 19/20 30
Luton T 20/21 4 FL
Exeter C 21/22 10 FL
Armadale 22/23

WATSON James Miller 6 caps
b. Motherwell 4.10.1877 d. Canada 1915
Burnbank A 95/96
96/97
Clyde 97/98 4
98/99 14 1
99/00 17
Sunderland 99/00 3 FL
00/01 32 FL
01/02 33 1 FL
02/03 30 FL
03/04 30 FL
04/05 30 FL
05/06 33 FL
06/07 21 FL
Middlesbrough 06/07 3 FL
07/08 38 FL
08/09 28 FL
09/10 36 FL
Shildon

WATSON John
b. Dundee 1877
Dundee W
New Brompton 96/97 15 SL
97/98 20 SL
98/99 20 2 SL
Dundee 99/00 6
Everton 99/00 3 FL
00/01 24 FL
01/02 20 FL
Tottenham H 02/03 13 SL
03/04 17 SL
04/05 25 SL
05/06 33 SL
06/07 12 SL
07/08 3 SL

WATSON John
b. Shotts c1907
Ayr U 27/28 6 D2
28/29 2

WATSON John G
Queen's Park
Port Glasgow A 02/03 14
Rangers 03/04 11
04/05 2
Port Glasgow A 04/05
05/06
Ayr Parkhouse 06/07 D2

WATSON Malcolm
b. Campbelltown (?)
Hamilton A
Falkirk 24/25 2

WATSON Martin
b. Cleland
Hamilton A 30/31 1
Queen of the South 31/32 D2
St Mirren 32/33
Dumbarton 33/34 D2

WATSON Philip
Bellshill A
Airdrieonians 34/35 22 6
35/36 8
Hamilton A 36/37 6 4

WATSON Philip Ross
b. Dykehead 29.4.1881 d. 1946
Shotts Hawthorn
Dykehead 00/01
01/02
Celtic 02/03 1
Dykehead L 02/03
Ayr 03/04 D2
04/05 D2
Dykehead L 04/05
Ayr 05/06 D2
Dykehead 06/07
Bathgate 07/08
Hamilton A 07/08 28 1
08/09 22 1
09/10 23
10/11 24 1
11/12 23
Motherwell 12/13
13/14 3
Dykehead 14/15
15/16

WATSON Philip Ross 1 cap
b. Dykehead 23.2.1907
Lakeland A
Wishaw YMCA
Hamilton A 27/28 33 2
28/29 36 2
29/30 38
30/31 38
31/32 29 2
Blackpool 31/32 15 1 FL
32/33 42 7 FL
33/34 42 1 FL
34/35 34 2 FL
35/36 33 FL
37/38 5 FL
Barnsley 37/38 5 FL
Queen of the South 37/38 8
38/39 15

WATSON Robert
Paisley Academicals
Queen's Park 09/10 6

WATSON Walter
b. Whifflet c1894
Wemyss A
Cambuslang R
Airdrieonians 11/12 2
Ashfield
Airdrieonians 13/14

WATSON Walter
b. Sheffield ?.11.1890
Worksop T
Aston Villa 11/12 3 FL
Rotherham T
Kilmarnock 13/14 15 1
Chesterfield T
Sheffield W
Worksop T

WATSON William
Cambuslang R
Motherwell 11/12 21 2
12/13 27 2
13/14 16 1
14/15 3
Dumbarton 14/15 11 3

WATSON William
b. Larkhall 29.7. d. Basildon ?.10.1950
Larkhall U
Airdrieonians 15/16 36
16/17 37
17/18 33
18/19 33
19/20 39
20/21 41
Bradford C 21/22 39 FL
22/23 35 FL
23/24 32 FL
24/25 33 FL
25/26 41 FL
26/27 29 1 FL
27/28 32 FL
28/29 41 FL
29/30 38 FL
30/31 10 FL
Walsall 31/32 35 FL

WATSON William
b. Catrine
Kilmarnock 20/21
Nithsdale W L 20/21
Kilmarnock 21/22 27 7
22/23 1
Galston 22/23
Dumbarton 22/23 D2
Ayr U 23/24
Vale of Leven 23/24 D2
24/25 D3
Galston 25/26 D3
Beith 26/27
27/28
Carlisle U 28/29 FL

WATSON William
b. Scotland c1902
Vale of Clyde
Ayr U 23/24 3
Vale of Leven
Coventry C 25/26 32 1
Bathgate
Clydebank
Bethlehem Steel 27/28 3 ASL
New Bedford Whalers 28/29 3 ASL
Providence Clamdiggers 28/29 39 4 ASL
29A 22 1 ASL
29/30 26 1 ASL
30A 26 ASL
Fall River 31S 17 2 ASL
New Bedford Whalers 31A 17 1 ASL
St Louis Stix,Baer & Fuller

WATSON William
Hamilton A 29/30 1

WATSON William
b. c1910
Stoneyburn Jnrs
Hibernian 30/31 19 2
31/32 D2
32/33 D2
33/34 25 1
34/35 36 1
35/36 9 1
Ayr U 35/36 8
Dundee U 35/36 8 1 D2
36/37 11 1 D2
Lincoln C 36/37 FL
New Allerton

WATSON William
Raith R
Dundee 36/37 2
Dundee U 37/38 24 D2
Airdrieonians 38/39 D2

WATSON William
East Stirlingshire 32/33 15

WATSON William
b. c1916
Renfrew Jnrs
Raith R 35/36 D2
36/37 D2
37/38 D2
38/39 2

WATT Clarence
Aberdeen 20/21 1

WATT Francis 4 caps
b. Beith 18.2.1866
Kilbirnie
Queen's Park
Clydesdale Harriers
Rangers 91/92 2

WATT H Munro
Arniston R
Heart of Midlothian 06/07 2

WATT Martin
b. Kilwinning
Morton 20/21 5 1
21/22 7
22/23 2
Ayr U T 22/23

WATT William W
Forthill A
Glossop
Cardiff C 10/11 10 2 SL
Airdrieonians 11/12 5

WATTERS John
b. Cathcart 24.9.1913 d. Glasgow 1989
Glasgow Perthshire 34/35
Ayr U 35/36 18 1
New Brighton 36/37 19 2 FL
Cowdenbeath 37/38 D2
38/39 D2
46/47 D2
Stockport Co 47/48 5 1 FL

WATTERS John
b. Waterside 5.9.1919
St Aloysius College
St Rochs
Celtic 36/37
37/38
38/39 9 4
46/47
Airdrieonians 47/48
48/49 D2

WATTIE Henry Benzie
b. Norwich 2.6.1893 K.I.A., Somme 1.7.1916
Tranent Jnrs
Aberdeen T 12/13
Heart of Midlothian 13/14 23 7
14/15 35 11
15/16 1

WAUGH Archibald
b. Falkirk
Falkirk 19/20 2
20/21 15
21/22 2
Kings Park 22/23 D2

WAUGH Archibald
Falkirk 26/27 1

WAUGH John
b. Dykehead
Heart of Midlothian 05/06 2
06/07 2
Ayr Parkhouse 07/08 D2
Dykehead 08/09
Hamilton A 09/10 30 3
10/11 28 7
11/12 29 5
12/13 23 6
Raith R 13/14 30 2
Motherwell 14/15 37 13
15/16 31 10
Newarthill Thistle
Vale of Clyde 16/17
Newarthill Thistle

WAUGH William 1 cap
b. Livingston Station 2.2.1910 d. 21.4.1974
Livingston Juveniles
Durhamtown R
Heart of Midlothian 28/29
29/30
Third Lanark L 29/30 D2
Heart of Midlothian 30/31
Third Lanark L 30/31 D2
Heart of Midlthian 31/32
Third Lanark L 31/32 33
Heart of Midlothian 32/33 2
33/34 2
34/35
35/36
Hibernian L 35/36 10
Heart of Midlothian 36/37 36
37/38 35
38/39 38

WEBB
b. Dublin
Ayr U 17/18 2 ?

WEBB Charles

b. Wellingborough 4.3.1879 d. Wellingborough ?.1.1939

Chesham Generals					
Higham Ferrers					
Rushden		98/99			
		99/00			
Kettering T		00/01	26	4	SL
Leicester F		01/02	32	3	FL
Wellingborough T		02/03	27	3	SL
Kettering T		03/04	33	4	SL
Southampton		04/05	17	4	SL
Blackpool		04/05			FL
Dundee		05/06	28	7	
		06/07	26	4	
		07/08	21	7	
Manchester C		07/08	11	3	FL
		08/09	11		FL
Airdrieonians		09/10	28	11	

WEBB William George

b. Shettleston 12.7.1906 d. Leicestershire

Cambuslang R					
Leicester C		25/26	1		FL
		26/27			FL
St Johnstone		27/28	10		
		28/29	30	6	
		29/30	29	4	
Bournemouth		30/31	19	4	FL
		31/32	20	2	FL
		32/33	18	1	FL
Ramsgate A		33/34			
Guildford C	T	34/35			
Bo'ness		36/37			
Hinckley U					

WEBSTER R A

Queen's Park		08/09	4		

WEIR

Cowlairs		90/91	3	1	

WEIR

Hibernian		19/20	1		

WEIR David

b. Shotts

Dykehead					
Rangers		25/26			
		26/27	2		
Third Lanark		27/28			
Morton		28/29			D2
		29/30	19		

WEIR Edward

b. Ireland c1911

Bonnybridge St Josephs					
Falkirk		29/30	1		
		30/31	2		
St Bernards	L	30/31			D2
Falkirk		31/32	4		
St Bernards		31/32			D2
		32/33			D2
		33/34			D2
		34/35			D2
		35/36			D2
		36/37			D2
		37/38			D2
Clyde		37/38	11		
		38/39	33		
Raith R					
Dundalk		48/49			LI

WEIR Gavin

Bedlay Jnrs					
Queen's Park		19/20	7		
		20/21	6		

WEIR H F

Dumbarton		94/95	1		
		95/96	10	6	
		96/97	2	?	D2

WEIR James

b. Muirkirk 23.8.1887

Benfoot Hill Thistle					
Dunaskin Lads					
Ayr		04/05			D2
		05/06			D2
		06/07			D2
Celtic		06/07	2		
		07/08	28		
		08/09	31		
		09/10	20	1	
Middlesbrough		10/11	35		FL
		11/12	33		FL
		12/13	32		FL
		13/14	8		FL
		14/15	5		FL
		19/20			FL

WEIR James

Wishaw Thistle					
Hibernian		09/10	1		

WEIR James

Kilwinning R					
St Mirren		09/10	33		
		10/11	27	2	
		11/12	8		

WEIR James

Grange R					
Falkirk		11/12	12	2	
Alloa A		12/13			

WEIR James

Falkirk		15/16	7	1	

WEIR James

b. Glasgow

Clydebank Jnrs					
Cowdenbeath		24/25	1		
		25/26	1		

WEIR James

b. Glasgow 12.6.1901 d. Glasgow 21.4.1984

Kilsyth R					
Kilmarnock		24/25	3		
		25/26	30	26	
		26/27	26	9	
		27/28	11	4	
Hamilton A	L	27/28	10	8	
Kilmarnock		28/29	8	1	
		29/30	3	1	
Queen of the South		29/30			D2
Norwich C		30/31	9		FL
Armadale		31/32			D2
Bo'ness		31/32			
Dunfermline A		32/33			D2
Dundee U		33/34	5	3	D2
Dunfermline A		33/34			D2

WEIR John

Renfrew					
Third Lanark		15/16	14	3	
		16/17	38	10	
		17/18	28	?	
		18/19	11	?	
Hamilton A	L	18/19	1	2	
Partick T	L	18/19	2		
Airdrieonians		19/20	16	3	
Armadale		20/21			
Kings Park		21/22			D2

WEIR Philip

b. Edinburgh d. 1963

Edinburgh Emmet					
East Fife		22/23	34	17	D2
		23/24	33	10	D2
		24/25	33	19	D2
		25/26	29	14	D2
		26/27	31	17	D2
		27/28	38	32	D2
		28/29	36	25	D2
		29/30	32	20	D2
		30/31	31	10	
		31/32	36	17	D2
		32/33	27	14	D2
		33/34	27	16	D2
		34/35	13	4	D2

WELDON Anthony

b. Glasgow 12.11.1900 d. Cumbernauld 20.9.1953

Croy Celtic					
Kilsyth R					
Airdrieonians		24/25	4		
		25/26	19	3	
		26/27	26	26	
Everton		26/27	9	3	FL
		27/28	38	7	FL
		28/29	20	3	FL
		29/30	3		FL
Hull C		30/31	31	6	FL
West Ham U		31/32	20	3	FL
Lovells A		32/33			
Dolphin		32/33			LI
Rochdale		33/34	28	6	FL
Bangor		34/35			IL
Distillery		34/35			IL
		35/36			IL
Bangor		36/37			IL
Distillery		37/38			IL
Larne		38/39			IL

WELFORD James William

b. Barnard Castle 27.3.1869 d. Renfrew 17.1.1945

Barnard Castle					
Bishop Auckland					
Mitchells St George		92/93			
Aston Villa		93/94	19		FL
		94/95	26		FL
		95/96	24	1	FL
		96/97	10		FL
Celtic		96/97			
		97/98	16		
		98/99	11		
		99/00	11		
Belfast Celtic	L	99/00			IL
Distillery		99/00			IL
		00/01			IL
Hamilton A		01/02			D2
		02/03			D2

WELSH

Heart of Midlothian		05/06	1		
		06/07			
Bo'ness		07/08			

WELSH Charles

Maryhill					
Clyde		14/15			
		15/16	6	1	

WELSH Fletcher

b. Galashiels 16.8.1893 d. Glasgow 1963

Tranent Jnrs					
Leith A					
Raith R		14/15	14	6	
		15/16	1		
Heart of Midlothian		15/16	24	18	
Raith R		16/17	8	4	
		19/20	19	23	
Sheffield W		19/20	9	4	FL
		20/21	3		FL
Third Lanark		20/21	15	14	
		21/22	2		
East Stirlingshire					

WELSH George

St Bernards					
Falkirk		21/22	3	1	

WELSH James

Cambuslang R					
Clyde		15/16			
Renton		15/16			
		16/17			
		17/18			
Clyde		18/19	6	?	

WELSH John

Clydebank Jnrs					
St Johnstone		31/32	36		D2
		32/33	37		
		33/34	20		
		34/35	31		
		35/36	25		
		36/37	30		
		37/38	34		
		38/39	32		

WELSH William

St Mirren		00/01	7		

WELSH William

Douglas Water Thistle
Motherwell 10/11 2
Royal Albert
Hamilton A 12/13 5
Royal Albert

WELSH William
b. Douglas Water 2.5.1904 d. Aviemore 9.11.1978
Lanark Technical College
Douglas Water Thistle
Heart of Midlothian 22/23 1
23/24 14 5
24/25 1
25/26 1
Dundee U 25/26 23 7
26/27 34 10
Charlton A 27/28 24 7 FL
28/29 4 FL
Wigan B 28/29 24 8 FL
29/30 31 9 FL
Southport 29/30 11 3 FL
Newport Co 30/31 6 1 FL
Connahs Quay L 30/31
Wrexham 30/31 9 1 FL
Gateshead 31/32 28 16 FL
32/33 28 6 FL
33/34 1 FL
Hartlepools U 33/34 4 FL
Jarrow

WELSH William A

Third Lanark 13/14 1

WEMYSS Thomas

St Anthonys
Bangor 33/34
34/35
Dundee 34/35 2
35/36 4
Ards 36/37 IL

WEST James L

Queen's Park 12/13 2
13/14 2
14/15 4
15/16
16/17
17/18
18/19
19/20
20/21 5

WESTLAND Douglas George
b. Aberdeen 5.2.1915
Banks o'Dee
Aberdeen 34/35 2
35/36 8
Stoke C 36/37 1 FL
37/38 1 FL
38/39 3 FL
Belfast Celtic 41/42 IL
Barlaston St Giles
Raith R 48/49 D2
49/50 2

WESTLAND James
b. Aberdeen 21.7.1916 d. Newcastle Under Lyme
Inchgarth
Banks o'Dee
Aberdeen 33/34 2 2
34/35 1
Stoke C 35/36 14 4 FL
36/37 21 4 FL
37/38 23 7 FL
38/39 2 1 FL
Mansfield T 46/47 10 FL

WESTWATER William
b. Edinburgh d. Burlington 16.3.1987
Heart of Midlothian 18/19 1 1
19/20 3 2
Toronto All Scots
Montreal Carsteel
New Bedford Whalers 24/25 17 12 ASL
Boston Wonder Workers 25/26 20 10 ASL
Montreal Carsteel

WHALMSLEY

Abercorn 91/92 3

WHARRIER Percy
b. Sheffield
Dumbarton Harp 10/11
11/12
Third Lanark 12/13 3
13/14 8
Renton 13/14
Third Lanark 14/15 4
15/16 8
16/17 1
17/18 2
Vale of Leven L 17/18
Ayr U L 17/18 1
Third Lanark 18/19
19/20
Dumbarton 20/21 14

WHIGHTMAN William

Queen's Park 13/14 1
14/15 4

WHITE

Renton 93/94 5
94/95 14 D2
95/96 2 D2

WHITE

Raith R 16/17 1

WHITE David R

St Mirren 06/07 5
07/08 12
08/09 10
09/10 2
10/11 5 1
11/12 25
12/13 6

WHITE Desmond
b. c1910
Edinburgh C 30/31 D2
31/32 D2
32/33 D2
Queen's Park 33/34
34/35 8
35/36 34
36/37 30
37/38 33

WHITE Gibson
b. c1916
Grange R
Falkirk 36/37 6
Leith A 37/38 D2
38/39 D2
East Stirlingshire 38/39 D2

WHITE J

Rangers 90/91 2

WHITE James
b. Airdrie 21.8.1899
Loanhead Mayflower
Bedlay Jnrs
Albion R 19/20 8
20/21 13
21/22 32 2
Maidstone U 22/23
Motherwell 23/24 37
24/25 19
Fall River Marksmen 25/26 39 33 ASL
26/27 39 16 ASL
27/28 46 21 ASL
28/29 49 22 ASL
29A 20 5 ASL
29/30 23 10 ASL
30A 27 4 ASL
New York Yankees 31S 17 4 ASL
New Bedford Whalers 31A 21 9 ASL

WHITE John
b. Galston
Kilmarnock
St Mirren 92/93 5 1
93/94 8
94/95 10
Clyde 95/96 16
Newcastle U 96/97 28 FL
97/98 21 1 FL
Galston 98/99
Dundee 98/99
Leicester F 99/00 FL

WHITE John 2 caps
b. Airdrie 27.8.1897 d. ?.2.1986
Bedlay Jnrs
Clyde * 14/15
Albion R 19/20 16 10
20/21 37 5
21/22 38 14
Maidstone U 21/22
Heart of Midlothian 22/23 35 30
23/24 38 16
24/25 33 21
25/26 31 18
26/27 26 15
Leeds U 26/27 16 2 FL
27/28 41 21 FL
28/29 28 9 FL
29/30 17 4 FL
Heart of Midlothian 30/31 34 11
31/32 29 5
32/33 31 21
33/34 27 17
Margate 34/35
35/36
Leith A 35/36 D2

WHITE Nicholas

Heart of Midlothian 09/10 2

WHITE Robert

Mossblown Strollers
Ayr U 11/12 D2
12/13 D2
13/14 D2
14/15 5
15/16
16/17 6
Stevenston U

WHITE Thomas

Falkirk 21/22 7

WHITE Thomas
b. Airdrie
Harthill A
Heart of Midlothian 22/23 3
23/24 3
24/25 3
25/26
26/27
Alloa A 26/27 D2
27/28 D2
Arthurlie 28/29

WHITE William
b. 1877
Broxburn A
Heart of Midlothian 96/97 3
Woolwich Arsenal 97/98 23 6 FL
98/99 17 11 FL
New Brompton 98/99 2 SL
West Calder 99/00
QPR 99/00 20 7 SL
00/01 SL
Liverpool 01/02 6 1 FL

WHITE William
b. Broxburn
Dundee 02/03 20 6
Middlesbrough 03/04 6 FL
Motherwell 04/05 5
Aberdeen 04/05

WHITE William Collins
b. Kerry Cowdie 5.3.1895 d. Glasgow 28.11.1974
Bedlay Jnrs
Hamilton A 19/20 31
20/21 42
21/22 38
Heart of Midlothian 22/23 30
23/24 37
24/25 37
25/26 35
26/27 18
27/28 3
Southampton 28/29 40 FL
29/30 40 FL
30/31 13 FL
31/32 8 FL
Aldershot 32/33
Weymouth
Wellington T

WHITECROSS Robert

Pumpherston
Falkirk 22/23 3
23/24
Broxburn U 24/25 D2

WHITEHEAD George
b. Galashiels 24.2.1890
Dalkeith Thistle
Newtongrange Star
Heart of Midlothian 11/12 12 3
12/13 13
13/14
Celtic L 13/14 7 2
Motherwell 13/14 18 11
14/15 10 2
Newtongrange Star
Cowdenbeath L 20/21
Newtongrange Star 21/22
22/23
Falkirk 23/24 3
St Bernards 24/25 D2

WHITEHILL
Clyde 18/19 1 ?

WHITELAW Andrew 2 caps
b. Jamestown 19.5.1865 d. Mansfield 2.1.1938
Vale of Leven 86/87
87/88
88/89
89/90
90/91 8
Heanor T
Notts Co 91/92 11 FL
92/93 30 FL
Heanor T 93/94
Leicester F 94/95 16 FL
Heanor T 95/96
96/97
Ilkeston T 97/98

WHITELAW John
b. Falkirk
Douglas Water Thistle
St Mirren 23/24 20 4
24/25 18 7
25/26 5 1
Stockport Co 25/26 8 2 FL
Rhyl A 26/27
Ebbw Vale 27/28
Stockport Co 27/28 12 3 FL
USA
Rhyl A
Chorley 29/30
Barrow T 30/31 FL
Rochdale T 31/32 1 FL

WHITELAW John
b. Cowdenbeath 1914
Lochgelly Celtic
Dunniker Jnrs
Inverkeithing Jnrs
Cowdenbeath 34/35 D2
35/36 D2
Racing Club de Calais 36/37
York C 36/37 10 4 FL
Raith R 37/38 34 26 D2
38/39 35 18
St Bernards

WHITELAW Robert
b. Stonehouse 2.11.1903 d. Kidderminster 1965
Larkhall Thistle
Doncaster R 26/27 7 FL
27/28 8 FL
28/29 9 FL
29/30 7 1 FL
Celtic 30/31 10
Albion R L 30/31 D2
Celtic 31/32 7
Bournemouth 32/33 10 2 FL
Glentoran (?) 33/34 IL
Queen of the South 33/34 D2
Celtic 33/34
Coleraine 33/34 IL
Linfield 33/34 IL
Cowdenbeath 34/35 D2
Hamilton A L 34/35
Albion R 35/36 16 3
Glentoran * 35/36 IL
Southampton 36/37 20 1 FL
Kidderminster H 37/38

WHITLOW Frederick William James
b. Bristol 3.9.1904 d. Bristol 6.1.1978
Barry YMCA
Barry T
Cardiff C
Charlton A 27/28 3 1 FL
Dundee 27/28 2
Charlton A 28/29 35 23 FL
29/30 32 27 FL
30/31 25 10 FL
Exeter C 31/32 23 15 FL
32/33 32 33 FL
33/34 28 13 FL
Cardiff C 34/35 7 1 FL
Barry T

WHITNEY Thomas John Black
b. At sea 6.3.1910
St Marys BG
Dalry Thistle
Bridgetown Waverley
Celtic 31/32 4 1
Stenhousemuir L 31/32 D2
Celtic 32/33
Larne 33/34 IL

WHITTIERS James
Newton Villa
St Mirren 30/31 3
31/32
Bo'ness 32/33 D2

WHITTLE William Cameron
b. Pollokshields
Pollok Thistle
Pollok Bluebell
Pollok Jnrs 10/11
Cambuslang R 11/12
Third Lanark 11/12 13 5
12/13 27 6
Kilmarnock 13/14 24 11
Partick T 14/15 28 19
15/16 14 7
16/17 23 7
17/18 27 8
18/19 31 10
19/20 11 2
Broxburn U 20/21
Alloa A

WHYTE
Port Glasgow A 08/09 1 1

WHYTE Albert
b. Edinburgh
Heart of Midlothian 20/21 1
21/22 3 1
22/23 1
23/24 2
24/25 4

WHYTE Campbell
b. Auchterderran 27.6.1907 d. 1984
Inverkeithing Jnrs
Denbeath Star
Lochgelly Celtic
Third Lanark
Cowdenbeath 27/28 4
28/29 7 2
Third Lanark
Gillingham 29/30 24 3 FL
Northampton T 30/31 5 1 FL

WHYTE George
Dundee 98/99 3

WHYTE George
b. Cowdenbeath 24.3.1909 d. Lincoln 23.10.1922
Kelty R
Dunfermline A 27/28 16
Rhyl A 28/29
Accrington S 29/30 35 5 FL
30/31 38 10 FL
Lincoln C 31/32 40 6 FL
32/33 25 1 FL
33/34 32 3 FL
34/35 42 3 FL
35/36 41 6 FL
36/37 42 FL
37/38 42 5 FL
38/39 31 1 FL
Gainsborough T

WHYTE Henry
Hibernian 95/96 4 3
Hamilton A

WHYTE James
Coatbridge Rob Roy
Third Lanark 10/11 3
11/12 1

WHYTE James
Hibernian 13/14 1

WHYTE James
Third Lanark 14/15 14

WHYTE John
b. Leven 1906
Denbeath Star
East Fife Jnrs
St Johnstone 24/25 30
25/26 30
26/27 21 1
Blackburn R 26/27 7 FL
27/28 18 2 FL
28/29 1 FL
Everton 29/30 FL
Dundee 30/31 7
31/32
32/33
33/34
34/35

WHYTE Philip
Heart of Midlothian 16/17 8 1

WILKIE Archibald
Yoker A
Third Lanark 16/17 13 2

WILKIE G
Falkirk 22/23 2

WILKIE James
East Fife
Partick T 06/07 20 2
Lochgelly U
East Fife
Reading 09/10 SL

WILKIE James G
Crossgates Primrose
Cowdenbeath 33/34 16 1

WILKIE John
b. Govan
Partick T 94/95 16 4 D2
Blackburn R 95/96 18 4 FL
96/97 27 7 FL
97/98 29 7 FL
Rangers 98/99 3 2
99/00 11 6
Middlesbrough 00/01 25 8 FL
Rangers 01/02 14 3
02/03
Partick T 03/04 14 5
04/05 17 6
Hibernian 05/06 7 2
Ayr Parkhouse 05/06

WILKIE John Cummings
Crossgates Primrose
Cowdenbeath
Clyde 37/38 7 1
38/39
East Fife 38/39 D2
Morton
Coleraine 46/47 IL

WILKIE Thomas
b. Edinburgh 1876 d. Perth, Australia 8.1.1932
Heart of Midlothian 93/94 1
94/95 3
Liverpool 95/96 20 1 FL
96/97 25 FL
97/98 10 FL
98/99 2 FL
Portsmouth 99/00 21 SL
00/01 28 SL
01/02 19 SL
02/03 23 SL
03/04 13 SL

WILKIE Thomas

Clyde		96/97	1		
		97/98	9		
St Bernards		97/98	1		
		98/99	15		
		99/00	5		
Partick T		00/01	17		
Preston NE	L	00/01	3		FL
Partick T		01/02	11		D2
Rangers	L	01/02			
Partick T		02/03	13		
		03/04	9		
		04/05	5		

WILKIE William

b. Glasgow 3.10.1903

East Fife					
Partick T		27/28	11	1	
Raith R		28/29	8	1	
Partick T		29/30	6		

WILKINSON George S

Crook T					
Falkirk		32/33	2		

WILKINSON J

Queen's Park		08/09	4		

WILKINSON James

Vale of Clyde					
Kilmarnock		11/12	8	1	

WILKINSON James Hector

b. Uphall

Vale of Grange					
Hibernian		27/28	8		
		28/29	16	1	
		29/30	36		
		30/31	32		
		31/32			D2
		32/33			D2
		33/34	33		
		34/35	38		
		35/36	35		
Dundee U		36/37	8		D2

WILKINSON John

b. Dumbarton

Bathgate		21/22			D2
Partick T		22/23	20		
Arbroath		23/24	35		D2
East Stirlingshire		24/25			D2

WILKINSON Joshua Hardisty

b. Anderston 1897 d. Hillhead 14.11.1921

Dumbarton Academy					
Rangers		19/20			
Renton		20/21			
Dumbarton		21/22	16		

WILLACY David Lewis

b. Barrow 13.6.1916 K.I.A. 1.9.1941

Greenbrae Juveniles					
Queen of the South		34/35	1		
		35/36			
		36/37	8		
		37/38			
Preston NE		38/39	1		FL

WILLIAMS

Third Lanark		94/95	1	1	

WILLIAMS

Heart of Midlothian		06/07	8		

WILLIAMS

Clyde		26/27	2		

WILLIAMS Alfred Stanley

b. S Africa 1.5.1919

Cape Town Railway					
Aberdeen		37/38	1		
		38/39	5	3	
		46/47	23	5	
		47/48	17	6	
		48/49	26	6	
Plymouth A		49/50	35	4	FL
Dundee		50/51	21	3	
		51/52	7	1	

WILLIAMS Fred

Bradford PA					
Dumbarton		17/18	1		

WILLIAMS Horace Frederick

b. Pembroke 1.1.1900 d. Mold 29.10.1960

Liverpool Regt					
Hibernian		18/19	8	?	
St Johnstone		19/20			
Hibernian		20/21	18	2	
St Johnstone		20/21			
Dundee Hibs		21/22	23	13	D2
Gillingham		22/23	26	10	FL
St Bernards					
Mold T					
New Brighton		26/27	41	34	FL
		27/28	5	4	FL
Blackpool		27/28	5	3	FL
Peterborough U		27/28			
Macclesfield T	T	28/29			
Caernarvon A	T	28/29			
Lovells A	T	28/29			
Hereford U		28/29			
		29/30			
Tunbridge Wells R		29/30			
		30/31			
Connahs Quay		30/31			
Abergele		31/32			
Lucerne					
Denbigh Mental Hospita		33/34			

WILLIAMS Robert

K.I.A., France 31.8.1916

Newmilns					
Airdrieonians		10/11	12		
		11/12	25	3	
		12/13	18		
		13/14	17	1	
		14/15	26	4	
		15/16	17	4	

WILLIAMS William

Darvel					
Kilmarnock		06/07	8		
Nithsdale W		07/08			
		08/09			
Tottenham H		09/10			FL
Nithsdale W					

WILLIAMSON

St Mirren		15/16	2		

WILLIAMSON James

b. Glasgow d. 1982

Ardrossan Winton R					
Kilmarnock		27/28	2		
		28/29	12	4	
		29/30	19	7	
		30/31			
		31/32	2		
		32/33	18	2	
		33/34	34	7	
		34/35	31	12	
		35/36	34	10	
		36/37	21	6	
Partick T		37/38	24	4	
		38/39	5	1	
Stenhousemuir					

WILLIAMSON James Russell

b. Carmunnock 1895 d. 11.10.1927

Burnbank A					
Bellshill A					
Hibernian		12/13	13	5	
		13/14	15	4	
		14/15	1		
Armadale		14/15			
Hibernian		19/20	6	?	
		20/21	33	22	
Tranmere R					
Ellesmere Port Cement Works					
Poulton V					

WILLIAMSON John

b. Manchester

Ancoats Lads Club					
St Mirren		11/12	17		
		12/13	8		
		13/14			
		14/15			
Manchester U		19/20	2		FL
		20/21			FL
Bury		21/22	12		FL
Crewe A		22/23	15	2	FL
British Dyestuffs					

WILLIAMSON John Robert

b. Paisley 19.1.1905

Paisley Jnrs					
Partick T		26/27	2	1	
		27/28	3	1	
Arbroath		28/29	35	8	D2
Partick T		29/30			
Arbroath		29/30	29	11	D2
		30/31	37	9	D2
Coleraine		31/32			IL
		32/33			IL
Coleraine Caledonians					

WILLIAMSON Robert

Clydebank		20/21	7		
		21/22	2		

WILLIAMSON Thomas Robertson

b. Dalmuir 8.2.1901 d. Norwich 1.4.1988

Kirkintilloch Rossdhu					
Kirkintilloch Rob Roy		20/21			
		21/22			
Blackburn R		22/23	4		FL
		23/24	15	1	FL
Third Lanark		24/25	37		
		25/26			D2
Stoke C		26/27	22	5	FL
		27/28	40	2	FL
		28/29	33	3	FL
		29/30	37	3	FL
		30/31	14	1	FL
Norwich C		31/32	40	2	FL
		32/33	41	1	FL
		33/34	1	1	FL
Frosts A					

WILLIAMSON Walter

Queen's Park		35/36	1		

WILLIAMSON William

Rutherglen Glencairn					
Heart of Midlothian		02/03	18	5	
		03/04	1		
Clyde		04/05			D2
Heart of Midlothian		05/06	6		
		06/07	3	2	

WILLIAMSON William

Clyde		07/08	20	1	

WILLIAMSON William Gallacher (born William GALLACH

b. Pollokshaws 7.4.1900 d. Dunfermline 19.4.1976

Glencraig Celtic					
Lochgelly U		20/21			
Broxburn U		21/22			D2
Heart of Midlothian		21/22			
		22/23	17	5	
		23/24	13	5	
		24/25	2		
Portsmouth		24/25	11	3	FL
		25/26	1		FL
Hamilton A		25/26	22	15	
		26/27	14	6	
Dunfermline A		26/27	14	3	
Crystal Palace		27/28	6	1	FL
Dunfermline A		27/28	15		
Ebbw Vale		28/29			
Montrose		28/29			D2
Clyde		28/29	11		
Shirebrook		29/30			
Dundee U		30/31	36	17	D2
Accrington S		31/32	27	14	FL
Southport		31/32	8		FL
		32/33	2		FL
Rochdale		32/33	8	2	FL
Montrose		32/33			D2
Distillery		33/34			IL
Alloa A		34/35			D2
		35/36			D2
Leith A		36/37			D2
Montrose		37/38			D2

WILLIS David

b. Leith

Musselburgh Bruntonians					
Ayr U		30/31	22		
		31/32	9		
		32/33	17		
Rochdale	T	33/34			FL
Dundee U		33/34			

WILLIS Joseph D

b. Gorebridge

Bo'ness		19/20			
Dumbarton	L	19/20	2		
Bo'ness		20/21			
East Fife		21/22			D2
Gala Fariydean		21/22			
Arniston R		22/23			
Kilmarnock		23/24	35	3	
		24/25	9		
Gala Fairydean					

WILLIS Robert Smith

b. Tynemouth 31.1.1901 d. Blackpool 13.5.1974

Shankhouse					
Blyth Spartans					
Dundee		21/22	15		
		22/23	2		
Rochdale		23/24	39		FL
		24/25	21		FL
		25/26	4		FL
Halifax T		26/27	2		FL

WILLOCKS David King

b. Arbroath 6.1.1871

Arbroath					
Bolton W		92/93	21	8	FL
		93/94	11		FL
Burton Swifts		94/95	29	15	FL
		95/96	29	10	FL
Dundee		96/97	17	9	
		97/98	18	6	
Brighton U		98/99	24	7	SL
		99/00	5	1	SL
Arbroath					

WILLOX Samuel

Aberdeen		03/04	6		D2
		04/05	2		D2
		05/06	5		
		06/07	1		

WILLS G

Third Lanark		90/91	5	1	
		91/92	1		

WILSON

Abercorn		90/91	1		

WILSON

Dumbarton		90/91	5	1	

WILSON

Heart of Midlothian		90/91	2		

WILSON

Third Lanark		90/91	7	2	
		91/92	1		
		92/93	2		
		93/94	7		

WILSON

Clyde		91/92	4		
		92/93	1		

WILSON

Abercorn		92/93	3		

WILSON

Dumbarton		92/93	2		
		93/94	1		

WILSON

Leith A		92/93	7		
		93/94	14	2	
		94/95	5		

WILSON

Renton		92/93	1		

WILSON

Renton		92/93	1		

WILSON

St Mirren		93/94	1		

WILSON

St Mirren		96/97	1		

WILSON

Clyde		99/00	2		

WILSON

Clyde		14/15	1		

WILSON

St Mirren		16/17	1		
		17/18	1	?	
		18/19	1	?	
		19/20	3	1	

WILSON

Hibernian		19/20	1	?	

WILSON A

Falkirk		22/23	3		

WILSON Alexander

b. Muirkirk 9.4.1883

Newmains Thistle					
Cambuslang R		01/02			
		02/03			
		03/04			
		04/05			
Morton	T	04/05			
Celtic		04/05			
Ayr	L	04/05			D2
Celtic		05/06	5		
Ayr	L	05/06			D2
Celtic		06/07	9		
Kilmarnock		07/08	28		
Hamilton A		08/09	20	2	

WILSON Alexander Adams

b. Wishaw 29.10.1908 d. Boston, USA 16.3.1971

Overton R					
Morton		29/30	35		
		30/31	25		
		31/32	37		
		32/33	21		
Arsenal		33/34	5		FL
		34/35	9		FL
		35/36	37		FL
		36/37	2		FL
		37/38	10		FL
		38/39	19		FL
St Mirren					
Brighton		47/48	1		FL

WILSON Allan

Renfrew Jnrs					
Morton		24/25	10	2	
		25/26	16		

WILSON Andrew

b. Strathclyde

Strathclyde					
Sunderland		96/97	2		FL
Partick T		97/98	17		
		98/99	13		
		99/00	18		D2
Motherwell		99/00	18	?	D2
		00/01	13	?	D2
Partick T		00/01	8		
		01/02	21		D2
		02/03	17		
		03/04	23		
		04/05	5		
Motherwell					

WILSON Andrew

Vale of Clyde					
St Mirren		06/07	2		

WILSON Andrew

St Mirren		11/12	1		

WILSON Andrew

Stenhousemuir					
Dumbarton		14/15	1	1	

WILSON Andrew

b. Stromsay

Banks o'Dee					
Aberdeen		19/20	23	2	
		20/21	1		
St Johnstone		21/22	32	3	D2
Arbroath		22/23	29	3	D2
		23/24	32	1	D2
		24/25	36	1	D2
		25/26	30	1	D2
		26/27	32		D2
		27/28	19	1	D2
Forfar A		28/29			D2
		29/30			D2
		30/31			D2

WILSON Andrew G

Lauriston Villa					
Falkirk		11/12	1		

WILSON Andrew McCrindle 6 caps

b. Irvine 10.12.1879 d. Irvine 13.3.1945

Irvine Meadow					
Clyde		99/00	18	7	
Sheffield W		00/01	31	13	FL
		01/02	25	9	FL
		02/03	34	12	FL
		03/04	29	11	FL
		04/05	30	15	FL
		05/06	35	16	FL
		06/07	35	18	FL
		07/08	34	17	FL
		08/09	37	18	FL
		09/10	30	12	FL
		10/11	38	9	FL
		11/12	37	12	FL
		12/13			FL
		13/14	31	15	FL
		14/15	38	14	FL
		19/20	1		FL

WILSON Andrew Nisbet 12 caps

b. Newmains 15.2.1896 d. Fulham 15.10.1973

Cambuslang R					
Middlesbrough		14/15	9	5	FL
Hamilton A		16/17	1		
		17/18	3		
Heart of Midlothian		17/18	7	3	
		18/19	22	20	
Dunfermline A		19/20			
		20/21			
Middlesbrough		21/22	35	32	FL
		22/23	29	11	FL
		23/24	13	8	FL
Chelsea		23/24	19	5	FL
		24/25	36	10	FL
		25/26	23	7	FL
		26/27	24	3	FL
		27/28	38	11	FL
		28/29	21	9	FL
		29/30	39	10	FL
		30/31	34	4	FL
		31/32	4		FL
QPR		31/32	20	3	FL
Nimes		32/33			
		33/34			
Clacton T					

Played some games for Hearts under the name Nisbet

WILSON Bert

Dundee		93/94	1		

WILSON Dale

Queen's Park		00/01	1		

WILSON David 1 cap

b. c1886 K.I.A. 28.12.1916

Queen's Park		00/01	20	7	
		01/02	16	4	
		02/03	15	4	
		03/04	8	2	
		04/05	16	5	
		05/06	3	2	

WILSON David (born WOOD)

b. Hebburn 23.7.1883 d. Leeds 27.10.1906

Black Watch					
Raith R		02/03			
Dundee		03/04	13	8	
		04/05	10	3	
Heart of Midlothian		04/05	4		
Hull C		05/06	10	3	FL
Leeds C		05/06	14	13	FL
		06/07	6		FL

WILSON David
b. Lochgelly 1883
Lochgelly U 00/01
Buckhaven U 01/02
Lochgelly U 01/02
Gainsborough T 01/02 15 FL
Cowdenbeath 02/03
East Fife 03/04
Heart of Midlothian 03/04 5 3
04/05 19 5
05/06 22 5
Everton 06/07 5 FL
Distillery 06/07 IL
Portsmouth 07/08 7 1 SL

WILSON David 1 cap
b. Irvine 14.1.1884
Irvine Meadow
St Mirren 02/03 2 1
Hamilton A 03/04 5
Bradford C 04/05 5 1 FL
04/05 7 FL
Oldham A 05/06 38 2 LC
06/07 38 3 FL
07/08 38 FL
08/09 38 2 FL
09/10 38 2 FL
10/11 34 2 FL
11/12 35 FL
12/13 38 2 FL
13/14 38 4 FL
14/15 42 FL
19/20 28 1 FL
20/21 34 3 FL
Nelson 21/22 30 FL
22/23 31 FL
23/24 24 FL

WILSON David
Airdrieonians
Liverpool FL
Hamilton A 06/07 1
Albion R

WILSON David
Beith
Kilmarnock 11/12 1
Third Lanark 12/13
13/14
Beith 14/15

WILSON David
b. Hebburn c1908 d. Glasgow 22.2.1992
Hebburn Colliery
Hamilton A 28/29 9 2
29/30 21 15
30/31 30 22
31/32 29 23
32/33 23 21
33/34 37 28
34/35 34 32
35/36 34 20
36/37 38 35
37/38 37 28
38/39 37 30
Stranraer

WILSON Francis
b. Motherwell 1904
Motherwell Jnrs
Mid Annandale
Motherwell 26/27 7 1
27/28 3
Hamilton A 28/29 37 3
29/30 34 4
30/31 28 2
31/32 18 1
32/33 33 4
Preston NE 33/34 6 1 FL
Falkirk 34/35 21 2
Glentoran 35/36 IL
Alloa A 36/37 D2
Rochdale 37/38 7 1 FL

WILSON George
St Bernards 95/96 6

WILSON George
Aberdeen University
Aberdeen 06/07 11 4
07/08 7
08/09 18 2
09/10 29 1
10/11 32
11/12 30
12/13 31 5
13/14 24

WILSON George
Rutherglen Parish Church
Bridgeton Waverley 34/35
Clyde 35/36 5 2
36/37 32 21
37/38 26 13
Third Lanark 38/39 4
Cowdenbeath

WILSON George B
b. Inverurie
Queen's Park 27/28 3
28/29 3
Kilmarnock 29/30 2
30/31
Airdrieonians 31/32 2
Partick T 31/32
32/33 10 3
Airdrieonians 33/34 12
34/35 15
35/36 2

WILSON George T
b. Hull 1912
Dreghorn
Galston
Ayr U 33/34 21
34/35 3
York C 35/36 39 FL

WILSON George Williamson 6 caps
b. Lochgelly 1884 d. Vancouver 2.6.1960
Thompson R
Lochgelly U 01/02
Buckhaven U
Cowdenbeath 02/03
Heart of Midlothian 03/04 22 8
04/05 22 8
05/06 28 10
Everton 06/07 27 3
Distillery 07/08 IL
Newcastle U 07/08 12 6 FL
08/09 28 5 FL
09/10 29 4 FL
10/11 19 1 FL
11/12 31 2 FL
12/13 23 3 FL
13/14 27 4 FL
14/15 6 FL
Raith R 15/16 23 2
16/17 14
17/18
18/19
19/20 19 1
East Fife 20/21
Albion R
Vancouver St Andrews

WILSON Henry
b. c1880 d. Hillhead ?.4.1934
Petershill
Partick T 03/04 23
04/05 15
05/06 21 1
06/07 12
07/08 19
08/09
Vale of Leven 09/10 D2

WILSON Hugh 4 caps
b. Mauchline 18.3.1869 d. 7.4.1940
Mauchline
2nd ARV (Hurlford)
Newmilns
Sunderland 90/91 21 2 FL
91/92 22 8 FL
92/93 29 7 FL
93/94 27 2 FL
94/95 25 3 FL
95/96 23 1 FL
96/97 27 1 FL
97/98 28 9 FL
98/99 25 6 FL
Bedminster 99/00 25 7 SL
Bristol C 00/01 28 7 SL
Third Lanark 01/02 18 1
02/03 21 2
03/04 22 10
04/05 24 4
05/06 24 10
06/07 26 9
Kilmarnock 06/07 1
07/08 21 3

WILSON J
Queen's Park 14/15 1

WILSON Jack
b. Ayrshire 1870
St Bernards 93/94 6 4
94/95 15 6
95/96 16 7
New Brompton 95/96 9 SL
Lincoln C 96/97 29 FL
97/98 5 FL
Manchester C 97/98 1 FL
Small Heath 98/99 FL
Swindon T 99/00 17 4 SL

WILSON James 4 caps
b. c1878 d. 28.2.1900
Vale Wanderers
Vale of Leven 87/88
88/89
89/90
90/91 9
91/92 6

WILSON James
b. c1883
St Mirren 00/01 15 1
01/02 7 2
02/03 22 3
03/04 23 6
Preston NE 03/04 4 FL
04/05 23 4 FL
05/06 34 3 FL
06/07 34 8 FL
07/08 27 6 FL
08/09 32 11 FL
09/10 4
10/11 5
Oldham A

WILSON James
b. Mauchline
Newmilns
Kilmarnock 02/03 10 2
Galston 03/04

WILSON James
St Mirren 06/07 24 5

WILSON James
St Mirren 06/07 20 5
07/08 15 3
08/09 20
Reading 09/10 SL
Abercorn 10/11 9 D2

WILSON James
Glasgow Ashfield
Motherwell 10/11 9 1
11/12 33
12/13 25
13/14 30

WILSON James
b. Glasgow 1894
Townhead Emerald
Cambuslang R
Celtic 13/14
Vale of Atholl L 13/14
East Stirlingshire L 14/15
L 15/16
Celtic 16/17 36
17/18 11
Dumbarton L 17/18
Celtic 18/19
Vale of Leven L 18/19
Albion R 18/19
19/20 29
East Stirlingshire 20/21
Kent Mills, Philadelphia

WILSON James
b. Glasgow
Kilbarchan A
St Mirren 22/23 2
Ayr U T 23/24

WILSON James
b. Glasgow
Moss Park Amateurs
Kilbirnie Ladeside
Rangers 32/33
Airdrieonians 33/34 6 2
St Mirren 34/35 4 1
Raith R 34/35

WILSON James G
Queen's Park 14/15 29
15/16 12
16/17 1
17/18
18/19 1

WILSON John

Queen's Park 00/01 3 2

WILSON John

Queen's Park 07/08 4 1

WILSON John

Penicuik Jnrs
Raith R 09/10 D2
10/11 4
11/12 14
12/13 4
Peebles R

WILSON John

Newarthill Hearts
Hamilton A 12/13 2
13/14 2
Peebles R

WILSON John
b. c1889 d. Paris 20.9.1914
Dumbarton 13/14 2
Vale of Leven 14/15

WILSON John

Raith R 14/15 1

WILSON John
b. Sunderland
Newmilns Jnrs
Heart of Midlothian 15/16 37 12
16/17 5
17/18
18/19 23
19/20 27
20/21 29
21/22 10
22/23 33
23/24 37
24/25 24
Dunfermline A 25/26 D2
26/27 35
27/28 37 4
Hamilton A 28/29 22 1
29/30 33 3
30/31 35 3
St Johnstone 31/32 36 D2
Penicuik A 32/33

WILSON John
b. Airdrie
Burnbank A
Bathgate
Hamilton A 15/16 7 1
16/17 5
Albion R 17/18

WILSON John

Clydebank 23/24 1

WILSON John
b. Paisley
Cambuslang R
Aberdeen 27/28 5
28/29 9 2

WILSON John

Cambuslang R
Bristol R T
East Fife 30/31 12 1

WILSON John Grant
b. Edinburgh 1908
Dalkeith Thistle
Plymouth A 31/32 2 FL
Cowdenbeath 32/33 1
St Bernards
Banbury Spencer

WILSON Mark

Stirling Emmet
Kilmarnock 20/21 2

WILSON Matthew
b. Glasgow
Queen's Park
Partick T 19/20 2
20/21 13 1
21/22 27 2
22/23 35 1
23/24 24 1
East Fife 24/25 D2
25/26 D2
Clyde 26/27 7
New York Nationals 27/28 28 ASL

WILSON Maurice

Queen's Park 10/11 1
11/12 12
12/13 16
13/14 28 1
14/15 1

WILSON Neil
b. Stevenston 1.9.1904
Ardrossan Winton R
Saltcoats V
Kilmarnock 24/25 8 1
Nithsdale W 25/26

WILSON Norman Henry
b. Bishop Auckland 1901 d. Aldershot 13.2.1945
New Delaval Villa
Blyth Spartans 22/23
23/24
Dundee 24/25 3
Bury 25/26 13 FL
Accrington S 26/27 32 FL
Aldershot 27/28 32 SL
28/29 22 1 SL
29/30 13 SL
30/31 3 SL
31/32 13 SL

WILSON Peter 4 caps
b. Beith 26.3.1905 d. Beith 13.2.1983
Beith Amateurs
Beith Jnrs 22/23
Celtic 23/24 11
Ayr U L 23/24
Celtic 24/25 33 4
25/26 38
26/27 34 1
27/28 38 4
28/29 36
29/30 36 3
30/31 25 1
31/32 32 1
32/33 36
33/34 25
Hibernian 34/35 34 1
35/36 28
36/37 20 1
37/38 6
Dunfermline A 38/39 D2

WILSON Robert

Maryhill
Partick T 08/09 26 1
09/10 21 1
10/11 20
11/12 27
12/13 26 1
13/14
Chelsea 13/14 FL

WILSON Robert
b. Chicago d. ?.11.1918
Kirkintilloch Rob Roy
Hibernian 13/14 20 4

WILSON Robert

Raith R 15/16 12

WILSON Robert

Burnbank A
Airdrieonians 18/19 9 3

WILSON Robert
b. Cambuslang 1896
Cambuslang R
Third Lanark 21/22 7
22/23 30 2
23/24 3
Bradford PA 24/25 FL
Shawsheen Indians 25/26 20 3 ASL
Fall River Marksmen 25/26 14 3 ASL
26/27 29 1 ASL
27/28 31 ASL
J & P Coats 28/29 8 3 ASL

WILSON Robert
b. Blantyre c1916
Bellshill A
Blackburn R T 37/38 3 FL
Falkirk 38/39 13
Nelson

WILSON Robert L
b. Broxburn
Raith R 21/22 4

WILSON Robert L

St Johnstone 24/25 4 1
25/26 15 1
South Shields

WILSON Ronald
b. Berwick (?) c1922
Wemyss A
Morton 24/25 8

WILSON T

Vale of Leven 91/92 12

WILSON T

Renton 93/94 5

WILSON Thomas F
b. Barrhead
St Mirren 30/31 9
31/32 2
32/33 1
33/34 33
34/35 31
35/36 D2
36/37 7
37/38 11
38/39 23

WILSON W

Rangers 90/91 1

WILSON W A

Queen's Park 05/06 4

WILSON William

Rangers 95/96 3

WILSON William

Clyde 99/00 18 7
00/01 7 ? D2

WILSON William

Helensburgh Amateurs
Dumbarton 17/18 24
18/19 7 ?

WILSON William
b. Port Seaton 7.9.1900
Musselburgh Bruntonians
Peebles R
Newcastle U 25/26 40 FL
26/27 42 FL
27/28 32 FL
28/29 13 FL
Millwall 29/30 17 FL
30/31 22 FL
31/32 42 FL
32/33 42 Fl
33/34 25 FL
Duns 34/35
Dunfermline A 35/36 5
36/37
Peebles R 36/37
Penicuik A 37/38

WILSON William
b. Kelty
Third Lanark 28/29 24 19
Queen of the South 29/30 D2

WILSON William Rose
b. Edinburgh c1891 d. Manchester (?) 1956
Dalry Primrose
Arniston R
Heart of Midlothian 10/11 8 1
11/12 4
12/13 24 16
13/14 24 1
14/15 28 10
15/16 17
16/17 2
17/18
18/19 12 3
19/20 34 4
20/21 34 9
21/22 34 5
22/23 33 4
Cowdenbeath 23/24 D2
24/25 38 6
25/26 36 10
26/27 33 5
27/28 33 2
28/29 24 4
Darwen

WINGATE Thomas
Dumbarton
Kirkcaldy
Clyde 99/00 6 1

WINNING Alexander
b. Glasgow
Shawfield Jnrs
Rangers 33/34
34/35 1
35/36 12 1
36/37 2
37/38 27
Clyde 38/39

WINNING William
b. Burnbank
Burnbank Shamrock
Parkhead Jnrs
Petershill
Raith R 13/14 37
14/15 24
Royal Albert 15/16
Raith R 16/17 25

WINTERS William
b. c1900
Benburb
Motherwell 23/24 7
24/25

WIPFLER Charles John
b. Trowbridge 15.7.1915 d. Petts Wood 1.6.1983
McCalls
Trowbridge T
Bristol R 34/35 18 5 FL
Heart of Midlothian 35/36 9 5
36/37
Watford 37/38 12 5 FL
38/39 10 2 FL
Frickley Colliery
Canterbury C
Watford 46/47 13 1 FL
Gravesend U 47/48

WISEMAN William S 2 caps
b. Wartle 18.10.1896
Aberdeen University
Queen's Park 21/22 1
22/23 31 D2
23/24 35
24/25 22
25/26 36
26/27 34
27/28 35
28/29 37
29/30 33

WISHART James W McNab
b. 1886
Darvel Jnrs
Kilmarnock 05/06 8 1
06/07 14 1
Carlisle U 07/08
08/09
Sheffield U 09/10 2 FL
Carlisle U

WISHART William D
b. Port Glasgow
Kilmarnock 25/26 7 2
26/27 11 2
27/28
Third Lanark 27/28
Albion R 27/28 D2

WOMBWELL Richard
b. Nottingham 1877
Red Hill
Bulwell 98/99
Ilkeston T 98/99
Derby Co 99/00 29 5 FL
00/01 34 9 FL
01/02 20 4 FL
Bristol C 02/03 34 11 FL
03/04 34 6 FL
04/05 24 4 FL
Manchester U 04/05 8 1 FL
05/06 25 2 FL
06/07 14 FL
Heart of Midlothian 06/07 10 1
Brighton 07/08 20 3 SL
Blackburn R 07/08 10 FL
Ilkeston U

WOOD A
Third Lanark 08/09 6 1

WOOD Alexander
b. Glasgow c1906
Greenock Overton
Airdrieonians 26/27 7 1
Albion R L 26/27 D2
Airdrieonians 27/28 12 2
Brentford 28/29 1 FL
Charlton A 29/30 1 FL
Fulham 30/31
Larne 31/32 IL

WOOD Alexander M
St Bernards 96/97 7
97/98 11
98/99 10
99/00 18
Sheffield U 00/01 3 FL
01/02 2 FL
St Bernards

WOOD Arthur Basil
b. Southampton 8.5.1890 d. Merton 17.5.1977
St Marys A
Eastleigh A
Fulham 11/12 2 FL
12/13 5 FL
13/14 9 1 FL
14/15 4 FL
Gillingham 19/20 31 12 SL
20/21 10 5 FL
21/22 19 5 FL
Hamilton A 22/23 8 2
Northfleet
Newport Co 22/23 13 3 FL
QPR 23/24 19 FL
24//2 1 FL
Regent Palace Hotel Staff

WOOD Daniel
Renfrew Jnrs
St Mirren 38/39 4
Motherwell 38/39

WOOD George
Lugar Boswell Jnrs
Ayr U 13/14
14/15
15/16
16/17
17/18
18/19
19/20 2

WOOD John
b. Birkenhead
Southern U
Derby Co 05/06 11 3 FL
06/07 26 5 FL
Manchester C 07/08 22 4 FL
08/09 6 2 FL
Plymouth A 09/10 23 3 SL
Huddersfield T 10/11 10 FL
Aberdeen 11/12 32 7
12/13 16 5
13/14 6 1
Hibernian 13/14 14 3

WOOD John
b. Leven 17.2.1894 (?) d. ?.9.1971
Montraive Jnrs
Black Watch
Hibernian 18/19 6 ?
19/20 34 7
Dunfermline A 20/21
Lochgelly U 20/21
Dumbarton 21/22 36 25
Manchester U 22/23 15 1 FL
Lochgelly U 23/24 D2
St Mirren 23/24 17 13
24/25 11 3
East Stirlingshire 25/26 D2
Hamilton A
Cowdenbeath
East Fife 25/26 D2
26/27 D2
27/28 D2
Alloa A T 28/29 D2

WOOD John
b. Glasgow
Overton R
Albion R 25/26 D2
26/27 D2
Airdrieonians 27/28 3
28/29 29 4
29/30 27 3
30/31 14
Albion R 31/32 D2
Bo'ness 32/33 D2

WOOD John
Wishaw Thistle
Clyde 32/33 36 1
33/34 38
34/35 30
35/36 30
36/37 5

WOOD John G
b. Paisley
Kilbarchan A *
Falkirk 18/19 1 ?
19/20 21 10
20/21
21/22 3
22/23 22 2
23/24 7

WOOD Robert
b. Glencraig
Falkirk
Alloa A 20/21
21/22 D2
22/23 35 2

WOOD William
Motherwell 05/06 9 2

WOOD William
Portsmouth
Airdrieonians 10/11 1

WOODBURN
Third Lanark 91/92 21 8

WOODBURN
Clyde 92/93 4 3

WOODBURN Hugh
b. Kilmarnock
Kilmarnock Rugby XI
Ashfield T 98/99
Kilmarnock Rugby XI 99/00
Kilmarnock 00/01 6
Stevenston U 01/02
Beith 02/03
Canada
Beith 06/07

WOODBURN John
b. Glasgow
Vale of Clyde 19/20
Ayr U 20/21 9
21/22 3
22/23 10
23/24
24/25 12
25/26 36 D2
26/27 36 D2
27/28 2 D2

WOODBURN William Alexander 24 caps
b. Edinburgh 8.8.1919
Edinburgh Ashton
Musselburgh A
Queen's Park Victoria
Rangers 38/39 12
46/47 18
47/48 23
48/49 30
49/50 29
50/51 28 1
51/52 27
52/53 27
53/54 21
54/55 1

WOODLOCK John
Motherwell
Carfin Emmett
Aberdeen 02/03
Rangers 03/04
Hibernian 04/05
Bathgate
Dykehead
Cowdenbeath
Hamilton A 06/07 8

WOODS George
b. Lugar c1892 d. 8.2.1938
Kilmarnock Jnrs
Auchinleck Talbot
Lugar Boswell
Ayr U 13/14 10
West Ham U 14/15 SL
Ayr U 18/19 4
Clydebank L 18/19 1
Ayr U 19/20
Queen of the South 20/21
21/22
Aston Villa T 21/22 FL
Queen of the South 22/23
23/24 D3
24/25 D3

WOODS Samuel
Dumbarton 95/96 5 1

WOOLLEY Gordon Horace Alfred
b. Rutherglen 5.6.1912
Larbert Amateurs
East Kilbride Thistle
Vale Ocoba
Partick T 35/36 6 2
36/37 11 1
Blackburn R 37/38 1 FL
Dundee U T 38/39 3 2 D2
Morton 38/39
East Kilbride Amateurs

WORKMAN Thomas
b. Paisley 31.5.1909 d. Paisley 8.1.1934
Paisley Carlisle
St Mirren 26/27
Bridgeton Waverley 27/28
28/29
29/30
30/31
St Mirren 31/32 36 9
32/33 31 5
33/34 20 4

WOTHERSPOON John
Queen's Park 21/22 1

WRIGHT Alexander
b. Aberdeen
Aberdeen East End
Aberdeen 13/14 11
14/15 6 1
15/16
16/17 1
17/18
18/19
19/20 42 2
20/21 26 4
21/22 40 2
Heart of Midlothian 22/23 33 1
23/24 28
24/25 23
25/26 36
26/27 7 2
Morton 27/28 D2
Queen of the South
Cowdenbeath 31/32

WRIGHT David
b. Kirkcaldy 5.10.1905 d. Holdeness ?.8.1953
Dunniker Jnrs
Raith R
East Fife 24/25 17 5 D2
25/26 34 21 D2
Cowdenbeath 26/27 34 18
Sunderland 27/28 32 5 FL
28/29 10 1 FL
29/30 10 1 FL
Liverpool 29/30 1 FL
30/31 15 6 FL
31/32 35 13 FL
32/33 30 14 FL
33/34 12 2 FL
Hull C 34/35 32 11 FL
Bradford PA 35/36 20 1 FL

WRIGHT Edward
b. Ireland
Shotts U
Hamilton A 31/32 35
32/33 23

WRIGHT Harold
Ashfield
Airdrieonians 13/14 2
Vale of Leven

WRIGHT Jack
Dumbarton A T 19/20
Aberdeen T 19/20 2

WRIGHT John
b. Hamilton 4.2.1873 d. Southend 1946
Hamilton A
Motherwell
Hamilton A
Clyde 94/95 18 4
Bolton W 95/96 30 3 FL
96/97 26 4 FL
97/98 22 4 FL
98/99 7 3 FL
Sheffield W 98/99 19 3 FL
99/00 33 24 FL
00/01 32 11 FL
01/02 19 3 FL
Hamilton A 02/03
Bolton W 02/03 19 FL
03/04 15 5 FL
Plymouth A 04/05 17 6 SL
05/06 30 4 SL
06/07 28 3 SL
Watford 07/08 27 SL
Southend U 08/09 36 7 SL
09/10 20 3 SL

WRIGHT John
Seaforth Highlanders
St Mirren 04/05 4
05/06 16 6

WRIGHT John G
b. Alva
Alva Albion R
Hibernian 20/21 4

WRIGHT John Stewart
Port Glasgow Jnrs
Morton 11/12 34
12/13 33
13/14 33 4
14/15 24 2
15/16 37 4
16/17 37
17/18 32 8
18/19 29 4
19/20 11
20/21 14
21/22 31 1
22/23 35 1
23/24 29 2

WRIGHT William Laird
Queen's Park 34/35 12 2
35/36 17 3
36/37 16 4
37/38
38/39 17 5

WRIGHT William Pountney
b. Seaforth 1892 d. Crosby 1945
Egremont
Everton 12/13 FL
13/14 FL
14/15 2 FL
South Liverpool
St Mirren 19/20 11 1
Tranmere R 19/20
Exeter C 20/21 17 9 FL
Huddersfield T 20/21 9 4 FL
Mid Rhondda 21/22
Yeovil T

WYKES Arthur
b. Wolverhampton
Dundee T 10/11
Third Lanark 10/11 1

WYLIE
Abercorn 91/92 1

WYLIE
Third Lanark 91/92 1

WYLIE George McHarg
b. Alloway 22.1.1913
Rankinston Seaview
Partick T 30/31 2 4
31/32 8 5
32/33 6 4
33/34 13 10
34/35 7 1
35/36 30 21
Airdrieonians 36/37 D2
Inverness Thistle T 37/38
Inverness Caledonian 37/38

WYLIE John
b. Maybole 1914
Glenafton A
Partick T 33/34 5
34/35 1
35/36 12 1
Ayr U 35/36 8 5
Partick T 36/37
Bury T 36/37 FL
Lincoln C 37/38 FL
Notts Co 38/39 1 FL
Stranraer L 38/39

WYLIE Robert
Cambuslang R
St Johnstone 32/33 9
33/34 35
34/35 32
35/36 32
36/37 38
37/38 38
38/39 38

WYLIE Thomas
Motherwell 02/03 D2
03/04 6
Clyde

WYLIE Thomas
b. Linwood 10.11.1907
Benburb
Motherwell 31/32 5 4
32/33 1
33/34 4 3
34/35 2 1
35/36 18 11
Sunderland 36/37 7 3 FL
Queen of the South 37/38 7
Peebles R

WYLIE William
Jarrow Croft
Dundee 10/11 1
11/12 11 3
12/13 32 4
13/14 19 1
Aberdeen 13/14 11 2
14/15 25 1
15/16 31 3
16/17 34 3
17/18
18/19
19/20 18 3

WYLLIE Alexander
b. Kilmarnock 1870 d. Kilmarnock ?.4.1902

St Mirren		90/91	13	5	
		91/92	22	4	
		92/93	16	5	
		93/94	7	2	
		94/95	16	1	
		95/96	17	7	
		96/97	17	6	
		97/98	16	10	
		98/99	15	8	
		99/00	17	4	
		00/01	6	2	

WYLLIE David
b. Hurlford 1880
Renfrew V

St Mirren		04/05	17	5	
		05/06	28	9	
		06/07	25	13	
		07/08	7	3	
		08/09	1		
Fulham		08/09	7		FL
Dunfermline A		09/10			
		10/11			
St Mirren		11/12			

WYLLIE James G
b. Hurlford

Kilmarnock		99/00			
		00/01	9		
		01/02			
Queen's Park		02/03	6	2	
Kilmarnock					

WYLLIE James McKean
b. Riccarton 1916

Cambuslang R		37/38			
Kilmarnock		38/39	11		
Petershill					

WYLLIE John Stewart
b. Riccarton 1884 d. Aberdeen 23.11.1940
Kilmarnock Deanpark

Kilmarnock		01/02	12	2	
		02/03	11	1	
		03/04	21		
		04/05	2	2	
Rangers	L	04/05			
Maxwelltown Volunteers		05/06			
Ayr Parkhouse		06/07			D2
		07/08			D2
Ayr		08/09			D2
Hurlford		08/09			
Clyde		09/10	13	3	
Aberdeen		10/11	30	2	
		11/12	34	4	
Bradford C		12/13			FL
Aberdeen		13/14	32	8	
		14/15	34	4	
		15/16	30	3	
		16/17	12	4	
		17/18			
		18/19			
		19/20	8	1	
St Johnstone		20/21			
		21/22	33	4	D2
Forfar A		22/23			D2

WYLLIE T

Clyde		16/17	1		

WYLLIE Thomas G
b. Maybole 5.8.1870 d. Bristol c1955
Maybole

Rangers		88/89			
		89/90			
		90/91	4		
Everton		90/91	4	4	FL
		91/92	16	1	FL
Liverpool		92/93			
Bury		93/94	16	13	LL
		94/95	30	9	FL
		95/96	26	9	FL
		96/97	17	2	FL
Bristol C		97/98	16	3	SL

WYNESS George Dow
b. Monkwearmouth 12.8.1907 d. Sunderland 26.6.1993
Tyzack

Jarrow		26/27			
Houghton CW		27/28			
Leicester C	T	27/28			FL
Falkirk		28/29	7	1	
Southport		29/30	19		FL
		30/31	19		FL
		31/32	14		FL
		32/33	36		FL
Chester		33/34	8		FL
Rochdale		34/35	33		FL
		35/36	37		FL
Notts Co		36/37	10		FL
Gateshead		37/38			
Jarrow		37/38			

WYPER Henry Thomas Hartley
b. Coatbridge 8.10.1900 d. Eagle Point, Aus 30.1.1974
Glengarnock Vale

Southport		21/22	7		FL
Motherwell		22/23	2		
Southport		22/23	2		FL
Burnley	T	23/24			FL
Wallasey U		23/24			
Burscough R		24/25			
Accrington S		25/26	36	10	FL
		26/27	25	4	FL
Hull C		26/27	17	1	FL
		27/28	23	1	FL
Arsenal	T	28/29			
Charlton A		28/29	39	4	FL
		29/30	15	4	FL
		30/31	28	4	FL
QPR		31/32	11		FL
Chester		31/32	11	3	FL
		32/33	12	3	FL
Bristol R		32/33	11	2	FL
Accrington S		33/34	29	7	FL
		34/35			FL
Crewe A		34/35			FL
Rossendale U		35/36			

WYSE Charles

Darlington St Augustines					
Albion R		09/10			D2
Clyde		09/10	10	1	

YARDLEY A

Third Lanark		36/37	28	14	

YARDLEY James
b. Wishaw 16.4.1907 d. Carluke 24.9.1959
Lorne Thistle
Overton R
Bellhaven Oak

Clapton Orient		24/25	3		FL
		25/26	10	2	FL
		26/27	16	1	FL
Luton T		26/27	6		FL
		27/28	39	23	FL
		28/29	40	17	FL
		29/30	40	15	FL
		30/31	28	13	FL
		31/32	20	10	FL
Charlton A		31/32	13	11	FL
		32/33	29	11	FL
		33/34	9	4	FL
Millwall		33/34	18	5	FL
		34/35	36	15	FL
		35/36	22	4	FL
Third Lanark		36/37	28	14	
		37/38	6		
Ayr U		37/38	13	9	
		38/39	25	15	
Morton					

YARNALL Herbert George
b. Goole 1892 d. Oswestry 1.10.1943
Kidsgrove Wellington

Blackpool		14/15	9	1	FL
Airdrieonians		16/17	33	39	
		17/18	13	6	
Clydebank		17/18	13	5	
Dumbarton		18/19	14	?	
		19/20			
Reading		20/21	3	1	FL
Oswestry T					

YATES James

Accrington S		12/13			
		13/14			
Third Lanark		14/15	17	2	

YATES William
b. Birmingham 1883
Witton Shell Shop
Erdington

Aston Villa		03/04			FL
		04/05			FL
Brighton		05/06	33	4	SL
Manchester U		06/07	3		FL
Heart of Midlothian		06/07	5	3	
		07/08	7	2	
Portsmouth		07/08	6	1	SL
		08/09	26		SL
		09/10	34		SL
		10/11	38		SL
Coventry C		11/12	38		SL
		12/13	38	1	SL
		13/14	30		SL

YELLOWLEES George

Hibernian		14/15	1		

YEUDALL John
b. Dennistoun 1885

Queen's Park		14/15	1		

YORK Charles H
b. Edinburgh 1882

Reading		01/02	5	1	SL
Derby Co		02/03	22	6	FL
		03/04	2		FL
Sunderland		03/04	2		FL
Heart of Midlothian		04/05	2		
Southampton		04/05			SL
		05/06			SL
Sheppey U		05/06			
South Farnborough		06/07			

YORKE Robert Johnstone
b. Haddington 8.3.1911
Rosyth Dockyard
Thornton R

Ayr U		29/30	13		
		30/31	26	1	
		31/32	8		
Dunfermline A		31/32			D2
Aldershot		32/33	6		FL
		33/34	8		FL
Dundee U		34/35	33	9	D2
Hull C		35/36	9		FL
		36/37			FL
Dundee U		37/38	30	1	D2
Montrose		38/39			D2

YORSTON Benjamin Collard 1 cap
b. Nigg 14.10.1905 d. Chelsea ?.11.1977
Kittybrewster
Aberdeen Mugiemoss

Alloa A	T				
Aberdeen Richmond					
Hibernian	T	25/26			
Montrose		26/27			D2
Aberdeen		27/28	28	17	
		28/29	31	22	
		29/30	38	38	
		30/31	28	16	
		31/32	18	8	
Sunderland		31/32	17	12	FL
		32/33	18	7	FL
		33/34	13	6	FL
Middlesbrough		33/34	12	7	FL
		34/35	19	7	FL
		35/36	42	13	FL
		36/37	21	7	FL
		37/38	25	8	FL
		38/39	33	12	FL
		39/40	2		FL

YOUNG

Heart of Midlothian		91/92	1		

YOUNG

Abercorn		92/93	4	2	

YOUNG Alexander
b. Yoker
Clydebank Jnrs

Hamilton A		32/33	8		
		33/34	14		
		34/35	8	1	
		35/36	17		
Dumbarton		36/37			D2

YOUNG Alexander Simpson 2 caps
b. Slamannan 23.6.1880 d. Portobello 17.9.1959
St Mirren 99/00 17 6
Falkirk 00/01
Everton 01/02 30 6 FL
02/03 19 5 FL
03/04 22 11 FL
04/05 31 13 FL
05/06 30 13 FL
06/07 33 30 FL
07/08 33 16 FL
08/09 23 9 FL
09/10 24 2 FL
10/11 30 7 FL
Tottenham H 11/12 5 3 FL
Manchester C 11/12 12 2 FL
South Liverpool

YOUNG Andrew
b. Campsie
Clyde 26/27 25 8
27/28 36 11
28/29 10 2
29/30 14 4
Dumbarton 30/31 D2

YOUNG Archibald C
b. Barrhead
Armadale
Hibernian 19/20 10 4
20/21 8
21/22 17 10
22/23 2
Armadale 22/23 D2
Hamilton A 23/24 4
St Bernards 23/24 D2

YOUNG D
St Mirren 24/25 5

YOUNG David
St Mirren 13/14 2
Stevenston U 14/15

YOUNG David Jeffrey L
b. Milngavie 1908
Milngavie Jnrs 28/29
29/30
Kilmarnock 30/31 2

YOUNG Edwin
Kincardine Jnrs
Falkirk 36/37 31 6
37/38 3
38/39 2
East Stirlingshire 39/40

YOUNG F
b. Glasgow
Dunfermline A 27/28 1

YOUNG Frank
Dundee Arnot
Dundee 12/13 8

YOUNG G
Hibernian 38/39 3 1

YOUNG Gavin
Galston
Newmilns
Kilmarnock 02/03 12 4
Ayr Parkhouse 03/04 D2
04/05
05/06
Galston

YOUNG George
b. Kirkintilloch 1880
Dumbarton
Beith 99/00
00/01
Rangers 01/02 1
Beith 02/03
Portsmouth 03/04 26 SL
04/05 24 SL
WBA 05/06 17 FL
West Bromwich Strollers
Worcester C

YOUNG George B
Beith Amateurs
St Mirren 09/10 1
10/11 2

YOUNG H
Queen's Park 11/12 1 1

YOUNG James
Clyde 94/95 2
95/96 13 2
96/97 4

YOUNG James 1 cap
b. Kilmarnock 10.1.1882 d. Kilmarnock 4.9.1922
Lilliemount Juveniles
Dean Park
Kilmarnock Rugby XI
Kilmarnock T 01/02
Stewarton 01/02
Shawbank 01/02
Barrow 01/02
Bristol R 02/03 19 SL
Celtic 02/03
03/04 17
04/05 19 2
05/06 19 2
06/07 32 5
07/08 29 1
08/09 31
09/10 34
10/11 31
11/12 34
12/13 33 1
13/14 34 2
14/15 38
15/16 35 2
16/17 5

YOUNG James
Cambuslang Hibs
Port Glasgow A 01/02 D2
02/03 19 1
03/04 20 3
04/05
Manchester C 05/06 1 FL
Port Glasgow A 06/07
07/08
08/09 6
St Johnstone 09/10
10/11
11/12 D2

YOUNG James
Darvel Jnrs
Airdrieonians 06/07 2
07/08 20
08/09 11
09/10 13
10/11 33
11/12 19

YOUNG James
Glencraig Celtic
Lochgelly U 16/17
Third Lanark 16/17
Lochgelly U 17/18
Raith R L 17/18
Kilmarnock L 17/18 2 1
Celtic L 17/18 1
Rangers 17/18 4
Dumbarton 18/19 5 ?

YOUNG James
Alloa A 19/20
20/21
21/22 D2
22/23 6
23/24 D2
24/25 D2
Clackmannan 24/25

YOUNG James
b. Newton Mearns
Hurlford U
Thornliebank
Ayr U 30/31 12
Lancaster T 31/32

YOUNG James
Leith A 30/31 32 4
Dunfermline A 31/32 D2
Leith A 32/33 D2
33/34 D2

YOUNG James
Dunfermline A 35/36 1

YOUNG John
Leith A 91/92 1
92/93 6
93/94 8
94/95 4
95/96 9 D2

YOUNG John
b. Kilmarnock
Kilmarnock Shawbank
Hurlford
Newcastle U 04/05
Kilmarnock 05/06 26 12
Hurlford
Bristol R 06/07 33 13 SL
Notts Co
Norwich C 07/08 24 6 SL
Kilmarnock 07/08 3
08/09 3 1
Hurlford 08/09
Crystal Palace 09/10 15 7 SL
Hurlford 10/11
11/12
12/13
13/14
14/15
15/16
16/17
17/18
18/19

YOUNG John
b. 1888
Strathclyde Jnrs
Celtic 08/09
Morton L 08/09 15 3
Celtic 09/10 2
Ayr L 09/10 D2
Celtic 10/11 1
Alloa A L 10/11
Dundee Hibernian 11/12 3 D2

YOUNG John
b. Burnbank
Burnbank A
Bradford C 10/11 9 8 FL
11/12 1 FL
Sunderland 11/12 13 2 FL
Port Vale 12/13 18 11 CL
Hamilton A 13/14 5 1

YOUNG John
Petershill
Morton 18/19 33
19/20 28
20/21 9
Clydebank
Barrow 21/22 13 FL

YOUNG John
Loanhead Mayflower
Lochgelly U
Dunfermline A 26/27 30

YOUNG John M
Motherwell 13/14 8
Partick T 14/15 6
15/16 1
Kings Park

YOUNG John William
b. Kilmarnock 26.12.1903
Auchinleck Talbot
Cowdenbeath 24/25 3 1
25/26 1
26/27
Rhyl A 26/27
Cowdenbeath 27/28 4 1
Southampton 28/29 FL
Crewe A 28/29 6 FL

YOUNG R
Clyde 18/19 1 ?

YOUNG R
b. Grangemouth
Falkirk 28/29 1

YOUNG R M
Motherwell 18/19 2 1

YOUNG Robert
Duntocher Jnrs
Motherwell 38/39 2

YOUNG Robert H

Queen's Park		04/05	1	1	

YOUNG Robert M

b. Catrine 1894

Queen's Park		12/13			
		13/14			
		14/15			
		15/16			
		16/17			
		17/18			
Albion R	L	17/18			
Airdrieonians		18/19	1		
Albion R		19/20	22		
Ayr U		20/21	14		
		21/22	2		
South Shields		21/22	1		FL
Sleekburn A					
Kings Park *		22/23			D2

YOUNG Robert M

Queen's Park		05/06	3		
		06/07	10		
		07/08	21		
		08/09	10		
		09/10	4		
		10/11	12		
		11/12			
		12/13	1		
		13/14	20		
		14/15	3		
		15/16			
		16/17			
		17/18	1		
		18/19	3	1	
		19/20	16		
		20/21	25		

YOUNG Robert Mackie

b. Stewarton d. Boston, Mass ?.1.1916

Stewarton Jnrs					
Kilmarnock		02/03	1		
		03/04	3		
		04/05	5		
		05/06	10		
Queen's Park	L	05/06			
Kilmarnock		06/07	16		
		07/08	20		
St Cuthberts W					
Motherwell		08/09	28		

YOUNG Robert Thomson

b. Stonehouse 7.9.1886 d. Scotland 1955

Swinhill Hearts					
Larkhall Thistle					
St Mirren		05/06	8		
		06/07	1		
West Ham U		07/08	32	1	SL
		08/09	9		SL
Middlesbrough		08/09	10		FL
		09/10	24	5	FL
Everton		10/11	31	6	FL
		11/12	7	2	FL
Wolverhampton W		11/12	25	5	FL
		12/13	34	3	FL
		13/14	8	2	FL

YOUNG Samuel

b. Belfast 14.2.1883 d. Belfast 28.11.1954

Linfield		04/05			IL
		05/06			IL
		06/07			IL
		07/08			IL
Airdrieonians		08/09	31	4	
		09/10	33	3	
		10/11	32	14	
		11/12	30	11	
		12/13	5		
Portsmouth		12/13	13	3	SL
Linfield		13/14			IL
		14/15			IL
		15/16			IL

YOUNG T S

Queen's Park		08/09	2		

YOUNG Thomas

Clyde		99/00	1		

YOUNG Thomas

Queen's Park		35/36	4		
		36/37	5		
		37/38	2		
Queen of the South		37/38			

YOUNG W

Dunfermline A		27/28	32		

YOUNG William

b. Paisley 1916

Mossvale YMCA					
Clydebank Jnrs					
Blackburn R		36/37	6		FL
St Mirren		37/38	5		
		38/39	34		
Dumbarton		46/47			D2

YOUNG William B

Kilsyth R					
Motherwell		15/16	8	1	
Kilsyth R					
Albion R		20/21	8	2	
		21/22	16	2	
Kings Park		22/23			D2
Hamilton A		23/24	6	1	
Lochgelly U					

YOUNGER

Cambuslang		91/92	1		

YUILL Duncan

b. Shettleston 19.3.1901 d. Winnipeg 19.12.1977

Clydebank Jnrs					
St Mirren		22/23	1		
		23/24			
		24/25			
		25/26	2		
Dumbarton		26/27			D2
Rangers		27/28	3		
Aberdeen		28/29	34		
		29/30	36		
Millwall		30/31	20		FL
		31/32			FL
		32/33			FL
		33/34	17		FL
		34/35	42		FL
		35/36	36		FL
		36/37	33		FL
		37/38	22		FL
		38/39	17		FL
		39/40	3		FL
Dumbarton					

YUILL John Crawford

b. Coltness 1917

Coltness U					
Falkirk	T				
Huddersfield T		34/35			FL
		35/36	1		FL
Arbroath		36/37	2		
Distillery		37/38			IL

YUILLE

St Mirren		98/99	2		

YUILLE James G M

Rangers		95/96	1		
		96/97			
		97/98	1		

YUILLE William

Ashgill R					
Rangers		08/09	3	2	
		09/10	5	2	
		10/11	6	1	
		11/12			
Peebles R		12/13			

YULE Robert

b. Aberdeen

Aberdeen Richmond					
Aberdeen		19/20	13	1	
		20/21	9		
		21/22	5		
Fore River		22/23			
Brooklyn Wanderers		23/24	17	1	ASL
		24/25	42	3	ASL
		25/26	25	5	ASL
		26/27	28	7	ASL
		27/28	36	6	ASL
		29A	16	6	ASL
		29/30	26	12	ASL
New York Giants		30A	23	7	ASL
Fall River		31S	8		ASL
New York Yankees		31S	7	2	ASL

YULE Thomas

b. Douglas Water 4.2.1888

Douglas Water Thistle					
Portobello					
Lincoln C		09/10	37	5	FL
		10/11	26	2	FL
Wolverhampton W		11/12	25	6	FL
		12/13	8	1	FL
Port Vale		13/14	35	8	CL
		14/15	18	5	CL
Ayr U		16/17	12		